LITERARY STRUCTURES OF RELIGIOUS MEANING IN THE QUR'ĀN

CURZON STUDIES IN THE QUR'ĀN

Editor: Andrew Rippin, University of Calgary

In its examination of critical issues in the scholarly study of the Qur'ān and its commentaries, this series targets the disciplines of archaeology, history, textual history, anthropology, theology and literary criticism. The contemporary relevance of the Qur'ān in the Muslim world, its role in politics and in legal debates are also dealt with, as are debates surrounding Qur'ānic studies in the Muslim world.

LITERARY STRUCTURES OF RELIGIOUS MEANING IN THE QUR'ĀN
Edited by Issa J. Boullata

THE DEVELOPMENT OF EXEGESIS IN EARLY ISLAM
The Authenticity of Muslim Literature from the Formative Period
Herbert Berg

LITERARY STRUCTURES OF RELIGIOUS MEANING IN THE QUR'ĀN

Edited by

Issa J. Boullata

CURZON

First Published in 2000
by Curzon Press
Richmond, Surrey
http://www.curzonpress.co.uk

Typeset in Baskerville by LaserScript Ltd, Mitcham, Surrey
Printed and bound in Great Britain by
T.J International Ltd, Padstow, Cornwall

British Library Cataloguing in Publication Data
A catalogue record of this book is available from the British Library

Library of Congress Cataloguing in Publication Data
A catalogue record for this book has been requested

ISBN 0–7007–1256–9

Contents

PART II LITERARY APPROACHES TO SELECTED SŪRAS OF THE QUR'ĀN

PART III LITERARY APPRECIATION OF THE QUR'ĀN: PAST AND PRESENT

Acknowledgements

I should like to take this opportunity publicly to thank all the contributors to this volume as I thanked them earlier in private communication. This volume would not have materialized if they had not accepted my invitation to write on the literary structures of religious meaning in the Qur'ān, a topic they daringly endorsed when it was only a compelling idea in my mind. Specialists in Qur'ānic studies and literary criticism, they honoured me by their contributions and were very helpful in making my editing responsibilities agreeable and accepting my imposition of consistency on their individual contributions to preserve uniformity in the volume as a whole.

A special note of appreciation is due to Professor A. Üner Turgay, Director of the Institute of Islamic Studies at McGill University, who encouraged me to proceed with the project of this book by granting me some financial support to supplement my spare means to hire assistance. I am also grateful to Siti Fathimah for making her computer expertise available to me and for assisting me in preparing the essays for publication by putting the edited texts of the contributors' variant diskettes on a single wordprocessing system to facilitate the work of the publisher and the typesetter. Her help is also gratefully acknowledged in the preparation of a collective bibliography for the volume.

List of Contributors

Kamal Abu-Deeb, School of Oriental and African Studies, University of London, London

Mahmoud M. Ayoub, Department of Religion, Temple University, Philadelphia

Issa J. Boullata, Institute of Islamic Studies, McGill University, Montreal

Soraya M. Hajjaji-Jarrah, Institute of Islamic Studies, McGill University, Montreal

Anthony H. Johns, Department of Pacific and Asian History, Australian National University, Canberra

Navid Kermani, Orientalisches Seminar, Bonn University, Bonn

Jane Dammen McAuliffe, Department of the Study of Religion, University of Toronto, Toronto

Mustansir Mir, Department of Religious Studies, Youngstown University, Youngstown

Angelika Neuwirth, Director, Orient-Institut der Deutschen Morgenländischen Gesellschaft, Beirut

Yusuf Rahman, Institute of Islamic Studies, McGill University, Montreal

Andrew Rippin, Department of Religious Studies, University of Calgary, Calgary

Michael Sells, Department of Religion, Haverford College, Haverford

Irfan Shahîd, Department of Arabic Language, Literature, and Linguistics, Georgetown University, Washington

Alford T. Welch, Department of Religious Studies, Michigan State University, East Lansing

A.H. Mathias Zahniser, Asbury Theological Seminary, Wilmore

Introduction

Issa J. Boullata

In the course of a public lecture delivered in 1930 on classical Arabic prose, the influential Egyptian litterateur Ṭāhā Ḥusayn (1889—1973) said, in his characteristic and articulate style:

> But you know that the Qur'ān is not prose and that it is not verse either. It is rather Qur'ān, and it cannot be called by any other name but this. It is not verse, and that is clear; for it does not bind itself by the bonds of verse. And it is not prose, for it is bound by bonds peculiar to itself, not found elsewhere; some of those bonds are related to the endings of its verses and some to that musical sound which is all its own. It is therefore neither verse nor prose, but it is "a Book whose verses have been perfected then expounded, from One Who is Wise, All-Aware." We cannot therefore say it is prose, and its text itself says it is not verse.
>
> It has been one of a kind, and nothing like it has ever preceded or followed it.[1]

Coming from a prominent literary historian and critic deeply conversant with Arabic prose and verse, this quote – for all it is worth – highlights the unique character of the Qur'ān, which is neither verse nor prose in Ṭāhā Ḥusayn's opinion; furthermore, as he says expressing the belief of all Muslims, "nothing like it has ever preceded or followed it." However, it should be noted that the uniqueness which is ascribed to the Qur'ān here is based on two things: first, its literary structures; and second, its provenance. With regard to the former, two of the structural elements that Ṭāhā Ḥusayn calls "bonds" (*quyūd*, singular *qayd*) by which the Qur'ān binds itself are referred to, namely, (1) the rhyming and assonant ends of its verses, and (2) the peculiar musical sound of its wording. With regard to its provenance, the Qur'ān is said to be a Book "from One Who is Wise, All-Aware," a Book "whose verses have been perfected then expounded" as indeed the Qur'ān says of itself (Q. 11:1). This reference to the Qur'ān's divine source is a matter of faith that is not our concern now; but its power should not be ignored, for it is quite significant in determining the attitude of Muslims to their Scripture.

However, literary structures are not limited to the two elements that Ṭāhā Ḥusayn summarily referred to in the above-quoted passage which, after all, is not from a study of the Qur'ān as such. Literary structures have many elements to them including diction, phonology, morphology, syntax, rhythm, rhetoric, composition, and style, in addition to matters related to tone, voice, orality, imagery, symbolism, allegory, genre, point of view, intertextuality, intratextual resonance, and other literary aspects – all of which are set within a historic epistemology and cultural ambiance. These elements combine with one another in the Qur'ān in different, multifunctional ways to produce the total meaning which it contains and which many generations have tried to comprehend.

By studying the Qur'ān's literary structures, this book hopes to contribute to the recently growing interest in Qur'ānic studies in the West and respond to the need for further development in them. Its intention is to concentrate on the literary structures of the Qur'ān in order to elucidate how they produce religious meaning, because such an approach has not been given sufficient attention. The literary structures of the Qur'ān are not ornamental elements in it that can be dispensed with; they are part and parcel of its meaning and without them that meaning is lost. It is, therefore, incumbent that the text of the Qur'ān be studied in its integrity as canonically received and as universally accepted by Muslims, and that scholarly efforts to reconstruct its text in accordance with a putative origin be disregarded for this purpose. The validity of historical-critical approaches to the origin of the Qur'ān is not at issue here but these approaches do not directly serve the aim of this book.

It is worth keeping in mind, right from the beginning, that Arabic is the language of the Qur'ān. The Arabic language is thus the most important aspect of the Qur'ān's literary expression. A translation of the Qur'ān into any other language cannot really be *the* Qur'ān, regardless of the accuracy and faithfulness of the translation; for every language has its own characteristics, its own cultural background, its own way of conveying meaning, its own structures to establish communication, its own idiom. Of course, the Arabic language existed for centuries before the Qur'ān was first recited piecemeal by Prophet Muḥammad to his contemporaries in about twenty-three years between A.D. 610 and 632. But the Qur'ān's use of the Arabic language is unique and worthy of special study at a variety of levels, not least being that of literary structures with which this book is concerned.

Now all monuments of great literature stand out because of their special use of language to convey meaning. In Arabic, the Qur'ān stands out additionally in a unique position because of its centrality in Arab culture on account of its distinctive use of Arabic, nothing like which is believed to have ever preceded or followed it. As the Speech of God for Muslims of Arabic and other national languages, it also occupies a unique position of centrality in their faith: it has a power that has shaped their lives and culture for centuries and it continues to affect their minds and hearts with its meaning couched in a special Arabic language. This special use of Arabic in the Qur'ān is the vehicle of the literary structures of its religious meaning, and it is these literary structures that are the subject of study in this book.

In the last few decades, a number of schools of literary criticism and theory have arisen in the continued scholarly effort to further understand literary texts and learn, under new lights, how meaning is produced in them. Ways of textual interpretation have recently multiplied at a dizzying pace, introducing subtle and continuing change in hermeneutical assumptions, but they have often been useful in showing that the meaning of a text cannot be taken for granted. Meaning has been shown to depend on so many elements in the text and its context, as well as in the relationship of both to other texts and contexts, that a single interpretation can no longer be considered to be sufficient or claim finality for itself. The cultural and socio-political circumstances of the receptors of a text have also been shown to create a horizon of understanding which constitutes an additional element in the production of meaning. Knowledge of all these elements continues to grow with the help of inquisitive minds developing new scholarly approaches and hermeneutical theories even as intellectual, scientific disciplines keep exploring further ways of understanding the world and human existence.

It is not claimed that this book will study all the literary structures of religious meaning in the Qur'ān, nor that its contributors will use all the methods of the contemporary schools of literary criticism and theory applicable to the Qur'ān. In fact, each contributor has been left to choose his or her own topic as well as his or her own method best suited for it. The overarching organization of the book has been planned by the editor to encompass three areas of literary structures singled out for study: (1) the Qur'ān as a whole, (2) individual sūras of the Qur'ān, and (3) Muslim literary appreciation of the Qur'ān. The commitment accepted by all the scholars invited to contribute to the book so planned is to shed new light on topics of their choice within one of these three areas in order to elucidate the literary structures of the Qur'ān's religious meaning. Some of these contributors are literary scholars interested in the Qur'ān and some are Qur'ānic scholars interested in literary criticism, but all are scholars who value the Qur'ān as one of humankind's most influential books and are competent to discuss its literary structures. Some of the contributors are established scholars whose publications are well-known in their field and some are younger scholars whose publications are very promising, but all are scholars who are eager to advance Qur'ānic studies by offering new perspectives. Each contributor is of course responsible for his or her own perspective, but the book as a whole hopes to be a worthy, collective addition to scholarship.

With these facts in mind, the reader will realize that this book is attempting to break new ground, on one hand, and to consolidate recently acquired knowledge, on the other. It is not to be compared with such books as *The Literary Guide to the Bible* edited by Robert Alter and Frank Kermode.[2] This latter work, for one thing, set out to offer studies of the books of the Bible contained in the Old Testament and the New Testament, in addition to relevant essays of a general nature, whereas our present book does not offer studies on each one of the Qur'ān's 114 sūras. It rather offers studies on selected sūras of the Qur'ān and a number of essays of a general nature on the whole Qur'ān or large segments of it. But like *The Literary Guide to the Bible*, our book draws attention to the literary aspects of Scripture and shows how religious meaning is produced by literary structures. Like it also, our book is written partly by literary scholars and partly by scholars of religious texts, all of whom are interested in studying these texts under new lights by using recent hermeneutical theories and literary methods. Our hope is that our book will encourage other scholars to broaden and deepen Qur'ānic studies by its effort to open new horizons of research, especially in this and related areas in need of further attention. If it does, it will have accomplished its purpose and will thus have helped keep Qur'ān interpretation an ever new discipline, an ever fresh endeavour, as continuous generations of Muslim exegetes have realized in the last fourteen centuries since *Iqra'* (Q. 96:1), the first of the Qur'ān's words, was initially heard and recited.

NOTES

1 From a lecture entitled "Prose in the Second and Third Centuries after the Hijra," delivered at the Geographical Society in Cairo on December 20, 1930, and published in Ṭāhā Ḥusayn, *Min Ḥadīth al-Shi'r wa 'l-Nathr,* 10th printing (Cairo: Dār al-Ma'ārif, 1969. First printing, 1936), 25.

2 Cambridge, MA: The Belknap Press of Harvard University Press, 1987; first Harvard University Press paperback edition, 1990.

PART I

FORM, MEANING, AND TEXTUAL STRUCTURE IN THE QUR'ĀN

Chapter 1

A Literary Approach to the Hymnic Sūras of the Qur'ān: Spirit, Gender, and Aural Intertextuality

Michael Sells

The hymnic sūras that are placed, for the most part, in the latter section of the written text of the Qur'ān are associated by tradition with the earliest period of Muḥammad's prophecy.[1] These are the passages that are learned first in Qur'ānic schools and frequently memorized. They contain, in brief, key aspects of Qur'ānic spirituality and theology. And they have attracted both strong aesthetic praise and strong aesthetic disapprobation from Western scholars. This essay constitutes a literary exploration of the early hymnic sūras, with special attention to *Sūrat al-Zalzala* (The Quaking, Q. 99) and *Sūrat al-Shams* (The Sun, Q. 91).[2] The essay will range over the early Meccan sūras as a whole and at times will bring in aspects of other Qur'ānic passages to reinforce certain points. The focus is upon aural intertextuality as a key to literary effect. The thematic area that links these passages together most closely is the Qur'ānic conception of spirit.

In framing the issue in this manner, I use a word, spirit, from everyday language but also at the heart of the world's religious traditions. Among the many common meanings of the word "spirit" are: "an animating or vital principle"; "a supernatural being"; "a temper or disposition, especially when vigorous or animated"; "the immaterial intelligent or sentient part of a person"; and "an inclination, tendency, mood."[3] The English word derives from the Latin *spirare* (to blow, breathe) and the English inspiration means literally a "breathing into." There is no doubt that Qur'ānic recitation is based on breath patterns and has an effect of slowing and modulating the breathing. Modulation of breathing is an aspect of almost all meditative traditions, and Qur'ānic reciters are trained rigorously in breath control.

Beyond the effects of breathing and on breathing, there is a quality to the sound of the Qur'ān which anyone familiar with it in Arabic can recognize. Qur'ānic commentators have discussed the power and beauty of this sound, what they call the *naẓm* of the Qur'ān – the composition, or more loosely but perhaps more richly translated, the Qur'ānic "voice." In turn, the concept of *naẓm* is one of the key aspects of the science of analyzing *i'jāz al-Qur'ān* (the inimitability of the Qur'ān) which is a standard feature of Qur'ānic commentary. Yet, while a rich history of testimonies exists regarding the power and beauty of the Qur'ānic voice, few explanations have been offered for how that voice works in relationship to the sound of the Qur'ān.[4] Here I will discuss the elusive issue of the relationship of sound to meaning in the Qur'ān by focusing upon the Qur'ānic understanding of spirit (*rūḥ*), a word that in Arabic as well is related to words for breath. While one could attempt to define the spirit as a particular being – as Gabriel, or another great angel, or yet another delimited entity,[5] the Qur'ānic language of spirit is most powerfully heard, through aural intertextuality, when the boundary between seemingly known and discrete entities is broken down.

The aural intertextuality of the Qur'ān is based upon the sound figure. This figure is particularly subtle in that it is developed within particular sūras (intratextually), but also across sūras that might be widely separated in the written version of the Qur'ān (intertextually). The Qur'ānic sound figures occur in connection with three moments: prophecy, creation, and the day of reckoning. These are boundary moments, points of contact between the eternal and the temporal realm, in which the structures of language (with temporality built into them) are transformed through contact with a realm beyond temporality; a transformation that manifests itself in the deeper sound figures. In each moment, the Qur'ān invokes the spirit (*rūḥ*).[6]

In temporal sequence the three moments are separate.[7] But the three moments are embedded, rhetorically and acoustically, within one another. Passages which may be separate in the written version of the Qur'ān echo, allude to, or offer variations of one another in a manner that ties them together. In a tradition as deeply oral and recitative as that of the Qur'ān, in which people have heard these passages recited thousands of times, one text will provoke the reader – through a sound figure shared with a passage from a different part of the written Qur'ān – into hearing the second passage as an undertone. As the various passages on each boundary moment weave themselves into one another through sound figures, the three boundary moments are brought into more intimate connection. The Qur'ānic references to spirit occur at center points or matrices of such inter-embedding.

Gender is a vital aspect of Qur'ānic sound figures and the Qur'ānic passages on spirit. Like all sacred texts of the classical period of religious revelations, the Qur'ān was revealed in a society in which the public voice of leadership was largely male, and thus the social context of the revelation, as with the Bible or the Vedas, was largely a male domain. Yet the gender dynamic within the Qur'ān is one of extraordinary gender balance, a balance constructed and modulated through sound figures. These patterns create partial personifications – of a woman giving birth, of a woman conceiving, suffering, experiencing peace, or grieving at the loss of her only child. The sound figures that create the implicit personifications also have the impact of interjections (that is, expressions of feeling, wonder, contentment and sorrow) in which the sound itself is intertwined completely with the meaning. These sound visions occur at theologically critical moments in the Qur'ān and are vital to its suppleness and beauty in the original Arabic. It may be no coincidence that spirit (*rūḥ*) is one of the few words in Arabic that can be both masculine and feminine; in the Qur'ān, at least, the role of spirit is both to highlight and to bring together polarities like temporality and eternity, male and female, night and day – polarities the Qur'ān refers to as signs or symbols (*āyāt*) of the deeper reality – and in some cases to point to union or unity transcending such polarities. The loss of such sound visions in translation is particularly damaging because of the way Islam has been caught up in stereotypes about gender and the role of women in society.

In order to show the gender figures and how the key texts intertwine, brief passages from early Meccan sūras as well as other passages in the Qur'ān will be considered. The focus here is on sound figures necessary to the intertextual evocation of spirit, with special attention to the Arabic sound *hā* – a sound that ties together a female pronoun; interjections of surprise, wonder, and sorrow; and key rhymes and acoustic features. The goal is to present enough of the sound figures of the original Arabic to give a feeling for the concept of *spirit in* the Qur'ān, and also an essential aspect of the *spirit of* the Qur'ān, that is, the distinctive manner in which the Qur'ān intertwines sound and meaning.[8]

PROPHECY

The notion of revelation contains an enigma. If the source of revelation is transcendent to the world and time, how can its word be communicated within time (at a particular moment in history) and within language (which is structured according to temporal categories of past, present, and future)? In this sense, the language of revelation is caught in the dilemma of the boundary moment; the goal is to express the timeless, but language has within itself ingrained patterns of temporality. Arabic verbs, for example, are either perfect (completed time) or imperfect (ongoing time). But the notion of eternity transcends such a division, and any effort to use language with temporal structures to discuss the eternal inevitably temporalizes the eternal in the process. In many traditions the language depicting the moment of revelation within sacred texts is transformed through the encounter with the subject of timelessness.[9] In the Qur'ān, a rapid shift back and forth between the perfect tense, in which something has been completed, and the imperfect tense, in which something is ongoing, destabilizes the normally mutually exclusive division between completed time and ongoing time. In addition, the Qur'ān, through its sound figures, melds the three moments of revelation, creation, and day of reckoning. The spirit is the agent of such meeting, and mention of the spirit is a sure indication that boundary moment transformations of language are taking place.

Spirit and prophecy are linked in the two prophetic missions of Muḥammad and Jesus, and are specifically related to the work of the spirit. Muḥammad is associated with the "spirit of transcendence," *rūḥu l-qudus* (Q. 16:102), while in the case of Jesus, son of Maryam, the spirit is said to be a support or assistance to his prophecy (Q. 2:87; 2:253; 5:110). However, in another passage, the relation of the spirit to Jesus is put into more emphatic terms: Jesus himself is called *spirit* (Q. 4:171). The spirit-as-support-for-Jesus passages and the Jesus-as-spirit passage echo, in sound quality and vocabulary, the Qur'ānic account of the conception of Jesus.

The account of Maryam's conception of Jesus (Q. 19:16–27) offers a view into the gender issues involved with the spirit. In one of the more extended passages on Maryam in the Qur'ān, the angel Gabriel appears to Maryam in human form and announces that she has conceived a child. Her reaction to Gabriel is clearly the reaction of a woman in the presence of a male outside of social propriety. She is worried about his intentions when she encounters him. Then she is astounded and fearful when he tells her she is pregnant. As she is about to give birth, she is in physical and emotional pain, feeling she will be a disgrace to her family. She states that she wishes she never existed. At that point, she is directed to eat of the fruit of a tree dangling above her, which gives her sustenance and strength. Typical of passages from the later periods of the Qur'ān, the passage in Sūra 19 offers a more developed narrative form, though still with strong acoustical effects of rhyme and assonance.

In Sūra 19, the spirit takes on the form of a human being (*bashar*) and speaks and acts accordingly. In another account of the role of spirit in Maryam's conception of Jesus, God states: "We breathed into her some of our spirit" (*nafakhnā fīhā min rūḥinā*). The phrasing of this statement, and especially the use of the terms *fīhā* and *rūḥ*, provide a clue that will link this sūra to other sūras involving prophecy. In Sūra 16:2 the Qur'ān proclaims that God "sends down the angels, with the spirit, from his order to whichever of his servants he wills." The passage contains four sections:

(1) The sending down of the angels by the deity.
(2) The appearance of the spirit in some connection with that sending down of the angels. However, the exact connection is not clear from the Arabic syntax. It could be "He sends down the

angels with the spirit," or something else, as will be explained below.

(3) The angels, with or through (*bi*) the spirit, are sent down from or with or out of the command of God. Again the syntax is open and the exact nature of the phrase (from his order or command) has been the object of centuries of discussion by commentators.

(4) This sending down can occur to whomever God wills.

This same fourfold phrase, with similar wording and syntactical ambiguities, appears in verse 4 of the Sūra of Destiny (*al-Qadr,* Q. 97): "The angels and the spirit come down on it by permission of their Lord from every order." In both verses there is a coming down (*tanazzul*) of the angels. In this descent the exact role of the spirit is unspecified, yet crucial. The descent occurs in accordance with the order (*amr*) of the deity, with the permission of (*bi idhni*) the deity, and upon whomever the deity wills (*man yashā'*).

The first parts of these two verses are almost identical:

(Q. 16:2)	*yunazzilu*	*l-malā'ikata*	*bi*	*r-rūḥi*
	he sends down	the angels	through/by/with	the spirit

(Q. 97:4)	*tanazzalu*	*l-malā'ikatu*	*wa*	*r-rūḥu fīhā*
	they come down	the angels	while/and/as	the spirit upon it/her

To follow how such parallel passages facilitate the creation of a sound figure, we return to the full Sūra of Destiny, at the heart of which is the phrase "the spirit upon it/her" (*ar-rūḥu fīhā*)

We sent him/it down on the night of destiny
And what could tell you of the night of destiny
The night of destiny is better than a thousand months
The angels come down – the spirit upon her
  by permission of their Lord from every order
5 Peace she/it is until the rise of dawn.

(Sūra of Destiny, *al-Qadr,* Q. 97)

Elsewhere I have argued in detail that the Sūra of Destiny is based upon an only partially completed personification of the night as a woman.[10] This personification is never made explicit in a way that would allow us the use of gendered English pronouns (she/he) without reservation. Yet the partial personification is so vital to the texture and beauty of the sūra, that to use the English "it" neuters the gender dynamic within the text. In verse 1, for example, the Arabic pronoun *hu* can be translated as either him or it. Commentators who view *hu* in a personal, gendered way interpret the referent of the pronoun as Gabriel. God, speaking as "we," states that he has sent him [Gabriel] down on the night of destiny. Gabriel is generally viewed as carrying the message of the Qur'ān from the deity to Muḥammad. Those commentators who view the referent as inanimate interpret it as the Qur'ān, interpreting the verse to mean: "We sent it [the Qur'ān] down" on the night of destiny. At the heart of the most dramatic moment of the sūra, the moment with the key verbal action, and at the rhythmic and rhetorical center of the sūra, are three words: *rūḥu* (spirit) *fī* (in/upon) *hā* (her/it/them). The phrase is shaped by the structure of the sūra into a sound figure, with intimations of the night as a feminine personification receiving the spirit.

As we read further in the Sūra of Destiny, we can sense even stronger intimations that the sūra involves such a personification of "conception." A strong clue occurs in the way in which verse 4 interacts with verse 5. Verse 4 stands out in the sūra as longer and more linguistically diffuse than the other verses. It contains more words and syllables than the other verses, along with a run of three subordinate clauses. By the end of these clauses, several ambiguities have been raised. What is the relation of the spirit to the coming down of the angels? Is the referent of the *hā* in *fī hā* (in it/them/her) the angels or might it be the night? What is the relationship of this process of coming down to the divine order? Does the "coming down" occur as a result of the divine command or in harmony with it? These ambiguities, based upon very loose syntactical relations among key words, build up a linguistic tension. In other words, the various possibilities for interpreting the referent of *hā* leave the hearer of the recitation in a state of anticipation rather than allowing the normal sense of closure that occurs at the end of an unambiguous sentence. In addition, the tight rhythms of verses 1–3 have temporarily been replaced in verse 4 by a loose series of prepositional phrases that leave the verse in rhythmic and syntactic tension. The resulting tension puts enormous pressure on the word *fīhā* in verse 4 and high expectation on the last verse.

The final verse begins with the word *salāmun* (Peace) which is usually followed in the Qur'ān and in everyday Islamic greetings by the word *'alaykum* (upon you), to form the greeting "Peace upon you" (*salāmun 'alaykum*), when expectation of such a greeting following the initial word *salāmun* is overwhelming. But, in the final verse that expectation is broken. The next word is not *'alaykum*, but *hiya* (she, it); the verse thus begins on a dramatic note of seeming familiarity, then suddenly breaks the expectations it has created and shifts to *hiya*.

The emphasis on *hiya* is compounded by the complex question concerning its grammatical antecedent. In other words, what does *hiya* (she/it) refer to? There is controversy and disagreement among commentators over this question. However, with the gendered aspect of the pronouns highlighted throughout the sūra by sound emphasis and the implicit personification of night, the dominant aspect of the verse in literary sensibility is gendered: "Peace she is, until the rise of dawn." Most importantly, the occurrence of *hiya* interferes with the possibility in the previous phrase (v. 4) that the *hā* (her/it/them) refers to the angels. A clear and consistent reading of the referent of *hā* as the angels would keep the *hā* from becoming a sound figure for a feminine, singular personification "her." However, *hiya* cannot refer grammatically to a plural (the angels), but only to a single animate being or a single object with feminine grammatical gender, and thus the appearance of *hiya* in verse 5 makes the argument that the *hā* in verse 4 refers to the angels difficult to sustain, and thereby gives more weight to the possibility of reading the *hā* as "her."

The possibility of an implied personification is also reinforced by the very close similarity between the word for night *layla* and one of the more common women's names in Arabic, *Laylā* – a name that was at the time of the Qur'ān, and still is, associated with one of the famous beloveds in the Arabic poetic tradition. Although *layla* clearly is a word for night and not a proper name, its aural similarity to the proper name Laylā might operate on the subliminal level of undertones as a kind of implied pun. Anyone whose name has close sound similarity to other words knows how deeply ingrained such sound similarities are in the mind of those hearing the original name or word. The word for night, *layla,* is particularly predisposed through the homonymic relation to Laylā and the prominence of Laylā within the tradition of expressive speech to being personified.

The final clue of such an implicit personification of the night occurs when the Sūra of Destiny is read along with passages referring specifically to Maryam's conception of Jesus. In Q. 21:91, God, speaking as "we," states of Maryam's conception of Jesus:

nafakhnā	**fīhā**	min	**rūḥ**inā
We breathed	into her	(some) of	our spirit[11]

These are the exact key words that occur in the Sūra of Destiny, *rūḥ/fīhā* only in a different order. And in this case there is no doubt that the *fīhā* refers to the spirit entering the virgin Maryam and impregnating her with Jesus, the bearer of prophecy. The implicit metaphor in the Sūra of Destiny is night, personified as a woman, conceiving the prophetic message through the spirit. This conception by the night of destiny echoes the conception by Maryam of Jesus through the spirit. The personification of the night is never direct or blatant, but is articulated through the most subtle sound figures and undertones.

CREATION

What occurred before the creation of the world? This question is a central theme in the mythic language of creation throughout human culture.

However, the question itself contains a contradiction since time is part of the world. To ask what happened *before* the creation of the world is to impose a category of time as a "time before time." Thus, discussion of a time before time involves a limitless series of paradoxes. Mystical writers used these paradoxes to stretch the limits of language. Philosophers have used them to critique the mythic understanding of creation. In the Qur'ān, the enigma of the origin of time, of the time before time, is a second vital boundary moment in which language itself, through sound figures, challenges or puts into question its own structures.

The creation of the world is mentioned in the Qur'ān frequently in reference to the world as a sign of the deeper reality of its creator. Explicit description of creation, however, is most focused upon the creation of Adam. In the Qur'ānic passages depicting the creation of Adam, the deity first shapes (*sawwā*) the primordial human being (*insān* or *bashar*) and then brings the form to life by breathing into it the spirit. In Q. 15:29 and Q. 38:71–2, the deity states that:

sawwaytuhu	*wa*	*nafakhtu*	*fīhi*	*min*	*rūḥī*
I shaped him/it	and	breathed	into him/it	(some) of	my spirit.

In Q. 32:9, the deity uses the same formula, this time referring to itself in the third person:

sawwāhu	*wa*	*nafakha*	*fīhi*	*min*	*rūḥihi*
he/it shaped him	and	breathed	into him/it	(some) of	his/its spirit

One of the key aspects of divine creativity is expressed by the Arabic word *sawwā*, a word that means "to knead," "to mold," "to form," or "to shape." Thus, just before breathing into the shape of Adam, the deity refers to his shaping of Adam with the term *sawwā*. Indeed, the term *sawwā* is intimately linked to the spirit; when something is first shaped, the spirit is then breathed into it. This term serves as a clue to the intertextual links among passages concerning creation.

One early Meccan passage referring to the "shaping" of the human creature consists of the first ten verses of the Sūra of the Sun (*al-Shams,* Q. 91). These verses are series of oaths that evoke the creative aspect of the deity through a strongly gendered language. Throughout the sūra, each verse ends with the rhyme *hā* which is the Arabic pronoun that can mean "her" or "it." The end-rhyme in *hā* was exploited in early Arabic poetry to play upon the various meanings of the pronoun: personal, impersonal, singular, and plural. In the Mu'allaqa of Labīd, for example, the end-rhyme in *hā* can refer to the stations of the beloved Nawār, to Nawār herself, and to a more unspecified referent, often slipping with ambiguity or ambivalence among these various possibilities. In the journey section, it can refer to the desert animals (the *nāqa,* the oryx, and the onager) as well as the various features of the desert. In the boast, it can refer to the enemies of the tribe, to the camel-mare that is ritually slaughtered, and to a variety of other features.

The Sūra of the Sun uses the end-rhyme in a manner as complex and as powerful as the Mu'allaqa of Labīd, but because the Qur'ānic verses are not composed in poetic meter, the assonance and the end-rhyme take on even more importance in the overall aural effect. The verses all end in the assonance/rhyme *āhā* and the long-*ā* sound is intensified by previous phrases such as *wa mā* or *idhā*. The *hā* is the grammatically feminine pronoun for "her" that is used first to refer to the sun (verses 1–2); the night and day, perhaps also with a possible reference back to the sun (verses 3–4); the heaven and earth (verses 5,6) and the soul (verses 7–10). This ending in *hā* was also used by early Arabic poets, and it allows a combination of personal references with grammatically feminine objects, facilitating a sound figure for the feminine, an intimation of personification. The intimation is so strong in this sūra that I have chosen to translate the *hā* as her. Because of the way in which the *hā* is emphasized in the sūra at the end of each verse, and the way in which it echoes other sūras that create an implicit feminine personification from *hā*, I have used the feminine pronoun "her" in the English version:

By the sun and her morning light
By the moon when it follows in her
By the day when it displays her
By the night when it veils her
5 By the sky and what constructed her
By the earth and what spread her out
By a soul and what shaped her (*sawwāhā*)
and revealed to her her degradation and her faithfulness
Whoever honors her will prosper
10 Whoever degrades her will find failure

(Sūra of the Sun, Q. 91:1–10)

This lyrical passage reflects the Qur'ānic theme that the heavens and the earth, the day and the night, the sun and the moon, are signs (*āyāt*) just as the verses of the Qur'ān are signs – signs of a reality that cannot be directly expressed but only understood through a sustained process of reading and interpreting. Here the reference to "a soul and what shaped her (*sawwāhā*)" repeats the same technical term used in the Qur'ānic passages on the creation of Adam, linking the two passages in a formal and explicit fashion. This explicit link facilitates the more subtle links between the two passages that make use of sound patterns centered around *hā*.

The implicit personification of the sun, the day and night, the heaven and earth, and the soul, are reminiscent of the personification of wisdom (*hokhma*) and the portrayal of her in cosmic terms found in the Biblical

Book of Wisdom. But, the sound figure does not offer a narrative portrayal of "her" that brings the personification out as explicitly as we would find in the *hokhma* passages of the Book of Wisdom. The partial personification remains hymnic, lyrical, and implied, rather than articulated through a narrative that would portray "her" (*hā*) as a female actor in more anthropomorphic terms.

The overall effect of the use of the rhyming *hā* in the sūra is a referential suppleness. As the sound of the *hā* anchors the sūra and as it is repeated, it creates a sense of a feminine-gendered presence within a set of sliding or shifting referents (the sun; the sky and the earth and/or the sun; and then the soul).[12] The objects evoked are marks of wonder and signs of their underlying source. As with other sūras where there is a partial personification, the translator into English is forced to choose between the neuter "it" and the personal "her," neither of which can bring across the full tension of the partial personification. I believe that either choice can be defended in any given situation, as long as the translator recognizes the problem and balances one choice in one passage with another choice in another passage to avoid overcharging the Qur'ānic text in one direction or another. Pickthall has translated the *hā* in *Sūrat al-Shams* as "him"[13] on the grounds that the sun is personified as masculine in the English tradition.

To understand what may lie behind the expurgation of the *hā,* we need to examine other rewritings of the Qur'ānic texts by translators that might show a pattern of censoring of the gender balance within the Qur'ān, particularly in reference to the Qur'ānic understanding of the concept of *āya* (sign). The sign refers not only to signs within the world but also self-referentially to the Qur'ān's own generation of meaning; thus verses of the Qur'ān are themselves called *āyāt.* In the following oath, the dynamic of gender is a sign both within the world and within Qur'ānic language:

wa l-layli idhā yaghshā
wa n-nahāri idhā tajallā
wa mā khalaqa dh-dhakara wa l-unthā

By the night when it shrouds
And the day when it reveals
And what (*wa mā*) made the male and the female
(The Sūra of the Night, *al-Layl,* Q. 92:1–3)

The relationship of sign to both gender and creation is also stressed in the story of Maryam's conception (Q. 21:91): "We breathed into her some of our spirit, and made her and her son a sign (*āya*) for all peoples." Yet, despite the critical importance of gender dynamic in the Qur'ānic understanding of creation and of signs, a number of popular translations follow the classical commentaries in interpreting the *mā* (what) in verse 3 above as a "substitute" for *man* (who).[14] In accordance with this tendency to convert all references to deity (and other sublime subjects) into the personal masculine, the substitution theory is used to justify the English rendering of the verse as "By Him who created the male and the female."[15] However, the substitution has no clear grounding in any early Arabic literature, and in addition, poses a theological absurdity. It is true that throughout the Qur'ān third person reference to Allah is made through the masculine/neuter *hu*. Neither the Qur'ān nor Islamic theology considers the one God to be differentiated sexually as male or female, however. It is thus conventional to translate the pronoun referring to the deity in most cases as masculine as "he." However, in the passage at issue, the subject is not just creation in general, but the *creation of gender*. The divine voice is swearing by that which creates the very categories of gender, of him and her. To translate that which is the creator of the male and female, and therefore necessarily transcendent to the male and the female, as "him" is to risk the loss of the transcendence of gender that is part of the Qur'ānic oath. The use of "him" also loses the syntactical ambivalence between the relative pronoun (what) and the interrogative pronoun (what?) that is another aspect of the power of the oath.[16] When the Qur'ān speaks of signs and the creation of signs, it most often brings together two polarities: day and night, and male and female. These polarities are affirmed as modalities of creation and signification.[17] It is thus no accident that the Qur'ānic gender balance and partial personification occurs powerfully in sūras connected to the imagery of day and night (Q. 91, Q. 92), so powerfully that it has given rise to an effort within some classical commentators and modern translators to in effect edit the text and replace it with what appears to those commentators and translators as a more comfortable monotonically masculine-gendered language. Given the stereotypes concerning gender within the polemics between Islamic and anti-Islamic militants, a retrieval of the gender dynamic within the Qur'ānic text is particularly important.

The second section of the Sūra of the Sun (Q. 91) shifts from the lyrical to the epic, with a recapitulation of the story of Thamūd and its slaughter of the *nāqa* of God.[18] Here the end-rhyme is torn out of its lyrical context and refers to the tribe of Thamūd; the *nāqa* of God; the tribesmen who are obliterated by God in punishment; and the generalized situation in which the Lord does not fear any consequences. Here the long-*ā* builds toward an intensity in the phrase "The messenger of God said to them: the camel-mare of God" (verse 13). The phrase "camel-mare of God" (*nāqata llāhi*) receives a special emphasis as it comes in the middle of the longest verse in the sūra, at the moment of greatest dramatic urgency, and its long-*ā* sounds allow the reciter to bring out that urgency with special resonance.

The people of Thamūd called truth a lie
  in their inhumanity
when they sent out their worst

The messenger of God said to them:
  God's camel-mare
  give her water

They called him liar
  and hamstrung her for the slaughter
15 Then their Lord rumbled down upon them condemnation
  for their crime and wiped them away
with no fear of what came after.

The word for the deity's obliterating of the sacrilege-committing tribe of Thamūd is *sawwāhā*, the exact word that was seen above to be central to creation mythology, here coming back to refer to annihilation. The metaphor of the creation, the deity molding the form of Adam from mud seems to imply here that the deity, like an artisan working with still wet clay, can roll back the formed into the formless. While the Qur'ān contrasts with early Arabic poetry in fundamental manners, it is worth noting here how the ritualized sacrilege of the *nāqa*-slaughter comes after the more *nasīb*-like homage to the feminine-gendered day, night, earth, heaven, and soul. The dramatic shift in tone between the two sections is reinforced by aural effects. In the words of verse 14, for example, "Then their Lord rumbled down upon them condemnation for their crime and wiped them away," a feature of *tajwīd* called *iqlāb* is used. The word *dhanb* (crime, fault, sin) is pronounced as *dhamb*, with a substitution of the "m" for "n" and a nasalization of the consonant cluster *mb*. This allows the weight of the consonants to sound through with a sense of foreboding.

The aural intratextuality (the assonance and acoustic plays within the Sūra of the Sun) heightens the effects of its intertextual resonances with other sūras. (See Figure # 1, opposite, for a transliteration of the sūra, with key sound effects noted in italics and boldface). The role of the spirit in prophetic revelation during the night of destiny showed echoes of its role in the Qur'ānic account of the conception of Jesus through the breathing into Maryam of the spirit. Similarly, the account of the formation and creation of Adam shows an intertextual resonance with the inbreathing of the spirit or inspiriting that we find in the Maryam passage. After shaping Adam, the deity breathes into Adam some of its spirit.

(Q. 38:72)	*nafakhtu*	**fīhi**	*min*	**rūḥī**
	I (Allah) breathed	into him/it	(some) of	My spirit.
(Q. 32:9)	*nafakha*	**fīhi**	*min*	**rūḥihi**
	He (Allah) breathed	into him	(some) of	His spirit

1	wa sh-shamsi by the sun			**wa** and		**ḍuḥāh ā** her morning light
2	wa l-qamari by the moon			**idhā** when		**talāh ā** it follows her
3	wa n-na**hā**ri by the day			**idhā** when		**jallāh ā** it displays her
4	wa l-layli by the night			**idhā** when		**yaghshāh ā** it veils her
5	wa s-sa**mā**'i by the sky			**wa mā** and what		**banāh ā** constructed her
6	wa l-arḍi by the earth			**wa mā** and what		**ṭaḥāh ā** spread her out
7	wa nafsin by a soul			**wa mā** and what		**sawwāh ā** shaped her
8	fa alhama**h ā** and revealed to her			**fujūrahā** her degradation		**wa taqwāh ā** and her faithfulness
9	qad aflaḥa would prosper			**man** whoever		**zakkāh ā** honors her
10	wa qad **khā**ba would fail			**man** whoever		**dassāh ā** degrades her
11	kadhdhabat denied	thamūdu Thamūd		bi through		**ṭaghwāh ā** their oppression
12	idhi when	nba'atha was sent forth				**ashqāh ā** their worst
13	fa **qā**la lahum rasūlu **llā**hi so said to them the messenger of God:		**nā**qata **llā**hi "The camel mare of God		wa so	**suqyāh ā** give her water"
14	fa and	kadhdhabūhu they denied him	fa 'aqarū**h ā** and hamstrung her			
	fadamdama 'alayhim so poured forth upon them		rabbuhum their Lord	bi dhanbihim for their crime	**fa sawwāh ā** and wiped them away	
15	wa lā and did not	yakhāfu fear		**'uqbāh ā** the consequence		

Figure # 1: The Sūra of the Sun (Q. 91)

Similarly, in describing the conception of Jesus, God states, here using the first person plural "we": "We breathed into her (some) of our spirit."

(Q. 21:91)	*nafakhnā*	**fīhā**	*min*	**rūḥinā**
	We breathed	into her	(some) of	Our spirit

The concept of a formed or shaped human being and the exact term used for it create another tie between the conception of Jesus and the creation of Adam. In Q. 19:17, the deity proclaims that "We sent to her our spirit who took the appearance before her as a human being that had been shaped."

fa	*arsalnā*	**ilayhā**	**rūḥanā**
so	We sent	to her	Our spirit

fa	*tamaththala*	*lahā*	**basharan**	**sawwiyyan**.
which	took the appearance	to her	as a human	shaped

The phrase *basharan sawwiyyan* (a human that had been shaped) is the exact phrase used in the story of Adam's creation to indicate the human form brought to life by the inbreathing of the spirit. In the Maryam story, the human (*bashar*) becomes the form taken by the spirit which in the other accounts of the conception of Jesus was breathed into Maryam. Once again, a gender dynamic is elicited by a discussion of the activity of the spirit. In the creation of Adam it is the human (*insān* or *bashar*) who *receives* the spirit. In this passage, the pronoun used for Adam is him/it (*hi*).[19] In the other case it is Maryam who receives the spirit that personifies itself (*tamaththala*) as a human (*bashar*). The context of social threat and Maryam's clear discomfort make it clear that the human form of the angelic figure is a male form. The pronoun used for Maryam as *receiver* of the spirit is *hā* (her, it); there is a complementarity between the two pronouns, masculine and feminine, used for the being that receives the spirit, further heightening the issue of gender that surrounds the spirit.

These parallels between the breathing of the spirit into the shape of Adam and the breathing of the spirit into Mary in the conception of Jesus link the two processes in a way that is never explicit, but which is nevertheless robust:

(Q. 38:72) ... *fīhi* (Adam) *min rūḥī*
(Q. 32:9) ... *fīhi* (Adam) *min rūḥihi*
(Q. 21:91) ... *fīhā* (Maryam) *min rūḥinā*
(Q. 97:4) ... *rūḥu fīhā* (the Night of Destiny)

These parallels place the full weight of Qur'ānic intertextuality around the key phrase in the Sūra of Destiny, "the spirit in/upon her." That intertextuality heightens the sense of implicit personification and gender interplay in the Sūra of Destiny. Through such intertextuality, sound figures can be heard that intimate the personification of night as feminine, conceiving the prophetic message through the spirit. In the context of such an implied personification, the night could be interpreted to convey peace, conceive peace, or be peace until the rise of dawn.[20]

RECKONING

Just as the time before time (creation) is an essential enigma, so the end of time and the afterworld (time after time) are enigmas. Like creation, the day of reckoning is a boundary moment, an intersection of time and eternity that cannot be directly expressed in the temporally structured patterns of normal language. As with creation, so with the day of reckoning, spirit is the agent that brings together the eternal and the temporal:

Someone asked about the pain that will fall
Upon those who rejected, a pain that cannot be warded off
From God of the ascending stairways
Angels ascend – and the spirit – to Him
on a day whose span is fifty thousand years.
5 Be patient, patience most fine
They see it from afar
We see it near
A day the sky will be like molten copper
and the mountains like fluffs of wool

(Sūra of the Stairways, *al-Ma'ārij,* Q. 70:1–9)

In the passage above concerning the day of reckoning, the language has multiple parallels with other passages on the reckoning. The mountains like fluffs of wool are almost identical to the mountains-as-fluffs-of-wool in the Sūra of the *Qāri'a* (Q. 101). The exact phrase "pain will fall" (*'adhāb wāqi'*) occurs in another day of reckoning passage:

By the mount (Sinai)
By a book inscribed
on rolls of parchment most fine
By the house brought to life
5 By the roof raised high
By the sea boiled over
The pain of your Lord will fall
None can ward it off
On a day the sky will sway
and the mountains slide away

(Sūra of the Mount, *al-Ṭūr,* Q. 52: 1–10)

The role of the spirit in the day of reckoning both echoes and inverses the role of the spirit on the night of destiny. In the passage quoted above (Q. 70:4): "Angels ascend – and the spirit – to Him on a day whose span is fifty thousand years." On the day of reckoning, therefore, the angels "rise" – in some relationship to the spirit – to Him (God). On the night of destiny, the angels descend – in some relation with the spirit – to or upon the night or the world. When it is asked what could tell us about the night of destiny, the answer is that it is "better than a thousand months." (Q. 97:4) Similarly, the day of reckoning is compared to a long span of time, "a day whose span is fifty thousand years." (Q. 70:4) These parallels in imagery and meaning are further strengthened by sound and syntax parallels:

Q. 70:4	*ta'ruju*	*l-malā'ikatu*	*wa r-rūḥu*	*ilayhi*
	there rise	the angels	and the spirit	in/upon Him/it
Q. 97:4	*tanazzalu*	*l-malā'ikatu*	*wa r-rūḥu*	*fīhā*
	there descend	the angels	and the spirit	in/upon her

The "coming down" of the angels in connection with the activity of the spirit on the night of *qadr* is balanced by the "rising" of the angels in connection with spirit on the day of reckoning; in addition, the feminine indirect object (*hā*) is balanced by the masculine indirect object (*hi*). The intertwining of the two passages, one on the night of destiny, the other on the day of reckoning, intimate something undefined and perhaps undefinable hidden within the imagery of daybreak. The ambiguity in both these passages concerning the role and relationship of the spirit in the "rising" and "descending" of the angels creates an openness of meaning that keeps the spirit from being limited to a particular finite being or form.

The day of reckoning and the night of destiny are brought together not only by the language of spirit, but also by gendered sound figures. While in the night of destiny, the sound figure intimates a woman conceiving in peace and joy, in the Sūra of the Quaking (Q. 99), the day of reckoning is depicted in a manner that suggests the personification of the earth as a woman giving birth in crisis:

When the earth is shaken, quaking, shaking
When the earth gives up her burdens
And someone says "What is with her"
At that time she will tell her news
5 That your Lord revealed to her
At that time people will straggle forth
  to be shown what they have done
Whoever does a mote's weight good will see it
Whoever does a mote's weight wrong will see it.

(The Sūra of the Quaking, *al-Zalzala,* Q. 99)

As in the Sūra of the Sun, the rhyme word is *hā* (her/it). Verses 1–5 of Q. 99 are based upon a highly fluid and complex end rhyme in *ālahā,* with the variant *ārahā* in verse 4. The fluidity of this combination of long-*ā* and "h" contrasts with the sharp consonant quality of the central part of the

1	**idhā**	zulzilati	l-arḍu	żil**zālahā**	
	when	quakes	the earth	in her quaking	
2	wa	akhrajati	l-arḍu	ath**qālahā**	
	and	bears forth	the earth	her burdens	
3	wa	qāla	l-in**sā**nu	**mā lahā**	
	and	says	the human	"what is with her"	
4	yawma'idhin	tuḥaddithu		akh**bārahā**	
	on that day	she will tell		her news	
5	bi'anna	rabbaka		aw**ḥā lahā**	
	– that	your Lord		revealed to her	
6	yawma'idhin	yaṣduru	n-**nā**su	ash**tā**tan	
	on that day	will go forth	people	scattered	
				li yuraw	a'**mālahum**
				to be shown	their deeds
7	fa man	ya'mal	mith**qā**la dharratin	khayran	yarah
	so whoever	does	the weight of a mote	good	will see it
8	wa man	ya'mal	mith**qā**la dharratin	sharran	yarah
	and whoever	does	the weight of a mote	wrong	will see it

Figure # 2: *Sūrat al-Zalzala* (Q. 99)

verses: *zulzilati l-arḍu* (v. 1), *akhrajati l-arḍu* (v. 2). These staccato combinations of consonants build up a sense of tension that is released at the end of each verse with the final *hā*.

The earth is portrayed as being caught up in a cosmic shaking. After two verses based upon /ā/ and the *lahā* rhyme, the third verse shows a powerful phonetic parallelism both with the surrounding verses of the sūra: *wa qāla l-insānu mā lahā* (v. 3). The most cosmic moment is combined with the most intimate speech, as if a person were asking about the state of a woman's birth pangs: "and a human will ask 'what is with her.'" The verses that follow bring the semantic and acoustical charge of the /ā/ and the final end-rhymes (*-zālahā, -qālahā, mā lahā, -bārahā, -ḥā lahā*) to the breaking point, allowing the *mā* of *mā lahā* a strong resonance as an undertone.

The last verses, with their cosmic reversal, place the long-*ā* sound in the center instead of at the end, and offer a contrast to the preceding sound patterns, which gives a particular emphasis to the final two verses. Indeed, the words spoken about the earth – "what is with her" (*mā lahā*) – are of a familiar and intimate quality that would be asked by those concerned about a woman in suffering. The depictions of earth in feminine constructions such as "bearing forth her burden" and telling "her news" create a partial and implicit, but nonetheless powerful personification of the earth as a woman giving birth.

After the earth bears forth her burden and tells her news, and after the quaking (which in the birth metaphor might correspond to labor), there occurs the ontological reversal that is key to the day of reckoning. What seems secure and solid turns out to be ephemeral, and what seems small or insignificant, a mote's weight of good or a mote's weight of evil, is what one will see as one's eternal reality and destiny. The last two words of verses, *khayr***an** *yarah* (good will see it) and *sharr***an** *yarah* (evil will see it), contain an effect called *idghām*, in which the final "n" of the penultimate word is elided with the following "y" and given a partial nasalization. This effect amplifies the tone of warning and foreboding with which the sūra ends.[21]

The interplay between the consonant/short-vowel staccatos and the long-*ā* sounds is precisely inversed in the Sūra of the Tearing (*al-Infiṭār,* Q. 82). There, the verse endings (*infaṭarat, intatharat, fujjirat, bu'thirat*) were staccato, while the central axis of the verses featured the long-*ā* (*samā',* *kawākib, biḥār*). In the Sūra of the Quaking (Q. 99), on the other hand, the staccato sets (*zulzilat, akhrajat,* etc.) occur in the central part of the verse, while the long-*ā* sounds (*zilzālahā, athqālahā,* etc.) occur at the end. Then, in verse 6, the sūra opens in a long, assonance-filled lament: "Oh, O human being, what has deceived you about your generous Lord" (*yā ayyuhā l-insānu mā gharraka bi rabbika l-karīm*) (Q. 82:6). After this interlude, verses 7–8, turn back to a more staccato and rhythmically taut locution:

When the sky is torn
When the stars are scattered
When the seas are poured forth
When the tombs burst open
5 Then a soul will know what it has given
  and what it has held back
Oh, O human being
  what has deceived you about your generous Lord
who created you and shaped you and made you right
In whatever form he willed for you, he set you

(*Sūrat al-Infiṭār,* Q. 82)

1	idha	s-sa**mā**'u	nfaṭarat
	when	the sky	is torn
2	wa idha	l-ka**wā**kibu	ntatharat
	and when	the stars	are strewn
3	wa idha	l-bi**ḥā**ru	fujjirat
	and when	the seas	are poured forth
4	wa idha	l-qubūru	bu'thirat
	and when	the tombs	are burst open

5	‘alimat	nafsun	**mā** qaddamat	wa akhkharat
	then will know	a soul	what it has given	and held back
6	**yā** ayyuha	l-insānu	mā gharraka	bi rabbika l-karīm
	Oh, O	human	what has deluded you	from your generous Lord
7	al-ladhī	khalaqaka	fa saw**wā**ka	fa ‘adalak
	Who	created you	then formed you	then set you right
8	fī ayyi	ṣūratin	**mā shā’**a	rakkabak
	in whatever	form	He wished	He set you

(*Sūrat al-Infiṭār,* Q. 82)

The Sūra of the Qāri‘a (Q. 101) does not contain an overarching implied metaphor such as the earth giving birth. Instead, it builds with strong gender dimensions toward a moment of grief and passion. The two mysterious words in the sūra, *qāri‘a* and *hāwiya,* are both feminine. And, although *hā* is not the rhyme word throughout the sūra, it is used in a particularly condensed manner to create a sound figure.

The *qāri‘a*
What is the *qāri‘a*
What can tell you of the *qāri‘a*
A day humankind are like moths scattered
5 And mountains are like fluffs of wool dyed and carded
Whoever's scales weigh heavy
His is a life that is pleasing
Whoever's scales weigh light
His mother is *hāwiya*
10 What can tell you what she is (*mā hiya*)
Raging fire.

(*Sūrat al-Qāri‘a,* Q. 101)

The *hāwiya* – a mother who has lost her child, an abyss, a fall, or desire – occurs here in a manner that brings out an expression of grief. The grief and sense of loss occur with finality but are not frozen into spatial and temporal limits. Instead, we have the refrain "what can tell you what she is" (*mā hiya*), followed by the phrase "raging fire." Notice the syntactical ambiguity between the two verses. Is she fire, or is fire something that can tell us what she is? This ambiguity prevents a facile interpretation of the sūra and allows a continuing echo of the sound of loss, the loss of a mother who has lost her only child, or the loss of someone who realizes – at the end of a wasted life – that "his mother is *hāwiya.*" The gender associations of *hā* are heightened by the rhyme and are parallel to previous *mā hiya* (what she is) in the following verse, even as the *mā hiya* reminds us of the *mā lahā* (what is with her) of the Sūra of Destiny.

At this moment, it is as if the language were shattered under the impact of the revelation; the word *hāwiya,* while remaining as a single word, is in the undertones of the verse, broken into parts. As the Qur'ānic reciter chants the word *hāwiya,* the syllable *hā* – which is part of the gendered sound figure in the passages on the spirit as "her" – is also heard in another key: the sound *hā* is part of several Arabic interjections of urgency, grief, or wonder. One very common interjection in the Qur'ān, for example, is *yā ayyuhā* ("Oh, O you"), an expression in which the long-*ā* is elongated into a mournful lament through the *tajwīd* recitation. As the word *hāwiya* is recited, its first syllable sounds with lyrical intensity, gender intimation, and high emotion both as a separate unit of sound and meaning and as part of the word *hāwiya.*

CONCLUSION

A key element of the early Meccan sūras is aural intertextuality. This element is found throughout the Qur'ān, but is reinforced by the hymnic nature of the early Meccan material. Aural intertextuality is based upon (1) the heighening of key acoustic features within a particular passage; (2) the connection of those sound features with key emotions, gender dynamics, or semantic fields; (3) the forming of "sound figures" from this connection between acoustical features and a supple use of emotions, gender, and semantics – sound figures that are not limited to a definite or lexically determinate figure of speech such as onomatopoesis, but rather reach across and through normal lexical boundaries; and (4) the intertextual play of such sound figures with similar or identical sound figures in other sūras.[22]

In this essay, these sound figures have been examined in connection with the Qur'ānic conception of spirit, with gender dynamic, and with the three boundary moments of prophecy, creation, and reckoning. It is through the modulation among sound figures that the spirit achieves its sense of openness, that gender balance and implicit personifications are constructed, and that the three boundary moments, discrete in linear times, are shown to be (and are performed as) embedded within one another in a manner that breaks down temporal boundaries.

NOTES

1 One exception is *Sūrat al-Zalzala,* Q. 99, which some consider a Medinan sūra, on thematic rather than literary grounds. For a fine translation and the discussion of the final section of the Qur'ān, see *The Awesome News, Interpetation of Juz' 'Amma – The Last Part of the Qur'ān,* by Mahmoud M. Ayoub (n.p.: World Islamic Call Society, second edition, 1997).

2 M. Sells, "Sound, Spirit, and Gender in *Sūrat al-Qadr,*" *Journal of the American Oriental Society* 111, 2 (1991):239–59; "Sound and Meaning in Sūrat al-Qāri'a,"

Arabica 40 (1993):403–30; *Early Islamic Mysticism* (New York: Paulist Press, 1996), 29–46. A full treatment of these issues is included in Michael Sells, *Approaching the Qur'ān: The Early Revelations* (Ashland: White Cloud Press, 1999).

3 *Webster's Ninth New Collegiate Dictionary* (Springfield, MA: Merriam Webster, 1986).

4 Bāqillānī ignores Sūras such as *al-Zalzala* (Q. 99) and *al-Qāri'a* (Q. 101), which most resemble *Sūrat al-Qadr* (Q. 97) in their acoustical and semantic resonances. He also ignores *Sūrat al-Qadr* itself. Cf. Abū Bakr Muḥammad ibn al-Ṭayyib al-Bāqillānī, *I'jāz al-Qur'ān*, ed. by Al-Sayyid Aḥmad Ṣaqr (Cairo: Dār al-Ma'ārif, 1981). Zamakhsharī discusses some of these passages, but from a largely rhetorical perspective: Maḥmūd ibn 'Umar al-Zamakhsharī, *Al-Kashshāf 'an Ḥaqā'iq Ghawāmiḍ al-Tanzīl wa 'Uyūn al-Aqāwīl fī Wujūh al-Ta'wīl* (Beirut: Dār al-Kitāb al-'Arabī, 1947). In his *Faḍā'il al-Qur'ān*, Ibn Kathīr relates traditions concerning the importance of proper recitation and the power of sound quality, but does not integrate such issues into his *tafsīr* proper: Ismā'īl ibn 'Umar ibn Kathīr, *Tafsīr al-Qur'ān al-'Aẓīm*, 7 (Beirut: Dār al-Fikr, 1966). Cf. Muḥammad ibn Ismā'īl al-Bukhārī, *Ṣaḥīḥ* (Cairo: Muṣṭafā al-Bābī, 1953), 3:162–9. For a translation of Abū Ḥāmid al-Ghazālī's discussion of the *faḍā'il*, see Muhammad Abul Quasem, *The Recitation and Interpretation of the Qur'ān: Al-Ghazālī's Theory* (London: Kegan Paul, 1982), 18–33.

5 For a discussion of *rūḥ* in the Qur'ān see Thomas O'Shaughnessy, *The Development of the Meaning of Spirit in the Koran* (Rome: Pont. Institutum Orientalium Studiorum, 1953). Earlier treatments include D.B. MacDonald, "The Development of the Idea of Spirit in Islam," *Acta Orientalia* 9 (1931):307–51; and E.E. Calverley, "Doctrines of the Soul (*Nafs* and *Rūḥ*) in Islam," *Moslem World* 33 (1943):254–65, a revision of Wensinck's article *Nafs* in EI^1 3:827–30.

6 The word for spirit (*rūḥ*) occurs less than two dozen times in the Qur'ān. O'Shaughnessy, lists 20 instances with the Arabic citations and translations: O'Shaughnessy, *The Development of the Meaning of Spirit in the Koran*, 13–5. 'Abd al-Bāqī's *Al-Mu'jam al-Mufahras* (Cairo: Kitāb al-Sha'b, n.d.), 326, gives the same citations, only numbers them as 21 separate references, giving a separate citation to the two occurrences of the word in Q. 17:85.

7 Q. 32, for example, begins with a mention of Muḥammad's prophecy (vv. 1–3). It moves suddenly to creation and the breathing of the spirit into the primordial human (vv. 4–9), and then, in a final sudden shift, to the day of reckoning (vv. 10–1). These are discrete verses, but even here they are brought into close connection. Through intertextual echoes, even verses distant from one another in the Qur'ān are inter-embedded.

8 In the articles cited above (n. 2), I have engaged more specifically the classical *tafsīr* tradition. Among the commentaries consulted, I have found two to be particularly useful: Fakhr al-Dīn al-Rāzī, *Al-Tafsīr al-Kabīr* (Cairo: Iltizām 'Abd al-Raḥmān Muḥammad, n.d.), 32:27–37 and Muḥammad ibn Aḥmad al-Qurṭubī, *Al-Jāmi' li-Aḥkām al-Qur'ān* (Cairo, n.p., 1962), 28:130–8.

9 For the Hindu and Christian tradition, for example, see the study of David Carpenter, *Revelation, History, and the Dialogue of Religions: a study of Bhartrhari and Bonaventure* (Maryknoll, NY: Orbis Books, 1995). For mystical interpretations of the way in which the Qur'ān, the Book of Exodus, and the first verses of the Gospel of John shatter normal structures of language, see M. Sells, *Mystical Languages of Unsaying* (Chicago: University of Chicago Press, 1994). Cf. Bernard McGinn, *The Presence of God: The Foundations of Mysticism* (New York: Crossroad, 1991), especially the chapter on Origen.

10 "Sound, Spirit, and Gender in *Sūrat al-Qadr*," cited above, n. 2.

11 Q. 66:12 offers a more graphic version, we breathed into it (*fīhi*) some of our spirit, the *hi* referring back to the word *farj* (vagina) earlier in the verse where Mary is said to have remained chaste, that is, in the idiom, "guarded her vagina."

12 In Arabic poetry, a final *hā* can also take on this sliding or shifting reference. A classic example is the Mu'allaqa of Labīd, in which the end-rhyme in *hā* sometimes refers to the beloved, Salmā, sometimes to various grammatically feminine objects, sometimes to plurals for groups of wild animals, and finally and very importantly, to an unspecified referent that seems to refer to the entire context. See M. Sells, *Desert Tracings: Six Classic Arabian Odes* (Middletown: Wesleyan University Press, 1989); Labid ibn Rabiah, *The Golden Ode*, translated with an Introduction and Commentary by William R. Polk (Chicago: University of Chicago Press, 1974); Suzanne Stetkevych, *The Mute Immortals Speak* (Ithaca: Cornell University Press, 1993), chapter 1.

13 See Marmaduke Pickthall, *The Meaning of the Glorious Coran*, (Bilingual edition) (Beirut: Dār al-Kitāb al-Lubnānī, 1970), 808.

14 al-Razī, *Al-Tafsīr al-Kabīr* (The Great Commentary) 32:198 is most-matter-of fact in making the substitution: *mā bi-ma'nā man* ("*mā* with the meaning of *man*"). Pickthall renders the last verse as "And by Him who made the male and the female," and translates the *mā* similarly in Q. 95:7 and Q. 91:5. Ahmad Ali translates the verse as "And what He created of the male and female." While grammatically possible, this interpretation not only creates the theological difficulty of a male being creating gender, but must create an antecedent for the subject of *khalaqa* that is not only not in the text, but also seems to go against the oath style. See also *al-Qur'ān: a Contemporary Translation* by Ahmed Ali (Princeton: Princeton University Press, 1988), 539.

15 Pickthall, *The Meaning of the Glorious Coran*, 809.

16 The *mā* also resonates with the "long-*ā*" sound of *unthā*, and the strong end-assonance of *yaghshā* and *tajallā* in the previous verses. This assonance focused on the "long-*ā*" sound is the key feature of the sound figures in the Sūras of Destiny (Q. 97), the Quaking (*al-Zalzala*, Q. 99), and the Calamity (*al-Qāri'a*, Q. 101). We also find in the *wa mā* of *wa mā khalaqa* the *aCā* sequence that was a major sound pattern of the Sūra of Destiny (*salā*, *malā*, and, precisely, *wamā*). In each of the three moments, the semantic, emotive, and acoustic energies fall upon units of sound and meaning that are complex and gender-charged. When it is not dismissed through the substitution of *man* for *mā*, the *mā* in the Sūra of Destiny can be heard in its interplay between animate and inanimate, and relative and interrogative, while its acoustical correspondences with other passages give it the highest emotive charge.

17 In the Sūra of the Dawn (*al-Fajr*, Q. 89), the polarity of day and night is evoked, as in the Sūra of Destiny; and, in both Sūras, that polarity is expressed in verses ending with a difficult rhyme in "r". The Sūra of the Dawn begins:

By the dawn
and ten nights
and the even and the odd
and the night when it is dispelled
is there not in that an oath for one of insight (*ḥijr*)?

(Sūra of the Dawn, Q. 89:1–5)

18 For a study of the *Thamūd* story in the Qur'ān, its Biblical parallels, and its reflection in early Islamic literature, see Jaroslav Stetkevych, *Muḥammad and the Golden Bough: Reconstructing Arabian Myth* (Bloomington: Indiana University Press, 1996).

19 Phyllis Trible's demonstraton of the gender nonspecificity of the Biblical Adam in the first creation account might have some bearing on issues in Qur'ānic interpretation as well. See Phyllis Trible, *God and the Rhetoric of Sexuality* (Philadelphia: Fortress Press, 1978); idem, *Texts of Terror: Literary-Feminist Readings of Biblical Narratives* (Philadelphia: Fortress Press, 1984).

20 The early twentieth-century scholar Richard Bell made the following elliptical comment on the Sūra of Destiny: "In some ways what is here said of it [the night of *qadr*] suggests that some account of the Eve of the Nativity may have given rise to it." Bell does not give his reasons for making such a speculation and Bell's intuition has not been further developed. The above analysis suggests that there is indeed connection between the night of destiny and the Eve of the Nativity. That connection, however, runs counter to the frequent treatment of Qur'ānic themes as borrowings from Biblical traditions. Through aural intertextuality, the Qur'ān seems to have evoked a sound figure for the experience of *bushrā* (bearing of good news) similar to that found in the *xaire kexaromene* (Hail, blessed one) of Luke 1:28. This figure is not announced on the level of surface semantics. It is not "borrowed" from the Biblical text, but it is created throughout the Qur'ān through a distinctive use of language. See Richard Bell, *The Qur'ān, Translated, with a Critical Re-arrangement of the Surahs* (Edinburgh: T. & T. Clark, 1937, 1960), 2:669.

21 The effects of *tajwīd* are not additions to the Qur'ānic text, but are an integral part of the text as it is performed. For a useful summary of the basic rules of *tajwīd,* see Muhammad Surty, *A Course in 'Ilm at-Tajwīd The Science of Reciting the Qur'ān* (Leicester, UK: Islamic Foundation, 1988). Surty's text is accompanied by audio-cassettes demonstrating the rules of recitation.

22 Clearly aural intertexuality cannot be perceived through silent reading of the text, but is heard through its recitation. The availability of the major Qur'ānic reciters on CD and the proliferation of excellent Qur'ān programs on CD-ROM, with written and recited text performed simultaneously, should allow make such features more accessible, especially for classroom purposes. My *Approaching the Qur'ān* (cited above, n. 2) includes a CD with examples of recitation and sound charts of five key texts to accompany the recitations.

Chapter 2

Major Transitions and Thematic Borders in Two Long Sūras: *al-Baqara* and *al-Nisā'*

A.H. Mathias Zahniser

In discussing the Qur'ān as literature, Mustansir Mir argues for "taking the Qur'ān in its finished form as a starting point for literary investigation."[1] Although, as Mir admits, "the Meccan sūras, with their greater narrative and dramatic element, are best suited for such a study,"[2] each of the major literary qualities of the Qur'ān he discusses could be exemplified to some extent from the longer Medinan sūras. Although these qualities could be discussed without reference to the unity and coherence of the sūras in which they are found, any meaningful literary study, as Mir suggests, "assumes that the discourse possesses a certain degree of unity and coherence."[3]

According to most critics, however, the long Medinan sūras exhibit little or no obvious unity and coherence. These sūras present the analyst with a more expository and excursive discourse and feature a greater abundance of parenthetical passages and a looser and more ambiguous structure than their Meccan counterparts.[4] Angelika Neuwirth, also a contributor to our appreciation of the composition of Qur'ānic sūras as coherent units, has described the Medinan "long sūras," such as sūras two (Q. 2, *al-Baqara*) and four (Q. 4, *al-Nisā'*), as lacking any comprehensive compositional schema. They serve, in her words, as "collection baskets for isolated verse groups."[5]

As early as the fourteenth century of our era, Badr al-Dīn Muḥammad al-Zarkashī (1344–1391), recognizing its difficulty, reported that few scholars have taken up the task of discovering the relationship between the verses of these long sūras.[6] And Mir believes that scholars who deny the Qur'ān order and coherence do so, not out of firm conviction, but out of only partial success at discovering that order and coherence.[7]

In his contribution to an anthology identifying current ways scholars approach the Qur'ān, Mir discusses six twentieth-century interpreters who view the Qur'ānic sūras as unified discourse. "If so many Qur'ān exegetes, belonging to different parts of the Muslim world, hold the view that the quranic *sūras* are unities, and then apply this understanding to the Qur'ān," he concludes, "it would be reasonable to infer that the view has taken root. It is remarkable that there is hardly any evidence that, in holding this view, some of the exegetes have been influenced by others."[8]

An experienced trial lawyer once told me that, in interpreting the testimonies of trial witnesses, he always assumes they are telling the truth – even when the information they contribute to the proceedings appears contradictory. More often than not, according to him, the situation is clarified as a result of struggling to discover how two conflicting testimonies could both be true. It is my conviction that it is the same with the interpretation of the long sūras of the Qur'ān. Though the order and coherence of these "collection baskets" may be difficult to identify, being convinced of its presence and pursuing it diligently will in the end bear fruit.

Three scholars writing in English: Mustansir Mir, representing the work of the contemporary Pakistani Qur'ān interpreter Amīn Aḥsan al-Iṣlāḥī,[9] Neal Robinson,[10] and I,[11] have attempted to demonstrate the unity and coherence for at least one Medinan long sūra.

DEMONSTRATING THE UNITY AND COHERENCE OF MEDINAN LONG SŪRAS

In several publications, Mustansir Mir provides windows into the work of Iṣlāḥī.[12] His book *Coherence in the Qur'ān* represents, as indicated by its subtitle, a study of Iṣlāḥī's concept of coherence or *naẓm* .[13] Mir's chapter in the volume *Approaches to the Qur'ān*, "The *Sūra* as a Unity," surveying the work of twentieth-century exegetes who treat sūras as unities, culminates in a description of Iṣlāḥī's work.[14] In each of these two publications, Mir has laid out in summary form Iṣlāḥī's method and his analysis of a Medinan sūra. By careful and repeated reading, Iṣlāḥī is able to discern a sūra's compositional units and the breaks between them. He then discerns, on the basis of the thematic content of its units, a sūra's core theme. This core Iṣlāḥī calls the sūra's *'amūd* ("pillar" or "hub"). The *'amūd* unites the diverse sections of the sūra, revealing its compositional unity.[15] Mir believes it is precisely Iṣlāḥī's search for thematic links between the various parts of a sūra that enables him to discover the compositional unity prevailing in it.[16] Iṣlāḥī tries to include within a section as many verses as can possibly be understood to participate in a common idea. He tends to locate the transition between sections only where there is a clear break in the thematic continuity.[17]

In *Coherence in the Qur'ān*, Mir summarizes the structure of Q. 4. In his chapter "The Sūra as a Unity" he has done the same for Q. 2. Very briefly, he structures Q. 2, the longest sūra of the Qur'ān, as follows:

§1 Introduction	vv. 1–39
§2 Address to the Israelites	vv. 40–121
§3 The Abrahamic Legacy	vv. 122–162
§4 The Sharī'a or Law	vv. 163–242
§5 Liberation of the Ka'ba	vv. 243–283
§6 Conclusion	vv. 284–286

Although Mir does not precisely state the core theme or *'amūd* of Q. 2, it is clearly something like "preparation for liberating the Ka'ba."[18] Iṣlāḥī divides Q. 4 into three main sections:

§1 Social Reform	vv. 1–43
§2 The Islamic Community and Its Opponents	vv. 44–126
§3 Conclusion	vv. 127–176

The *'amūd* unifying these parts is "factors that make for cohesion in a Muslim society."[19] The reforms laid out in §1 give rise to the opposition dealt with in §2 against a backdrop of the necessity of communal solidarity. Section 3 rounds off the sūra by answering questions, amplifying what has already been said, issuing a final warning, and consoling the Messenger.[20]

In a recent book, *Discovering the Qur'ān: A Contemporary Approach to a Veiled Text,*[21] Neal Robinson describes the salient features of the Medinan sūras, demonstrating these features by laying out the content and structure of Q. 2 in some detail. Although he is influenced by Iṣlāḥī and draws from his results, Robinson goes beyond a thematic analysis, giving considerable attention to such formal criteria as verse and verse-group types (for example, polemic, eschatology, narrative, and signs); position of verses in a sūra; repetition – especially of stock phrases; comparison and contrast; and rhyme clauses containing attributes of God. For example, these latter are not always simply refrains required by the rhyme pattern, but can also mark the end of a sūra's subsection, ground a statement in the divine nature, protect the hearer from misunderstanding, or contribute to the cohesion of a sūra or one of its parts. Rare rhyme clauses may even occur in a sūra to indicate a relationship between two or more of its thematic units.[22] This line of investigation proves fruitful.

By means of a painstaking analysis, Robinson finds – along with Iṣlāḥī – six sections in Q. 2. These sections are unified under the theme of creating a Muslim community in the light of the change in the direction of prayer from Jerusalem to Mecca.[23] Topics in §1 (vv. 1–39), his "prologue," include revelation, belief and unbelief, and the story of Adam.[24] In §2 (vv. 40–121), often by means of "the metaphor of the bad business transaction,"[25] Jews and Christians of Arabia come under criticism. A prominent feature of §2 is a collection of brief narratives about the Children of Israel under the leadership of Moses. The next of the six major sections of the sūra (§3) (vv. 122–152) represents a summons to the Children of Israel to unite with the Muslim community around Abraham, the two communities' common ancestor. In §3, the Ka'ba plays an important role, along with the change of *qibla*. The fourth and longest division of the sūra (§4) provides legislation for the newly constituted "middle nation" (v. 143) of Islam. According to Robinson, §4 extends from v. 153 through v. 242. Here he differs from Iṣlāḥī who would begin §4 at v. 163. The penultimate section of Q. 2 (§5) (vv. 243–283) deals with the process required to liberate the Ka'ba as a ritual center for the new community. Finally, the sūra ends with an epilogue (§6) (vv. 284–286).

My analysis of Q. 4 was completed before I had any contact with Iṣlāḥī's work on it.[26] I also found that identifying blocks of verses according to theme yielded the best understanding of the sūra's structure. I identified these thematic units by keywords.[27] For example, I identified a "battle block" made up of vv. 71–104 as a basic unit of Q. 4, based on keywords for fighting in vv. 71–93 and other terms associated with fighting in the cause of God in vv. 94–104. This theme does not occur in any other part of the sūra. Like Robinson, I also considered more formal criteria such as formulas of address and repeated verses. My divisions turned out to be similar to those of Iṣlāḥī, with the major exception that I found two additional major breaks in the discourse as a result of identifying the battle block mentioned above. I did not try to discover an *'amūd* or central core idea around which the various parts of the sūra can be understood to cluster. But I did find meaning in the sūra's overall structure. The biggest problem I faced was deciding on the exact borders of thematic units.

DISCERNING THEMATIC UNIT BORDERS

I offer this study of the transitions in sūras two and four to help readers of the Qur'ān's long sūras discern the borders between thematic units.

The common ground for Iṣlāḥī, Robinson, and me has been the conviction that long sūras possess overall unity and meaningful coherence. For the two longest sūras of the Qur'ān, we have a summary of Iṣlāḥī's conclusions about their structure and core theme. In addition, for Q. 2 we have the analysis of Robinson, and for Q. 4 my analysis. Robinson and Iṣlāḥī agree on four of the five points of transition between the major sections of Q. 2. Robinson places the end of §3 at v. 152, while Iṣlāḥī extends the section through v. 162. Iṣlāḥī and I agree on locating major divisions for Q. 4 between vv. 43 and 44 and between vv. 126 and 127.[28] This makes six long-sūra transitions between major thematic units agreed upon by two interpreters. In addition, the point of transition between §3 and §4 of Q. 2 disputed by Iṣlāḥī and Robinson offers an example of the ambiguities of Qur'ānic transitions. Finally, since Mir suggests that Iṣlāḥī might just as well have made the second of his main caesuras for Q. 4 between vv. 134 and 135 rather than between vv. 126 and 127,[29] we can examine a second disputed transition. In this chapter, therefore, the following transitions between major thematic units of the longest two sūras of the Qur'ān will be examined: Q. 2 vv. 39/40, 121/122, 152/153 (162/163), and 242/243; Q. 4 vv. 43/44, and 126/127 (135/136). The transition at Q. 2 vv. 283/284 will be treated briefly with Q. 2 vv. 121/122.

The conclusions presented here must be used heuristically for three reasons: (1) the results are based on the work of only three interpreters and focused on only six transitions; (2) I am proceeding on the *assumption* of the unity and coherence of the discourse under discussion; I do not interact systematically with the arguments and evidence for its lack of unity and coherence; and (3) the procedures I am using for analysis are recursive, that is, capable of yielding different valid results for different analysts.

FORMULAS OF ADDRESS

The first transition between major sections of Q. 2 (vv. 39 and 40) is one of the simplest and most obvious kinds of transition found among the long sūras. First of all, §2 (vv. 40–152/162) begins with a formula of address: "O Children of Israel" (*yā banī isrā'īl*).[30] Although obvious attention-getting caesuras such as this do not always indicate a major division in Qur'ānic discourse, they often do. Of the five major transitions in Q. 2 as analyzed by Robinson, three begin with formulas of address: §2 and §3 begin with "O Children of Israel" and §4, according to Robinson, (vv. 153–243) opens with the formula "O ye who have believed" (*yā ayyuhā lladhīna āmanū*). The formulaic question, "Hast thou not considered?" (*a-lam tara*) opens §5 (vv. 243–283) and is repeated in v. 246. Even §6, the epilogue, starts with an oft-repeated formula or refrain, "To God belongs what is in the heavens and what is on the earth" (*li 'llāhi mā fi 's-samāwāti wa mā fi 'l-arḍ*) (v. 284).

In two other long sūras I have examined, some sections begin with formulas of address. Q. 3 (*Āl 'Imrān*) has four main sections: §1, a prologue (vv. 1–18); §2, a long section, including a narrative addressing primarily People of the Book (vv. 19–101); §3, a long section addressing primarily the Believers (vv. 102–189); and §4 an epilogue (vv. 190–200). Only §3 in which the primary addressees are the Believers begins with a formula: "O ye who have believed" (v. 102). The formula appears in v. 100 and is repeated three more times throughout §3 (vv. 118, 130, and 156).[31]

Only §1 of Q. 4, according to Iṣlāḥī's analysis, begins with a formula of address, the familiar, "O humankind" (*yā ayyuhā 'n-nās*) (v. 1).[32] His §2 begins with a frequently occurring refrain mentioned above in connection with Q. 2: "Hast thou not considered?" (v. 44).[33] V. 71 begins with "O ye who have believed." While for Iṣlāḥī this formula begins a rather brief subsection (vv. 71–76) of his §2, according to my analysis, it marks the beginning of a major section of the sūra (vv. 71–104), focusing on the topic of fighting in the way of God.[34]

Care must be exercised in identifying formulas of address with the beginnings of major sections of a long sūra. Excluding the formula "Hast thou not considered?" (vv. 243, 246, and 258), sixteen verses in Q. 2 begin with formulas of address (vv. 21, 40, 47, 104, 122, 153, 168, 172, 178, 183, 208, 254, 264, 267, 278, and 282). Only three of these begin major sections of the sūra in Robinson's analysis, but two in that of Iṣlāḥī. In Q. 4, exclusive of "Hast thou not considered?" (vv. 44, 49, 51, 60, and 77), of fourteen verses with formulas of address (vv. 1, 19, 29, 43, 47, 59, 71, 94, 135, 136, 144, 170, 171, and 174), only two (vv. 1, 71) begin main sections in my analysis and only one (v. 1) in that of Iṣlāḥī.[35] Obviously other factors must be considered in addition to formulas of address in determining transitions between units of discourse in the long sūras.[36]

Nevertheless, these formulas do represent interruptions in the flow of the discourse and can help in discerning transitions between major units. In addition to careful attention to formulas of address, one must look for evidence of sizable thematic units on either side of the formula. V. 40 represents the first time the Children of Israel have been addressed in Q. 2. And they turn out to be the major implied receptors,[37] other than the Prophet himself, from v. 40 until at least v. 104. By means of the formula of address, "O ye who have believed," at v. 104, the believing Muslims become the implied receptors until at least v. 109. From v. 110 through v. 118, it is unclear whether the primary implied receptors are the Muslims or their Prophet, but he is clearly the primary implied receptor in vv. 119 and 120. At any rate, §2 (vv. 40–121) is clearly united under the theme of the Children of Israel, vv. 40–103 speaking primarily *to* them and vv. 104 through 121 speaking primarily *about* them. In fact, from this first transition point throughout the first half of the sūra, the Children of Israel specifically, or the People of the Book in general, provide referential coherence for the discourse.

Looking at §1, we find a solid coherent span of dialogical narrative from v. 30 through v. 39. This cluster of narratives involves the topic of Adam, the father of humankind and first prophet. It climaxes the first thirty nine verses of the sūra, verses dealing with humankind in general, especially the Prophet's challengers. This broad category of receptors of the message is referred to as *al-nās* or "humankind."[38] Adam stories seem thematically appropriate for a section focusing on humankind in general. Moses stories (vv. 47–74) occur in §2 where the Children of Israel are urged to remember the grace of God in their history. Abraham stories (vv. 124–133) adorn §3 which accents the common ground between People of the Book and the Muslim community. The location of these Adam, Moses, and Abraham stories supports the divisions both Robinson and Iṣlāḥī propose for the first three parts of Q. 2.

In short, this transition takes the receptor from the first main section of the sūra to the second by means of a clearly defined thematic unit climaxing §1 and a formula of address introducing the theme of §2. Interestingly enough, this same formula of address begins §3. We now turn to that transition – also a transition agreed upon by Robinson and Iṣlāḥī.

INCLUSIO AND WRAP-UP UNITS

One feature of the transition at vv. 121/122 in Q. 2, its formula of address, "O Children of Israel," has already been discussed in treating the preceding section. The fact, however, that the same formula of address begins both sections suggests a question: In so far as the two formulas form an *inclusio* for §2, why not consider the closely related vv. 122 and 123 the final verse group of §2? Answering this question will help us understand the nature of some Qur'ānic transitions.

For one thing, unlike the transition at vv. 39/40, these transitions are preceded by a common feature of Qur'ānic transitions I call *wrap-up* units. They function at the verse-group level the way a rhyme clause functions for many verses. Wrap-up units reinforce the content of the passages they cap off, act as motivational support for them, or reinforce the worldview of the Qur'ān in general.[39] Note that v. 119 begins with the attention-getting element *inna* not preceded by a conjunction. It begins by confirmation of the Messenger's mission; it comforts him in the face of the challenge of the People of the Book; and it ends with a typical positive/negative verse: "Those to whom we have given the Book and who recite it as it should be recited – they believe in it; those who disbelieve in it – they are the losers" (v. 121).

The last transition in Q. 2 (vv. 283/284) is a simple one with a wrap-up unit and so can be discussed briefly here. It occurs just three verses short of the sūra's end, forming a conclusion or epilogue. Syntactically unconnected with the verse preceding it, v. 284 begins with a refrain that has occurred before in Q. 2 and occurs frequently and at important places in other long sūras: "To Allah belongeth what is in the heavens, and what is in the earth" (*li 'llāhi mā fī 's-samāwāti wa mā fī 'l-arḍ*). The verse of this "sovereignty refrain" goes on to the topic of "hiding and concealing" also found at other points in the sūra. The theme is related to the last verse of the previous section where the faithful are enjoined not to hide testimony in cases of recording debts on a journey, reminding them – based on what was stressed in the rhyme clauses of vv. 282 and 283 – that God knows everything, keeps accounts of their deeds, and will forgive or punish according to His own will. Its rhyme clause seems appropriate: "Allah over everything hath power" (*wa 'llāhu 'alā kulli shay'in qadīr*) (v. 284).[40]

In other words, what is developing in the epilogue of the sūra is a wrap-up unit for both the final section of the sūra and for the entire sūra. V. 285 combines the themes of the content of the faith and obedience to the Messenger by identifying the content of the Messenger's faith and then quoting the Believers, "We hear and obey. . . ." After a brief statement, also common in the Qur'ān as follow-up for a series of laws and divine punishment, that God's requirements are tailored to a person's capacity, the sūra ends with a model prayer, suggesting the proper response of faith to divine revelation and stipulation. The prayer ends with this petition: "Pardon us and forgive us, and have mercy upon us; Thou art our patron (*mawlānā*), so help us against the people of unbelievers" (*al-qawmi 'l-kāfirīn*). Thus the epilogue ends on a topic central to the purposes of the sūra, according to Iṣlāḥī and Robinson: the struggle to liberate the Ka'ba from its control by "those who stand against faith."[41] Other examples of transitions in sūras two and four preceded by wrap-up units include Q. 2 vv. 152/153, 162/163, 242/243 and Q. 4 vv. 42/43. For sūras three and five, several occur: Q. 3 vv. 32/33 and 64/65; Q. 5 vv. 40/41, and 86/87.

Another factor arguing for placing a major thematic border between vv. 121 and 122 – in spite of the possible *inclusio* formed by vv. 40 and 122–123 – is the clear connection between vv. 122–123 and the verses following them.[42] The narrative passages focused on Abraham immediately follow. Given what they have already encountered in the previous section, receptors of the sūra will connect the Abraham experiences with the goodness or grace of God which the Children of Israel are commanded to remember in v. 122. This Abraham topic takes the discourse beyond the narratives to v. 141, at which point only one more verse group remains (vv. 142–152) – a thematic unit of obvious coherence – in §2, according to Robinson's analysis. Add to this the interesting correspondence between the theme of each of the first three sections of the sūra and the narratives featured in each, and a section division at vv. 121/122 seems certain.

This does not mean, however, that v. 122 cannot function with v. 40 as an *inclusio* for §2 and at the same time help effect a caesura between it and §3. The three-fold repetition of this formula at the beginning of vv. 40, 47, and 122 is an instance of a fairly common structure of formulas and refrains, especially in shorter passages. The structure can be represented with the following figure: FaFa–aF[a]. *F* stands for a formula or refrain, *a* indicates a short span of a given topic or theme, and *a* – *a* represents a longer span of the same theme, sometimes spilling over the formula. In this way the formula or refrain can provide borders for a thematic unit. Some examples include Q. 3 vv. 8, 9, and 16; Q. 4 vv. 135, 136, and 144; Q. 5 vv. 7, 11, and 20; and – a case in reverse (Fa–aFaF) – Q. 4 vv. 126, 131, and 132.[43]

This brings us to the place in the sūra where Iṣlāḥī and Robinson differ as to the point of transition. Robinson begins §4 with the now familiar formula of address in v. 153: "O ye who have believed." Iṣlāḥī carries his §3 beyond this point to v. 162, beginning his §4 with the creedal verse: "And your God is one God; there is no god but He, the Merciful, the Compassionate" (v. 163).[44] According to H. Van Dyke Parunak, a student of transitional techniques in the Bible, "Disagreement on where verses belong is often a sign that they are transitional."[45] Possibly Iṣlāḥī and Robinson disagree on the break between sections three and four of Q. 2 because the disputed territory is itself a transition.

A TRANSITIONAL HINGE

Like vv. 39/40 of Q. 2, the transition at vv. 152/153 features a formula of address following immediately upon the end of a clearly defined, unified, and coherent thematic unit (vv. 142–152). This unit finishes up §3 by responding to the question of some "stupid people" (*as-sufahā'u mina 'n-nās*), "What has turned them from the *qibla* they have been observing?" (v. 142). This topic moves toward the legislation of §4 of the sūra which will deal again with the *qibla* in v. 177. Thus, it would be logical to start the second main section as Robinson does with v. 153, especially since Believers are there addressed with the formula: "O ye who have believed." This formula, repeated nine times in §4 and §5, contributes to the referential coherence of the remainder of the sūra.

On the other hand, this formula of address can certainly not of itself indicate a new main section – after all, out of sixteen formulas of address in the sūra, as mentioned above, only three begin sections agreed on by Robinson and Iṣlāḥī as being main divisions. In fact, neither Robinson nor Iṣlāḥī appears to give much attention to formulas of address as indicators of thematic unit boundaries in their analyses. Both, however, register some sense of the importance of attention to receptors of the discourse.[46]

Iṣlāḥī, in fact, does not begin his section on legislation for a new community of faith at v. 153. Rather, he begins it with v. 163, "And your God is one God; there is no god but He, the Merciful, the Compassionate." Iṣlāḥī begins here, at least in part, because communal legislation – characteristic of the remainder of the sūra – must begin with the singularity, sovereignty, and omnipotence of God.[47] This verse is appropriately followed by a hymnic passage about God's generous gift of life and its sustenance through the bounty of the created things of heaven and earth (v. 164). Focus on the world as God's creation leads naturally to a critique of idolatry (vv. 165–167), followed by a kind of legislation opening with a formula of address, "O humankind, eat of what is in the earth as lawful and good" (v. 168). Before the reintroduction of the formula of address, "O ye who have believed" (v. 172), introducing legislation for the believers about dietary permissions and restrictions, this passage closes in controversy with unbelievers, quite likely from among "the people," over the revelation of God and the traditions of their fathers (vv. 169–171).[48]

Thus, before Robinson's point of division we have a clearly defined thematic unit (vv. 142–152) and after that of Iṣlāḥī we have a clearly defined thematic unit (vv. 164–171). The earlier unit commands the faithful to pray toward the Sacred Mosque and the later one featuring the oneness of God permits the eating of all permitted and good food (v. 168).[49] The one begins in controversy with "the people": "The stupids among the people will say..." (v. 142). The other ends in controversy with unbelievers who very well could be the people as well: "When one says to them, 'Follow what Allah hath sent down,' they say: 'Nay, we will follow what we found our fathers doing'" (v. 170). We must now look at the verses between v. 152, the place where Robinson would end §3, and v. 163, the place where Iṣlāḥī would begin §4.

First, vv. 153–157 do not contain legislation typical of §4. Rather, they consist of an appeal related to the content of §5, dealing with the liberation of the Ka'ba (vv. 243–283, especially vv. 243–252).[50]

153a O ye who have believed, seek help in patience and the Prayer;
b verily Allah is with those who patiently endure.[51]
154a Say not of those who may be killed in the way of Allah, "Dead";
b nay, (they are) alive, only ye are not aware.
155a We shall surely try you with some experience of fear and hunger
b and defect of property and persons and fruits;
c so give (thou) good tidings to those who patiently endure.
156a Who when misfortune falls upon them
b say: "Verily we are Allah's, and to Him do we return."
157a Upon such are blessings and mercy from their Lord;
b such are the (rightly) guided.[52]

Second, according to Robinson, even though it has thematic connections with v. 125 through rituals linked to the Ka'ba, "the relationship of v. 158 to the five āyahs which precede it and the four which follow it is not immediately obvious."[53] He resolves the issue by suggesting a setting in the life of the Qur'ānic community in which vv. 153–162 might appropriately fit with v. 158 and the verses following it. I have no quarrel with such a setting for these verses. Rather, I have another interest – an interest in the role of v. 158 within vv. 153–162. The topic of this verse, isolated from its immediate context, is Ṣafā and Marwa, sites in Mecca associated with the Ka'ba and the Pilgrimage. Thematically, it offers permission for Muslim pilgrims to participate in the ritual activities connected with them.

158a Ṣafā and Marwa are amongst the manifestations of Allah;
b so if anyone performs the pilgrimage to the House or the *'umra,*
c it is no fault in him
d that he makes the circuit of them;
e if one does good spontaneously,
f Allah is Grateful, Knowing.[54]

The verse does connect, indirectly however, with subsection vv. 142–152 which, as we have seen, is governed by the topic of the *qibla* (v. 142) and the theme expressed in the question, "What has turned them from the *qibla* which they have been observing?" Within that section, "the Sacred Mosque" (*al-masjid al-ḥarām*) as the focus of prayer or *qibla* is mentioned three times in almost identical words (vv. 144, 149, and 150). V. 158 is connected with the *qibla* and the *masjid al-ḥarām* by the obvious fact that the *bayt* or "House" mentioned in it and to which one is to make *ḥajj* or "Pilgrimage" is the Sacred Mosque; and the rites associated with Ṣafā and Marwa and enjoined in v. 158 are performed during the Pilgrimage, a significant part of which centers on the Ka'ba. Finally, both vv. 142–152 and v. 158 end on a note of thankfulness: "So remember Me and I shall remember you; show *thankfulness* to Me and do not act ungratefully towards Me" (*wa 'shkurū lī wa lā takfurūni*) (v. 152); "If one does good spontaneously, Allah is *Thankful*, Knowing" (*shākirun 'alīm*) (v. 158).[55] Nevertheless, in no other place in the sūra are Ṣafā and Marwa mentioned, and thus the reader or reciter of the Qur'ān notes the way v. 158 is isolated from the verses immediately preceding and following it. By virtue of its focus on Ṣafā and Marwa, the verse looks forward to the liberation-of-the-Ka'ba theme of the second half of the sūra. Iṣlāḥī defines §5 of the sūra by means of this topic, in all likelihood because the section begins with the most thorough passage devoted to the topic (vv. 243–252) and because the rest of §5 flows out of this beginning thematic unit and is related to it in some way. The theme also occurs in §4 (vv. 177, 190–195, and 216–219).

Third, a number of interesting phenomena show up in the passage between vv. 158 and 163 linking it to the first half of the sūra. For one thing, "those who conceal revelation" is the topic of these verses. This would seem to indicate that the section refers to the Children of Israel or the People of the Book, the topic of §2 and a prominent theme of §3. The same word for concealing occurs in the rhyme clause of v. 33 where, after teaching the names of things to Adam, God announces to the angels, "I know what ye reveal and what ye have been concealing" (*taktumūn*). In v. 42, God charges the Children of Israel not to "conceal (*wa-[lā] taktumū*) the truth knowingly"; and a party of those who have been given the scripture are charged with knowingly concealing the truth in v. 146 (*yaktumūna 'l-ḥaqqa wa-hum ya'lamūn*). The same subject also turns up as the topic of vv. 174–176: "Those who conceal (*yaktumūna*) what of the Book Allah hath sent down," the theme of which is the severe punishment awaiting those who conceal what God has revealed. In spite of this one reference in §4, the theme of concealing the truth, as it comes to the receptor, serves to link the passage immediately after v. 158 with a topic of the first half of the sūra.[56]

In addition, the form of the divine address in the final colon of v. 160 represents a link with another feature of the first half of the sūra. Even though vv. 159–162 start with divine self-reference in the plural, "what We have sent down" (*mā anzalnā*) (v. 159), in the rhyme clause of v. 160, God speaks in the first-person singular: "I am the Relentant, the Compassionate" (*wa anā 't-tawwābu 'r-raḥīm*). In fact, if we were to follow Iṣlāḥī's analysis, v. 160 would be the final instance in a series of first-person singular divine references in the first half of the sūra. The Adam narratives in vv. 30–39 feature a drama in which participants speak in their own voices. In these verses, as a participant, God speaks to the angels, to Adam, and to humans in general in the first person. But God, as the narrator of the drama, uses the first-person plural for self-reference. Following immediately in vv. 40 and 41, the Children of Israel are addressed by God in the first person on the basis of a graced covenantal relationship: "O Children of Israel, remember My grace[57] which I have graced you with; fulfill My covenant and I shall fulfill your covenant; so to Me give reverence." Vv. 47 and 122 are almost identical. They say in part: "I gave you preference over all creation."[58] The one verse outside Q. 2 beginning "O Children of Israel" (Q. 20:80) does not feature first-person singular divine voice.[59]

At the end of §3, according to Robinson's structure, the first-person singular divine address is used again, this time in relation to the Muslim community: "Fear them not [that is, the people who have done wrong] but fear Me (*wa 'khshawnī*); and in order that I may perfect My favour (*ni'matī*), upon you and mayhap ye will be guided" (v. 150b); "So remember ye Me and I will remember you; show thankfulness to Me and do not act ungratefully towards Me" (*fa 'dhkurūnī adhkurkum wa 'shkurū lī wa lā takfurūni*) (v. 152). Robinson sees this first-person divine voice as significant: "In constituting the Muslims a 'middle nation', God was giving them the same status as that previously enjoyed by the Children of Israel. This is implied by His intimate use of the first-person singular 'I' when addressing them; the reference to His 'favour' towards them; and the injunction to 'remember' Him."[60] In the verses between vv. 152 and 160, references to God are confined to the third-person singular.

The sūra contains one more of these intimate passages. In one short verse in the midst of a legal portion of the sūra offering guidance about fasting (v. 186), God speaks to the Messenger personally in the first-person singular: "When My servants ask thee about Me, lo, I am near to answer the call of the caller when he calls upon Me; so let them respond to Me and believe in Me; mayhap they will go straight."[61] The first instance of intimate divine first-person singular discourse occurs in connection with Adam in the introductory portion of the sūra. In the last occurrence, the intimate form is used for communication with the Messenger. The others fall within §2 and §3. The second section, itself described by Robinson as an address to the Children of Israel, begins with the formula "O Children of Israel" (v. 40), a formula repeated in v. 47. The formula also begins §3. All three of these instances of the formula are accompanied by intimate, first-person singular discourse from God.

Since vv. 153–157 point toward the second half of the sūra and vv. 159–162 point back to the first half of the sūra, we could very well be exploring what Parunak calls an *inverted hinge.*[62] Parunak shows how a link or transition between major spans of discourse can be effected by a smaller middle or *hinge* span. According to his analysis, span A (in this case Q. 2 §3) is followed by the linking panel or hinge (in this case vv. 153–162) to which it contributes something like itself (in this case vv. 158–160). The linking panel is then followed by panel B (in this case §4) which contributes something like itself to the linking panel (in this case vv. 153–157). Parunak expresses the structure of an inverted hinge thus: A/ba/B.[63] One key feature of a true hinge, according to Parunak, is the presence of a clear caesura between the hinge and its surrounding blocks of discourse. The fact that Robinson puts a major caesura between vv. 152 and 153 and Iṣlāḥī places one between vv. 162 and 163 provides evidence for a significant caesura on each side of the hinge.

In summary, vv. 153–157 thematically refer forward to §4 and §5 of Q. 2, and vv. 159–162 refer back thematically to its §2 and §3. The references to the pilgrimage to the House and the two ritual sites, Ṣafā and Marwa, connected with it in v. 158 point both forward and backward. They point back to verses 142–152 by means of their connection with the *qibla.* They point forward because it is precisely Mecca as a ritual center for the new faith that the struggle, thematic in the remaining sections of the sūra, aims to liberate. It looks as though we have detected a hinge of transition in the territory disputed by the two interpreters Iṣlāḥī and Robinson. We also note with Robinson, however, the thematically isolated character of verse 158 – in spite of its connections with both halves of the sūra. Is there anything further we can say about this verse? Looking at the transitions between §4 and §5 of Q. 2 and that in Q. 4 between §1 and §2 will provide a clue.

CONCATENATION AND ISOLATED VERSES

Since the formula, "Hast thou not considered?" (*a-lam tara*) makes a clear syntactic break in the discourse at v. 243 and since the topic of the discourse clearly changes from issues involving women, particularly divorce (vv. 222–241), to fighting in the way of God, Robinson and Iṣlāḥī appropriately consider this caesura the point of transition between §4 and §5 of Q. 2. v. 242, the last one in §4, though brief, exhibits a typical wrap-up topic, namely, confirmation of revelation: "Thus doth Allah make clear to you His signs, mayhap ye will understand." Major sections of Qur'ānic discourse sometimes end on this note.[64]

This transition would be a simple one similar to the one between §5 and §6 of the same sūra if it were not for the presence just before the end of §4 of a curious two-verse parenthetical passage (vv. 238 and 239):

238a Remember the prayers, the middle Prayer included,
b and stand (in worship) to Allah reverently.
239a If ye fear (danger), pray either on foot or mounted,
b then, when ye are in security, remember Allah
c according as He hath taught you what ye did not use to know.[65]

The verses following these two (vv. 240 and 241) cohere thematically with the broad theme of the span beginning at v. 222 in that they deal with the maintenance of widows and divorced wives. The final wrap-up unit of the section is mentioned above. These parenthetical verses command the maintenance of prayer. Although Robinson can relate them to the exhortation to prayer and patience at the outset of §4 as he defines it (a further bit of evidence for his analysis),[66] they are truly isolated from their *immediate* context. In fact, the circumstance or condition in v. 239 fits the governing topic of §5, fighting in the way of God (vv. 243–260):[67] "If ye fear (danger), pray either on foot or mounted."[68] This foreshadowing represents a typical feature of Qur'ānic discourse recognized by all of the analysts upon whose work this chapter depends. Robinson considers it "a common feature of Qur'anic style for a subject to be introduced briefly and then amplified at a later point."[69] Iṣlāḥī's analytic method involves recognizing a germ idea in one span of discourse that foreshadows the main idea in a subsequent span, "a characteristic feature of Madīnan sūrahs."[70] This feature is certainly a form of concatenation, a characteristic transitional device of all oral discourse.[71] Speakers may anticipate an approaching section of their discourse by advancing a thematic element from that next section. They may also include an element from the previous section in the early part of the section they have moved into.[72] Concatenation sometimes indicates a transition from one main sūra section to another. But what of the fact that we have found an isolated verse contributing to the transition between sections 3 and 4 and between sections 4 and 5 of Q. 2? And what about the fact that some kind of ritual activity turns out to be the topic of both v. 158 and vv. 238–239? The transition between §1 and §2 of Q. 4 contributes to a tentative answer to both questions.

Like the last half of Q. 2, §1 of Q. 4 (vv. 1–43) provides legislative guidance for the Muslim community. It deals with women and related concerns: orphans, marriage, dowry, inheritance, sexual offenses, concubines, and other relations between men and women. At the beginning of v. 36, with the exhortation, "Serve Allah, and do not associate anything with Him," a transition is begun to the content of §2 (vv. 44–126) where the focus at its beginning and at its end is upon idolatry. V. 48 warns the People of the Book, "Allah will not forgive the association of anything with Himself, though He forgives anything short of that to whom He willeth; he who associates anything with Allah has strayed into error far."[73] Further on, a virtually identical v. 116 presents the same warning to unbelievers. In v. 36, five parallel imperatives follow in rapid succession the command to serve God and to shun association. They all deal with matters related to the topic of §1. The final colon of v. 36 grounds the set of exhortations in the nature of God: "And verily Allah loveth not any crafty boaster."[74] In doing so, it has two movements: it forms an *inclusio* with the focus on God in the first colon of the verse; and it makes a transition to the subject of God, the topic of the last subsection (vv. 37 [36g]–42) of §1. This final subsection, like the final colon of v. 36, grounds the legislation of §1 in God's nature: God responds to niggardliness with punishment and humiliation (v. 37); of ostentation and the unbelief accompanying it God is fully aware (vv. 38–39). This concept of God's awareness leads to an exposition on God's nature and relation to His Messenger that ends with the claim that "those who disbelieve and oppose the messenger ... from God will not be able to conceal anything" (v. 42). Thus we have a wrap-up unit similar to the one identified above at Q. 2 vv. 121/122. But following the wrap-up unit, this verse occurs:

43a O ye who have believed,
b come not nigh the Prayer when ye are intoxicated,
c until ye know what ye say;
d nor (when ye are) polluted,
e unless ye be travelers on the road, until ye wash yourselves –
f if ye be sick, or on a journey,
g or if one of you come from the privy,
h or if ye have touched women,
i and do not find water,
j sand yourselves with dry good (sand),
k and rub your faces and your hands;
l verily Allah hath become disposed to overlook and forgive.[75]

This verse makes a significant break in the discourse with its address, "O ye who have believed," and radical change of topic to prayer, mentioned in the second colon. It will be noted that the word *women* does occur in it. I included it therefore, as does Iṣlāḥī,[76] with the section on women, even though it has a topic all its own (v. 43b). In this regard, it is the opposite of Q. 2 vv. 238–239, since these verses point forward toward the next topic of discourse. As mentioned above, concatenation, as a transition device of oral discourse, may consist of an item anticipating an approaching section or consist of an item related to a previous section. In the case of Q. 4 v. 43, though it is too isolated from the section immediately following it to be a part of that section, the inclusion of a lexical link with the preceding section gives it the transitional force of concatenation like that of Q. 2 vv. 238–239. The topic of the two transition devices are also the same: prayer.

The theme of v. 43 is "things that make prayer invalid or difficult" such as intoxication, pollution, sickness, travel, or the absence of water. The verse following v. 43, beginning with a familiar formula, changes the topic again, "Hast thou not seen those to whom a portion of the Book has been given buying error and wishing that ye would err as regards the way?" (v. 44). The People of the Book become the topic around which the first part of Iṣlāḥī's §2 (vv. 44–126) is configured.

Apparently, isolated verses assist receptors of Qur'ānic oral discourse in recognizing a significant change in the topic of the discourse. If this judgment is correct in the cases of Q. 2 vv. 238–239 and Q. 4 v. 43, then it may also be the case in Q. 2 v. 158. If so, then we have in the middle of Q. 2 an elaborate transition indeed. V. 158, like these other two sets of isolated verses, deals with a set of guidelines for a ritual activity, changes the subject rather abruptly, and has some links with an adjacent section of discourse. V. 239 links to §5 of Q. 2, as stated above, only through indicating extenuating circumstances relaxing the requirements of prayer which the receptor would naturally connect with fighting in God's way, a major topic in that section. V. 43 of Q. 4 casts its shadow behind into §1 merely by the mention of women. V. 158 features references to ritual activity connected with the Ka'ba and Pilgrimage relevant to both §3 and §4 of Q. 2 and contains a lexical link with v. 152 of §3 through its ascription of gratefulness to God.

If the span of discourse composed of vv. 153–162 consists of an inverted hinge, as indicated earlier, and an isolated verse similar to Q. 2 vv. 238–239 and Q. 4 v. 43, it represents an elaborate transition device between §3 and §4 of Q. 2. With such an elaborate transition at its center, Q. 2 might be suspected of falling into essentially two major sections divided by the transition passage. Although no fully convincing case can be made for this change in understanding its overall structure, some corroborating evidence, both internal and external, can be adduced. Internally, the content of Q. 2 supports this analysis (See Figure 1).

In fact, the topic of the span made up of §2 and §3 is the relationship between the Muslims and People of the Book (vv. 40–152), and the topic of the unit composed of §4 and §5 (vv. 163–283) is the strengthening of the Muslim community for the recovery of the Holy Land. The macro

Islam	Islam is for People of the Book			Law and Liberation		
Universal	Children of Israel	Unite		Communal Guidance	Free Ka'ba	
§1 Prologue	§2	§3	Hinge	§4	§5	§6 Epilogue

Figure 1. The Structure of *al-Baqara*, Q. 2

structure of Q. 2 would then consist of a prologue stressing the universal implications of the new faith (§1), an elaborate hinge (vv. 153–162) linking two major wings of the sūra, finished off by a final epilogue (§6). One of the wings, composed of §2 and §3, would be essentially an invitation to the People of the Book to Islamic faith and to make common cause with the Muslims under Abraham, their common spiritual father. The other wing, made up of §4 and §5, would consist of guidance for Believers on a number of topics related to recovery of Mecca as a ritual center for the new and final faith. This structure is supported externally by its analogue in Q. 3

Q. 3 is similarly structured into two major parts: §2 (vv. 19–101) dealing with People of the Book and §3 (vv. 102–189) addressed to the community of Muslim believers.[77] The last four verses of §2 (vv. 98–101) appear to serve both as its wrap-up unit and as a unit of transition to the second major part of the sūra. These verses are marked off by three second-person singular imperatives, *qul* ("Say!") at the outset of vv. 98, 99, and 100 – v. 101 being syntactically and semantically an extension of v. 100. The formula of address "O People of the Book" follows each imperative in vv. 98 and 99, linking the transition verses with the major topic of §2 of the sūra. The formula "O ye who have believed" follows the imperative in v. 100, linking the transition verses with the primary receptors in §3. Thus, vv. 98–101 form what Parunak calls a "direct hinge" (A/ab/B).[78] The change in mood from declarative to singular imperative between vv. 97 and 98 and the change from singular to plural imperative along with the introduction of the formula of address between vv. 100/101 and 102 meet the requirement of a significant break in the discourse on either side of the hinge.

Iṣlāḥī's and Robinson's disagreement over the location of the divide between §3 and §4 of Q. 2 led to this discovery of several dimensions of transition in the long sūras of the Qur'ān. We now look at another controversial point of transition in the two sūras under investigation with a similar hope.

STRUCTURE AND COHESION OF THEMATIC UNITS

As I mentioned early in the chapter, Iṣlāḥī and I agree on a major division of Q. 4 between vv. 126 and 127. He divides the sūra into three main parts: §1 (vv. 1–43), dealing with social reform; §2 (vv. 44–126), focusing on the Islamic community and its opponents; and §3 (vv. 127–176), concluding with explanatory and supplementary material, consoling the Messenger and issuing a final warning. Although I, working independently, divided the sūra into more major divisions than did Iṣlāḥī, we both discerned major divisions at vv. 43/44 and 126/127.

For me, two simple factors turned out to be decisive in establishing the caesura between vv. 126 and 127: the structural cohesion of vv. 116–126 and the thematic cohesion of vv. 127–134.[79] Here we have an example of a major caesura and a simple transition.

In modern texts, graphic symbols such as indentation, unit headings, capital letters, and italics make divisions between structures of discourse clear. Oral discourse such as the Qur'ān must, in contrast, rely on other means of indicating structure such as rhyme cola at the end of verses, formulas of address, thematic coherence, and concatenation. Ring structures or chiasms and alternations also represent devices for indicating the beginning and end of a meaningful span of oral discourse.[80] An alternation such as vv. 150 through 152 of Q. 4 gives a clear sense of the end of its span:

150a Those who disbelieve in Allah and His messengers
b and wish to make a distinction between Allah and His messengers,
c and say: "We believe in some but disbelieve in others,"
d and wish to take between (this and) that a way –
151a These are the unbelievers in very truth
b and we have prepared for the unbelievers a humiliating punishment.
152a But to those who have believed in Allah and His messengers
b and have made no distinctions between any of them –
c these We shall in the end give their hires[81]
d and Allah is Forgiving, Compassionate.[82]

A 150a *Those* (*alladhīna*) who disbelieve in Allah and his messengers
B 150b and wish to *make a distinction* (*yufarriqū*) between Allah and His messengers . . .
C 151a *these* (*ulā'ika*) are the unbelievers in truth
D 151b and We have prepared for the unbelievers a humiliating punishment
A' 152a But *those* (*alladhīna*) who have believed in Allah and His messengers
B' 152b and have *made no distinctions* (*wa lam yufarriqū*) between any of them,
C' 152c *these* (*ulā'ika*) We shall in the end give their wages
D' 152d and Allah is Forgiving, Compassionate.[83]

The progression A–D allows cola A' to set up in the receptor's mind the expectation – increased with each successive utterance of B' through C' – of D' and also of closure for the unit. The two extra cola in B, "and say, 'We believe in some but disbelieve in others,' and wish to take between (this and that) a way," represent amplification of 150b and make clear that B is the theme of the construct, giving the amplification prominence, stressing that there is no middle ground between belief and unbelief.[84]

Ring structures or chiasms function in much the same way. The thematic unit (vv. 116–126) immediately preceding the caesura under discussion represents such a structure:[85]

116a God will not forgive the association of anything with Himself,
b though He forgives anything short of that to whom He willeth;
c he who associates anything with Allah
d has strayed into error far.
117a Short of Him they only call upon female beings,
b and they only call upon a Satan rebellious.
118a Allah cursed him
b and He said: "Surely of Thy servants will I take an appointed portion;
119a I will lead them astray, and fill them with desires;
b I will give them command
c and they will cut the ears of camels,
d and I will give them command
e and they will alter the creation of Allah."
f He who takes Satan for his patron apart from Allah
g has suffered manifest loss.
120a Who makes promises to them and fills them with desires;
b but Satan promises them only delusion.
121a These – their abode is Gehenna,[86]
b from which they will not find a place to flee to.
122a But those who have believed and worked the works of righteousnes
b We shall cause to enter Gardens
c through which the rivers flow,
d to abide therein for ever –
e the promise of Allah in truth,
f and who is more truthful than Allah in what He says?
123a It is not by your dogmas,
b and not by the dogmas of the People of the Book.
c Whoever does evil will be requited for it,
d and will not find for himself, apart from Allah, either patron or helper.
124a But whoever does works of righteousness,
b be it male or female, and is a believer –
c these – they will enter the garden
d and not be wronged a speck.
125a Who is better as regards religion
b than he who surrenders himself to Allah,
c doing good meanwhile,
d and follows the creed of Abraham as a hanif
e Allah took Abraham as a friend.

126a To Allah belongs whatever is in the heavens and whatever is in the earth;
b of everything hath Allah become comprehending.[87]

The ring structure can be laid out as follows:

A	116	Warning against association	4[88]
B	117–118a	Calling on lesser beings (Satan)	3
C	118b–119e	Satan deceives believers	6
D	119f, g	Satan as patron (*waliyy*)	2
E	120	Satan makes false promises (✓W'D)	2
F	121	Punishment = Gehenna	2
F'	122a–c	Reward = Gardens	3
E'	122d–e	God keeps promises (✓W'D)	2
D'	123	There is no patron (*waliyy*) . . . but God	4
C'	124	God rewards fairly	4
B'	125	Submitting to God (Ibrāhīm)	5
A'	126	Affirmation of God's sovereignty	2

Like the alternation, the chiasm creates expectations reinforced as the figure unfolds. Immediately, with the utterance of the first element, F', of the second panel, receptors could very well be expected to anticipate the discourse's covering the territory of the first panel again in a contrasting mode – in a contrasting mode because the two middle elements, F and F', represent obvious and familiar matched contrasts. The chiasm does focus upon contrast throughout: idolatry contrasts with divine sovereignty, Satan's deceits with God's rewards, Satan's false promises with God's fair rewards, the destiny of those who take Satan as a patron with the destiny of those who believe. Receptors intuit by the time they hear v. 126 (A') that the matter of idolatry is settled by the model behavior of Abraham and the sovereign adequacy of God. They would, therefore, be expecting the onset of something new.[89]

What they get is a new topic sentence for the next thematic unit: "And they ask you for a deliverance [*fatwā*] about women" (*wa yastaftūnaka fī 'n-nisā'*) (v. 127). The next four verses (26 cola) represent the requested declaration on the topic of women. These verses are followed by four more (14 cola) on the topic of the sovereignty of God in which the sovereignty refrain, "To Allah belongs whatever is in the heavens and whatever is in the earth," is repeated three times (vv. 131a,e, and 132a). This is the refrain occurring in the final element (A') of the chiastic structure vv. 116–126, where it signals a transition through concatenation.

At this point we confront once again the ambiguities presented by the loose structure of long sūras. Mustansir Mir, in summarizing Iṣlāḥī's structuring of Q. 4, suggests a possible revision of the point of transition between his §2, called "The Islamic Community and Its Opponents" (vv. 44–126), and §3, the sūra's conclusion (vv. 127–176). According to Mir, "The division of the sūrah into three main parts seems to be justified by the major shifts that occur in the sūrah at vss. 44 and 127, *although it may be asked whether vs. 135 does not make as good a point of division as vs. 127.*"[90]

Although Mir does not go into any detail as to why he considers v. 135 an alternative to v. 127 as the first verse of the last division of the sūra, we can imagine his reasoning.

Rather than serving as a concatenating device for transition between sections, the sovereignty refrain in v. 126, repeated three times near the end of the proposed §2 (vv. 44–134), could serve as a hinge linking the thematic units vv. 116–126 and vv. 126–135 by means of its Fa–aFaF structure mentioned above and discussed in note 43. Furthermore, the transition at vv. 134/135 is a more elaborate one than the one at vv. 126/127. The short span of response to the request for a declaration about women goes only through v. 130, though vv. 131–134 represent a wrap-up extension of this thematic unit. These four verses stress divine sovereignty and revelation, warn against unbelief, and remind "humankind" (*al-nās*) that if they disbelieve, they can be replaced (v. 133). Furthermore, v. 127 begins with a conjunction, while the Mir alternative would begin the last section of Q. 4 (vv. 135–176) with a formula of address, "O ye who have believed." One would have to say, based on the small sampling of verses beginning with formulas of address mentioned above, that formulas of address and refrains are more likely than conjunctions to begin major units of long sūras. Furthermore, many thematic units end with wrap-up verses, often dealing with revelation and/or obedience to God and his Messenger.[91] Finally, if Q. 2 v. 158 qualifies as an isolated verse and aids in the major transition in the middle of Q. 2, then vv. 135 and/or 136 qualify as isolated verses and deserve to be considered in the transition Mir suggests. Vv. 127–130 call believers to the requirements of Islamic order regarding some women issues. V. 135 follows up vv. 131–134 stressing the importance of obedience with an elaborate exhortation to honesty and justice in human relations – a kind of summary of Islamic practice, climaxing an answer to a question about practice. V. 136, in contrast, summarizes Islamic faith, initiating a span of discourse dealing with various kinds of unbelief (vv. 137–175). The ingredients of a good transition clearly abound around v. 135. In the passage between the disputed endpoints of Q. 2's §3, we discerned an elaborate transition involving an inverted hinge. Do we find any such thing for the passage between vv. 126 and 135 under discussion here?

It looks as though we do not, principally because the thematic unit on women (vv. 127–130) hardly seems a candidate for part of a hinge. In any case, it seems that a case for a hinge here, if it could be made at all, is much weaker than the case outlined immediately above for a transition at vv. 135/136. In the case of the center of Q. 2, we did not have to decide between the judgment of Iṣlāḥī and Robinson. Rather we made use of both insights. How do we decide between placing a transition with Iṣlāḥī at vv. 126/127 and placing it at vv. 134/135 where Mir thinks it could just as legitimately be put?

Although the point here is to illustrate the factors entailed in identifying major transitions in the long sūras of the Qur'ān and not to defend a particular choice, let me conclude the discussion of this disputed transition with a summary of my argument for putting the caesura between vv. 126 and 127, in spite of the conjunction at the outset of v. 127 and the strong case for identifying the break between §2 and §3 with the break between vv. 134/135. In addition to the evidence presented above from the structure of the thematic units on both sides of the caesura, considerations relating to the overall structure of Q. 4 support its location at vv. 126/127 and not at vv. 134/135. Allowing the span of 26 cola on the topic of women (vv. 127–130/134) to begin the last division of the sūra, helps us interpret the position of the sūra's last verse (v. 176), an isolated verse consisting of 12 cola dealing with inheritance of sisters, a topic related to the women themes of the sūra's first main division as well as to the themes of vv. 127–130/134. It begins with a refrain or formula almost identical to the one beginning the thematic unit 127–130/134, and since it also shares in the women theme with these verses, it forms an *inclusio* with them for the last fifty verses of the sūra. Furthermore, this *inclusio* encompasses §3, a unit that balances §1, a major section which, like the *inclusio*, is devoted to women and related matters.[92]

What conclusions may we draw from this examination of major transitions and thematic borders in the long sūras of the Qur'ān?

CONCLUSIONS

Although this chapter has been written on the basis of the assumption that the long sūras of the Qur'ān in their canonical form possess a coherent unified order, I do not intend to deny their obvious loose structure, their parenthetical verses and verse groups, their laconic compactness or their frequent digressions, or even that they may be a collection of independently composed verses and verse groups, and that "the distinctness of the separate pieces ... is more obvious than their unity."[93] This chapter is part of an ongoing attempt to discern what careful study of the long sūras would yield if carried out on the assumption of their coherence.

This chapter conveys some of what I have learned about the borders between major sections of long sūras and the transitions that cross them. By referring to those borders of major sections of Q. 2 and Q. 4 agreed on by two interpreters, I have been able to limit the scope of the chapter to a discussion of transitions at thematic unit borders on which there is at least some agreement.

One obvious conclusion of the study is that these transitions exhibit a significant variety of features. Thus in looking for borders and transitions, interpreters will pay careful attention to roles of formulas of address as well as other refrains and repeated phrases breaking the flow of the discourse. They will expect what I have called wrap-up verses and verse groups to precede caesuras in the discourse that might divide major sections. Wrap-up verses and verse groups involve motifs reinforcing the dominant themes of the sūra or even more likely the worldview of the Qur'ān as a whole. Such verses and verse groups will often include positive/negative reminders of the ultimate destiny resulting from choices and loyalties of receptors. Wrap-up material may involve consolation of the Messenger and/or his followers, especially in the form of confirmation of divine revelation. Since transition may involve some kind of linking to signal receptors of a significant change of topic or theme, interpreters may take notice when a motif appears isolated from its semantic or formal environment, knowing that such anticipatory or retrospective embedding is frequently used to signal receptors that a change has occurred or might be coming. I hope readers of this chapter will be on the lookout for the connection between an isolated verse or verse group with thematic unit borders and transitions, since such parenthetical passages may occur near the border of thematic units to signal a rupture in the flow of the discourse and a transition to a new topic.

The findings of the chapter also require certain caveats. For one thing, the very variety of transition devices employed in moving from one main section of a sūra to another should make interpreters cautious about establishing main sections prematurely by virtue of their presence. For another, since these several features can all be found in transitions occurring between minor thematic units, interpreters will obviously need to add other criteria to their analysis. For another, the limitations of the study itself mentioned in the chapter's introduction – the restriction of the study to three interpreters and six transitions; the assumptions of unity and coherence, not the proof of it; and the recursive nature of this kind of analysis of discourse – mean the results will yield most fruit if used heuristically.

Finally, the identification of major sūra divisions in these loosely structured long sūras depends most upon identifying the major thematic units themselves primarily through such procedures as thematic analysis, attention to implied receptors, and observation of the position and repetition of a variety of discourse elements. But since once the bulk of such units has been identified the problem will arise as to exactly where the borders between them are located, I hope that this exercise in describing thematic borders and their transitions will prove useful.

NOTES

Author's note: I wish to thank Georg Krotkoff and Neal Robinson for reading drafts of this chapter and for making useful suggestions.

1 "The Qur'an as Literature," *Religion and Literature* 20 (1988):53.

2 Ibid.
3 Ibid., 50.
4 Mustansir Mir, *Coherence in the Qur'ān: A Study of Iṣlāḥī's Concept of* Naẓm *in* Tadabbur-i Qur'ān (Indianapolis, IN: American Trust Publications, 1986), 42.
5 Angelika Neuwirth, "Vom Rezitationstext über die Liturgie zum Kanon: Zu Entstehung und Wiederauflösung der Surenkomposition im Verlauf der Entwicklung eines islamischen Kultus," in Stefan Wild, ed. *The Qur'an as Text,* Islamic Philosophy, Theology, and Science: Texts and Studies 27 (Leiden: E. J. Brill, 1996), 98.
6 *Al-Burhān fī 'Ulūm al-Qur'ān,* 4 vols. in 2, ed. Muḥammad Abū Faḍl Ibrāhīm (Cairo: 'Īsā al-Ḥalabī wa Shurakā'uhu, 1957–58), I:38; cited in Mir, *Coherence,* 17.
7 Mir, *Coherence,* 31.
8 "The *Sūra* as a Unity: A Twentieth Century Development in Qur'ān Exegesis," in G. R. Hawting and Abdul-Kader A. Shareef, eds., *Approaches to the Qur'ān,* Routledge/SOAS Series on Contemporary Politics and Culture in the Middle East (London and New York: Routledge, 1993), 217.
9 *Coherence*; "The Qur'an as Literature"; and "The *Sūra* as a Unity." Amīn Aḥsan al-Iṣlāḥī's major work is *Tadabbur-i Qur'ān* (8 vols. [vols. 1–2: Lahore: Dār al-Ishā'āt al-Islāmiyya, 1387–1391/1967–1971; vols. 3–4: Lahore: Anjuman-i Khuddām'ulqur'ān, 1393–1396/1973–1976; vols. 5–8: Lahore: Fārā Foundation, 1398–1400/1977–1980]).
10 *Discovering the Qur'ān: A Contemporary Approach to a Veiled Text* (London: SCM Press, 1996), 201–23.
11 "The Word of God and the Apostleship of 'Īsā: A Narrative Analysis of Āl 'Imrān (3):33–62," *Journal of Semitic Studies* 37 (1991):77–112; and "Sūra as Guidance and Exhortation: The Composition of *Sūrat al-Nisā',*" in Asma Afsaruddin and A. H. Mathias Zahniser, eds. *Humanism, Culture, and Language in the Near East: Studies in Honor of Georg Krotkoff* (Winona Lake, Indiana: Eisenbrauns, 1997), 71–85.
12 *Coherence*; "The Qur'an as Literature"; "The *Sūra* as a Unity"; and "The Qur'ānic Story of Joseph: Plot, Theme, and Characters," *The Muslim World* 76 (1986):1–15.
13 *Coherence.*
14 "The *Sūra* as a Unity," 215–7.
15 Ibid., 215; *Coherence,* 34 and 38. Iṣlāḥī got the concept of *'amūd* from his mentor, Ḥamīd al-Dīn 'Abd al-Ḥamīd al-Farāhī (1280–1349/1863–1930), two volumes of his commentary have been published in Arabic: *Dalā'il al-Niẓām* (Azamgarh, India: Al-Dā'ira al-Ḥamīdiyya wa Maktabatuhā, 1968) and *Al-Takmīl fī Uṣūl al-Ta'wīl* (Azamgarh, India: Al-Dā'ira al-Ḥamīdiyya wa Maktabatuhā, 1968). Iṣlāḥī published all Farāhī's commentary, translated into Urdu, in *Majmū'a-yi Tafāsīr-i Farāhī,* tr. Amīn Aḥsan Iṣlāḥī (Lahore: Anjuman-i Khuddāmu'lqur'ān, 1973).
16 *Coherence,* 50.
17 Ibid., 71–2.
18 "The *Sūra* as a Unity," 216.
19 *Coherence,* 47.
20 *Coherence,* 48–9.
21 See note 10 above.
22 *Discovering the Qur'ān,* 200–1.
23 Robinson bases his conclusion about the overall purpose of the sūra partly on the conviction that the statement, "Thus we have made you a community in the middle" (*ummatan wasaṭan*) (Q. 2 v. 143), occurs in the middle verse of the sūra and in the subsection dealing with the *qibla* (Ibid., 201).

24 Ibid., 202–6.
25 Ibid., 206.
26 Zahniser, "Sūra as Guidance." Although this essay was published after those of Mir allowing me to refer to Iṣlāḥī's analysis in the notes, I completed the analysis of Q. 4 independently and prior to reading Mir's *Coherence.*
27 The notion *keyword* as H. Van Dyke Parunak uses it refers to any material placed in a span of discourse to unite it with other spans of discourse. The keyword does not have to be a word as such. It could be a formula of address, a rhyme clause, one of a set of parallel cola, or a repeated verse ("Transitional Techniques in the Bible," *Journal of Biblical Literature* 102 [1983]:529–30).
28 As mentioned above, I identified an additional "battle block" (vv. 71–104) within vv. 44–126, giving me two more transitions. "Sūra as Guidance," 76 and 77.
29 *Coherence,* 58–9.
30 I am using the translation of Richard Bell (*The Qur'ān: Translated, with a Critical Re-arrangement of the Surahs,* 2 vols. (Edinburgh: T. & T. Clark, 1937) because of its accuracy and its use of an older English showing singular and plural in the second person.
31 For a discussion of the central transition in Q. 3, see below. My analysis here differs somewhat from my analysis in "The Word of God," 84–7.
32 Bell translates *nās* "people." He translates *ahl* and *qawm* "people" as well. With Robinson, I am using "humankind" in the expression "O humankind" to emphasize the broad scope of this term. This rendering will not, however, fit all occurrences of *nās.*
33 Bell translates *a-lam tara* here "Has one not seen?" I see no reason for this change from his "Hast thou not considered?" in Q. 2 v. 243. Bell may be reflecting the fact that Qur'ānic addresses in the second person singular can be taken as if written to the individual receptor, as well as to Muḥammad (See Robinson, *Discovering the Qur'ān,* 242).
34 "Sūra as Guidance," 76–7. Three main transitions may be identified in Q. 5 (*al-Mā'ida*): vv. 40/41, 86/87, and 108/109. Two of these begin with formulas of address: "O thou messenger" (*yā ayyuhā 'r-rasūl*) (v. 41) and "O ye who have believed" (v. 87).
35 Only four of Iṣlāḥī's subsections for Q. 4 begin with formulas of address (vv. 19–22, 29–33, 71–76, and 135–152). Mir lists the subsections in *Coherence,* 46–7.
36 In some cases formulas of address may intervene in the flow of discourse because a passage is parenthetical. For example, Ibn 'Āshūr points out that the formula *yā ayyuhā lladhīna āmanū,* "O ye who have believed," signals that the first part of v. 2 of Q. 5 is parenthetical. Muḥammad al-Ṭāhir Ibn 'Āshūr, *Tafsīr al-Taḥrīr wa al-Tanwīr,* 17 vols. (Tunis: al-Dār al-Tunisiyya li-al-Nashr, 1971), 6:81.
37 I am using *receptor* as a term to include both readers and hearers of the Qur'ān.
38 According to Fakhr al-Dīn al-Rāzī, *al-nās* represents all those in general to whom the regulations of the sūra apply. What he offers in support of this point in connection with Q. 4:1 would seem to apply here: (1) *al-nās* is a collective noun in the definite state, conveying the idea of completeness; (2) the formula is connected with Adam; and (3) the charge to revere (in this case worship [Q. 2:21]) is the right of all people (*Al-Tafsīr al-Kabīr,* 33 vols. [Cairo: al-Maṭba'a al-Bahiyya, 1938], 9:157–8).
39 Robinson, *Discovering the Qur'ān,* 200–1. For further analysis of the nature and function in Qur'ānic discourse of rhyme clauses (clausels), including the fact that rhyme clauses also function at the verse-group and thematic unit level, see Angelika Neuwirth, *Studien zur Komposition der mekkanischen Suren* (Studien zur

Sprache, Geschichte und Kultur des islamischen Orients, Neue Folge, Band 10) (Berlin and New York: Walter de Gruyter, 1981), 157–70; and idem. "Zur Struktur der *Yūsuf*-Sure," in Werner Diem and Stefan Wild, eds., *Studien aus Arabistik und Semitistik: Anton Spitaler zum siebzigsten Geburtstag von seinen Schülern überreicht* (Wiesbaden: Otto Harrossowitz, 1980), 148–52.

40 Robinson shows how this rhyme clause gives coherence to the sūra as a whole (*Discovering the Qur'ān*, 201).

41 A. Yusuf Ali's translation of *al-qawmi 'l-kāfirīn*. Q. 3 ends with a similar wrap-up unit (vv. 196–200). Another interesting feature of the relationship between the wrap-up units of Q. 2 and Q. 3 is that Q. 3 vv. 190–195, a span of text just before the wrap-up unit, is very much like the wrap-up unit of Q. 2. It starts with the sovereignty refrain, *wa li 'llāhi mulku 's-samāwāti wa 'l-arḍi wa 'llāhu 'alā kulli shay'in qadīr* (v. 189), and ends with a set of prayers featuring three instances of the invocation of the divine: *rabbanā* (vv. 192, 193, and 194).

42 Vv. 122 and 123 obviously form a unit. The positive proposal, "protect yourselves," with which v. 123 begins represents a parallel proposal to "remember the good" of v. 122.

43 In Q. 3:8–16 *rabbanā* initiates prayers of believers that surround a unit dealing with unbelief; the unit features rhyme deviation, further supporting its distinct character. Q. 4:135–144 surrounds a nice thematic unit featuring a ring structure (vv. 137–143). Even though v. 20 lies in the midst of Mūsā's discourse, Q. 5:7–20 comprises a unit bounded by the phrase "remember the goodness [grace] of God (*ni'mata llāhi*) towards you." The unit contains examples of God's grace, but goes on to make an elaborate transition to a law about killing a person for illegitimate cause. For a discussion of this transition, see Ibn 'Āshūr, *Tafsīr al-Taḥrīr*, 6:168. The reverse case is interesting because, both Iṣlāḥī and I make a major section break at Q. 4:126/127, and yet 126–132 fits the pattern we are discussing in reverse. Here again, as in the case of Q. 2:122, there is no reason why Q. 4:126 cannot function as both the final verse of a main section and as a component of a structure such as the one discussed here. The sovereignty refrain, "To Allah belongs whatever is in the heavens and whatever is on the earth," gives boundary to a passage (Q. 4:127–132) devoted to issues related to women, one of the three passages in the sūra devoted to such issues. See Zahniser, "Sūra as Guidance," 76 and the discussion about Q. 4:126/127, 135, and 136 below.

44 *wa ilāhukum ilāhun wāḥidun lā ilāha illā huwa 'r-raḥmānu 'r-raḥīm.* Bell does not start his translation of this verse with "and." But because so few sections of sūras begin with "and," it seems important to include the conjunction in the translation where it exists in the Arabic.

45 "Transitional Techniques in the Bible," 539.

46 Robinson is interested in the implied receptor in connection with the special addressee addressed in the second person singular (*Discovering the Qur'ān*, 240–3); and Mir reports the importance of the receptor of the entire sūra to Farāhī and gives no evidence that Iṣlāḥī thought differently (*Coherence*, 41).

47 Mir, "The Sūra as a Unity," 216. V. 163 begins with the conjunction *wa*. Major divisions of sūras do not usually begin with a conjunction. None of the other divisions suggested by Iṣlāḥī and Robinson for Q. 2 begins with a conjunction. Some do, however. For example, one of my major divisions for Q. 4 begins with a conjunction (v. 127). On this choice Iṣlāḥī agrees. None of my other major subdivisions for Q. 4 begins with a conjunction. Several minor subdivisions do.

48 Iṣlāḥī maintains that "the subject [of Law] is not taken up until vs. 177." Cited in Mir, *Coherence*, 88.

49 It is clearly a characteristic of the Qur'ān to combine legislation and exhortation or guidance. All the long sūras do both. See, for example, Iṣlāḥī's suggestion that Q. 4 is both legislation and guidance (*Tadabbur-i Qur'ān*, 2:16; cited in Mir, *Coherence*, 55).

50 The liberate-the-Ka'ba material is not limited to §5, but is distributed as follows: vv. 114–115, 177, 190–195, 216–219, and 243–252. The related vv. 142–152 and 158 deal with the *qibla* and Ka'ba but not with fighting in the way of God. Because this final and significant passage begins the last major span of the sūra and because it leads into, and is connected with, the other spans within the last major span, it determines the content of the section. Fighting in §5 (vv. 243–252) leads to the topic of spending (vv. 254–274). This leads into the economics of lending (vv. 275–283).

51 This recalls v. 45 in §2 devoted to the Banū Isrā'īl.

52 Q. 2 vv. 153–157 *yā ayyuhā lladhīna āmanū 'sta'īnū bi 'ṣ-ṣabri wa 'ṣ-ṣalāti inna llāha ma'a 'ṣ-ṣābirīn • wa lā taqūlū li-man yuqtalu fī sabīli llāhi «amwātun» bal aḥyā'un wa lākin lā tash'urūn • wa la-nabluwannakum bi-shay'in mina 'l-khawfi wa 'l-jū'i wa naqṣin mina 'l-amwāli wa 'l-anfusi wa 'th-thamarāti wa bashshiri 'ṣ-ṣābirīn • alladhīna idhā aṣābathum muṣībatun qālū: «innā li 'llāhi wa innā ilayhi rāji'ūn» • ulā'ika 'alayhim ṣalawātun min rabbihim wa raḥmatun wa ulā'ika humu 'l-muhtadūn.*

53 Robinson, *Discovering the Qur'ān*, 211.

54 Q. 2:158 *inna 'ṣ-ṣafā wa 'l-marwata min sha'ā'iri llāhi fa-man ḥajja 'l-bayta awi 'tamara fa-lā junāḥa 'alayhi an yaṭṭawwafa bihimā wa man taṭawwa'a khayran fa-inna llāha shākirun 'alīm.*

55 I changed Bell's "grateful" for *shākirun* in v. 158 to "thankful" to highlight the parallel with v. 152.

56 The notion of the futility of hiding anything from God shows up in the epilogue (v. 284). This does not, however, necessarily refer to hiding scripture.

57 Bell translates *udhkurū nīmatī llatī an'amtu 'alaykum* "remember the good which I have bestowed upon you."

58 Bell's translation of *al-'ālamīn* ("the worlds") in *annī faḍḍaltukum 'alā 'l-'ālamīn* is misleading in that what is meant is more like the orders of creatures, animals, humans, angels, etc., or possibly even "people" or "peoples." Al-Ṣābūnī must take it as 'nations' because he says about the phrase, "I preferred your ancestors to the nations of their times (*'ālamī zamānihim* [v. 47]; *sā'iri 'l-umami fī zamānihim* [v. 122]) by sending apostles. . . ." (Muḥammad 'Alī al-Ṣābūnī, *Ṣafwat al-Tafāsīr: Tafsīr al-Qur'ān al-Karīm*, 3 vols. [Beirut: Dār al-Qur'ān al-Karīm, 1980], 1:55 and 92).

59 This formulation is used in Q. 61:6, but there it is within a statement made by 'Īsā.

60 Cf. vv. 47 and 122 (*Discovering the Qur'ān*, 211). See also Robinson's more thorough discussion of divine first-person address in Ibid., 230–4.

61 Q. 2:186 *wa idhā sa'alaka 'ibādī 'annī fa-innī qarībun ujību da'wata 'd-dā'i idhā da'āni fa-l-yastajībū lī wa-l-yu'minū bī la'allahum yarshudūn.*

62 "Transitional Techniques," 540–2. A hinge is a form of double concatenation. See note 71 below.

63 A direct hinge, in contrast, can be represented A/ab/B. The hinge, or middle panel, can also contain material of its own in addition to the material related to panels A and B: A/xbxax/B (Ibid.). We encounter a direct hinge below in sūra 3.

64 For example, see Q. 5:89. For the terms *Qur'ān-Bestätigung* or *Offenbarungsbestätigung*, see Angelika Neuwirth, "Zur Struktur," 139, and idem. *Studien*, 250–3.

65 Q. 2:238–239 *ḥāfiẓū 'alā 'ṣ-ṣalawāti wa 'ṣ-ṣalāti 'l-wusṭā wa-qūmū li-llāhi qānitīn • fa-in khiftum fa-rijālan aw rukbānan fa-idhā amintum fa 'dhkurū llāha kamā 'allamakum mā lam takūnū ta'lamūn.*

66 *Discovering the Qur'ān*, 215.

67 The topic of vv. 261–274 is clearly contributing wealth in the cause of God, even though it contains some material related to giving that is charitable. Note the references to "the way of God" in vv. 244, 246, 261, 262, and 273.

68 V. 240 contains a purely lexical link with §5 through the phrase *in kharajna* ("if they [the widows] go out [of their houses]"). V. 243 begins with this sentence: "Hast thou not considered those who went forth (*kharajū*) from their dwellings?" Such purely lexical correspondences do sometimes link adjacent spans of Qur'ānic discourse. Robinson relates v. 243 to v. 85 and the biblical Exodus. Receptors would recognize that after leaving their homes in Egypt, the Children of Israel would be involved in fighting to occupy the Promised Land (*Discovering the Qur'ān*, 215 and 216).

69 Ibid., 205.

70 Mir, *Coherence*, 53–4 (with examples).

71 Parunak, "Transitional Techniques in the Bible," 526 and 530–2. Parunak offers terminology to describe different types of concatenation. Angelika Neuwirth observed that rhyme change and alteration in the Meccan sūras plays a significant role in indicating structure. Often the transition from one structural unit indicated by a given rhyme scheme to another structural unit indicated by a different rhyme scheme is signaled by concatenation. That is, the rhyme scheme change does not take place immediately at the break between the two units of discourse, but a verse or a few verses before or after it (*Studien*, 113).

72 For example, consider some concatenation occurring in Q. 4. The introductory formula, "Hast thou not considered?" the repetition of which contributes to the coherence of vv. 44–70, occurs again in v. 77 of the following section (vv. 71–104). The sovereignty refrain in v. 126 anticipates the refrain's providing coherence for the following section (vv. 127–175) (Zahniser, "Sūra as Guidance," 78).

73 As mentioned above, I organize the section vv. 44–126 into three main parts. The large central section devoted to struggle in the way of God is flanked by two shorter sections in which idolatry is prominent (vv. 44–70, 104–126) ("Sūra as Guidance," 76–84). But this difference with Iṣlāḥī is not significant for the topic of this chapter.

74 Many Qur'ānic verses, especially in the Medinan period, feature a collection of commands grounded through a rhyme clause in the nature of God.

75 Q. 4:43 *yā ayyuhā lladhīna āmanū lā taqrabu 'ṣ-ṣalāta wa-antum sukārā ḥattā ta'lamū mā taqūlūna wa lā junuban illā 'ābirī sabīlin ḥattā taghtasilū wa in kuntum marḍā aw 'alā safarin aw jā'a aḥadun minkum mina 'l-ghā'iṭi aw lāmastumu 'n-nisā'a fa-lam tajidū mā'an fa-tayammamū ṣa'īdan ṭayyiban fa 'msaḥū bi-wujūhikum wa aydīkum inna llāha kāna 'afuwwan ghafūrā.*

76 *Tadabbur-i qur'ān*, 2:9–10; cited in Mir, *Coherence*, 46–7.

77 §1 of Q. 3 is its prologue (vv. 1–18). Although the message of Q. 3 to the community of believing Muslims extends to v. 200 where the formula, "O ye who have believed," is repeated, the sūra clearly climaxes with an eleven-verse conclusion or epilogue (§4) (vv. 190–200). In addition to its content – including an elaborate prayer and assurance of divine response (vv. 191–196), a brief verse of consolation to the Messenger (v. 196), a negative-positive pair of wrap-up verses (vv. 197–198), a message of hope for the People of the Book recalling the first half of the sūra (v. 199), and a final brief challenge to those who have believed (v. 200) – the unit is marked off by an elaborate change in rhyme pattern -*ā*C, where C is *bā'*, *dāl*, or *rā'*, similar to that of vv. 1–20. Vv. 21–23 represent an interesting transition with wrap-up verses (vv. 21–22)

and the familiar formula "Hast thou not considered?" (v. 23). In fact, I believe the wrap-up unit begins with verse 19, the prologue consisting of vv. 1–18.

78 See note 63 above.

79 Iṣlāḥī also identifies vv. 116–126 and vv. 127–134 as distinct thematic units (cited in Mir, *Coherence*, 47).

80 H. Van Dyke Parunak, "Oral Typesetting: Some Uses of Biblical Structure," *Biblica* 62 (1981):153–5.

81 I added *these* to Bell's construction in keeping with the extraposition of *ulā'ika* in the colon and in parallel with 151a. The extraposition of the second *ulā'ika* preserves the structural balance of the coordinated clauses and thus the contrast between the destinies of the two groups represented in the verses. The first *ulā'ika* represents the subject of the main clause. In this case the whole of verse 150 is an extraposed clause requiring the resumptive *ulā'ika* to preserve the balance mentioned in the previous sentence. See Geoffrey Khan, *Studies in Semitic Syntax* (London Oriental Series, 38) (New York, Oxford, Toronto: Oxford University Press, 1988), 46 and 48.

82 Q. 4:150–152 *inna lladhīna yakfurūna bi 'llāhi wa rusulihi wa yurīdūna an yufarriqū bayna llāhi wa rusulihi wa yaqūlūna «nu'minu bi-ba'ḍin wa-nakfuru bi-ba'ḍin» wa yurīdūna an yattakhidhū bayna dhālika sabīlā • ulā'ika humu 'l-kāfirūna ḥaqqan wa a'tadnā li 'l-kāfirīna 'adhāban muhīnā • wa 'lladhīna āmanū bi 'llāhi wa rusulihi wa lam yufarriqū bayna aḥadin minhum ulā'ika sawfa yu'tīhim ujūrahum wa-kāna llāhu ghafūran raḥīmā.*

83 I have altered Bell's translation here to make the parallels between panels of the alternation more clear. These parallels still come out much better in the Arabic transliteration. See notes 81 and 82.

84 Amplification involves the repetition of a proposition or other unit of discourse with something added. When the unit of discourse is a proposition or cluster of propositions as it is here, then the amplification is made prominent (John Beekman, John Callow, and Michael Kopesec, *The Semantic Structure of Written Communication*, 5th ed. [Dallas, TX: Summer Institute of Linguistics, 1981], 96; Robert E. Longacre, *The Grammar of Discourse* [Topics in Language and Linguistics, ed. Thomas A. Sebeok and Albert Valdman] [New York and London: Plenum Press, 1983], 119–20). In this case, 150c being the repetition of 150b, the colon, *wa yurīdūna an yattakhidhū bayna dhālika sabīlā* ("and wish to take between (this and) that a way"), is made prominent. This prominence is fully congruent with the semantic impact of the whole alternation, since the phrase appears to mean essentially, "There is no middle ground between belief (152a–d) and unbelief (150a–151b)" (See Ṣābūnī, *Ṣafwat al-Tafāsīr*, 1:315). Direct speech such as that in 150c also contributes to the prominence of the particularization (150b–d) of "those who disbelieve in Allah and His messengers" (150a). In the passage soon to be analyzed below (vv. 116–126), Satan is made prominent by a disproportionate allotment of space including a narrative with direct address from him (vv. 118b-e). This in turn makes prominent the comment in 119f–g, "He who takes Satan for his patron apart from Allah has suffered manifest loss."

85 The awareness of the structure for vv. 116–126 helps us opt with Iṣlāḥī for a division between thematic units 105–115 and 116–126. Al-Ṭabātabā'ī who is more interested than most interpreters of the Qur'ān in overall sūra structure considers vv. 105–126 all one unit (Mir, *Coherence*, 72). My analysis agrees with that of Iṣlāḥī in finding a sub-division of vv. 105–126 at vv. 115/116, but my analysis is congruent with al-Ṭabāṭabā'ī in making vv. 105–126 a major unit of the sūra ("Sūra as Guidance," 77).

86 Here and in 124c I extraposed a *these* in keeping with the extraposition of *ulā'ika* in these cola. Here the extraposed pronoun does not achieve balance but emphasizes the destiny of the particular group to whom Satan makes promises. See note 81.

87 Q. 4:116 *inna llāha lā yaghfiru an yushraka bihi wa yaghfiru mā dūna dhālika li-man yashā'u wa man yushrik bi 'llāhi fa-qad ḍalla ḍalālan ba'īdā* • 117 *in yad'ūna min dūnihi illā ināthan wa in yad'ūna illā shayṭānan marīdā* • 118 *la'anahu llāh* • 119 *wa-qāla «la-attakhidhanna min 'ibādika naṣīban mafrūḍan wa la-uḍillannahum wa la-umanniyannahum wa la-āmurannahum fa-la-yubattikunna ādhāna 'l-an'āmi wa la-āmurannahum fa-la-yughayyirunna khalqa llāhi» wa man yattakhidhi 'sh-shayṭāna waliyyan min dūni llāhi fa-qad khasira khusrānan mubīnā* • 120 *ya'iduhum wa-yumannīhim wa mā ya'iduhumu 'sh-shayṭānu illā ghurūrā* • 121 *ulā'ika ma'wāhum jahannamu wa lā yajidūna 'anhā maḥīṣā* • 122 *wa 'lladhīna āmanū wa 'amilū 'ṣ-ṣāliḥāti sanudkhiluhum jannātin tajrī min taḥtihā 'l-anhāru khālidīna fīhā abadan wa'da llāhi ḥaqqan wa man aṣdaqu mina llāhi qīlā* • 123 *laysa bi-amāniyyikum wa lā amāniyyi ahli 'l-kitābi man ya'mal sū'an yujza bihi wa lā yajid lahu min dūni llāhi waliyyan wa lā naṣīrā* • 124 *wa-man ya'mal mina 'ṣ-ṣāliḥāti min dhakarin aw unthā wa huwa mu'minun fa-ulā'ika yadkhulūna 'l-jannata wa lā yuẓlamūna naqīrā* • 125 *wa man aḥsanu dīnan mimman aslama wajhahu li 'llāhi wa huwa muḥsinun wa 'ttaba'a millata ibrāhīma ḥanīfan wa 'ttakhadha llāhu ibrāhīma khalīlā* • 126 *wa li 'llāhi mā fī 's-samāwāti wa mā fī 'l-arḍi wa kāna llāhu bi-kulli shay'in muḥīṭā.*

88 This column indicates the number of cola in each element of the chiasm.

89 In fact, with both the alternation and the chiasm, an interruption or deviation in the structure would call attention to itself and thus emphasize the content of the deviating element. As in the case of the alternation, the expanded proportion of discourse given to Satan, including direct address by him would seem to make him prominent in the structure. See Parunak, "Oral Typesetting," 166–67 (with examples) and note 84 above.

90 *Coherence*, 48. I have supplied the emphasis. See also Ibid., 58–59 where it is more clear that Mir means for §3 to begin at v. 135.

91 Q. 2:39 and 242 are similar to Q. 4:131–134 on a smaller scale. Q. 2:119–121 is a little more specific, but still quite similar to Q. 4:131–134. Q. 2:159–162 seems close in type of material to Q. 4:134–136. Q. 4's §1 ends with an attribute of God and an encouraging word for his Messenger. Q. 4:69 and 70 deal with obedience to God and his Messenger in wrapping up section 44–70.

92 More space is given to this argument in Zahniser, "Sūra as Guidance," 76–85. See also Mir's discussion of Iṣlāḥī's argument for the placing of vv. 127–134 and v. 176 in *Coherence*, 58–59.

93 W. Montgomery Watt, *Bell's Introduction to the Qur'ān* (Islamic Surveys, 8) (Edinburgh: University of Edinburgh, 1970), 74.

Chapter 3

Text and Textuality: Q. 3:7 as a Point of Intersection

Jane Dammen McAuliffe

As a field, Qur'ānic studies must inevitably encompass issues that arise from the interpretive encounter with texts, i.e., hermeneutical issues. In its traditional signification hermeneutics connotes that activity that identifies the principles and procedures requisite to the interpretation of texts. It provides the methodological propaedeutic to the explication or exegesis of texts. Within the Islamic tradition the pre-eminent text is, of course, the Qur'ān. For Muslims, it is God's full and final revelation to his Prophet Muḥammad. As such, and in common with other texts deemed revelatory by their respective communities, the Qur'ān has presented its potential interpreter with certain hermeneutical boundaries. With God as the direct author of the scripture, discussions of cultural borrowing or authorial development are pre-empted. Lexical and grammatical analysis have proceeded within the assumption of the divinely-wrought perfection of the text. Matters of canonical formation and structure became theological postulates during the very first centuries of the community's growth. Moreover, within that canon itself are to be found certain self-reflective statements that must necessarily guide the exegete in the elaboration of his exegetical approach. The Qur'ān, in other words, makes reference to itself, characterizes itself in various ways, and defines (in at least a preliminary way) what might be termed the exegetical relationship that coheres between God, the Prophet and the faithful. These reflexive characterizations were of central importance in charting the development of a specifically Qur'ānic hermeneutics. In commenting upon them, individual exegetes revealed the systemic perspectives of their exegetical methodologies.

A key element in the totality of such Qur'ānic self-reflection is Q. 3:7. Occurring, as it does, in one of the initial *sūras* of the Qur'ān, this verse provided commentators with an opportunity early in their commentaries (*tafsīr*) to address some basic methodological issues. Chief among these are questions such as: (1) Is the Qur'ān uniform in genre or diverse? (2) Are all parts of the text equally accessible to interpretation or are there variations of translucence and opacity? (3) If analogical explication plays any role in Qur'ānic hermeneutics, how broad or limited is its scope? (4) What sort of individuals is potentially capable of exegetical activity? (5) Of what ultimate value is the effort of exegesis?

In recent years, several scholars have worked on Q. 3:7, providing selected exegetical surveys, each from a different perspective or motivated by a different set of questions. The most recent contribution, that of Stefan Wild, focuses explicitly on Q. 3:7 as an index of Qur'ānic self-referentiality.[1] In 1985, Michel Lagarde published an article in *Quaderni di studi arabi* [2] on the various significations of the Qur'ānic terms *muḥkam* and *mutashābih* as culled from a selection of classical exegetical works. Three years later Leah Kinberg's more extensive classification was published in *Arabica*.[3] Both of these articles, as well as earlier work by John Wansbrough in his *Quranic Studies*,[4] provide very useful accounts of the taxonomic activity which Q. 3:7 has generated during the long history of exegesis.[5] Certainly, the classical interest in the analysis and categorization of Qur'ānic contents found motivating force in this passage. Taken together, these several studies provide an excellent foundation for the closer examination of enduring exegetical concerns that emerge from this crucial verse, concerns that can be classified as intratextual and as intertextual.[6]

The present study will explore some significant lines of interpretation that repeatedly issue from the *tafsīr* tradition on this verse. It will do so, however, in a manner that translates the language of traditional hermeneutical reflection into a more contemporary idiom. The language or languages of late twentieth-century critical discourse have opened new ways of construing the relationship between textual production and textual reception. One particularly useful instance of this may be drawn from the writings of the French theorist, Gérard Genette, who uses the vocabulary of transtextuality to illumine and explain an interconnecting range of textual relations. Others, such as Paul Ricoeur, Michael Riffaterre, the Anglo-American reader-response critics and the German *Rezeptionsgeschichte* theorists offer additional and complementary perspectives. The point of reflecting upon the exegetical history of Q. 3:7 in light of these contemporary critical insights is not simply to conduct an exercise in retrieval and reformulation. Rather, the intent is to discover whether a new language allows us to explore levels of the tradition or points of intersection that have not been found before or that have been insufficiently understood. Or to put it interrogatively: Can we construct cultural bridges between medieval commentaries and contemporary theories that approach the Qur'ān and its exegetical elaboration as a literary artifact?

I INTRATEXTUALITY AND TRANSTEXTUALITY: THE CLASSICAL SOURCES

To introduce this exploration, I want to move back in time from the fully developed schemes of classification and categorization, as represented by the summative works of, for example, al-Zarkashī[7] (d. 793/1392) and al-Suyūṭī[8] (d. 911/1505), to much earlier exegetical strata. To do so, I will draw on sources, some published rather recently, which purport to transmit the *tafāsīr* of Mujāhid b. Jabr (d. 100/718), Zayd b. 'Alī (d. 120/738), Muqātil b. Sulaymān (d. 150/767), Sufyān al-Thawrī (d. 161/777), Abū 'Ubayda (d. 210/825), and 'Abd al-Razzāq al-Ṣan'ānī (d. 211/827). I use the term 'purport' to signal the complex and still-unresolved issues surrounding the confident attribution of these works, issues which, however, may be bracketed for present purposes. The intent of this study is not the archaeolgy of attribution but the excavation and assay of exegetical elements.

Examining this early exegetical material in light of the tremendous elaboration which this verse eventually receives, it is interesting to note both what is said and what is not said in response to Q. 3:7. For those early commentaries that amount to little more than lexical glossing and periphrasis, the key words are not so much *muḥkamāt* and *mutashābihāt*, the paired terms that garnered much of the subsequent exegetical attention, but *zaygh* and *fitna*. For *zaygh*, Mujāhid, Zayd b. 'Alī, and Abū 'Ubayda offer only single synonyms, either *shakk*/doubt[9] or *jawr*/oppression.[10] For *fitna*, they suggest either 'the means by which they wreck havoc'[11] or *kufr*/disbelief.[12]

Where *muḥkamāt* and *mutashābihāt* are mentioned, however, the expected equations begin to emerge. Representations of the *muḥkamāt* have a decidedly juridical focus as, for example, in (1) 'Abd al-Razzāq's identification of them as those verses upon which action can be based,[13] (2) or Mujāhid's more succinct equation of them with the *ḥalāl* and *ḥarām*,[14] or (3) Sufyān al-Thawrī's correlation of *muḥkam* and the abrogating/*nāsikh*.[15] While the last-mentioned finds its anticipated equivalent among semantic designations of the *mutashābihāt*, this latter term is not regularly defined, in these early works, in paired relation with *muḥkamāt*. Both Abū 'Ubayda and Mujāhid characterize the *mutashābihāt*, in quite a general fashion, as those verses that resemble one another or confirm the truth of one another.[16]

The most restrictive application of the term *mutashābih* – and the one with which the summative *mufassir* Abū Ja'far b. Jarīr al-Ṭabarī (d. 310/923) ultimately sides – is that which assigns it only to the *fawātiḥ*/*muqaṭṭa'āt*, the so-called 'mysterious letters', leaving everything else in the Qur'ān to be described as *muḥkam*.[17] Clearly, what this foundational layer of exegetical identification emphasizes is the use of *muḥkam* and *mutashābih* as taxonomic categories.[18] The earliest exegetes, in the main, used these terms as a means of classifying varieties of Qur'ānic material. Debate among them, addressed to the apparent elasticity of categories thus created, was conducted over the issue of how best to divide and label the contents of the Qur'ān in order to fill the two categories created by these Qur'ānic designations.

After al-Ṭabarī's fixation of this primordial layer of exegetical material, however, a shift of perspective occurs. Attention turns from the taxonomic to the hermeneutic. Classification by genre gives way to categorization by exegetical potential. The pivot for such a shift may, in fact, be that most restrictive designation of *mutashābih* just mentioned. What is distinctive about the 'mysterious letters' is that they are exegetically opaque. Even the most educated *'ālim* cannot crack the code. Here is a class of Qur'ānic material whose interpretation is accessible to God alone.

Certainly, the evidence for such a shift in post-Ṭabarī commentary is persuasive. While most of the *mufassirūn* whom I have surveyed recapitulate the inaugural taxonomy, when professing their own views they unanimously support an understanding of *muḥkam/mutashābih* in hermeneutical terms. Nevertheless, within this general perspective, a Shī'ī and Sunnī specification may be distinguished. Beginning with 'Alī b. Ibrāhīm al-Qummī's (fl. mid 4th/10th) formulaic definition of *muḥkam* as "that whose *ta'wīl* is its *tanzīl,*" Shī'ī commentaries accented the transparent intelligibility of *muḥkam* verses as contrasted with the need for explanation displayed by the *mutashābih.*[19] Yet, in the view of al-Qummī and his successors, Muḥammad b. al-Ḥasan al-Ṭūsī (d. 460/1067) and al-Faḍl b. al-Ḥasan al-Ṭabarsī (d. 548/1153), the latter are ultimately intelligible. They may require supporting demonstration and their significations may be multiplex but they are not, finally, inexplicable.[20]

By contrast, the Sunnī exegetical tradition on this verse appears more tentative in assessing the ultimate intelligibility of the *mutashābihāt.* Al-Zamakhsharī refers to such verses as "endowed with dubiety (*mutashābihāt*) and with possibility (*muḥtamalāt*)"[21] while Ibn Kathīr insists that the *mutashābihāt* are those "verses in which there is doubt about the meaning for many people or some of them."[22] In by far the most sophisticated analysis of *muḥkam* and *mutashābih* as hermeneutical divisions, Fakhr al-Dīn al-Rāzī (d. 606/1210) develops a full-scale description of linguistic signification.[23] But he, too, prefaces this excursus with a defintion of the *mutashābihāt* that stresses their inherent ambiguity: "Since it is of the nature of any two *mutashābih* that man cannot distinguish between them, everything to which man cannot with certainty find his way is called *mutashābih* by applying the name of the cause (*sabab*) to the effect (*musabbab*)."[24]

But, taxonomic and hermeneutical concerns do not exhaust the exegetical energies expended on this verse. From a very early period transtextual issues emerged, issues that explore the literary terrain captured by the concepts of 'connection' and 'reception'. The notion of connection surfaces at least as early as the *Tafsīr* of Muqātil b. Sulaymān. This eighth-century traditionist, who was born in what is now Afghanistan, implicitly situates the Qur'ānic text within the broader literature of written revelation. The intertextual connections between the Qur'ān and its scriptural precedents open, for Muqātil, another semantic horizon, one which may conveniently be dubbed 'comprehensive scriptural stability'.

To understand his exegetical move here, it is necessary to sketch the framing sections of Muqātil's work on Q. 3:7. He opens his remarks on the third sūra with a *sabab al-nuzūl* that focuses upon the Christians of Najrān[25] and orients the interpretation of its first several verses to Jewish and Christian concerns. Coming to the *āyāt muḥkamāt* as the *umm al-kitāb*, he immediately makes the connection with *al-lawḥ al-maḥfūẓ*[26] and then adds: "These are the things made sacrosanct (*muḥarramāt*) for all peoples in their book. They are called the *umm al-kitāb* simply because they are written in all the books which God sent down on all the prophets. No people of any religion have not been charged with them."[27] Later, in his *aḥkām* commentary, Muqātil repeats this interpretation and adds the definitive statement: "Nothing in all the books abrogates these *muḥkamāt* verses. They are *muḥkamāt* for the entirety of the children of Adam, all of them. They are the *umm al-kitāb*, i.e. the *aṣl al-kitāb*. They are called the *aṣl al-kitāb* simply because they are written in *al-lawḥ al-maḥfūẓ* and in all of the books."[28]

This is a fascinating assertion, one which throws the whole interpretive agenda into a cross-traditional perspective. Muqātil's hermeneutical horizon has expanded to include not only the Qur'ān but such previous revelations as the Tawrāh and the Injīl, in fact, "all the books which God has sent down on all the prophets." Unequivocally, he posits a revelatory core to which people of any religion will be held accountable. Issues of 'centre' and 'periphery' lurk beneath these pronouncements as do those of scriptural abrogation, issues which eventually spawned their own literature of polemics and apologetics.[29]

Muqātil, commenting specifically on the *mutashābihāt*, ignores the general definitions attributed to Abū 'Ubayda and Mujāhid and restricts their signification to four sigla, the particular letter combinations which precede thirteen Qur'ānic sūras.[30] Interestingly, the equation is not with all the *fawātiḥ/muqaṭṭa'āt* but only with a subset of them. According to the full account as found, for example, in al-Suyūṭī's *Itqān*, these figured in a discussion which Muḥammad had with a certain Jew about the foretold length of the Prophet's sovereignty and the appointed time of his community.[31] Muqātil's understanding of *ta'wīl* in the phrase *seeking the ta'wīl of it* accords with this. The term carries none of the hermeneutical connotations which it eventually acquired but means simply the extent and *terminus ad quem* of Muḥammad's hegemony. Given this signification of *ta'wīl*, Muqātil's understanding of the subsequent phrase, *no one knows the ta'wīl of it but God*, is a foregone conclusion.[32]

With the phrase *al-rāsikhūn fī l-'ilm*, "those deeply rooted in knowledge," as it is normally rendered, Muqātil remains within his broader hermeneutical horizon, at least that portion of it which focuses upon the Jews. He certainly does not anticipate the future exegetical focus of this phrase which, with virtual unanimity, relates it to the Muslim *'ulamā'*, because he makes it applicable only to such Tawrāh people as 'Abdallāh b. Salām and his associates. Of the select group of early *mufassirūn* who have functioned as the foundational exegetical stratum for this analysis, he is alone in doing so. Others, however, propose equivalences which permit entrée into another exegetical trajectory from Q. 3:7, that concerned with 'reception', whether that concept is construed in terms of the varying capacities, both intellectual and moral, of those who 'receive' the Qur'ān or in terms of the value to be found in the variant accessibility of the Qur'ānic contents themselves.

Much of the first part of this pair hinges upon the understanding of *wāw*, an issue that has been well surveyed in previous studies. For example, unlike Muqātil's insistence on inceptive *wāw* (*wāw al-ibtidā'*), Mujāhid opts for conjunctive *wāw* (*wāw al-'atf*) so that the *al-rāsikhūn fī l-'ilm* share – at least partial – knowledge with God. Abū 'Ubayda goes further, melding the scholarly with the spiritual, by characterizing those thus designated as "deeply rooted in both *'ilm* and *īmān*."[33] The second part of the paired conceptualization of 'reception', however, deserves more extended treatment. It has prompted some fruitful reflection on what today might be termed the utility or purpose of textual investigation or, to use explicitly religious language, the spiritual value of scriptural scholarship.

Among the earliest to develop this matter more fully was Ibn Qutayba (d. 276/889), a great polymath of the third/ninth century who spent most of his life in Baghdād. He is one of the first to expose and express the theological conundrum contained in this verse. "What," he straightforwardly asks, "did the One who wanted the Qur'ān to be guidance and elucidation for his servants intend by sending down the Qur'ān's *mutashābih[āt]*?"[34] What purpose could they serve? Ibn Qutayba prefaces his response with some apposite remarks about the way the Arabic language works and about the multiple rhetorical strategies that it has at its disposal. He then makes an argument that strikes at the heart of contemporary egalitarianism. If the entire Qur'ān were of what one might term 'equal semantic accessibility' (*ẓāhir*), the ignorant and the educated would be on the same footing. Intellectual competition (*tafāḍul*) would be nullified and the mind's activity (*khawāṭir*) would cease to exist.[35]

Ibn Qutayba proceeds to buttress this with both a pedagogical and an epistemological argument. In his estimation pedagogy is a hierarchically structured process. Every branch of learning, he continues, includes matters of greater and lesser importance. This provides those who study a particular subject with the opportunity to advance, level by level, until they reach the highest degree, thereby acquiring the talents of analytical reflection and inferential deduction.[36] Taking another tack, he argues that positing the concept of internally undifferentiated fields of knowledge would erase not only the distinction between scholar and student but that between logical contrarieties, thus rendering cogitation impotent. To secure his argument Ibn Qutayba expands the domain well beyond that of Qur'ānic discourse to include such verbal productions as *ḥadīth,* poetry and even sermons. All of these genres, he maintains, incorporate different levels of what I have labeled 'semantic accessibility' and include subtleties of signification (*al-ma'nā al-laṭīf*), "about which even the advanced scholar can become confused and the individual of surpassing intellect can remain incapable of comprehending."[37]

It is worth recalling that the frequently unexpressed provocation of such efforts to justify the presence of *mutashābihāt* are the recurrent Qur'ān's references to itself with such terms as *mubīn, uḥkimat,* etc.[38] Nor was the need for such justification restricted to Sunnī *tafāsīr.* Al-Ṭūsī presents a number of what were to become standard exegetical vindications of the Qur'ānic *mutashābihāt.* His list of reasons includes (1) the need "to motivate the kind of investigation that real knowledge demands as opposed to relying on unexamined information," and (2) the importance of displaying the expertise of the *'ulamā'.*[39] Without the *mutashābihāt,* al-Ṭūsī argues, there would be no gradations of Qur'ānic accomplishment: "Whoever speaks the Arabic language would be a scholar of it [the Qur'ān]."[40] The Mu'tazilī *mufassir* Maḥmūd b. 'Umar al-Zamakhsharī (d. 538/1144) adds to this inventory the argument that the *mutashābihāt* are a test of faith because "when the believer, who believes that there is no inconsistency (*wa-lā munāqaḍa*) in the discourse of God and no variation (*wa-lā 'khtilāf*), sees there what is contradictory when understood literally (*fī ẓāhirihi*) and is thus keen to search for what would create reconciliation and cause it to flow in one channel, he ponders and has recourse to himself and others. God inspires him, explaining the *mutashābih*'s conformity to the *muḥkam,* increasing the confidence of his belief and the vigour of his conviction."[41]

A contemporary of al-Zamakhsharī's, though far removed from him geographically, was the Andalusian *mufassir* Abū Bakr Muḥammad b. al-'Arabī (d. 543/1148) who studied in both Damascus and Baghdad but lived most of his life in Seville. Ibn al-'Arabī repeats Ibn Qutayba's earlier defense of the *mutashābihāt* but with considerable restriction. Although he does not discuss this verse in his *aḥkām tafsīr,*[42] in his commentary on al-Tirmidhī's *Ṣaḥīḥ* he does address the question of the '*fawā'id*/benefits' to be derived from the Qur'ānic presence of the *mutashābihāt.* For this scholar as well, a Qur'ān in which all verses were equally clear would be a revelation that provided no means of differentiating degrees of knowledgeability.[43] But the degrees that interest Ibn al-'Arabī are not so much those between the learned and the ignorant but the distinctions that can be made among the *'ulamā'* themselves. Here, his explanation of *those deeply rooted in knowledge* proves interesting. Working within a rather elaborate and extended architectural trope, he describes the construction and consolidation of new knowledge on the foundations of past intellectual achievements by those whose learning is so secure that "the winds of remonstrations (*riyāḥ al-i'tirāḍāt*)" will not rock them.[44]

Abū Muḥammad 'Abd al-Ḥaqq b. 'Aṭiyya (d. 546/1151), was an Andalusian contemporary of Ibn al-'Arabī's and, like the latter, served as *qāḍī* for a period. A generation ago he became better known to Western scholars through Arthur Jeffery's publication of two *muqaddimāt,* that of the anonymous *Kitāb al-Mabānī* and that of Ibn 'Aṭiyya's *tafsīr.*[45] Although he does not treat this topic in that *muqaddima,* Ibn 'Aṭiyya offers a developed *tafsīr* of the full verse in the body of his commentary and, not unexpectedly, associates his remarks about 'benefits' with the phrase *those deeply rooted in knowledge.* Here, he probes the notion of 'deep-rootedness' (*rusūkh*), arguing that the very concept carries a comparative sense. "In what," he asks, "does their being deep-rooted consist if they know nothing more than anyone else?"[46] In his estimation the *mutashābihāt* within the Qur'ānic revelation necessitate and, indeed, cultivate a special class of people, one particularly equipped with a combination of native aptitude and extensive preparation, to comprehend such semantic multivalence. Their comprehension is, of course, not complete. That distinction is reserved for the divine intelligence. And even to characterize their partial comprehension, Ibn 'Aṭiyya is careful to use gradation language, acknowledging the variance of individual capability.[47] Intellectually, this class is a midpoint between God, who comprehends all, and the ordinary individual whose intellectual range is limited to the *muḥkam.*

For a classical Shī'ī perspective on this issue, al-Ṭabarsī provides a developed argument. Like his predecessor al-Ṭūsī (d. 460/1067), he ordinarily organizes his *tafsīr* on a particular verse, or group of verses, by subject matter, i.e. dealing separately, and sequentially, with issues of etymology, inflection, sentence structure, and, of course, meaning. At the very close of his lengthy treatment of Q. 3:7, al-Ṭabarsī poses the now-familiar question, "Why did God send down the *mutashābih[āt]* in the Qur'ān? Why did He not make all of it *muḥkam?*" While his response, summarizing in part that of al-Ṭūsī,[48] incorporates the factor of intellectual differentiation/hierarchy, it includes two additional elements. One strikes directly at the most conservative adherents of *al-tafsīr bi l-mā'thūr.* "Had God made the Qur'ān entirely *muḥkam,*" al-Ṭabarsī contends, "then everyone would have relied on the transmitted interpretation (*khabar*) and would have dispensed with close, reflective examination (*naẓar*) [of the text]."[49] Consequently, – and this is the second element – "the reward (*thawāb*) for close examination and for pursuing various lines of thought (*ittibāʿ al-khawāṭir*) to find out the meaning would not have accrued to them."[50]

Yet to forestall any criticism that he considers the Qur'ān maimed by ambiguity, al-Ṭabarsī quotes the Shāfiʿī *faqīh* ʿAlī b. Muḥammad al-Māwardī (d. 450/1058) to the effect that on the basis of Q. 11:1,[51] God has described the Qur'ān as entirely *muḥkam* and on the basis of Q. 39:23[52] as entirely *mutashābih*. The definitions of these terms which al-Ṭabarsī then cites from al-Māwardī are, not unexpectedly, capable of sustaining this tension. For al-Māwardī, the *muḥkam* verses, proceeding etymologically, are those secured and protected from the intrusion of any imperfection. Correlatively, the *mutashābih* are those verses which resemble each other with respect to goodness, truth, freedom from contradiction and imperfection, etc.[53] Obviously, from this meta-level of definitional inclusivity the dichotomy dissolves.

Although the renowned thirteenth-century *khāṭib* Abūl-Faraj b. al-Jawzī (d. 587/1200) devotes almost 100 pages of his *Funūn al-afnān* to classifying the Qur'ānic *mutashābihāt*, he does not address the issue of their utility. In his *musalsal* commentary *Zād al-Masīr*, however, he provides a convenient summary of the now multiple responses to the recurring question of 'why should there be *mutashābihāt*?' Expanding on the notion of reward or merit, one now finds mention of the *mutashābihāt* as a divine test (*mukhtabar*, cf. *imtiḥān* in other sources) for the believer.[54] And to earn that reward, believers, especially scholars, had better get busy. One of the pleasures of reading Ibn al-Jawzī is his propensity to seize upon a precise and pithy way of putting matters, and this instance is no exception. He says quite straightforwardly that God wanted scholars to occupy themselves with referring the *muḥkam* to the *mutashābih*. This would get them thinking long and hard, would spark their investigative interests and would thus allow them to be rewarded for their intellectual toil, just as for their other religious duties.[55]

To bolster these assertions, he quotes directly from the Ibn Qutayba passage that has already been discussed.[56] It is from Ibn al-Anbārī (d. 328/940),[57] however, that he adopts what I would like to call the 'pedagogical psychology' argument for the presence of the *mutashābihāt*: "People of every field of endeavour set forth abstruse concepts (*maʿānī ghāmiḍa*) and subtle issues in their areas of expertise so that by means of them they can make things difficult for their students and can train them to extract the right answer. This is because when students can handle the abstruse, they will be [yet] more capable of dealing with the obvious. Since the *ʿulamāʾ* consider that to be a good way of proceeding, it may be that God's sending down the *mutashābih* operates analogously."[58]

These two exegetical trajectories of 'connection' and 'reception' converge in *al-Tafsīr al-Kabīr* of Fakhr al-Dīn al-Rāzī (d. 606/1210). His commentary on this verse is certainly the most extensive of any in the corpus of classical exegetical works and a significant portion of it is addressed to the advantages or benefits of the *mutashābihāt.* I can only summarize some of the principal points that he makes. (1) The greater effort expended in trying to understand them will secure a greater reward.[59] (2) They provide an opportunity to test and clarify diverse theological views. (3) The need to use reason frees one from 'the darkness (*ẓulma*) of *taqlīd*'. (4) They require the cultivation of exegetical skills, such as knowledge of language, grammar and *uṣūl al-fiqh.*[60] (5) Finally, and most importantly, the *mutashābihāt* suit the Qur'ān to the differences in human capacity to receive it, allowing sufficient variety in the modes of revelation to accommodate both the learned and the ignorant.

Al-Rāzī's commentary on this verse also underscores the textual awareness that emerged in Muqātil's *Tafsīr,* the concept of what I have called 'comprehensive scriptural stability.' Despite the silence of much of the intervening exegetical tradition in al-Rāzī, one hears an echo of this theme. After citing a number of the Salafī *ḥadīth*s on the definitions of *muḥkam* and *mutashābih,* al-Rāzī presents his own view: "The obligations which come from God are divided into two parts. One part is that which cannot change from one dispensation (*shar'*) to another. That would be like the command to obey God, to guard against injustice, deceit, ignorance, and killing people without justification. Another part is that which differs from one dispensation to another, like the number of prayer periods, or the amounts of obligatory alms or the conditions governing commercial activity and sexual relations, etc."[61] For al-Rāzī, then, as for Muqātil, there are elements of revelation that remain constant from one *da'wa* to the next and these are the *muḥkamāt*. Conversely, there are those that God makes incumbent upon a particular people and these are the *mutashābihāt.*

II TRANSLATION AND TRANSFORMATION: CONTEMPORARY CRITICAL THEORY

To introduce the final section of this article, it is worth recapitulating the four fundamental nodes of discursive analysis with which this exegetical study has been concerned. The first directed attention to scholastic efforts at categorization or classification, while the second opened issues of what could be called exegetical potential, hermeneutic accessibility or, simply, interpretability. Both of these operate at the intratextual level, keeping the commentator tied tightly to the text as a lexical and linguistic artifact. The other two nodes, however, move beyond the text, opening into the much larger cognitive arena that, following Genette, I would specify as 'transtextual'. The third pushes to prominence the questions of scriptural connection and intertextuality, while the fourth acknowledges a variability in the interplay between text and recipient, one that can be construed as a function of semantic opacity or intellectual/moral capacity or both.

Ordinarily, Q. 3:7 has been treated as essentially a taxonomic or hermeneutical directive. The *tafsīr* on this verse, and the subsequent study of that *tafsīr*, have focused on the intratextual concerns expressed in my first two nodes, especially on the way that the particular lexemes relate to their meaning and use in other Qur'ānic passages and on the extent to which centuries of interpretation have clustered around particular themes and preoccupations. Another rehearsal of this would serve no useful purpose. But, through the exegesis of this passage, larger literary issues have also surfaced. Some lines of interpretation of Q. 3.7 raise transtextual issues, pushing the discussion beyond the canonically-inscribed boundaries of the Book.

The sense of 'connection' captured by commentators like Muqātil b. Sulaymān and Fakhr al-Dīn al-Rāzī, as they posit a revelatory core that perdures from one dispensation to another, introduces a number of intertwined concerns. Foremost, of course, is the question of how the Qur'ān connects with or relates to other scriptures. What are the ratios of similarity and difference? Are there prescribed limits, either chronological or cultural, to the diffusion of prior scriptures? Can the tension between Qur'ānic abrogation and the predictive value of previous revelations be sustained?

Yet, another aspect of this notion of connection is the explicit evidence of genre recognition. Such recognition inevitably involves definition, an act of identification expressed in terms of common elements. The Qur'ān makes specific and repeated statements of genre self-perception. It sees itself as a revealed book and thereby situates itself as part of an identifiable literary genre. Further, the Qur'ān is a self-authorizing narrative. Unlike much of later Islamic literature, it does not seek to ground its authority in earlier texts or authors. No *imprimatur* of attribution buttresses its claim to authority. Previous revelations and scriptures do not authenticate the Qur'ān. Rather, the Qur'ān mandates how they are to be read and received, thereby providing what partial authorization or authentication it chooses to bestow. Some earlier revelations may be permitted predictive value, but even this degree of authentication is an act of retrojection, not of authorizing attribution.

In addressing aspects of this notion of connection, some contemporary literary theorists make a useful distinction between the world behind the text and the world in front of the text.[62] It is the former, the world behind the text, that interests me here; the latter will be the subject of a subsequent section. To speak of the world behind the text is to speak of the world that generated and produced the text and this, in fact, has been subject of much Western scholarship on the Qur'ān for the last century and a half. Philological-historical criticism, largely drawn from the models of biblical scholarship, has explored the production history of the text, posing all of the expected queries about textual antecedents, oral and literate form conversion, stages and processes of redaction, etc. The epistemology underlying such lines of inquiry tends to view language as referential and informative and to see meaning as stable and determinate, passively awaiting discovery and disclosure, uncovering and conveyance. In the words of Paul Ricoeur, "The illusion is endlessly reborn that the text is a structure in itself and for itself and that reading happens to the text as some extrinsic and contingent event."[63]

Yet, the connection that Muqātil and others have created between the Qur'ān and earlier revelations is a function of Muqātil as reader/hearer. It reflects an experience of intertextuality, an awareness of the echoes between literary/scriptural composites, an instance of the anticipatory and retroactive construction of meaning that preoccupies contemporary reading theory.[64] That experience of 'connecting', of creating cognitive links with the world behind the text, occurs, of course, within the production of an explicitly intertexual work. A commentary, by its very nature, is an avowedly intertextual product. To elaborate, for a moment, on Genette's concept of transtextuality may help to clarify this. Genette defines transtextuality as "tout ce qui le met en relation, manifeste ou secrète, avec d'autres textes."[65] Within this overarching designation, he sets metatextuality as the specific text/commentary category. For him, the commentary or metatext embodies the *critical* relationship "par excellence."[66]

References to Genette and to contemporary reading theory provide a useful prelude to the other transtextual consideration that evolves from the commentary tradition on Q. 3:7, that of 'reception'. The notion of reception brings us to what I have previously referred to as the world in front of the text. It shifts the accent from those earlier poles of literary scholarship, text and context, to a more recent emphasis, a concentration upon the reader/hearer. (Despite its awkwardness, I use such a paired terminology as 'reader/hearer' or 'reader/hearer-centered criticism' to underscore the enduring pre-eminence of Qur'ānic aurality. To speak only of the Qur'ānic 'reader' would, I fear, subtly undermine this distinction).

Much of the discussion in the mid-century emergence of this phase of contemporary literary scholarship centered on the question of 'who is the reader?'.[67] The various taxonomies and theoretical perspectives suggested, such as those of Chatman, Booth and Iser, offered a more insightful way of understanding the relation between text and hearer/reader.[68] The work of Wolfgang Iser, for example, supplies us with a phenomenology of reading, one that takes its essential interactivity as fundamental. Arguing that reading/hearing is not a one-way process, not a passive internalization,

Iser contends that the configurative meaning of the text "is not given by the text itself; it arises from the meeting between the written text and the individual mind of the reader with its own particular history of experience, its own consciousness, its own outlook."[69]

Such analyses intersect with the exegesis of Q. 3:7 at those points where receptive plurality is fully acknowledged. There are gradations of intellect, of scholastic ability and accomplishment and, by extension, of psycho-spiritual formation. To use Iser's idiom "the degree to which the retaining mind will implement the perspective connections inherent in the text depends on a large number of subjective factors: memory, interest, attention, and mental capacity all affect the extent to which past contexts become present."[70] Nor is the act of reception necessarily a single, non-repeated event. Listeners listen again; readers read again. The repetition of textual receptivity is, in fact, an inescapable condition of the critical, exegetical turn. The semiotician Michael Riffaterre even speaks of two stages of reading, a first heuristic reading or sequential decoding and a second, retroactive reading. Only the second opens a truly hermeneutic perspective because it operates within a grasp of the text's comprehensive structure.[71]

From a related perspective, some rather recent work within this field of literary studies underscores the temporal linearity of the reading/listening event and appreciates the transformative quality of that experience. The reader/hearer is changed through the event and brings that transformed consciousness back to the text in an ever-adjusting series of reciprocally transformative exchanges. Again, such insights correlate well with the 'gradation' language or the 'stages-of-study' language that some *mufassirūn* have used to justify the Qur'ānic presence of *mutashābihāt.* The transformative potential of the text is actualized in the exegetical engagement with the *mutashābihāt.* A profounder understanding emerges from the encounter and the hearer/reader brings that more enriched consciousness to the next textual confrontation in a continually reiterative process.

Yet, boundaries for that reiteration are set, in the phrase Stanley Fish made popular, by the "interpretive community" within which the act of reading/listening takes place.[72] Seeking to break the impasse between the objectivist position that the text dominates by imposing a single, unitary meaning on its hearers/readers and the subjectivist view that locates meaning entirely within the whim of the individual recipient, Fish looks at the sociology of the reception experience. Particular communities shape and form readers/hearers, providing the institutional or paradigmatic framework within which interpretive accountability operates.[73] Meaning, then, is neither entirely objective or subjective. Rather, it is shared by members of particular social and cultural groups.[74]

Translation of these insights into the language of classical Qur'ānic exegesis requires little adjustment. Taken collectively, the commentators are nothing if not an 'interpretive community', one both defined by a textual tradition and constrained by its communal assumptions and methodologies. Yet, even within the confines of these assimilated assumptions, the individual *mufassir* meets the text anew and creatively shapes the continuing permutation of the critical community.

Tracing that evolution both synchronically and diachronically has captured the attention of a related form of literary criticism, the *Rezeptionsgeschichte* or *Rezeptionsästhetik* linked most closely with the work of Hans Robert Jauss.[75] Where Iser's listener/reader remains de-historicized or transhistorical, the reception theory of Jauss presents a more historically sensitive understanding of this process, one that accounts for the 'horizon of expectations' operative within a particular historical period.[76] For Jauss, the method of historical reception, which is "indispensable for the understanding of literature from the distant past," entails the reconstruction of the horizon of expectations in the face of which a work was created and received in the past."[77]

Reacting to criticisms that the notion of 'interpretive communities' remains too abstract and hypothetical, or too static and homogeneous, and that both the theory and practice of 'reception history' have been insufficiently attentive to inequities of power and social control, more recent voices have begun to focus on the coercive power of interpretive communities, on the realization that textual control can also be socio-political control.[78] In light of such equations, it is not difficult to see that grappling with the duality of *muḥkamāt/mutashābihāt* forces the *mufassirūn* to ask about the location of authority for interpretation, to raise the question of exegetical hegemony.

Ideological analysis has thus joined the arsenal of literary scholarship as critics strive self-consciously to situate their own receptive postures and to uncover the politics of interpretation in previous acts of listening/reading. Steven Mailloux, for example, wants to refocus attention from reception as individually experienced to reception as socially located. What he calls 'rhetorical hermeneutics' would track the "exchanges among interpreters within specific historical contexts," recognizing that these take place within traditions of argumentation and that these traditions are "themselves part of the micropractices making up culture at any historical moment."[79]

Yet, more inclusively, reading the exegetical tradition on Q. 3:7 through the lens of contemporary reader/hearer-oriented criticism recasts the foundational semantic equation. A perception of meaning as stable and determinate is replaced with an awareness of meaning as something created in the activity of reception, in the interplay of text and recipient. Language as influential and operative, as rhetoric that achieves its effect through the experience-in-time of hearing/reading, supersedes more static conceptions.

The inescapable dynamism and fluidity of 'reception' as a literary-critical category points to what I would call the morphogenesis of meaning, viewing textual comprehension as created and recreated in the interactive encounter of hearer/reader and text. The language of levels or gradations of understanding, specifically where it appears in the exegesis of Q. 3:7 but also more generally within the history of Qur'ānic *tafsīr*,[80] implicitly credits the continually creative nature of this interaction. As audience-oriented criticism concentrates more intensely on the congeries of activities that can be collected under the rubrics of hearing/reading, noting that such processes as preview and review, looking forward and looking back, anticipation and adjustment or correction are inescapably part of any text/recipient encounter, it echoes some basic exegetical insights. Classical dictums like the adjuration to "interpret the Qur'ān by the Qur'ān"[81] recognize the inherent intratextuality of the exegetical endeavour and understand that the hearer/reader brings a continuously formed and re-formed comprehension to that endeavour.[82] Expanded from the individual to the corporate level, one can speak of 'reading formations' that relate the reader/listener and the text within a particular discursive practice, one that is culturally-constructed and continually modified by the incessant interaction of text and recipient within an ever-changing context.[83]

Finally, aspects of the exegetical tradition on Q. 3:7, particularly that which dwells upon the advantages or benefits of the Qur'ānic *mutashābihāt*, exhibit a profound appreciation for the persuasive power of Qur'ānic language. Even those most casually acquainted with the Qur'ān recognize that it is a highly interactive text, one that frequently addresses the listener directly, seeking to persuade, to influence, to transform. The rhetorical affectivity of the Qur'ān challenges any notion of receptive passivity, any sense that hearing or reading it can be a matter of the mere conveyance of meaning. For the classical commentators, the juxtaposition of *muḥkamāt* and *mutashābihāt* within the Qur'ānic corpus provides a pre-eminent opportunity for the kind of full intellectual, moral and spiritual engagement that the text incessantly demands.

NOTES

1 Stefan Wild, "The Self-Referentiality of the Qur'ān: Sūra 3,7 as an Exegetical Challenge," forthcoming in *With Reverence for the Word: Medieval Scriptural Exegesis in Judaism, Christianity and Islam*, ed. J. McAuliffe et al.

2 Michel Lagarde, "De l'ambiguïté (mutašābih) dans le Coran: tentatives d'explication des exégètes musulmans," *Quaderni di studi arabi* 3 (1985):45–62.

3 Leah Kinberg, "*Muḥkamāt* and *Mutashābihāt* (Koran 3/7): Implication of a Koranic Pair of Terms in Medieval Exegesis," *Arabica* 35 (1988):143–72.

4 John Wansbrough, *Quranic Studies: Sources and Methods of Scriptural Interpretation* (Oxford: Oxford University Press, 1977). For the collected citation of earlier

work, see Rudi Paret, *Der Koran. Kommentar und Konkordanz* (Stuttgart: W. Kohlhammer, 1980), 60–1.

5 Of related interest is an article by Mahjoub Ben Milad that sketches a general theory of polarity in Arab culture and understands the 'seven *mathānī*' as the seven basic polarities which subsume all of the ambiguous verses. "Ambiguïté et *mathani* coraniques," in *L'ambivalence dans la culture arabe*, ed. P. Alexandre, R. Arnaldez et al. (Paris: Éditions Anthropos, 1967), 366–81.

6 The term 'intertextuality,' whose coinage is regularly attributed to Julia Kristeva, has collected multiple definitions. In general, it points to the fact that texts do not operate as closed systems but that both their production and reception occur within the noetic ambience of other texts. For a pertinent collection of essays, see *Intertextuality: Theories and Practice*, ed. Michael Worton and Judith Still (Manchester: Manchester University Press, 1990).

7 Badr al-Dīn Muḥammad b. 'Abdallāh al-Zarkashī, *al-Burhān fī 'Ulūm al-Qur'ān*, ed. Muḥammad Abū al-Faḍl Ibrāhīm (Cairo: Dār al-Turāth, n.d.).

8 Jalāl al-Dīn 'Abd al-Raḥmān al-Suyūṭī, *al-Itqān fī 'Ulūm al-Qur'ān*, ed. Muḥammad Abū Faḍl Ibrāhīm (Cairo: Dār al-Turāth, 1985/1405).

9 Mujāhid b. Jabr, *Tafsīr Mujāhid*, ed. 'Abd al-Raḥmān al-Ṭāhir b. Muḥammad al-Sūrtī (Islamabad: Majma' al-Buḥūth al-Islāmiyya, n.d.), 1:122.

10 Zayd b. 'Alī, *Tafsīr Zayd b. 'Alī al-Musammā Tafsīr Gharīb al-Qur'ān*, ed. Muḥammad Taqī al-Ḥakīm (Cairo: Dār al-'Ālamiyya, 1412/1992), 107; Abū 'Ubayda Ma'mar b. al-Muthannā, *Majāz al-Qur'ān*, ed. Muḥammad Fu'ād Sizkīn (Beirut: Mu'assasat al-Risāla, 1401/1981), 1:86; cf. Muqātil b. Sulaymān, *Tafsīr Muqātil b. Sulaymān*, ed. 'Abdallāh Maḥmūd Shiḥāta (Cairo: al-Hay'a al-Miṣriyya al-'Āmma lil-Kitāb, 1979), 1:264.

11 *al-halakāt allāti ahlakū bihā*. Mujāhid, *Tafsīr*, 1:122.

12 Zayd b. 'Alī, *Tafsīr*, 107; Abū 'Ubayda, *Majāz al-Qur'ān*, 1:86; cf. Muqātil, *Tafsīr*, 1:264.

13 'Abd al-Razzāq b. Hammām al-Ṣan'ānī, *Tafsīr al-Qur'ān*, ed. Muṣṭfafā Muslim Muḥammad (Riyadh: Maktabat al-Rushd, 1410/1989), 1:115.

14 Mujāhid, *Tafsīr*, 1:121.

15 Sufyān al-Thawrī, *Tafsīr Sufyān al-Thawrī*, ed. Imtiyāz 'Alī Arshī (Beirut: Dār al-Kutub al-'Ilmiyya, 1403/1983), 75.

16 Abū 'Ubayda, *Majāz al-Qur'ān*, 1:86, *yushbihu ba'ḍuhā ba'ḍan*, and Mujāhid, *Tafsīr*, 1:121, *yuṣaddiqu ba'ḍuhā ba'ḍan*, respectively.

17 Abū Ja'far Muḥammad b. Jarīr al-Ṭabarī, *Jāmi' al-Bayān 'an Ta'wīl Āy al-Qur'ān*, ed. Maḥmūd Muḥammad Shākir and Aḥmad Muḥammad Shākir (Cairo: Dār al-Ma'ārif, 1954–68), 6:169–82.

18 Further to al-Ṭabarī's treatment of *muḥkam* and *mutashābih*, see Jane Dammen McAuliffe, "Qur'ānic Hermeneutics: The Views of al-Ṭabarī and Ibn Kathīr," in *Approaches to the History of the Interpretation of the Qur'ān*, ed. A. Rippin (Oxford: Clarendon Press, 1988), 50–4.

19 'Alī b. Ibrāhīm al-Qummī, *Tafsīr*, ed. Ṭayyib al-Mūsawī al-Jazā'irī (Qumm: Dār al-Kitāb li 'l-Ṭibā'ah, 1202 [solar]), 1:96–7.

20 Muḥammad b. al-Ḥasan al-Ṭūsī, *al-Tibyān fī Tafsīr al-Qur'ān*, ed. Aḥmad Ḥabīb Qaṣīr al-'Amalī (Beirut: Dār Iḥyā' al-Turāth al-'Arabī, n.d.), 2:394–8; al-Faḍl b. al-Ḥasan al-Ṭabarsī, *Majma' al-Bayān fī Tafsīr al-Qur'ān*, intr. Muḥsin al-Amīn al-Ḥusaynī al-'Āmilī (Beirut: Dār Maktabat al-Ḥayāh, 1380/1961), 3:14–7.

21 Maḥmūd b. 'Umar al-Zamakhsharī, *al-Kashshāf 'an Ḥaqā'iq al-Tanzīl wa-'Uyūn al-Aqāwīl fī Wujūh al-Ta'wīl*, ed. Muḥammad Mūsā 'Āmir (Cairo: Dār al-Muṣḥaf, 1397/1977), 1:162.

22 Ismā'īl b. 'Umar b. Kathīr, *Tafsīr al-Qur'ān al-'Aẓīm* (Beirut: Dār al-Fikr, 1389/1970), 2:5. Cf. McAuliffe, "Qur'ānic Hermeneutics," 58–62.
23 Fakhr al-Dīn al-Rāzī, *al-Tafsīr al-Kabīr* (*Mafātīḥ al-Ghayb*) (Beirut: Dār al-Fikr, 1401/1981), 7:179–93.
24 al-Rāzī, *Tafsīr,* 7:181.
25 The consistent *sabab al-nuzūl* for this verse is the delegation of Najrān disputing with the Prophet about Jesus and using Qur'ānic terms like *kalima* and *rūḥ* to justify their Christology. This was deemed to be *mā tashābaha minhu.* Additionally, there are recurrent allusions to Q. 3:59: "The likeness of Jesus in God's eyes is the likeness of Adam. He created him from dust. Then he said to him 'Be' and he was."
26 A.J. Wensinck and C.E. Bosworth, EI^2 s.v. "Lawḥ" which notes that the idea of heavenly tablets of revelation and of tablets of fate or God's decisions are contained in the Book of Jubilees.
27 Muqātil, *Tafsīr,* 1:264.
28 Muqātil b. Sulaymān, *Tafsīr al-Khams Mi'at Āya min al-Qur'ān,* ed. I. Goldfeld (Shfaram: Dār al-Mashriq, 1980), 275. Cf. Claude Gilliot, "Muqātil, grand exégète, traditionniste et théologien maudit," *Journal asiatique* 279 (1991):39–92.
29 On various aspects of intrascriptural relations see Jane Dammen McAuliffe, "The Abrogation of Judaism and Christianity in Islam: A Christian Perspective," *Concilium* (1994/3), 154–63; "The Qur'ānic Context of Muslim Biblical Scholarship," *Islam and Christian-Muslim Relations* 7 (1996):141–58; "Ṭabarī's Prelude to the Prophet," forthcoming in *Al-Ṭabarī: A Medieval Muslim Historian and his Work,* ed. Hugh Kennedy (Princeton: Darwin Press); "Assessing the *Isrā'īliyyāt*: An Exegetical Conundrum," in *Story-telling in the framework of non-fictional Arabic literature,* ed. S. Leder (Wiesbaden: Harrassowitz Verlag, 1998), 345–369.
30 *alif-lām-mīm, alif-lām-mīm-ṣād, alif-lām-mīm-rā', alif-lām-rā'.*
31 al-Suyūṭi, *Itqān,* 3:25–6. For a related discussion of Jewish connections with the Prophet's chronology see Uri Rubin, *The Eye of the Beholder: The Life of Muḥammad as Viewed by the Early Muslims* (Princeton: Darwin Press, 1995), 189–214.
32 Muqātil, *Tafsīr,* 1:264: "how many years they will rule, meaning the *umma* of Muḥammad who will rule until the day of resurrection except for the days in which God will test them with *al-dajjāl.*" 'Abd al-Razzāq, *Tafsīr,* 1:116, also recognizes disjunction, signaling this by transposing *yaqūl* to avoid any ambiguity.
33 Abū 'Ubayda, *Majāz al-Qur'ān,* 1:86.
34 'Abdallāh b. Muslim al-Dīnawarī b. Qutayba, *Ta'wīl Mushkil al-Qur'ān,* ed. al-Sayyid Aḥmad Ṣaqr (Beirut: Dār al-Kutub al-'Ilmiyya, 1401/1981), 86.
35 Ibid. For the negative linkage of Q. 3:7 with the Qur'ānic censure of *jadal,* see Jane Dammen McAuliffe, "The Genre Boundaries of Qur'ānic Exegesis" forthcoming in *With Reverence for the Word: Medieval Scriptural Exegesis in Judaism, Christianity and Islam,* ed. J. McAuliffe et al.; "'Debate with Them in the Better Way': The Construction of a Qur'ānic Commonplace," forthcoming in *Aspects of Literary Hermeneutics in Arabic Culture: Myths, Historical Archetypes and Symbolic Figures in Arabic Literature, Beiruter Texte und Studien,* eds. A. Neuwirth, S. Gunther, M. Jarrar (Wiesbaden: Franz Steiner).
36 Ibn Qutayba, *Ta'wīl Mushkil,* 86.
37 Ibid. Interestingly, Muḥammad b. Muḥammad al-Māturīdī's (d. 333/944) definitions of the *tafsīr/ta'wīl* pair in the introduction to his commentary

parallel some of those which other *mufassirūn* have offered for *muḥkam/mutashābih.* For example, he repeats the saying that "*tafsīr* is for the Companions and *ta'wīl* is for the *fuqahā'*" in order to restrict *tafsīr* activity to actual eye witnesses of the Qur'ānic period. *Tafsīr,* therefore, is univalent while *ta'wīl* is multivalent. Muḥammad b. Muḥammad b. Maḥmūd al-Māturīdī al-Samarqandī, *Ta'wīlāt Ahl al-Sunna* (also *Ta'wīlāt al-Qur'ān*), ed. Muḥammad Mustafīḍ al-Raḥmān (Baghdad: Maṭba'at al-Irshād, 1404/1983), 6.

38 E.g. Q. 5:15, Q. 11:1, Q. 12:1; also Q. 22:52, *thumma yuḥkimu 'llāhu āyātihi.*

39 al-Ṭūsī, *al-Tibyān,* 2:396.

40 Ibid.

41 al-Zamakhsharī, *al-Kashshāf,* 1:162. On al-Zamakhsharī's exegesis of Q. 3:7 see Ignaz Goldziher, *Die Richtungen der islamischen Koranauslegung* (Leiden: Brill, 1920), 127–9.

42 Muḥammad b. 'Abdallāh b. al-'Arabī, *Aḥkām al-Qur'ān,* ed. Muḥammad 'Abd al-Qādir 'Aṭā' (Beirut: Dār al-Kutub al-'Ilmiyya, 1408/1988).

43 Muḥammad b. 'Abdallāh b. al-'Arabī, *'Āriḍāt al-Aḥwadhī bi-Sharḥ Ṣaḥīḥ al-Tirmidhī* (Beirut: Dār al-'Ilm li 'l-Jamī', 1972), 11:115.

44 Ibid., 11:119.

45 Arthur Jeffery, *Two Muqaddimas to the Qur'anic Sciences: the Muqaddima to the Kitab al-Mabani and the Muqaddima of Ibn 'Atiyya to his Tafsir,* edited from the MSS in Berlin and in Cairo, 2nd ed. revised by 'Abdullāh Ismā'īl al-Ṣāwī (Cairo: Maktabat al-Khānijī, 1392/1972). For a Karrāmī attribution of the *Kitāb al-Mabānī,* see Aron Zysow, "Two Unrecognized Karrāmī Texts," *Journal of the American Oriental Society* 108 (1988):577–87. For the genre of *muqaddimāt al-tafāsīr,* see Jane Dammen McAuliffe, "Ibn al-Jawzī's Exegetical Propaedeutic: Introduction and Translation [of the *muqaddima* to *Zād al-Masīr fī 'Ilm al-Tafsīr*]," *Alif: Journal of Comparative Poetics* 8 (1988):101–13; "Creating a Genre: Explorations in *muqaddimāt al-tafāsīr,*" forthcoming in *Qur'ānic Studies on the Eve of the 21st Century,* ed. J.J.G. Jansen and Nasr Abu Zaid.

46 'Abd al-Ḥaqq b. 'Aṭiyya al-Gharnāṭī, *Al-Muḥarrar al-Wajīz fī Tafsīr al-Kitāb al-'Azīz,* ed. Aḥmad Ṣāriq al-Mallāḥ (Cairo: al-Majlis al-A'lā li 'l-Shu'ūn al-Islamiyya, 1399/1979), 1:341.

47 E.g. "to the extent that he is capable" and "each according to his capability." Ibid., 1:340 and 341, respectively.

48 al-Ṭūsī, *al-Tibyān,* 2:396.

49 Similarly, but at greater length, al-Zamakhsharī, *al-Kashshāf,* 1:162.

50 al-Ṭabarsī, *Majma' al-Bayān,* 3:17.

51 "*Alif-lām-rā'.* A book the verses of which are fortified (*uḥkimat*) and then set forth in detail (*fuṣṣilat*), from the One who is wise, informed."

52 "God has sent down the best of statements, a book *mutashābih, mathāniya* which makes the flesh of those who fear their Lord shudder so that their flesh and their hearts soften to God's reminder. That is God's guidance by which He guides those whom He wishes. For the one whom God sends astray there is no guide."

53 Ibid. For an example of contemporary exegetical controversy about Qur'ānic *mutashābih,* see J.J.G. Jansen, "Polemics on Mustafa Mahmud's Koran Exegesis," *Proceedings of the Ninth Congress of the Union Européenne des Arabisants et Islamisants, Amsterdam, 1st to 7th September 1978,* ed. R. Peters (Leiden: E.J. Brill, 1981), 110–22.

54 'Abd al-Raḥmān b. 'Alī b. al-Jawzī, *Zād al-Masīr fī 'Ilm al-Tafsīr* (Beirut: al-Maktab al-Islāmī, 1404/1984), 1:353.

55 Ibid.

56 Ibid. He includes, with supplementary explanation, the same proverb which Ibn Qutayba cited: "'The defect of wealth is that it bequeaths simple-mindedness while the virtue of poverty is that it evokes clever thinking.' Because when one is in need, one becomes clever."

57 Abū Bakr Muḥammad b. al-Qāsim b. al-Anbārī was a traditionist and theologian who wrote works on *aḍdād*, on *waqf* and *ibtidā'*, and on Qur'ānic orthography. *EI*^{2}, s.v. (C. Brockelmann).

58 Ibn al-Jawzī, *Zād al-Masīr*, 1:353.

59 al-Rāzī, *al-Tafsīr*, 7:185. He supports this with Q. 3:142, "Do you reckon that you will enter the Garden while God has not yet known those of you who have made great effort (*alladhīna jāhadū minkum*) and those who are steadfast?"

60 al-Rāzī, *al-Tafsīr*, 7:184–5.

61 al-Rāzī, *al-Tafsīr*, 7:183.

62 In an influential essay entitled "The Hermeneutical Function of Distanciation," Paul Ricoeur makes this distinction, not in relation to scriptural texts, but in the more restricted context of authored works of fiction and poetry. Paul Ricoeur, *Hermeneutics and the Human Sciences*, ed. and trans. John B. Thompson (Cambridge: Cambridge University Press, 1981), 131–44.

63 Paul Ricoeur, *Time and Narrative*, trans. Kathleen Blamey and David Pellauer (Chicago: University of Chicago Press, 1988), 3:164.

64 Notions of 'echo' and 'pretext' figure in Angelika Neuwirth's "Intertextuality and 'Intrinsic Exegesis': Sūrat ar-Raḥmān between its Biblical Pretext and its Implied Audience," forthcoming in *With Reverence for the Word: Medieval Scriptural Exegesis in Judaism, Christianity and Islam*, ed. J. McAuliffe et al.

65 Gérard Genette, *Palimpsestes: la littérature au second degré* (Paris: Seuil, 1982), 7. English trans., Channa Newman and Claude Doubinsky (Lincoln: University of Nebraska Press, 1997). This definition is actually closer to the way I have been using the term 'intertextual'. Genette prefers to reserve the idea of intertextuality for the more restricted range of textual co-presence found in such activities as quotation, plagiarism and direct allusion.

66 Genette, *Palimpsestes*, 10. It is tempting to graft Genette's distinction between the 'hypotexte' and the 'hypertexte' onto the hermeneutical relationship but Genette confines these terms to literary transformations of earlier works. He does, however, realize that a hypertext often functions as a commentary. A parody, for example, frequently critiques its precursor text.

67 Retrospective surveys often mark 1980 as a summative moment in post-war reader-response and reception theory because that year saw the publication of two important anthologies, Susan R. Suleiman and Inge Crossman, eds., *The Reader in the Text: Essays on Audience and Interpretation* (Princeton: Princeton University Press, 1980) and Jane P. Tompkins, ed., *Reader-Response Criticism: From Formalism to Post-Structuralism* (Baltimore: Johns Hopkins University Press, 1980) as well as Stanley Fish's influential *Is There a Text in This Class? The Authority of Interpretive Communities* (Cambridge: Harvard University Press, 1980).

68 Seymour Chatman, *Story and Discourse: Narrative Structure in Fiction and Film* (Ithaca: Cornell University Press, 1978) and Wayne Booth, *The Rhetoric of Fiction*, 2nd ed. (Chicago: University of Chicago Press, 1983).

69 Wolfgang Iser, *The Implied Reader: Patterns of Communication in Prose Fiction from Bunyan to Beckett* (Baltimore: Johns Hopkins University Press, 1974), 284. Originally published as *Der Implizite Leser: Kommunikationsformen des Romans von Bunyan bis Beckett* (Munich: Wilhelm Fink, 1972). Iser has been criticized for lack of exemplification, i.e. for providing few instances of dissimilar or

conflicting interpretations of particular texts. See Steven Mailloux, *Interpretive Conventions: The Reader in the Study of American Fiction* (Ithaca: Cornell University Press, 1982), 49.

70 Wolfgang Iser, *The Act of Reading: A Theory of Aesthetic Response* (Baltimore: Johns Hopkins University Press, 1978), 118. Originally published as *Der Akt des Lesens. Theorie ästhetischer Wirkung* (Munich: Wilhelm Fink, 1976).

71 Michael Riffaterre, *Semiotics of Poetry* (Bloomington: Indiana University Press, 1978), 5–6. Two recent studies on rereading are: Marcel Cornis-Pope, *Hermeneutic Desire and Critical Rewriting: Narrative Interpretation in the Wake of Poststructuralism* (Basingstoke: Macmillan Press, 1992) and Matei Calinescu, *Rereading* (New Haven: Yale University Press, 1993).

72 Fish, *Is There a Text*, 304.

73 "Again the point is that while there are always mechanisms for ruling out readings, their source is not the text but the presently recognized interpretive strategies for producing the text." Fish, *Is There a Text*, 347.

74 For S. Fish on the relationship between the theory of interpretive communities and change see his *Doing What Comes Naturally: Change, Rhetoric, and the Practice of Theory in Literary and Legal Studies* (Durham: Duke University Press, 1989), 141–60.

75 Hans Robert Jauss, *Toward an Aesthetic of Reception*, trans. Timothy Bahti (Minneapolis: University of Minnesota Press, 1982); and *Aesthetic Experience and Literary Hermeneutics*, trans. Michael Shaw (Minneapolis: University of Minnesota Press, 1982). The former is a collection of previously published essays and the latter was originally published as *Ästhetische Erfahrung und literarische Hermeneutik I* (Munich: Wilhelm Fink, 1977).

76 Robert Holub, who first introduced 'reception theory' to a more general, English-speaking audience, criticized Jauss for never adequately defining this 'horizon of expectations'. *Reception Theory: A Critical Introduction* (London: Methuen, 1984), 58–63. See also *Holub's Crossing Borders: Reception Theory, Poststructuralism, Deconstruction* (Madison: University of Wisconsin Press, 1992). Broadly understood, however, it appears to correspond with both the genre expectations alive in a specific cultural moment and, more negatively, to what Mohammad Arkoun would call the *impensé* and the *impensable* of any individual cultural configuration. Mohammad Arkoun, *Ouvertures sur l'Islam*, 2nd ed. (Paris: Jacques Grancher, 1992), 33. Arkoun develops this notion of the *impensable* in various of the essays to be found in his *Lectures du Coran* (Paris: Maisonneuve and Larose, 1982) and *Pour une critique de la raison islamique* (Paris: Maisonneuve and Larose, 1984).

77 Jauss, *Toward an Aesthetic*, 28. In an engaging essay entitled "First Steps Toward a History of Reading," the historian Robert Darnton highlights cultural variety when he asks whether reading is "different for Chinese, who read pictographs, and for Westerners, who scan lines ... for Southeast Asians whose languages lack tenses and order reality spatially... for the holy man in the presence of the Word and for the consumer studying labels in a supermarket?" Darnton concludes that the "differences seem endless, for reading is not simply a skill but a way of making meaning, which must vary from culture to culture." *The Kiss of Lamourette: Reflections in Cultural History* (New York: Norton, 1990), 171.

78 Edward Said, for example: "If, as we have recently been told by Stanley Fish, every act of interpretation is made possible and given force by an interpretive community, then we must go a great deal further in showing what situation, what historical and social configuration, what political interests are concretely entailed by the very existence of interpretive communities." *The World, the Text, and the Critic* (Cambridge: Harvard University Press, 1983), 26.

79 Steven Mailloux, "Power, Rhetoric, and Theory: Reading American Texts," in *Making Sense: The Role of the Reader in Contemporary American Fiction*, ed. Gerhard Hoffmann (Munich: Wilhelm Fink, 1989), 115. Cf. his earlier, "Learning to Read: Interpretation and Reader-response Criticism," *Studies in the Literary Imagination* 12 (1979):93–108. Mailloux's more developed exposition of 'rhetorical hermeneutics', with its insistence upon "rhetorical histories ... histories that are interpretive, institutional, and cultural," actually brings him quite close to the agenda of Jauss. See Mailloux, *Rhetorical Power* (Ithaca: Cornell University Press, 1989), 19.

80 For recent work on the 'senses of scripture' in Qur'ānic exegesis, see Gerhard Böwering, "The Scriptural 'Senses' in Medieval Sufi Qur'ān Exegesis," forthcoming in *With Reverence for the Word: Medieval Scriptural Exegesis in Judaism, Christianity and Islam*, ed. J. McAuliffe et al.

81 For classical expositions of a sequential exegetical methodology, see Jane Dammen McAuliffe, "Ibn Taymiyya's *Muqaddimatun fī Uṣūl al-Tafsīr*," in *Windows on the House of Islam: Muslim Sources on Spirituality and Religious Life*, ed. John Renard (Berkeley: University of California Press, 1998), 35–43; and "Qur'ānic Hermeneutics," 55–58.

82 For example, anticipated connections with such Qur'ānic vocabulary of *mubīn*, *uḥkimat*, etc., both expressed and inferred, animate the commentary on *muḥkam/ mutashābih*, Q. 3:7.

83 Tony Bennett contends that "such interaction would be conceived of as occurring between the culturally activated *text* and the culturally activated *reader*, an interaction structured by the material, social, ideological, and institutional relationships in which both text and readers are inescapably inscribed." "Texts, Readers, Reading Formations," in *Modern Literary Theory: A Reader*, ed. Philip Rice and Patricia Waugh, 2nd ed. (London: Edward Arnold, 1992), 216. Bennett's article was originally published in *The Bulletin of the Midwest Modern Language Association* 16 (1983):3–17.

Chapter 4

Formulaic Features of the Punishment-Stories

Alford T. Welch

If they call thee [Muḥammad] a liar, so too before them the people of Noah called him a liar, as did 'Ād and Thamūd, and the people of Abraham, the people of Lot, and the people of Madyan. Moses also they called a liar. And I indulged the unbelievers, then I seized them, and how [terrible] was My retribution!

Sūrat al-Ḥajj (Q. 22) mentions here in verses 42–44[1] the peoples of seven of Muḥammad's predecessors who appear frequently in the Qur'ān in accounts often called "punishment-stories," "Straflegenden," etc. Anyone reading these accounts or hearing them recited is immediately struck by their formulaic features – repeated elements that convey added force to passages that are already powerful in their warnings to those who reject God's messengers.

A wide variety of formulaic elements occur frequently throughout the Qur'ān, consistent with its essentially oral nature. Formulaic introductory statements, refrains, and repeated rhyme phrases are just a few examples.[2] Among the most memorable formulaic introductory statements are those that comprise entire identical verses, such as the praise formula that occurs at the beginning of sūras *Al-Ḥadīd* (Q. 57), *Al-Ḥashr* (Q. 59), and *Al-Ṣaff* (Q. 61): "All that is in the heavens and the earth magnifies God; He is the All-mighty, the All-wise."[3] One example of the many refrains that punctuate major themes of the Qur'ān is the statement, "Woe on that day to those who call it a lie!," which occurs ten times as separate verses in *Sūrat al-Mursalāt* (Q. 77), a sūra with fifty verses. The refrain that occurs most frequently in a single sūra of the Qur'ān is the rhetorical question, "O which of your Lord's bounties will you two [jinn and man] count false (*tukadhdhibān*)?,"[4] that (after the introductory passage) occurs as virtually every other verse in *Sūrat al-Raḥmān* (Q. 55), which has 78 verses. Among the many types of formulaic statements that serve as rhyme phrases in the Qur'ān, the most conspicuous are the hundreds that end with two divine epithets, such as "God is All-forgiving, All-compassionate," "God is All-knowing, All-wise," and "God is All-mighty, All-wise." The first of these occurs over fifty times as a rhyme formula in the Qur'ān, and the other two occur over twenty times each.

These formulaic features of the Qur'ān and others all come together in versions of the "punishment-stories." Expressions that occur frequently in the descriptions and discussions below to designate the formulaic features of the punishment-stories will be used according to the following definitions. The terms "formula" and "formulaic" are used to refer to any verse or statement in one account that appears verbatim in another, and also to individual terms or phrases that serve the same significant function in a series of accounts. Thus an "introductory formula" could be an entire verse, the opening statement or phrase of a verse, or a single word that introduces several accounts in the same group of punishment-stories. The term "refrain" is used for one or more entire verses that occur at the ends of two or more accounts in the same series. The expression "schematic form" refers to verses, statements, or other extensive wording that occurs verbatim in two or more accounts in the same series.

Most of the so-called punishment-stories are not stories in the usual sense or even narratives, although it is not unusual for them to occur along with "prophet stories" that have narrative form, and in some sūras one or more in a group of punishment-stories are fully developed as narratives.[5] Their basic plot is that God sends or selects a messenger from among the people of a tribe or town, who urges his people to serve only the true God, warns them that they will be destroyed if they reject his message, which the majority do, and then God rescues the messenger and those who believe him and destroys those who do not. Punishment-stories occur in groups, usually featuring four or more peoples or towns that were destroyed after most of the people rejected a messenger sent by God from among themselves. They rarely occur singly, and no more than one group occurs in the same sūra. The emphasis is on the peoples and towns destroyed rather than on the messengers, who often are not even mentioned. One notable exception involves Noah, since his people are virtually always called simply "the people of Noah" or "his people." The major formulaic elements, such as refrains, of no two groups are identical. It is not uncommon, however, for an isolated formula in a punishment-story in one sūra to occur also in one or more other sūras.

Among the many groups or series of punishment-stories, those in four sūras stand out as the most illuminating examples of this distinctive literary genre employed by the Qur'ān to convey one of its major themes.[6] The groups of punishment-stories in the first four sūras discussed below contain patterns of formulaic features that are far more complex than they appear when first read or heard. Since these features are best understood within the broader context of the accounts in each sūra, and in comparison and contrast with versions of the same accounts in other sūras, brief comments will be made on the contents or structure of each of these four sūras before the formulaic features of their punishment-stories are discussed. These four will be discussed in two separate sections because they exemplify two distinctive types of schematic form.

PARALLEL SCHEMATIC FORM

1. In *Sūrat al-Shu'arā'* (Q. 26)

The "Sūra of the Poets" contains a group of punishment-stories with the most fully developed "schematic form" of any in the Qur'ān in terms of having the largest number of consecutive verses, and thus rhyme words, that are repeated in the same series of accounts, a pattern that can be called "parallel schematic form." Five punishment-stories in this sūra all begin with a five-verse introductory passage in this form, with the rhyme words *mursalīn, tattaqūn, amīn, aṭī'ūn,* and *'ālamīn,* and end with two verses with the rhyme words *mu'minīn* and *al-raḥīm.* The rhyme for the entire sūra is introduced in verse 1, which consists entirely of three Arabic consonants, *ṭā', sīn,* and *mīm,* examples of what are traditionally called "the Openers (*al-fawātiḥ*)"[7] and in modern writings, "the mysterious letters."[8] Another feature that stands out in *Al-Shu'arā'* is its large number of very short verses (227), which makes the rhetorical effect of its punishment-stories all the more dramatic.

After the "mysterious letters" (v. 1) and a frequently occurring formula that refers to the heavenly Book (v. 2),[9] *Al-Shu'arā'* begins with a five-verse passage addressed to Muḥammad, assuring him that those who reject his message will suffer the same punishment as former unbelieving peoples. Two long prophet stories and the five schematic punishment-stories mentioned above then comprise the heart of the sūra. These seven accounts are followed by a long passage addressed to Muḥammad (vv. 192–227) that stresses his role as one of the warners, and applies the main point of the punishment-stories to his hearers, with explicit references to them, as in verse 208: "We never destroyed a town (*qarya*) without [first sending] to it warners (*mundhirūn*)."[10]

The first two stories in this sūra, involving Moses and Abraham, are much longer than the other five accounts and do not share their schematic form. The first (vv. 10–66) is in narrative form and is among the longest and most detailed of the many Moses stories in the Qur'ān. It contains several statements that are characteristic of the punishment-stories, such as the last two verses of the story, "We rescued Moses and those with him, all together, and We drowned the others." The Abraham story (vv. 69–102), on the other hand, contains none of the typical elements of a punishment-story. Like the Moses story, it is in narrative form and is one of the longest of the Qur'ān's many Abraham stories. One of its main themes is his rejection of the idols (*aṣnām*) worshipped by his father and his people (*qawm*), but Abraham is not sent by God as a messenger, and his people are not destroyed for their idolatry. These two stories are each followed by what appears at first to be a two-verse refrain.

The series of five punishment-stories that share the same "parallel schematic form" follows these two long narratives. Each of these five accounts is comprised of three distinct parts: the five-verse schematic introductory section mentioned above, a middle section that differs in each account, and a refrain. In the following quotations from the first two accounts, the elements of parallel schematic form are indicated by italics:

105 The people of Noah ***accused the Envoys of lying***
106 ***when their brother*** Noah ***said to them, "Will you not be godfearing?***
107 ***I am for you a faithful Messenger.***
108 ***So fear God and obey me.***
109 ***I ask of you no wage for this. My wage falls only upon the Lord of all Being.***
110 **So fear God and obey me**"
111 They said, "Shall we believe thee, whom the lowest follow?"[11]
. . . .
115 [He said,] "I am only a plain warner."
116 They said, "If thou cease not, Noah, thou shalt surely be one of the stoned."
. . . .
119 So We rescued him and those with him in the laden Ark [cf. Q. 7:64].
120 Then afterwards We drowned the rest.
121 ***Surely in that is a sign, yet most of them are not believers.***
122 ***Surely thy Lord, He is the All-mighty, the All-compassionate.***
123 'Ād ***accused the Envoys of lying***
124 ***when their brother*** Hūd ***said to them, "Will you not be godfearing?***
125 ***I am for you a faithful Messenger.***
126 ***So fear God and obey me.***
127 ***I ask of you no wage for this. My wage falls only upon the Lord of all Being.***
128 What, do you build on every prominence a sign, sporting,
129 and do you take to you castles, perhaps to dwell forever?
130 When you assault, you assault like tyrants!
131 **So fear God and obey me.**
132 And fear Him who has aided you with flocks and sons, gardens and fountains.
. . . ."
139 So they accused him of lying, and then We destroyed them. ***Surely in that is a sign, yet most of them are not believers.***
140 ***Surely thy Lord, He is the All-mighty, the All-compassionate.***

These two accounts illustrate well the formulaic pattern called "parallel schematic form." One conspicuous feature of this form in these two accounts is that the names of the people and the messenger sent by God differ in each account, but the first five verses are otherwise identical. This same feature occurs in the other three schematic punishment-stories, involving the (tribe or people of) Thamūd in verses 141–59, "the people of Lot (*qawm Lūṭ*)" in verses 160–75, and "the people of the Thicket (*aṣḥāb al-ayka*)" in verses 176–91. A surprising aspect of this five-verse introductory section is that it contains none of the distinctive elements of a punishment-story. The statement in the opening verse that the people accused God's messengers of lying occurs frequently in the Qur'ān in contexts other than the punishment-stories, for instance, in reference to Muḥammad.

The middle portions of these five schematic accounts vary in length from nine to thirteen verses. Except for the nine verses of this section in the Lot account, all of which are devoted to his story, only two or three verses of the middle sections mention elements of the distinctive stories of the peoples who are punished or destroyed by God: the last two verses (119–20) in the middle section of the Noah account, the first three (128–30) in that of 'Ād, the last three (155–57) in that of Thamūd, and the first three (180–82) in that of "the people of the Thicket". The other verses in these middle sections consist of either general statements that occur in other punishment-stories or specific accusations that in other parts of the Qur'ān are directed against Muḥammad by his opponents.[12] The formulaic statement that appears as the fourth verse of the schematic introductory section, "So fear God and obey me (*fa 'ttaqū llāh*[a] *wa aṭī'ūni*)," is repeated in the middle sections of three of the five accounts: as the first verse (110) in that of the Noah account, the fourth verse (131) in that of 'Ād (both in bold type above), and the fifth verse (150) in that of Thamūd.[13]

The second prominent formulaic feature in *Al-Shu'arā'* is not easily explained. At first glance it appears to be a two-verse refrain at the end of the Noah account (vv. 121–22). These same two verses also occur at the ends of the Moses and Abraham stories (as vv. 67–68 and 103–4) and the last two of the five schematic accounts. These five (the two prophet stories and three of the schematic accounts) appear to have a two-verse refrain. But the same two verses also occur just after the introduction to the sūra (as vv. 8–9), where it is doubtful that they serve as a refrain. The first three occurrences of this pair of verses (after the introduction and each of the prophet stories) seem more like section or story dividers, rather than repetitions of a refrain.[14] Furthermore, the first of these two formulas, "*Surely in that is a sign, yet most of them are not believers,*" does not constitute a separate verse in two of the five schematic accounts, those about 'Ād

(v. 139b, above) and Thamūd (v. 158b). That this statement is formulaic is clear, but in these two accounts it is not the first part of a two-verse refrain. It can be argued that these two formulas do constitute a single refrain when they appear as complete, contiguous verses, but it seems best – especially in light of a similar but more convincing case of an apparent two-verse refrain in the next sūra to be discussed – to interpret all five schematic accounts in *Al-Shu'arā'* as having only a one-verse refrain, preceded by a formulaic statement that occurs in different positions, similar to the formula, "So fear God and obey me" (which occurs in different positions in three of the five accounts), and the many other formulas that occur repeatedly in other groups of punishment-stories discussed below.

2. In *Sūrat al-Qamar* (Q. 54)

The "Sūra of the Moon" is one of the few sūras devoted almost exclusively to a series of punishment-stories. They involve "the people (*qawm*) of Noah" (vv. 9–17), the tribe or people referred to simply as "'Ād" (vv. 18–22), the people referred to only as "Thamūd" (vv. 23–32), "the people (*qawm*) of Lot" (vv. 33–40), and "the folk (*āl*) of Pharaoh" (vv. 41–42). The first eight verses of this sūra treat primarily the Day of Resurrection, and thus appear not to serve as an introduction to the punishment-stories. The sūra ends with a thirteen-verse concluding passage warning Muḥammad's contemporaries that those who reject his message could suffer the same fate as the peoples of the punishment-stories. *Al-Qamar* has several interesting literary features, some of which are unique. The last word of the first verse, after which the sūra is named, establishes a pattern that occurs in the final syllable of all of its fifty-five verses, with words ending with the consonant "r" preceded by a short vowel, "a," "i," or "u". These verse end-words do not constitute a true rhyme or assonance,[15] but can be regarded as having a "weakened assonance," since they have unstressed short vowels before the final consonant. That *Al-Qamar* is the only sūra in the Qur'ān that has this particular assonance (short vowel + "r") throughout is one example of the extent to which the major groups of punishment-stories are each unique in some way.[16]

The major formulaic features of the punishment-stories in *Al-Qamar* constitute another example of parallel schematic form. This series of accounts also contains two elementary stages of what can be called "cumulative schematic form," discussed below. The first stage is indicated by italics, and formulas that occur in other parts of these accounts or in punishment-stories in other sūras are indicated by bold type in the first and second punishment-stories in this sūra:

9 The people of Noah ***rejected [the warnings] as lies*** before them. They accused Our servant of lying, and said, "A man possessed!" And he was rejected.
10 And so he called to his Lord, saying, "I am overcome. Help me!"
11 Then We opened the gates of heaven until water poured out,
12 and We made the earth to gush with fountains, and the waters met for a predestined purpose.
13 And We bore him upon a vessel made of planks and nails,
14 which sailed under Our eyes – a reward for him who was rejected.
15 And We left it as a sign, **but is there any who remembers?**
16 ***How then were My chastisement and My warnings!***
17 ***Now We have made the Qur'ān easy to remember, but is there any who remembers?***
18 'Ād ***rejected [the warnings] as lie***s. **How then were My chastisement and My warnings!**
19 We let loose upon them a roaring wind on a day of constant calamity,
20 which carried off the people as if they were stumps of uprooted palm-trees.
21 ***How then were My chastisement and My warnings!***
22 ***Now We have made the Qur'ān easy to remember, but is there any who remembers?***

These two accounts appear to have a two-verse refrain, but the rhetorical statement with its implied threat, "*How [terrible] then were My chastisement and My warnings!*" (in vv. 16 and 21), occurs as an independent formula in verse 18 of the 'Ād account, and, more significantly, is separated from the final verse in the third account, involving Thamūd, where these two occur as verses 30 and 32, and thus do not constitute a two-verse refrain.

The expression in italics in verses 9 and 18 translated as "***rejected [the warnings] as lies***" consists of a single word in Arabic, ***kadhdhabat***, the first word in the Noah and 'Ād accounts, and also in the Thamūd and Lot accounts that follow. The formulaic nature of this expression and its fuller meaning, indicated by the interpolation in the first two accounts, become clear in the opening verses of the third and fourth accounts, which begin "Thamūd ***rejected as lies*** **the warnings**," (v. 23) and "The people of Lot ***rejected as lies*** **the warnings**" (v. 33). The addition of the expression ***bi-n-nudhur*** to the introductory formula, ***kadhdhabat***, of the Noah and 'Ād accounts constitutes a second stage of cumulative schematic form. This second stage, the one-verse refrain from the first stage in the Noah and 'Ād accounts, and a new formula that appears twice can be seen in the fourth punishment-story in *Al-Qamar*.

33 The people of Lot ***rejected as lies*** **the warnings,**
34 We let loose upon them a squall of pebbles, except for the family (*āl*) of Lot. We rescued them at dawn,

35 a blessing from Us. Even so We recompense him who is thankful.
36 He had warned them of Our assault, but they disputed the warnings.
37 Even his guests they had solicited of him, so We blinded their eyes, saying, ***"Taste now My chastisement and My warnings!"***
38 Early in the morning a settled chastisement came upon them:
39 ***"Taste now My chastisement and My warnings!"***
40 ***Now We have made the Qur'ān easy to remember, but is there any who remembers?***

The exclamation in verse 39 replaces the similar formula that appears just before what can now be regarded as a one-verse refrain in the first four accounts in this sūra (in vv. 16, 21, 30, and 40). It also occurs in verse 37, and is thus a repeated formula. Verses 39–40, however, can hardly be regarded as a two-verse refrain, since they occur together only in this account. The punishment-stories in *Al-Qamar* end with a brief account about the "folk (*āl*) of Pharaoh" (vv. 41–42) that incorporates formulaic elements from earlier accounts. As in other sūras, the lesson of the punishment-stories is then applied to Muḥammad's contemporaries in verse 43: "What, are your unbelievers better than those?" The main formulaic features in these groups of accounts in *Al-Shu'arā'* and *Al-Qamar* serve as just two examples of "parallel schematic form," which also occurs in other punishment-stories and in other contexts in the Qur'ān.

CUMULATIVE SCHEMATIC FORM

In some ways even more striking than the parallel schematic form that is developed most fully in *Al-Shu'arā'* is another type that can be called "cumulative schematic form," that is, two or more stages of schematic form that are introduced one at a time and are then repeated in later accounts. The first stage usually occurs in the first account in the series and is repeated in the following account or accounts. A second stage is then introduced, usually in the second or third account, and is repeated in other accounts. A third stage occurs often, and a fourth one occasionally. In most cases the wording of each stage is repeated verbatim – or with changes in one or two key words or phrases, such as the names of the people and the messenger – in parts of the account or accounts that immediately follow the one in which it is introduced, but patterns of repetition vary in different sūras that share this form. Unlike parallel schematic form, which usually includes entire verses and thus establishes patterns of repeated rhyme or assonance words, cumulative schematic form usually does not continue to the ends of the verses. The following sūra contains the most fully developed example of cumulative schematic form, with three or four stages.

3. In *Sūrat al-Aʿrāf* (Q. 7)

The "Sūra of the Heights" is the fourth longest sūra in the Qur'ān and contains the third largest number of verses.[17] It begins with a unique group of "mysterious letters," ALMṢ, followed by a one-verse reference to the heavenly Book being sent down to Muḥammad as a warning and "as a reminder to the believers." The sūra then has four main parts: (1) a series of admonitions to people in general on a variety of themes (vv. 3–58), with the address "O Children of Adam" occurring several times; (2) a group of five punishment-stories (vv. 59–93), with a concluding passage (vv. 94–102); (3) what appears to be a composite Moses story (vv. 103–56); and (4) a long section with a variety of disparate themes (vv. 157–206), with some passages being addressed to Muḥammad and his followers. The overall composition of this sūra is difficult to explain (partly because of the wide variety of topics treated, with no indication that they form a whole or provide a major theme for the entire sūra[18]) and the role of the punishment-stories within this complex sūra is not clear. They comprise only one fifth of the sūra and appear to have little connection with its other themes, but they constitute one of the most important and rhetorically powerful versions of these accounts in the Qur'ān.

In the following quotations from the first two accounts, the first stage of the cumulative schematic form of *Al-Aʿrāf* is indicated by italics, the second stage by underlining, and some of the formulas that occur verbatim in punishment-stories in other sūras are in bold type:

59 **And We sent Noah to his people** [= Q. 11:25a], and ***he said, "O my people, serve God! You have no god other than He.*** **Surely I fear for you the chastisement of a** dreadful (*ʿaẓīm*) **day**" [cf. Q. 11:26b].

60 ***Said the Council of his people, "We see thee in*** clear error."

61 ***Said he, "My people, there is no*** error ***in me, but I am a Messenger from the Lord of all Being.***

62 ***I deliver to you the messages of my Lord,*** and I give sincere advice to you, for I know from God what you know not.

63 ***What, do you wonder that a reminder from your Lord should come to you by the lips of a man from among you, that he may warn you,*** that you may be godfearing, that perhaps you may find mercy?"

64 But they accused him of lying, ***so We rescued him and those with him*** in the Ark [cf. Q. 26:119], ***and We*** drowned ***those who called Our signs lies.*** Surely they were a blind people.

65 ***And to*** ʿĀd [***We sent***] ***their brother*** Hūd. ***He said, "O my people, serve God! You have no god other than He.*** Will you not be godfearing?"

66 ***Said the Council*** of the unbelievers ***of his people, "We see thee*** [= Q. 11:27a] ***in*** folly, and we think you are one of the liars."

67 ***Said he, "My people, there is no*** folly ***in me, but I am a Messenger from the Lord of all Being.***
68 ***I deliver to you the messages of my Lord,*** and I am a faithful sincere adviser to you.
69 ***What, do you wonder that a reminder from your Lord should come to you by the lips of a man from among you, that he may warn you?*** **And remember when He appointed you as successors after** the people of Noah and increased you in stature broadly. Remember God's bounties; perhaps you will prosper."

. . . .

72 ***So We rescued him and those with him,*** by a mercy from Us, ***and We*** cut off the last remnant of ***those who called Our signs lies.***

The majority of the 'Ād account consists of statements that occur verbatim in the Noah account, giving the impression that in these two punishment-stories rhetorical effect takes precedence over the distinctive elements of each story. The difference of a single word in verses 61 and 67 catches the attention especially of those who hear these accounts recited. In the first, Noah says to his people, "there is no error (*ḍalāla*) in me," while in the second, Hūd says to his people, the 'Ād, "there is no folly (*safāha*) in me," in both cases denying accusations made in the preceding verses. Formulas that are not part of the schematic form of this sūra also stand out, since they also occur in other versions of the punishment-stories and are familiar to some hearers and readers of the Qur'ān. The second stage in the cumulative schematic form of this series of punishment-stories consists of two formulaic elements introduced in verses 65 and 69 in the 'Ād account. The first, "And to ... [We sent] their brother ...," is repeated at the beginning of the Thamūd and Madyan stories. The second, a statement that gives some indication of the chronological order in which the peoples in these accounts lived, "And remember when He appointed you as successors after ...," is repeated only in the Thamūd account, where a third stage, indicated by underlined italics, is introduced:

73 And to Thamūd [We sent] their brother Ṣāliḥ. ***He said, "O my people, serve God! You have no god other than He. There has now come to you a clear sign from your Lord.*** This is the she-camel of God, to be a sign for you. Leave her that she may eat in God's earth, and do not touch her with evil, lest you be seized by a painful chastisement.
74 And remember when He appointed you as successors after 'Ād and lodged you in the land, taking to yourselves castles of its plains, and hewing its mountains into houses ...."
75 ***Said the Council of those of his people who waxed proud*** to those who were abased, "Do you know that Ṣāliḥ is an Envoy from his Lord?" ....

76 The ones who waxed proud said, "As for us, we are unbelievers in the thing in which you believe."
77 So they hamstrung the she-camel and turned in disdain from the commandment of their Lord, saying, "O Ṣāliḥ, bring us what thou promisest us, if thou art an Envoy."
78 ***So the earthquake seized them, and morning found them in their habitation fallen prostrate.***
79 ***So he turned his back on them and said, "O my people, I have delivered to you the message of my Lord, and I gave sincere advice to you***, but you do not love sincere advisers."

The close relationship between the Thamūd and Madyan accounts in terms of the extent to which they share several stages of schematic form is clear in the following quotations from the latter, which contain a formulaic statement (in underlined bold type) that could be interpreted as a fourth stage of schematic form:

85 And to Madyan [We sent] their brother Shu'ayb. ***He said, "O my people, serve God! You have no god other than He. There has now come to you a clear sign from your Lord.*** So fill up the measure and the balance, and diminish not the goods of the people ....
86 And do not sit in every path, threatening and barring from God's way those who believe in Him .... **So see the nature of the end of those who caused corruption!"**

....

88 ***Said the Council of those of his people who waxed proud***, "We will surely expel thee, O Shu'ayb, and those who believe with thee from our town (*qarya*) unless you return to our creed". He said, "What, even though we detest it?

...."

91 ***So the earthquake seized them, and morning found them in their habitation fallen prostrate.***
92 Those who accused Shu'ayb of lying became as if they never dwelt there . . .
93 ***So he turned his back on them and said, "O my people, I have delivered to you the messages of my Lord, and I gave sincere advice to you.*** How should I grieve for a people of unbelievers?"

When comparing the formulaic features and other aspects of these four punishment-stories in *Al-A'rāf* (examples of cumulative schematic form) with the versions of the same accounts in *Al-Shu'arā'* (examples of parallel schematic form) several significant differences stand out. The equally powerful effect of the recitation of these two versions of the same punishment-stories is also quite different. In *Al-A'rāf* the Thamūd and Madyan accounts are longer than those of Noah and 'Ād, and are more in the form of complete stories, rather than consisting almost exclusively of shared formulaic statements. The elements of the third stage of the schematic form of this sūra are introduced in verses 73, 75, 78, and 79 in the Thamūd story, and are repeated in verses 85, 88, 91, and 93 in the Madyan story. One significant aspect of this third stage is that two refrain-like formulas that appear in contiguous verses in the Thamūd story are separated by one verse in that of Madyan, similar to the two formulas that occur together in the Noah and 'Ād accounts in *Al-Shu'arā'* (in vv. 16–17 and 21–22), but occur separately in the Thamūd account (in vv. 30 and 32). This flexibility in the repetition of formulaic statements within the same group is a characteristic feature of the punishment-stories.

Al-A'rāf contains an excellent example of another type of variation in the formulaic elements of a group of punishment-stories that adds to their dramatic effect: several stages of development or change in the wording of a key phrase or statement in the accounts. In references to "the Council (*al-mala'*)" of the people to whom a messenger is sent, the simple statement in verse 60 of the Noah account, "*Said the Council of his people,*" is expanded to "*Said the Council* of the unbelievers *of his people*" in verse 66 in the 'Ād account, and then becomes part of the third stage of this sūra's cumulative schematic form in the Thamūd story, as the fuller formula at the beginning of verse 75, "*Said the Council <u>of those</u> of his people <u>who waxed proud</u>,*" which is then repeated verbatim in verse 88 of the Madyan story.[19] These closely related Thamūd and Madyan stories, the third and fifth in *Al-A'rāf* (in vv. 73–79 and 85–93), are separated by a Lot account (vv. 80–84) that breaks the connection between them. The Lot account is quite different in form and content from the others in this series, containing none of the characteristic elements of this sūra's schematic form.

After a section that serves as a conclusion to these five accounts (vv. 94–102), a Moses story (vv. 103–56) begins, "We sent after them Moses with Our signs to Pharaoh and his Council," and contains in the last verse the statement spoken by God, "I smite with my chastisement whom I will." Between this formulaic introductory statement and the reference to punishment at the end of the story, most of the long intervening section relates the familiar story of Moses and the Exodus, with only occasional elements of the punishment-stories. The first verse of this story repeats the formulaic statement (in underlined bold type) in verse 86 of the Madyan story. This statement could be taken as a fourth stage of the cumulative schematic form of the punishment-stories in *Al-A'rāf*, but this repeated formula occurs in a story that comes after the conclusion to the other accounts.

4. In *Sūrat Hūd* (Q. 11)

The "Sūra of Hūd," the name of God's messenger to the people called 'Ād, begins with a four-verse introduction (with the consistent rhyme "-īr") stating that the Book (of God) is being revealed to Muḥammad, who is to be both a warner (*nadhīr*) and a bringer of good tidings (*bashīr*). The section that follows (vv. 5–24), addressed mostly to Muḥammad, appears to be composite, with passages on different topics and rhymes, alternating between "-ūr/-īr" and "-ūn/-īn/-īm," a flexible rhyme that occurs far more frequently in the Qur'ān than any other. The main part of the sūra consists of a series of four punishment-stories (vv. 25–68 and 84–95) and two "prophet" stories, one about the supernatural "messengers (*rusul*)" who visit Abraham and Lot (vv. 69–83), the other a short version of the story of Moses and Pharaoh (vv. 96–99). The sūra ends with what again appears to be a composite passage (vv. 100–23), containing lessons to be learned from these punishment and prophet stories.

Except for *Sūrat Nūḥ,* "the Sūra of Noah" (Q. 71), which is not in the form of a punishment-story, *Sūrat Hūd*[20] is the only sūra in the Qur'ān named for an "envoy (*mursal*)" or messenger who is associated primarily with the punishment-stories. As is typical of the ways sūras are named, the story of Hūd and the destruction of his tribe, the 'Ād (vv. 50–60), is no more prominent than the other stories in this sūra.[21] The name of *Sūrat Hūd* may, however, be an indication of the centrality of the punishment-stories within the sūra. Its rhyme changes several times, including once in the middle of the 'Ād account. The frequently occurring "-ūn/-īn/-īm" rhyme begins in verse 13, continues through the first punishment-story (about Noah, in vv. 25–48), and ends in verse 56. The rest of the 'Ād account and all of the other punishment and prophet stories in this sūra (through v. 95) have a flexible assonance pattern that consists of verses ending with "ū" or "ī" followed by any consonant. This pattern continues through verse 112, and then the remainder of the sūra goes back to the "-ūn/-īn/-īm" rhyme. The changing rhyme and assonance patterns of *Sūrat Hūd,* especially the fact that the major change in the entire sūra occurs within the series of punishment-stories, constitute one of several characteristics that distinguish this series from those in other sūras.

The four punishment-stories in *Sūrat Hūd* contain three stages of cumulative schematic form and a number of formulaic statements and phrases that occur verbatim in other versions of the same stories, especially in *Al-A'rāf* and *Al-Shu'arā'.* In the quotations below, the first stage of the cumulative schematic form of the punishment-stories in *Sūrat Hūd* is indicated by italics, the second stage by underlining, and the third stage by underlined italics. Other formulaic elements in these accounts that also occur verbatim in punishment-stories in other sūras appear in bold type. The following is only the beginning of the first account in this series:

25 **And We sent Noah to his people** [= Q. 7:59a], [saying] "Surely I am for you a clear warner.[22]

26 Serve none but God. **Surely I fear for you the chastisement of a painful** (*alīm*) **day**" [bold = Q. 7:59b].

27 **Said the Council of the unbelievers of his people, "We see thee** [= Q. 7:66a] only as a mortal like ourselves, and we see only the lowest among us following thee, without reflecting. We see in you [pl.] no superiority over us. Indeed, we think you are liars [cf. Q. 7:66b].

28 ***He said, "O my people, what do you think? If I stand upon a clear sign from my Lord, and He has given me mercy from Him***, while it has been obscured for you, shall we compel you to it while you are averse to it?

29 ***O my people, I ask of you no*** wealth [*māl*] ***for this. My wage*** [*ajr*] ***falls only upon*** God [cf. Q. 26:109]. I will not drive away those who believe. They will surely meet their Lord. But I see you are an ignorant people.

Most of the remainder of this account, which continues through verse 48, does not have the distinctive characteristics of a punishment-story. Verses 30–36, although mentioning Noah twice, treat the same challenges and accusations from opponents that in other parts of the Qur'ān are directed against Muḥammad. Punishment-story themes resume in verse 37 and appear to end in verse 44, with the enigmatic, concluding formula: "Away with the people of the evildoers (*bu'd*^{an} *li-l-qawm*^{i} *ẓ-ẓālimīn*)." This formula appears in an abbreviated form at the end of the 'Ād, Thamūd, and Madyan accounts in *Sūrat Hūd*, as seen below.[23] All of the formulaic elements of the Noah account as a punishment-story, except for the *bu'd* formula in verse 44, occur in the verses quoted above. One significant difference between the cumulative schematic form of the punishment-stories here in *Sūrat Hūd* and that of *Al-A'rāf* is that only one part of the first stage (in v. 29) is repeated in the second account, while the other part (in v. 28) is repeated in the third and fourth accounts. This innovation in the repetition of formulaic features and also the introduction of the second stage are shown in the following quotations from the second and third accounts:

50 And to 'Ād [We sent] their brother Hūd He said, "O my people, serve God! You have no god other than He [= 7:65a]. You are but forgers.

51 ***O my people, I ask of you no*** wage [***ajr***] ***for this. My wage*** [***ajr***] ***falls only upon*** [cf. Q. 26:127[24]] Him who originated me. **Will you not understand?** [= Q. 37:138].

52 And O my people, ask forgiveness of your Lord, and then repent to Him, He will loose heaven in torrents (of rain) upon you. And He will increase you strength upon strength. And turn not your backs as sinners."

. . . .

58 **And when Our Command came, We rescued Hūd and those who believed with him, by a mercy from Us.** We rescued them from a harsh punishment.
59 That was ʿĀd. They denied the signs of their Lord and rebelled against His messengers, and followed the command of every obstinate tyrant.
60 So a curse was made to follow them in this world and on the Day of Resurrection. Surely ʿĀd disbelieved in their Lord. So away with ʿĀd, the people of Hūd!
61 And to Thamūd [We sent] their brother Ṣāliḥ. He said, "O my people, serve God! You have no god other than He [= 7:73a]. He brought you forth from the earth and has given you life therein. So ask forgiveness of Him, and then repent to Him. Surely my Lord is near and answers prayer."
62 They said, "Ṣāliḥ, thou hast hitherto been a source of hope among us. What, dost thou forbid us to serve what our fathers served?..."
63 ***He said, "O my people, what do you think? If I stand upon a clear sign from my Lord, and He has given me mercy from Him,*** who will help me against God if I rebel against Him? You would do nothing for me except increase my loss.
64 O my people, this is the she-camel of God, to be a sign for you. Leave her that she may eat in God's earth, and touch her not with evil, lest you be seized by a near chastisement" [cf. Q. 26:155–56].
65 But they hamstrung her [= Q. 26:157a], and then he said, "Enjoy life in your dwelling three days. That is a threat that will not be belied."
66 And when Our command came, We rescued Ṣāliḥ and those who believed with him, by a mercy from Us, from the humiliation of that day. Thy Lord is the All-strong, the All-mighty.
67 ***And the evildoers were seized by the Cry, and morning found them in their dwellings fallen prostrate***
68 ***as if they had never dwelt there.*** Surely Thamūd disbelieved in their Lord. So away with Thamūd!

A story about supernatural messengers[25] visiting Abraham and Lot (vv. 69–83) is interjected into the series of schematic punishment-stories at this point. This narrative could be interpreted as two stories, since its two parts have identical introductory formulas: "Our messengers came to Abraham" (v. 69) and "Our messengers came to Lot" (v. 77),[26] but Lot appears prominently in the first part of the story (in vv. 70 and 74). The Lot portion of the story (vv. 77–83) does not contain the standard features of a punishment-story (he is not sent to his people with a message from God, does not issue a warning, is not rejected as a liar, etc.), but punishment elements do appear, for instance in the statements in verses 81–82, "so set forth with thy family (*ahl*) during the night," and "so when

Our command came, We overturned it and rained upon it stones of baked clay."[27] This Abraham-Lot story can be interpreted as a prophet story with some terrestrial punishment themes. Its intrusion between the third and fourth schematic punishment-stories in *Sūrat Hūd* is conspicuous since it contains none of their formulaic elements, and it separates the closely related Thamūd and Madyan accounts. The following portions of the Madyan account show its integral place among the four accounts in which the cumulative schematic form of the punishment-stories of this sūra develops:

84 And to Madyan [We sent] their brother Shu'ayb. He said, "O my people, serve God! You have no god other than He. And diminish not the measure and the balance.

. . . .

87 They said, "O Shu'ayb, does thy prayer command thee that we should leave what our fathers served, or to do as we will with our goods? . . ."

88 ***He said, "O my people, what do you think? If I stand upon a clear sign from my Lord, and He has*** provided me with fair provision ***from Him***, and I desire not to go behind you, taking for myself what I forbid to you.

. . . .

94 And when Our command came, We rescued Shu'ayb and those who believed with him, by a mercy from Us, ***and the evildoers were seized by the Cry, and morning found them in their dwellings fallen prostrate***

95 ***as if they had never dwelt there***. So away with Madyan, even as Thamūd were done away!

This account shares all three stages of the schematic form that occur in the Thamūd account (vv. 61–68), making clearer the impression that the story about Abraham and Lot (vv. 69–83) breaks up this sūra's four schematic punishment-stories and weakens their dramatic and rhetorical effects.[28] The brief version of the story about Moses and Pharaoh (vv. 96–99) that follows the Madyan account focuses on the Day of Resurrection and the chastisement of the afterlife rather than terrestrial punishment. Then follows what appears to be a two-part conclusion, the first part referring to the punishment-stories, the second to the Moses account. The first part (vv. 100–2) begins: "That is of the tidings of the towns (*al-qurā*) We relate to thee [Muḥammad], some of which are (still) standing and some (are) reaped (*ḥaṣīd*)." The second part (vv. 103–9) begins: "Surely in that is a sign (*āya*) for those who fear the chastisement in the world to come."

As in *Al-A'rāf*, so also here in *Sūrat Hūd* a group of punishment-stories is set within a wider context that applies their main themes to Muḥammad's hearers. Specific references to Muḥammad and passages addressed to him occur before and after the groups of punishment-stories in both of these sūras. This aspect of the role of these accounts within the Qur'ān is present in the wider contexts of several other groups of punishment-stories, and is even more prominent in many passages that contain brief statements about them, or simply mention the peoples or messengers who appear in them. As in the preceding section, the sūras discussed here contain just two examples of groups of punishment-stories that illustrate a specific type of schematic form. Elements of cumulative schematic form, usually involving only two stages, occur in a number of other versions of these accounts.

MIXED FORMS AND CONTENTS

Other sūras contain groups of punishment-stories in which the formulaic features are not so fully developed. Accounts in some of these groups are largely derivative in terms of their formulaic elements and other punishment-story features. Some are brief, but include details of the stories not found in longer versions. Several sūras contain accounts of widely varying length, including verses with little more than lists of communities or towns that were destroyed for rejecting messengers sent by God. In other sūras, including one with a four-verse sequence of parallel schematic form, only two or three of the punishment-stories occur with several "prophet" stories. These shorter and mixed groups of accounts contribute to a better understanding of the formulaic features of the punishment-stories and their role and significance in presenting a major theme of the Qur'ān.

A. Accounts with Derivative Formulaic Elements

1. *Sūrat al-Mu'minūn*, "the Sūra of the Believers" (Q. 23), contains a group of punishment-stories that departs from those discussed above in having accounts that are largely derivative, that provide some indication of the order in which the destroyed peoples lived, and in having one fully developed punishment-story that omits the names of the people and the messenger. As is usually the case, an account about the people of Noah occurs first:

23 **And We sent Noah to his people**, and he said, "O my people, ***serve God! You have no god other than He. Will you not be godfearing?***"
24 ***Said the Council of the unbelievers of his people*** [= Q. 7:66], "***This is only a mortal like yourselves*** who desires to gain superiority over you . . .
25 He is only a man bedeviled. So wait on him for a time."
26 ***He said, "O my Lord, help me, for they call me a liar."***
27 Then We suggested to him, "**Build the Ark under Our eyes and inspiration** [= Q. 11:37]

> ... And address Me not concerning those who have done evil. They will be drowned."

A first stage of the cumulative schematic form of the punishment-stories in this sūra (in italics) occurs in the first four verses of this Noah account, which continues through verse 30. The first verse is completely derivative. The rhetorical question at the end, "*Will ye not be godfearing?*," appears in the second verse of the five-verse introduction to the five schematic accounts in *Al-Shu'arā'.* All of the rest of this verse (i.e., the beginning part) occurs verbatim in Q. 7:59, and also in two parts in the punishment-stories in *Sūrat Hūd*, with the first part, "And We sent Noah to his people," introducing the first account (in v. 25)[29] and the remainder occurring in the introductions to three other accounts (in vv. 50, 61, and 84). Since the beginning of the second verse is also derivative, occurring verbatim in Q. 7:66 (as is indicated in the quotation above), this means that all of the schematic elements in verses 23–24a consist of formulas that also appear in punishment-stories in other sūras. This is not the case with verse 26, the last part of this first stage, since this formula (repeated in v. 39 below) does not occur in any other sūra. All of the first stage of schematic form that was introduced in the account about the people of Noah is repeated in the second account – one that appears to be unique in the Qur'ān – where a second stage, indicated by underlining, is introduced:

31 Then after them We raised up another generation (*qarn*) [cf. Q. 6:6],
32 and We sent to them a messenger from among themselves, saying, ***"Serve God! You have no god other than He. Will you not be godfearing?"***
33 ***Said the Council of the unbelievers of his people***, ... ***"This is only a mortal like yourselves***, who eats what you eat and drinks what you drink.
34 If you obey a mortal like yourselves, then you will be losers.
....
38 He is only a man who has forged against God a lie, and we will not believe him."
39 ***He said, "O my Lord, help me, for they call me a liar."***
40 He [God] said, "In a little while they will be remorseful."
41 And the Cry seized them justly, and We made them as rubbish. So away with (*fa-bu'd*^{an}) the people of the evildoers! [= Q. 11:44].

The elements of the first stage of the cumulative schematic form of the accounts in this sūra that occur in verses 32–33 are derivative, since they are identical with those in the Noah account, and the rhetorical statement at the end of verse 41 appears to be derived from *Surat Huḍ*[30] The most striking feature of this second account, however, is that, unlike every punishment-story quoted and discussed above, it does not mention the name of the people (in v. 31) or the messenger (mentioned anonymously in v. 32). Although it contains none of the distinctive elements of any particular punishment-story, certain evidence suggests that it might refer to the people called 'Ād. In the four major groups of punishment-stories discussed in the first two sections above (and in several lists, such as in Q. 9:70, Q. 14:9, and Q. 22:42–44), an 'Ād account always follows immediately after that of the people of Noah. In the 'Ād account in *Al-A'rāf*, verse 69 contains the formula: "And remember when He appointed you as successors after the people of Noaḥ" Here in *Al-Mu'minūn* this second account begins: "Then after them [the people of Noah] We raised up another generation, and we sent to them a messenger from among themselves, saying. . . ." The formulaic wording that follows "saying" occurs in only one other context in all of the Qur'ān, in verses 65–66 of the 'Ād account in *Al-A'rāf*. This evidence is not conclusive, and the second account in *Al-Mu'minūn* can be interpreted in various ways. Its omission of the names of the people and the messenger could be related to the brief but important summary passage that follows it:

42 Then after them We raised up other generations.
43 **No nation hastens its appointed time** [= Q. 15:5], nor do they postpone it.
44 Then We sent Our messengers successively. Whenever its messenger came to a nation, they called him a liar [cf. Q. 22:42–44], so We caused some of them to follow others, and We made them as but tales. So away with a people who do not believe!

The first part of verse 43 – referring to a key concept in the Qur'ān, the "term of life (*ajal*)" appointed by God for each person and nation (*umma*) –appears to be derived from *Sūrat al-Ḥijr* (Q. 15), and virtually all of verse 44 repeats themes and formulas from other punishment-stories. Although these three verses contain the second stage of the cumulative schematic form of the punishment-stories in this sūra, they do not constitute a story. Instead, they provide a summary statement about "generations (*qurūn*)" or peoples who rejected messengers sent by God. That this passage mentions no peoples or messengers by name might explain why neither is named in the preceding account, but it still raises the question as to why this three-verse summary occurs before rather than after the fourth and last account in this series, which mentions both:

45 Then **We sent Moses** and his brother Aaron **with Our signs and a clear authority**
46 **to Pharaoh and his Council** [bold = Q. 11:96–97a]. **But they waxed proud** [= Q. 29:39b] and were a lofty people.
47 And they said, "What, shall we believe in two mortals like ourselves [cf. Q. 11:27], whose people are our servants?"
48 So they called them liars [cf. Q. 22:44], and they were among the destroyed.

The only formulaic element this concise punishment-story shares with other accounts in this group is the very first word, "then (*thumma*)," which serves an important function by indicating a chronological sequence between the time of Noah and the time of Moses. The remainder of this Moses account is derivative, consisting of formulaic language that appears in several other versions of the same story. Thus, *Al-Mu'minūn* contains three punishment-stories: one involving Noah, one that can be interpreted as referring to 'Ād, and one about Moses. The formulaic statement "then after them (*thumma min ba'di-him*) We raised up other generations" at the beginning of the three-verse summary passage that occurs just before the Moses account, with the occurrence of *thumma* at the beginning of the Moses account, suggests that the "other generations" who rejected God's messengers lived between the times of Noah and Moses. This same pattern and the same formulaic introductions occur in *Sūrat Yūnus* (Q. 10), which has a Noah account (vv. 71–73), a summary statement about unnamed peoples and their messengers that begins "then after him [Noah] (*thumma min ba'di-hi*) We sent ..." (v. 74), and then a long Moses story (vv. 75–93) that begins: "Then after them (*thumma ... min ba'di-him*) We sent after them Moses and Aaron ...."[31]

2. *Sūrat al-'Ankabūt*, "the Sūra of the Spider" (Q. 29), contains a series of punishment-stories that begins and ends with the same messengers as in *Al-Mu'minūn* and *Yūnus*, but differs from these two sūras in having accounts that name the peoples, and sometimes the messengers, who apparently are presented as having lived between the times of Noah and Moses. The first account consists of only two verses:

14 Indeed, **We sent Noah to his people** [= Q. 7:59a, Q. 11:25a], and he tarried among them a thousand years, all but fifty. So the Flood seized them while they were evildoers.

15 So We rescued him and those who were in the ship [cf. Q. 7:64], **and We made it a sign to all beings.**

This concise account is largely derivative in terms of its formulaic elements, but it also includes details about the Noah story that other accounts do not provide. The formulaic statement at the end of verse 15 occurs also in Q. 21:91.[32] The brevity of this Noah account is made more conspicuous by the length of the section about Abraham and Lot (vv. 16–35) that follows it. As in other sūras, an Abraham story appears with a group of punishment-stories and contains none of their distinctive elements. Here the same formula introduces Abraham and Lot passages in the first part of the story:

16 ***And*** (***remember***) Abraham, ***when he said to his people*** (***qawm***), "Serve God and fear Him. That is better for you, if you only knew.

....

28 ***And*** (***remember***) Lot, ***when he said to his people*** (*qawm*), "Surely you commit such indecency as never any being in all the world committed before you.
29 What, do you approach men and bar the way [to offspring?], and commit in your assembly dishonor?" But the only answer of his people (*qawm*) was that they said, "Then bring us the chastisement of God, if thou speakest truly."
30 He said, "My Lord, help me against the people who work corruption."

The specific reference to the people (*qawm*) of Abraham in a formulaic statement within a group of punishment-stories is rare. The Abraham portion of the story still serves only as a prelude to a Lot punishment-story, but the formulaic connection ties it more closely to the other accounts than is the case in other sūras. The construction of the section of this sūra that deals with Abraham and Lot is not clear. Verses 18–23 appear to be addressed to Muḥammad's followers, and then the Abraham story resumes in verses 24–27. Verses 31–35 could be interpreted as a continuation of the Abraham story, but it seems more likely that at one time they comprised a separate account:[33]

31 ***And*** (***remember***) ***when Our messengers came to*** Abraham with the good tidings [that he was to have a son], they said, "We will destroy the people (*ahl*) of this town (*qarya*). Surely its people (*ahl*) are evildoers."
32 He said, "But Lot is in it." They said, "We know very well who is in it. **Surely We will rescue** him **and** his **family, except for** his **wife. She has become of those who tarry**."
33 ***And*** (***remember***) ***when Our messengers came to*** Lot, he was troubled on their account and felt distress for them. But they said, "Fear not, neither sorrow, for **surely We will rescue** thee **and** thy **family, except for** thy **wife. She has become of those who tarry**."
34 We [God] will send down upon the people (*ahl*) of this town wrath out of heaven for their ungodliness.
35 And indeed We have left there a sign, a clear sign, to people who understand.

The presence of two introductory formulas for the Abraham and Lot passages (one in vv. 16 and 28, and another in vv. 31 and 33) and the difference of terms used for the "people" of Abraham and those of Lot support the view that verses 31–35 once constituted a separate punishment-story.[34] The formulaic elements in verses 32 and 33 introduce details of the Lot story that other accounts do not provide. As in groups of punishment-stories in others sūras, a Lot account is followed by one about Madyan:

36 **And to Madyan [We sent] their brother Shu'ayb, who said, "O my people, serve God** [= Q. 11:84] and look for the Last Day, and do not mischief in the land, working corruption."
37 But they called him a liar, **so the earthquake seized them, and morning found them in their habitation fallen prostrate** [= Q. 7:91].

The first half of verse 36 appears to be derived from the Madyan account in *Sūrat Hūd*, and the last part of verse 37 appears to be derived from the Madyan account in *Al-A'rāf*. The reference to "the Last Day" in verse 36 alludes to punishment in the afterlife rather than physical destruction in this world, and thus adds a second element of warning to the people of Madyan. Unlike every other group of punishment-stories discussed above, references to 'Ād and Thamūd here in *Al-'Ankabūt* follow rather than precede accounts involving the people of Lot and the people of Madyan. The first part of verse 38 states cryptically: "And [remember] 'Ād and Thamūd. [Their fate] is clear to you from [the ruins of] their dwelling-places (*wa 'Ād^{an} wa Thamūd^{a} wa qad tabayyana la-kum min masākin^{i}-him*)." Here 'Ād and Thamūd, two of the most prominent peoples in the major groups of punishment-stories discussed above, do not even receive separate verses. Just mentioning their names and their fate is sufficient as a warning to those who reject God's messengers.

In a single verse devoted to Moses (v. 39), two additional recipients of his message of warning are mentioned along with Pharaoh: "And (remember) Korah (*Qārūn*), and Pharaoh, and Haman (*Hāmān*). Moses came to them with clear signs, but they were boastful in the land. And they did not win."[35] Verse 40 then declares that the unbelieving peoples were responsible for their own fate: "Each [community] We seized for [their] sin. And of them against some We loosed a squall of pebbles, and some were seized by the Cry (*al-ṣayḥa*), and some We drowned. God would never wrong them, but they wronged themselves." This concluding verse is unique in providing a summary of the methods used by God in destroying earlier peoples who rejected his messengers.

These accounts in sūras *Al-Mu'minūn* and *Al-'Ankabūt* provide just two examples of punishment-stories in which the major formulaic elements are largely derivative, that is, based on portions of earlier versions of the same stories. Each of the four major groups of punishment-stories discussed in the first two sections above has its own unique formulaic patterns and contents, but most of the other numerous groups appear to be formed from a common body of formulas, themes, and key terms, in such a way that many accounts share some of the same elements, but no two accounts in the Qur'ān are identical.

B. Groups with Short and Mixed Accounts

Several sūras contain groups of short punishment-stories, sometimes with accounts that have only one or two verses. In some cases two or more of the peoples who are destroyed in the punishment-stories are mentioned in a single verse. These groups of short accounts sometimes involve the same peoples and messengers who appear in the longer ones, sometimes omit some of them, sometimes present the peoples in a different order, and sometimes include additional peoples or individuals. The contexts in which they occur often include verses that address or refer to Muḥammad, sometimes giving the impression that a primary purpose of these short punishment-stories and references to them is to stress his role as a warner.

1. Groups with Short Accounts and Lists

Sūrat Al-Dhāriyāt, "the Sūra of the Scatterers" (Q. 51), contains short accounts of four of the five most prominent punishment-stories (those in *Al-Shu'arā'* that share the same schematic form), omitting one about Madyan but (as in several other groups) including one about Moses and Pharaoh. The accounts are not in the usual order, but begin with, or are preceded by, a much longer story about Abraham and Lot, apparently addressed to Muḥammad, beginning: "Hast thou received the story of the honored guests of Abraham?" (Q. 51:24–25). The narrative continues with Abraham preparing a feast for his guests, who give him the good news that he is to have a son, and then a variation on the Lot punishment-story follows, with Abraham addressing his supernatural guests:

31 He said, "And what is your business, envoys (*mursalūn*)?"
32 They said, "We have been sent to a people (*qawm*) of sinners
33 to loose upon them stones of clay,
34 marked with thy Lord for the prodigal."
35 So We [God] brought forth those in it who were believers (*al-mu'minūn*),
36 but We found only one house (*bayt*) of those who surrendered (*al-muslimūn*).
37 Therein We left a sign to those who fear the painful chastisement [the hell-fire].[36]

This narrative differs from the standard plot of the punishment-stories in several ways. Supernatural messengers replace the human "envoys" sent by God from among the people. Lot is not even mentioned, and thus does not deliver a message from God that his people reject, and several other distinctive elements of the Lot story are not present.[37] It is only after this longer Abraham-Lot narrative that four short punishment-stories are presented, the first three sharing a concise introductory formula that implicitly refers back to the statement in verse 37, "therein We left a sign (*āya*)":

38 ***And in*** [***the story of***] Moses [***is a sign***], when We sent him to Pharaoh, with a clear authority,
39 but he turned his back, with his court, saying, "A sorcerer or a man possessed!"
40 So We seized him and his hosts, and We cast them into the sea, and he was blameworthy.
41 ***And in*** [***the story of***] 'Ād [***is a sign***], when We loosed against them the withering wind
42 that left nothing it came upon, but made it as dust.
43 ***And in*** [***the story of***] Thamūd [***is a sign***], when it was said to them, "Take your enjoyment for a while!"
44 Then they turned in disdain from the commandment of their Lord, and the thunderbolt overtook them, even as they looked,
45 and they were not able to stand upright, and were not helped.
46 And [remember] the people of Noah before. Surely they were an ungodly people.

A striking feature of this group of short accounts is that it ends with a single verse on the people of Noah, which does not have the concise introductory formula "And in (*wa fī*)" that ties the three former accounts together. His diminished position here is notable since in all of the more fully developed groups the Noah accounts occur first, making them the most prominent, and they often introduce the distinctive formulaic features of each group. These five accounts are followed by a "sign-passage"[38] that culminates with two verses (vv. 50–51) that tie Muḥammad's role to that of the messengers in the punishment-stories, through a formula that occurs twice: "Surely I am a clear warner from Him to you (*in-nī la-kum min-hu nadhīr*^{un} *mubīn*)." Then follows a passage (vv. 52–55) that connects Muhammad to the punishment-stories in a different way, by repeating (in verse 52) an accusatory formula that appears in verse 39 in reference to Moses: "A sorcerer or a man possessed!" The fact that the group of punishment-stories in this sūra is preceded and followed by "signs" of God in nature suggests that the statement in the last verse of the Abraham-Lot account, "Therein We left a sign" – implied in the introductory formula of the Moses, 'Ād, and Thamūd accounts – has special significance in this sūra, incorporating these punishment-stories into a series of sign-passages.

Another group of very short punishment-stories and references to past people destroyed for their unbelief that share the same pattern of leading up to statements about Muḥammad's role as a warner or a messenger occurs in *Sūrat al-Furqān*, "the Sūra of the Criterion" (Q. 25):

35 We gave Moses the Book and appointed with him his brother Aaron as minister (*wazīr*),
36 and We said, "Go to the people who have called Our signs lies." Then We destroyed them utterly.
37 ***And*** [***remember***] the people of Noah, when they called the messengers liars. We drowned them and made them to be a sign to the people. And We have prepared for the evildoers a painful chastisement [in the hell-fire].
38 ***And*** [***remember***] 'Ād and Thamūd, and the people of al-Rass,[39] and between them many generations.
39 We made examples of each, and each We ruined utterly.
40 Surely those [who have rejected Muḥammad] have passed by the city on which a fatal rain was sent down. What, have they not seen it? No, but they look for no resurrection.
41 And when they see thee [Muḥammad], they take thee in mockery only: "What, is this he whom God sent as a messenger?"

The brevity of these accounts and the way some are introduced give the impression that the fuller punishment-stories were already known by Muḥammad's hearers when he first recited this passage. The "people of al-Rass" are mentioned in only one other context in the Qur'ān, one of the shortest passages with the longest list of peoples destroyed by God, including one tribe or people not encountered above. This passage of only three verses occurs in *Sūrat Qāf*, "the Sūra of [the letter] Q" (Q. 50):

12 The people (*qawm*) of Noah called [the messengers] liars before them, [as did] the people (*aṣḥāb*) of al-Rass, and Thamūd,
13 and 'Ād, Pharaoh, the brothers (*ikhwān*) of Lot,
14 the people (*aṣḥāb*) of the Thicket, and the people (*qawm*) of Tubba' They all accused their messengers of being liars, so My threat came true.

Unlike the brief accounts in *Al-Dhāriyāt*, this list names or refers to the peoples, rather than their messengers. The expression "the brothers of Lot" is unique here. This expression and the various terms for "people" in the punishment-stories, some of which are indicated in parentheses in this passage from *Sūrat Qāf*, are significant and will be discussed in the Conclusion. The people of Tubba' are mentioned only here and in Q. 44:37, neither context providing any indication as to their identity.[40]

Sūrat al-Najm, "the Sūra of the Star" (Q. 53), contains a passage with references to four punishment-stories that, like the short accounts in *Al-Dhāriyāt*, occur within a broader context of "signs" of God in nature. These verses include a designation for a destroyed people not yet encountered. Also, as in *Al-Dhāriyāt* and *Al-Furqān*, a series of references to past peoples destroyed by God leads to a declaration that Muḥammad is also one of the warners:

50 And [were they not told] that He destroyed 'Ād, the ancient,
51 and Thamūd, whom He did not spare,
52 and the people of Noah before – surely they were exceedingly evil and insolent.
53 And Al-Mu'tafika He cast down,
54 so that it was overwhelmed by what overwhelms.
55 Then which of thy Lord's bounties dost thou dispute?
56 This [Muḥammad] is a warner like the warners of old.

This last verse is a clear statement that Muḥammad is to be regarded as a warner (*nadhīr*) just like those in these stories. The term *al-mu'tafika*, which occurs in the Qur'ān in the singular only here, means "that which is overthrown or turned upside down." This expression in its plural form, al-Mu'tafikāt, is traditionally regarded a designation for the "cities of Lot."[41] It occurs in verse 70 of *Sūrat al-Tawba*, "the Sūra of Repentance" (Q. 9), which contains a list of past peoples destroyed by God: "Has there not come to them the report of those before them – the people (*qawm*) of Noah, 'Ād, Thamūd, the people (*qawm*) of Abraham, the people (*aṣḥāb*) of Madyan, and Al-Mu'tafikāt. Their messengers came to them with clear signs. God would not wrong them, but they wronged themselves." One difference between this list and that in Q. 22:42–44 (quoted at the beginning of this article) is that Al-Mu'tafikāt appears here in place of "the people of Lot," as appears also to be the case in Q. 53:50–53 above, where the singular form appears. In all three of these lists only the peoples are named, not the messengers. The passages quoted and discussed in this section contain only a few examples of numerous groups of short punishment-stories and verses with little more than lists of their peoples and messengers that appear throughout the Qur'ān.

2. *Groups with Punishment and Prophet Accounts*

Punishment-stories sometimes occur in contexts in which those who read the Qur'ān or hear it recited are apt not to recognize them as such, since only two or three are embedded in passages that contain accounts and references to a larger number of prophets or messengers who are not connected with punishment-stories in the Qur'ān. One such context, which names sixteen prophets altogether, occurs appropriately in *Sūrat al-Anbiyā'*, "the Sūra of the Prophets" (Q. 21). After a short Moses account (vv. 48–49) that begins "*And surely We gave to* Moses and Aaron the Criterion (*al-furqān*)" and a long Abraham story (vv. 51–73) that begins "*And surely We gave to* Abraham of old his proper course" (and vv. 71–72 mentions Lot, Isaac, and Jacob), a series of eight short passages follows, all of which begin with a concise introductory formula that requires an implied verb such as "remember" or "mention." The first two contain punishment-story themes and introduce formulaic statements that are repeated in later passages in the series:

74 ***And*** [***mention***] Lot, to whom We gave judgment and knowledge. And We rescued him (*wa najjaynā-hu*) from the city (*min[a] l-qarya*) that had been doing deeds of corruption. They were an evil and licentious people.
75 ***And We brought him into Our mercy***. He was one of the righteous.
76 ***And*** [***mention***] Noah, when he cried out before. And (*fa-*) **We answered him** and (*fa-*) **[We] rescued him (*fa-najjaynā-hu*) and his family from the great distress** [bold = Q. 37:76].
77 And We delivered him (*wa naṣarnā-hu*) from the people (*min[a] l-qawm*) [cf. v. 74b] who called Our signs lies. Surely they were an evil people, so We drowned them all.

Passages about David and Solomon (vv. 78–82) and Job (vv. 83–84) follow, and then the formulaic statements in the Lot and Noah accounts are repeated in the next four verses, which mention four prophets or messengers who do not appear in the punishment-stories:

85 ***And*** [***mention***] Ismāʿīl (Ishmael), Idrīs, Dhū-l-Kifl, all of whom were of the steadfast.
86 ***And We brought them into Our mercy***. They were among the righteous.
87 ***And*** [***mention***] Dhū-l-Nūn, when he went forth enraged and thought We had no power over him. Then he cried out in the darkness saying, "There is no God but Thee. Glory be to Thee! Surely I have done evil."
88 And (*fa-*) We answered him and (*wa*) rescued him [cf. v. 76 above] out of grief, and We rescue the believers.

These verses are followed by two about Zachariah and his son John (vv. 89–90) and then one about Jesus and his mother Mary (v. 91), neither of whom is named. Thus, of the seventeen men and Mary who are mentioned in these accounts, only two appear in contexts with punishment-story themes. Verses 85–88 are quoted above to illustrate the extent to which such accounts, including the complete but brief Noah punishment-story (vv. 76–77), are sometimes difficult to recognize, partly because of formulaic elements they share with other accounts. For instance, the statement "So We answered him and rescued him" appears in both the Noah and Dhū-l-Nūn accounts, but in the latter it is not a punishment-story theme.

Sūrat al-Ṣāffāt, "the Sūra of Those who Stand in Ranks" (Q. 37),[42] contains a unique set of accounts that are among the most instructive for understanding the formulaic features of the punishment-stories and their role within the teachings of the Qur'ān. As in *Al-Anbiyā'*, punishment and prophet accounts are intermixed and do not occur in chronological order according to later Islamic Sacred History. Four of the six accounts share the most fully developed "parallel schematic form" in the Qur'ān after that in *Al-Shu'arā'*, and five contain additional formulaic features:

75 Noah called to Us –and how excellent were the answerers –
76 and (*wa*) **We rescued him and his family from the great distress** [bold = Q. 21:76b]
77 And We made his seed the survivors,
78 ***and left upon him among those of later times*** [***the saying***]:
79 ***"Peace be upon*** Noah among all beings!"
80 ***Thus We recompense those who do good.***
81 ***He was among Our believing servants.***
82 Then afterwards We drowned the rest.

Once again, a Noah account occurs first and introduces this sūra's schematic form. The second account is about Abraham (vv. 83–113), and, as in several other sūras, it is much longer than the others in the series. Except for the name of the recipient of the peace greeting, the schematic verses in the Noah account occur verbatim in one about Abraham (vv. 108–11), which typically contains no punishment-story themes. This Abraham account differs from other versions in being separated from one about Lot in the same series. The schematic form of the third account differs slightly from that of the others in having dual pronominal suffixes:

114 We also favored Moses and Aaron,
115 and **We rescued** them and their people **from the great distress** [cf. Q. 21:76 and Q. 37:76]
. . . .
118 And We guided them in the straight path,
119 ***and left upon*** them ***among those of later times*** [***the saying***]:
120 ***"Peace be upon*** Moses and Aaron!"
121 ***Thus We recompense those who do good.***
122 They were ***among Our believing servant***s.

Dual pronominal suffixes also occur in the formulaic statement in verse 115, along with the term "people (*qawm*)," instead of "family (*ahl*)," which appears in the Noah and Lot accounts in the same sūra. The pivotal fourth account, about Elijah, is transitional in that it continues the parallel schematic form of the first three accounts and also introduces a formula that occurs at the beginning of each of the last three:

123 Elijah (Ilyās) <u>too was one of the Envoys</u>,
124 **when he said** to his people, **"Will you not be godfearing?**[43]
125 Do you call on Baal and abandon the best of creators?"
. . . .

129 ***and* [*We*] *left upon him among those of later times* [*the saying*]:**
130 ***"Peace be upon*** Elijah (Ilyāsīn)!"[44]
131 ***Thus We recompense those who do good.***
132 ***He was among Our believing servants.***
133 Lot too was one of the Envoys,
134 when **We rescued him and his family all together,** [= Q. 26:170]
135 **except for an old woman among those who tarried.** [= Q. 26:171]
136 **Then We destroyed the others.** [= Q. 26:172]
137 And you pass by them in the morning
138 and in the night. **Will you not understand?** [= Q. 11:51]
139 Jonah too was one of the Envoys,
140 when he ran away to the laden ship,
....
147 Then We sent him to a hundred thousand or more,
148 and they believed. So We gave them enjoyment for a while.

What a fascinating group of punishment and prophet stories! Although the first four – about Noah, Abraham, Moses and Aaron, and Elijah – share the parallel schematic form of five punishment-stories in *Al-Shuʿarāʾ*, only one (that of Noah) is among those five. The second and last verses of the Noah account contain typical punishment-story themes, but the four schematic verses do not. The other three schematic accounts in *Al-Ṣāffāt* are prophet stories, with only one verse, the second in the Moses account, having a punishment theme. Thus, although elements of the punishment-stories occur in two of the four schematic accounts, the dominant theme of the four as a whole involves the roles of these five men (including Aaron) as prophets.

The Lot account in *Al-Ṣāffāt* contains none of this sūra's schematic form, but three of its six verses occur verbatim in the Lot account in *Al-Shuʿarāʾ*. Curiously, these three verses do not occur in the schematic portions of *Al-Shuʿarāʾ*, but in the middle section of the Lot account there. Another anomaly about the Lot account in *Al-Ṣāffāt* is that it is the best example of a punishment-story in this sūra, containing most of the crucial elements in a concise form, whereas in most groups of punishment-stories the accounts about the people of Lot are often atypical and omit essential elements of the "plot." It is also notable that it is only in this series of "mixed" accounts in *Al-Ṣāffāt* that Lot is explicitly said to have been "one of the Envoys (*al-mursalūn*)" – a term associated especially with the messengers in the punishment-stories – and that this statement about Lot (in v. 133) is part of the introductory formula that also appears in the Elijah and Jonah accounts (in vv. 123 and 139), which contain no punishment themes. One other remarkable connection between the formulaic elements of *Al-Ṣāffāt* and *Al-Shuʿarāʾ* is that the second verse of the five schematic accounts in the latter appears in the Elijah account in

Al-Ṣāffāt (v. 124), and not in one of the punishment-stories there, as would be expected.

The formulaic features of the six accounts in *Al-Ṣāffāt* and their relationships with the punishment-stories in other sūras are complex and multifaceted, but one point seems clear: the dominant theme of these six accounts as a whole, not just the four schematic ones, is expressed in the penultimate verse of the passage that contains the parallel schematic form of this series, "Thus We recompense those who do good" (vv. 80, 110, 121, and 131). Thus, the meaning of the accounts that have punishment themes is influenced by their broader context within the series. This is also the case with those in the group of "mixed" accounts in *Al-Anbiyā'*, discussed above. One difference is that the punishment themes in *Al-Ṣāffāt* become ancillary to the primary focus of the entire group in that sūra, while the two brief accounts about Lot and Noah in *Al-Anbiyā'* remain essentially punishment-stories.

One distinctive feature shared by all of the accounts in these two sūras that sets them apart from groups and lists that involve only punishment-stories is that they focus on prophets or messengers, rather than on peoples and towns. This is clearest in *Al-Ṣāffāt*, where the four verses that share the same parallel schematic form and contain no punishment elements dominate the first four accounts or express their main theme, while the Jonah story deals only with him. Among the accounts in *Al-Anbiyā'* (that mention sixteen prophets by name), only those about Lot and Noah mention their city (*qarya*) or people (*qawm*) as having been evil or as having been destroyed. Even though these two brief accounts retain their distinctive character as punishment-stories, the emphasis in these versions of the stories is on the messengers and not their peoples. The two verses on Lot, for instance, do not even mention that the evil people of his city were destroyed.

CONCLUSIONS

This cursory analysis of the major formulaic features of the "punishment-stories" of the Qur'ān has made clearer the impressions received by those who recite or read them: their purpose is not to entertain, to relate history, nor even to teach, but to warn, threaten, convince, and even to reassure. They provide examples of past towns and peoples who were destroyed by God for rejecting messengers selected from among themselves. Although the dominant theme of their basic plot is to warn, the specific purpose of different groups of accounts varies. This is reflected in some of their formulaic features, in their broader contexts within individual sūras, and in certain key terms and concepts that make clear that these warnings are addressed to different audiences in different times and places. Some groups of punishment-stories that appear to be addressed to Muḥammad's opponents – probably both during his years in Mecca before the Hijra in 622 C.E. and during the last ten years of his life in Medina – have the purpose of threatening their destruction if they reject the message he brings from God. The purpose of others, especially the shorter accounts and the lists, appears to be to convince Muḥammad's hearers, both believers and non-believers alike, that they should accept him as a warner like the warners of old (Q. 53:56). Other passages reassure his followers that he is indeed a messenger of God sent as a warner (*nadhīr*) to those who might reject him and as "a bearer of good tidings (*bashīr*)" to those who accept the one true God (Q. 11:2).

This study has also yielded new insights into the roles and importance of the punishment-stories and references to them as a way of presenting a major theme of the Qur'ān over an extended period of time. What appear to be the earliest versions of these accounts, some with highly developed formulaic features, date from fairly early in the period of Muḥammad's public activities in his native city of Mecca, while references to them occur in lists in some of the latest parts of the Qur'ān, such as in Q. 9:70. A related insight is that the punishment-stories play a much larger role in the Qur'ān's portrayal of Muḥammad's ever-changing circumstances, including his growing power and position among his followers and within the communities in which he lived, than is recognized or acknowledged in writings about him and about the Qur'ān. This portrayal includes overlapping stages in his public life as a warner, a messenger sent by God to his own people, and a prophet in a long line going back at least to Noah.[45] This close relationship between Muḥammad and the punishment-stories can be seen in the broader contexts where their main theme is explicitly applied to his hearers, usually in passages that immediately follow the punishment accounts, as in Q. 26:208: "We never destroyed a town without first sending to it warners," Q. 54:43: "What, are your unbelievers better than these?," and Q. 54:43: "This [Muḥammad] is a warner like the warners of old.[46]

In groups of punishment-stories, but not always in lists and in groups where prophet and punishment accounts appear together, Noah consistently appears as the first of "the warners of old." Yet, in what appear to be the earlier versions, the impression is given that the chronological order in which God sent the warners is of no significance.[47] Later, special attention is given to the chronological order in which the peoples and messengers in the punishment-stories lived. This can be seen in several of the groups and lists discussed above (as well as in many others), but is most clear in certain explicit formulaic statements, in temporal particles that serve as introductory formulas, and also in certain temporal prepositions. An example of the first type occurs in Q. 7:69 and Q. 7:74, "<u>And remember when He appointed you</u> ['Ād] <u>as successors after</u> the people of Noah," and "<u>And remember when He appointed you</u>

[Thamūd] as successors after ʿĀd." An example of the second type is the particle *thumma* (then) that occurs in Q. 23:31 at the beginning of the account after that of Noah, and then at the beginning of the brief accounts that follow it, in verses 42, 44, and 45. Two examples of the third type occur in Q. 14:9: "Has the story of those before you (*min qabl*^{i}*-kum*) reached you: the people of Noah, ʿĀd, Thamūd, and those after them (*baʿd*^{i}*-him*)."[48] The temporal expression "before them" (*min qabl*^{i}*-him*) occurs frequently after the name Noah in punishment accounts and lists and in other contexts in the Qur'ān.

The significance of the different terms for "people" or "tribe" in the punishment-stories and in lists is not always clear. The term *aṣḥāb* (literally, "companions") occurs consistently for the people of al-Rass and for the people of the Thicket, while *qawm* always appears for the people of Noah, and virtually always for the people of Lot.[49] The term *ahl* usually occurs for Lot's "family," who are rescued,[50] but in Q. 29:31–34 *ahl* occurs three times for the "people" of Lot who are evildoers (*ẓālimūn*) and whom God is about to destroy (v. 31), and twice for Lot's "family," who are to be rescued (vv. 32–33).[51] The expression "the brothers (*ikhwān*) of Lot" in Q. 50:13 is unique, occurring nowhere else in the Qur'ān. The distinctive element of the Lot story that serves as the reason for the destruction of his people suggests that this term is best interpreted as referring not to his *qawm* in general, but only to those men who in Q. 7:80–81 and Q. 27:54–55 are said to "commit indecency" and "lust after men instead of women."

A basic core of four tribes or peoples to whom God sent warners appears to have been the basis of the earlier groups of punishment-stories: the people of Noah, ʿĀd, Thamūd, and the people of Lot, whose accounts occur in this order in *Al-Qamar, Al-Shuʿarā', Al-Aʿrāf,* and *Sūrat Hūd*. One other tribe or people appears to have joined this core fairly early, and their account occurs fifth in the last three sūras just mentioned. They are sometimes called Madyan (as in *Al-Aʿrāf* and *Sūrat Hūd*, and in the lists in *Al-Ḥajj* and *Al-Tawba*) and sometimes "the people of the Thicket" (as in *Al-Shuʿarā'*, and in the list in *Sūrat Qāf*). What ties these two names of peoples together is that their messenger is consistently said to be Shuʿayb. They do not appear in *Al-Qamar* or in the vast majority of references to the punishment-stories, either in the groups of short accounts or in the many partial lists. The uncertain position Madyan and their messenger Shuʿayb may be related to the important, but atypical and variable, accounts that center on Pharaoh and Moses. In some groups of punishment-stories (such as those in *Al-Qamar, Al-Dhāriyāt,* and *Al-Ṣāffāt*) and in some lists (such as that in *Al-Ḥāqqa*), accounts about Pharaoh and Moses appear to have taken the place of those about Madyan and Shuʿayb. This interesting possibility may be related to the close connection between Moses and the geographical area called Madyan (in the northern Sinai) or the town called Madyan Shuʿayb.[52] For instance, in the long Moses story in *Sūrat al-Qaṣaṣ,* "the Sūra of the Story" (Q. 28), verses 21–29 relate how Moses escaped from the land of Pharaoh, settled in the land of Madyan (Midian), married there, and worked for his father-in-law for eight or ten years.[53]

In any case, Moses came to have a special relationship to the punishment-stories. His accounts, however, differ from the others in a variety of ways. Even those that most closely resemble others in the same group omit basic elements of the plot of the punishment-stories. Moses is not called an "envoy" and is not sent to his own people, or even to a tribe or people at all. He is usually said to be sent simply to Pharaoh, but sometimes to "Pharaoh and his Council (*mala'*)." The Moses accounts never contain the more fully developed schematic forms of others in the same series. Those in the form of long narratives that occur before groups of formulaic or schematic accounts (as in *Al-Shu'arā'*), those in the form of short accounts that occur after such groups (as in *Al-Qamar, Al-A'rāf* and *Sūrat Hūd*), those that occur after groups of short accounts (as in *Al-'Ankabūt*), and references in some lists (as Q. 22:44): all give the impression of having been attached to groups of punishment-stories or appended to lists that had already existed earlier. Significant in a different way are the cases where only Noah and Moses are named, in the first and last accounts in a group, with indications (such as the use of the temporal particle, *thumma*) that unnamed messengers in the intervening accounts lived between their times (as in *Al-Mu'minūn* and *Sūrat Yūnus*). Whenever Moses stories occur in the same contexts with punishment-stories, they share some of the formulaic features of the other accounts, such as the two-verse ending in *Al-Shu'arā'* and the numerous formulaic statements where only one or two formulas are usually involved.

Some groups of accounts appear to have been revised or expanded to address different audiences during the changing circumstances of the life of Muḥammad and the emergence of the Muslim community. Formulaic elements and other indications make clear that one audience of the punishment-stories was the Meccan polytheists, who were threatened, at least implicitly, with the destruction of their city. Some verses that do not occur within the punishment-stories make this point explicitly, such as Q. 47:13: "How many a city (*qarya*) that was stronger than thy city (*qarya*), which expelled thee [Muḥammad], have We destroyed, and they had no helper." The expression "thy city" no doubt refers to Mecca, and "How many a city ... have We destroyed" implies physical destruction. The phrase "which expelled thee" is only one of many indications that punishment-story themes, directed against Muḥammad's native city, continued to be a part of the message of the Qur'ān after he and his followers settled in Medina. The same point is made in a passage addressed to Muḥammad that serves as a conclusion to the punishment-stories in *Al-Furqān:* "We made examples of each .... and surely they [the unbelievers of Mecca] have passed by (*ataw*) the city (*al-qarya*) on which

We sent down a fatal rain[54] . . . . And when they see thee [Muḥammad] they only mock thee" (Q. 25:39–41).

The more fully developed versions of the punishment-stories we now have in their final form serve as excellent examples of basic tenets of modern critical scholarship regarding the Qur'ān. Nineteenth- and early twentieth-century scholars who specialized in the study of the Arabic text of the Qur'ān established an elementary foundation for current research. The present study has shown that literary features of the punishment-stories call for further analysis. For instance, strong evidence suggests that some groups of accounts were recited on different occasions with different formulaic features, such as the refrains in *Al-Shu'arā'* and *Al-Qamar.* It is not implausible that authorities on the Qur'ān during Muḥammad's lifetime, such as Ibn Mas'ūd, memorized groups of the punishment-stories such as those in *Al-Shu'arā'* and *Al-Qamar* with one refrain – directly from the mouth of the Prophet, as Ibn Mas'ūd later claimed – while others memorized the same accounts or Muḥammad dictated them to his secretaries with a different refrain. What appear to be two (or more) refrains in these two sūras contain language and themes that are characteristically Meccan in one case and Medinan in another. Most of the groups of more fully developed punishment-stories contain evidence that is clear to those who know the Arabic text of the Qur'ān well and apply to it modern methods of historical and literary criticism that many of the revelations were fluid during Muḥammad's lifetime, in accordance with modern oral formula theory.

It is not unreasonable to conclude that Muḥammad recited the punishment-stories in different forms on different occasions from a common body of key terms, phrases, and formulas in such a way that their basic plot and primary theme could be presented to his ever-changing audience in an almost endless variety of forms – to address the different circumstances of his hearers. Such a conclusion is not inconsistent with clear statements in the Qur'ān or with traditional Islamic teachings.[55] The formulaic nature of the main groups of punishment-stories supports the view that the Qur'ān is basically oral in nature. The dominant theme of the punishment-stories is strengthened by the fact that the same message is presented repeatedly to the same or different audiences in a wide variety of interesting and indeed fascinating forms.

NOTES

1 In this article all references to sūra names and verse divisions and numbers are to those of the 1342 A.H. Cairo edition of the Qur'ān, sometimes called the "Egyptian standard edition." Sūra names, verse divisions, and verse numbering systems (even when the verse divisions are the same) vary in different modern editions of the Arabic text and in translations. See A. Spitaler, *Die Verszählung*

des Koran nach islamischer Überlieferung (Munich: Verlag der Bayerischen Akademie der Wissenchaften, 1935) and Alford T. Welch, "Ḳur'ān," in *The Encyclopaedia of Islam,* New Edition, 5:411.

2 See Welch, "Ḳur'ān," 420.

3 The first part of this praise formula occurs also at the beginning of sūras 62 and 64. Classical writers refer to this group of five sūras (57, 59, 61, 62, and 64) as *al-musabbiḥāt,* since they all begin with *sabbaḥa li-llāh* or the synonymous wording *yusabbiḥu li-llāh.* See Welch, "Sūra," in *The Encyclopaedia of Islam,* New Edition, 8:887, where names of other groups are also mentioned.

4 On the identification of the subjects of this dual-form verb, see vv. 14–15 and 33, both of which are preceded and followed by this refrain. The first tells of the creation of man and jinn, and the second begins, "O company of jinn and man . . . ." The commentators often connect this verb (*tukadhdhibān*) at the end of the refrain with *thaqalān* ("you two burdensome companies") in v. 31, which they interpret as referring to jinn and man. See Bayḍāwī, *Anwār al-Tanzīl wa Asrār al-Ta'wīl,* 5 vols. bound in two (Beirut: Dār al-Jīl, n.ḍ) and Zamakhsharī, *al-Kashshāf 'an Ḥaqā'iq al-Tanzīl Aqāwīl fī Wujūh al-Ta'wīl,* 4 vols. (Cairo: al-Ḥalabī and Associates, 1972) on Q. 55:31, and Jalāl al-Dīn al-Maḥallī and Jalāl al-Dīn al-Suyūṭī, *Tafsīr al-Jalālayn* (Beirut: Dār Ibn Kathīr, 1994) on Q. 55:13.

5 For recent discussions of definitions and characteristics of narratives, see Casare Segre, *Introduction to the Analysis of the Literary Text,* trans. John Meddemmen (Bloomington: Indiana University Press, 1988), 223–35; also: F. K. Stanzel, *A Theory of Narrative,* trans. Charlotte Goedsche (Cambridge and New York: Cambridge University Press, 1984) from the 2nd ed. of *Theorie des Erzählens* (Göttingen: Vandenhoeck and Ruprecht, 1982); Mieke Bal, *Narratology: Introduction to the Theory of Narrative,* trans. Christine van Boheemen (Toronto: University of Toronto Press, 1985) from the 2nd ed. of *De theorie van vertellen en verhalen* (Muiderberg: Coutinho, 1980).

6 The punishment-stories do not constitute a "genre" in the sense of a distinctive category of literary composition as a whole, since they occur within various sūras that treat other topics, nor as having a distinctive literary style, but they can be considered as a genre in the sense of sharing the same plot and other characteristic features. While some groups share one distinctive form, others share another, or have no specific form at all. Thus, it is on the basis of their contents rather than their form that the punishment-stories can be regarded as a discrete genre. Another complicating factor is that they are basically oral in nature and contain several distinct formulaic features that vary in different groups. For a succinct account of the history of the concept "genre" and various recent literary theories about them, see Segre, *Introduction to the Analysis of the Literary Text,* 199–222.

7 So-called because they occur at the very beginning of 29 of the 114 sūras. For traditional views: Jalāl al-Dīn al-Suyūṭī, *al-Itqān fī 'Ulūm al-Qur'ān,* 2 vols. (Cairo: al-Ḥalabī and Sons, 1951), 2:105–7 and P.J.E. Cachia, "Bayḍāwī on the *Fawātiḥ,*" *Journal of Semitic Studies* 13 (1968):218–31.

8 So-called because their meaning has never been satisfactorily explained (see Theodor Nöldeke and Friedrich Schwally, *Geschichte des Qorāns,* 3 vols. (Hildesheim: Georg Olms Verlag, 1970), 2:68–78; R. Blachère, *Introduction au Coran,* 2nd ed. (Paris: G.-P. Maisonneuve et Larose, 1977), 144–49; W.M. Watt, *Bell's Introduction to the Qur'ān, Completely Revised and Enlarged* (Edinburgh: Edinburgh University Press, 1970), 61–65; and Welch, "Ḳur'ān," 412–14). Sūras 26–28 form a triad called in the classical writings *ṭawāsīn,* since they are the only ones in the Qur'ān that begin with the "mysterious letters," *ṭā' sīn.* They

appear to have been kept together for this reason when the Qur'ān was collected and arranged (see Watt, *Bell's Introduction,* 40–44 and Welch, "Ḳur'ān," 404–6).

9 On this characteristic feature of the "mysterious letters" as being followed immediately by a formula referring to the heavenly Book, the source of the revelation being sent down to Muḥammad, see Welch, "Ḳur'ān," 413–14.

10 When first person verb forms and pronominal suffixes appear in the Arabic (usually in the plural), a frequently occurring feature of the text of the Qur'ān, the speaker (usually "We" in translation) is virtually always God and the pronouns (in translation) also refer to God – except in stories or narratives, where speaker and referent are usually clear from the context.

11 The archaic English terms "thou," "thee," and "thy" and corresponding verb forms, such as "shalt" and "art," are used throughout this article to make clear that second person singular forms occur in the Arabic. The immediate contexts usually indicate the persons being addressed in the punishment-stories, but frequently passages in the wider contexts that affect their meaning or purpose address Muḥammad. This would not be clear without the use of these archaic pronouns (see Welch, "Muhammad's Understanding of Himself: The Koranic Data," in *Islam's Understanding of Itself,* ed. Richard G. Hovannisian and Speros Vryonis, Jr. (Malibu: Undena, 1983), 17, and the many examples in that article that demonstrate how frequently Muḥammad is addressed in the Qur'ān, and how important it is to indicate this in translations).

12 Examples include: "Shall we believe thee, whom the lowest follow," addressed to Noah in Q. 26:111, and "Thou art merely one of those who are bewitched, no one but a mortal like us," addressed to Ṣāliḥ in vv. 153–54, and to Shu'ayb in vv. 185–86.

13 This precise formula, typical of parts of the Qur'ān that refer to Muḥammad after his rise to power in Medina, occurs only two other times in the Qur'ān, in 3:50 and 43:63. Two similar formulas occur seven times: "Obey God and His Messenger" in 8:1, 20, 46, and 58:13, and "Obey God and obey the Messenger" in 24:54, 47:33, and 64:12, both referring to Muḥammad.

14 This interpretation is reflected in Arberry's translation of the Qur'ān (*The Koran Interpreted,* 2 vols. London: George Allen & Unwin, 1955) by the way these verses are set apart from the introduction and the stories that precede them.

15 A true rhyme is marked by complete correspondence of terminal syllables, such as *ṣadrak, wizrak,* and *ẓahrak* in Q. 94:1–3. A true assonance is a partial rhyme in which the consonants at the ends of the words differ, but the preceding vowel, which is stressed and thus in Arabic is a long vowel, is always the same, such as *majīd, 'ajīb,* and *ba'īd* in Q. 50:1–3.

16 One exception is the very short, three-verse *Sūrat al-Kawthar* (Q. 108). The only other groups of verses in the Qur'ān with this specific "weak assonance" ("r" preceded by a short vowel) occur in two sūras: eighteen verses out of fifty-six in Sūra 74 (vv. 1–7, 18–37, and 42) and seven verses out of forty in Sūra 75 (vv. 7–13).

17 See Watt, *Bell's Introduction,* 206.

18 Welch, "Sūra," 887–89, provides evidence for rejecting recent theories that support the modern concept of the "coherence" of the sūras, each of which is said to have a central theme that unifies the entire sūra. On the concept "theme" in contemporary literary theory, see Segre, *Introduction to the Analysis of the Literary Text,* 277–99.

19 *Al-A'rāf* contains an example of a similar feature of some groups of the punishment-stories: variations in the wording of key phrases or statements that

are not themselves formulaic in nature, but are related to statements in the same series of accounts that are. The statement at the end of the formulaic part of Q. 7:79 and Q. 7:93, "and I gave sincere advice to you (*wa naṣaḥtu la-kum*)," is a simple variation of "and I give sincere advice to you (*wa anṣaḥu la-kum*)" in v. 62 of the Noah account. A somewhat fuller form, "and I am a faithful sincere adviser to you (*wa anā la-kum nāṣiḥun amīn*)" occurs in v. 68 in the 'Ād account. These statements, although not formulaic, produce an effect for the hearer that is similar to that of cumulative schematic form, since they constitute stages of development of the same theme – and, in this case, involve verb and noun variations of the same Arabic root.

20 This sūra will be called *Sūrat Hūd* throughout the article in order to avoid ambiguity, since the messenger Hūd is also mentioned frequently, while other sūras that are discussed and mentioned often are referred to in the text of the article simply by their Arabic titles, such as *Al-A'rāf* and *Al-Shu'arā'*. In the notes, for clarity, partly because they are separated from the text, sūras are referred to by their ordinal numbers, such as Sūra 7 and Sūra 26.

21 See Welch, "Ḳur'ān," 410.

22 Arberry made two errors in translating the last part of Q. 11:25. Instead of "Surely I am for you a warner (*in-nī la-kum nadhīr*^{un} *mubīn*)," he has: "I am for you a warner, and a bearer of good tidings." He thus adds a phrase that is not in the Qur'ān, in either the Egyptian standard edition or that of Gustav Flügel (*Concordantiae Corani arabicae,* Leipzig, 1841). He also omits the rhyme word in the expression at the end of the verse, "a clear warner (*nadhīr*^{un} *mubīn*)." With these two mistakes it appears that Arberry was influenced by the statement referring to Muḥammad near the beginning of this sūra, in Q. 11:2: "Surely I am to you a warner from Him and a bearer of good tidings (*inna-nī la-kum min-hu nadhīr*^{un} *wa-bashīr*)." The only other occurrence of a similar statement in the Qur'ān also refers to Muḥammad, in Q. 7:188: "I am only a warner and a bearer of good tidings (*in anā illā nadhīr*^{un} *wa bashīr*)."

23 Bell suggests that the *bu'd* formula (which he translates, "Ho, away with ... ") is best interpreted as being pronounced at the Last Judgement, a view that is supported by the fact that the Day of Resurrection is mentioned in the same verse (Q. 11:60) just before this formula in the 'Ād account.

24 In all of the five schematic punishment-stories in Sūra 26, the first part of this formula reads "I ask of you no wage [*ajl*] for this," just as here in 11:51. It is only in 11:29 in the Noah account above that the term "wealth" (*māl*) occurs.

25 The commentators identify these messengers (*rusul*) here as angels (*malā'ika*), e.g. Zamakhsharī and Bayḍāwī on Q. 11:69.

26 Richard Bell, *A Commentary on the Qur'ān,* ed. C.E. Bosworth and M.E.J. Richardson, 2 vols. (Manchester: Manchester University Press, 1991), 1:363–64.

27 Interpretations differ as to the precise referent of the pronominal suffixes in the statement "We overturned it and rained upon it ... (*ja'alnā 'āliya-hā sāfila-hā wa amṭarnā 'alay-hā*)" in Q. 11:82, although the majority view is that they refer to the city or the cities of Lot. Pickthall (*The Glorious Koran, a Bi-lingual Edition with English Translation, Introduction and Notes,* Albany: State University of New York Press, 1976) interprets it (in parentheses) as Lot's "township" (his rendering of *qarya,* usually translated as "town" or "city"), a view shared by most European translators (Blachère: "la ville", as his translation of *-hā*; Julio Cortes (*El Coran, edición, traducción y notas,* Madrid: Editora Nacional, 1979): "la ciudad," in a footnote; Paret (*Der Koran: Übersetzung,* Stuttgart: W. Kohlhammer, 1962): "Stadt Lots," in a footnote, and "die Stadt (*qarya*) Lots," in his *Der Koran: Kommentar und Konkordanz* (Stuttgart: W. Kohlhammer, 1977, 241). Curiously, it

is the Muslim commentators who often interpret this reference to the city of Lot (consistently referred to in the Qur'ān by the singular term, *qarya*) in light of the Biblical tradition: Ibn Kathīr (*Mukhtaṣar Tafsīr Ibn Kathīr,* 2 vols. Beirut: Dār al-Ma'rifa, 1983) says simply that it refers to *Sadūm* (Sodom), but others interpret the fem. sing. pronominal suffixes in Q. 11:82 as referring to Lot's "cities" or "towns," in the plural, e.g., Bayḍāwī says *madā'in,* and *Jalālayn* says *qurā,* while Yusuf Ali (*The Holy Qur'ān: Text, Translation and Commentary,* Lahore: Muhammad Ashraf, 1979) renders *-hā* in his translation as "the cities" and adds in a footnote "the Cities of the Plain," with a reference to Gen. 19:26.

28 These facts provide additional support for the view that the story of Abraham and Lot was added later than the time of the original recitation of the four schematic punishment-stories in this sūra, since it "breaks the connection that binds the group together" (Bell, *The Qur'ān, Translated with a Critical Re-arrangement of the Surahs,* 2 vols. Edinburgh: Edinburgh University Press, 1937–39, 204); see also Bell, *Commentary,* 1:363–64.

29 This formula also occurs in Q. 7:59, Q. 29:14, and Q. 71:1.

30 The exact order in which the groups of punishment-stories were first recited by Muḥammad, as well as the dating of later versions of the same accounts, cannot be known (see Watt, *Bell's Introduction,* 89–101, and Welch, "Ḳur'ān," 417–19). It is possible, however, through a careful analysis of the vocabulary, major themes, contexts, and Qur'ānic usage of key terms, to determine that certain accounts and lists are considerably earlier and others much later than the most fully developed groups discussed in the first two sections above.

31 A portion of Sūra 40 is similar to this pattern in sūras 23 and 10. A punishment-story in vv. 5–6 begins, "The people of Noah and the parties after them called the messengers liars," and later states, "then I seized them, and how [terrible] was My retribution." Then a Moses story (vv. 23–46) includes a passage in which a believer among the people of Pharaoh says he fears that his people will meet the same fate as "the people of Noah, 'Ād, Thamūd, and those after them [i.e. before the time of Moses]" (vv. 30–31).

32 A similar formula that has essentially the same meaning, "surely it is but a reminder to all beings (*in huwa illā dhikrā li-l-'ālamīn*)," occurs in Q. 6:90, Q. 12:104, Q. 38:87, and Q. 81:27, and, with *wa mā* in place of *in* at the beginning, in Q. 68:52.

33 Bell, *The Qur'ān, Translated,* 387, suggests a third possibility for interpreting the construction of a Lot punishment-story in this sūra.

34 The use of italics (rather than underlining) in the quotation of vv. 31–35 reflects the interpretation that these verses constitute an independent account that at some point was inserted into, or combined with, the Abraham-Lot story in vv. 16–17 and 24–30. Such an interpretation need not be inconsistent with traditional beliefs, since the Qur'ān itself acknowledges that changes were made in the revelations (e.g., Q. 2:106, Q. 16:101–2). For brief comments on this issue and these verses, see Welch, "Ḳur'ān," 404.

35 These three to whom Moses is said to have been sent (Korah, Pharaoh, and Haman) are mentioned together only in this verse (Q. 29:39) and in Q. 40:24. Haman's name appears in the Qur'ān four other times, always with Pharaoh: three times in a story in Sūra 28 (vv. 6, 8, and 38) and once in Sūra 40 (in v. 36). Korah is mentioned (twice) in only one other passage in the Qur'ān, Q. 28:76–79, which says he was "of the people of Moses."

36 The expression, "painful chastisement (*'adhāb alīm*)," usually indefinite, but occasionally (as here) with definite articles, occurs in the Qur'ān almost seventy times, always (or virtually always, since the meaning is ambiguous in a

few contexts) referring to punishment in the afterlife. Some of the commentators, however, interpret this expression in Q. 51:37 as referring to terrestrial punishment. Bayḍāwī, for instance, says it involves destruction with "stones (*aḥjār*)" or "boulders (*ṣakhr*)".

37 Compare this Abraham-Lot story in Sūra 51 with the similar but even longer story in Q. 29:16–35, where Lot does appear as a messenger addressing and warning his people.

38 See Watt, *Bell's Introduction,* 121–27.

39 The term *rass* means "well," but the identity of this group called literally "the people of the Well" has not been satisfactorily explained. Ibn Kathīr says "the people (*aṣḥāb*) of al-Rass are a family (*ahl*) of a city (*qarya*) of the cities (*qurā*) of [the people of] Thamūd" (2:156). The *Lisān* says al-Rass is a wadi or a place in the Najd (Ibn Manẓūr, *Lisān al-'Arab,* 6 vols. Cairo: Dār al-Ma'ārif, n.d., 1642), and others have said it is in Yamāma. *Jalālayn* (on Q. 25:38) says al-Rass could be the name of "their prophet."

40 The term Tubba' is known to have been the title of the rulers of the tribe or people called Ḥimyar, who lived in South Arabia, just as "Pharaoh" was the title of the rulers of ancient Egypt. Whether the expression "the people of Tubba'" refers simply to the people of Ḥimyar or to some specific tribe or people remains uncertain.

41 The use of the Arabic term Al-Mu'tafikāt ("those that were overthrown or turned upside down") as a designation for the cities of Lot may have been influenced by verses of the Qur'ān such as Q. 11:82: "So when Our command came, We overturned it (*'āliya-hā sāfila-hā*) and rained on it stones of baked clay." The Qur'ān consistently refers to Lot's town or city (*qarya*) in the singular (as in Q. 7:82, Q. 21:74, Q. 27:56, Q. 27:86, and Q. 29:31). *Jalālayn* and others interpret the sing. form, *al-mu'tafika,* in Q. 53:53 as "the town (*qarya*) of the people (*qawm*) of Lot," while other commentators interpret the sing. pronominal suffixes in Q. 11:82 as referring to the "cities" of Lot (see note 27 above). It is largely because Al-Mu'tafika and Al-Mu'tafikāt (which occurs only in Q. 9:70 and Q. 69:9) have become designations for the city or cities of Lot that these terms are left untranslated in this article.

42 The title of this sūra is usually interpreted as referring to a celestial scene. Commenting on Q. 37:1, Zamakhsharī and *Jalālayn* say the title refers to ranks of angels lined up worshipping God (near his Throne in heaven). Bayḍāwī mentions ranks of celestial angels first, but then offers other possible interpretations, including ranks of demons.

43 The formulaic rhetorical question at the end of this verse and also the frequently-occurring introductory formula appear in the second of the five verses that constitute the first stage of the "parallel schematic form" in Sūra 26, occurring in vv. 106, 124, 142, 161, and 177. The only difference in Q. 37:124 is the middle expression, "to his people (*li-qawmi-hi*)," where the accounts in Sūra 26 have *idh qāla la-hum akhū-hum* followed by the name of one of the five messengers, Noah, Hūd, Ṣāliḥ, Lot, and Shu'ayb. The beginning and the end of all six verses have the wording, *idh qāla ... a-lā tattaqūn.*

44 The most reasonable explanation for this change in the spelling of the Arabic name for Elijah is that the second occurrence serves as a rhyme word. It is not unusual in the Qur'ān for a word to have a different spelling when it serves this function. The name Elijah occurs in only one other verse of the Qur'ān, Q. 6:85, where it is spelled Ilyās.

45 This later stage appears in a number of verses such as Q. 33:7: "When We took a pledge from the prophets (*al-nabiyyūn*), and from thee [Muḥammad], from

Noah, Abraham, Moses, and Jesus son of Mary, We took a solemn pledge." See also Q. 3:33, Q. 4:163, Q. 19:58, and Q. 42:13, among a number of similar contexts.

46 For an analysis of Muḥammad's roles in the Qur'ān as warner, messenger, prophet, and several others, see Welch, "Muhammad's Understanding," 41–46.

47 For instance, Sūra 53 mentions the "scrolls of Moses and Abraham" and then 'Ād, Thamūd, the people of Noah, and then Al-Mu'tafika (the city of Lot), and Sūra 69 mentions Thamūd, 'Ād, Pharaoh, Al-Mu'tafikāt (the cities of Lot), and then alludes to Noah in v. 11, "Lo, when the waters rose We bore you in the ship." This indiscriminate order in which the Qur'ān mentions past messengers of God in contexts that appear to be fairly early can be seen in a number of passages not related to the punishment-stories, such as Q. 6:83–87, which mentions Abraham, Isaac, Jacob, Noah, David, Solomon, Job, Joseph, Moses, Aaron, Zachariah, John, Jesus, Elijah, Jonah, and Lot, and ends: "We chose them and guided them upon a straight path."

48 The last part of this quotation from Q. 14:9, involving the people of Noah, 'Ād, and Thamūd, occurs verbatim in Q. 40:31, and a similar statement occurs in Q. 40:5: "The people of Noah and those after them (*min ba'd^{i}-him*). ..." Even more common in the Qur'ān is the expression in Q. 50:12, "the people of Noah before them (*qabl^{a}-hum*)," and the variation in Q. 51:46, "the people of Noah before (*min qabl^{u}*)."

49 For instance, in Q. 7:80, Q. 11:70, Q. 22:43, Q. 26:160, and Q. 29:28, all referring to the people of Lot.

50 Two other expressions (*āl* and *bayt*) refer to the family of Lot: *āl lūṭ* (Lot's "family") in Q. 27:56, and *bayt min al-muslimīn* (one household of those who surrender) in Q. 51:36. In both of these contexts the "people" of Lot who are destroyed are referred to as his *qawm*.

51 The use of *ahl* (usually meaning "family" in the Qur'ān) in place of *qawm* (the term that occurs most frequently in the punishment-stories for "people" or possibly "tribe") is not at all unique in this Lot account. In the Madyan punishment-story in Sūra 7, verse 96 says: "If the people of the towns (*ahl al-qurā*) had believed and kept from evil, We would have sent down on them blessings from heaven." This same expression, also referring to those about to be destroyed, occurs in vv. 97 and 98, and *ahl* occurs with the same meaning in v. 94. This term also occurs for the unbelievers of Thamūd and Pharaoh in punishment-stories, and in a number of passages addressed to Muḥammad.

52 See C.E. Bosworth, "Madyan Shu'ayb in Pre-Islamic and Early Islamic Lore and History," *Journal of Semitic Studies* 29 (1984):53–64.

53 See also Q. 20:40 where God tells Moses: "You tarried for years among the people (*ahl*) of Madyan." Sūra 28 (which says Moses lived in Madyan for eight or ten years) begins with the "mysterious letters," "Ṭā' Sīn Mīm," which introduce the rhyme of the 135–verse sūra, a common feature of the "mysterious letters" (see Welch, "Ḳur'ān," 414).

54 *Jalālayn* says the verb *ataw* means "the unbelieving (ones) of Mecca passed (*marra kuffār^{u} makka*)" and *al-qarya* here refers to "the cities of Lot (*qurā lūṭ*)." Ibn Kathīr, *Mukhtaṣar,* 2:156, says *al-qarya* here in Q. 25:40 refers to "the city of the people of Lot" and adds that it is Sodom (*Sadūm*), which Ibn Manẓūr (*Lisān,* 1977) says is near Ḥimṣ.

55 For Qur'ānic references and an analysis of "Evidences of Revision and Alteration" in the Qur'ān, see Watt, *Bell's Introduction,* 89–101.

Chapter 5

"Desiring the Face of God": The Qur'ānic Symbolism of Personal Responsibility

Andrew Rippin

Centuries of theological discussion and many scholarly studies have drawn attention to the centrality of the theme of "personal responsibility" in the Qur'ān. Clearly linked to the conception of God, the issue has been framed primarily in terms of free will versus predestination: human responsibility versus God's fore-knowledge.[1] The issue is, however, far more fundamental to the Qur'ān and to religious language in general. It sits as an issue which is embedded in the implications of much of the symbolism which is present in the text of the Qur'ān. By considering the example of the idea of "desiring the face of God," this point will be illustrated and some insights will be gained into the particular contribution of the Qur'ān to the discussion of monotheism and its ethos in the Near East. Overall, the point is to discuss the way in which the idea of "personal responsibility," a theme central to the monotheistic traditions, is embedded in a variety of symbolic expressions: the aim, notice, is not to "explain" what the symbolism "means," for symbolism means what it says, but to explore the symbolism used in discussing certain ideas, in order to see the way in which language mediates certain human experiences, ideas and ideals which would otherwise be inexpressible.

The historical experience of exile from the land promised by God provoked the prophets of ancient Israel to an exploration of the theme of individual responsibility and Yahweh's protective guidance. The demand that Israel find for itself "a new heart and a new spirit" (Ezekiel 18:31) is matched by the promise that Yahweh will provide that new heart and spirit (Ezekiel 36:26) in order to protect his "holy name."[2] This theological theme of the tension between power and mercy is often seen to be the central problem of the monotheist tradition; it is certainly one which both Christianity and Islam inherit and to which they both suggest resolutions.

The terms in which the Qur'ān discusses this problem are not those of Ezekiel. For Ezekiel, as with other ancient Israelite prophets, the crisis is caused by the loss of the land of Israel, perceived to be due to the lack of faith and obedience. The emphasis is on the disasters which have befallen Israel which are proffered as a rationale for the exile which is being experienced. While the Qur'ān recounts the stories of the ancient communities and their subsequent failures, thus matching the historical emphasis of the Biblical tradition, the stress within the Qur'ān falls elsewhere. The alienation of the individual from God appears to be the Qur'ānic focal point. The metaphor of the pathway becomes the most consistent expression: people have strayed from the straight path, but God will guide them back.

A good deal of scholarly attention[3] has been paid to the expression *aslama wajhahu li' l-lāhi*, "He submitted his face to God," concerning which many writers agree with M.M. Bravmann's opinion that "*wağh* 'face' [is used here] instead of the more regularly used noun *nafs* 'soul'."[4] The crucial differences of opinion concerning this phrase have related more to what *aslama* might mean in this and other contexts. On the other hand, the use of the phrase "desiring the face of God" or "seeking the face of God" has not attracted as much attention, although it certainly has been remarked upon.[5] The assumption seems to have been, in agreement with Muslim tradition, that this is an "anthropomorphism" in which *wajh* should be taken to mean something like *dhāt*, "essence" or "presence."[6]

But a question lingers: put reductively, it would ask, why *wajh*? That is, if *wajh* here means something other than "face," then why is that "something other" not used? That manner of expressing the question, however, does not really allow any particular access into the religious message of the Qur'ān: it asserts only the philological impulse of seeking the background to the word or it invites a dogmatic response regarding the literary style of the Qur'ān. Certainly it cannot be denied – Bravmann has demonstrated the point quite fully – that ancient Arabic used expressions regarding "submitting the face" in a broad range of contexts with specific meanings. But the overall question of the significance of *wajh* in the Qur'ān can be pursued within a broader semantic and religious – perhaps theological – context. The word "face" carries with it an entire structure of discourse, some of it mythical, some of it strictly theological. The goal of a study such as this becomes, in fact, not the "meaning" of "face" but what the word conveys. The use of the word *wajh* becomes the key to its significance, not the meaning.

Central to this study is the need to view the use of "face" within a broader cultural setting of monotheism. It has, after all, been remarked on numerous occasions also that "the face of God" is an ancient expression. The Qur'ān participates within the monotheistic discourse of the Near East through its very use of such symbolism.

However, the citation of parallels to the Qur'ān from the Bible is a procedure fraught with difficulties and a method viewed with deep suspicion. Yet it is, I would claim, absolutely essential if we are to understand the religious message of the Qur'ān. The images used in the Qur'ān of God in relation to humanity have an ancient heritage. In asserting that, however, we must be clear about how to separate these insights from those of the philological method. The tendency is to see the assertion of a past usage as meaning that the past represents the original and true usage and that all later usages are derivatory. Such are the traps into which many studies of the Qur'ān have fallen. However, a comparative approach can be of some significance if the aims and the limitations of the method are clearly kept in mind. A successful (that is, meaningful) comparative methodology involves analogical comparisons in terms of systems, not in terms of isolated "bits and pieces" with an understanding that analogous processes within parallel cultural situations are likely to produce similar results. Comparisons need not involve the questions of "origins" of particular items: the focus of interest must be on cultural patterns and symbolic systems. Once again, it is not, in this instance, the "meaning" of *wajh* which is to be determined within a comparative framework: rather, the word itself, when situated comparatively, gives us a view into the religious system of the Qur'ān. For our purposes here, the Bible presents, like the Qur'ān, a (relatively) static tradition of the expression of Near Eastern monotheism. The Bible cannot be presumed to define the range of the symbolism said to be analogical to a text such as the Qur'ān, even less to provide the normative example by which all others may be compared. It does, however, furnish a convenient textual source from which comparative insights may begin.

Samuel Balentine[7] in his book *The Hidden God* has argued persuasively for understanding there to be a relationship between the theological notion of the "hiddenness of God" and the expression "hide the face." The Biblical writers expressed the benevolence of God through the presence of his face: for example, see Deuteronomy 4:37, "Because he loved your fathers and chose their children after them, he himself [literally, with his face] brought you out of Egypt by his great strength" and Exodus 33:14, "And he said, 'My face will go and I will lighten your burden'." However, alongside that idiom developed the motif of God's turning away his face, of his face being hidden, when the lack of favour on the nation of Israel was evident. God is spoken of as hiding his face 26 times in the Bible, 12 times in the Psalms alone. Isaiah 54:8 has God say of himself, "In slight anger for a moment I hid my face from you, but with kindness everlasting I will take you back in love." Psalm 10:11 pictures the wicked, arrogant man thinking, "God is not mindful, he hides his face, he never looks." The lament of the hiddenness of the face of God is to be traced back to Sumerian and Akkadian prayers.[8]

The expression *biqqesh pene yahweh* as found in the Bible,[9] meaning "to seek the face of God," has been cited in scholarly literature on the Qur'ān because of the significance of its parallelism to the Qur'ānic statement.[10] Here we see precisely the danger of the citation of parallels. The expectation comes about that by finding a parallel expression we have somehow solved the problem of the "meaning" and "background" to the expression. The discovery of the parallel leads to speculation over how it is that the phrase "passed" to Muḥammad. Baljon in his article "'To seek the face of God' in Koran and Hadith" puts it this way: "In my opinion there can be no objection against assuming that the expression of the O[ld] T[estament] has been translated into pure Arabic idiom, either by Mohammed himself (supposing he could understand Hebrew) or by Jews of his neighbourhood."[11] Certainly, there can be no necessary objection to such speculation, but the point must be made that we have not really accomplished very much by the mere juxtaposition of the facts. We do not understand the Qur'ān any better for knowing that parallel. What is needed is an investigation which will situate both the Biblical usages and the Qur'ānic usages in terms of their overall symbolic, mythological and theological impact.

~

The word *wajh* and its plural *wujūh* are used 72 times in the Qur'ān. Seven times, the idea of believers "seeking the face of God" or "desiring the face of God" is expressed: Q. 2:272, *ibtighā' wajh Allāh* ; 6:52, *yurīdūna wajhahu* ; 13:22, *ibtighā' wajh rabbihim* ; 18:28, *yurīdūna wajhahu* ; 30:38, *yurīdūna wajh Allāh* ; 30:39 *turīdūna wajh Allāh* ; and 92:20, *ibtighā' wajh rabbihi.* The "face of God" is also present in prayer according to Q. 2:115, in which *wajh* is generally glossed as *qibla* : "Wherever you turn, there is the face of God." It is also spoken of in a rather mystifying manner with regards to charity in Q. 76:9: "[The pious say] 'We feed you [the needy, the orphan, the captive] for the face of God'."[12] Two other passages have proven significant in Muslim eschatological speculation and are clearly to be related to the other passages: Q. 28:88 asserts that only "His face" survives in the end (all else has perished, *hālik*) and, similarly, Q. 55:27 holds forth the promise that "the face of your Lord" will abide for eternity (*yabqā*) alone.

The significant aspect of these verses is that they speak, for the most part at least, from the human perspective. That is, it is humans who search for or who are promised the "face of God": that "face" is available and, what is more, people want to know of its presence. Despite the presence of suffering in the world which might suggest an absent God, the Qur'ān is suggesting that it is not so much that God has not hidden his face, but rather that it is his people who must find his face. "Face," it may therefore be said, is intimately connected to an expression of the will of the individual, the need for the human being to seek God. This is also conveyed in other uses of the word "face" in the Qur'ān.

On a number of occasions it is quite clear that "face" means just that. There can be little doubt that verses which speak of wiping the face for prayer make reference to the physical part of the body, as in Q. 4:43 and 5:6, and Q. 48:29 with its reference to the mark of prostration on the face. Other passages were clearly taken that way by the juristic tradition in Islam although, in a number of verses, the human face may also be seen as a reflection of the divine face (see Q. 2:144, 149, 150, 177 which are all regarding the *qibla* to which one should turn one's face). This also occurs in many other passages, for example Q. 6:79 in which Abraham says, "I have turned my face to him who created the heavens and the earth, and I shall never be a polytheist" (also see Q. 7:29, 10:105, 12:9, 12:93, 12:96, 22:72, 30:30, 30:43, 67:22, 67:27). As I have suggested, these passages do not necessarily mean solely the physical face, although they have generally been interpreted that way: there is also a sense in which the human face is a reflection of the divine face in its longing for God.

Additionally, the use of "face" in eschatological passages is noticeable. It is the face which bears the brunt of punishment as in Q. 3:106–7, "On the day when some faces will be white and some faces will be black" (also see Q. 4:47, 8:50, 10:26–7, 14:50, 16:58, 17:97, 18:29, where punishment in hell consists of being "succoured with water like molten copper that shall scald their faces"; additionally see Q. 20:111, 21:39, 23:104, 25:34, 27:90, 33:66, 39:24, 39:60, 43:17, 47:27, 54:48, "the day on which they are dragged on their faces to the fire," and Q. 75:22, 75:24, 80:38, 80:40, 83:24, 88:2, 88:8). The punishment of one's face also occurs in non-eschatological passages as in smiting one's face in Q. 51:29, disfiguring the face in Q. 17:7, and turning one's face in Q. 22:11 and elsewhere. These uses of the punishment of the face may be thought of as the human equivalent of the Biblical notion of God hiding his face: displeasure induces a response via the face.

The other major use of *wajh* is in "submitting one's face" to God. As noted earlier, Bravmann has suggested an Arab background to this expression but it seems to me that there are, perhaps, a number of images associated here of a mythic nature. There may be in this phrase a reflection of an image of presenting one's self before the king: the humble servant before the majestic king, hiding the face by bowing so as not to gaze into the face of the king, in keeping with an overall picture of God as king.[13] "Averting the eyes" might be an image associated with "submitting one's face." The Qur'ān pictures such averting of the face as a way of avoiding the truth, for example in Q. 18:101 where the unbeliever is he "whose eyes were covered against my remembrance" and this may be compared to the way God watches the world with his eyes in Q. 11:37 and 23:27 where the Ark is made under his eyes and Q. 54:14 where it floats under God's eyes (also see Q. 20:39, Moses is raised under God's sight, and Q. 52:48, "you are before our eyes"). Overall, the royal imagery of the submitted face cannot be isolated from the general sense of the face in the

Qur'ān in the sense that the emphasis falls upon the human responsibility for submitting to God.[14]

The suggestion to be made here, then, is that the expression "desiring the face of God" and associated usages of "face" in the Qur'ān embody a part of the special emphasis of the message of the Qur'ān: the human personal responsibility before God. The emphasis is on the human action of desiring or seeking the face of God. Now, another way of illustrating this is to be shown in the use of the notion of "hiding" in the Qur'ān: who is it that hides? While God is spoken of as the *bāṭin* certainly, in the same breath he is the *ẓāhir*, of course (Q. 57:3). God may be equated with the *ghayb*, the "unseen," the "hidden," but God is also the one who gives humans knowledge about that "unseen" as in Q. 12:102. The emphasis in the Qur'ān, expressed through a wide variety of vocabulary, is that God knows what is hidden, he knows the secrets, he knows what is concealed. While some of these hidden things are facets of nature or God's plan (specifically "the Hour," Q. 20:15, knowledge of which is "hidden" by God who says of the hour, *akādu ukhfīhā*, "I would conceal it"[15]), for the most part they are the actions of human beings which they try to hide from God (and from one another as in *katama*, "God knows what you reveal and what you hide," Q. 24:29, for example). As well God once declares, in the context of the general story of human creation, that "We were not absent (*ghā'ib*)" (Q. 7:7). Thus, once again, and flowing from the idea of the "face" of God, it is not God who hides in the Qur'ān but humans who hide (vainly of course) from God, but ultimately, as within the eschatological use of "face," they cannot hide anything and the "face" reveals all. In that sense, one might suggest that submitting one's face provides a sense of being open, just as God's face suggests his being open to humans. But the emphasis falls on personal responsibility and this is conveyed, at least in part, through the symbol of the face.

Additionally, one may wish to argue that the absence of the hiddenness of God as a motif also conveys some significant aspects of the Qur'ānic understanding of divine existence and divine activity. Considering recent discussions of Old Testament theology, this point has tremendous significance. It was Pascal who suggested that a religion which does not affirm that God is hidden "cannot be true." Divine sovereignty is affirmed by God's ability to conceal himself: the claim is made that the "elusive" presence of God is a key to understanding the Bible such that Biblical faith affirms "an active and sustaining hiding with emphasis on divine freedom and sovereignty."[16] The Hebrew God does not always conceal himself by any means, but from Isaiah's lament that "Yahweh concealed his face from the house of Israel" as in Isaiah 8:17, to modern Jewish theological reflection on the Holocaust, the elusiveness has been felt. The Christian perception of the absence of God was solved in a radical way, by non-Jewish notions: an embodiment of God in human form symbolized in sonship, although even there Jesus's lament on the cross, quoting Psalm 22, "My God, my God, why hast thou forsaken me," allows for much discussion over God's absence. For Islam, the tables are turned on the reader. God is declared present for the human who seeks him. The human presence is the one demanded. The discussion does not entertain the absence of God.

There are also certain aspects of the symbolism of God as portrayed in the Qur'ān that need to be noted in this regard. The affirmation of the family in the symbolism of the Biblical divine-human relationship[17] can lead to the lament over the absence of the parent as in Deuteronomy 32:6, "Is he not your father who formed you?". The Qur'ān rejects all such symbolism and thus the significance of the expression of that alienation from one's family is remarkably absent. In the Qur'ān, God is not the father of his people, he is not married to his people, nor do his sons populate the earth. The absence of this realm of divine symbolism in the Qur'ān – for reasons probably quite outside issues of personal responsibility but rather related to the rejection of the Christian embodiment of the "son" of God – has resulted in silence in the discussion of his presence and absence in terms of the family. The Qur'ān's use of symbolism in language is not just a mirror of Biblical imagery, but a coherent theological vision in which the emphasis falls on human personal responsibility towards God and in which the absence of God, however much humans may feel that to be so, is denied as a significant issue.

However, such an explanation is not quite a full representation of the data and a certain tension remains. For one, the very existence of the text of the Qur'ān implies the absence of God: his word must be represented in writing because he is not present; we may compare here, for example, the Jewish understanding of the Torah as "a letter from one's absent father," although there it is significant to notice that the image of parent occurs once again. Most overwhelmingly, the presence of evil in the world suggests a hidden and uncaring God. But the Qur'ān asserts constantly that the signs of God's presence and involvement in the world are all around; indeed the Qur'ān itself is one of those signs. Divine presence is affirmed, but ultimately that would not seem to be the point. Rather, the Qur'ānic stress falls on the responsibility of human beings for their own actions in their search for a life in relationship with God. This is expressed, in a common Near Eastern symbol, through speaking of the "face of God" being available to those who seek it out.

NOTES

1 Consider the summation of De Lacy O'Leary, *Arabic Thought and its Place in History* (London: Luzac, 1922), 184, as quoted by Daud Rahbar, *God of Justice: A Study in the Ethical Doctrine of the Qur'ān* (Leiden: E. J. Brill, 1960), 180: "... Islam made a strong appeal to the motive of fear, an appeal not based on divine

severity so much as on divine justice, and on man's consciousness of his own sinfulness and unworthiness, and on the fleeting passage of the life lived in the present world."

2 See Paul Joyce, *Divine Initiative and Human Response in Ezekiel* (Sheffield: JSOT Press, 1989), 11.

3 Helmer Ringgren, *Islām, 'Aslama and Muslim* (Uppsala: Almqvist, 1949), esp. 22–4. Ringgren gives a good summary of the thoughts of earlier scholars, 2–9; D. Z. H. Baneth, "What Did Muhammad Mean When He Called His Religion 'Islam'? – the Original Meaning of *Aslama* and Its Derivatives," *Israel Oriental Studies* 1 (1971):183–90; Meir M. Bravmann, *The Spiritual Background of Early Islam. Studies in Ancient Arab Concepts* (Leiden: E. J. Brill, 1972), 22–3; idem, "Arabic *Aslama* (*Islām*) and Related Terms," in his *Studies in Semitic Philology* (Leiden: E. J. Brill, 1977), 434–54.

4 Bravmann, "Arabic *Aslama*," 434.

5 Otto Pautz, *Muhammeds Lehre von der Offenbarung. Quellenmässig Untersucht* (Leipzig: J. C. Hinrichs'sche Buchhandlung, 1898), 155; J. M. S. Baljon, "'To Seek the Face of God' in Koran and Hadith," *Acta Orientalia* 21 (1953):254–66; Kenneth Cragg, *The Mind of the Qur'ān* (London: George Allen and Unwin, 1973), 165–6; Muhammad Abdel Haleem, "The Face, Divine and Human, in the Qur'ān," *Islamic Quarterly* 34 (1990):164–79.

6 Notice the concern of Abdel Haleem to situate his discussion within the framework of Ash'arite-Mu'tazilite debate over anthropomorphism.

7 Samuel E. Balentine, *The Hidden God. The Hiding of the Face of God in the Old Testament* (Oxford: Oxford University Press, 1983).

8 See the evidence for this in Geo Widengren, *The Accadian and Hebrew Psalms of Lamentation as Religious Documents* (Uppsala: Almqvist 1936).

9 See Aubrey R. Johnson, "Aspects of the Use of the Term פנים [penim] in the Old Testament," in *Festschrift Otto Eissfeldt zum 60. Geburtstage 1. September 1947*, Johann Fück, ed. (Halle: Max Niemeyer Verlag, 1967), 155–9.

10 Baljon, "'To Seek the Face of God'," 261; Rudi Paret, *Der Koran: Kommentar und Konkordanz* (Stuttgart: W. Kohlhammer, 1977), ad Q. 2:272.

11 Baljon, "'To Seek the Face of God'," 261.

12 See Abdel Haleem, "The Face, Human and Divine,"169–70, who considers this expression as one with "desiring the face of God."

13 I have developed this theme in my "'God is King': Studying the Qur'ān and Talking of God," unpublished paper presented at a colloquium in honour of Mohammed Arkoun, Carthage, 1993, which will form a chapter of my long-delayed *Reading the Qur'ān*, forthcoming from Darwin Press, Princeton.

14 "Turning one's back" may be seen as the opposite of this as in Q. 33:15 ("they had made covenant with God before that, that they would not turn their backs") adding to that sense of averting one's face from God.

15 Thus translated by A. J. Arberry, *The Koran Interpreted* (London: George Allen and Unwin, 1955); others (e.g., Maulawī Sher 'Alī, *The Holy Qur'ān* [Rabwah, Pakistan: Quran Publications, 1971] translate it with the opposite meaning, "I am going to manifest it."

16 Balentine, *Hidden God*, 174, citing Samuel Terrien, *The Elusive Presence. Toward a New Biblical Theology* (San Francisco: Harper and Row, 1978), 251 but also see 320–6. The need for humans to search for God is, of course, not neglected in the Bible.

17 See Eva Maria Lassen, "Family as Metaphor: Family Images at the Time of the Old Testament and Early Judaism," *Scandinavian Journal of the Old Testament* 6 (1992):247–62.

Chapter 6

Fawātiḥ al-Suwar: The Mysterious Letters of the Qur'ān

Irfan Shahîd

ن ق ص حمٓ يسٓ طسٓ طه عسق

كهيعص الر الم طسم المر المص

Of the three principal Qur'ānic dogmas, its Arabness, Eternity and Incomparability, the last is the most important and the most controversial. To those who doubted, even denied the truth of Muḥammad's Prophethood, the Qur'ān's Incomparability was the reply, it was the Prophet's miracle. As to what the incomparability,[1] the *i'jāz*, consisted in, this is a question that has been asked and answered in a variety of ways in the course of the last fourteen centuries or so.[2] *Jumhūr al-mufassirīn,* however, have understood this Incomparability in literary terms, and the latest contribution on this issue has endorsed this conception of *i'jāz* and has added the thought that the key to unlocking the secret of *i'jāz* is the Sūra of the Poets, (Q. 26) especially verse 226.[3]

وَأَنَّهُمْ يَقُولُونَ مَا لَا يَفْعَلُونَ

Those who have understood the Incomparability in literary terms went into great details illustrating various aspects and elements of this literary excellence. One of these elements was for some, *Fawātiḥ al-Suwar,* those mysterious alphabetical letters found at the beginning of 29 sūras of the Qur'ān.[4] These *Fawātiḥ,* however, have proven to be related to *i'jāz* in the literal sense, namely, they have reduced those who have tried to solve their problem to a state of helplessness. In spite of the many gallant attempts to understand these *Fawātiḥ* and in what sense they are part of the concept of Incomparability, no consensus has been reached on either score. Hence this article in a volume titled *Literary Structures of Religious Meaning in the*

Qur'ān, hopefully as a contribution to a fresh understanding of these mysterious letters.

Before presenting the new perspective, it is well to state the two main conceptions of these *Fawātiḥ.* The first views them not as part of the Qur'ānic Revelation but as part of the editorial work that went into the production of the authoritative 'Uthmānic text. The second considers the *Fawātiḥ* part of the Revelation and this is the view of most Muslim and non-Muslim scholars alike, going back to the early days of Islam.[5] The former view, if true, will eliminate the *Fawātiḥ* as is relevant to the problem of Incomparability and the literary aspect of the Qur'ān while the latter will retain them as relevant. The present article does not take a stance as to which position is valid. It only presents a new perspective on the spectrum of the many and various proposed solutions to this crux on the assumption that the latter view is correct.

It will be argued that these mysterious letters were sounds of the Revelation that the Prophet did not hear distinctly because he was not ready or prepared to receive the *waḥy,* and consequently they appear in this unintelligible form. His honesty and care to reflect exactly what he had heard made him leave them as he had heard them.[6] In support of this position, the following arguments may be presented and they fall into two main categories.

I

Arguments that derive from appeal to the Qur'ān and the Tradition (Ḥadīth) on matters relevant to the problem of the *Fawātiḥ.*

1. The first clue as what these mysterious letters are or may be is the fact that these letters appear neither in the middle nor at the end of the sūras but at the beginning.[7] This chimes well with the view that they were sounds indistinctly heard and consequently incomprehensibly grasped. There must have been situations when the *āya*s (verses) would suddenly start to be revealed while the Prophet was not ready to receive them and so he would miss the initial portion or would not grasp it in its entirety. In such situations the initial portion is the one likely to be missed.
2. The Qur'ān has a number of verses that are addressed to the Prophet directly in the second person, in which matters related to receiving Revelation and preserving it correctly are indicated. Especially relevant and significant are the following:
   a. *Sūrat Ṭāhā* (Q. 20), verse 114: "*lā ta'jal bi 'l-Qur'āni min qabli an yuqḍā ilayka waḥyuhu*", "Do not make haste in the recitation of the Qur'ān."
   b. *Sūrat al-Qiyāma* (Q. 75), verse 16: "*lā tuḥarrik bihī lisānaka li-ta'jala bihi*", "Do not move your tongue with it so that you may make haste in reciting it."[8]

c. *Sūrat al-A'lā* (Q. 87), verse 6: "*sa-nuqri'uka fa-lā tansā*", "we shall teach you its recitation so that you will not forget."

3. Tradition (Ḥadīth) also describes the psychological state of the Prophet when Revelation would descend on him. Often it speaks of perspiration, fear, trembling and the sound of bells in his ears.[9] Conceivably such states sometimes were not conducive towards a clear reception of the Revelation, especially, at the inception of the *waḥy*; hence the initial portion of a sūra that has been revealed under such circumstances could have been received incompletely and thus retained in an imperfect state of preservation, consisting of some sounds represented by these alphabetical letters.
4. One of the features of Qur'ānic Revelation, to which reference is reiterated in the Holy Book is that the Qur'ānic message is crystal clear with no ambiguity which would be difficult to understand by the Arabs in Mecca and Medina. It is utterly inconsistent with this, that the Qur'ānic Revelation would contain deliberately something that is incomprehensible as these *Fawātiḥ* which have exercised the ingenuity of scholars for some fourteen centuries. The position taken in this article on the *Fawātiḥ*, thus, relieves them of being evidence to the contrary and relieves the Qur'ān of the charge of incomprehensibility by explaining it away as only apparent and accidental. It was only incident to such rare occasions as described above when conditions of reception were not ideal and so prevented the Prophet from hearing distinctly and transmitting clearly the divine message.

II

The second category of arguments in support of this position on the *Fawātiḥ* consists in an appeal to one particular sūra of the Qur'ān, which possibly holds the key to the mystery of the *Fawātiḥ* in much the same way that the Sūra of the Poets holds the key for unlocking the secret of *i'jāz*, incomparability. This approach is consonant with the exegetical principle that the Qur'ān explains itself through itself.[10]

The sūra in question is *al-Muzzammil*,[11] the relevant verses are the first seven and especially the sixth, and within it the phrase *wa aqwamu qīlā*.

يَٰٓأَيُّهَا ٱلْمُزَّمِّلُ ﴿١﴾ قُمِ ٱلَّيْلَ إِلَّا قَلِيلًا ﴿٢﴾ نِّصْفَهُۥٓ أَوِ ٱنقُصْ مِنْهُ قَلِيلًا
﴿٣﴾ أَوْ زِدْ عَلَيْهِ وَرَتِّلِ ٱلْقُرْءَانَ تَرْتِيلًا ﴿٤﴾ إِنَّا سَنُلْقِى عَلَيْكَ قَوْلًا
ثَقِيلًا ﴿٥﴾ إِنَّ نَاشِئَةَ ٱلَّيْلِ هِىَ أَشَدُّ وَطْـًٔا وَأَقْوَمُ قِيلًا ﴿٦﴾ إِنَّ لَكَ فِى
ٱلنَّهَارِ سَبْحًا طَوِيلًا ﴿٧﴾

It is generally recognized that this sūra is one of the earliest of all sūras, possibly even the third or so; that it was revealed after the *fatra*, hiatus, when the *waḥy* ceased to descend on the Prophet; that he had been in Ḥirā' when the *waḥy* started to return to him. The Tradition goes on to state that he went home to his wife, Khadīja, who covered him with a mantle, hence the title of the sūra, *al-Muzzammil*, the one covered with a mantle. Thus the Tradition associates this sūra clearly not with *tahajjud* (vigil, nocturnal prayer) but with *waḥy* (revelation).

The external evidence of the Tradition is supported by the internal evidence of the sūra:

A

1. The first verse addresses the Prophet as the *Muzzammil*, the one enwrapped. That state of being mantled, given prominence and mentioned in the opening verse, is unlikely to have been referred to in the context of *tahajjud* (nocturnal prayer) which is performed daily but it is more appropriate in the context of something else, more important, such as the Tradition says it was, following the experience in the cave of Ḥirā'. Being *muzzammil* seems irrelevant to the routine performance of prayers.
2. Then there is verse (4): *wa rattili 'l- Qur'ān tartīlā*, usually interpreted as a reference to the recitation of the Qur'ān during the night. Interpreted <u>without</u> reference to the background of the sūra, preserved in the Tradition and without reference to the context of the seven verses within which it lies, the verse can certainly refer to nocturnal prayers and *tahajjud*. But if interpreted in the context to which it belongs, it could refer to the *nuzūl* of the *waḥy* and how the Prophet should receive it and articulate it slowly and surely for its better retention and transmission. Furthermore the verse itself sits uneasily in the sūra. The occurrence of the term "Qur'ān," in it is noteworthy; it is the first occurrence of the term for the Holy Book of Islam and in this context it clearly does <u>not</u> refer to the Qur'ān in its entirety but only to that portion that had been revealed, a few short sūras, not more than three. This could suggest that this verse does not belong to this sūra, and that its allocation to it was inspired by the allocation of the last verse (20) to the same sūra. The sūra is composite, not entirely Meccan but partly Medinan and so is, possibly, this verse (4).
3. The last verse (verse 20), is the one that most probably swayed the *mufassirūn* in favor of interpreting the verses as related to *tahajjud*. But this verse has no value whatsoever for the exegesis of the first seven verses. It is universally agreed that the length of this verse and its reference to such matters as the *zakāt*, allocates it to the Medinan sūras and so it is utterly irrelevant to the exegesis of this early Meccan one.

B

In addition to these arguments deriving from the text of the sūra pertaining to the three verses, other arguments may be advanced:

1. *Ṣalāt* as one of Islam's five *arkān*, pillars, was instituted later than this early Meccan period to which belongs this early sūra associated with *nuzūl al-waḥy*, traditionally dated A. D. 610. This is even more true of this type of *ṣalāt* namely, *tahajjud.*
2. Related to this is the fact that at this stage only a few sūras and very short ones at that, had been revealed.[12] It is quite unlikely that the Prophet at this critical stage in his Prophetic career, when he had to wrestle with many more important problems related to himself and his position vis-à-vis the Quraysh, would have been given divine instruction related to *tahajjud* and to the *tartīl* of the Qur'ān, especially as only a few *āyāt* had by then been revealed. *Tahajjud* and *tartīl* are relatively matters of details at this stage, and are more relevant to a later stage in Muḥammad's Prophetic career.
3. The cluster of sūras that belong to this period are only a few, three, and they are closely related to *nuzūl*, and *al-Muzzammil* 's first verse implies it. Interpreting the first seven verses in devotional rather than Revelational terms allocates them to the wrong context and takes them out of the right one vouched for by *asbāb al-nuzūl.*
4. The nocturnal prayers and indeed all the later five canonical prayers can be performed in a very short period. An injunction to stay awake all night or half of it cannot be related to performing a prayer which can be done in a very short time.[13] The injunction to spending the night awake must have been for the sake of something more important, which makes the long vigils of the night intelligible, namely, awaiting the *nuzūl* of the *waḥy* lest the Prophet should miss it, since there was no way of determining exactly when at night it would descend.

Now that *tahajjud* has been ruled out as the theme of these seven verses, it is time to state the case for the theme as *nuzūl al-waḥy*; and a few preliminary observations are necessary before coming to grips with the seven verses and the crucial one, the sixth:

1. Doubts on the truth or accuracy of the Tradition with its account of the background of the sūra, are dispelled by the first verse of the sūra with its address to the Prophet as *al-Muzzammil*, "the one wrapped in a mantle" already discussed in an earlier context.[14]
2. It will also be noted that in these seven (verses) which have been thought to be an exhortation for *tahajjud*, only the Prophet is addressed unlike verse (20), where the Prophet and the community of believers are addressed in the plural and where the context is clearly

that of *ṣalāt*. In these seven verses only, the Prophet is addressed and this is consonant with the fact that he is the only Muslim who is the recipient of the Revelation in his capacity as the Prophet and that what was involved in the seven verses that address him exclusively was *nuzūl* not *tahajjud*.

III

Perhaps the foregoing paragraphs with their arguments have clearly indicated that the first seven verses of *Sūrat al-Muzzammil* refer to the coming down, the descent of Revelation, *nuzūl al-waḥy*. This has set the stage for the intensive examination of the crucial verse within this cluster of verses, namely, verse 6, the one most relevant to the theme of this article, namely, the *Fawātiḥ*, the mysterious letters of the Qur'ān. The verse has always been interpreted as a reference to *tahajjud*:

إِنَّ نَاشِئَةَ ٱلَّيْلِ هِيَ أَشَدُّ وَطْـًٔا وَأَقْوَمُ قِيلًا

Nāshi'at al-layl, interpreted as the nocturnal prayer, is further described in two phrases that follow, as "more powerful in impact," *ashaddu waṭ'an*, and "more straight or correct in discourse or enunciation," *wa aqwamu qīlā*. It will be argued that what is involved in this verse, is not *tahajjud*, but the coming down, the descent of *waḥy* at night and that this is the denotation of *nāshi'at al-layl*. The following arguments may be advanced in support of this position:

A

1. As a preliminary observation, it may be said that the verses before and after it all relate to *waḥy* at night; *ṣalāt* would have been an egregiously dissonant and incomprehensible note, if the verse is interpreted as expressing *tahajjud*. The *contextualization* of the verse is the first pointer in the direction of its correct exegesis.
2. Another preliminary observation relates to the efforts of early exegetes to improve the text of the verse. Two of them were evidently uneasy about the verse: one, none other than Ibn 'Abbās, apparently pondered this curious interpretation of the verse, and in support of it as *tahajjud*, which he swallowed, went the length of thinking that *nāshi'at* was not an Arabic but an Ethiopic word; another, Anas ibn-Mālik, also must have felt some uneasiness and suggested instead of *aqwamu*, such terms as *aṣwabu* and *ahya'u*![15]
3. On the most basic lexical and semantic level, *nāshi'at* as prayer or reference to prayer has to be rejected. The unnatural meaning given to

this common and clear Arabic term, in the morphological pattern of the *nomen agentis*, militates against this unnatural interpretation and no amount of ingenuity in manipulating the word can make it yield the meaning related to *ṣalāt*. *Ṣalāt*, one of the five *arkān*, is used many times in the Qur'ān with the proper verb *aqāma* ; the verb *nasha'a*, if applied to it, will appear as a bizarre *hapax legomenon* standing in splendid isolation. Of the twenty-eight instances[16] in which the verb *nasha'a* or its derivatives are used, only one is used of human beings while the rest are always used with God as subject. *Nāshi'at*, when interpreted as related to nuzūl, is thus in good company as a Qur'ānic term that is associated with God and not with Muḥammad or any Muslim agent.

4. The two descriptive phrases that follow *nāshi'at* are inapplicable to it if interpreted as *ṣalāt/tahajjud*. *Waṭ'* ("treading", "impact") is meaningless if applied to *ṣalāt* and one can only "concoct" a meaning or explanation to make it applicable, while it is singularly applicable to *nāshi'at* when interpreted as *waḥy*. The use of the elative (*ashaddu* and *aqwamu*) in both phrases implies that prayers during daylight time are less *shadīda* and *qawīma* than those performed at night. But it is impossible to believe that three of the five canonical prayers (instituted later) can be so described and contrasted with *tahajjud*.

B

The negative arguments or observations for the rejection of *nāshi'at* as related to *tahajjud* may now be followed by positive arguments for relating it to *nuzūl al-waḥy*.

1. The preceding verse, 5, *innā sa-nulqī 'alayka qawlan thaqīlā*, "verily we shall throw upon you a heavy discourse," unmistakably points to the interpretation of *nāshi'at* as *waḥy* and not at all as *ṣalāt/tahajjud*, and the verse speaks for itself. What is more, the two words, *qawlan thaqīlan*, are directly related to the two descriptive phrases of verse 6. *Thaqīlan*, heavy, is clearly related to the first phrase with its *waṭ' shadīd*, "heavy impact," while *qawlan*, is even closer, being almost identical with *qīlā*. So this verse, 5, both introduces verse 6 and also controls its interpretation as *waḥy* not *ṣalāt*. The slight variation from *qawl* to *qīl* may be non-significant but it may also reflect a nuanced shift from simple discourse and recitation of *waḥy* to its careful and clear enunciation, to be grasped, retained and repeated by the Prophet.
2. The term is a *nomen agentis* and if it is construed as singular it can refer to the sūra, *suwar*, *āya/āyāt* that are revealed by night. Its denotation can be the singular, or the plural of sūra and *āya*. In relating *nāshi'at* to Revelation, the verb *nasha'a* takes on its natural meaning within the context of Qur'ānic lexicology. Of the twenty-eight instances of its

occurrence in the Qur'ān, 26 are definitely related to God, one to a human being, and the one in this verse to the Prophet. Now this one in the verse is dissociated from its referent as the Prophet performing *tahajjud* and is returned to God as the force behind the Revelation, its inspirer.

3. Morphologically, *nāshi'at* can also be construed as a substantive in the plural, and so it is used in Arabic for the young generation, *al-nāshi'at.* What nuance it had in 7th century Arabic when the Qur'ān was revealed is not clear. As a plural substantive, *nāshi'at* could possibly have as its referent the angels, the *malā'ika* whose function in this context is related to the verb *nasha'a,* used mostly of God in the Qur'ān and possibly also of those associated with him in his work, the angels. What commends this interpretation of *nāshi'at* as applying to the angels is the fact that these are instruments of Revelation in the Qur'ān and its transmitters to the Prophet, before Gabriel became the chief transmitter, and the sūra, *al-Muzzammil,* does belong to this early, very early period. The function of angels as transmitters of Revelation is clearly stated in *Sūrat Maryam* and *Sūrat al-Qadr,* and the latter sūra is more relevant than the former since their function as transmitters is performed by night, thus recalling *nāshi'at al-layl* in this verse, (6), of *al-Muzzammil.* Even more relevant are verses 1–6 in *Sūrat al-Mursalāt* (Q. 77), applied to the angels. Especially important and relevant is verse (5) *al-mulqiyāt dhikran,* which brings to mind verse (5) in *Sūrat al-Muzzammil* with its *innā sanulqī 'alayka qawlan thaqīlan.*[17]

C

An alternative way of interpreting *nāshi'at* as *waḥy* can be related to *al-qirā'āt,* the variant readings of the Qur'ān, especially important in the study of a Holy Book that was compiled and put together by Caliph 'Uthmān at a time when writing materials in Mecca were rather primitive consisting, *inter alia,* of hides and camel bones, and, what is more important, when only the consonantal skeletons of words were written with no vowels or diacritical points. Although the crucial word, *nāshi'at* as re-interpreted and applied to *waḥy* has lost much of the difficulties that attached to it when applied to prayer, and so can be considered perfectly acceptable, yet it is possible that *nāshi'at* may have been originally another word, even more appropriate one for *waḥy,* and the word *nāzilat* comes to mind as possibly the original correct reading. In support of this, the following may be advanced:

Nāzilat has the same morphological pattern as *nāshi'at;* so the process of transcriptional transformation into *nāshi'at* is not difficult. It is easy to see how the process of transformation worked: the (z) of *nazilat* coalesced with its (l), which became shorter and so appeared as the kursī, the chair of a new letter, the hamza of *nāshi'at*. And it is of course the right and the most common word for Revelation, the Qur'ān itself being called the *tanzīl*.

So then the referent would be the *āyāt* or *suwar* that came down, *nazalat* at night and this makes possible the reading *nāzilat al-layl*.

D

The conclusion that *nāshi'at* refers not to *Ṣalāt/tahajjud* but to *waḥy*, makes necessary a return to the Qur'ānic terms that precede and follow *nāshi'at al-layl*. A close examination of these terms will corroborate the conclusion on *nāshi'at al-layl* as Revelation and will show how incongruous is an interpretation of *nāshi'at* as *Ṣalāt/tahajjud*.

1. The two descriptive phrases, that follow *nāshi'at al-layl*, already shown to be inapplicable to *Ṣalāt/tahajjud* can now be seen to be singularly applicable to *nāshi'at* as Revelation:
   a. *Ashaddu waṭ'an*: "more powerful or stronger in impact or incidence" goes perfectly well with the descent of the *waḥy* from above, and recalls what the Tradition says on the power of the *waḥy* and its effect on the Prophet. Noteworthy is the word *waṭ'*, expressing something coming from above and weighing heavily on the Prophet.
   b. *wa aqwamu qīlā*: "more correct in enunciation" is even equally applicable to *waḥy* that descends from above and expresses the notion that *waḥy* revealed at night is clearer and so can be heard more distinctly than *waḥy* coming during daylight time, a matter of great importance to the Prophet who, as recipient, can thus comprehend it better and transmit it accurately.
2. The fourth verse, *wa rattili 'l-Qur'āna tartīlā*, which has suggested to the *mufassirūn* that what is involved in the crucial verse is *ṣalāt* and the recitation of the Qur'ān may now be understood in the new light of the Revelation and its descent. The injunction goes well with the phrases *aqwamu qīlā* and *ashaddu waṭ'an* which describe the descent of Revelation at night. The Prophet is asked to grasp accurately the *waḥy*, that came down under ideal circumstances at night and so to remember it and recite it slowly and surely to ensure its safe transmission.[18]

IV

Now that *Sūrat al-Muzzammil* with its first seven verses, especially the sixth, has been shown to be related not to *ṣalāt* but to *waḥy* and its *nuzūl*, Revelation, its relevance to unlocking the secret of the *Fawātiḥ*, the mysterious alphabetical letters may now be discussed.

A

The gist of the seven verses is that the night is the best time for the reception of *tanzīl* since what is revealed during the night is clearer to hear and grasp and so to retain and transmit. In addition to the general statement, there is the crucial verse, (6), which is even more specific when it describes *nuzūl* as more powerful in impact and so easier to grasp and comprehend; even more significant is the second phrase *wa aqwamu qīlā*, "more straight and distinct in its enunciation." The relevance of all this to the *Fawātiḥ*, which, it has been proposed in this article, were sounds indistinctly heard and so left in that incomprehensible state is clear. But the relevance is clearer in the *implication* of the two phrases, namely, that there were occasions and times when the *nuzūl* was not or would not be *qawīm* in *qīl* and not *shadīd* in *waṭ'* or at least not as *shadīd* and *qawīm* as *nuzūl* at night. It provides a good setting for understanding why some initial portions of the Revelation were not grasped distinctly by the Prophet and so were left in this incomprehensible manner – as broken letters of the alphabet – *al-Muqaṭṭa'āt*.

What these occasions or circumstances were can only be guessed and inferred from the first six verses of *Sūrat al-Muzzammil*. In these six, night is contrasted with daylight time, Arabic *nahār*, while verse (7) clearly expresses it; it mentions *nahār* explicitly as the time of the day not ideal for the *nuzūl* because of its distractions and involvements, which divert the attention of the Prophet from concentrating on hearing and comprehending what he hears.[19]

B

Emphasis on the night as the ideal time for *nuzūl al-waḥy* naturally yields the conclusion that it is better than daylight time. Consequently, it may be maintained that the twenty-nine sūras or some of them that have these unintelligible letters were revealed during daylight time. But was daylight time the only explanation for the incomprehensibility of the *Fawātiḥ*? Perhaps not. One can venture the thought that there were also other causes. There were occasions when the Prophet was in a psychological state, perturbed and agitated, by events or encounters that were not favorable to a good reception of *waḥy*. This may be briefly illustrated as follows:

1. It has been noted that these *Fawātiḥ* occur in sūras where some reference to the Holy Book of Islam is involved. This is the most significant clue to follow for understanding the mystery of these letters. The Qur'ān, as a divinely inspired Holy Book, a *tanzīl* from heaven, was presented to Mecca but was received with total rejection and

sometimes with ridicule, entailing the rejection of Muḥammad's Prophethood. Thus, the Qur'ān was the great issue that separated Muḥammad from the incredulous Meccan opposition. Its rejection must have deeply perturbed the Prophet. So, perhaps the *Fawātiḥ* or most of them were revealed after some bitter encounters with Meccans involving the Qur'ān, when the Prophet was left despondent and agitated and hence not in a state that enabled him to grasp distinctly the *waḥy* when the *nuzūl* started.

2. Another occasion which might have induced in the Prophet an agitated state of mind was the Persian invasion of the Near East and the Fall in A. D. 614 of Jerusalem, the *qibla* of his prayers while he was in Mecca. That invasion resulted in the occupation of Bilād al-Shām for some fifteen years. Its effects on Arabia are little known but they have been pointed out, so far as the Prophet was concerned, in a recent publication where it has been argued[20] that the *hijra* to Abyssinia (the emigration) took place because of it in A. D. 614, or at least was related to it in some way. The mood of the Prophet and the early Muslims who were on the side of Christian Byzantium and against Zoroastrian Persia is recorded in *Sūrat al-Rūm* (Q. 30), which appropriately for the theme of this article and the present argument opens with one of those combination of mysterious letters namely, *Alif, Lām, Mīm.*
3. The association of *Sūrat al-Rūm* and its mysterious letters with a major historic event and its consequences on the Prophet's state of mind in Mecca, can easily lead to further probing of the relation of this and other events to other sūras that are prefaced by the *Fawātiḥ*. In this article only the Persian invasion and occupation of Bilād al-Shām will be briefly discussed amplifying what has been said in the previous paragraph, since it has not received sufficient attention, although it is important for both Muḥammadan and Qur'ānic studies.
   a. The Persian invasion of Bilād al-Shām ushered in a period of convulsions and dislocations in the Near East and a series of repercussions in the Arabian Peninsula and Mecca, a caravan city with important trade relations with Bilād al-Shām and Egypt, all occupied by the Persians. As far as Muḥammad was concerned, now a Prophet and no longer a caravan leader, which he had been before his Call, what mattered was the fall of Jerusalem, the *qibla* of his prayers, while the defeat of Byzantium represented the disheartening defeat of the Monotheism he was preaching by the Zoroastrianism of the Persians, anathema to him.[21] And it has been argued that just as the invasion occasioned panic in various parts of Bilād al-Shām and a flight to Egypt, it may have done the same in the neighboring parts of Arabia especially in Mecca, among the members of the new faith that Muḥammad was preaching and that

ranged the early Muslims on the side of Monotheistic Byzantium. One consequence, it has been argued, was the *hijra* to Abyssinia.

b. *Sūrat al-Rūm* is a very important Meccan sūra for such major themes as Christian-Muslim relations and Arab-Byzantine relations *inter alia*. Its importance in this context of the *Fawātiḥ* is that it is the one Meccan sūra that can be dated accurately to A. D. 614, since it can be interlocked with a major historical event, and so, its date is firmly established. This will correct Nöldeke's dating, which he assigned to the late, third Meccan period.[22] Not only must this sūra be predated but it also could represent the end of the first or early period of the Meccan sūras and the beginning of the second or middle one and this is the added attraction of this sūra datable to A. D. 614.[23]

c. The relevance of *Sūrat al-Rūm* and its date to a better understanding of the problem of the *Fawātiḥ* should by now be clear. It has been generally thought that these sūras prefaced by the *Fawātiḥ* belong to the late Meccan and early Medinan periods.[24] The date of *Sūrat al-Rūm* withdraws the dating of these sūras to the middle Meccan period and even as early as its inception in A. D. 614, the year that witnessed a cataclysm in Bilād al-Shām and a major event in the life of the nascent Muslim community in Mecca – the *hijra* to Abyssinia.[25] So this must be the earliest or one of the earliest of the twenty-nine sūras with *Fawātiḥ*.

d. Finally, it has been noted that stylistically the sūras of the early Meccan period are prefaced by a series of oaths and that these are seldom used in the second, middle period.[26] Perhaps the *Fawātiḥ*, which start to appear in the Qur'ānic Revelations in the middle Meccan period,[27] may now be considered a stylistic feature of the Qur'ān, following the virtual disappearance of the oaths of the early Meccan period.

CONCLUSION

The investigation of the *Fawātiḥ* has led to a detailed analysis of the first seven verses of *Sūrat al-Muzzammil*. In the introductory part of this article the present writer has indicated that he is putting a new perspective on the *vexata quaestio* of the *Fawātiḥ*, only if they are part of the Revelation, and so the truth about them is still for him an open question to which one could append *Allāh a'lam*. Not so, the detailed analysis of *Sūrat al-Muzzammil* with the conclusion that it has nothing to do with prayer but that it is about Revelation, and so is the radical interpretation of verse 6 in that sūra. If the *Fawātiḥ* finally turn out to be editorial and not Revelational, the new exegesis of the sūra will not be affected by this eventuality and so the discussion of the *Fawātiḥ* will still have been fruitful because it has led to the reexamination of the exegesis of the sūra and presenting it under an entirely new light. This reexamination can be presented and maintained independently of the *Fawātiḥ*.

NOTES

1 *'Arabiyya, Qidam,* and *I'jāz.*

2 That the problem has not been laid to rest is evidenced by books and articles on *i'jāz* that have appeared in fairly recent times, especially reflected in two massive volumes by 'Abd al-Karīm al-Khaṭīb, *I'jāz al-Qur'ān* (Cairo: Dār al-Fikr al-'Arabī, 1964); the problem has been treated more recently by the present writer for which, see "Medieval Islam: the Literary-Cultural Dimension," in *Religion and Culture in Medieval Islam,* ed. Richard G. Hovanissian and Georges Sabagh, Cambridge University Press, (forthcoming).

3 See the present writer in "Another Contribution to Koranic Exegesis: the Sūra of the Poets," *Journal of Arabic Literature* 14 (1983):1–21. The article was written in consonance with the principle of Qur'ānic *tafsīr,* that says "the Qur'ān explains itself through itself," *al-Qur'ān yufassir ba'ḍuhu ba'ḍan* for which, see Ṣubḥī al-Ṣāliḥ, *Mabāḥith fī 'Ulūm al-Qur'ān* (Beirut: Dār al-'Ilm li 'l-Malāyīn, 1982), 299–312. A reprise of the examination of the problems presented by the Sūra of the Poets in light of recent publications may be read in an article by the present writer, titled "The Sūra of the Poets Re-visited: Some Final Observations" (forthcoming).

4 The *Fawātiḥ* were welcomed by those devotees of such occult sciences as *'Ilm al-Ḥurūf* and *Jafr* and also by the mystics of Islam. For all these, the *Fawātiḥ* are part of the Islamic Revelation, and, so, have been inextricably woven into the texture of these "sciences" although the problem of the *Fawātiḥ* is still *sub judice.*

5 For a clear and succinct statement of the problem see W. M. Watt, *Bell's Introduction to the Qur'ān* (Edinburgh: Edinburgh University Press, 1970), 61–65. For a more recent statement of the problem and a very competent presentation, see A. Welch, in the *EI*[2], s.v. "Ḳur'ān," 5:412–14, and its bibliography, 428, where the views of Qur'ānic scholars who have dealt with the problem are critically discussed: Muslim scholars such as 'Ikrima, Ibn 'Abbās, al-Suyūṭī, H. A. 'Ali, N. al-Ṭāhir; and Western scholars such as Nöldeke, Loth, Schwally, Hirschfeld, Bauer, Goossens, Seale, Jones and Bellamy. Welch brings the discussion to a close with some perceptive remarks of his own on the *Fawātiḥ* to the effect that they most probably belong to the Qur'ānic Revelation. One of the strongest arguments in favor of this position is the fact that the Prophet himself at the battle of *Ḥunayn* is said to have uttered one of these *Fawātiḥ* (*Ḥā Mīm*) to encourage his followers. To this may be added, that the Caliph 'Alī at the battle of Ṣiffīn did the same, and 'Alī is not likely to have been fooled *à propos* of these *Fawātiḥ*.

The most recent discussion since Welch's treatment in 1978 is by Keith Massey; see his "A New Investigation into the Mystery Letters of the Qur'ān," *Arabica* 43 (1996):497–501, where the author goes back to the Abbreviated Letters theory.

6 Muḥammad was described by his people even before his Call as al-Amīn, the honest one. The term recurs in the Qur'ān, applied mostly to the Prophets, including the Arabian ones, celebrating their honesty and integrity. It occurs five times in the Sūra of the Poets (26) applied to Prophets and once to Gabriel. In the context of transmitting accurately what is revealed to him,

relevant is the verse in *Sūrat al-Isrā'* (Q. 17) verse 45 which says that severe punishment would await the Prophet if he were to transmit erroneously or deviate what God reveals to him.

7 Unlike certain similar terms in the Bible, such as Selah, which appears 71 times, e.g. Psalm 44, verse 9, and which is interpreted as a liturgical direction.

8 Verses 18 and 19 in *Sūrat al-Qiyāma* (Q. 75) are intriguing: *fa idhā qara'nāhu fa' ttabi' Qur'ānah; inna 'alaynā bayānahu.*" "When we recite (the Revelation) then follow this recitation; on us falls its explanation." Was this an injunction that the Prophet should transmit whatever he hears, irrespective of whether he understands it or not, since God will later explain it? Could this apply to the *Fawātiḥ*?

9 For these, see Ṣ. al-Ṣāliḥ, *Mabāḥith fī 'Ulūm al-Qur'ān,* 39–40.

10 On this, see *supra,* n. 3.

11 Sūra 73, "The Mantled, Enwrapped."

12 In Nöldeke's chronological arrangement of the Qur'ān, *al-Muzzammil* is the 23rd of the early Meccan sūras. The Muslim tradition, however, assigns it to a much earlier date; it is considered the first sūra after the *fatra,* the hiatus in the *nuzūl* of *waḥy,* and was followed by *al-Muddaththir* (Q. 74). Before that *fatra* only two sūras, according to tradition had been revealed, *al-'Alaq* (Q. 96) and *al-Qalam* (Q. 68); see Yusuf 'Ali, *The Holy Qur'ān* (Kuwait: Dhāt al-Salāsil, 1984), 1632 and also that excellent modern *tafsīr* by M. 'I. Darwaza, *al-Tafsīr al-Ḥadīth* (Cairo: 'Īsā al-Bābī al-Ḥalabī, 1962), I:5.

13 Even if *tahajjud* is interpreted to mean not the actual nocturnal prayer but keeping the vigils of the night in reading the Qur'ān and in contemplation.

14 *Supra.* Those hypercritical of the authenticity of the early Islamic sources are likely to say that the tradition on the *waḥy* at the Cave of Ḥirā' was a later *tafsīr* intended to explain the first verse in the sūra. However, there is no cogent reason for rejecting the tradition. Moreover, the sūra revealed immediately after *al-Muzzammil,* namely, *al-Muddaththir,* (Q. 74) a term synonymous with *al-Muzzammil,* cannot but point to an authentic tradition about the background of the two sūras.

15 For Ibn 'Abbās, see the commentary of Ibn Kathīr, *Tafsīr al-Qur'ān al-'Aẓīm* (Beirut: Dār al-Ma'rifa, 1987), 4:464. The Codex of Anas ibn Mālik has *aṣwatu* and *aṣwabu* but not *ahya'u;* see A. Jeffery, *Materials for the History of the Text of the Qur'an* (Leiden: Brill, 1937), 217. The reading *ahya'u,* is an *ijtihād* from Anas according to George Schoeler's article in which he quotes Ṭabarī; see his "Schreiben und Veröffentlichen. Zu Verwendung und Funktion der Schrift in den ersten islamischen Jahrhunderten," *Der Islam* 69 (1992):25 and n. 127.

A. Jeffery does not consider *nāshi'at* as an Ethiopic word and so it does not appear in his *The Foreign Vocabulary of the Qur'an* (Baroda: The Oriental Institute, 1938).

16 See M. 'Abd al-Bāqī, *al-Mu'jam al-Mufahras li-Alfāẓ al-Qur'ān al-Karīm* (Beirut: Dār al-Fikr, 1992), 872. The one exception occurs in *Sūrat al-Zukhruf* (Q. 43) verse 18.

17 Many referents for the opening verse of *Sūrat al-Mursalāt* (Q. 77) have been suggested: winds, clouds, and angels; verse 5 *al-mulqiyāt dhikran* can only refer to angels not to clouds or winds, thus tipping the scales in favor of angels; it is so understood by Muslim exegetes; see Darwaza, *al-Tafsīr al-Ḥadīth,* 1:19.

18 It has been suggested that this verse may possibly not belong to this sūra, *supra,* 128. However, verse 5 already analyzed, does, and is relevant to the argument of this section on the verses that precede and follow the crucial one (6) including the two phrases that describe *nāshi'at al-layl.*

19 The traditional commentary on this verse (7) relates it to prayer and how during daylight time, involvement and preoccupations do not allow the Muslim or, in this case, Muḥammad himself, to perform it free from distractions.

20 See the present writer in "The *Hijra* (Emigration) of the Early Muslims to Abyssinia: The Byzantine Dimension," *To Hellenikon, Festschrift Speros Vryonis, Jr.*, ed. Milton v. Anastos (New Rochelle, New York: Aristide D. Caratzas, 1993), 2:203–13.

21 Ibid., 207–9.

22 The chronological arrangement of the sūras undertaken by Nöldeke is conveniently reproduced in Watt, *Bell's Introduction,* 110–11; for sūra (30) *al-Rūm,* see ibid., 110.

23 The chronological arrangement of Nöldeke left the Meccan sūras divided into early, middle, and late periods, without any specific dates that reflected the inception or duration of these three periods. Owing to the certain date that *Sūrat al-Rūm* can be assigned to, this sūra enables the sequence of three periods to be provided with a chronological framework. A. D. 614, the date of the Fall of Bilād al-Shām and Jerusalem and also the Emigration to Abyssinia, could thus terminate the first early Meccan period and open the second, middle one. A major event in the life of the Prophet and the Muslim community later than the *hijra* to Abyssinia and earlier than the *hijra* to Medina may also be sought for the termination of the second and the inception of the third, late Meccan period; possibly the death in one and the same year, A. D. 619, of both his wife, Khadīja, and his uncle, Abū Ṭālib, the two pillars of strength that supported Muḥammad.

24 Watt, *Bell's Introduction,* 64. Loth was the first to suggest these periods; Welch, "Ḳur'ān," 412.

25 The 29 sūras, dated also to the late Meccan and early Madinan periods, all, with only two exceptions, share the fact that the Qur'ān is referred to after the *Fawātiḥ* at the beginning of the sūras. It would be fruitful to examine the *nuzūl* of each of these sūras to establish whether the *Fawātiḥ* appeared after an encounter with the opposition concerning the Qur'ān, an encounter that would leave the Prophet perturbed, and consequently not in an ideal situation to receive the *waḥy* accurately. *Sūrat al-Baqara* could illustrate this. The Prophet had expected the Jews of Medina to believe in his Prophethood and the Qur'ān; their rejection of both could have left him deeply hurt and perturbed; hence the three mysterious letters at the beginning of the sūra, *Alif. Lām. Mīm,* followed by reference to the Book. The tradition is not silent on such encounters as when the *mushrikūn* in Mecca after hearing the Qur'ān ", . . . , cursed it, the One who revealed it and the one who transmitted it;" see *Ṣaḥīḥ al-Bukhārī* (Cairo: 'Abd al-Salām Ibn Muḥammad Ibn Shaqrūn, 1314 H), 9:153, line 13.

If encounters with the opposition concerning the Qur'ān can be successfully established, this will solve the problem of why so many different sūras, 29, share the same feature – the *Fawātiḥ*. It will be a tribute to Loth who first noted the relation between the appearance of the *Fawātiḥ* and the reference to the Qur'ān.

26 Watt, *Bell's Introduction,* 110.

27 After *Sūrat al-Rūm* has been assigned to it, dated A. D. 614.

PART II

LITERARY APPROACHES TO SELECTED SŪRAS OF THE QUR'ĀN

Chapter 7

Referentiality and Textuality in *Sūrat al-Ḥijr*: Some Observations on the Qur'ānic "Canonical Process" and the Emergence of a Community

Angelika Neuwirth

0 THE PROBLEM OF THE QUR'ĀNIC CANON

0.1 Canonization: Social and Cognitive Dimensions

Several recent studies on the Qur'ān have focused anew on the problem of its canonization, raising it to a central issue in Qur'ānic research.[1] What these studies have called into question is the traditional account about the redaction and publication of a unified and for once authorized final version of the Qur'ān corpus through which the text came to occupy the rank of a Scripture bearing an intrinsic logic of its own. By focusing on this final phase, by ranking it as the crucial event in Qur'ānic genesis, however, an epistemological course has been set: The literary image of the Qur'ān reflecting a text still in progress, indeed, displaying a unique microstructural diversity due to its evolution out of an extended process of a liturgical communication, becomes blurred, being eclipsed by its macrostructural weight, by the *social* importance of the henceforth normative corpus and its ideological implications for the construction of the community's identity. Andrew Rippin has lately proclaimed the macrostructural approach an appropriate basis for the "reading (of) Scripture in the 21st century,"[2] a manifesto which in my view overleaps important steps of inquiry still badly missing. The issue of the canonicity of the Qur'ān will therefore be taken up anew, though with the changed objective of shedding light on its implications for the text itself. Too little attention, it seems, has been paid until now to the *cognitive* aspects of canonization: Does canonization necessarily mark a punctually definable turning-point in the development of the text, whose growth has thereby come to an end? Or may canonization be understood as an extended process which should even appear mirrored in the text itself? What essentially new qualities does the corpus in the community's view acquire after its literary fixation, after the authorization of a final version?

Let us consider the last question first: According to the dominating Islamic tradition,[3] the Qur'ān owes its authoritative final version to the redaction carried out by a committee summoned by the third caliph, 'Uthmān b. 'Affān. The codex thus coming into existence, does, it is admitted, impose on the sūras a sequence which until then had not been fixed; in many cases it also accommodates passages that had been transmitted isolatedly into completely new contexts. However, the committee clings faithfully to the text material whose authenticity is warranted by reliable oral and/or written tradition, considering all the revelations still available at the time, thus tacitly following the 'canon formula' "to leave out nothing and to add nothing".[4] The performance of the committee is, therefore, traditionally identified with the act of a collection, *jam'*, in perfect accordance with the concept of its commissioner, 'Uthmān, who is reported to have imposed on the redactors – apart from the observing of some linguistic cautelas – no further task than the gathering of all still available parts of the Qur'ān. The presentation of the events as tradition reports them is not offbeat at all;[5] at least, it fits well into the findings offered by the text itself, since the new codex, which does not claim any chronological or theological justification for the sequence of the single texts (sūras and parts of sūras) which it encompasses, but which it arranges at least apparently[6] according to merely technical, exterior criteria, does display inexstinguishable traces of its compilation as a *collection,* or even an *anthology* of texts. It presents itself as a corpus of unconnected texts of diverse structure not allowing for an immediate classification under one single particular genre.

The admitted fact that the collection had been carried out somewhat hastily and thus had to proceed in a rather mechanical fashion, is duly explained and justified in the traditional reports by political constraints. Still the outcome gave rise to a problematic development: The joint codification of loosely composed passages and often unframed, conceptually isolated communications – so characteristic of the long sūras – together with complex polythematic structures and mnemotechnically sophistical pieces that make up the short and middle-sized sūras resulted in a most heterogenous ensemble – a fact that did not remain without consequences. Once these elements melted to form a comprehensive and closed corpus, a codex, *muṣḥaf,* they became neutralized as to their liturgical 'Sitz im Leben' and their communicational context in the emergence of the community. Previously defined text units distinguishable through reliable devices such as introductory formulas and markers of closure were, it is true, retained by the redaction as such, and labelled 'sūra'. They lost, however, much of their significance. For along with them in the same codex there were other units bearing the same label 'sūra' whose single passages had not come to form a coherent literary structure and thus invalidated the structural claim raised by the neatly composed sūras. These latter ceased to be conceived of as individual literary units transporting messages of their own and mirroring individual processes of communication relevant as stages of a development.[7] On the contrary, once all parts had become equal in rank, arbitrarily selected texts could be extracted from their sūra context and used to explain arbitrarily selected others. Having thus become virtually *de-contextualized,* they were stripped of the tension they once partook of within their original units. Genuine text units thus had lost their literary integrity and could therefore be mistaken to present mere repetitions of each other.[8]

Thus, with its final canonization the Qur'ān as such had become *de-historicized.* Not *the process* of its successive emergence as mirrored in the text, but the timeless, eternal quality of its message had become its brand. This made the understanding of the Qur'ān all the more dependent on the *Sīra,* a corpus that although transmitted and codified separately has been grafted on the Qur'ān by its readers and listeners from early times onward.[9] Prophetic tradition, developing, as it did, haggadic metahistory, thus took the place that intra-Qur'ānic history should legitimately have occupied, i.e. the history, however scarce in chronological evidence, of a liturgical and social communication process, that distinctly took textual shape in the Qur'ān.[10] To reveal the still traceable traits of that history which has an important bearing on the porblematic raised in the first question, a systematic literary investigation of the microstructure of the Qur'ān remains an urgent desideratum.

The following discussion of *Sūrat al-Ḥijr* (Q. 15) is meant to be a step in that direction. It is at the same time an attempt to comply with a provoking demand proffered by A. Rippin, that the Qur'ān should finally be studied by (a) "situating ... (it) in its literary tradition" and (b) by "situating ... (it) at the focal point of a reader-response study."[11] But diverging from Rippin's proposal we will not (a) go so far as to replace an immediately traceable intra-Qur'ānic context by a *speculative Biblical* or post-Biblical one to provide the appropiate 'literary tradition'. Nor shall we embark on (b) reconstructing a *post-Qur'ānic reader-response* from the exegetical literature. What we shall rather analyze on the basis of an individual sūra is the Qur'ānic communication process as taking place between speaker and listeners, the place of the reader-response thus being taken by a *listener-response,* the literary concept of the "implied reader" being modified into that of the "implied listener"(b).[12] The "situating the Qur'ān in its literary tradition" (a) will be realized through the investigation of its peculiar referentiality, not stopping short, however, with noting particular instances of a Biblical background, but proceeding to examine the position of the sūra as a stage in an extended *'canonical process'.*

0.2 Two Complementary Models to be Tested on the Qur'ān: 'Canon from Below'/'Canonical Process'

It appears promising for our assessment of the Qur'ānic canon problem, to adopt the typological distinction made by Aleida and Jan Assmann between a 'canon from *above*' and a 'canon from *below*'.[13] Particularly the old sūras seem to mirror a development which in its essential traits reflects a 'canonization from below' as characterized by Aleida and Jan Assmann: "Perhaps it is true that the 'canon from below' particularly underlines the *social* aspect, whereas the 'canon from above' rather focuses on the *cognitive* aspect. We shall juxtapose two canons: a canon to be described as *power-oriented*, and a canon, that relies on a particular *source of meaning*. By 'source of meaning' we understand phenomena, that have been conceptualized in social studies as 'charisma', that is a truth not warranted by an institution, but by a person (or sometimes by a situation). A charismatic situation needs at least two protagonists: the bearer of charisma, i.e. the leader, and his followers, a group of the faithful, who submit themselves to his word as being ultimately binding. This relation is diametrically opposed to the *norms* of the socio-political surroundings. ... Whenever the message is preserved to survive beyond the situation in which the original group was directly interacting, it will usually undergo a profound change in structure. The message gains a new appearance through scripturalization and moreover through institutionalization." These observations, on the one hand, may serve as a useful impulse to move the Qur'ānic canon problem back to the genesis of the text itself and deter from onesidedly localizing it with the first official edition of the codex. On the other hand, the case of the Qur'ān could provide some not irrelevant modifications to the above-mentioned model which appears to have been primarily deduced from the New Testamental Scriptures. Thus, in the case of the Qur'ān the phenomenon of the aura emanating from 'the bodily contact of the charismatic leader'[14] so essential for the Gospels, is totally absent, its place being taken by the aura of the spoken and the aurally received word.

In the case of the Qur'ān, then, a 'canon from below' precedes the 'canon from above'. The latter only comes about with the authoritative final redaction, which became necessary to counteract the pressure of a reactionary tendency towards provincialization and fragmentarization. The 'canon from below' has thereby changed into a 'canon from above' – a development well comparable to that in Early Christianity when the official church contracted a pact with political power.[15]

What textual signs of a developing canon from below does the Qur'ān text display? To discern these we may draw on new approaches developed in recent Biblical studies, essentially due to the American scholar Brevard Childs who has proposed to understand the genesis of a canon as a process of growth. 'Canon' in this context does no longer cover the officially codified final form of a text, but rather means 'the consciousness of a binding covenantal character deeply rooted in the texts' that is affirmed by continuous references of later emerging text units to a text nucleus and by recurrent instances of intertextuality mirrored in the text units developing around the nucleus. "Even at the point where the genesis of a text conceived as a 'canonical process' has come to a close with the end the text's growth, its final form will not offer a harmonical form but leave the roughness caused by the organic growth unleveled. The final shape only re-locates interpretation, which until then took place in productive additions or changes within the text, and which henceforth takes place through exegesis and interpretation separate from the text."[16]

On the basis of these concepts of 'canon' we will try in the following to escape the dilemma of the two presently dominating positions so infelicitously blocking each other: a traditional position of Qur'ānic interpretation relying heavily on the *Sīra* and thereby unduly re-historicizing the Qur'ān[17] on the one hand and a counter-position oriented towards Formgeschichte or semiological approaches, that not only dismisses the *Sīra,* but also rigorously de-historicizes the Qur'ān, and which confining itself to the macrostructure of the canonized final version disregards the distinctive internal literary structures of the Qur'ān. This paper argues for a third way: a Qur'ān reading that respects the redactionally warranted unit 'sūra' as a literary text, studying it as a communicational process. Its striking pattern of *debate*[18] will thus occupy the focus of interest: The sūra will not be considered as a *message* of a speaker moving *linearly* in the direction of the addressee, but as a communication between a larger number of *dramatis personae* involved in the process of the emergence of a community. Since, however, this communication as documented in the Qur'ān is not conveyed in a protocol-like fashion, but appears in a 'literarized' form, having been condensed by the force of an artistic objective to form a discourse of its own, it deserves to be studied as a literary phenomenon.

1 A CASE STUDY: *SŪRAT AL-ḤIJR* (Q. 15) AS A LITERARY TEXT[19]

1.0 Preliminary Remarks

What recommends this particular sūra as the basis for a revision of the canon problem is its particularly striking *self-referentiality* : it is the only sūra to mark explicitly its particular position within the growing mass of Qur'ānic pericopes. Still on a further level this text mirrors itself: the crucial development attested in the sūra, the *emergence of a community*, the confrontation of two parties, *antum/hum,* ideologically no longer compatible, is aetiologically traced back to a divine plan developed in pre-existence and 'quoted' in the sūra. The *cultic* dimension of this socio-religious development, again, is reflected on the structural level of the text where particular formulas point to *a liturgic* 'Sitz im Leben', to the sūra's being intended as a scriptural pericope in the framework of a religious service. This impression is further enhanced by the projections of nearly all the verses of the Muslim communal prayer, *al-Fātiḥa*, which appear interspersed in the text. We will first survey the literary composition of the sūra (part 1), then turn to its communicational structure (part 2) and finally (part 3) present some conclusions to be drawn from the double dimension of the Qur'ān as a literary text and as a communication process.

1.1 The Sūra and Its Subdivisions: a Descriptive Survey

The sūra may be subdivided into five single passages, texts 1–5. These will be described in short as to the course of the argument and the *dramatis personae* involved.

Verse 1 constitutes a liturgical *introduction*, consisting of a metatextual formula, which qualifies the entire following speech as part ("set of signs", *āyāt*) of an authorized comprehensive text ("codex", *kitāb*) and specifies its function as a ceremonial recitation (*qur'ān*). The sender figures indirectly, represented by his emblems: scripture, signs and pericope. The message is presented as immediately enacted speech (*qur'ān*), at the same time – since reproducing a textually fixed source (*āyāt al-kitāb*) – as speech extended in time and space.[20]

Text 1 (vv. 2–15): Consolation interwoven with polemics:[21] Debate about the urgency to face the imminent catastrophe

Dramatis personae:
1. sender (we),
2. addressee/transmitter (you)
3. (absent from stage, but commented upon and quoted verbally:) a group of ridiculers

Vv. 2–10: The *text* thus ceremonially announced opens with a lament about the deficient acceptance of the message: The sender admonishes the addressee to separate from those that refuse to accept the message (*alladhīna kafarū*): in their unrestrained enjoyment of wordly life (v. 3: *ya'kulū, yatamatta'ū*) and their refusal to realize the imminence of the end of time (v. 5: *ajal*) they are building on *elusive* hopes (v. 3: *amal*), they will discern truth through the eschatological catastrophe itself (v. 3: *ya'lamūn*). For the sender, at once Lord of History (v. 4: *ahlaknā min qaryatin*), has set fixed terms for all communities (v. 4: *kitāb ma'lūm*). The refusers, however, insinuate that it is the transmitter (v. 6: *alladhī nuzzila 'alayhi*) who is deluded, being possessed by demons and thus afflicted by a disturbed mind (v. 6: *majnūn*), that he falsely claims to owe his message to superior powers (vv. 7ff.: angels). Their demand for empirical proof is strictly rejected by the sender.

Vv. 11–15 recollect earlier dispatchments of messengers who were equally ridiculed, thus confirming a fixed pattern of stubborn refusal on the side of the non-believers who take unambiguous evidence, even autopsia, for *illusion* (v. 15: *sukkirat abṣārunā/bal naḥnu qawmun masḥūrūn*).

Text 2 (vv. 16–25): *Paraenesis* on cosmology and intra-cosmical communication[22]

Dramatis personae:
1. sender, at the same time: warrant of creation and preservation,
2. plurality of listeners, at the same time beneficiaries,
3. addressee called upon as a personally addressed witness (v. 25: *anta* vs. *hum*).

Continuation of the debate about the origin of the message: the *heavens* are fortified (v. 16: *burūj*) and protected from demons, eager to listen and surreptitiously communicate supernatural knowledge to humans,[23] *communication* of such knowledge via demons thus being precluded. Knowledge is reserved to the sender: The *earth* warrants the preservation of humans according to His pre-mediated schemes of distribution (v. 19: *mawzūn*, v. 21: *bi-qadrin ma'lūm*, v. 24: *wa qad 'alimnā*). It is particularly, subdued to the limits He has set in time (vv. 23–25); His pre-existing knowledge implying his exclusive disposition of time (v. 23). The threatening statement of the irreversibility of the end of each community (from v. 5) is translated positively (v. 24) to assure the listeners already convinced (*antum*) of divine providence. Yet the passage ends up in a polemic comment on the deniers absent from the scenario (*hum*).

Text 3 (vs.26–48): Mythic narration about the heavenly deal[24] concerning man's destiny

Dramatis personae in the process of transmission:
1. sender = narrator (*naḥnu/rabbuka*),
2. addressee (*anta*)
3. convinced listeners

Dramatis personae in the narrated interaction:
1. mythic creator,
2. obedient servants (angels),
3. antagonist (Iblīs),
4. God-fearing humans of the future (*muttaqīn*).

The sender presents himself in the guise of a mythic[25] creator, who delegates part of his power over the humans that will be the progeny of the newly created first man to a negatively connotated rival figure, Iblīs, whose refusal to obey the divine order to prostrate himself before Adam arouses divine wrath, but who is still conceded an active role: he is allowed to delude humans by *disturbing* the clarity of their knowledge (v. 39). The option thus opened to humans between following guidance and passing to seduction makes true believers discernible from deluded disbelievers. The Meccan *community* and their opponents alike thus appear to have been preconceived as such already *in pre-existence.* The narration not only presents an aetiology for the *social* reality experienced by the listeners but also reassures these listeners of a fair recompense in the hereafter presented as decreed for each group already in pre-existence. The sender assumes a simultaneous double role – acting as a protagonist in the mythic narration and addressing the community as a legislator; thus his speech within a dialogue in the primordial story can merge with his annunciation of eschatological remuneration to the community in the present.

Text 4 (vv. 49–84): Narration from salvation history[26]

Dramatis personae in the process of transmission:
1. sender,
2. addressee/transmitter,
3. community (*'ibād*);

Dramatis personae in the narrated interaction:
1. narrator (=sender, whose speech directly ends up in that of the messengers),
2. anonymous, apparently superhuman messengers,
3. Ibrāhīm,
4. Lūṭ,
5. people of Lūṭ

The narration is introduced by a metatextual formula: a liturgical annunciation of the 'recitation', commissioned to be read to the community (*'ibādī*) through an explicit instruction by the sender. It exemplifies the two alternatives of divine response to man: mercy or severe punishment – thus translating the agreement arranged with Iblīs in pre-existence into eschatological terms. The two stories of Ibrāhīm and his angelic guests, and of the people of Lūṭ respectively present opposite examples of human response to the divine offer of guidance.

The narrated plot, again, merges into *metatextual* appeals to a plurality of listeners, urging them to use their reason (v. 75, v. 79) to decipher for themselves the signs implied in the narration, which are even presented once as posing a kind of riddle.[27] The narration about the two options of divine grace and divine retaliation is extended by additional summary negative examples ending up in a statement about due punishment (v. 84). Thus the anticipation aroused by the *metatextual* annunciation of a 'text within the text', a pericope about *raḥma* and *'adhāb* (vv. 49f.) to be read before the community has been fulfilled.

Text 5 (vv. 85–99): Consolation of the addressee through the affirmation of the continuance of communication

Dramatis personae:
1. sender
2. addressee

The addressee is reassured through the affirmation of eschatological truth[28] and the recollection of the fact that an amount of messages has already been received;[29] he is advised to turn away from the deniers, following Lūṭ's example, who turned away from his sinful city. He is encouraged to devote himself to liturgical services, following the positive example of the angels,[30] not the negative example of Iblīs.[31] The sūra closes with the instruction to continue the communication with the sender until the definite clarification will occur.

1.2 The Literary Composition of the Sūra and the Achievement of Textual Coherence between Its Heterogeneous Parts

Already a descriptive reading of the sūra reveals a striking heterogeneity of its single parts. It is composed from different sorts of texts: consolation, paraenetical recollection, mythic narration, narration from salvation history. These elements would hardly form a convincing ensemble, were it not for a device of forcefully re-establishing coherence, namely Qur'ānic referentiality. On the one hand, central *ideas* are *reiterated,* such as the concept of the delusiveness of enjoyment in worldly life, *matā',*[32] a concept that connects text 1 (v. 3) with text 5 (v. 88); or the idea bridging text 1(v. 1) and 5 (v. 86) of insight (*'ilm*)[33] evolving too late. In another case it is a grave *incident* in the community's social life, like the insinuation of a demon to be the transmitter of the message from text 1 (v. 6) which is re-assumed in the context of a consolation in text 5 (v. 94);[34] or like the painful experience of the debasement of messengers (*istihzā'*), which appears to follow a fixed pattern[35] binding text 1 (v. 11) to text 5 (v. 95). On the other hand, a past event may be recollected to encourage a *mimesis* in the present, such as the self-prostration practiced in pre-existence by the angels (text 3, vv. 29–33) and demanded in the present from the addressee (text 5, v. 95);[36] or the segregation from the opponents, demanded in the past from Lūṭ (text 4, v. 65), and resumed in the present by the addressee (text 5, v. 94).[37] Finally, a key concept (*'ibād,* text 3, v. 49) can even acquire the function of a mythic foundation for the social conditions of the community in the present.[38]

Still higher significance for the coherence of the sūra, indeed the rank of a *Leitmotiv*[39] can be claimed by one particular sequence of arguments, which – bridging all the partial texts – translates the concept of belief/ disbelief into a problem of the acuteness of human realization: the disbelievers regard truth as *delusion,* resulting from a disturbance of mind. They cling to *elusive* hopes (text 1), they have been *deluded* - as resolved from the mythic account of creation (text 3) – by Iblīs, who again had been *deluded* and thus creates – in accordance with the agreement in pre-existence – disturbance and *delusion.* Accordingly the people of Lūṭ act out of a disturbance of mind and thus delusion (text 4); still, clear sight will prevail in the end (text 5). *Sūrat al-Ḥijr* thus appears as a compact composition whose coherence is warranted by multiple referentiality.

2 TEXT-REFERENTIALITY AS A CHARACTERISTIC OF THE COMMUNICATIONAL STRUCTURE OF THE QUR'ĀN

2.0 Preliminary Remarks

The efficiency of this kind of referentiality, however, is in no way confined to the *literary* function of rendering the composition of the sūra more close-knit. It is moreover a medium to integrate the listeners into the *communication* : referentiality by no means always refers to ideas already stated explicitly before; on the contrary, it is often left to the listeners to connect the referent with the signified, as becomes apparent from the appeals urging the listeners to think about what they had just been hearing.[40] Since we are confronted with a debate about a novel, eschatologically determined *concept of time,* it is little surprising that the *present* is dismissed as insignificant and the issue is mostly about the *past*– understood as salvation historical past providing exempla for the ongoing argument,[41] or as mythic past bearing an impact on the worldview of the listeners[42] – and about the eschatological *future.* Whenever the issue of the present reality of the transmitter is raised, it is done with reference to what has already been said in the text.[43] More than once, moreover, the text is mirrored in a metatext, such as the recollection of previous refusals to accept the message or by the triumphal statement that the text communicated to the transmitter has already grown to constitute a corpus.[44] The spacial and temporal realm outside the text, where believing and opponent listeners could still meet and communicate, lurks through only rarely, and in those cases exclusively under a negative, indeed condemning aspect.[45]

Thus, a new world of 'converts'[46] emerges, which deserves the predicate of a 'textual world', since it is a world which permanently draws on textual testimonies, a counter-world to the reality inhabited by those not prepared to convert where enjoyment, 'eating', and thoughtlessness attest the elusive confidence in its stability. The textual world is conditioned by the extreme pressure of tense temporal constraints; its herald is, moreover, pressed under a heavily weighing covenant tying him to the sender of the message. It is a world beleaguered by powerful opponents appearing as ridiculers, or at least as deniers.

What strategies does the beleaguered text use to assert itself, in spite of its incompatibility with the still triumphant, and seemingly untroubled world that does without a constraining textual superstructure? In *Sūrat al-Ḥijr* we are witness to a debate, the explicit part of which, the sender's message, presents itself as the communication of signs, *āyāt,* as an impulse for and an appeal to the listeners to re-orient themselves.

2.1 Metatextual References to the Genesis of a Scripture in Progress

Let us cast a look at the metatexual parts of the sūra: the sūra identifies itself through its introductory verse as a 'set of signs' from a pre-existing more extensive text, as an excerpt from 'the Scripture', *al-kitāb.* Such a book, obviously imagined as being unchangeable and comprehensive presupposes a stream of tradition to have come to a standstill[47] and thus frozen to constitute a store of warranted knowledge. Qur'ānic reference to Scripture thus presupposes a certain extent of signs as existing in previously fixed form and dispatched by the sender in single portions (single *āyāt*) to form neatly composed pericopes – '*qur'ān*'.[48] The ceremonial formula of the opening v. 1 announces such a new individual pericope – 'Qur'ān(in)' – to follow in the shape of the ensuing text. The sūra returns again in its final part to the text form of *qur'ān*[49] which now appears in the grammatically determined form as *al-qur'ān.* Here the transmitter is reminded of his already disposing of significant portions of Scripture, 'the mighty corpus of pericopes, the mighty lectionary' (*al-qur'ān al-'aẓīm*). What does this part of the text look like, judged from the vantage point of Q. 15? The question is complex and can be answered in terms of quantity as well as quality.

Let us turn to the latter aspect first: How does *qur'ān* manifest itself? What is it that the transmitter has been credited with as a token of the truth of his being addressed by a superhuman speaker?

2.2 Qualitative Aspects of 'al-Qur'ān al-'Aẓīm' (v. 87): "Qur'ān" as a Code

2.2.1 Qur'ān-Code as a Medium to defamiliarize Customary Perception

We follow Naṣr Ḥāmid Abū Zayd[50] in stating that the Qur'ān is a coded text, a text, that is, that responds through the code underlying its form to the historically and culturally conditioned capacities of its first receiver and the public addressed by him directly. Since the message is meant to be understood by them, its linguistic system (*niẓām lughawī*) should be tailored to fit the addressees. How does the Qur'ānic text proceed in order to assert its set of signs, its referents to a *textual world*, as against the rivalling set of signs referring to a *real world* charged with dynamics that move towards widely different ends?

Presupposing that Qur'ānic texts are not meant primarily as messages directed solely to the person addressed by 'you', but are rather as new interpretations of the world to be reflected upon again and again by a plurality of receivers, and thus clad in the form of literary texts,[51] we have to inquire about the anticipations of these listeners. How to come closer to a 'listeners' response'? We are confronted in the Qur'ān, we have to remember, with a text generated by an extraordinary communication process: in Abū Zayd's terminology – adopted from the Qur'ān itself – by *waḥy*, usually translated as 'revelation', though 'suggestion' would be a more precise rendering. The text form resulting from *waḥy* is characterized by the fact that it appears enigmatic, hardly understandable to the outsider, being, however, immediately accessible to the addressee who is also endowed with the capacity to 'translate' it to others. But even once this work of 'translation' has been carried out, and the message communicated through *waḥy* has received a linguistically clear form, the text retains a code distinguishing it from all other texts of its time. The sūras, particularly the early ones that introduce the new message for the first time must have shocked their listeners in view of the extreme claim implied in the Qur'ānic communication: the sūras, demanding from the converts no less than the renunciation of an existing *consensus*, their *new code* being intended to exstinguish a familiar old code. Abū Zayd already stresses that Qur'ānic speech creates a code of itself, which reconstructs in a new way the elements of the original system of meaning.[52] A familiar way of living comes to be regarded from a new perspective. But isn't there still more at stake? In fact, familiar social interaction comes to be reinterpreted as being extended to accommodate a new 'mythic' participant, hierarchically more elevated, who plays the role of a 'stage director'. Not only is the message apt to modify the familiar vision of social interaction substantially, but the mode of communication itself claims to encompass the participation of the dominant new protagonist, thus emerging as the speech of a transcendant sender. Insofar as this sender is at once an ever-present actor in the scenario of the new textual world, communication as reflected in the Qur'ān in a decisive way transcends the analogon adduced by Abū Zayd,[53] namely *waḥy* as existing in soothsaying, *waḥy al-kahāna*. *Waḥy* in the Qur'ān, then, is not only the transmission of an enigmatic message from a supernatural sphere, as it may present itself to the transmitter prepared to receive it (*anta*). It is at the same time –

seen from the angle of the listeners who have still to be convinced (*antum, hum*) – the truly revolutionary suggestion of a divine 'stage director' existing behind all human acts and interactions.[54] Since he is presented as a king, the Qur'ān speaks in a language which transports the hierarchic superiority of the sender, a language that is clearly ceremonially imprinted.[55]

It is a language, moreover, which – instead of adapting itself smoothly to the horizon of the understanding of the listeners – calls familiar understanding into question. Already in text 1 this codation appears striking. Thus the analytical "*alladhīna kafarū*" (v. 2) serves to defamiliarize a circle of persons well known individually; equally, the formula "*alladhī nuzzila 'alayhi 'dh-dhikru*" (v. 6) in the reproduction of the opponents' polemics comes to replace the individual addressing of a figure who is well known to the speakers by his name. Both these oblique references are understandable as means of a codation of a world, whose real processes and interrelations are dismissed as irrelevant as against the scenario of the newly implemented textual world, and whose individuality is therefore considered insignificant, allowing for its signs to be blurred. The place of a scenario of interaction informed by reality has been taken over by a scenario of interaction informed by texts. The peculiarly Qur'ānic style based on the use of clausulas that is to emerge later but is already foreshadowed in our text (Q. 15:75: *inna fī dhālika la-āyātin li 'l-mutawassimīn* and the like), highlights the most powerful device of de-individualizing facts.[56] But the issue is in no way only limited to formal matters.

Semantic key terms, as well, like the classification of those that submit themselves to the divine demand of rendering account as "*muslimīn*" (v. 2) or the imposition of a *kitāb ma'lūm* (v. 4), a term for rendering account fixed by writing, or the notion of a time-span granted to the community collectively, *ajal* (v. 5), or finally the concept of an ultimate eschatologically informed truth, *al-ḥaqq* (v. 8), attest a radical re-interpretation of familiar reality.

Such key terms have been proved by Izutsu, Arkoun und Abū Zayd as basic elements of the Qur'ānic discourse; in our particular context, however, since we are concerned with textual strategies, it is not the system they constitute on the macrostructural level, but rather their being anchored – tightly or loosely – in the communication process itself. We may assume that in the eyes of the receivers, the sūra under investigation, whose style still betrays earlier Meccan features, should have appeared as a fairly novel form of communication with a linguistic code still unfamiliar. It is not irrelevant, then, that the terms "*muslimūn*" and "*ajal*" as well as the word "*kitāb*" in the sense of a term in time in *Sūrat al-Ḥijr* appear for the first time and that "*al-ḥaqq*" with its eschatologic connotation is still not known from more than two older sūras.

2.2.2 The Qur'ānic Code as a Medium to defamiliarize the Coordinates of Space and Time

The re-encoding of a reality dismissed as insignificant into terms of a durable, eschatologically informed textual world is thus progressing, provoking irritation on the part of the listeners still bound to worldly life. This applies in particular to the re-interpretation of the world in terms of space and time: The world inhabited by men and demons now appears isolated from the heavens – reserved for the divine entourage – by barriers to be no longer overcome by demons (*jinn*)[57] but exclusively by angelic intermediaries, whose crucial function concerning humankind altogether will be fulfilled in the end of time (cf. Q. 69:17). The scenario of the textual world thus supersedes a traditional vision; the irritating effects on the still unbelieving listeners are clearly reflected in their provocative demand directed to the transmitter to present to them those angelic beings who have been made responsible for his inspiration[58] so as to prove his sincerity. The rejection of such a control to be imposed upon the textual world by the rules of the 'real' world, again, relies on texts. A previously presented Qur'ānic passage, Q. 89:22, is evoked, which speaks of the eschatological function carried out by the angels which will affect every man and thus eventually also fulfil the provocative demand.

Not only has a *cosmico-spacial* extension of the image of the world taken place, but also the new textual world has introduced a broadening of the horizon in terms of time as well, primarily, but not solely, through introducing the new eschatological vantage-point of the *future:* In *Sūrat al-Ḥijr* a mythic past is introduced in narrative form for the first time, presenting the creator in pre-existence as delegating particular power to a creature of his. The narrative is not told with an abstract *aetiological* perspective, but it serves to *explain* the social situation as existing in the present: it culminates in the vision of an elected *community* (*'ibād*), and the abandonment of the unconvinced adherents of wordly life to the seducer. This projection of present developments, already associated with their eschatological retribution, to the mythic past achieves to imprint the empirically observable situation with the character of a timeless necessity. No less is the narrative about the dispatchment of messengers which translates the vision of an all-comprehensive book, the source of the salvation historical accounts, into a Qur'ānic manifestation, opening up a novel discourse; it is one of the first full-fledged narratives in the Qur'ān.[59] It leads back into a remote *past* antedating the events known to the listeners from local ancestral tradition;[60] still, with its account about the messengers sent to reassure Ibrāhīm and Lūṭ, it is meant to serve as a *mirror* for the present: the badly harrassed just in the Lūṭ story are typological forebears of the addressee and his listeners, having been taken by surprise by a communication from the "textual world" which now renders their subsistence in their surroundings most problematic. This story with its *mirror* effect is marked by introductory formulas as destined to be a liturgical reading before an emerging *community*, that is before those mirrored in the narrative themselves, a phenomenon until then unique in the Qur'ān.

To sum up the observations about the quality of what was termed as *qur'ān* in v. 87: we are confronted – as was already underlined by Abū Zayd – less with a mass of texts than with a particular *code* which encodes familiar reality in such a way as to make it discernible as its more authentic counter-form, as a textual world.[61] This Qur'ānic code does not, however, draw primarily on the collective memory shared by the receiver and the rest of the Meccans, but draws predominantly on a different memory warranted by the Book and shared by the recipients to some extent with earlier figures of salvation history. Still, the Qur'ān does refer – if even with a de-familiarizing intention – to Meccan reality. It does not evaporate into a space exclusively filled by Biblical reminiscences. One might therefore speak of textual referentiality – or 'textuality' – dominating but not exclusively expleting the Qur'ān.[62] Both worlds, 'reality' as inhabited by the majority focused on the enjoyment of the present, and the vision of an apocalyptic time disturbed by eschatological tension, as shared by the addressee and his adherents relate to each other in such a radically contrary way that they appear to exclude each other. They are presented as two unequally successful readings, as two unequally acute realizations of one and the same indisputable truth, which some, the clear-sighted, are able to discern, whereas the others, in consequence of their disturbed state of mind,[63] are confined to its distorted realization until the event of the catastrophe will make their sight acute.[64]

Both codes to read reality, thus, according to the Qur'ān, do not differ so much as to the psychologic preconditions or the inclinations of their adherents, but rather as to the different degrees of *exactness*. The Qur'ānic code is a medium to discern reality in a more acute way.

2.3 Quantitative Aspects of "al-Qur'ān al-'Aẓīm" (v. 87)

We now turn to the question of what could be intended materially by the expression "*al-qur'ān al-'aẓīm*", what amount of texts it should allude to. Obviously, the novel code, the vision of a textual world, manifests itself in *Sūrat al-Ḥijr* not for the first time; the addressee should have communicated his appeal to revise the vision of reality already several times previously. The triumphal statement (v. 87): *Innā ātaynāka sab'an min 'l-mathānī wa 'l-qur'āna 'l-'aẓīm*, is made in a phase of development when a host of images, of new conceptual coinages, of figures of thought, indeed, a complete textual world has emerged that enabled the addressee to evoke intensive echoes with every new pronunciation of his. How is this echo effect to be traced? There is hardly an alternative to registering all those verses presenting parallels to a particular verse in *Sūrat al-Ḥijr* in terms of contents or argument, of the codation of persons or figures of thought, that can be traced in older sūras, i.e. those sūras that display the stylistic features of early close-knit, *saj'*-informed Qur'ānic texts. Considering all the material that bears a relation of the above-mentioned kinds to individual verses of *Sūrat al-Ḥijr* one might conclude that "*al-qur'ān al-'aẓīm*" of v. 87, i.e., the Qur'ānic material presupposed to have been promulgated when *Sūrat al-Ḥijr* was composed, was made up by the following sūras:[65]

> 111, 109, 106, 105, 96, 94, 89, 88, 87, 86, 85, 84, 83, 81, 80, 78, 77, 75, 74, 73, 70, 69, 68, 65, 56, 55, 54, 53, 52, 51, 50, 37. These sūras contain at least one, but more often several verses that should have been conceived – in view of their close lexical, phraseologic or blatant semantic similarity – as resounding in individual verses of *Sūrat al-Ḥijr*. Sūras 52, 51 and 50, that share identical verses with *Sūrat al-Ḥijr*, should be regarded as particularly closely related to our text.

2.4 The Problem of the Nucleus of the Emerging Canon

Though a positive stringent proof for the existence of this particular 'partial corpus' as a background for *Sūrat al-Ḥijr* cannot be provided, still the construction has some plausibility to boast of. Let us return to the model mentioned earlier of the canonical process as a continuous growth of a text corpus from a nucleus. It is evident that *Sūrat al-Ḥijr* presents a continuation of previous texts, to mention but the most striking examples: it unfolds the story of Ibrāhīm and Lūṭ, which was related as a monopartite story in Q. 51, into an idpartite account, not without quoting from the previous version verbally. Furthermore, *Sūrat al-Ḥijr* develops the idea of the doublefold creation of both men and demons which was proclaimed in Q. 55 as a short manifesto, through the unfolding of the Iblīs-myth, into a full-fledged narrative. In addition, single verses clearly refer to an existing text nucleus beyond their sūra, thus, v. 74, mentioning an event of collective annihilation known from the local Meccan history, presupposes the knowledge of Q. 105, and even provoke the listeners to draw on that knowledge, appealing to their acuteness (*mutawassimīn*, v. 75) and to establish the relation to that text themselves. In the story of Ibrāhīm, the issue of the protagonist's embarrassment shown towards the angelic guests relies again on the explanation given in the earlier version of the story in Q. 51 where Ibrāhīm's shocking experience of the hierophany is dwelt on. Other verses become unambiguous only when related to an explicit statement in a previous sūra such as v. 2, whose eschatological dimension becomes clear only through the more explicit Q. 51:60 *fa-waylun li 'lladhīna kafarū min yawmihimu 'lladhī yū'adūn*. Equally, the abstract menace in v. 3 *dharhum ya'kulū wa yatamatta'ū wa yulhihimu 'l-amalu fa-sawfa ya'lamūn* relies on Q. 70:42 *fa-dharhum yakhūḍū wa yal'abū ḥattā yulāqū yawmahumu 'lladhī yū'adūn* and an almost similar expression in Q. 52:45.

The emergence of central elements of the new code become clearly discernible only against this background: the all-comprising Book from v. 1, alluded to in the early oath Q. 52:2: *wa kitābin masṭūr,* which in *Sūrat al-Ḥijr* appears as the source of the Qur'ānic pericopes, had been identified as such already in Q. 56:78f: *innahu la-qur'ānun karīm/ fī kitābin maknūn,* but nowhere else in the early sūras. Heavenly books figuring in earlier sūras consisted rather of registers of human deeds: Q. 83:8f: *kallā inna kitāba 'l-fujjāri la-fī sijjīn/ wa mā adrāka mā sijjīn/ kitābun marqūm,* and similarly Q. 83:20f; a hypothetical, terrestrial book was mentioned as an instance of self-legitimation in a current dispute in Q. 68:37: *am lakum kitābun fīhi tadrusūn.*[66] As to "*qur'ān*" in the sense of pericope, it has been mentioned only twice before *Sūrat al-Ḥijr,* Q. 85:21f: *bal huwa qur'ānun majīd/ fī lawḥin maḥfūẓ,* and Q. 56:78f *innahū la-qur'ānun karīm/ fī kitābin maknūn.* The rest of the old sūras associate with the term "*qur'ān*" rather the process of recitation.[67] than the text itself. Our sūra thus, sheds new light on the Book as the source on which the new textual world draws and on the Qur'ānic pericope as an excerpt from that Book put at the disposition of the recipients.[68]

As against that, the insinuation of mental disturbedness, *junūn,* appears to have been put forward more frequently in previous sūras,[69] equally the pretext to be deluded, encharmed.[70] The concept of a community (*'ibādī*), however, is new altogether; its cosmogonic aetiology attests its significance. A number of arguments from Q. 15, concerning the position of a single Qur'ānic pericope in the process of revelation, or concerning the conclusions to be drawn from the ever worsening social constraints of the community as reflecting on the structure of the communal service, will be taken up again in later sūras: Q. 37 and Q. 17.[71] *Sūrat al-Ḥijr* thus marks, an important stage in the canonical process, not only betraying an organic growth out of the nucleus of preceding texts but also opening the intra-textual discussion about that process of growth. It is a text no longer anchored in positive everyday reality, but in a textual world which relies on the newly established hermeneutic fact of the Qur'ānic code.

2.5 Emerging Canon and Emerging Cult: Communicational and Liturgical Coherence between the Single Texts

This model having been proposed as a vantage point for Qur'ānic investigations in general, the question arises how to trace the growth of the nucleus through the single sūras. It has to be demonstrated that the sūras with their reiterated patterns do not constitute mere repetitions, but rather build upon each other, their elements proving functional in creating ever new ensembles with new focuses of meaning. What is the particular focus of every single sūra, in our case of *Sūrat al-Ḥijr*?

Since the literary style of Q. 15 allows to localize the text with some probability after a number of sūras discernibly older as to their literary features and before a number of others obviously dependent on Q. 15 and thus later, a certain control of the familiarity or lack of familiarity of repetition and innovation becomes possible. It was argued that the mythic account of the distribution of power in pre-existence was represented for the first time, as was the (second half of the) account about the dispatchment of messengers focusing on the harrassed just forebears of the Meccan community. In addition, the concept of a comprehensive Book encompassing the Qur'ānic pericopes altogether was shown to have been rendered more precise in the sūra, to denote a source of pericopes. A number of important issues are new then. Why do they merge in this particular sūra?

I would venture to answer: because a new discourse has emerged which raises the sūra to the rank of a remarkable self-portrayal of a charismatic leader and his adherents[72] – a discourse which is due, it seems, to a particularly significant phase in the general development of the 'Qur'ānic event'.

The expression *'ibādī* (my servants, my community) appears to be the keyword here. It emerges – if one leaves aside a passage in Q. 89 which is presumably a later addition – as a new term organically adjusted to the code of the textual world: the servants are directly assigned to the sender (as expressed through the possessive suffix) thus entering a relation analogous to that between the addressee and the sender ever reaffirmed through the self-manifestation of the latter as *rabbuka*. *'Ibādī* appears for the first time in the creation myth of *Sūrat al-Ḥijr*, which projects the division of created beings into adherents of the creator and adherents of the seducer into pre-existence. The myth, which is retold in several later sūras, only here carries the function of affirming the community of the present as conceived and elected in pre-existence. The notion of the community in its full meaning, not only as a group of adherents of a charismatic leader but as participants in one and the same cult, is affirmed immediately by the ensuing instruction given to the addressee, to recite to them an *exemplum* : a story about their spiritual forebears, a group of harrassed just in the past put before the option between acceptance and rejection of adherence to the creator. The entire sūra may be conceived as an appraisal of the emerging community: Being conceived as a community in pre-existence (text 3), the *'ibād* are mirrored in an account from salvation history (text 4) and are thus affirmed in the option they have taken. At the same time their suffering (text 1, 5) is filled with meaning attesting their succession to their forerunners. The community conceived within the cosmogonic process has taken concrete shape in the present.

2.6 The Sūra Looked upon as an Enactment of Liturgy

The focus put in this sūra on the idea of a community seems to point to a new consciousness. There is more to affirm this impression: not only does the cosmic foundation of a community of faithful believers (*mukhlaṣūn*) occupy the central part of the sūra, but the sūra also translates the cultic dimension of that social development into *theatrical* terms. The sūra, indeed, may be read as an enactment of a service: It is opened by a liturgical introductory formula authorizing the ensuing speech as an excerpt from (heavenly) Scripture and at the same time destining it for a festive recitation (v. 1), thus raising it to a *ceremonial* level. The formula takes the place of an introductory hymn, an *introitus* in monotheistic services. What follows is a communication between the sender and the addressee. However, if the listener does not hear except the replica of the one actor, i.e. the sender, he will not fail to realize that it refers – sometimes even through the quoting of the addressee's lament – to thoughts belonging to that latter, thus leaving the impression of a dialogue. This bipolar communication would in terms of extra-Islamic monotheist services match an ectenia, the *responsorium* between community or deacon and priest, which conveys prayers to the divine addressee who is assumed present though not speaking. Though in the Qur'ānic case this part is not a prayer, it still mirrors, in the divine speaker's response to the unspoken pleas of the transmitter, the hardships and needs of the community. The centre of the sūra is occupied by two accounts from the store of salvation historical knowledge. The first is a cosmogonic myth, introduced by a pathetical reference to a previous text, an extended quotation of a most expressive statement about creation from Q. 55, evoking the very source of the tension existing between the opposite principles of truth and delusion. The rivalry between the adherents of the creator and those of a demonic seducer, preconceived in the narrative, conveys to the account the value of a *cosmic* aetiology for the emergence of the community. The second account, explicitly marked by an introductory formula as a Scriptural recitation, portrays Biblical figures in a situation of tribulation, thereby mirroring the situation of the Meccan believers. Both accounts retelling Biblical or aprocryphal stories come up to the expectation of monotheistic worshippers, and demand that the central position of a service should be occupied by the reading of Scriptural texts as is customary in other monotheistic services. A further *responsorium* closely related to the first, and merging into a closing exhortation of the addressee would have a counterpart in the closing *responsorium* of a monotheistic service,[73] though again "with exchanged roles", the divine partner in the Qur'ān being not the addressee but the speaker. Deducing from the complete absence of the opponents from among those addressed in the text, their physical absence from the scenario, one tends to presuppose that the staging of this performance should have taken place in a space reserved for the community and no longer in a shared framework with the opponents' cultic ceremonies at the Ka'ba. Thus, *Sūrat al-Ḥijr,* it appears, reflects a new cultic situation, in which the form of liturgical service has come very close to the pattern familiar from other monotheistic communities.

2.7 A 'Text within the Text': Reminiscences of al-Fātiḥa as the Fullfilment of the Annunciation of the Seven Litany Verses (Sab' min al-Mathānī) Mentioned in v. 87

A monotheistic service is, of course, by no means completey represented through the elements that were found reflected in the structure of the sūra. What is felt missing, in particular, are liturgical contributions presented by the community itself such as a profession of faith and prayer. These observations bring us back to the triumphant statement about the breakthrough reached by the transmitter in communicating the textual world: *innā ātaynāka sab'an mina 'l-mathānī wa 'l-qur'āna 'l-'aẓīm,* whose first element, the allusion to a veiled text, has not yet been given due attention. An earlier attempt to collect arguments in favour of the interpretation of *sab' min al-mathānī* as referring to 'the seven litany verses' of *al-Fātiḥa*[74] – an interpretation already held by a major group of classical exegetes – need not be reiterated here. As will be shown *al-Fātiḥa,* known in pre-redactional context as "*al-Ḥamd*", lurks through our text in more than one passage, indeed it constitutes a kind of subtext.

Its individual parts seem to be dispersed over the entire sūra: The old name *al-Ḥamd,* at once the first word of the text of *al-Fātiḥa,* Q. 1:2, seems to be echoed in the closing exhortation of the recipients to perform liturgical practices (Q. 15:98): *fa-sabbiḥ bi-ḥamdi rabbika* – an exhortation that would, if taken without the awareness that it alludes to the name of a prayer, sound tautological as it would in two other early sūras closely related to *Sūrat al-Ḥijr,* Q. 50:39 and Q. 52:48. In each of these instances *al-Ḥamd* is evoked at the end of the sūra, a position that appears to point to an ensuing recitation of the prayer. The essential function of the *Fātiḥa,* as a communal prayer to accompany the *ritual* performances, the *sujūd,* of the service, is evoked in *Sūrat al-Ḥijr* in diverse passages that raise the issue of prostration: vv. 29–33, v. 98. V. 2 of *al-Fātiḥa* is evoked in v. 70, where particular humans, apparently viewed as anonymous, are termed *'ālamīn,* an unusual use of the lexeme which otherwise only appears in formulaic combinations, previous to *Sūrat al-Ḥijr* twice in the phrase *dhikrun li 'l-'ālamīn* : Q. 68:52, Q. 81:27 and three times in *rabbu 'l-'ālamīn* : Q. 83:6, Q. 81:29, Q. 69:43. The predicate "*ar-raḥīm*" from Q. 1:3 reappears – presumably for the first time[75] – in the programmatic annunciation of the exemplary account about divine grace and severity: Q. 15:49. Remarkably, *yawmi 'd-dīn* from Q. 1:4 has been dwelt upon no less than eight times before Q. 15:35. Derivatives from ʻBD (cf. *naʻbudu*, Q. 1:5) had been used already in Q. 109 and Q. 106 (both focusing on the Kaʻba worship), in Q. 15:99 the form *fa ʻbud* in the sense of a personal adoration functions prominently as the closing imperative of the sūra. Q. 1:6: *aṣ-ṣirāṭ al-mustaqīm* appears – after Q. 67:22 – for the second time in the Qur'ān in Q. 15:41, in the creator's affirmation of Iblīs's claim: *hādhā sirāṭun ʻalayya mustaqīm.* Q. 1:7 *aḍ-ḍāllīn* is evoked in Q. 15:56, where Ibrāhīm defies the predicate of a *ḍāll.* Thus, apart from the *basmala* all the verses of the *Fātiḥa* are reflected in *Sūrat al-Ḥijr* through one lexeme or phrase at least.

The reference to the two tokens of confidence received by the addressee from the superhuman sender: the mighty *qur'ān* and the 'seven litany verses', resounds the triumphal assertion that the recipients have reached a substantially new self-awareness. In the case of "*al-qur'ān al-ʻaẓīm*" the significance of this new development manifests itself in the efficiency of the communication made possible through the new code, in the positive acceptance of the new reading of reality by the emerging community. As demonstrated in the summary comparison of our sūra with several older ones, the concept of a cultic group of adherents of the speaker, of *ʻibād*, was new, as was the notion of a comprehensive Book, *kitāb*, as the source of the 'Qur'ān' pericopes. Indeed both belong together: Text-referentiality, the assumption of a text corpus to be the central instance of reference, can reach the degree of replacing reality-oriented referentiality only on the condition that it is assisted and maintained by a circle of 'fellow-converts'. These need a powerful collective self-expression. The *Fātiḥa* attests the believers' awareness of being bound to the textual world, of acting in a scenario, that includes among its *dramatis personae* the divine actor as an omnipotent and ubiquitous stage director.

Through multiple devices: through the Qur'ān code re-coining reality, and the resounding of the strongly text-referential self-articulation of the community in the *Fātiḥa*, *Sūrat al-Ḥijr* proves to be uniquely connected with the process of the emergence of a community. The sūra reflects that process on three levels: in the cosmogonic and salvation historical topics treated in its central parts, in its structure mirroring a monotheistic service and in its intertextuality, the instances of interspersed reminiscences of *al-Fātiḥa.* It can thus be justly claimed that the text is situated in the very heart of a growing canon.

3 THE DOUBLE DIMENSION OF THE QUR'ĀN AS A LITERARY TEXT AND AS A COMMUNICATION – CONCLUSIONS TO BE DRAWN FOR QUR'ĀNIC SCHOLARSHIP

Two complementary approaches have been applied to Q. 15: The sūra has been surveyed a*s a literary* text, a first step that led to the discovery of a mass of regular features warranting a close-knit composition. In the case of *Sūrat al-Ḥijr,* this composition clearly betrays an aesthetic objective – in Abū Zayd's terms: it attests the efficient decoding of the message as achieved by the transmitter. Now, such an observation would, in Abū Zayd's macrostructural view, hold true for text units other than the sūra as well. In insisting on the *sūra,* we consciously transcend Abū Zayd's frame. Only by taking the sūra as an intended unit for granted, we are demanded to embark on the *second* step, the inquiry into the sūra's context by cautiously tracing its *textual referentiality,* its links to other Qur'ānic texts. This step can be dispensed with if the unit of the sūra is – as in the structuralist, the semiological or form-critical approach – not credited with literary and thus historical significance, but regarded as a merely technical device to divide the text into portions. Only when acknowledging the sūras heuristically as individual pericopes ("*qur'ānun*") of the Qur'ān, i.e. speech units developing around a *particular* focus and producing a particular *tension* in arranging the diverse motifs and stereotypical elements, only when acknowledging the sūras as liturgical texts with the power to arouse the remembrance of certain others, the researcher is urged to inquire about the situation of a sūra in the process of the growth of the corpus and its situation in the process of the emergence of community. The venture is, however, worth while undertaking. Only the quest for the "context", i.e. the text nucleus which can be assumed as underlying every sūra (except for the very short monopartite ones), and which conveys to it – to borrow a musical term – a kind of *tonus rectus,* will enable the researcher to fathom the uniqueness of a given sūra as a piece of art[76] and as a liturgical *communication,* which *per definitionem* for its commemoration is heavily dependent on the evocational force of the texts recited.

Thus, to remain faithful to historico-critical procedures in Qur'ānic research should not be taken as an obsession for the idea of an 'original intention' and therefore be disqualified as 'ultimately meaningless'.[77] It is undeniable that the procedure proposed here, as long as it is applied to single texts only, produces results tinted with uncertainty. Only the consequent investigation into all the sūras as literary texts and as liturgical communications, as an ensemble of pronunciations growing out of each other, will allow to definitely verify the heuristical basis or to falsify it. Until then, the attempt to achieve an approximate localization of the sūras in the canonical process is worth pursuing – no less indeed than the same procedure is regarded necessary as applied to the Psalms, where it is attested as a self-evident step of investigation even in the latest contributions to Biblical studies.

NOTES

1 According to John Wansbrough, *Quranic Studies, Sources and Methods of Scriptural Interpretation* (Oxford: Oxford University Press, 1977), who initiated the debate, the final canonization of the text not only marks the decisive caesura in the history of the text but also constitutes the vantage point for the construction of a history of the Islamic community, cf. Andrew Rippin, "Literary Analysis of *Qur'ān, Tafsīr,* and *Sīra:* The Methodologies of John Wansbrough," (in Richard C. Martin (ed.), *Approaches to Islam in Religious Studies,* Tucson: The University of Arizona Press, 1985, 151–63), 161: "Canonization and stabilization of the text of the Qur'ān goes hand in hand with the formation of the community. A final, fixed text of the scripture was not required, nor was it totally feasible, before political power was firmly controlled; thus the end of the second/eighth century becomes a likely historical moment for the gathering together of oral tradition and liturgical elements leading to the emergence of the fixed canon of scripture and the emergence of the actual concept, 'Islam'". For a diametrically contrary hypothesis put forward at the same time by John Burton, *The Collection of the Qur'an* (Cambridge: Cambridge University Press, 1977), see the review by the present writer in: *Orientalische Literaturzeitung* 76 (1981):372–80. Wansbrough's approach has influenced scholars beyond Qur'ānic studies, see the recent paper by Aziz al-Azmeh, "The Muslim Canon from Late Antiquity to the Era of Modernism" (unpublished).

2 See his "Muhammad in the Qur'ān. Reading Scripture in the 21st Century" (unpublished).

3 See the summary of the traditional reports by A. Neuwirth, 'Koran', in Helmut Gätje (ed.), *Grundriß der arabischen Philologie, II: Literaturwissenschaft* (Wiesbaden: Dr. Ludwig Reichert Verlag, 1987), 96–130.

4 For codification processes in antiquity where this principle, which finally goes back to an ancient Egyptian prototype, has been observed and often explicity articulated, see Jan Assmann, *Das Kulturelle Gedächtnis. Schrift, Erinnerung und politische Identität in frühen Hochkulturen* (Munich: Beck, 1992, second edition, 1997).

5 J. van Ess (Re. Wansbrough, in *Bibliotheca Orientalis* 35 (1978):353) comments on Wansbrough's hypothesis, which dismisses the redaction commissioned by 'Uthmān as a mere exegetical construction: "Generelly speaking I feel that the author has been overwhelmed by the parallel case of Early Christianity. Islam comes into being at a time and in surroundings where religion is understood as religion of the Book. This understanding had been prepared by the developments in Judaism and Christianity, as well as in Manichaeism. Canonization was no longer something novel; it was expected to happen. This, in my view, suffices as a justification for the process in Islam taking place so rapidly." Though in van Ess's view the first redaction should have taken place early, he follows Wansbrough in his observation that canonization in the case of the Qur'ān has been implemented in a rather mechanical sense, without due consideration of the fact that such a measure should not precede, but rather follow the acknowledgement of the authoritative stance of Scripture which in the case of the Qur'ān was still in process. See J. van Ess, *Theologie und Gesellschaft im 2. und 3. Jahrhundert der Hidschra* (Berlin: de Gruyter, 1991), 1:34f. Since the present study is based on those Qur'ānic elements that apparently do have a rooting in liturgy, and thus should have enjoyed an authoritative stance from very early times onward, this verdict which is mainly based on juridically significant texts, should have no bearing on our material and thus not

contradict the approach chosen here. Also G. Schoeler takes the early final redaction for granted, see "Writing and Publishing. On the Use and Function of Writing in the First Centuries of Islam," *Arabica* 44 (1997):423–35.

6 Concerning the exceptional cases of sūras forming groups already in the pre-'Uthmānic corpus, see the references adduced by Neuwirth in "Koran."

7 The sūra as a unit bearing meaning has been rediscovered, as Mustansir Mir has stressed, by Muslim exegetes only more recently, see "The *Sūra* as a Unity. A Twentieth Century Development in Qur'ān Exegesis," in G.R. Hawting and Abdul-Kader A. Shareef (eds.), *Approaches to the Qur'ān* (London: Routledge, 1993), 211–24. An attempt at explaining the missing interest in the sūra as a unit arguing from textual history has been made by the present author in "Vom Rezitationstext über die Liturgie zum Kanon. Zu Entstehung und Wiederauflösung der Surenkomposition im Verlauf der Entwicklung eines islamischen Kultus," in S. Wild (ed.), *The Qur'ān as Text* (Leiden: E.J. Brill, 1996), 69–105.

8 This development may have been preceded by a previous change in the vision of the concept of 'sūra'. If any of the long texts which obviously are collections of chronologically heterogenous smaller units should have been edited as 'sūras' by the Prophet himself, then the official redaction committee would only have acted in accordance with a new discourse developed already in the later phase of the Qur'ān genesis: that of an archive of texts meant to be drawn upon for public recitation by the Prophet or his representatives at various occasions. 'Sūra' as applied to those texts, then, would represent a kind of sub-corpus of divinely authorized communications meant to be read again and again in front of the community, but as a collection without any claim to an underlying literary or structural pattern, see Neuwirth, "Zu Entstehung."

9 The relation between *Sīra* and the Qur'ān is considered no less controversial than the Qur'ānic genesis itself. For a novel attempt to discuss *Sīra* in its own right, see U. Rubin, *The Eye of the Beholder. The Life of Muhammad as Viewed by the Early Muslims* (Princeton: Darwin Press, 1995).

10 Traces of such a history – like those of a literary structure – are denied in macrostructural research; cf. A. Rippin, "Even within many of the chapters themselves there would appear to be, in a surface reading, no particular thematic, historical, literary or didactic unity. A given chapter of the Qur'ān will talk of salvation in general, then turn abruptly to the ancient Hebrew prophets, then discuss points of law for the Muslim community, and finally, summarize polemical discussions taking place in the Near Eastern sectarian religious milieu. In literary form, then, the Qur'ān is nothing like the Bible, for example," in "The Qur'ān as Literature: Perils, Pitfalls and Prospects," *British Society for Middle Eastern Studies Bulletin* 10 (1983):38–47, particularly 39. More recently a counter-movement to macrostructural Qur'ānic studies seems to arise; a new interest in the sūra as a unit has newly been aroused; see, for example, M.A.S. Abdel Haleem, "Context and Internal Relationships: Keys to Quranic Exegesis. A Study of *Sūrat al-Raḥmān* (Qur'ān Chapter 55)," in G.R. Hawting and A. Shareef (eds.), *Approaches to the Qur'ān*, 71–98; A. Neuwirth, "Symmetrie und Paarbildung in der koranischen Eschatologie. Philologisch-Stilistisches zu *Sūrat al-Raḥmān*," in Louis Pouzet (ed.), *Mélanges M. Allard et P. Nwyia* (Beirut: Dar el-Machreq Sarl, 1985); A. Neuwirth, "Erste Qibla – Fernstes Masǧid? – Jerusalem im Horizont des historischen Muhammad," in F. Hahn, F.L. Hossfeld, H. Jorissen and A. Neuwirth (eds.), *Zion – Ort der Begegnung. Festschrift für Laurentius Klein* (Bodenheim, Hain: Athenäum; Hainstein, 1993), 227–70 (ad *Sūrat al-Isrā'*). M. Zahniser, "Sura as Guidance and Exhortation: The Composition of *Sūrat al-Nisā'*," in *Humanism, Culture and*

Language in the Near East. Studies in Honor of Georg Krotkoff (Winona Lake, Indiana: Eisenbrauns, 1997), 71–85; M. Sells, "Sound and Meaning in *Sūrat al-Qāri'a,*" *Arabica* 40 (1993):403–30. There is also interest in particular elements such as the narration, see, for example, A.H. Johns, "The Quranic Presentation of the Joseph Story," in G.R. Hawting and Abdel-Kader Shareef (eds.), *Approaches to the Qur'ān,* 37–70; Mustansir Mir, "The Qur'ānic Story of Joseph: Plot, Themes and Characters," *The Muslim World* 56 (1986):1–15; A. Neuwirth, "Zur Struktur der *Yūsuf*-Sure," in W. Diem and S. Wild (eds.), *Studien aus Arabistik und Semitistik Anton Spitaler zum 70. Geburtstag* (Wiesbaden: Harrassowitz, 1980), 123–52. M.S. Stern, "Muhammad and Joseph: A Study of Koranic Narrative," *Journal of Near Eastern Studies* 44 (1985):193–202. The problem of the genre in general is taken up by M. Zahniser, "Discourse Analysis and the Qur'ān" (forthcoming). Historico-philological approaches thereby converge with discourse analysis, much as is the case in modern Biblical scholarship, see particularly the commentary on the Psalms compiled by E. Zenger and H.L. Hossfeld, a work which is based on historico-critical and form-critical principles and which at the same time takes communicational aspects into consideration. (So far, only vol. 1 appeared: *Kommentar zum Alten Testament mit der Einheitsübersetzung. Die Psalmen. Psalm 1–50* (Würzburg, 1993).

11 A. Rippin, "The Qur'ān as Literature," 46. One would agree principally with Rippin on his observation (ibid., 44): "The Qur'ān is quite clearly a reading – with the full implications of that word intended – of the biblical tradition among the other strands of thought and literature. It stands as one point in the historical continuum of response to the Bible." He argues, however, tacitly, on the hypothesis of a later dating of the Qur'ān and thus of the hybridity of its textual composition when claiming its being situated in an exclusively biblical context and portraying the early listeners to be as well-versed in biblical matters as Talmudic scholars in Judaism, see "Methodologies," 159.

12 Cf. S.R. Suleiman and I. Crossman (eds.), *The Reader in the Text. Essays on Audience and Interpretation* (Princeton: Princeton University Press, 1980).

13 Aleida and Jan Assmann, "Kanon und Zensur als kultursoziologische Kategorien," in Aleida and J. Assmann (eds.), *Kanon und Zensur. Archäologie der literarischen Kommunikation II* (Munich: Fink, 1987), "Einleitung," 7–27.

14 Ibid., 22.

15 Ibid., 23.

16 See B.S. Childs, *Biblical Theology of the Old and New Testaments. Theological Reflection on the Christian Bible* (London: SCM Press, 1992); and Chr. Dohmen and M. Oeming, *Biblischer Kanon warum und wozu?* (Freiburg: Herder, 1992), 25. This model has been applied in a summary way in the general survey of the Qur'ānic development given by A. Neuwirth, "Vom Rezitationstext."

17 See, for instance, A.T. Welch, "Muhammad's Understanding of Himself: The Koranic Data," in R.G. Hovannisian and S. Vryonis Jr (eds.), *Islam's Understanding of Itself* (Malibu, Calif.: Undena Publications, 1983), 15–51; and N.A. Newman, *Muhammad, the Qur'ān and Islam* (Hatfield, PA.: Interdisciplinary Biblical Research Institute, 1996); a severe critique has been raised by A. Rippin, "Muhammad in the Qur'ān," see note 2.

18 See J. van Ess, *Theologie und Gesellschaft,* 48; and J. McAuliffe, "'Debate with Them in the Better Way': The Construction of a Qur'ānic Commonplace," to appear in A. Neuwirth, S. Guenther, B. Seekamp and Maher Jarrar (eds.), *Myths, Historical Archetypes and Symbolical Figures in Arabic Literature* (forthcoming).

19 For a summary analysis of the composition of Q. 15, see A. Neuwirth, *Studien zur Komposition der mekkanischen Suren* (Berlin: Walter de Gruyter, 1982), 264–66.

20 For the concept coined by K. Ehlich, see "Text und sprachliches Handeln. Die Entstehung von Texten aus dem Bedürfnis nach Überlieferung," in A. Assmann, J. Assmann and Chr. Hardmeier (eds.), *Schrift und Gedächtnis. Archäologie der literarischen Kommunikation I* (Munich: W. Fink, 1983), 24–44.

21 The single elements of the composition of the Meccan sūras have been discussed by Neuwirth, *Studien.*

22 It integrates the motif of "Schöpfungsāyāt" (signs implied in creation) which is very frequent in the oldest sūras, see ibid., 187ff.

23 For the function of the *shayāṭīn* as transmitters of supernatural knowledge, cf. Q. 81:25 *wa mā huwa bi-qawli shayṭānin rajīm.*

24 This myth is discussed by Heinrich Speyer, *Die biblischen Erzählungen im Koran* (Gräfenhainichen o.J., ca. 1936, reprint Hildesheim: G. Olms, 1961). See more recently Peter J. Awn, *Satan's Tragedy and Redemption. Iblis in Sufi Psychology* (Leiden: E.J. Brill, 1983).

25 The term 'myth' should be taken in Qur'ānic context with due reservation. Myth in the context of Scripitures has gone through a transformation. What Gerd Theissen has stated for myth in the New Testament does apply to the Qur'ān as well: "First: Myths are no longer Tales of Origin, treating primordial times, but are related to historical events, such as exodus ... and exile ... that assume the function of those basic events taken to have happened at the beginning of time and bearing an everlasting imprint on history... Second: Biblical stories are not stories about deities. There is only one God who does not have a common history with other gods, male or female, but with man alone ... Third: The synthetic form of thinking, i.e. the assumption of a mythic divine presence in the Bible focuses on the 'word'. Thus Abraham is not present in his progeny due to their physical originating from him but due to the word he received. ... It is through the word that God is present in man ... This word always is doublefold, being at once promise and demand, good tidings and law. Mythic divine presence in Biblical belief becomes efficient only when ethical imperatives are taken seriously." See Gerd Theissen, "Mythos und Wertrevolution im Urchristentum," in Dietrich Harth and Jan Assmann (eds.), *Revolution und Mythos* (Frankfurt: Fischer Taschenbuch Verlag, 1992), 2–81, particularly 72f.

26 The retaliation legends are discussed by J. Horovitz, *Koranische Untersuchungen* (Berlin: de Gruyter, 1926).

27 V. 75 *inna fī dhālika la-āyātin li 'l-mutawassimīn* is a challenge of the acuteness of the listeners, who are invited to connect the punishment mentioned here (the throwing of *ḥijāratun min sijjīl*) with the appropriate precedent case, i.e. the *aṣḥāb al-fīl* familiar from local history.

28 For *al-khalq bi 'l-ḥaqq* in v. 85, cf. *mā nunazzilu 'l-malā'ikata illā bi 'l-ḥaqqi* v. 8 (text 1), *wa laqad khalaqnā 'l-insāna min ṣalṣālin min ḥama'in masnūn/ wa 'l-jānna khalaqnāhu* vv. 26f. (text 2). For *as-sā'atu ātiyatun* in v. 85, cf. *wa inna rabbaka huwa yaḥshuruhum* v. 25 (text 2). For *yaqīn* in v. 99 cf. *wa yulhihimu 'l-amalu wa sawfa ya'lamūn* v. 3 (text 1).

29 For *wa laqad ātaynāka sab'an min al-mathānī wa 'l-qur'āna l-'aẓīm* in v. 87, cf. *tilka āyātu 'l-kitābi wa qur'ānin mubīn* v. 1 (text 1).

30 For *wa kun mina 's-sājidīn* in v. 98, cf. *fa-qa'ū lahu sājidin / fa-sajada 'l-malā'ikatu kulluhum ajma'ūn,* vv. 29f. (text 3).

31 Cf. *illā Iblīsa abā an yakūna ma'a 's-sājidīn,* v. 31.

32 For *dharhum ya'kulū wa yatamatta'ū wa yulhihimu 'l-amalu* in v. 3 (text 1), cf. *lā tamuddanna 'aynayka ilā mā matta'nā bihi azwājan minhum,* v. 88 (text 5).

33 For *dharhum ya'kulū ... wa sawfa ya'lamūn* in v. 3 (text 1), cf. *alladhīna yaj'alūna ma'a 'llāhi ilāhan ākhara fa-sawfa ya'lamūn,* in v. 96 (text 5).

34 For *wa qālū yā ayyuhā 'lladhī nuzzila 'alayhi 'dh-dhikru innaka la-majnūn* in v. 6 (text 1), cf. *wa laqad na'lamu annaka yaḍīqu ṣadruka bi-mā yaqūlūn* in v. 97 (text 5).
35 For *wa mā ya'tīhim min rasūlin illā kānū bihi yastahzi'ūn* in v. 11 (text 1), cf. *innā kafaynāka 'l-mustahzi'īn* in v. 95 (text 5).
36 See vv. 29–33 (*sajda*) in text 3 and v. 99 in text 5.
37 See v. 65 (a demand enhanced through the word *amr*) in text 4 and v. 94 in text 5.
38 See v. 40 (*'ibādī*) in text 3 and v. 49 in text 4.
39 In this text it may be justified to speak of the emergence of a conceptual matrix: the dichotomy between disturbed and clear realization of reality is a motif which extends all over the sūra – a phenomenon comparable to the matrix of a dominant image which appears to underlie some old sūras discussed by A. Neuwirth, in "Der Horizont der Offenbarung. Zur Relevanz der einleitenden Schwurserien für die Suren der frühmekkanischen Zeit," in U. Tworuschka (ed.), *Gottes ist der Orient – Gottes ist der Okzident. Festschrift für Aboldjavad Falaturi zum 65. Geburtstag* (Köln: Böhlau, 1991), 3–39; see also the same author, "Images and Metaphors in the Introductory Sections of the Makkan *Sūras*," in G.R. Hawting and Abdul-Kader A. Shareef (eds.), *Approaches to the Qur'ān*, 3–36.
40 See vv. 75, 76, 77, 79. Paraenetic clausulas have been discussed by Neuwirth, *Studien*, 157ff.
41 See v. 4f. (*ihlāk qarya*) and vv. 49ff. (story of *Ibrāhīm/Lūṭ*).
42 This applies to text 2 in general.
43 So e.g., v. 87: affirmation of a revelation, cf. v. 1; v. 88: *matā'* for the opponents, cf. v. 3; v. 94: recommendation of segregation, cf. v. 3; v. 95: debasement, cf. v. 11; v. 97: idle talk, cf. v. 6; v. 99: anticipation of clearness, cf. v. 3.
44 V. 87 "*al-qur'ān al-'aẓīm*," see below part 2.
45 V. 3 and v. 88 raise the issue of the luxurious way of life of the contemporaries, v. 4 recollects the annihilation of communities not unlike the Meccan *qurā*.
46 In trying to situate the communication as reflected in the sūra, one might speak of a process of collective conversion, a change in worldview, the adoption of a vision that is diametrically opposed to the norms of the socio-political surrounding. This conversion is performed by a group of the dramatis personae figuring in the Qur'ānic discourse, in opposition to another group equally involved that insists on the customary norms. See for the model Th. Luckmann, "Kanon und Konversion," in Aleida and Jan Assmann, *Kanon und Zensur*, 38–46.
47 See J. Assmann, *Das kulturelle Gedächtnis*, 94.
48 *Qur'ān* cannot be taken in this verse as referring to a mass of already codified texts at the disposition of the speaker, a Qur'ān in nuce, as becomes clear from verses like Q. 56:78; 52:2f and Q. 85:21.
49 From among the two references we have to dismiss one – vv. 90f – which is apparently not preserved integrally; see for attempts to emendations Neuwirth, *Studien*, 265f.
50 Cf. Naṣr Ḥāmid Abū Zayd, *Mafhūm al-Naṣṣ. Dirāsa fī 'Ulūm al-Qur'ān* (Cairo: al-Hay'a al-Miṣriyya al-'Āmma li 'l-Kitāb, 1990). See also S. Wild, "Die andere Seite des Texts. Naṣr Ḥāmid Abū Zaid und der Koran," *Die Welt des Islam* 33,2 (1993):256–61. A most lucid critical analysis has been given by Navid Kermani, *Offenbarung als Kommunikation. Das Konzept waḥy in Naṣr Ḥāmid Abū Zayd, Mafhūm an-naṣṣ* (Frankfurt: Lang, 1996).
51 Here a glance at the genre of the love poem may prove helpful. The *ghazal* is addressed to a 'you', the beloved person, it finds; however, since claiming to be a literary work and not an exclusively pragmatic pronunciation, its recipients

are not primarily in the figure addressed as 'you', but rather in a group of outsiders. See the convincing argument by Thomas Bauer, "Liebe und Liebesdichtung in der arabischen Welt des 9. und 10. Jahrhunderts. Eine literatur- und mentalitätsgeschichtliche Studie des arabischen Gazal," (Unpublished habilitation thesis submitted to the University of Erlangen, 1996).

52 Abū Zayd, *Naqd al-Khiṭāb al-Dīnī* (Cairo: Sīnā li 'l-Nashr, 1992), 194 (following Kermani, *Offenbarung*, 10f).

53 The deficiency of the *waḥy al-kahāna* is, however, stressed. See *Mafhūm al-Naṣṣ*, 44; Kermani, *Offenbarung*, 48f

54 Assuming the perspective of the contemporary listeners, A. Noth has demonstrated the difficultly acceptable demand entailed in the Qur'ānic message exemplifying the call to *jihād*. See his "Früher Islam," in Ulrich Haarmann (ed.), *Geschichte der arabischen Welt* (Munich: C.H. Beck, 1987), 11–100.

55 In assuming – as Wansbrough and his disciples have done – a merely inter-monotheist debate, it is difficult to vindicate the plausibility of the ever-preserved role of the speaker, the double role of the sender as the acting protagonist of salvation history and a kind of polemical commentator in sermons by far exceeding the extent familiar from the Biblical prophetic books.

56 For the often didactic clausulae juxtaposing positively and negatively evaluated comments, see Neuwirth, *Studien*, 157–66, and particularly Neuwirth, "Zur Struktur der *Yūsuf*-Sure." These devices in my view presuppose a public that has still to be indoctrinated with monotheistic ideas.

57 See for the Qur'ānic cosmology in general Speyer, *Die biblischen Erzählungen*.

58 Here the allusion might be to the account about a vision in Q. 53.

59 The only narration preceding this account of the dispatch of messengers is the narrative of Ibrāhīm in Q. 51.

60 An event still recollected through the ancestral memory is reflected in one of the oldest sūras, *Sūrat al-Fīl* (Q. 105).

61 *Mafhūm al-Naṣṣ*, 27; Wild, "Die andere Seite des Texts," 257.

62 For an application of this differentiation to modern literature, see Priska Furrer, "Fenster zur Welt oder selbstreflektierender Spiegel? Referentialität und Textualität in der modernen türkischen Erzählliteratur," *Asiatische Studien* 50/2 (1996):321–38.

63 Cf. *sukkirat abṣārunā*, v. 15, *sakra*, v. 72, *masḥūr*, v. 15.

64 Cf. *fa-sawfa ya'lamūn*, in v. 3 and v. 96.

65 The relation of *Sūrat al-Ḥijr* to an already existing nucleus of texts might best become clear through the parallels listed below. They do, however, only present an excerpt out of a far broader spectrum of 'old' verses which might be felt resounding as echoes in our sūra. The principle behind the selection of the testimonies is to present at least one verse out of each of the old sūras that possibly resound in *Sūrat al-Ḥijr* ; all further parallels can easily been drawn from the concordance.. However, if single sūras from among the ones listed might not have come down to us in their pre-redactional form, the verses quoted have still to be regarded on the basis of their structure as 'old':

For Q. 15:84 *fa-mā aghnā 'anhum mā kānū yaksibūn*, cf. Q. 111:2: *mā aghnā 'anhu māluhu wa mā kasab*;

For Q. 15:99: *wa 'bud rabbaka ḥattā ya'tiyaka 'l-yaqīn*, cf. Q. 106:3: *fa l-ya'budū rabba hādhā 'l-bayt* ('BD otherwise in Q. 109);

For Q. 15:74: *wa amṭarnā 'alayhim ḥijāratan min sijjīl*, cf. 105:4: *tarmīhim bi-ḥijāratin min sijjīl* (cf. also Q. 51:33);

For Q. 15:98: *wa kun mina 's-sājidīn,* cf. Q. 96:19: *wa 'sjud wa 'qtarib* (SJD otherwise in Q. 84:21);

For Q. 15:97: *wa laqad naʿlamu annaka yaḍīqu ṣadruka bi-mā yaqūlūn,* cf. Q. 94:1: *a-lam nashraḥ laka ṣadrak;*

For Q. 15:7: *law mā ta'tīna bi 'l-malā'ikati,* cf. Q. 89:22: *wa jā'a rabbuka wa 'l-malaku ṣaffan ṣaffā;*

For Q. 15:50: *wa anna ʿadhābī huwa 'l-ʿadhābu 'l-alīm,* cf. Q. 88:24: *fa-yuʿadhdhibuhu 'llāhu 'l-ʿadhāba 'l-akbar* (*ʿadhāb* otherwise 18x);

For Q. 15:98: *fa-sabbiḥ bi-ḥamdi rabbika,* cf. Q. 87:1: *sabbiḥi 'sma rabbika 'l-aʿlā* (*sabbiḥ* attested in old sūras another 5x);

For Q. 15:2: *rubbamā yawaddu 'lladhīna kafarū law kānū muslimīn,* cf. Q. 86:17: *fa-mahhili 'l-kāfirīna amhilhum ruwaydā* (KFR otherwise 8x);

For Q. 15:16: *wa laqad jaʿalnā fī 's-samā'i burūjan,* cf. Q. 85:1: *wa 's-samā'i dhāti 'l-burūj;*

For Q. 15:1: *tilka āyātu 'l-kitābi wa qur'ānin mubīn,* cf. Q. 85:21f: *bal huwa qur'ānun majīd/fī lawḥin maḥfūẓ* (*qur'ān* in the sense of 'lectionary' only in Q. 56:78);

For Q. 15:36: *qāla: rabbi fa'anẓirnī ilā yawmi yubʿathūn,* cf. Q. 83:4f: *alā yaẓunnu ulā'ika annahum mabʿūthūn / li-yawmin ʿaẓīm;*

For Q. 15:17: *wa ḥafiẓnāhā min kulli shayṭānin rajīm,* cf. Q. 81:25: *wa mā huwa bi-qawli shayṭānin rajīm;*

For Q. 15:6: *wa qālū: yā ayyuhā 'lladhī nuzzila ʿalayhi 'dh-dhikru innaka la-majnūn,* cf. Q. 81:22: *wa mā ṣāḥibukum bi-majnūn* (*majnūn* otherwise 6x);

For Q. 15:22: ... *fa-anzalnā mina 's-samā'i mā'an,* cf. Q. 78:14: *fa-anzalnā mina 'l-muʿṣirāti mā'an;*

For Q. 15:3: *dharhum ya'kulū wa yatamattaʿū* (MTʿ another 2x), cf. Q. 77:46: *kulū wa tamattaʿū qalīlan, innakum mujrimūn* ;

For Q. 15:15: *la-qālū: .... bal naḥnu qawmun masḥūrūn,* cf. Q. 74:24: *fa-qāla: in hādhā illā siḥrun yu'thar;*

For Q. 15:8: *mā nunazzilu 'l-malā'ikata illā bi 'l-ḥaqqi,* cf. Q. 69:17 *wa 'l-malaku ʿalā arjā'ihā;*

For Q. 15:2: *rubbamā yawaddu 'lladhīna kafarū law kānū muslimīn,* cf. Q. 68:35: *a-fa-najʿalu 'l-muslimīna ka 'l-mujrimīn* (*muslim* otherwise in Q. 51:36);

For Q. 15:47: *ikhwānan ʿalā sururin mutaqābilīn,* cf. Q. 56:15f: *ʿalā sururin mawḍūna/ muttaki'īna ʿalayhā mutaqābilīn;*

For Q. 15:26f: *wa laqad khalaqnā 'l-insāna min ṣalṣālin min hama'in masnūn/ wa 'l-jānna khalaqnāhu min qablu min nāri 's-samūm,* cf. Q. 55:14f: *khalaqa 'l-insāna min ṣalṣālin ka 'l-fakhkhār/ wa khalaqa 'l-jānna min mārijin min nār;*

For Q. 15:4: *wa mā ahlaknā min qaryatin illā wa lahā kitābun maʿlūm,* cf. Q. 54:51: *wa laqad ahlaknā ashyāʿakum;*

For Q. 15:74: *fa-jaʿalnā ʿāliyahā sāfilaha,* cf. Q. 53:53: *wa 'l-mu'tafikata ahwā;*

For Q. 15:3: *dharhum ya'kulū wa yatamattaʿū,* cf. Q. 52:45: *fa-dharhum ḥattā yulāqū yawmahum* (*dharhum* otherwise 1x: Q. 70:42);

For Q. 15:2: *rubbamā yawaddu 'lladhīna kafarū law kānū muslimīn,* cf. Q. 51:60: *fa-waylun li 'lladhīna kafarū min yawmihim;*

For Q. 15:45: *inna 'l-muttaqīna fī jannātin wa ʿuyūn* = Q. 51:15;

For Q. 15:89: *innī anā 'n-nadhīru 'l-mubīn,* cf. Q. 51:50: *innī lakum minhu nadhīrun mubīn;*

For Q. 15:23: *wa innā la-naḥnu nuḥyī wa numītu wa naḥnu 'l-wārithūn,* cf. Q. 50:43: *innā naḥnu nuḥyī wa numītu wa ilaynā 'l-maṣīr;*

For Q. 15:19: *wa 'l-arḍa madadnāhā wa alqaynā fīhā rawāsiya* = Q. 50:7.

66 See Arthur Jeffery, *The Qur'ān as Scripture* (New York: R.F. Moore Co., 1952).

67 Cf. Q. 84:21: *wa idhā quri'a 'alayhimu 'l-Qur'ānu lā yasjudūn,* and Q. 55:1–2: *ar-raḥmān/ 'allama 'l-qur'ān;* Q. 54:40f: *wa laqad yassarnā 'l-qur'āna li 'dh-dhikri/ fa-hal min muddakkir,* Q. 75:17f: *inna 'alaynā jam'ahū wa qur'ānah/ fa-idhā qara'nāhu fa 'ttabi' qur'ānah.*

68 See the detailed presentation by Neuwirth, "Vom Rezitationstext."

69 See Q. 81:22, 68:2, 54:9, 52:29, 51:39, 51:52, and cf. Neuwirth, "Der historische Muhammad im Spiegel des Koran – Prophetentypus zwischen Seher und Dichter?" in W. Zwickel (ed.), *Biblische Welten. Festschrift für Martin Metzger zum 65.Geburtstag* (Göttingen: Vandenhoeck & Ruprecht, 1993), 83–108.

70 See Q. 74:24, 54:2, 52:15, vgl. ibid.

71 An attempt to situate a sūra closely related to *Sūrat al-Ḥijr,* namely *Sūrat al-Isrā'* (Q. 17) in the genetic development of the Qur'ān, has been presented by Neuwirth in "Erste Qibla – Fernstes Masǧid," 227–70. The debate, which is pursued in these sūras in a particularly pathetic way, is centred around the possibility of an ascension. The intensive use of text-references can best be explained by the transition from oral transmission to the use of writing, see Neuwirth, "Vom Rezitationstext."

72 It is striking that in this early account of a dispatchment of messages the situation of the transmitter is mirrored primarily in the situation of Lūṭ, whereas the accomplishment of the listeners, namely to believe even against reason appears mirrored in Ibrāhīm's way of behaviour. Both are surprised by supernational messages; like the addressee (Q. 15:88: *wa 'khfiḍ janāḥaka li 'l-mu'minīn*), Lūṭ has oligations to fulfill towards clients (precisely: *ḍayf*).

73 The sūra is in no way an isolated case; for further sūras that allow to be read as 'liturgies', as services, see Neuwirth, "Vom Rezitationstext."

74 See A.u.K. Neuwirth, "*Sūrat al-Fātiḥa.* 'Eröffnung' des Text-Corpus Koran oder 'Introitus' der Gebetsliturgie?" in W. Gross, H.Irsigler and T. Seidl (eds.), *Text, Methode und Grammatik. Wolfgang Richter zum 65. Geburtstag* (St. Ottilien: EOS Verlag, 1991), 331–57, containing a list of the reminiscences of the *Fātiḥa* in *Sūrat al-Ḥijr.*

75 Q. 73:20 and Q. 52:28 may be considered as later additions, see Neuwirth, *Studien,* 206–7 and 213–214; they are, therefore dismissed here.

76 This argument is based on the author's experience with the Meccan sūras; an investigation of the Medinan sūras is still a desideratum

77 See Rippin, "Methodologies," 158f.

Chapter 8

Irony in the Qur'ān: A Study of the Story of Joseph

Mustansir Mir

The Qur'ān is a theological text – chiefly, but not exclusively. In a very fundamental sense, it is literature, too. It is not that the Qur'ān is not regarded as a literary masterpiece. It is, by non-Muslims as well as by Muslims. The problem, however, is that the discussion of the literary aspect of the Qur'ān usually remains confined to the narrow framework of the Qur'ān's challenge to the unbelievers to produce a work like it if they thought it was human and not divine speech.[1] The Qur'ān's claim to inimitability was later developed into an elaborate doctrine by Muslim scholars. But, although the claim was interpreted to mean that the Qur'ān is inimitable in point of style and language, the doctrine resulting from the attempts to vindicate that claim was, in its spirit and structure, not literary but theological.

This "theologization" of the literary aspect of the Qur'ān was unfortunate in two ways. First, it made appreciation of literature contingent upon subscription to dogma, an unwarranted precondition since it was the unbelievers, not the believers, who had been challenged by the Qur'ān to produce the like of it – something they could not be expected to attempt if they had not recognized any literary excellence in the Qur'ān. Second, it obscured the very merit and beauty of the Qur'ān which, it had sought to prove, could not be matched or even approximated. This is evident from many of the works that were written to establish that the literary beauty of the Qur'ān is unsurpassable. One of the standard texts on the subject of the inimitability of the Qur'ān is the *I'jāz al-Qur'ān*[2] of Abū Bakr Muḥammad ibn al-Ṭayyib al-Bāqillānī (950–1013). But while this book presents a theological doctrine with a vengeance, it can hardly be described as offering a keen analysis of the literary and rhetorical aspects of the Qur'ān.[3]

The need to study the Qur'ān as literature proper thus remains. The present article, by focusing on a single literary element – irony – in a single sūra of the Qur'ān – the twelfth – is offered as a small contribution toward the fulfillment of that need.

There is rich and deep irony in *Joseph.* To my knowledge, the irony has not been studied and its scope in the sūra not properly identified.[4] The following treatment of the subject is divided into four parts. Part I summarizes the story of Joseph as told in the Qur'ān. Part II cites and examines comments found in selected *tafsīr* works about irony in the sūra. Part III analyzes the Qur'ānic story. Part IV compares, from the standpoint of irony, the Qur'ānic version of the story with the Biblical. Part V states the conclusions of the study.

PART I: THE STORY[5]

Joseph dreams that eleven stars and the sun and the moon[6] have bowed down to him. He relates the dream to Jacob, who advises him not to tell it to his jealous brothers. The brothers nevertheless plot to get rid of Joseph and, having talked Jacob into sending him with them on a pleasure trip, cast him into a well, telling Jacob that a wolf has devoured him. Jacob, unconvinced, decides to bear misfortune patiently. Meanwhile a caravan takes Joseph out of the well and sells him to one the Qur'ān calls *'azīz* ("powerful [official]"); we will refer to him by his Biblical name, Potiphar. Potiphar's wife tries unsuccessfully to seduce Joseph, and a similar attempt by other ladies of the Egyptian nobility fails, too.[7] Joseph is imprisoned. He interprets the dreams of two prison-mates, but the one whose release is foretold by him forgets to mention him to the king, thus prolonging his stay in prison. The king sees a dream and Joseph interprets it to mean that seven years of plenty will be followed by seven years of famine; Joseph also suggests a plan to provide for the difficult years. The king orders his release, but Joseph would first have the truth about the scheming ladies revealed. Declared guiltless, he is made the virtual ruler of Egypt. When conditions of famine bring Joseph's brothers to Egypt in search of grain, he instructs them to bring Benjamin[8] with them on the next trip. Jacob only reluctantly agrees to send Benjamin with the brothers, whom he distrusts. When Benjamin arrives, Joseph uses a stratagem to detain him in Egypt, letting the others return home. A sorrow-stricken Jacob sends the brothers back in search of Joseph and Benjamin. Joseph reveals his identity to the brothers, forgiving them for their conduct toward him, and the entire family is reunited in Egypt, where Joseph's dream is fulfilled as the members of his family bow down to him.

PART II: EXEGESIS

I would like to make two observations on the Muslim exegetical treatment of the Qur'ānic story of *Joseph.*

1. There is no doubt that several Qur'ān commentaries note the existence of elements of irony in *Joseph.* A good example is the following passage from Qurṭubī. Commenting on the phrase *wa 'llāhu ghālibun 'alā amrihī* ("And God is in complete control of His affairs" = God's decree always prevails), Qurṭubī writes:

> The sages have said in regard to this verse: "God is in complete control of His affairs" in that Jacob instructed him [Joseph] not to relate his dream to his brothers, but the decree of God prevailed, so that he did relate the dream. Then his brothers planned his murder, but the decree of God prevailed, so that he became a king and they bowed down before him. Then the brothers wished to secure the exclusive attention of their father, but the decree of God prevailed, so that their father's heart became disinclined to them, and even after seventy or eighty years he thought of him, saying, "Alas for Joseph!" Then they thought of becoming righteous after him [after getting rid of Joseph] – that is, of repenting – but the decree of God prevailed, so that they forgot their sin, persisting in it, until, in the end, after seventy years, they made an admission [of their guilt] before Joseph, saying to their father: "Indeed we were the ones at fault." Then they tried to deceive their father by means of crying and by means of the [bloodied] shirt, [but the decree of God prevailed], and he was not deceived, and he said: "Rather, you are the victims of self-deception." Then they used a strategem, trying to remove his love from their father's heart, but the decree of God prevailed, and the love and affection he had in his heart [for him] increased. Then the wife of the *'azīz*, contriving, thought that if she could preempt him in speech, she would get the better of him, but the decree of God prevailed, so that the *'azīz* said [to his wife]: "Ask forgiveness for your sin; indeed you are the one at fault." Then Joseph devised a plan to secure his release from prison by having the butler mention [Joseph to the king], but the decree of God prevailed, and the butler forgot [to mention Joseph to the king], and so Joseph remained in prison for several years.[9]

This is a fine example of knitting the various parts of the sūra together by means of a central insight, which also represents one of the major themes of the sūra. Unfortunately, such examples are only rarely found in Muslim Qur'ān exegesis. The example just quoted stands out in Qurṭubī precisely because it is an isolated example. Moreover, there is hardly an attempt made by Qurṭubī – or others – to discuss the use of irony as a literary device in the sūra.

2. In several cases in the exegesis on *Joseph,* irony is seen to reside not in the Qur'ānic text itself, but in the extra-Qur'ānic material brought to bear on that text. An example is the following report emanating from Mujāhid

in which Joseph, responding to the two prison-mates' profession that they admire and love him, pleads with them not to love him:

> I implore you, in God's name, not to love me! For, by God, not one person ever loved me without my suffering some kind of misfortune on account of his love. My aunt loved me, and I suffered a misfortune on account of her love. Then my father loved me, and I suffered a misfortune on account of his love. Then the wife of my master loved me, and I suffered a misfortune on account of her love. So do not love me, may God bless you![10]

That Joseph might have uttered this semi-comical protest is, given the chain of circumstances in his life, plausible. The only problem is that this speech of Joseph's is not found in the Qur'ān. According to another report, which, too, has no basis in the Qur'ānic text, the two prison-mates subsequently tell Joseph that they had made up their dreams in order to test Joseph's ability to interpret dreams, whereupon Joseph remarks, with ominous irony, that his interpretation of the dreams will materialize regardless.[11] Incidentally, even in the passage quoted from Qurṭubī above, the statement that Joseph, either forgetting or disobeying Jacob's explicit instructions, related the dream to his brothers, is not Qur'ānic.[12]

It is perhaps unfair to criticize Muslim Qur'ān exegesis for its failure to see the pervasiveness of irony in *Joseph,* or for its failure, especially, to note the use of irony as a literary device in the sūra. The concerns of the exegetes as also their methods of analysis constrained them in certain ways, and we cannot always expect them to read the Qur'ānic text in ways we find satisfying or possible. What we can do, however, is read the Qur'ānic text afresh, from new perspectives we may have developed and employing new tools of analysis we may have acquired.

PART III: THE IRONY

The Irony and Its Function

The essential irony of *Joseph* may be summed up in the statement that evil intended by human beings is turned into good by God. The very attempt of the brothers to consign Joseph to oblivion becomes a means of raising him to the pinnacle of fame and power. And those who conspire to dispose of Joseph are in the end thrown at his mercy.

To the thesis that evil intended by humans is turned into good by God is opposed in the story another thesis: that innocence sometimes comes to undeserved harm, though, in the end, the harm gives way to good. But the latter thesis is overshadowed in the story by the first, and both are resolved into a master thesis, namely, that ultimate control belongs to God, who inevitably fulfills His purposes. As v. 21 says: "God is in complete control of His affairs, but most people do not know that."[13]

That God is dominant and always fulfills His purposes is a theme that is not peculiar to *Joseph* but is expressed in many other places in the Qur'ān. What is peculiar to *Joseph* is the way in which the theme is brought home – through a sustained use of irony. Irony is built on contrast – contrast between hope and outcome, will and incapacity, reality and one's perception of it. By establishing contrasts of various types that are resolved in accordance with what is finally recognized to be a divine plan, *Joseph* basically makes an indirect rather than a direct statement. It is by negating the dominance of other beings that it lets the conclusion emerge that God alone is dominant.

In a sense *Joseph* has no losers: the forsaken Joseph becomes the ruler of Egypt, the sorrowful Jacob regains his lost eyesight, and the proud and jealous brothers in the end see the light. The happy ending of the story means that the irony in *Joseph* is not tragic. And yet the irony has driven a few lessons home, lessons briefly verbalized in the sūra but amply illustrated by the developing story. Two of these lessons may be stated as follows: God does not abandon those who resolutely place their trust in Him (Joseph and Jacob; see the last portions of vv. 67, 90), and He gives those who have committed wrongs an opportunity to correct their mistakes (the brothers; see vv. 92, 97–98). These statements describe an important aspect of the Qur'ānic conception of the relationship between God and humans, and it is through the vehicle of irony that this aspect is expounded in the sūra.

We can now look at specific instances of irony that convey the above-stated themes. We will begin by noting that there are two main types of irony in *Joseph*. These may be identified, borrowing terms used by A. R. Thompson, as the irony of event and the irony of speech.[14]

Irony of Event

This type of irony, as found in *Joseph,* is marked by a contrast either between the components of a single situation or between two situations. The contrast may take the form of hopes that are thwarted or fears that turn out to be unfounded (as in 1, 2.b, 3.b, c, 5 below); misperception of the true nature of a situation (2.a, c); capacity to perform well in one situation but not in a similar other situation (3.d); inability to prevent danger one has awareness of (4); conflicting forces producing the same result (3.a).

1. The brothers' hatred of Joseph stems from the fact that they consider themselves to be an *'uṣba* or "powerful group." The importance of physical might in tribal life being what it is, the brothers feel that, as the pride of the family, it is they who should be the principal object of their father's

affections, and not Joseph, who has only one (real) brother and thus lacks *'uṣba*. They believe that if they somehow get rid of Joseph, they will replace Joseph in their father's eyes. As events unfold, their analysis of the situation turns out to be woefully simplistic and their scheme against Joseph, which is born out of that analysis, not only proves abortive, but produces results exactly opposite to those they have anticipated. For they succeed only in further alienating Jacob, who still hopes to meet Joseph and becomes even more attached to him. Joseph, whose presence has piqued the brothers, even in his absence turns the tables on them.

2. The story of Benjamin accompanying the brothers to Egypt is in several ways an ironic replication of the story of Joseph accompanying them on the excursion.

a. The brothers take Joseph away from Jacob on their own initiative and with the intention of getting rid of him; Benjamin they have to take along because it is a question of their own survival. In the former case, they consider themselves to be the masters of Joseph's fate – and are mistaken about it; in the latter, they are like pawns in the hands of Joseph – and are unaware of it.

b. The brothers' attempt to protect Benjamin fails no less than does their attempt to harm Joseph. In asking Jacob to allow Joseph to accompany them, they say, first, that they are Joseph's well-wishers (v. 11), and, second, that they will protect him against any danger (v. 13), and they know that they mean neither of the two. But when they ask Jacob to send Benjamin with them, they do not claim to be Benjamin's well-wishers, for they know that, in view of what they have done to Joseph, their words would not carry much weight with Jacob. But grain has to be brought from Egypt, and, to that end, Benjamin must come with them. And so, with a show of confidence that barely hides their sheepishness, the brothers promise to protect Benjamin (v. 63). But all their efforts to save him from being detained by the Egyptian authorities fail (vv. 77–80).

c. The trip on which the brothers take Joseph hides a conspiracy, and the conspiracy is so effectively disguised that even the wary Jacob is prevailed upon rather easily by the brothers. But the trip on which they take Benjamin, although not a conspiracy, has, to Jacob, all the trappings of one (v. 64).

3. Irony touches the life of Joseph.

a. The traders who pick him up are described as being very indifferent to his fate (v. 20). Their utter lack of interest in Joseph is contrasted with the interest, a little too great, soon to be taken in him by Potiphar's wife. Needless to say, neither kind of interest serves Joseph too well.

b. If, upon being thrown into the pit, Joseph despairs of his life, his fears will prove to be unfounded, for he will soon be rescued. If, upon arriving in the house of Potiphar, Joseph feels a sense of security, he will be disappointed.

c. Potiphar refuses to believe his wife's allegation against Joseph. In fact he immediately perceives that the fault is his wife's, and so he reprimands her, asking Joseph to forget about the whole incident.[15] But right at the moment when he feels he has been cleared of the charge, Joseph is dispatched to prison. For the incident must soon have become the talk of the town and the honor of Potiphar's house put on the line; Joseph has to be put behind bars in the hope that people would either forget all about it or start thinking that Joseph was at fault and has been duly punished.[16] At any rate, it is the innocent Joseph who gets punished.

d. Again, Joseph is adept at interpreting dreams. He correctly interprets the dreams of his prison-mates. Later his interpretation of the king's dream saves Egypt from certain economic ruin. And yet the man who prevents the misfortune of Egypt is unable to prevent his own as the prison-mate he thinks will be released forgets to mention him to the king (v. 42). Of course the Qur'ān means to point out that Jospeh's gift of interpreting dreams was God-given and that he was unable to see into the future on his own, for, to use Joseph's words in Gen. 40:8, "Do not interpretations belong to God?"[17] But some irony still attaches to the fact that the man who helps avert a national disaster is unable to see what the future holds for himself. And perhaps on occasion Joseph has wondered about the dream he saw in Canaan. Is it true that dreams go by contraries? If at all he has thought so, then there is irony in that, too, for good luck will be generated out of the very misfortunes he has suffered.

4. While in the case of Joseph the irony consists in that he can watch out for others but not for himself, in Jacob's case it consists in that Jacob knows exactly what to watch out for but is unable to; his theoretical awareness of danger does not equip him to cope with danger in practice. Jacob is keenly aware of the possibility that the jealous brothers would seize any opportunity to bring Joseph to harm. So real to him is this possibility that, upon hearing Joseph's dream, his first reaction is to caution him against relating it to his brothers (v. 5), and only afterwards (v. 6) does he comment on the dream. And yet Jacob is unable to see through the plot against Joseph. As in the case of Joseph, so in the case of Jacob the irony is meant to highlight the familiar Qur'ānic theme that a person's distinction or excellence is, ultimately, a gift from God, the use of that gift always being subject to the will of God.[18]

5. The Egyptian ladies' criticism of Potiphar's wife implies a boast that they would have fared much better with Joseph had they been in her place. But they give up sooner (v. 31) than does Potiphar's wife (v. 51).

Irony of Speech

Supplementing the ironic episodes in *Joseph,* and thus heightening their effect, are a series of ironically used words and expressions.

1. As we noted, the brothers are proud of being an *'uṣba,* and it is this pride that leads them to conspire against Joseph. By the time the story draws to a close, their pride in being an *'uṣba* has been effectively humbled and they are thrown at the mercy of Joseph, who lacks *'uṣba.*

Besides this humbling of the pride in the broader context of the story, the word *'uṣba* itself is used ironically. The word is used twice, each time by the brothers and in the construction *wa naḥnu 'uṣba,* "And we are a powerful group." It first occurs in v. 8: "Recall the time when they said, 'Joseph and his brother are dearer to our father, whereas we are an *'uṣba;* indeed our father is in plain error.'" The words *wa naḥnu 'uṣba* are here used *before* the plot against Joseph has been hatched and, as such, betokens pride born of self-confidence. Soon afterwards, when the plot has been formed and Jacob asked to send Joseph along on the trip, the brothers try to allay Jacob's fears about Joseph's safety by saying: "If a wolf should devour him, we being the *'uṣba* that we are, then we will certainly prove to be losers" (v. 14). Here the words *wa naḥnu 'uṣba* have a false ring of confidence since the conspiring brothers know that they do not mean what they are saying. The *wa naḥnu 'uṣba* of v. 14 thus becomes an ironic comment on the same expression in v. 8. Further, when they have to take Benjamin with them to Egypt and must reassure Jacob that they will take good care of him, the brothers discreetly avoid any mention of being an *'uṣba* and content themselves with saying: "And we shall be his protectors" (v. 63). Finally, the brothers' statement that their failure to protect Joseph would make them losers contains more truth than they realize. For the chain of events that begins with Joseph's disappearance does reduce them to the status of losers.

2. The brothers believe that once Joseph is out of Jacob's sight, he will soon be out of Jacob's mind (v. 9): *yakhlu lakum wajhu abīkum,* "you will then have the exclusive attention of your father." As we saw, their hopes turn out to be fanciful. Here we will note that there is possible irony in their use of the word *wajh,* "face," in v. 9. As a result of his intense grief at the disappearance of Joseph, Jacob loses his eyesight (v. 84) and is thus unable to even look at the brothers. Instead of turning his "face" toward them, he, so to speak, turns it completely away from them,[19] as if he cannot even "bear the sight" of them. It is as though Joseph alone was worthy of being looked at. And, to be sure, Jacob regains his sight only when he receives Joseph's tunic and is assured of meeting him again (vv. 93–96).

3. After forsaking Joseph in the wilderness, the brothers come back to Jacob and lie to him about Joseph. Seeing Jacob disinclined to believe them, they add in protest: "You will not believe us even if we were telling the truth" (v. 17). This is ironic in two senses. First, *wa law kunnā ṣādiqīn,* "even if we were telling the truth," is, grammatically, hypothetical conditional. As such, it is a non-committal remark made by men with an

uneasy conscience, and is probably followed by an unexpressed aside: "And we know we are not telling the truth." It is thus an ironic comment on the report they give to Joseph. Second, the verse is proleptic. When, at a later time, they explain to Jacob why they have failed to bring Benjamin back from Egypt, the brothers are, to the best of their knowledge, telling the truth (vv. 81–2), and yet Jacob would not believe them. With biting irony, the statement "you will not believe us even if we were telling the truth" has turned out to be true. The brothers are not unlike the boy who has cried wolf a little too often.

4. A highly strategic use of the preposition *fawqa* ("over") occurs in v. 36. The king's baker, narrating his dream to Joseph, says that he saw himself carrying bread *fawqa ra'sī* ("over my head"). One feels that *'alā* ("on") would have been more appropriate than *fawqa*, and Ṭabarī does say that *fawqa* has been used here in the sense of *'alā*. But this, perhaps, is too easy a solution. It seems that *fawqa* in this verse has an ironic potential that *'alā* would not have had. To describe a man as carrying a load *over* his head rather than *on* his head is to describe a man who is moving fast, with arms in full vertical extension, for only a load raised from his head will allow him to move quickly.[20] With baked bread in a basket carried *over* his head and moving nimbly, the baker could only be rushing to serve his master, his assiduousness ostensibly meriting praise and reward. As we learn from Joseph's interpretation of the dream, however, the baker is only rushing to his own death.

5. Joseph instructs the brothers to bring Benjamin with them on the next trip, and the brothers promise to try their best to do so, saying: "We will persuade our father in regard to him" (v. 61). The Arabic word used for "we will persuade" is *nurāwidu*, a Form III word with the root *R-W-D*. Other words from the same root and Form have already occurred in the sūra several times, each time with the connotation of trickery. Thus it has been used in connection with the attempted seduction of Joseph by Potiphar's wife and the Egyptian ladies (vv. 23, 26, 30, 32, 51). By using the word, then, the brothers align themselves with the scheming characters of the story.

6. The brothers tell Jacob that they stand to gain an extra amount of grain if Benjamin would accompany them to Egypt.[21] They say: *dhālika kaylun yasīr,* "This is a measure [= camel-load of grain] easily obtained" (v. 65).[22] In fact the measure proves to be anything but "easily obtained."

7. In the incident of the recovery of the cup from Benjamin's sack, considerable wordplay is involved. One of the words played on is *saraqa,* "to steal." The brothers are accused of stealing, but the reference is not to their stealing of the cup but to their "stealing" of Joseph from Jacob. After the cup has been recovered and Benjamin held responsible for the "theft," the brothers try to defend themselves by using fallacious reasoning. If Benjamin has committed a theft, they argue, then he takes after his real

brother, Joseph, who, too, committed theft. Little do they know that they are talking to Joseph himself and that, far from shifting the blame from themselves, they have furnished yet another piece of evidence against themselves.

PART IV: COMPARISON WITH THE BIBLICAL STORY

The Biblical story of Joseph is very rich in irony. The essential irony of the story, namely, that evil intended by man is turned into good by God is summed up toward the end of Genesis (50:20): "As for you, you meant evil against me; but God meant it for good. . . ."[23] And this irony is instantiated through numerous incidents and expressions. It is not my intention, however, to give details of that irony, which has been ably studied by several Biblical scholars.[24] I shall confine myself to making some comparative observations on irony as found in the two books, since the Qur'ānic story of Joseph differs from the Biblical in some important respects.[25]

Since the element of irony is strong in both accounts, the differences between them would naturally result in each having its own points of strength. The Biblical story has a larger canvas, the situations have greater variety, and the characters are generally more fully drawn and there is greater interaction among them, and there is much greater detail – all of which allows for the irony in the story to develop on a truly grand scale. On the other hand, the Qur'ānic account also has its strengths, and it is to these that we will now turn. It goes without saying that the following comparative remarks are only meant to stimulate further thought on the subject.

As a preliminary remark I would like to say that where the irony in the Qur'ān seems to have a particularly sharp edge, it is due largely to the differences in the plot and in the conceptions the Qur'ān and the Bible have of the relationships between the principal characters of the story.

1. A major difference in the plot is that in the Bible the brothers' attempt to dispose of Joseph is a spontaneous one whereas in the Qur'ān it is premeditated. In Genesis, since the conspiracy is hatched on the spur of the moment and away from home, Jacob is left out of the picture altogether. In Genesis the brothers take advantage of Jacob's ignorance, in the Qur'ān they use the method of deception: in order to put a smooth face on the conspiracy, they seek Jacob's approval to take Joseph out on a picnic. This difference between the two versions results in some twists of irony that are peculiar to the Qur'ān. The Qur'ānic incident involving Benjamin's travel to Egypt, for example, may be taken to be a rich ironic replication of the similar incident involving Joseph, related earlier in the sūra. The same cannot perhaps be said of the corresponding Genesis incident involving Benjamin's travel to Egypt.

2. The relationship of Joseph with his father and his brothers is conceived in the Qur'ān very differently than it is in the Bible. In Genesis, Jacob, while he must know about the brothers' hatred of Joseph, does not seem to entertain seriously the possibility that the brothers would actually try to harm Joseph. In the Qur'ān, on the other hand, the brothers do not enjoy the trust of Jacob. Accordingly, while in Genesis Jacob can send Joseph in search of the brothers (37:13–14), the incident would have been out of place in the Qur'ān and so does not occur in it at all.[26] As we saw, Jacob in the Qur'ān has a keen theoretical premonition that Joseph's brothers might do him harm, which becomes ironic when, in actual practice, Jacob is found to be incapable of warding misfortune off from Joseph. The character of the Qur'ānic Jacob, it would appear, is somewhat more complex than that of the Biblical – for one thing, he is less credulous – and this makes for pungent irony in the Qur'ānic incidents involving him.

3. In the Bible one of the reasons given for the brothers' hatred of Joseph is that "Joseph brought an ill report of them to their father" (Gen. 37:2). The Qur'ān does not contain any mention of this; it presents Joseph as a completely innocent person who falls victim to the sheer malevolence of his brothers. Now if, according to the Bible, Joseph used to bring Jacob evil reports about his brothers, then even though it would in no way justify the brothers' cruel treatment of him, the brothers' hostility toward him would become somewhat understandable, especially if Joseph used to indulge in that reprehensible habit very often. This would seem to blunt slightly the edge of the irony.

4. According to the Qur'ān, Joseph was Jacob's favorite not "because he was the son of his old age" (Gen. 37:3) but because Jacob saw in him potential that he found wanting in the other brothers. It was Joseph who appeared to be the best-equipped to carry on the legacy of Abraham and Isaac after Jacob. When, therefore, Joseph tells Jacob about his dream, Jacob predicts: "In this way shall your Lord choose you, teach you to fathom the reality of matters, and complete for you and for the family of Jacob the blessing He previously completed for your ancestors, Abraham and Isaac; indeed your Lord is All-knowing, All-wise" (v. 6). And it is not at all unlikely that the Qur'ān is here suggesting that, deep inside their hearts, the brothers, too, are aware of the real reason behind Jacob's great affection for him. If so, then it would seem that the brothers, in the beginning, consciously refuse to acknowledge that God has singled Joseph out for a special favor. In the end, however, they cannot deny Joseph his merit. When Joseph discloses his identity, they admit: "God has indeed accorded you preference over us; indeed we were the ones at fault" (v. 91).

Now all this imparts a profound religious character to the irony in the Qur'ānic story, a character that a modern Qur'ān commentator calls a "spiritual tenor."[27] It is true that, in the last analysis, the irony in the

Biblical account, too, has to be construed in religious terms. But it will be admitted that the religious element in the story is not very pronounced. As E. A. Speiser observes, "The theme is essentially personal and secular ... the theological component has been kept discreetly in the background."[28] And as Gerhard von Rad remarks about the Biblical Patriarchs in general: "Above all, one must ask where and in what sense Abraham, Jacob, or Joseph are meant by the narrator to be understood as models, by virtue of their own actions or of divine providence."[29] Running through the Qur'ānic narrative of Joseph, on the other hand, is a strong religious motif that, without ever becoming obtrusive, enriches the drama and gives the Qur'ānic story its distinctive color.[30]

5. The Genesis story, essentially, looks backward: it recounts the fates and fortunes of the family of Jacob. The Qur'ānic story, to use Shakespeare's words, looks before and after.[31] In summarizing the story in the beginning, we left out the introductory and concluding verses of the sūra, though we noted that these verses serve to relate the sūra to the then prevailing situation in Mecca. Muḥammad is identified with Joseph, and the tribe of Quraysh, to which Muḥammad belonged and which had turned hostile to him, with Joseph's brothers. In addition, the story predicts that just as Joseph finally triumphed over the obstacles put in his way by his brothers, so Muḥammad will eventually emerge a victor in his struggle against the Quraysh. When, in 630, Muḥammad conquered Mecca and the Quraysh anxiously waited for the verdict on their fate, Muḥammad addressed them, asking them how they expected him to treat his former enemies. Their plea for mercy was made in the form of praise: "You are a noble brother and the son of a noble brother." Muḥammad issued a general amnesty, saying: *lā tathrība 'alaykumu 'l-yawm*, "No blame rests on you today." These words were taken from v. 92 of the twelfth sūra of the Qur'ān – *Joseph.*[32] The story had worked itself out in history. And so had the irony.

PART V: CONCLUSIONS

If we leave aside the introductory and concluding portions of *Joseph,* we are left with a story that has a coherent plot and is completely free from digressions and loose joints. But we have now seen that those portions bear a close relationship to the story, for by means of them the Qur'ān brings out the relevance of the story to the Meccan situation of Muḥammad's time. This being the case, *Joseph* in all likelihood represents a single revelatory event.[33] In fact, if there is one Qur'ānic sūra of substantial length that decidedly gives no impression of being composed of parts or fragments revealed at different times, it is probably *Joseph.* But if *Joseph* possesses organic coherence, then it raises an important question about the composition of the Qur'ān: Do the other sūras (especially those which, like *Joseph,* were revealed as wholes and not in parts) also possess such coherence? The limits of this article prevent us from pursuing this question, though we will note that several modern Muslim scholars have argued that the Qur'ān is a well-knit and integrated work,[34] and it is not at all unlikely that some of the impetus in this regard was provided by sūras like *Joseph.*

A more immediately pertinent question has to do with the Qur'ānic outlook. When we notice that irony in *Joseph* is pervasive, we are led to ask whether irony has methodical significance in the Qur'ān. A sustained, rather than random, use of irony in a text is proof of the presence of an indwelling ironic outlook. If so, then it is likely that irony has been as a means of communicating thought not only in *Joseph* but also in other parts of the Qur'ān, an inference for which a careful study of the Qur'ān might provide support. But if, with all its remarkableness, the irony in *Joseph* has largely gone unappreciated, we can imagine how it must have been missed in those parts of the Qur'ān in which it is not so obvious or pronounced.

It was said at the beginning of the article that the Qur'ān may not be regarded as a book of theology only. But the cause for concern is not simply that the literary aspect of the Qur'ān is being overlooked in favor of its theological aspect, but that, in a great religious work like the Qur'ān, the two aspects are so intimately related that it is doubtful whether the theology of the text can be fully comprehended in disregard of its literary dimension. In a wider sense, therefore, the present paper may be taken as a plea for studying the Qur'ān as literature not only for the sake of cultivating a largely ignored area of Qur'ānic studies, but also for the sake of developing a better understanding of the content of the Qur'ān. The following remark, made by Edwin Good about the Hebrew Scriptures, may, with a slight modification, be made about the Qur'ān as well: "If the Old Testament writers sometimes express their ideas by irony, the possibility opens that they have said something different from, or more complex than, what we have supposed."[35]

NOTES

1 See Q. 2:23; 11:13; 17:88; 52:33–34.

2 Ed. Al-Sayyid Aḥmad Ṣaqr (Cairo: Dār al-Ma'ārif, [1954]).

3 See Mir, "Bāqillānī's Critique of Imru' al-Qays," in *Studies in Near Eastern Culture and History in Memory of Ernest T. Abdel-Massih*, ed. James A. Bellamy (Ann Arbor: Center for Near Eastern and North African Studies, University of Michigan, 1990), 118–31.

4 Isolated comments on some of the ironic reversals and ironic phrases in the sūra are found in classical exegesis of the Qur'ān, and modern Qur'ān scholars, too, sometimes note points of irony in the Joseph story (see below). No sustained discussion of the subject exists, however.

5 The following summary leaves out the introductory and concluding verses (1–3 and 102–111, respectively) of the sūra. These verses serve to relate the story to the Meccan situation at the time of the sūra's revelation and we shall come to them later.

6 The order in which the heavenly bodies are mentioned in the Qur'ān is different from that in the Bible; it is the eleven stars that are mentioned first, which gives us a clue to the character of Joseph. Having perceived that the members of his family are meant, Joseph would, out of respect, delay the reference to his parents, and that is why he mentions the stars – that is to say, his brothers – first.

7 I accept a somewhat unorthodox interpretation of the incident involving the Egyptian ladies. At a banquet given by her, Potiphar's wife has Joseph appear before her female guests, who, upon seeing Joseph, cut their hands with the knives they are holding. According to the standard interpretation, the ladies are so overwhelmed by Joseph's beauty that they do not realize that it is their hands, and not fruit, that they are cutting. But a contemporary exegete, Amīn Aḥsan Iṣlāḥī offers a different interpretation, which I take to be the valid one. According to Iṣlāḥī, the ladies' ridicule of Potiphar's wife (v. 30) contains the implicit boast that they are far better schooled in the art of love and, had they been in her place, would easily have persuaded Joseph to do their wish. It is to call the ladies' bluff that Potiphar's wife arranges the banquet. At the banquet, the ladies first try their charms on Joseph but to no avail. Becoming desperate, they threaten to kill themselves if Joseph would not yield, and, as a token of the seriousness of the threat, cut their hands. This interpretation is sufficiently attested in the Qur'ānic text. For details, see Mir, "The Qur'ānic Story of Joseph: Plot, Themes, and Characters," *Muslim World* 76, 1 (1986):1–2, n. 3.

8 Benjamin is not mentioned by name in *Joseph* or anywhere else in the Qur'ān. Neither is any of the other brothers for that matter.

9 Abū 'Abdallāh Muḥammad b. Aḥmad al-Anṣārī al-Qurṭubī, *Al-Jāmi' li-Aḥkām al-Qur'ān*, 20 vols. in 10 (Cairo: Dār al-Kātib al-'Arabī li 'l-Ṭibā'a wa 'l-Nashr, 1387–1967; Teheran reprint), 9:161.

10 Abū Jarīr al-Ṭabarī, *Jāmi' al-Bayān fī Tafsīr al-Qur'ān*, 30 vols. in 12 (Būlāq, 1327 H; Beirut reprint), 12:127 (for an explanation of the misfortune involving Joseph's aunt, see ibid., 13:20). Maḥmūd b. 'Umar al-Zamakhsharī cites a report according to which Jacob, having dreamt that a wolf had attacked Joseph, expressed the fear that Joseph might be devoured by a wolf, thus ironically suggesting to the brothers an idea they could, and in fact did, use in explaining Joseph's alleged death. *Al-Kashshāf 'an Ḥaqā'iq al-Tanzīl wa-'Uyūn al-Aqāwīl fī Wujūh al-Ta'wīl*, 4 vols. (Beirut: Dār al-Ma'rifa, n.d.), 2:245. Zamakhsharī (2:256, 257) also quotes the report about the several people whose love for him led Joseph into trouble and the report about the prison-mates' comment that they had not really seen the dreams. Fakhr al-Dīn al-Rāzī quotes the second of the two reports. *Al-Tafsīr al-Kabīr* (Cairo: al-Maṭba'a al-Bahiyya al-Miṣriyya, 1353–1382?/1934–1962?; Teheran reprint), 18:97.

11 Ibid. 12:131.

12 Modern exegetes also note instances of irony in the Qur'ān, but there is hardly an attempt made, either by classical or by modern scholars, to study the irony from a literary perspective.

13 Here and elsewhere I give my own translation of the Qur'ānic verses. Biblical verses are cited from the Revised Standard Version of 1952.

14 In Gilbert Highet, *The Anatomy of Satire* (Princeton: Princeton University Press, 1962), 255–6, n. 51.

15 This, incidentally, is in marked contrast to Gen. 39:19–20 where Potiphar readily believes his wife's story and sends Joseph to prison because "his anger was kindled."

16 Amīn Aḥsan Iṣlāḥī, *Tadabbur-i Qur'ān* [Urdu; "Reflecting on the Qur'ān"], 8 vols. (Lahore: Dār al-Ishā'at al-Islāmiyya/Anjuman-i Khuddāmu 'l-Qur'ān/ Fārān Foundation, 1967–80), 3:454, 463.
17 Cf. Gen. 41:15–6.
18 In the sūra, Jacob tells the brothers that he knows something they do not (namely, that Joseph is alive), but he makes it clear that he owes this special knowledge to God (v. 86; also v. 96).
19 V. 84: *Wa tawallā 'anhum* ("And he turned away from them").
20 *'Alā* does not necessarily carry this meaning, and, in opposition to *fawqa*, may in fact connote restriction of movement. An Arabic proverbial phrase expressing motionlessness uses *'alā* – *fawqa* being inconceivable in this context: *Ka'anna 'alā ru'ūsihimu 'l-ṭayr* ("[They were so still that] it seemed as if there were birds perched on their heads").
21 There was probably a rationing system in force and a family's share was proportionate to the number of its members. Iṣlāḥī, 3:484–5.
22 *Yasīr* may also be interpreted to mean "small in amount," in which case the brothers would be referring to the amount of grain they have brought from Egypt and to which they hope to add by taking Benjamin to Egypt and getting him his share of grain.
23 Cf. Gen. 45:5, 7–8; 49:22–24.
24 See Edwin M. Good, *Irony in the Old Testament* (Philadelphia: The Westminster Press, 1965), 106–14; Donald B. Redford, *A Study of the Biblical Study of Joseph, (Genesis 37–50)* (Leiden: E.J. Brill, 1979; Supplements to Vetus Testamentum, Vol. XX), 72–4; and W. Lee Humphreys, *Joseph and His Family: A Literary Study* (Columbia, South Carolina: University of South Carolina Press, 1988), especially 108–16.
25 Among those who bring out the differences between the two versions are Abū 'l-A'lā Mawdūdī, *Tafhīm al-Qur'ān* [Urdu; "Explaining the Qur'ān"], 6 vols (Lahore: Maktaba-i Ta'mīr Insāniyat/Idāra-i Tarjumānu 'l-Qur'ān, 1947–72), Iṣlāḥī and Muhammad Asad, *The Message of the Qur'ān* (Gibraltar: Dār al-Andalus, 1980). For an extensive treatment, see Malik Bennabi, *Le Phénomène coranique* (Kuwait: International Islamic Federation of Student Organization, 1977), 119–66.
26 In Genesis, Jacob is certainly a little apprehensive about sending Benjamin with the brothers (42:29), but not in a way that would indicate any great distrust of the brothers.
27 Asad, 336.
28 E. A. Speiser, *Genesis* (Garden City, New York: Doubleday, 1982). The Anchor Bible Series.
29 Gerhard von Rad, *Genesis, A Commentary* (Philadelphia: The Westminster Press, 1972).
30 In a chapter on the subject, Humphreys tries to prove that the theological vision in the story is quite strong (Chapter 6), but he does not appear to succeed eminently.
31 "Sure He that made us with such large discourse,
Looking before and after ..." (*Hamlet*, IV.iv)
32 See Iṣlāḥī, 3:430–1,497.
33 Cf. Mawdūdī, 2:378.
34 Mir, "The *Sūra* as a Unity: A Twentieth Century Development in Qur'ān Exegesis," in G. R. Hawting and Abdul-Kader A. Shareef (eds.), *Approaches to the Qur'ān* (London: Routledge, 1993), 211–24.
35 Good, 10.

Chapter 9

Reflections on the Dynamics and Spirituality of *Sūrat al-Furqān*

Anthony H. Johns

Sūrat al-Furqān, in the *textus receptus* Q. 25, is a medium length sūra, consisting of 77 verses. By general consensus, it is late Meccan, apart from verses 68–70, which are attributed to Medina. In order of revelation it is variously put as 66 (Flügel)[1] and 68 (Blachère).[2] It presents, with a distinctive pattern in its distribution of emphases, the three great themes of the Qur'ānic revelation: Divine Unity, Prophecy, and the Resurrection. It elaborates this core with subtle variations of imagery, rhetoric, and dialectic that are characteristic of the Qur'ān as a whole.

Commentators in different periods have responded to it in individual ways. Muqātil b. Sulaymān,[3] for example, sees it at one level as foreshadowing the Battle of Badr, associating the title with the phrase 'the Day of *al-Furqān* (*Yawm al-Furqān*)' (Q. 8:41) when the Muslims defeated the Meccan unbelievers, and seeing the eponymous title as a metaphor for Muḥammad's victory over those who rejected him and the Qur'ān. Al-Bayḍāwī urges recitation of it as a support to faith in the Resurrection, and a smooth passage into Paradise.[4] Sayyid Quṭb sees its 'axis' as a comfort to the Prophet in face of the hostility of his tribe, the Quraysh.[5]

The sūra includes a rich cast of dramatis personae. It is a drama of voices: that of God Himself, of the Prophet, the unbelievers, those they take as gods, and the angels. These conflicting, altercating and complementary voices as they play their role in heaven, hell and on earth, carry the message of the sūra and articulate its emphases.[6] It reaches its climax with the proclamation of God, Allāh, as *al-Raḥmān.*

This essay attempts to clarify some of the internal structures that realize its unity and spiritual emphases, and to indicate some of the literary and rhetorical devices that generate its power. It is based on the premise that a genuine encounter with any sūra of the Qur'ān as much on a literary as a spiritual level involves an encounter with the Qur'ān as a whole, and involves a response that is at the same time personal, moral, literary, and aesthetic.

The approach is non-revisionist in the sense that it accepts the importance and contribution of the discipline of *balāgha* as a guide to the complexities and richness of its language, that is to say to an aesthetic appreciation of the text, and together with it the traditional understanding of the relationship between the Qur'ān and the *sīra* literature.

For the purposes of this essay, it is *sīra* literature that provides a social context for many of the pericopes of the Qur'ān, and serves as an indispensable guide to the primary inter-text of the Book: the relation between the Prophet and those to whom he presented it. This is how the mainstream exegetical tradition, beginning with Muqātil b. Sulaymān, has understood it and has sought for a perception of its allusions and ellipses on the basis of narrations attributed to the Companions and Followers compiled into the *asbāb al-nuzūl*, which are so widely distributed as to be regarded as part of its meaning.[7]

This twin tradition lays the foundation for an understanding both of the prose sense of the sūra and its literary dimension. In addition it contributes to an awareness of the dynamism and energy within it and the tensions held in equilibrium that define it as a unity.

In brief, the sūra is a network of interlocking binary oppositions: God – idols; believers – unbelievers; present and future, paradise and hell; general and particular brought together and separated by key formulae, orchestrated by musical resonances of recurring rhymes and vowel patterns. These awaken harmonic echoes and set chords sounding, which resolve into a pedal point underlying an inspiring peroration, a peroration that takes the hearer beyond these oppositions to the qualities by which the servants of *al-Raḥmān* are to be recognized and to the rewards they will enjoy.

Properly, the sūra is to be heard as an extended discourse, a 'master-narration' told by God, in which God speaks of Himself as third person other, and also in the first person, addressing now the Prophet, now the unbelievers, presenting the words of the participants, and introducing sub-plots with constantly changing shifts of perspective and emphasis.

For a closer appreciation, however, it is convenient to divide the sūra into building blocks or segments for a closer scrutiny by which better to appreciate the structure and significance of the whole. Such divisions of the sūra *into* segments are not intended to introduce arbitrary breaks into its unity but to facilitate the uncovering of elements in the structure of its rhetoric and the dynamics of proclamation of its message.

Accordingly I have divided it into nineteen segments, each marked by a heading which serves as a kind of short-hand guide to its character.

I Doxology vv. 1–3

This is an exordium, introducing themes central to the sūra:
The revelation God has made to the Prophet:

1 *Blessed be He who revealed the* Furqān [8] *to His servant*
that he might be a warner to all the worlds

The power and uniqueness of God:

2 *He to whom belongs dominion over the heavens and the earth*
and has not taken a son
Who has no associate in His dominion,
Who created all things,
fashioning them in proper measure

The non-entity of all other gods:

3 *They take beside Him gods – these create nothing*
being themselves created
they possess in themselves no capacity to help or harm,
they possess no power over death or life or resurrection.

God speaks of Himself as third person other, declaring Himself blessed by virtue of revealing the *Furqān* to His servant (Muḥammad) that he may be a warner to all the worlds. He tells of His dominion and power, and then of the gods taken by the unbelievers.

The language of these three verses is highly wrought, structured around a symmetric balance of antitheses. What is predicated of God is emphasized by its denial by the unbelievers. Against His strength is set the weakness of the gods they set alongside Him. He creates, they do not, they are created. He has dominion (*mulk*) over the heavens and the earth. They exercise none, having no dominion by which they might bring benefit to or ward off harm from themselves, let alone power over death, life, and resurrection.

The rhetorical effect of the passage is strengthened by parallel sentence structures that contrast what God does not do with what the unbelievers do. He does not take a son (*lam yattakhidh waladan,* v. 2); they have taken gods beside Him (*wa 'ttakhadhū ... ālihatan,* v. 2). That God should take a son is repugnant. He does not! It should be equally repugnant that they take gods beside Him. Yet they do!

The impact of such antithesis is strengthened by the balanced structure and rhythmic pulse of the verses: God *has* dominion ... He *does not* have a son ... He *does not* have an associate ... He created ... (v. 2) symmetrically juxtaposed with verse 3, telling of their gods: they create nothing ... they exercise no dominion on behalf of themselves ... they exercise no dominion over death, life, and resurrection (v. 3). The finality of this statement is emphasized by this triple beat of the ending of the verse, and the contrast of the final vowel changing from *ī* (vv. 1 and 2) to *ū*.

All these devices give a solemnity and dignity to the exordium. There are, however, other elements contributing to its power. These become apparent when the diction and motifs are heard against the background of reprises, echoes, ideas, and word forms that occur both elsewhere in the sūra and throughout the Qur'ān: variations, emphases and nuances ever-present in the minds of reciters and hearers alike. Such complementarities and relationships may be direct or oblique. An example within this doxology is the conclusion to verse 3, declaring that the gods of the unbelievers have no dominion over death, life, and resurrection. That God does have dominion over life is here affirmed by implication, as it is throughout the sūra. But it is in verse 50 that it is made explicit, and that God is celebrated as The Living, *al-Ḥayy*.

There are frequent references back to this exordium throughout the sūra. The resonances it carries of expressions of praise that resound through the Qur'ān as a whole, however, are equally numerous. The first word, *tabāraka* strikes a chord of exultation that generates a sense of awe on the two subsequent occasions on which it occurs in this sūra (vv. 10 and 61). The effect is multilayered due to the background of the occasions on which it occurs elsewhere in the Qur'ān, emphasizing or giving thanks for God's wonders and blessings. For example 'Blessed is He (*tabāraka 'l-ladhī*) in whose hand is Dominion, He having power over all things' (Q. 67:1); and 'And blessed is He (*wa tabāraka 'l-ladhī*) who has Dominion over the heavens and the earth and all that is between them' (Q. 43:85). Other examples of the use of this formula are Q. 23:14; 7:54; 40:64; 55:78.

The sense of devotional intensity is further enhanced by formulae with a parallel structure likewise exalting God, His Uniqueness and Might for the favours He has done His Prophet, that inevitably resonate along with it. Formulae such as *subḥāna* as in 'Exalted be He (*subḥāna 'l-ladhī*) who took his servant by night' (Q. 17:1), and 'So exalted be He (*fa subḥāna 'l-ladhī*) in whose hand is sovereignty' (Q. 36:83). Other examples are Q. 36:36 and Q. 43:82.

Formulae beginning with *al-ḥamd* contribute to the same effect, as 'Praise be to God to whom belongs (*al-ḥamdu li 'llāhi 'l-ladhī lahu*) what is in the heavens and what is in the earth' (Q. 34:1); and 'Praise be to God (*al-ḥamdu li'llāhi*) creator of the heavens and the earth' (Q. 7:43), and other instances such as Q. 17:111; 1:1; 10:10 *et passim*. All contribute to the grandeur and impact of the phrase *tabāraka 'l-ladhī*, both as the first words of the sūra, and the two subsequent occasions in the sūra on which it occurs.

Al-Furqān[9] doubles as the name of the sūra. It is a word of great power. Grammarians regard it as an intensive form of the verbal noun of the root *faraqa*, meaning to separate or divide. It has the sense both of the act of separating and the instrument of separation. In this context it is the latter, for the separation of good from evil and truth from error is the role of scripture, and as such of the Qur'ān *par excellence.* The word occurs on six occasions in the Qur'ān, Q. 8:29; 2:53; 2:176; 3:4; 21:48; 25:1. In most cases it signifies a scripture, i.e., a means of guidance, of separation of right from wrong, bestowed as a divine gift. In Q. 8:41, however, it signifies division, separation in a special sense, when the Battle of Badr is referred to as *Yawm al- Furqān,* when the Muslims were separated from the Meccans by victory over them. The word *Furqān* occurs only once in this sūra. But given the prominence of its position, these other attestations, the fact that it is both a name of the Qur'ān and fully rhymes with it and shares a common final long vowel with *al-Raḥmān,* it is enduringly fixed in the mind of the hearer. The association with the Battle of Badr may be a significant key element in the symbolic structure of the sūra, for a number of the individual foes of the Prophet identified in the *asbāb al-nuzūl* as referred to in it, were to be killed at or in the aftermath of that battle.[10]

'Abd has two senses: human creature, servant of God in general, and specially chosen servant as a title of honour for the prophets. Here, and on many other occasions, it designates the Prophet Muḥammad. Notable among them are the verses 'Glory be to Him who took His servant by night' (Q. 17:1) and 'Praise be to God who revealed to His servant (*'alā 'abdihi*) the Book' (Q. 18:1). And also notable is the verse referring to *Yawm al-Furqān* 'And what We revealed to Our servant (*'alā 'abdinā*) on the Day of *Furqān*' (Q. 8:41). Examples of its designation of other prophets are Job in Q. 38:44, Noah in Q. 17:3, Zakariyyā in Q. 19:2 *et passim.*

'Ālamīn likewise has a broad distribution. This word which occurs in the Qur'ān on over seventy occasions, carries the resonances of the universality of God's sovereignty throughout the book from *Sūrat al-Fātiḥa* (Q. 1) onwards.

Nadhīr, a warner, designates one of the duties of the messengers God sends to intervene in human history, ranking with other terms indicating the responsibilities of the role such as *nabī, rasūl* and *mubashshir.* It is a key word in the Qur'ān occurring over forty times. Here, its significance is heightened because it is in a prominent – final – position in the verse, carrying a rhyming long vowel.

Verse 1 then is multilayered in the richness of its associations. It is not an exaggeration to say that the principal themes of the Book resonate in it. The connotations and associations of each of these words *tabāraka, Furqān, 'abd, 'ālamīn* and *nadhīr* extend beyond the context in which they occur: they set sounding sympathetic chords elsewhere in the Qur'ān, and are imbued with a singular majesty and power that sets the groundwork for the spiritual architecture and design of the sūra.

Verse 2 is enriched in the same way by parallels and echoes from elsewhere in the Qur'ān. For example, 'and has not taken a son (*wa lam yattakhidh waladan*)' and 'has no associate in His dominion' (v. 2) is supported by *Sūrat al-Isrā'*, 'Praise be to God who has not taken a son, and has no associate in dominion (*l-ladhī lam yattakhidh waladan, wa lam yakun lahu sharīkun fi 'l-mulk'* (Q. 17:111), and in *Sūrat Maryam* 'It is not of God that He should take a son (*an yattakhidha min waladin*)' (Q. 19:35) *et passim.*

Verse 3 also has counterparts, heard sounding alongside it. For example 'and they take gods alongside Him (*wa 'ttakhadhū min dūnihi ālihatan*)' is complemented by a verse in *Sūrat Maryam* 'They have taken gods alongside God (*wa 'ttakhadhū min dūni 'llāhi ālihatan*) to be a [source of] strength for them' (Q. 19:81). The words 'They create nothing, rather they are created', has counterparts in *Sūrat Yā Sīn*, 'So exalted be He in whose hand is sovereignty over all things (*malakūtu kulli shay'in.*)' (Q. 36:83), and in *Sūrat al-Aḥqāf* 'Have you reflected on those you call on other than God. Show me what they have created (*arūnī mādhā khalaqū*) on the earth' (Q. 46:4).

The first verse, which sets the tone of the sūra, has a distinctive majesty and largeness of utterance. The opening word *tabāraka* establishes both the tone of a doxology and the atmosphere of a liturgical action of awe and praise. Together with the following two verses it forms an exordium packed with meaning, establishing the themes of God, Prophecy, and the Resurrection. The objections raised against them generate the tensions in the development of the sūra as the issues of the uniqueness of God, the truth of Muḥammad's message, and the coming of a day of resurrection are brought into confrontation by their denial.

II Objection and response vv. 4–9

The unbelievers (the implied subject of *wa 'ttakhadhū*, v. 2) put their objections to the Qur'ān and the Prophet:

4 *Those who disbelieved say*
This is nothing but a lie! He has made it up!
Others have helped him!

God responds:

5 *They perpetrate wickedness and a falsehood*
They say
It is stories of the ancients.
He has them written down, then they are dictated to him morning and evening.

God commands the Prophet:

6 *Say,*
The one who knows the secret of the heavens and the earth revealed it

saying of Himself:

He is one who pardons, is compassionate
7 *They say*
What sort of a prophet is this?
He eats, he walks through the markets.
Why isn't an angel sent to be a warner alongside him?
8 *Or a chest of treasure thrown down to him,*
or [why doesn't] he have a garden from which to eat?

They insult the Prophet's followers:

The wicked ones say
You are following one possessed

God responds:

9 *Consider how they make by-words about you*
– yet they go astray
for they can find no way [of proving you false]

Those objecting are identified first as 'those who disbelieve (*kafarū*)' (v. 4), and when they scoff at the Prophet's followers as 'the wicked ones (*al-ẓālimūn)*' (v. 8).

These insults are heard elsewhere in the Qur'an. For example in *Sūrat al-Aḥqāf,* 'And when Our clear signs are recited to them, those who disbelieve say ... "This is obvious trickery." *Idhā tutlā 'alayhim āyātunā bayyinātin, qāla 'l-ladhīna kafarū ... hādhā siḥrun mubīn* (Q. 46:7–8). There is a subtle play on the words *tutlā* (recited, Q. 46:7) telling of the recitation of God's signs, and *tumlā* (dictated, Q. 25:6), telling of the stories of the ancients allegedly dictated to the Prophet.

'Those who act wickedly keep secret counsel "Is this any other than a human being like yourselves"' – *wa asarrū 'n-najwā 'l-ladhīna ẓalamū hal hādhā illā basharun mithlukum* (Q. 21:3) in which the attempt of the evil doers to keep secret counsel is set against the knowledge of God, 'The One who knows the secret of the heavens and the earth – *al-ladhī ya'lamu 's-sirra ...*' (v. 6).

Such trans-sūra echoes and juxtapositions occur throughout the Qur'ān, each being complementary to the other. They thus have a significant function in the literary structure of the sūra, giving a stereophonic dimension to its content. Here these echoes suggest the intensity, the continuity and animus behind opposition to the Prophet, as well as the limited range of the arguments that can be brought against him.

The objections are in a naturalistic, demotic, language register that contrasts with that of the doxology with its carefully structured solemn liturgical tones. The scorn in them is communicated through the brief sense units, contemptuous in tone. In the sentence beginning *lawlā* (v. 7) it is possible to hear the sneer: 'Why isn't an angel sent down to be a warner alongside him ... or [why isn't, *lawlā*] a chest of treasure sent down to him ...or [why doesn't, *lawlā*] he have a garden from which to eat' (v. 8).

God's responses are measured and deliberate. They are given in various ways: In the first instance by an immediate denial that the Qur'ān is a lie, 'They perpetrate wickedness and a falsehood' (v. 4); in the second, by directing the Prophet how to respond, 'The One who knows the secret ... revealed it', and by the words 'Who pardons, is compassionate' (v. 6) which hint at the divine name, to take centre stage later in the sūra, when God is named as *al-Raḥmān.* In the third, (v. 7), when the Prophet's followers are said to be following one possessed, a direct answer to the questions is suspended, but words of encouragement and consolation are addressed directly to the Prophet, God telling him that He knows what the wicked ones say to his followers and assuring him that his enemies will never prove him false.

In each case God speaks without introduction. His words are identified by a break in the flow of discourse, and a sonority and authority of utterance in the language register which sets it apart from that of the unbelievers.

There is a constant variation of the pulse within and between verses. The first objection and response are in a single verse, the rebuttal following it immediately. The second objection occupies an entire verse, and likewise the response given to the Prophet to utter. The next objection, consisting of three questions occupies two verses. To this God responds, addressing the Prophet directly, with the command *unẓur* (consider) to introduce a single tautly structured verse.

There is an elaborate network of continuities between this segment, the doxology that it follows, and the segments yet to come. The words Muḥammad is commanded to utter, 'The One who knows the secret of heavens and the earth revealed it,' are complementary to 'He to whom belongs dominion over the heavens and the earth' in the doxology (v. 2). They carry an echo of *Sūrat al-Mulk*, 'Keep your thoughts secret or proclaim them, He knows what is in every breast (*wa asirrū qawlakum aw 'ijharū bihi, innahu 'alīmun bi-dhāti 'ṣ-ṣudūr*)' (Q. 67:13). Such complementarities occur throughout the Qur'ān. What has passed and what is to come have a point of reference in almost every verse.

The question the unbelievers ask about the Prophet, 'Why isn't an angel sent to be a warner (*nadhīr*) alongside him?' has a number of aspects. It is a sneer from the unbelievers confronted with Muḥammad's claim to be a warner (v. 1 *et passim*); the fact that he eats demonstrates his inferiority to angels, who do not eat; it draws attention to the futility of their imagining that an angel is needed to empower him when he has the Qur'ān, *al-Furqān*, revealed to him and is commanded, 'Wage the great struggle against them with it' (v. 52). No angel could empower him with such a weapon. At the same time, it gives a cue to the coming encounter of the unbelievers with the angels on Judgement Day, so dramatically and graphically elaborated in segment VI.

III Doxology v. 10

The final words of v. 9, '... for they can find no way [of proving you false],' introduces the next doxology:

10 *Blessed be He, who if He wills,*
can make for you better far than this,
gardens through which rivers flow
and set within them for you mansions.

The recurrence of the formulaic phrase, 'Blessed be He who ...' *tabāraka 'l-ladhī*), sets sounding again in the ear of the mind the opening words of the sūra, 'Blessed be He who revealed the *Furqān* to His servant that he might be a warner to all the worlds,' which are therefore heard as a background accompaniment to this verse. God, who as third person other, declared Himself blessed in His revealing *al-Furqān* to the Prophet (v. 1), now addresses him personally, declaring Himself blessed for He 'can make for you better far than this.' He says this to console him and to assure him that He, God, is not to be put to the test by the unbelievers. Nevertheless, He assures the Prophet that He, if He wills, can do far more for the Prophet than the Meccans demand as proof of his mission. They had asked, 'Why doesn't he have a garden?' God replies He could give him, not just a garden, but gardens through which rivers flow, with mansions set within them.

The verse then functions at two levels: as doxology with its echo of verse 1, and as consolation of the Prophet. At the same time, having referred back to the opening of the sūra, it looks ahead to the reward promised those who persevere. God is able to give the Prophet far more than the Meccans demand of him. And in the gardens and the mansions within them that He can give, is foreshadowed the palace, *al-ghurfa* (v. 75), promised to all His servants – *'ibād al-Raḥmān* – the prophets and those who conduct themselves as befits the servants of *al-Raḥmān*.

IV Excursus vv. 11–19

This segment is a continuation of God's address to the Prophet in v. 9, but is distinguished by the presentation within it of two mini-dramas: a punishment scene and a judgement scene.

The punishment scene presents the fate of those who disbelieve in the Resurrection:

> 11 *Indeed, they deny the Hour!*
> *We have prepared for whomever denies the Hour a Fire*
> 12 *When it sees them from afar off*
> *they hear its screams and cries.*
> 13 *When they are hurled, chained into a narrow space*
> *there do they cry out 'Destroy us.'*

The guardians of Hell reply:

> 14 *On that Day plead not for one destruction,*
> *plead for destruction many times over.*

Those who make up by-words about the Prophet and say the Qur'ān is a lie are those who deny the Resurrection. The sūra opened with God speaking of Himself as third person other. There is a switch (*iltifāt*) when He intervenes directly in the events, first to rebut the unbelievers, then to address the Prophet. Here, for the first time He speaks in the first person. Thus His utterance '*We* have prepared ... a Fire' (v. 11) has increased dramatic force as a warning of the punishment to be inflicted on those who deny the Hour!

The immediacy of this utterance is heightened by the personification of Hell. Even when they are still far off, Hell *sees* the unbelievers being herded towards it, and they *hear* its screams as it blazes up in anticipation of their arrival. They are hurled, chained, into the narrowest of spaces, and so they too cry out as they heard those already within it cry out when they were still at a distance.

Their pain is such that only death can give relief, and they cry out to be destroyed. But the guardians of Hell reply that one death alone will not be enough to put an end to their pains. They had better call for many deaths. Such verbal exchanges are an integral part of the dramatic character of the Qur'ān.[11]

There are other references to Hell later in the sūra. In verse 34, the evil-doers are taken there 'on their faces' (v. 34); and the *'ibād al-Raḥmān* utter the prayer text, 'Our Lord, avert from us the punishment of Hell' (v. 65).

Elsewhere in the Qur'ān are scenes of the evil-doers being escorted to Hell, the role of the guardians of Hell in taking them there, and the cries of pain. Thus in the *Sūrat al-Mulk*, 'For those who disbelieve in their Lord is the punishment of Hell. How terrible a destiny. When they are thrown into it they hear its braying as it boils up' – *li 'l-ladhīna kafarū bi rabbihim 'adhābu jahannama wa bi'sa 'l-maṣīr idhā ulqū fīhā sami'ū lahā shahīqan, wa hiya tafūru* (Q. 67:6–7).

Having presented this picture of the pains of Hell to the Meccans, God instructs the Prophet to address them:

15 *Say*
Is that better or the garden of eternity
promised to the devout,
theirs as a reward and destiny;
16 *theirs in it, all they desire, eternally,*
a promise your Lord may be called on [to keep.]

In so doing, the contrast between the destiny of the wicked and that of the devout, those who believe, is all the more striking. The garden of eternity – *jannatu 'l-khuldi* – alludes to the unbelievers' demand that the Prophet have a garden 'from which to eat' (v. 8). In verse 10, God assured him that if He so willed he could give to the Prophet not just a garden, but gardens, with mansions set within them. Here He promises the garden of eternity, *jannatu 'l-khuldi,* better than any earthly garden. In it, whatever they wish is theirs. The contrast with Hell has a certain symmetry. In the one, total constraint and agony, to be endured 'eternally' as they cry for destruction, and the scorn of the guardians of hell, telling them that one destruction will not be enough to put an end to their pains. In the other, the garden, there is amplitude and fulfillment of desires, whatever they wish for is theirs, a reward God's promise has sealed. This antithetic structure, highlighting one thing by setting it against its opposite is parallel to the antithesis so clearly presented (vv. 2 and 3) between the power of God and the non-entity of other gods in the opening doxology.

The second mini-drama presents the trial of those who have put other gods beside God. It is a Judgement Scene with God as Judge, the unbelievers as accused, and those they treated as partners of God as witnesses.

17 *The Day He assembles them*
with those they worship other than God, He will say,
'Did you lead my servants astray,
or did they wander astray [of their own will]?'
18 *They reply*
Glory be to You, we ought not to have taken
protectors other than You.

and say to God:

You gave them lee-time, as you did their forebears
[for time to repent], yet they forgot the scripture (dhikr)
and became a people who were in perdition

God addresses the accused:

19 *They have denied what you say,*
so you are unable to avert [punishment]
or obtain help.

and gives His verdict:

> *Whoever of you does wrong,*
> *We will make him taste a terrible punishment*

The dialogue is vivid, a vividness enhanced by the dramatic change of perspective. The question is directed first, not to the sinners, but to those wrongly worshipped. Did they ever ask to be treated as gods or intercessors? They deny it. They too condemn the sinners (the words put in their mouths are a pedagogical device), explaining that these have not taken advantage of the time to repent God allowed them, as He allowed it to their forebears also in vain, before disaster overwhelmed them. The verb *matta'a* – in this context 'to give lee-time' – has a significant role in the message of the Qur'ān. God is forbearing. He has been forbearing to many generations of sinners (Q. 43:29; 21:43–44; 26:205–6 *et passim*). The people of Jonah (Q. 10:98) took advantage of this lee-time but many others did not and were destroyed (as were those mentioned in verses 35–38 of this sūra). That God gives this lee-time is indicative of His mercy, and reference to it here is a cue to the presentation of God as *al-Raḥmān* in verse 26. However, though it may be long (Q. 26:205–206), this lee-time is not unlimited.

From another perspective, it is an oblique way of indicating why the punishment of the Meccans has not yet come. God has given them time to repent. But the implication is that its approach is inexorable. The Battle of Badr is not far off.

After this exchange, God addresses these sinners. Those you wrongly honoured 'have denied what you say, so you are unable to avert [punishment] or obtain help.' Here He speaks again in the first person, and addressing a wider audience, He assures punishment to whomever does wrong as these have done.

There is a subtlety in the difference in structure between the first person address here, 'Whoever of you does wrong *We* will make him taste...' – *wa man yaẓlim minkum nudhiqhu* ... – (v. 19) and 'We have prepared for whomever denies the Hour' – *a'tadnā li man kadhdhaba bi 's-sā'a* – (v. 11) the inversion from an object verb construction in the case of the one to a verb object in the case of the other sharpens the impact of the threat. The threat to make taste carries echoes of *Sūrat Ṣād* (Q. 38:8), 'Rather they have not yet tasted My punishment.'

The subject of the verb *yaẓlim* in 'Whoever of you does wrong' (v. 19) includes 'the wicked ones (*al-ẓālimūn*)' (v. 8) who tell the Prophet's followers that they are following a man possessed and are also threatened. The transformation of the root form of the verb highlights the meanings and brings out continuities at a deeper level.

Such dramatic realizations of religious concepts are a vital element in the Qur'ānic rhetoric of instruction and these two mini-dramas are classic examples of this mode of presentation. They focus on different sins: disbelief in the Resurrection, and association of creatures with God, attributing to them a power of intercession. The former tells of the punishment for this sin, the latter tells of an arraignment before judgement is passed. Such a transposition or hyperbaton adds to the drama and immediacy of the scenes presented, the pain of the punishment making its impact on the hearers before the judgement that leads to the infliction of such pain.

V Divine allocution v. 20

The following verse is structurally complex.

20 *We have never sent any messenger before you*
who did not eat or walk through the markets.
We have set some of you against others
as a test.
Can you persevere?
Your Lord is All-Seeing.

The opening of the verse is the suspended response to the objection that the Prophet 'eats, he walks through the markets' (v. 7). In the light of the two mini-dramas in the excursus, which in effect are directed against the unbelievers in verse 3 who take gods beside God, such a suspension has its literary wisdom. It serves to hold the attention and heighten expectancy.[12]

The verse, however, may fruitfully be considered from a number of other perspectives. Formally, it is a continuation of God's locution to the Prophet that began in verse 9, and may be seen as reaching a point of climax with this response.

Structurally, it has four parts, according as God shifts the direction of His address. First, He speaks to the Prophet, answering the objection that he eats and walks through the markets (v. 7). He then addresses the community as a whole, divided among themselves into believers and unbelievers, saying that this division in the community has come about because they have been put to the test. He then addresses a brief question to those who have accepted the Prophet's message, and face the hostility and taunts of the unbelievers, 'Can you persevere (*a-taṣbirūn*)?' In conclusion, He addresses again the Prophet, reassuring him, 'Your Lord is All-Seeing (*Wa kāna rabbuka baṣīran*)'. These final words may be heard as a continuation of the first words of the verse, 'We have never sent any messenger before you who did not eat or walk through the markets ... 'Your Lord is All-Seeing' [of the ways in which they react to you and the questions they put].'

The question, 'Can you persevere?' looks forward to the destiny of the devout who, at the end, will be rewarded for what they have endured (v. 75). There is a subtle emphasis on *a-taṣbirūn* because the final word of the verse *baṣīr* is a metathesis of its root, thus the one enriches the significance of the other.

These shifts of address indicate the importance of listening for speech rhythms in the movement of Qur'ānic syntax, an aid to which are the *jā'iz* pause markings after *aswāq, fitnatan* and *taṣbirūn* in the *muṣḥaf*, which indicate how the verse is recited and heard.

VI Objection and Response vv. 21–29

Here, disbelief in the resurrection and the demand for angels to be sent down are conjoined.

21 *Those who do not expect to meet Us say*
Why are not angels sent down to us,
or [why don't] we see our Lord?

God responds:

They are above themselves in arrogance.

The divine locution continues, God speaking in the first person, recounting the protestations of the unbelievers. The rhetorical level of the scorn is rising. In verse 7, the unbelievers had asked, 'Why isn't an angel sent to be a warner ...'. Now they demand not simply an angel to accompany the Prophet but the angels to be sent down to them, and to see God Himself. God's response is immediate. It impacts directly on the arrogant words of the unbelievers in the same verse, as did God's intervention when the Qur'ān was denounced as a lie in verse 5. Moreover, the weight and register of the language of the divine utterance with its measured pace and deep 'heavy' vowels contrast with that of the speech of the unbelievers in the same way. In verse 5, God's words were, 'They perpetrate wickedness and a falsehood (*fa-qad jā'ū ẓulman wa zūran*)' and here 'They are above themselves in arrogance (*fa-qadi 'stakbarū ... wa 'ataw 'utuwwan kabīran* ' (v. 21).

The divine response continues:

22 *On the day they see the angels, on that day*
there will be no welcome for the evil-doers.
[The angels] will say 'a forbidding barrier [for you].'
23 *We will visit all they have done*
and make it as scattered dust.
24 *Those of the Garden*
on that day will have a better abode
and fairer place of noon-day repose.

The evil-doers [here, all those who reject the Prophet, those who disbelieve (*kafarū*), those who deny (*kadhdhabū*), and the wicked ones (*al-ẓālimūn*) are subsumed under the term 'the evil-doers' (*al-mujrimīn*)] will indeed see the angels on the Judgement Day they deny but will receive no welcome from them.

The pericope is one of many that shares in and establishes the luminous presence of angels in the Qur'ān and outlines their various roles: taking the souls of humankind in sleep or in death, punishing them in hell, welcoming them into heaven, or participating in the overwhelming event of Judgement Day, as in *Sūrat al-Ḥāqqa* 'When a single blast is sounded on the trumpet, and earth and its mountains are lifted up and cast down, on that Day the Event will befall; the sky will split, for on that day it will be rent apart, angels will be on all sides of it, and on that day eight [of them] will bear the throne of your Lord', (Q. 69:15) and in *Sūrat al-Baqara*: 'Do they expect other than that God and the angels should come to them in the shadows of the clouds' (Q. 2:210, and 8:50; 13:23; 16:32; 21:103). The phrase *ḥijran maḥjūran* is understood as uttered by the angels, qualifying the phrase *lā bushrā*. Any welcome (*bushrā*) for them is prohibited. As though to say 'God has made *bushran* for you *ḥarām*.' The rhyme between *bushrā* and *maḥjūrā(n)* intensifies the effect. The phrase occurs again later in the sūra (v. 53). God then, speaking in the first person declares: 'We will reduce all they have done to scattered dust.'[13]

Alongside this account of the destiny of those who receive no welcome from the angels is set a vignette of those in the Garden, who on that day will have a better dwelling place (*mustaqarr*) and a better abode of noon-day repose. The word *mustaqarr*, suggesting stability of the blessed, may be seen as in a chiasmic relation to *habā'an manthūran*, the scattered dust of the works of those who disbelieve. The picture of the pain and disarray of the wicked is thus heightened by the contrasting image of the bliss of those in heaven.

When they see the angels

25 *It will be the day when the sky is riven with clouds*
and the angels descend in ranks;
26 *true dominion on that day belongs to the Merciful*
it will be a day grievous for the unbelievers.

The picture is succinct but vivid. It is filled with the harmonics of other Judgement Day scenes of the Qur'ān, telling of when the heavens and the earth are split, the angels descend, and peoples are brought to judgement; for example, 'When the sun is extinguished and the stars are darkened, when the mountains are moved and the pregnant she-camels neglected' (Q. 81:1–3) and 'When the heavens are split, when they harken to their Lord and receive their due' (Q. 84:1–2).

The phrase 'dominion (*mulk*) on that day belongs to the Merciful' awakes the resonances of verse 2 'He to whom belongs dominion over the heavens and the earth' and 'Who has no associate in His dominion' (v. 2) together with the account of the non-entity of those treated as associates to God, and brings the verse to a climax when God is presented as *al-Raḥmān* (the Merciful), the name foreshadowed earlier when God describes Himself as *ghafūran raḥīman* – Forgiving, Compassionate (v. 6). The dominating position of this name is realized by the rhythmic structure of the verse, but equally by the final rhyme shared with *al-Furqān*, the name of the sūra, and occupying so prominent a position in verse 1.

A paradox adds to the tension within the verse. God is *al-Raḥmān*, the Merciful. Nevertheless on that day, the state of those who disbelieve will be grievous (*'asīran*), a word all the more evocative because it is a metathesis of *sa'īran* (v. 11), the raging fire that is ravenous for them. The tension between the two words, *raḥmān* and *sa'īran*, drawn tight by the vowels they share, is not to be resolved until the phrase 'except those who repent' (*illā man tāba*) v. 70, towards the end of the sūra.

In the next pericope is an instance of another feature of the rhetoric of the Qur'ān, a shift of focus from the general to the particular (and vice-versa). Thus in the following verses there is a shift of focus away from the destiny of the unbelievers in general to that of an individual evil-doer,

27 *a day on which the wicked one will bite his fingers while saying*
28 *Would that my path had been with the Messenger,*
Woe is me! would that I had not taken such a one as a companion
29 *He led me astray from Guidance after it had come to me*

And God comments:

The devil is ever ready to abandon Man.

The wicked one (*al-ẓālim*) who speaks biting his fingers, regretting that he had been led astray by an unbelieving friend, is one of *al-ẓālimūn* (v. 8), one of those who act wickedly (*man yaẓlim*), (v. 19). In the tradition, although grammatically *al-ẓālim* is understood as a generic, he is also identified as 'Uqba, a man led astray by his unbelieving friend Ubayy, one of the enemies of the Prophet who denounced the Qur'ān as a lie (v. 4). 'Uqba is in Hell thanks to Ubayy, who now can do nothing to help him.'[14]

The moral of the incident is clear, whether the words 'The devil is ever ready to abandon Man' are understood as specific in their referentiality, *al-Shayṭān* being understood as 'Uqba, and *al-Insān* as Ubayy, or as generics – the Devil and Mankind respectively.

There are two further points in this extended discourse. One is the prominent role given to angels as instruments of the exercise of God's power, a response to the unbelievers who believed they could be called on by them to testify at their demand; the other is the constant repetition of the word day: the *day* on which they see the angels ... on that *day*... (v. 22); the *day* on which the sky is riven (v. 25), dominion on that *day*, ... it will be a *day* grievous ... (v. 26), a *day* on which the wicked one ... (v. 27), the word day recurring like an insistent drum beat, warning of the imminent and inexorable coming of the Day of Resurrection, the Day in which the evil ones refuse to believe.

VII Objection and Response vv. 30–34

Verse 30 introduces a different perspective. A complaint from the Prophet.

30 *The Messenger said*
My Lord, my people treat this Qur'ān
as something to be cast aside

God responds:

31 *Thus have We appointed to every prophet*
an enemy from among the evil-doers

assuring him:

Your Lord is sufficient as a Guide and a Helper

The objection:

32 *Those who disbelieve say*
Why isn't the Qur'ān revealed to him as a whole?

God replies:

It is in this wise that by it We strengthen your heart,
as We recite it clearly

He promises:

33 *They will not come up with any by-word about you*
without Our coming to you with the truth
and the best of explanations.

and assures him:

34 *Those [who disbelieve] will be brought*
on their faces to Hell.
They are in the worst of places and on a path
the most astray

The Prophet's complaint that the Qur'ān is rejected – *mahjūran,* may be heard as a cry of pain, resulting from the cumulative effect of continuous insults. The unbelievers have been saying of the Qur'ān, 'This is nothing but a lie! He has made it up! Others have helped him . . .!' (v. 4) It is 'stories of the ancients' (v. 4).

The word rendered as 'rejected', *mahjūran* has powerful resonances. It is evocative of the phrase *ḥijran maḥjūran* (vv. 22 and 53) and carries the connotations of the absoluteness and finality to which the phrase gives expression: the evil-doers will receive no welcome (v. 22), the salt and fresh waters will never intermingle (v. 53). The pejorative associations of the sound *ūr* in words such as *būran* (v. 18) *zūran* (vv. 4 and 72) and *kufūran* (v. 50) *ḥijran maḥjūran* (v. 22) and the echo of *thubūran* (v. 13) suggest the contempt with which the unbelievers regard it, and so reject it utterly.

The divine response echoes that given in verse 20. Just as every prophet God has sent eats and walks through the markets; so, every prophet has an enemy from among the evil-doers. The word rendered as 'an enemy', *'aduwwan,* suggests an individual, the individual identified in the tradition is Abū Jahl.[15]

The question he puts, 'Why isn't the Qur'ān revealed to him as a whole?' is raised a number of times in the Qur'ān, as in *Sūrat al-Isrā'* '... We have divided it into sections that you might recite it to humankind slowly and deliberately (... *faraqnāhu li taqra'ahu 'alā 'n-nāsi 'alā mukthin wa nazzalnāhu tanzīlan*)' (Q. 17:106) *et passim.*

It is introduced by the question marker *lawlā* as were the previous questions in 'Why isn't an angel sent down to be a warner alongside him? ... (*lawlā unzila ilayhi malakun*?)' (vv. 7–8). The divine response impacts immediately on the objection, as it does also in verses 4 and 21. It is followed by the assurance that anything the unbelievers say about the Prophet, God will answer, echoing 'Consider the by-words they make up about you' in verse 9.

That those who circulate such by-words be brought to Hell (*jahannam*) on their faces, the most demeaning of postures, is a fitting punishment for the arrogance of their demand that angels be sent down to them and they see their Lord (v. 21), when God says of them 'They are above themselves in arrogance.'

This final ground for objection to the Qur'ān, given after the statement that the Qur'ān is rejected, is another instance of a hyperbaton. As in the other instances, it heightens the dramatic effect of the events presented. The rejection of the Qur'ān creates a tension. How could it be so? Because it is not revealed as a whole! Prompting the implicit question, 'Why isn't the Qur'ān revealed to him as a whole?' The response, 'that by it We strengthen your heart,' – God speaking in the first person– is thereby all the more effective.

VIII Divine allocution vv. 35–42

Structurally, this is a continuation of God's first person address. He tells the Prophet of past prophets, and how they, like him, were rejected by the peoples to whom they were sent.

35 *We gave Moses the Book*
We set with him his brother Aaron as a helper,
36 *then We said*
Go the two of you to those who denied Our Signs!
We destroyed them utterly!
37 *[Tell of] the people of Noah*
When they denied the messengers
We drowned them.
We prepared a painful punishment for the evil-doers.
38 *[Tell of] 'Ād and Thamūd and those of al-Rass*
and the many generations between then and now.
39 *Each of them We made a by-word,*
Each of them We shattered utterly.
40 *They have passed by the township*
on which was rained the rain of death.
Have they not seen it [time and again]?
Yet still they have no hope of a resurrection!

Seven prophets are mentioned in this pericope: three of them identified by name, three by the people to whom they were sent, and the last, Lot, by the fate his people suffered, forming an outline of salvation history to demonstrate the essential and integral continuity of the experience of the prophets. The presentation of these figures and their rejection is brief and allusive, yet sufficient to awaken in the mind of the hearers more detailed accounts of them elsewhere in the Qur'ān. The excursus on former prophets in addition to being an assurance to him is also a consolation. As he suffers, so they suffered from rejection by their people.

The people to whom Moses and Aaron were sent 'denied (*kadhdhabū*) Our signs'; the people to whom Noah was sent 'denied (*kadhdhabū*) the messengers'; the peoples to whom Hūd, Shu'ayb, Ṣāliḥ and Lot were sent, did so likewise. The prophets were treated as liars because they preached the Resurrection, just as do the people to whom Muḥammad is sent. All had refused to believe that a Day of Retribution would overwhelm them. God said of them, 'We prepared a painful punishment for the evil-doers' (v. 37), and that punishment befell them.

Through Muḥammad, God warns those of Muḥammad's time, 'Those who disbelieved (*kafarū*)', (v. 4), 'the wicked ones (*al-ẓālimūn*)', (v. 8); 'those who deny (*kadhdhabū*) the Hour [Resurrection]', (v. 11), and 'those who do not expect to meet Us (*lā yarjūna liqā'anā*)', (v. 21), that 'We have prepared for whomever denies the Hour a Fire' (v. 11). The peoples before them had been destroyed. Destruction will surely come upon them if they continue to reject their Prophet.

The ruins of the township of Lot (v. 40), which the Meccans can see for themselves on their journeyings, provide the axis for a shift of perspective from the past back to the present. Muḥammad's contemporaries have passed by these ruins (v. 40), and so must know that such punishments took place. Yet still they do not hope for a Resurrection, (*lā yarjūna nushūran*) and continue to reject the Prophet's teaching. This pericope has a close counterpart in *Sūrat Qāf* 'The people of Noah disbelieved [in the Resurrection], and those of al-Rass, and 'Ād and Pharaoh and the brethren of Lot (Q. 50:13 – 16); and 'Were We wearied by the first creation? Yet they are in doubt of a new creation' (Q. 50:15).

The review of these great heroes of salvation history is of striking rhetorical power. One aspect of its style is the reiteration of the first person pronoun 'We' as God speaks: *We* gave Moses ... (v. 35); *We* said ... *We* destroyed ...(v. 36); *We* drowned them ...*We* prepared a painful punishment ...(v. 37); *We* made them a by-word ... *We* shattered utterly (v. 39), which rings through the passage with ringing anvil-like strokes.

His statement, 'Each of them We made a by-word (*amthāl*)', turns the tables on those who make a by-word (*mathal*) of the Prophet. It is the divine response to 'they make by-words (*amthāl*) about you' (v. 9) and 'They will not come up with by-words (*bi mathalin*) about you' (v. 33). God has made each of these past peoples a by-word for the punishment that befell them for their rejection of their prophets, and the Meccans too who reject the Prophet will become such a by-word.

The rhythmic pulse contributes to the unity and coherence of the pericope. This is particularly evident in verse 40. Even a casual listener can feel the strong triple beat of 'They have passed by the township ... have they not *seen* it [time and again]? Yet still they have no hope of a resurrection' as the Arabic words *wa laqad ataw 'alā 'l-qarya ... a-fa-lam yakūnu yarawnahā? bal kānū lā yarjūna nushūran* replicate in a naturalistic manner rhythms of the spoken language.

IX Objection and response vv. 41–44

God's locution to Muḥammad continues, but with a shift of focus that puts the Prophet and his experience of rejection centre stage. God reminds him of the contempt with which the Meccans treat him.

41 *Whenever they see you*
they take you as but a joke
'Is this the one God sent as a messenger?
42 *Indeed he almost led us astray from our gods.*
Had we not persevered in our devotion to them
[we would have abandoned them]'

God assures him:

They will find out when they see the punishment
the path of whom is more astray

and asks him:

43 *Have you reflected on the one who takes his whim as his god?*
Could you then be a guardian over him?
44 *Or do you think the greater part of them*
to listen or understand?
They are but like the beasts!
Rather they are more astray.

This locution to the Prophet represents another point of climax on a line of tension that began with the first insult (v. 4), and was tightened with the reference to Moses (v. 25). It is realized by a shift from the past back to the present, from the experience of prophets and communities over a period of centuries to the immediacy and particularity of the experience of Muḥammad as an individual, taken as a joke.

Pari passu with this shift of focus from the community of past messengers to the individual Messenger, the Prophet Muḥammad, is a shift from the peoples who rejected them to an individual among those who scoff at Muḥammad, 'Thus have We appointed to every prophet an enemy (*'aduwwan*)', (v. 31) one of those who 'take [him] as but a joke', and utters the sneer 'Had we not persevered in our devotion to them, [we would have followed him]'. In the tradition he is identified as Abū Jahl.[16]

Abū Jahl has an established place in the demonology of Islam. This pericope gives a vivid thumb-nail sketch of a group of the unbelievers laughing at the Prophet as Abū Jahl taunts him with these words. The ellipted apodosis of the clause introduced by the conditional *lawlā,* 'Had we not persevered ... [we would have abandoned them]' had there been a period of silence allowed it, would have added to the scorn, but the divine response cuts in directly mid-verse, effectively excluding the ellipted phrase from forming in the hearers' minds. As in the other instances (vv. 4 and 21) the divine response cuts in directly mid-verse, likewise distinguished by the sonority of its utterance, 'They will find out when they see the punishment (*wa sawfa ya'lamūna ḥīna yarawna 'l-'adhāb*)' (v. 42), for God knows what he is suffering.

And just as the earlier divine response turned the by-words of the Prophet's enemies against themselves, so, here, Abū Jahl's words 'Indeed he almost led us astray (*in kāda la-yuḍillunā*)', are turned against him when confronted by God's words saying they will find out 'the path of whom is more astray' (*man aḍallu sabīlan*).

The case of Abū Jahl is followed by that of another individual, identified as al-Ḥārith b. Qays al-Sahmī.[17] It was said of him, 'Whenever he found anything he liked, he worshipped it,' the intention of which is to make him appear ridiculous. How could the Prophet be responsible for such a one?

From these two individuals, the malevolent Abū Jahl and the foolish al-Ḥārith, the focus of the locution turns again to the Meccan community.

On the basis of his experience with these two, can the Prophet expect that the majority of them will listen or understand? 'They are but like the beasts! Rather they are more astray' (*bal hum aḍallu sabīlan*) (v. 44).

The expression, 'They are more astray' once again refers back to Abū Jahl's words 'Indeed he almost led us astray (*in kāda la-yuḍillunā.*) ...'. He and 'So-and So' (v. 28) and the greater part of the Meccans are like the beasts. 'Rather they are more astray.' They are like the beasts in their lack of reason. However, the image is complemented and clarified by the verse in *Sūrat al-Naḥl* 'Before God bows whatever is in the earth of the beasts and angels, they are not proud' (Q. 16:49). The beasts and angels do sin: angels because it is of their nature, and the beasts because they are without the gift of reason and so serve God as their God-given instinct guides them. The Meccans then are the more astray – *aḍallu* – in failing to learn from the ruined township, and refusing to believe. There is an insistent drum-like beat in this repetition of the various forms of the verb *ḍalla.*

These two verses (vv. 43 and 44) reveal a concern on the Prophet's part that he may be failing in his mission, and assure him he is not responsible for those who reject him. They express the same anxiety that God addresses in *Sūrat al-Shu'arā'*, 'Perhaps you are tormenting yourself that they do not believe'- *la'allaka bākhi'un nafsaka allā yakūnū mu'minīn* (Q. 26:3), and the consolation He gives him in *Sūrat 'Abasa*, 'It is not your responsibility that they do not purify themselves [of unbelief]' – *wa mā 'alayka allā yazzakkā* (Q. 80:7). Is he to expect (at this stage in his mission) that the majority of his hearers will listen and understand? Such verses show the Prophet's anxiety and his self-scrutiny. Such a revelation of his humanity is a significant aspect of the literary dimension of the sūra.

In this pericope is yet another instance of the role of a key word in establishing the unity of the passage and highlighting a significant theme. Here the root *ra'ā, see*, reflect on, or a word expressing a related idea, has such a function. The sequence begins in the last verse of the previous segment with the words 'Have they not *seen* it [time and again]', (v. 40) referring to the Meccans passing by the ruins of the township of Lot's people. The sight should give them reason to believe. The word is a cue for the shift of focus to the Prophet in verse 41. Yet 'whenever they *see* you (*wa idhā ra'awka*)...' (v. 41) i.e., whenever they *see* the Prophet, they take him as a joke. However, 'when they *see* the punishment (*ḥīna yarawna 'l-'adhāba*) ...' (v. 42), 'Have you seen (reflected on *a-ra'ayta*) ...' (v. 43) 'Do you think (*am taḥsab*)...'(a synonym of *ra'ā*) (v. 44), and then 'have you not seen (reflected on *a-lam tara*) ...' (v. 45), set up a new emphasis in the pericope, the power of God over nature.

There has been a progression from the unbelievers seeing the ruins, their seeing the Prophet and mocking him, the Prophet seeing and reflecting on them, the group and the individuals who reject him, and then his seeing and reflecting on the power of God demonstrated in His moving the shade.

This leads to an image of striking beauty.

45 *Have you not reflected on how your Lord*
stretched out the shade.
Had He wished, He could have held it still.
Then We appointed the sun to guide it,
Then We drew it gently towards Us.

The lexical meaning of *al-ẓill* is at first sight simple, a shadow cast by the sun. Shade, however, is a divine blessing, and the word is rich in its connotations: protection from the heat of the sun, comfort, peace, contentment and delight in this world (Q. 26:24; 4:57; 16:81) and in the hereafter (Q. 56:30; 13:35; 36:56). It is soothing, and there is a parallel between the physical comfort that shade gives and the balm of God's words applied to the pain inflicted on the Prophet by the Meccans' sarcasm. Shade represents an ideal: a mid-point between total darkness and dazzling brightness.[18]

The image is complemented by a verse from *Sūrat al-Naḥl*, 'Have they not seen (reflected on) the things God has created. Their shadows turn from the right and the left, as they pay homage to God, they are humble' (Q. 48:16), telling how the movement of the shadow is a symbol of obedience to God.

In this context, however, *ẓill* is to be understood not simply as the shadow of an individual object, or an area of quietude and peace, though it has these connotations, but something on a much broader scale. In the exegetic tradition it is glossed as *ṣafar*, the yellowish half-light of dawn, when the eastern sky has brightened but the sun not yet risen and shade still lies over the earth. At that time, looking westwards, the first rays of the sun can be seen to strike the highest point of the horizon, and from that moment on, the whole mass of shade gradually but inexorably rolls back as the sun rises. This word *ẓill* then creates an image of cosmic grandeur, showing the power of God on a vast scale over the processes of nature.

In first introducing this phenomenon, inviting the Prophet to reflect on it, God refers to Himself as third person other. ' ... your Lord stretched out the shade. Had He wished He could have held it still.' Then He switches to the first person, 'Then We appointed the sun to guide it,' and the effect is electrifying. The words are no longer an account of God's power but God Himself, telling of His exercise of that power and how all creation is in His charge.

The final word of the verse 'gently' (*yasīran*) (v. 46), telling how God moves the shade is profoundly significative, indicating the gentle sureness with which He exercises His power. The phonetic similarity of *yasīran,* gently, to *'asīran,* grievous, (v. 26.) and *sa'īran,* Fire (v. 11), words describing the destiny of the unbelievers, heightens the contrast between their meanings. It suggests that though His power is inexorable and His punishment severe, His mercy is close to those who repent. It is a subtle indication that He is *al-Raḥmān.*

The Prophet then is invited to see in the shade an image of divine power over the cosmos, and to consider how much greater is God's power over recalcitrant human beings. Men may refuse to listen to God; but nature, so much vaster than humankind, obeys him. In the shift of focus from wicked individuals to this demonstration of God's power, there is a dramatic broadening of focus, showing how puny indeed are Abū Jahl and al-Ḥārith, thus bringing solace to Muḥammad.

X Doxology vv. 47–50

The shade, in obedience to the sun, follows it in its day-long journey into night, and so vanishes, making way for another gift.

47 *He it is who made the night for you as a garment,*
sleep as rest
and made the day for stirring abroad.

It is an echo of *Sūrat al-An'ām* 'He it is who gathers you [to Himself] at night, knowing what you have done during the day, then He arouses you during the day, so that the term decreed for you be fulfilled. Then to Him is your return.' (Q. 6:60). Night is a time for rest. The following day again is a time for stirring abroad (*nushūran*). The word *nushūran* (v. 47) has two levels of meaning. In this context where day is contrasted with night, its primary meaning is 'stirring abroad' and day-time activities in general. But equally it signifies the Resurrection, as in 'Yet still they have no hope of a resurrection' (*nushūran*), (v. 40) and *passim* throughout the Qur'ān. As such it cues a double level of meaning in the other blessings yet to be told:

48 *He it is who sent the winds from His presence*
heralding His mercy.
We sent from the sky purifying water
49 *that We might bring to life with it a dead land*
that We might give it as drink
to the multitude of beasts and humankind
We have created.
50 *We have dispersed it among them that they might reflect,*
Yet most of humankind have refused
[everything] but ungratefulness.

'His mercy' is a metaphor for the rain that the winds bear and distribute. The pericope (v. 48) opens with God speaking of Himself as third person other, but in mid-verse there is a switch to Him speaking in the first person, thus 'activating' the second meaning of *nushūran.* '*We* sent from the sky purifying water'. This switch has a function analogous to that in mid-verse 45, telling of His control over the shade, 'Had He wished, He could have held it still. Then *We* appointed ...'.

That switch highlighted God's power, this one emphasizes both the gifts He gives and the reason for His bestowing them on beast and humankind (*an'āman wa anāsiyya*) alike (v. 49), so that humankind may reflect (*yadhdhakkarū*). Yet despite the miracle of the rain God sends to restore the dead earth to life, proof of His power to resurrect the dead, most of humankind refuse to reflect on this miracle and will not believe, being ungrateful disbelieving. The final verse echoes vv. 41–44, in which the unbelievers, led by Abū Jahl, scoff at the Prophet, and God comforts him by asking whether he thinks that the greater part of them will listen [to him] or understand [what he is saying].

God's words are uttered with ringing force: *We* sent ... purifying water (v. 48), that *We* might bring to life ..., that *We* might give it as drink ..., *We* have created (v. 49), *We* have dispersed it (v. 50), reiterating the word *We* with the same anvil-like strokes referred to earlier in verses 35–39, yet still they refuse to reflect. The consolation to the Prophet is that it is not only him they reject, but that despite all that God bestows, the movement of the shade, night, day, and the revival of the dead earth, they reject Him too, refusing to reflect on what He has shown them. The word rendered as reflect, *yadhdhakkarū*, points ahead to the qualities of the servants of *al-Raḥmān*. They are those who wish to reflect (v. 73).

XI Allocution

Kufūran, as the final word in verse 50, has a prominent position, and so cues this allocution to the Prophet in verses 51–52. It is brief and almost parenthetic.

51 *Had We wished*
We would have sent a warner to every township.
52 *Do not then give in to the unbelievers*
Wage the great struggle against them with it

There is a shift of focus from the general category of those who reject everything but ungratefulness, *kufūran*, to a particular individual, the Prophet, the object of their hostility. The unbelievers are many; their objections are many, likewise the townships where the message is to be preached. The greater part of humankind will not listen or understand. Is the task beyond any one man?

Here too the Qur'ān reveals something of the personal psychology of the Prophet. He is hurt by the pain of rejection and the number of problems he has to face. He grieves that so many refuse to accept God's message. Therefore God tells him: He could indeed have sent a warner to every township had He willed. But He did not. Accordingly, the Prophet is not to give in to the unbelievers, but to wage the great struggle against them 'with it', i.e., the Qur'ān, the very Qur'ān which they have described as 'a lie' (v. 4) and 'stories of the ancients' (v. 5).

There is a close interplay between the words *furqān* and *qur'ān*. The word *qur'ān* carries the resonances of *furqān* from verse 1 of the sūra wherever it is mentioned or referred to. As a name for the Qur'ān, it highlights its role as the instrument of separation (*furqān*) between believers and unbelievers, just as did the Day of *al-Furqān*, (Q. 8:41), the Battle of Badr. *Jāhid-hum* then, may be heard as bearing the connotation of this great encounter.

The word *nadhīr* (warner) too, brings to the consciousness of the hearers the universalistic vocation of Muḥammad announced in verse 1. In that verse, God appointed His servant a warner to all the worlds. Here, He declares that had He willed He could have sent a warner to every township, thereby stressing the momentousness of the act of divine will that made Muḥammad a Prophet.

Such a consideration draws attention to a parallelism between 'Had He wished, He could have held it [the shade] still' (v. 45) and 'Had We wished We could have sent a messenger to every township' (v. 51). It puts on an equal footing God's will to determine the movement of sun, moon, and stars, and His will to send one prophet to all the townships as part of His eternal wisdom.

XII Doxology vv. 53–55

The doxology continues, God speaking of Himself as third person other:

53 *It is He who let loose the two great waters*
this one sweet and fresh,
The other salt and bitter
and set between the two of them a barrier forbidding [any breaching of it];
54 *It is he who created humankind from [seminal] fluid,*
making it related through consanguinity and affinity,
your Lord being All-Powerful.
55 *Yet they worship alongside Him*
what can neither help them nor harm them,
and the unbeliever is an aid [to Satan] against his Lord.

God praises His power over the two great masses of water, the sweet and the salt. He has let them flow forth and encounter each other, but any breaching of the barrier between them is unthinkable. The phrase *ḥijran maḥjūran* here means that any breaching of this barrier is prohibited, prohibited as any welcome by the angels of those who disbelieve in the resurrection in v. 22 where the same phrase occurs.

The opening of the doxology may be seen as a re-presentation of verses 19–20 from Q. 55, *Sūrat al-Raḥmān,* differing only in the final phrase of the verse, *ḥijran maḥjūran* in place of *lā yabghiyān,* 'they do not come to a meeting point'. They at once evoke the name of that sūra, a cue to the coming climax of this sūra, where God is celebrated as *al-Raḥmān.*

God has the same power over the greatest masses of water as he has over the tiniest and can concentrate life in a drop of seminal fluid, from which are generated male and female. This demonstrates that He is All-Powerful, *qadīr,* by virtue of which He has 'dominion over the heavens and the earth' (v. 2). His dispositioning of this dominion is equally illustrated in the doxology of verses 45–50 in which He draws back the shade, bestows night and sleep, disperses the rain, as it is in His control over the masses of water great and small (vv. 53–54). Even so, the unbelievers worship alongside Him deities that can neither help nor harm them (v. 55), deities that cannot bring help to or divert harm even from themselves (v. 3).

Among these unbelievers is the individual, the disbeliever (*al-kāfir*) identified as Abū Jahl,[19] who continues to be an aid [to Satan] by his hostility to the Prophet. This shift of focus continues this basic rhythm of the Qur'ān in moving from great to small – from the great masses of water juxtaposed to the drop of seminal fluid, from the general, the community of unbelievers to the particular individual Abū Jahl.

God's power in segments XI and XII is shown as constantly active. From one perspective there is a movement from shade at early dawn, to night, sleep and rest, and back to day-time and stirring abroad, against the background of winds bringing life-giving rain to the dead earth as a sign of the Resurrection.

In them can be discerned a fecund image built from the elements of rain-drop, sea, and semen. Out of them one can uncover two parallel evidences of God's creative power, rain and the Resurrection, and semen and procreation. In the sequential ordering of events is again a hyperbaton. The proof of the second creation, i.e., the Resurrection demonstrated by the effect of rain on the dry earth, is set before the miracle of the first creation, i.e., conception and birth.

XIII Allocution to the Prophet vv. 56–58

The reference to the disbeliever *al-kāfir* (identified as Abū Jahl) in verse 55, itself an echo of *kufūran* (v. 50), cues this locution.

56 *We sent you only as a herald of good tidings, and a warner*
57 *Declare I ask nothing of you for it other than that whoever wishes should take a path to his Lord.*
58 *Place your trust in the Living One*
Who dies not, celebrate His praise.

In this address to the Prophet, God's utterance switches again to the first person. He defines the Prophet's mission, tells him what to say, and then what to do. As for the first, the word *mubashshir,* 'herald of good tidings,' complements his role as a *nadhīr,* a warner, announced in verse 1, for which God declares himself blessed. In addition, *mubashshir* has the same root as *bushrā* (v. 48) 'heralding', thus there is an association between the winds heralding God's mercy – the rain – and the Prophet bringing good tidings.

The Prophet is to tell the Meccans that the only recompense he is to ask for his preaching is that whoever of his hearers so wishes should take a path to his Lord. This needs to be heard against other occurrences of this verbal root: 'They take beside Him gods' (*wa 'ttakhadhū min dūnihi ālihatan.*) (v. 3); 'They take you as nothing but a joke' (*in yattakhidhūnaka illā huzuwan*) (v. 41); 'One who takes his whim as a god' (*mani 'ttakhadha ilāhan hawāhu*) (v. 43); contrasting with and highlighting with brilliant clarity the injunction: ' ... take a path to his Lord' (*yattakhidha ilā rabbihi sabīlan*) (v. 57). Finally, it tells what he is to do: Place his trust in the Living One and celebrate His praise.

The divine name *al-Ḥayy* (v. 58) dominates this pericope. Earlier (v. 54), God was honoured as *qadīr,* All-Powerful, in respect of His dominion over all things great and small. In verse 6 He was described as *ghafūr raḥīm* Forgiving, Compassionate. At the end of this verse He is designated *khabīr,* Fully-Knowing. Such names and attributes recur again and again throughout the Qur'ān in a veritable symphonic chorus, and the utterance of these names and attributes prepares the way for the name *al-Raḥmān* to sound as a pedal note that sustains its resonance for the remainder of the sūra.

XIV Doxology vv. 58–59

This segment begins at the mid-point of verse 58.

58 *He is fully knowing of the sins of His servants*
59 *He who created the heavens and the earth and what is between*
them in six days, then took His place on the throne, the Merciful,
so ask one fully knowing of Him.

In the previous segment the Prophet was commanded to celebrate God's praise (v. 58). This pericope continues with reasons why He should so be praised: because He is fully aware of the sins of His servants – *'ibādihi* – those who reject His Prophet, here the word *'abd* having its general meaning; because He created the heavens and the earth, then took His place on the throne; because He is the Merciful. So, if you wish to know all this about Him, ask one who is knowing of Him.

Al-Ḥayy (v. 58) may be heard as the subject of the verb 'created' in'who created the heavens and the earth'(v. 59). These words bring to mind the doxology of verse 2, praising God 'to whom belongs dominion over the heavens and the earth ... who created all things,' complementing it with the phrase 'in six days'. The phrase 'in six days' is a significant detail which awakes echoes of these words which occur so often throughout the Qur'ān in accounts of God as Creator. Together with 'then took His place on the throne' it leads to the centre and climax of the verse proclaiming God as *al-Raḥmān.*

There is an exquisite subtlety in the occurrence of the word *khabīr,* Fully Knowing, at the beginning of the segment (i.e., end of v. 58) telling of God's awareness of the sins of His servants, and at the close of this doxology, where the Prophet is singled out as the one to be asked of Him, he being fully aware [of God's Mercy]. The juxtaposition of God as *khabīr* of Man, and a man (the Prophet) being *khabīr* of God is an ending to the verse with a striking spiritual impact.

XV Objection v. 60

The celebration of God as *al-Raḥmān* provokes the final objection put by the unbelievers:

60 *When it is said to them*
'Bow before the Merciful',
they reply
'And what is the Merciful?
Are We to worship what you tell us?'

And God says of them:

It makes them ever more fugitive [from the truth].

These words of the unbelievers interrupt the doxology.

'And what is *al-Raḥmān*?' (v. 60) is the last of the series of objections to the Prophet which began with 'This is nothing but a lie!' (v. 4). In the question 'Are we to worship what you tell us' (v. 60) can be heard the sneer in the words addressed to Muḥammad, 'What sort of a prophet is this?' (v. 7) and the arrogance and contempt of Pharaoh's question to Moses, 'And what is the Lord of the universe' (*wa mā rabbu 'l-'ālamīn?*) (Q. 26:23).

In such questions are revealed the mentality, the attitude and the prejudices of those who accuse Muḥammad of making up the Qur'ān and peddling the stories of ancient times he has had written down; who complain that he eats and walks through the market as an ordinary human being and assert that his followers are possessed (v. 8). Why should they worship what he tells them? That God should be called *al-Raḥmān* is yet another reason to reject him.

XVI Doxology vv. 61–62

61 *Blessed be He who placed in the sky the constellations,*
and placed among them a lamp and a moon radiating light
62 *He it is who appointed the alternation of night and day*
for whomever so wishes to reflect or to be thankful.

This, the final doxology in the sūra, begins with the phrase that opened it – *tabāraka 'l-ladhī...*, here adding to God's celebration of the revelation of *al-Furqān* to the Prophet (v. 1) and His capacity to give the Prophet more than his opponents could ever imagine(v. 10), a celebration of God's power in establishing these mighty signs, the constellations with the sun and the moon, and ordering the alternation of night and day in comparison with which man is insignificant.[20]

Such signs were established that whoever so willed might reflect (*li man arāda an yadhdhakkara*) or be thankful (*shukūran*). This account of God's power exercised so that men might reflect is a variation of verse 50, in which God tells that He dispersed the rain among humankind reviving the dead earth so that they may reflect (*li yadhdhakkarū*), and realize the reality of the Resurrection. Yet the greater part of humankind refuse [to do so], being but ungrateful (*illā kufūran*) the antonym conceptually of *shukūran* and structurally of the same form. Between these two pericopes is the adjuration to the Prophet that his only recompense for preaching is that whoever wishes take a path to his Lord (v. 57).

And 'the alternation of night and day' (v. 62) is a variation of v. 47 'It is He who made the night for you as a garment, sleep as rest, and made the day for stirring abroad' with its *double-entendre* of the Resurrection.

XVII Response: The servants of al-Raḥmān vv. 63–74

The response to the question 'And what is *al-Raḥmān*?'

63 *The servants of al-Raḥmān (the Merciful) are*
those who walk humbly on the earth
and when the ignorant address them say 'Peace'.
64 *[They are] those who pass the night in prostration*
or standing before their Lord,
65 *[They are] those who say:*
Our Lord, avert from us the punishment of Hell
its punishment is eternal torment
66 *Indeed it is evil as an abode and dwelling place*
67 *[They are] those who in spending*
are neither ostentatious nor miserly,
between these two is a clear moderation.

68 *[They are] those who call on no other god beside God*
and slay none under God's protection
except with just cause,
and do not commit adultery.
Whoever does this will face the penalty.
69 *Punishment will be doubled for him*
on the Day of Resurrection,
he will be punished for ever, despised,
70 *– except for those who repent and believe*
and do good deeds.
For these, God will replace their evil deeds
with good ones
God is Forgiving, Compassionate
71 *Whoever repents and does good deeds*
it is he who has turned to God without reserve.
72 *[They are] those who do not look on evil deeds*
and if they pass by vanities,
do so with dignity.
73 *[They are] those, who, when the signs of their Lord*
are told them, do not bear themselves as deaf and blind before them,
74 *[They are] those who say*
Our Lord, give us contentment with our wives and posterity,
make of us an example for the devout.

The answer to the question is not given immediately. Rather it is developed step by step in the wake of an account of the qualities and the conduct defining His servants in relation to each other and to Him and His response to them, coming to a climax in verse 70, when the meaning of *al-Raḥmān* is defined. The preceding verses set out eight qualities by which the *'ibād al-Raḥmān* may be identified and they summate the ethical principles of Islam. These qualities are presented as an organic part of the sūra, engaged with it from its beginning. They realize and give specificity to its moral and ethical implication by a variety of devices, including the reiteration of keywords, phonetic similarities, parallelisms and networks of association and allusions.

As for the phrase *'ibād al-Raḥmān* : *'ibād* is the plural of *'abd,* a key word in v. 1 where God declares Himself blessed because He had revealed the Qur'ān to His servant (*'abdihi*), the Prophet Muḥammad, the servant of *al-Raḥmān par excellence.* But every servant, if he wills, may follow the example of the Prophet and be one of those who walk humbly on the earth, responding to insults with the word 'Peace.' This was the answer of the Prophet when the unbelievers said of the Qur'ān 'This is nothing but a lie,' and complained that he was like themselves in that he ate and walked (*yamshī*) (v. 8) through the markets. The common verb in both places *yamshī* (v. 8) and *yamshūna* (v. 63) is suggestive of this association. The servants of *al-Raḥmān* pray during the night, as did the Prophet. They pray to be delivered from the pains of Hell. They say: 'Our Lord, avert from us the punishment of Hell. Indeed it is evil as an abode and dwelling place.' The punishment of Hell is vividly described earlier in the sūra. It is a fire (*sa'īran,* v. 11), it is narrow (*ḍayyiqan,* v. 13), the state of the unbelievers in it is grievous (*'asīran,* v. 26). In it the unbeliever bites his fingers (v. 27). The intensity of the pain is heightened by the contrastive parallel structures telling of those in heaven in verse 24, 'they will have a better abode (*mustaqarr*) and fairer place of noon-day repose,' and v. 76, 'it is fair as an abode (*mustaqarr*) and dwelling place.'

They are moderate in all they do. They do not call on or worship other gods beside God as do the unbelievers (vv. 3 and 55).

They avoid the great sins of unlawful killing and adultery, sins which deserve the most severe punishment. The punishment for such sins is reiterated in *Sūrat al-Nisā'* (Q. 4) 'One who kills a believer by design, his penalty is hell, to be in it eternally. God will be angry with him, and prepare for him a terrible punishment' (Q. 4:93). But those who repent, believe, and do good deeds, the evil they have done will be changed to good, God being Forgiving and Compassionate, (*ghafūran raḥīman*) (vv. 70 and 6).

And this is the answer to the question 'And what is *al-Raḥmān*?' One who is Forgiving and Compassionate. The same definition is given in *Sūrat al-Zumar* (Q. 39), '... Do not despair of the mercy of God. God indeed will forgive all sins. He is indeed the Forgiving, the Compassionate (*Innahu huwa 'l-ghafūru 'r-raḥīm*) (Q. 39:53).

They 'do not look on evil deeds and if they pass by vanities ...' (v. 72) has a counterpart in *Sūrat Qaṣaṣ* 'When they hear vanity, they turn aside from it, and say, "We have our way of conduct and you have yours"' (Q. 28:55). But in Paradise, when they receive their reward, there will be no vanity, as it is put in *Sūrat Maryam* (Q. 19), 'They will not hear in it any vanity, but only [the greeting of] peace' (Q. 19:62)

When the signs of God are recited to them, they do not bear themselves as deaf and blind before them, behaving as do those who cannot be expected to listen or understand (v. 44).[21] Rather, their response is as described in *Sūrat Maryam* (Q. 19), 'When the signs of *al-Raḥmān* are recited to them, they fall prostrate and in tears (*wa idhā tutlā 'alayhim āyātu 'r-Raḥmāni kharrū sujjadan wa bukiyyan*) (Q. 19:58).[22]

XVIII Rewards to the servants of al-Raḥmān vv. 75–76

75 *These will be rewarded with a palace*
for their perseverance.
They will be greeted in it with the greeting of peace
76 *eternally, it is beauteous as an abode and dwelling place*

The palace, *al-ghurfa*, epitomizes the reward they are to receive. This is an echo of God's assurance that He can give the Prophet not simply a garden, but gardens with mansions (*quṣūr*) within them (v. 10); and to achieve which God asked them 'Can you persevere?' (*a-taṣbirūna?*) (v. 20) The palaces that they are to receive are also told of in *Sūrat Saba'* (Q. 34), 'They will have a twofold reward for what they have done, in palaces (*ghurufāt*) will they be secure' (Q. 34:37) and in *Sūrat al-Zumar* (Q. 39) 'But those who have been devout to their Lord, theirs will be palaces (*ghurafun*) over them, palaces built [for them], by which rivers flow' (Q. 39:20).

They receive this reward because they have persevered through difficulties and persecution, having given a positive answer to God's question, 'Can you persevere' (v. 20). The reward and victory they have received for this perseverance is also echoed in *Sūrat al-Mu'minūn* (Q. 22), 'Indeed today have I rewarded them for their perseverance (*bimā ṣabarū*). They indeed are the victors' (Q. 22:111).

They receive the greeting of peace (*salām*) because of the response of *salām* they gave to those who insulted them. This is the greeting (*bushran*) (v. 22) they receive from the angels who welcome them, the greeting denied to those who refused to believe in the Resurrection and demanded angels be sent down to prove Muḥammad's mission.

This promised reward to the servants of *al-Raḥmān* is reiterated in *Sūrat Maryam* (Q. 19), 'The Garden of Eden that the Merciful has promised His servants' (*wa'ada 'r-Raḥmānu 'ibādahu*) (Q. 19:61).

XIX Final Adjuration v. 77

77 *Say,*

My Lord will have no concern for you
Without your calling on Him,
for you disbelieved in Him!
and [without your call]
an ineluctable punishment will await [you].

This is a final appeal to the unbelievers: to all who rejected the Prophet, disbelieved his message, and denied the coming of Judgement Day as much as a warning to those who have sinned. They can still repent. Their evil deeds can be replaced by good deeds. They too can be among the *'ibād al-Raḥmān*; but since they have disbelieved, God will not be ready to accept them unless they call on him in prayer. The prayers that they are to utter are the two prayer texts in segment XVII, 'Our Lord, avert from us the punishment of Hell' (v. 65) and 'Our Lord, give us contentment with our wives and posterity, make of us an example to the devout' (v. 74).

A discussion of this kind cannot be based on a *tabula rasa* approach to the Qur'ān. Any exploration of a sūra is conditioned, consciously or unconsciously, by the explorers' encounter with the Qur'ān as a whole in the light of the exegetical tradition that has been their guide.

My understanding of the sūra is largely shaped by the *tafsīr* of Muqātil: his glosses, the trans-sūra echoes and complementarities he adduces, and the material taken from *asbāb al-nuzūl* that provide anecdotal information and on the basis of which he identifies individuals. Muqātil's work is significant, not because his understanding and overall perception of the sūra is necessarily more authentic than that of any later *mufassir*, but because it offers a frame of reference for understanding the Book which allows a wide range of options in the exploration of its dynamics, and lays the ground for the continuing development of mainstream Sunnī exegesis.

The literary structure of the sūra is not reducible to a formula, but is by no means inchoate. It presents a number of themes susceptible of differing degrees of emphasis: the majesty and power of God; the Meccan rejection of the Prophet, the pain this rejection causes him, the comfort that God gives him; the contrast between heaven and hell, and the presentation of *al-Raḥmān* as a name of God equal in status to Allāh, expressing an essential aspect of His nature.

These themes are presented through a number of voices which express the altercations and debates central to the sūra, and carry them to a point at which they are either resolved or transcended. They are set within the framework established by the opening and close of the sūra, and then distributed among a mosaic of situations and perspectives that cohere, though not structured according to conventional expectations of a narrative or time-line.

One element shaping the internal organization of the sūra is the dialect of challenge and response. The effect of the objections raised against the Prophet is cumulative, and the total impact may be realized when each is taken out of its individual context, and they are run together seriatim: This (the Qur'ān) is nothing but a lie; he has made it up. Others have helped him. It is tales of the ancients; he has them written down, then they are recited to him morning and evening (vv. 4–5). What sort of a Prophet is this? He eats and walks through the markets. Why isn't an angel sent down with him? [Why isn't] a treasure chest thrown down to him, or [why isn't] he given a garden? You are following nothing but a man possessed (vv. 7–8). Why aren't the angels sent down to us? [Why don't]we see our Lord? (v. 21) Why isn't the Qur'ān revealed to him as a whole? (v. 32) Is this the one God has sent as a messenger? He almost led us astray from our gods. If we hadn't persevered with them [we would have abandoned them](vv. 41–42). What is *al-Raḥmān*? Are we to worship what you tell us? (v. 60)

Those raising these objections are, in general, given group identities: Those who disbelieve (*kafarū*, vv. 4, 32); the wicked ones (*al-ẓālimūn*, v. 8), those who act wickedly (*man yaẓlim*, v. 19); those who have no hope of meeting Us (v. 21), who have no hope of the Resurrection (40); those who deny (*kadhdhabū*) the Hour (v. 11), and the signs of God (v. 36). As a class, they are evil-doers (*mujrimīn*, vv. 23 and 31).

Certain individuals, however, are singled out, though not by name: the wicked one (*al-ẓālim*, v. 27), So-and-So (*fulān*, v. 28), the disbeliever (*al-kāfir*, v. 55), and one who makes his whim into a god (v. 56).

Muqātil, and the tradition generally, identify these individuals. Thus one of the disbelievers who says that the Qur'ān is 'nothing but a lie' is al-Naḍr b. al-Ḥārith who names a 'gang of three' as helpers of the Prophet in compiling it.[23] Of those who 'have no hope of meeting Us' (v. 21), who ask for the angels to be sent down to them, or to see their Lord, Muqātil singles out 'Abd Allāh b. Umayya and al-Walīd b. al-Mughīra.[24]

Abū Jahl was one of the bitterest enemies of the Prophet. It is he who asks 'Why isn't the Qur'ān revealed all at once?' (v. 32); he who treats the Prophet as a figure of fun, and of whom God says, 'He will find out who is the more astray when he discovers the punishment in the world to come' (v. 42); he of whom God says to Muḥammad, 'We have appointed an enemy to every prophet' (v. 31). It is Abū Jahl who is referred to as *al-kāfir*, the disbeliever (v. 55), who is an aid to the unbelievers and who insolently asks, 'And what is *al-Raḥmān* ? Are we to worship what you tell us?' (v. 60) And the individual who treats his whim as a god and who, when he liked something, worshipped it, is al-Ḥārith b. Qays.[25]

These identifications are part of the meaning of the sūra in the sense that they contribute to a definition of its form and establish its relation to a social reality, providing a kind of hinterland to the speaking parts of the drama. They heighten the dramatic character of the discourse by telling us: This is how it was; these are the individuals, for whom and for the like of whom God says, 'We have prepared for them a Fire' (v. 11).

They have been handed down with the *muṣḥaf*, and are so closely associated with it as to be felt part of its meaning. They serve to clarify shifts of addressee. Thus, for example, once the question 'Can you persevere?' (*a-taṣbirūn*, v. 20) is heard as addressed to the disciples of the Prophet, such as Bilāl and Khabbāb b. Aratt, persecuted by the Meccans, the structure of this verse and the complexities of its levels of meaning are clear and fixed in the mind.[26] The identification of the wicked one (*al-ẓālim*) biting his fingers as 'Uqba, led away from the Prophet by his friend Ubayy, sets up a vignette of an incident in the life of the Prophet.

The fact that such individuals have become icons of good and evil, demonized or canonized within the tradition, add to the immediacy and vividness of the Qur'ānic message, with or against whom the hearers can identify or measure themselves.

It is not relevant in this context whether such identifications are part of history as it happened or literary devices. In any case these are not mutually exclusive. Certainly they have a literary function, for they serve to articulate the dramatic structure of the sūra, involve the hearer in the conflicts that are occurring, and clarify the syntactic relationships between word groupings in the verses. But they serve to concretize the situations, and so make possible the superimposition on them of a universalistic dimension.

These identifications highlight the humanity of the Prophet. He is shown as a person. Those accepting or rejecting his message are persons. The exchanges between them occurred in a place, Mecca, and at a particular time. And this knowledge of them as persons serves to generate dramatic vignettes packed with tension.

The dialectic of challenge and response, the challenges of the unbelievers and divine responses to them alike, are set within a lattice-work of doxologies, the first of which opens the sūra. The distribution of the others is indicated in the headings given above to segmental divisions of the sūra. In these doxologies, God declares Himself blessed for revealing the *Furqān* to His servant (v. 1) and for His power to bestow on the Prophet better than the unbelievers demand of him (v. 10). He celebrates His gift of night and day, the winds carrying the rain to bring to life the dead land and give drink to beast and humankind (vv. 47 – 49), His power over the great waters and the barrier set between them and His creation of humankind from seminal fluid (vv. 53–55), His knowledge of the sins of His servants, His creation of the heavens and the earth and all between them in six days (vv. 58–59), and finally, His placing in the sky the constellations, the sun and the moon, and appointing the alternation of night and day (vv. 61–62).

When heard against the language register of the doxologies and divine responses to objections raised against the Prophet, the distinctive register of the words of the unbelievers is immediately recognizable. The lightness of movement, the 'naturalistic' not to say demotic character of their discourse expressing their contempt for the Prophet contrasts with the sonority and dignity of God's words when speaking as God, with their broadness of utterance and their majesty of cadence.

There are a number of other features that characterize the discourse of the sūra, some of which have already been discussed in detail. One is the intensity generated by the reiteration of key words to emphasize a theme or drive home a point. An example is the repetition of the word for angel (*malak*) across a number of verses (and segments). The unbelievers demand that an *angel* be sent to accompany the Prophet (v. 7), they ask why are not *angels* sent down to them (v. 21). They are told that the day on which they see the *angels*, the *angels* [understood] will have no welcome for them (v. 22); when the skies are riven, the *angels* will descend in ranks

(v. 25). The Qur'ānic words hammer relentlessly at the Meccan expectation that the Prophet needs the support of an angel; that the angels be at their bidding; and firmly place them at the angels' mercy. Other such sequences have already been referred to: the word for day (vv. 22–30), the pronoun We (vv. 35–39 and vv. 48, 49, 50), the word for 'go astray' (vv. 41–44) the verb see/reflect (vv. 40, 41, 42, 43, 44, and 45). Each of these sequences has its own dramatic power and acoustic emphasis.

Attention has also been drawn to the electrifying and dramatic effect of the switches (*iltifāt*) from God speaking of Himself as third person other to speaking in the first person on His own authority (vv. 11, 19, 45, 48, 55–56).

Yet another feature, equally important, is the strong, more deliberate movement of rhythmic pulse created by the expansion and contraction of focus already referred to. Examples already given are the shifts from the community of prophets and those to whom they were sent (vv. 35–39) to the individual Prophet, Muḥammad; from the mass of unbelievers to the individual Abū Jahl; from the divine power over the winds and the rain and the great masses of water to the tiny sperm from which men and women are generated; from the foolishness of an individual such as al-Ḥārith b. Qays al-Sahmī, who takes any of his whims as a god, to the divine power exercised on a cosmic scale in drawing back the shade.

From an aesthetic point of view, this image of the movement of the shade over the vast tracts of earth in the tremulous half-light of early morning is breath-taking. It offers a challenge to the hearer or reader of the words to look at the phenomenon from a strategic position, to watch the shade as it rolls back eastwards and understand the power behind its movement and God's control over it.

All these elements contribute to the power of the sūra, which is realized by an elaborate interlocking of relationships between the dramatis personae, of theme words, motifs and images and which have their power through their relationship with each other, enhanced by echoes from elsewhere in the Qur'ān. Together they present the universalistic, timeless message that goes beyond the individuals who serve as the circumstances for the revelation of the divine logia. And they have a prime goal: to draw the hearer into the events and the situations the sūra portrays; to make him or her an eyewitness of them; to share the pain the Prophet feels at his rejection and to feel indignation at the scorn he endures; in fact, to participate in this intense drama of the confrontation between the evil-doers and the Prophet.

Two general remarks may conclude this 'exploration' of the sūra. One is that since the Qur'ānic canon is now complete, the sūra's reference points extend to the Book as a whole and are not limited to the time and circumstance of the revelation of any pericope. Thus the sūra looks forward to the migration to Medina, the Battle of Badr and beyond, as much as to the beginning of the mission of the Prophet. The listener to the divine words thus knows more of the individuals identified in it as enemies of the Prophet and their fate than they themselves knew at the moment of revelation. Thus there is a strong element of dramatic irony as a didactic element in the divine words. Abū Jahl who asked insolently, 'Why isn't the Qur'ān revealed to him as a whole?' (v. 32), and 'What is *al-Raḥmān*?' (v. 60), and sneered at the Prophet, saying, 'He almost led us astray from our gods' (v. 42), was killed at Badr. Al-Naḍr, to whom is attributed the words 'This is nothing but a lie' (v. 4) and 'Uqba (v. 27), who was seduced from following the Prophet by his friend Ubayy were taken prisoners at Badr, and subsequently executed.[27]

Badr, then, is to be seen as the punishment that the Meccan enemies of the Prophet were sure would never come upon them, because God had given them lee-time, as He had to those before them – the peoples of Moses and Aaron, Noah, Hūd, Ṣāliḥ and Lot (vv. 35 – 39). As these had become a by-word for the punishment they received and as the Meccans had made the Prophet a by-word, so at Badr the tables were turned, and they, the wicked ones, were made a by-word at Badr. Badr brought them death and the judgement of hell so graphically described (vv. 11–14).

The other remark has to do with the significance of *al-Furqān*, and again the concept of a lee-time to allow sinners an opportunity to repent. A dialectic between belief and disbelief is a core element in the structure of the sūra, and *al-Furqān* is the instrument by which truth is separated from error and defeats it. This dialectic, however, can be resolved. As for sinners, they can repent, and God as *al-Raḥmān* can exercise an act of mercy, He being 'Forgiving, Compassionate' (v. 6). Muqātil, in drawing attention to the repentance of Waḥshī, who killed Ḥamzah, the Prophet's uncle at the Battle of Uḥud, points out that his sins might be expected to test God's mercy to the limit. But he was forgiven.[28]

Thus those who are put to the test for their faith in the Prophet must persevere. Those who persecuted them, treated the Prophet as a joke (v. 41), and rejected the Qur'ān (v. 30) may repent. Muḥammad, by waging 'the great struggle against them with it' (v. 52) opens the way for reconciliation through repentance. Yet this involves two sides: God and man. God is knowing (*khabīr*) of men's sins. The Prophet is knowing (*khabīr*) of God's mercy (vv. 58–59). There is a reciprocity, a literary as well as a spiritual equation involved. God will not turn to them unless they turn to Him. As the sūra concludes (v. 77):

Say,
My Lord will have no concern for you
Without your calling [on Him],
for you disbelieved [in Him!]
and [without your call]
an ineluctable punishment [will await you].

NOTES

1 As listed in George Sale, *The Koran Translated into English from the Original Arabic* (London and New York: Frederick Warne and Co., n.d), xi–xiv (Numerous reprints).

2 Régis Blachère, *Le Coran, Traduction selon un essai de reclassement des sourates* (Paris: Maisonneuve & Co, 1949), 2: xv.

3 'Abdallāh Maḥmūd Shiḥāta, ed., *Tafsīr Muqātil ibn Sulaymān* (Cairo: al-Hay'a al-Miṣriyya al-'Āmma li 'l-Kitāb, 1984), 3:223–43.

4 Bayḍāwī, *Anwār al-Tanzīl wa Asrār al-Ta'wīl* (Beirut: Mu'assasat Sha'bān li 'l-Nashr wa 'l-Tawzī', n.d.), 4:100.

5 Sayyid Quṭb, *Fī Ẓilāl al-Qur'ān* (Cairo: Dār al-Shurūq, 1402/1982), 5:2543–582.

6 For a discussion of altercation as a literary feature of the Qur'ān, see F. Leemhuis, "A Koranic Contest Poem in Sūrat al-Ṣāffāt," in ed. G.J. Reinink and H.L.J. Vanstiphout, *Dispute Poems and Dialogues in the Ancient and Medieval Near East* (Leuven: Departement Orientalistiek: Uitgeverij Peeters, 1991), Orientalia Lovaniensia Analecta series 42, 165–77.

7 For a useful outline of Muqātil's use of *asbāb al-nuzūl*, see John Wansbrough, *Quranic Studies* (Oxford: Oxford University Press, 1977), London Oriental Series 31, 141. For a more detailed study of Muqātil, see Paul Nwyia, *Exégèse coranique et langage mystique* (Beirut: Dar el-Machreq, Recherches Série 1: Pensée Arabe et Musulmane, Tome xlix, 1970), 25–34.

8 *Furqān* is often rendered 'Criterion'. Since on the one hand this word has a number of unsatisfactory connotations, and on the other *al-Furqān* has the status of a proper name, it is left untranslated. The translation of the sūra in this essay is mine as well as other citations from the Qur'ān.

9 For a discussion of the significances and distribution of *Furqān* in the Qur'ān, see Paret's entry in EI^2 s.v. In the light of this sūra, it seems inappropriate to take *Furqān* primarily as a calque of an Aramaic word, in the semantics of which the Arabic root *faraqa* is simply 'another element'.

10 This point is to be taken up later and in the conclusion.

11 See Leemhuis, "Koranic Contest."

12 Bell regards this verse out of place, due to an error in copying. See Richard Bell, *The Qur'ān, Translated, with A Critical Re-arrangement of the Surahs* (Edinburgh: T.& T. Clark, 1939), 2:345–47.

13 The impermanence of even the good deeds of the unbelievers is referred to in Ibn Isḥāq's *sīra*.. See A. Guillaume, *The Life of Muhammad* (London, New York and Toronto: Oxford University Press, 1955), 142.

14 The story of 'Uqba shamed into insulting the Prophet and leaving his company is given in Guillaume, *Life*, 164–5.

15 In Muqātil's *Tafsīr*, 3:233, this verse is said to be revealed specifically apropos of Abū Jahl. The event is referred to in Guillaume, *Life*, 140–41. For further details on Abū Jahl, see Guillaume, *Life*, by index, (listed Jahl, abū).

16 Muqātil identifies Abū Jahl as the speaker of these words, *Tafsīr*, 3:235.

17 Identified by Muqātil, *Tafsīr*, 3:235–36.

18 The notion is exquisitely summated by Fakhr al-Dīn al-Rāzī in *al-Tafsīr al-Kabīr* (Beirut: Dār al-Kutub al-'Ilmiyya, n.d.), 24:88.

19 Identified by Muqātil, *Tafsīr*, 3:238.

20 For example: *Sūrat Yā Sīn*, 'Does not He who created the heavens and the earth have the power to recreate the like of them' (Q. 36:81).

21 In the *sīra*, the unbelievers are reported as saying in mockery, 'Our hearts are veiled, we do not understand what you say. There is a load in our ears so we cannot hear what you say ... '. See Guillaume, *Life*, 143.

22 See the account of the weeping of the Negus and the bishops in Abyssinia on hearing the recitation of *Sūrat Maryam,* in Guillaume, *Life,* 152.
23 Muqātil, *Tafsīr,* 3:226–27.
24 Muqātil, *Tafsīr,* 3:230–31.
25 Muqātil, *Tafsīr,* 3:235–36.
26 Muqātil, *Tafsīr,* 3:230.
27 Muqātil, *Tafsīr,* 3:232–33. See also W. Montgomery Watt, *Muḥammad at Medina* (Karachi, Oxford, New York, Delhi: Oxford University Press, 1981), 14.
28 Muqātil, *Tafsīr,* 3:241.

Chapter 10

The Enchantment of Reading: Sound, Meaning, and Expression in *Sūrat al-ʿĀdiyāt*

Soraya M. Hajjaji-Jarrah

Thumma naẓar, thumma ʿabasa wa basar, thumma adbara wa ʾstakbar, fa-qāla in hādhā illā siḥrun yuʾthar.[1]

These compendious verses describe with remarkable precision the pagan Meccans' stance toward the Qur'ānic *ʿArabiyya*:[2] a paradox of interlocked rejection and enchantment. In a milieu dominated by the power of the oral word, their haughty unwillingness to admit (*istakbar*) its divine source was precisely because they innately recognized its superiority in terms of style and content and hence its enthralling potentialities. Alarmed by such extraordinary arresting power, the Meccans described the Qur'ān, as the above verse testifies, as being sorcery inherited from predecessors. More frequently, however, the Meccans expressed their repudiation by labeling the Qur'ān as being poetry or the incantation of a soothsayer (*sajʿ kāhin*). Fired by such remarks, the Qur'ān emphatically rejects every possibility that it may be in any way the utterances of a *kāhin* or a *shāʿir*: Q. 69:41–42; 52:29–30; 37:36; 36:69;[3] for these remarks devalue the origins of the Qur'ān by attributing them to demonic beings that are not greater than a *jinn* or a *shayṭān*.

Despite all claims to the contrary by several Muslim scholars, many Qur'ānic sūras do possess the style of pre-Islamic and early Islamic *sajʿ*.[4] The similarities in structure and style between *sajʿ al-kuhhān* and a considerable section of the Qur'ānic revelation, particularly during the Meccan period, are conspicuous. Both are marked by short phrases, conjuration of natural phenomena, and recurrence of end-rhymes. But what stunned the early Arabs was the displacement of the Arabian *sajʿ* into a new context. In this setting, all the shared characteristics are borne by the Qur'ān to effectually underscore and support its new value system. It was the interplay between style, structure, sound, and sense of the Qur'ānic *ʿArabiyya* that caused an "explosion" in the minds of the early

Arabs. *Sūrat al-ʿĀdiyāt* (Q. 100) offers an excellent example of how the Qur'ānic *'Arabiyya* brings forth a dazzling assembly of word meaning and sound defying the conventions of both the Arabian *saj*ʿ and the literary rules of classical Arabic literature.[5] It represents the persuasive, arresting construction, pervasive rhythm, and important message of the Qur'ānic *'Arabiyya* which has selected and expressed these materials in just this way.

In attempting to elucidate, in this article, some of the components of the Qur'ānic distinct literary and aesthetic dimensions, as well as its world view, my approach to the sūra is determinate within the boundaries of studying the Qur'ān for its own sake. Without delving into the complex arenas of philology and syntax and without a priori theological premises, my treatment of the sūra is undertaken within what Boullata calls studying the Qur'ān "for itself and as a literary text, a scripture having its own referential system, and independently of any other consideration."[6] It follows, then, that the Qur'ānic intertextual resonances of the verses and their expressions constitute the most important measuring rod of this study. In other words, the Qur'ān is present *in toto* throughout the discussion.

However, this article goes beyond the boundaries of verses and expressions, intertextual echoes and reverberations. The prelude to the main part of the discussion offers a succession of verses from six different sūras held here to be developing a single subject or a sequential narrative (Q. 97:5; 77:1–5; 51:1–4; 79:1–5; 100:1–11; 37:1–3; 8–9; 165–166; 182). It is noteworthy, however, that my construction of the connections that bind certain verses in these different sūras is not based on the Islamic tradition regarding the chronological order of the sūras.[7] It is rather founded upon the verses' repetitive quality of an identical style and mode of discourse. Moreover, the verses' running rhythmic structure supports a swift flowing set of images that share a particular eschatological tone, as we shall see, which binds them further together.

Before engaging in the study, there is yet another important issue to be addressed. Since the vitality and rhetorical devices of the Qur'ānic *'Arabiyya* make their fullest impact through the auditory experience, the role of the spoken word here is imperative. Consequently, the discussion is built on the basis of oral recitation of *Sūrat al-ʿĀdiyāt,* for this was the manner in which it was originally presented by Muḥammad to the Meccans. I am not thinking here of *al-tajwīd* art of recitation, through which the Qur'ānic verses are read in accordance with established rules of pronunciation and intonation. I am rather thinking of oral reading where the emotive impact of the Qur'ānic discourse and of its intense images is transmitted in the dynamics of the reader's voice.[8] Additionally, since the impulse of alliteration constitutes an important segment in the Qur'ānic *'Arabiyya*'s auditory rhetorical repertoire, the pausal form (*al-waqf*) at the end-rhymes of the verses has a crucial importance. Indeed I am thinking, here, of the oral presentation of *saj'*, for even though reliable historical data is lacking, there is little doubt in my mind that the Prophet delivered the revelation to the Meccans in a *saj'* mode of oral recitation.[9] The importance of both the oral reading of the Qur'ānic *'Arabiyya* as well as the pausal form for the terminal rhymes of its verses will become clear in the course of the discussion.

"*Salāmun hiya ḥattā maṭla'i 'l-fajr.*"[10] Thus the Qur'ān concludes its revelation sūra par excellence (*Sūrat al-Qadr,* Q. 97) with a sense of threatening evil to follow the onset of dawn. An outbreak of some type and other forms of unexpected upheavals are alluded to in this verse, particularly in its final word, *al-fajr* (dawn), ending the *salām* (peace) of *Laylat al-Qadr* (The Night of Power).[11]

Assuming a sacred power, the Qur'ānic *fajr,* here, marks both the termination and the beginning of what Sells calls the Qur'ān's second and third key moments: Revelation and *Yawm al-Dīn* respectively.[12] The Qur'ānic accounts of *Yawm al-Dīn* (Judgment Day), however, are preceded by powerful images with a haunting beauty announcing the anarchy and alienation of man's physical world and the end of temporal time. These images declare the commencement of *Yawm al-Qiyāma,* the Day of Resurrection, which is succeeded by the Judgment Day.

Three introductory clusters of verses of three sūras condense the sublime reality of *Yawm al-Qiyāma,* and convey images of the upheaval implied by the Qur'ānic *fajr:* Q. 77: 1–5; 51: 1–4; 79: 1–5. In vigorous, intense, and short rhyming phrases, these verses give a vision of unidentified female agents (*fā'ilāt*) with unfettered energy. These *fā'ilāt* are pervasively cryptic and, for the most part, stubbornly resist identification.[13] Nevertheless, their impetuous movements and the connotations of some of their terms impose the sense of the natural world's exodus from its state of order, and the arrival of the cataclysm of *al-Qiyāma.*[14]

Allusions to powerful tortuous winds, precipitation of some kind, thunderstorms, and aimlessly fleeing animals demonstrate, through the verses, the beginning of the upheaval. The natural world, in these verses, appears to have been transformed into a mysterious alienating force. It seems to separate itself from being subservient to man and recaptures the essential dimensions of its existence: an *āya* (sign) of the divine command.

As the drama of *al-Qiyāma* unfolds throughout the three sūras, the introductory verses of *Sūrat al-Ṣāffāt* (Q. 37) announce the beginning of the Judgment Day (*Yawm al-Dīn*): Q. 37: 1–3. The vigorously moving *fā'ilāt* of the preceding introductory clusters of verses are replaced, in this sūra, by female agents with a stationary might. They are *al-ṣāffāt,* the forces of God, protecting the celestial council, registering the triumph of the divine promise, and chanting praise to God, *rabb al-'ālamīn.* In between the above tableau of the beginning of the cosmic upheavals of *Yawm al-Qiyāma* and the awesome panorama of the convening divine tribunal, *Sūrat al-'Ādiyāt*

(Q. 100) offers a condensed period of transition. Its few verses give a link between *Yawm al-Qiyāma* and *Yawm al-Dīn.*

Sūrat al-ʿĀdiyāt (Q. 100)

> *Wa 'l-ʿādiyāti ḍabḥan* (1) *fa 'l-mūriyāti qadḥan* (2) *fa 'l-mughīrāti ṣubḥan* (3) *fa-atharna bihi naqʿan* (4) *fa-wasaṭna bihi jamʿan* (5) *Inna 'l-insāna li-rabbihi la-kanūd* (6) *wa innahu ʿalā dhālika la-shahīd* (7) *wa innahu li-ḥubbi 'l-khayri la-shadīd* (8) *A-fa-lā yaʿalamu idhā buʿthira mā fī 'l-qubūr* (9) *wa ḥuṣṣila mā fī 'ṣ-ṣudūr?* (10) *Inna rabbahum bihim yawma'idhin la-khabīr.* (11).

The Sūra of *al-ʿĀdiyāt*[15]

> By the runners *ḍabḥan* (1) the strikers of *qadḥan* (2) and the raiders *ṣubḥan* (3) with which they roused up *naqʿan* (4) and cleaved with it the centre of a *jamʿan* (5) Surely man is ungrateful to his Lord (6) and to that He/he is indeed a witness (7) And intense is His/his love for the good (8) Knows he not when what is in the tombs is plundered (9) and what is in the breasts is extracted? (10) Verily, of them, on that Day, their Lord is the All-Knower (11).

There is almost a consensus among past and contemporary Muslim commentators that the female agents (*al-fāʿilāt*), depicted in the five introductory verses of this sūra, refer to a flock of horses whose riders are carrying out a raid (*ghazwa*) or a defensive attack (*jihād*), surprising the enemy in the morning. According to these commentaries the divine voice swears solemnly by the image of the charging horses that man,[16] (*al-insān*), who is tenacious (*shadīd*) in his intense love of worldly possessions, and hence avaricious, is ungrateful to his bountiful God. Such grasping man who shows no gratitude, the commentaries postulate, seems not only to be unaware that he will bear witness to his own ingratitude, on the Day of Judgment; he also ignores the fact that this dark side of his nature will be revealed, then, by the Almighty God, the All-Knower.[17]

Undoubtedly, the import of a *ghazwa* is present in the introductory five verses of the sūra. It is particularly clear in the term *al-mughīrāt* in v. 3, and in the sparse allusion to a raid in v. 5: *fa-wasaṭna bihi jamʿan.* However, to give the sūra a temporarily defined reading, in which the image of the introductory verses is merely assigned the role of a divine oath and the following verses are designated as the apodosis of the oath (*jawāb al-qasam*), is what Sells calls a "taming of the text."[18] It is a "subordination" of the Qur'ānic *ʿArabiyya* to the conventions of the atomism of the *tafsīr* genre and the rhetoric and grammar of classical Arabic literature. For even though the reading of these exegetes is syntactically correct and reduces, to a large degree, the ambiguity and inconsistency of the introductory profane image with the rest of the sūra, it obliterates its compelling literary drama and hence refracts its arresting enchantment. Furthermore such commentaries reduce the sūra's quasi-narrative to the level of near redundance by deleting its semantic relevance to the rest of the sūra.

Sūrat al-ʿĀdiyāt is fortified, as it were, with a wealth of the rhetorical features of the Qur'ānic *'Arabiyya*. Its quasi-narrative is dramatic and sparse, where details are at a bare minimum. The shifts in topic, tense, and locale, in the sūra decisively obliterate any relation between the sūra and any locale or historical time. Indeed these shifts presumably fragment the sūra. However, the specific arrangement, emphasis, and rendering of its literary materials, as will become evident, tie the sūra together and maintain its inner coherence.

At a preliminary reading, the profane introductory section of the sūra (vv. 1–5) does appear redundant and inconsistent with the spiritual purpose of the sūra. However, its intratextual conceptual links and intertextual resonances lend it striking eschatological colours, which renders a symbolic reading of this section compelling. For the continuation of the narrative in vv. 9–10 with its images of a violent sudden eruption of tombs and coercive plunder and rending of humans makes the eschatological significance of the sūra's introduction an irresistible logic. Furthermore, while on a first encounter the unit of vv. 6–8 appears distinct and separate from the eschatological drama, it is in fact a moral episode which sets the inner coherence of the sūra, as we shall see, into a bas-relief. With these three verses the whole drama of the sūra acquires an axis and a double interlocked conflict. The first is between ungrateful man and the bountiful God in v. 6 (*inna 'l-insāna li rabbihi la-kanūd*). The second is between this caring God who is overflowing with kindness, on the one hand, and the vigilant detached Judge, and All-Knowing God (*al-khabīr*) of v. 11, on the other.

The organic structure of the sūra swings from the rapidly moving scenes of a pseudo-narrative (vv. 1–5), climaxed by an unbearably tremendous scene of withered stunted humans (vv. 9–10). This whole drama evolves around a quiet and meditative orbit (vv. 6–8) and terminates by a triumphant majestic closing weight (v. 11), namely, the sound and meaning of *al-khabīr*. The sūra's phonic patterns, which are composed of a profusion of gutturals, compressed consonants, open syllables, and liquids contribute to its impact by offering a "sound-track" to the whole drama. For these sound patterns which are marked by roughness, rumble, vigorous beat, melancholy, solemnity, and grave sedateness correspond with an atmosphere of tumultuous and explosive chaos, ingratitude, unbelief, subjugation, and divine authority.

The sūra's assonance divides it acoustically into three rhythmic groups: vv. 1–5, 6–8, and 9–11. Apart from the first group which is tightly knit through an identical verse ending with *an*, the remaining two groups are loosely threaded by similar rhymes of *ūd, īd, ūr* and *īr*. The periodic rhymes (*fawāṣil*) of the entire sūra are set in the following phonic patterns:

an/an/an/an/an/ūd/īd/īd/ūr/ūr/īr. What remains now is to elucidate in more detail how the sūra's component parts evolve by an internal energy which derives from the interweaving of and tension between its words, expressions, images and sounds creating a meaningful whole. In dealing with this examination the sūra is divided into four units: vv. 1–5, 6–8, 9–10, and 11. The division by and large is based on the verses' rhythmization, conceptual parallelism, and syntactical structure.

VERSES 1–5

Wa 'l-'ādiyāti ḍabḥan (1) fa 'l-mūriyāti qadḥan (2) fa 'l-mughīrāti ṣubḥan (3) fa-atharna bihi naq'an (4) fa-wasaṭna bihi jam'an (5)

These short, rapidly moving scenes give a vivid picture of a dramatic action whose sole protagonists are the *fā'ilāt* or the feminine plural active participles that are left without a definite antecedent. These agents are depicted in quickened gallop charging violently into the middle of a crowd. The verses' rhetorical forcefulness of ascending drama is, however, interrupted at the climax (v. 5) giving the verses a quasi-narrative quality.

Syntactically this section of the sūra is composed of three simple, short nominal, sentences, vv. 1–3, followed by two verbal clauses, vv. 4–5. The five verses are held tightly together by their rhyming alliteration. Each verse ends with a strong metrical gesture of the closed syllable *an*. The beat of the stresses in their stream of sounds is based on the form of the verses' end-words: the accusative (*manṣūb*) adverbial noun. These heavy adverbial rhythms dominate the verses to the point of representing the upward springing movement of the female agents. The wording of the verses is marked by a driving energy, where the strength of expression (*jazālat al-alfāẓ*) and their harsh gutturals (*'a, ḥa, qa, gha*) enhance the dynamic force of the drama and transmit a strong sense of physical energy. For so it may be thought that some of this energy is released by the oral utterance of these words.

Each one of the verses begins by a particle (*ḥarf*); *wa* for the first verse and *fa* for the ensuing ones. While Muslim scholars hold that the *wāw* of the first verse (*wa 'l-'ādiyāti ḍabḥan*) introduces an invocation of a divine oath, intended to magnify the stature of horses, Bint al-Shāṭi' gives it a more convincing definition.[19] The oath particle *wāw* which commences several Qur'ānic verses, she argues, has departed from its original linguistic connotation. In such verses, she explains, the *wāw al-qasam* assumes a rhetorical role intended to provoke the intense attention of the listener to believe what follows the oath. Indeed this rhetorical definition fits quite well within the cumulative intensity of the sūra, for it intensifies the impact of such an oath as it takes the listener by surprise. It also reclaims the "dignity" of the introductory verses, not evident in their traditional treatments. In short, it brings the Qur'ānic *'Arabiyya* under its own dominion.

This literary "exodus", however, is not unique to the *wāw* of the first verse; it is also assumed by the particle *fa* which ushers the second verse (*fa 'l-mūriyāti qadḥan*). Rather than remaining within its confines of denoting succession of events, it takes up the role of connoting the simultaneity of actions in vv. 1 and 2. For both the actions of producing the nasal and vocal sounds (*al-ḍabḥ*) of v. 2 are brought forth by and occur concurrently with the rapid motion of the female agents (*al-'adw*) of v. 1.[20] These two verses and their assimilation into one scene hold the key to resolving the ambivalence of the *fā'ilāt* who dominate the entire unit under discussion. For even though the term *ḍabḥ* can be used for camels when in the motion of walking, it is used exclusively for horses engaged in the act of vigorous running (*'adw*).[21] The identity of the *fā'ilāt* is evidenced further by both the onomatopoeia of the expressions as well as by the rhythmic placement of the terms; this puts a special emphasis on their phonic makeup as the verse reenacts the action. Here the beat of sound ranges from the high guttural *'a* in *al-'ādiyāt*, to its low *dāl* and *ḍād* in *ḍabḥan*, and finally to its high guttural of *ḥan*. These acoustic elements which are replayed in vv. 2–3 relay the sense of the ascending and descending movements of horses engaged in *'adw*.

The second verse distinguishes the female active participles (*al-'ādiyāt*) from camels with a sharper demarcation line and provides a conclusive definitude. Here the act of kindling of sparks (*mūriyāti qadḥan*) accompanying the forceful contact between the hooves and a rocky terrain is indeed a characteristic of horses in quickened galloping rather than of camels. The word *qadḥan* in this verse with the proximity of its *dāl* and *ḥā'* imparts the sense of the heated friction and the powerful contact between the hooves of the *fā'ilāt* and the rocks, bringing to mind the extent of the force with which they are moving. Consequently the identity of the *fā'ilāt* as being female horses, mares, becomes logically compelling. In the final analysis, and interestingly, while the *fa* of v. 2 assimilates the actions of the two verses and assists in identifying *al-fā'ilāt*, it concurrently creates a buffer zone that grants each *āya* its own versicular independence. By contrast, the *fa*s which introduce vv. 3–5 reclaim the status of being coordinating conjunctions that denote the succession of events. The most important chronological sequence, for our purpose, is alluded to by both the sort of action referred to in v. 2 (*fa 'l-mūriyāti qadḥan*), and by the term *ṣubḥan*, morning, in v. 3 (*fa 'l-mughīrāti ṣubḥan*). In scene one of v. 2 the kindling of sparks is a key device to discerning the time the drama begins. Since these sparks can be striking and very visible in the darkness only, the motion of the mares, then, must have begun before the morning (*ṣubḥan*) of v. 3. Further, the quickening of the pulse of the five verses alludes to the chronological proximity of the episodes. The rapid galloping of the mares, therefore, would seem to have occurred immediately before the daylight of the morning. It then begins at dawn (*al-fajr*), bringing to mind the sense of ominousness alluded to in the last verse of *Sūrat al-Qadr.* And finally, the shortness of the verses, which underscores the quick succession of events, reflects also the Qur'ānic sense of time where the eschatological hour (*al-Sā'a*) has an imminent urgency as Q. 20:15 affirms: (*inna 's-sā'ata ātiyatun akādu ukhfīhā*).[22] In fact, according to the Qur'ān, the outbreak of the Hour can happen at any moment like the twinkling of the eye or quicker and nearer as Q. 16:77 says: *wa mā amru s-sā'ati illā ka-lamḥi 'l-baṣari aw huwa aqrabu* . . .

In contrast to the frictional sound relayed by the term *qadḥan* in v. 2, *atharna* of v. 4, with its consecutive series of vowels, transmits an acute sound of splattering, scattering and dispersion, ushering the climax of the drama. This sense of disintegration and the breaking up of a mass is picked by the verb *wasaṭna,* cleaved, of v. 5, where the *tajwīd* convention of *qalqala* emits "sound waves" of instability, tremor and agitation.[23] The cumulative effect of both *atharna* and *wasaṭna,* in the verses' swiftly moving scenes, is supposed to be a preface to the climax. Indeed the violent and vigorous thrust in the middle of a host, by the verses' unrestrained protagonists, spectacular disintegration, convulsion and commotion are expected to follow. But no sooner has the fifth verse reached the climax, than the Qur'ān suddenly shifts into what appears to be an unrelated topic in the ensuing verses (6–8). With this abrupt shift the episode of the five verses has now acquired the definition of a "cliff-hanger", whereby the lure of the unfinished narrative preserves the attention of the listeners.

Such swerving and divergence typify two characteristics of the Qur'ānic *'Arabiyya.* First, it fits neatly within the Qur'ān's style of relating events: outside the realm of recording events and hence without the conventional literary perspectives of linearity. And second, the Qur'ānic characteristic, intense, dramatic tension is unmistakably embedded in the interruption of a drama already haunted by suspense owing to its cryptic heroines and the ambivalence of the verses.

The semantic openness of the verses stems basically from the fact that the whole drama fluctuates between being a dramatic episode of a raid and being an image of female horses on the loose. For the image of the mares alternates between their being ridden and their being riderless. This can be argued for in various ways. The most obvious is the fact that the designation of the verses' protagonists as being *fā'ilāt* (sing. *fā'ila*), establishes their being the principal active subjects. The implicit partial autonomy regarding their movement haunts the verses beginning at the second verse (*fa 'l-mūriyāti qadḥan*). As the verses proceed, the sense of the mares' autonomy is conjured into a more pronounced expression in v. 4: (*fa-atharna bihi naq'an*). V. 5 gives a striking yet intriguing reference to both the mares' autonomy and lack of it: (*fa-wasaṭna bihi jam'an*).[24]

Nevertheless, this heightening of tension and ambivalence together with the semantic field of these verses' expressions remove this unit further from the rigidity of its traditional interpretation. They all contribute, as we shall see, to the atemporal "displacement" of the dramatic tableau of these verses. As already remarked, the term *ḍabḥan* of v. 1 denotes the quality of inhaling and exhaling rapidly and spasmodically; it, however, is not exhausted by its basic meaning. Al-Qurṭubī holds that it also describes animals affected by fear or exhaustion.[25] His definition is of particular importance here, as it brings a subtle shift of interpretation. For the attention is now drawn to the mares' environment where the cause of their fear or exhaustion could reside. A notable clue is found in the nature of horses themselves. Together with a well developed sense of smell and keen hearing, horses' instincts enable them to sense an approaching strong wind or heavy rain. When such distant danger interferes with their senses, they have the tendency to flee to avoid danger.[26] Now in light of this information, the mares would seem to be fleeing the approaching terrestrial upheaval alluded to in the introductory verses of Q. 77; 51; 79 which began by the breaking of dawn of *Sūrat al-Qadr* (Q. 97). In this context the expression *naq'an* of v. 4 (*fa-atharna bihi naq'an*) is important for our purpose, as its semantic openness redirects the whole drama from its literal context even further. For even though Qur'ānic commentaries, and English language rendering have always defined the term *naq'an* in this sūra as being dust, al-Zamakhsharī relates *ṣurākh,* loud outcries, as being one of its meanings.[27] More interestingly, however, Ibn Manẓūr gives *naq'* the main definition of something that is being soaked in water, and restricts its meaning of being dust solely to the context of v. 4 of *Sūrat al-'Ādiyāt.*[28] Evidently al-Zamakhsharī's reading and Ibn Manẓūr's main definition of the term *naq'an* play a crucial role in transposing the whole image of the unit under discussion from its material level. For both meanings appear appropriate to an environment undergoing some kind of a storm, where the fugitive mares splatter the drenched soil, and where the outcries of an aghast crowd are provoked by the sudden and frightening arrival of the unrestrained animals: v. 5 (*fa-wasaṭna bihi jam'an*).

Following the intertextual resonances of these verses and their expressions in the Qur'ānic field of meaning, their symbolic reading becomes more in evidence. The term *ṣubḥan,* mornings, in v. 3 demonstrates how the Qur'ānic *'Arabiyya* has transformed its basic meaning from denoting a time of day to being a key word that refers to *Yawm al-Qiyāma.* This word in v. 3, showing that the hostile incursion of the running mares occurs in the morning, *fa 'l-mughīrāti ṣubḥan,* echoes the Qur'ānic conceptual parallelism between the morning and *Yawm al-Qiyāma.* For instance, Q. 74: 34–36 reads: (*wa 'ṣ-ṣubḥi idhā asfar, innahā la-iḥdā 'l-kubar, nadhīran li 'l-bashar*).[29] *Sūrat al-Ṣāffāt* (Q. 37) which abounds with repeated references to the Day of Resurrection and the Judgment Day reiterates: Q. 37: 176–177: (*a-fa-bi-'adhābinā yasta'jilūn, fa-idhā nazala bi-sāḥatihim fa-sā'a ṣabāḥu 'l-mundharīn*).[30] Moreover, the arousing of the dead from their "sleep" without a warning is expressed in a verse like this: Q. 36:52 (*qālū yā waylanā man ba'athanā min marqadinā hādhā mā wa'ada 'r-raḥmānu wa ṣadaqa 'l-mursalūn*).[31]

More intriguing, however, is how the Qur'ān lends the last term in v. 5, *jam'an* (host, crowd) a special "meta-terrestrial" colouring. It is what Culler calls "the signal"[32] and it sets off and directs perception toward the link between the introductory metaphor and the explicit description of *Yawm al-Qiyāma* later on in the sūra. For in the new Qur'ānic conception this term is often associated with the awesome congregation at the final and mysterious destiny of the journey of mankind. *Sūrat al-Shūrā* (Q. 42) brings the term *jam'an* and the dispersion of v. 5 into a significant semantic union: Q. 42:7 (... *wa tundhira yawm al-jam'i lā rayba fīhi farīqun fī 'l-jannati wa farīqun fī 's-sa'īr*).[33]

Through such conceptual associations and repetitions of key words, the images of vv. 1–5 bring into human language the ineffable reality of *Yawm al-Qiyāma* which transcends all expressions. Their suggestiveness conjures a link between the specified and the unspecified. For even though the words and phrases of the verses describing the ferocious movement of the female agents have not changed in their original basic meaning, they have undergone a subtle but very profound inner semantic transformation. This remolding is a result of the images being put in a new place and in a new system. The Qur'ān in this sūra identifies a form of a familiar event, an attack of some kind, and places it in a metaphor. In this metaphor energy, urgency, surprise, plunder, anarchy, turbulence and subjugation are presented as common to all: the words, the metaphor, and *Yawm al-Qiyāma*. All blend into a total whole creating a mode emancipated from any spatial or temporal order.

VERSES 6–8

Inna 'l-insāna li-rabbihi la-kanūd (6) wa innahu 'alā dhālika la-shahīd (7) wa innahu li-ḥubbi 'l-khayri la-shadīd (8)

From within the mist of force and commotion of the introductory verses emerges a triad of sententious maxims presented in a different key. With such an abrupt shift in theme and rhythmic pattern, the preceding predominance of physical action is altered into a drama of characterization which brings home the Qur'ānic cardinal point: man's character and conduct. Consequently the intensity of the rapidly successive beat and oracular rhetoric of the first section of the sūra is substituted, as we shall see, by a lingering reflective mood and an authoritative discourse.

This tripartite section of the sūra is composed of a cluster of nominal sentences which have double the length of the previous verses and a more complex syntax. The untranslatable particle *inna* and *lām al-tawkīd*, which precedes the predicates, are intended to declare most emphatically the axiomatic value of the passages. Further, *inna* serves to initiate the sound break in the sūra that v. 6 appears as a "rhythmic explosion"[34] and release, after the tightly constructed introductory verses.

The first two words in v. 6, *inna 'l-insāna*, convey a variant sound order of *i/n/a/i/n/ā/n/a*. Such variation is augmented by the *tajwīd* recitation. For through the *ghunna* convention, the particle *inna* and the *in* of *al-insān* are lengthened, while the convention of *madd* lengthens the *ā* in *al-insāna*, thus creating the sound combination of *innn/innn/āāna*. The result is what Sells calls "an intricately intertwined series of echoes, partial echoes, tensions and releases".[35] This parade of acoustic polarities is semantically mirrored in the proximity of the two *lāms* in *li-rabbihi* and *la-kanūd* in v. 6 which creates a paradoxical sense of intimacy between man and God. For the Arabic root R-B-B of the term *rabb* is associated with a devout, nurturing guardian who is lovingly raising a dependent.[36] The root K-N-D of *kanūd*, on the other hand, connotes both the act of ingratitude toward a benefactor and the act of rejecting friendly and affectionate ties.[37] *Kanūd* is, then, antithetical to *rabb* and their proximity is in tension with the sense of release borne by their two *lāms*. But however paradoxical the sense of intimacy is, it illustrates one of the Qur'ānic structural characteristics. After flirting with chaos in vv. 1–5, the Qur'ān immediately follows it by a sense of rescue and safety which augments the value of deliverance.

As a Qur'ānic value-word, *kanūd*, meaning spiritual and moral bankruptcy, plays a pivotal role in the entire Qur'ānic view on human character and conduct. Its intertextual semantic resonances reveal that in several verses its basic meaning in classical Arabic has been blended with that of the Qur'ānic *'Arabiyya* so that the cumulative result leaves no doubt that a *kanūd* is admittedly a *kafūr*. The following two verses express this thought very clearly: Q. 17:83 (*wa idhā an'amnā 'ala 'l-insāni a'raḍa wa na'ā bi-jānibihi*); Q. 14:7 (*la-in shakartum la-azīdannakum wa la-in kafartum inna 'adhābiya la-shadīd*).[38] Returning to the whole passage (v. 6), we soon find how it remarkably conveys the Qur'ān's vision of the order of the relationship between the Qur'ānic two major poles: man and God. In this simple phrase the Qur'ān is insisting that the relationship has to be bilateral and reciprocal. God delivers grace and bounty; man simultaneously delivers moral and spiritual gratitude and commitment. In its majestic simplicity, the verse speaks in a voice with a pitch of sublime spiritual melancholy. This sound quality expresses the divine human drama where God's bounty and man's ingratitude confront one another.

The sound of vv. 7 and 8 is presented in identical keys. In contrast to the introductory verses which rely upon a few sound qualities, vv. 6–8 offer a variety of sound colours: contrasts of deep nasals at their beginnings (*inna/innahu/innahu*) and shallow liquids at their final words (*ūd/īd/īd*). These long syllables at the beginning and at the end of each verse create a balanced weight enhanced by short syllables in the middle of the verses. Their phonic pattern has a bas-relief based on the *i* sounds and the nasalization of the three verses' protasis section: *inna/innahu/innahu.* The cadence of the verses has an oblique assonance based on the sounds of *ūd/īd/īd* in *kanūd; shahīd; shadīd.* The acoustic alliteration of the passage is built upon the assonance between the *ghunna* convention of *tajwīd* at the beginning of the verses and the *madd* convention at the end of each verse.[39] These lingering tones intensified by the innately emotive sounds of *ūd/īd/īd* create a euphony that generates some sort of an emotional power and contemplation. Or better still, their sound qualities produce a melancholic melody, a lyric, and a departure from the melodrama of vv. 1–5.

It is the generation of emotion and contemplation through the passages' meditative rhythm which Frye describes as a rhythm that returns on itself,[40] where the reflective mood is held in clear perspective in the three verses. The replay of the two long syllables in v. 7 (*wa innahu 'alā dhālika la-shahīd*) further anchors the melancholic meditative atmosphere. A strong sense of sorrow over a loss that can be avoided is transmitted through the return of the rhythm and rhyme in each passage and their reverberations in the other two.

The semantic union of vv. 6–7 is built on the pronoun *hu* in *innahu* and the demonstrative pronoun *dhālika* in v. 7. Man's lack of moral and spiritual values and his conduct of ingratitude have an eye-witness who cannot be avoided. However, the air of ambivalence, which permeates vv. 1–5, begins to invade this tripartite cluster through the ambiguous reference of the pronoun *hu* in *innahu*: *wa innahu 'alā dhālika la-shahīd.* Determining its reference identifies the eye-witness or the Qur'ānic *shahīd.*[41]

Lisān al-'Arab makes it clear that *shahīd* is one of the divine names, and an emphatic form of *shāhid.* It connotes an aspect of the absolute divine knowledge (*al-'ilm al-muṭlaq*): His being ever aware of all esoteric matters (*al-umūr al-bāṭina*).[42] Still seen from the angle of the Qur'ānic *'Arabiyya,* the Qur'ān uses the term *shahīd* thirty-five times, out of which in four occasions only it is applied to man. None of these occasions describes man as an eye-witness who gives a testimony on his conduct on the Day of Judgment (*Yawm al-Dīn*).[43] In nineteen Qur'ānic verses the term *shahīd* is clearly used to refer to the absolute and ever present divine knowledge which encompasses everything now and in the Hereafter. The context of many of these usages is the divine knowledge of and God's testimony about man's conduct and character. This point is explicitly clear in the following verse Q. 33:55 (*wa 'ttaqīna 'llāha inna 'llāha kāna 'alā kulli shay'in shahīdan*).[44] Via these routes, then, the pronoun *hu* and *shahīd* in v. 6 are ultimately connected with God.

Innahu is replayed for the second time in v. 8 reinforcing the affirmative tone and building once more the ambivalent structure simultaneously: *wa innahu li-ḥubbi 'l-khayri la-shadīd.* Undoubtedly this replay of the emphatic and the indefinite preserves the attention of the listener and begins to heighten the sense of tension and suspense as a prelude to the succeeding verses.

In this replay the absence of an antecedent for the pronoun *hu* is more obscure than its counterpart in v. 7. In v. 7 it occurs at a point in the sūra where it is immediately preceded by two antecedents: man and God. Consequently the pronoun *hu*, depending on the context, can be applied to either one of them. In the case of v. 8, it is preceded by another *hu* pronoun in v. 7 whose antecedent can be considered arguable.[45] Moreover, the ambiguity continues to push deeper into the verse through its last two words: *al-khayr* and its predicate *shadīd* whose interpretation is interlocked with the antecedent of *hu* as we shall see.

The term *khayr* is one of the more recurring and comprehensive Qur'ānic expressions. It occurs more than one hundred and seventy times, of which in over one hundred occasions it is used as a value-judgment word and an antithesis of *sharr*, evil, from the point of view of the Qur'ān. It embraces both the secular and the religious spheres, worldly possession, desirable acts and events, as well as God and the Hereafter. In terms of our purpose, it is connected with God essentially for the intent of reshaping man's vision of God and of this world. In many verses *al-khayr* denotes the divine limitless bounty bestowed on man and as a superlative to the divine attributes. Others present *al-khayr* as a value-judgment word subordinating this life to the life to come in heaven. When *al-khayr*, meaning worldly possessions or wealth, occurs in the Qur'ān within the bounds of expenditure, it is strictly covered by the scope of homilies (Q. 2:272–73). On the other hand, when worldly wealth is brought within the context of man's acts of charity despite his love of his possessions, the Qur'ān recruits other expressions: *māl* and *ṭa'ām* (Q. 89:20; 76:8). Conversely and significantly, man's ethical vice of avarice and niggardliness is always linked by the Qur'ān with the term *al-khayr*. The Qur'ān describes the avaricious in the most emphatic forms of expression as a person who hinders, obstructs, blocks, and refuses to do any acts of good will. From the Qur'ānic vantage point, such a person is a sordid human being and the Qur'ān does not hesitate to refer to him as being the ultimate unbeliever (*kaffār*): Q. 50:24–25 *alqiyā fī jahnnama kulla kaffārin 'anīd, mannā'in li 'l-khayri mu'tadin murīb.*[46]

The antecedent of *hu*, thus, is contingent upon the meaning of the last word of the verse *shadīd*. This term is solidly anchored in the Qur'ān in contexts that intensely convey the meaning of severe action and potent force. These denotations stem from the term's root (SH-D-D) which means solidness and the unyielding nature of a thing or person. Most importantly, for our purpose, in the form of an adjective, it also means covetous and niggardly.[47]

V. 8, then, read in light of the above inquiry, takes a direction and a purpose "inherently" within the boundaries of the Qur'ānic *'Arabiyya* where the *hu* of this verse shifts into referring to man. There is enough evidence, therefore, to suggest an interpretation of v. 8 where the first *lām* in *li-ḥubbihi* emerges as a particle of causality, and the second in *la-shadīd* stands as an emphatic confirmation of the dark side of the human psyche. What v. 8 literally means, from this point of view, is that due to his love of all that is valuable and desirable, man is indeed covetous and hinderer of the good.

The Qur'ānic choice of the term *shadīd* in v. 8 rather than *mannā'* or *shaḥiḥ*, to describe man's covetous nature is self-evident: it fits neatly within the Qur'ānic idiom, on the one hand, and its "rhythmic ethos"[48] on the other. For the term *shadīd,* in its pervasiveness and its overtones of indefinite capacity for resisting, plays a central role in bringing a certain meaning to the foreground. In this light the word *shadīd* reflects the image of intense tight-fistedness and the grudging of others, the force to block acts of good will, greed, stubbornness, and consequently hate and jealousy, namely, the epic realm of the insolent. Moreover, its long syllable of *īd* continues the series of the meditative rhythm of vv. 6 and 7 penetrating mind and feeling.

Despite these three verses' absorbing and pondering mood, they are, as we shall see, a central axis of tension between the preceding five verses and the two that follow. The latter regather momentum with another unexpected thematic and syntactical shift.

VERSES 9–10

A-fa-lā ya'alamu idhā bu'thira mā fī 'l-qubūr (9) wa ḥuṣṣila mā fī 'ṣ-ṣudūr? (10)

The thought-provoking tranquillity generated by the meaning and sound of the preceding verses is shattered by vv. 9–10. A disturbing image of another dimension of reality suddenly drops from nowhere with these two verses: the eruption of *Yawm al-Qiyāma.* The unexpected appearance and juxtaposition of this tableau with what preceded it has the quality of surrealism. Also the atmosphere of the scattered contents of the graves whose occupants become places of forceful "excavations" has the intense irrational "reality" of a frightening dream.

The couplet's portrayal of disorder, violence and pillaging unfolds the climax of the first five verses. In so doing, it provides an expansion for the early metaphor from its original context where the symbol and the symbolized come together. The "new" image presses home the realities of *Yawm al-Qiyāma* upon the mind and emotions. Within the realm of this identification, the mind and imagination mingle and flow freely from the sudden raid to the animation of the climactic eruption. These operations intensify the unifying forces that hold the metaphor of vv. 1–5 to vv. 9–10, the terrestrial to the eschatological.

The two verses open a window into the beginning of the final journey of mankind. However, the view is from the realm of the fantastic. In the violent breaking out of the graves of v. 9, the sleeping dead are ejected and forcefully ousted. Their sudden and tormenting awakening brings to mind v. 5 *fa-wasaṭna bihi jam'an.* It also comes explicitly in Q. 36:52 (*qālū yā waylanā man ba'athanā min marqadina*).[49] The term *bu'thira* of v. 9 picks up, through its semantic markings, the sense of volcanic eruption where "matter" is upturned and overthrown suddenly and violently. This is further suggested by the lexical sign *mā* which, contrary to its lexical usage, refers in the verse to rational beings: the dead humans. Its combination with the term *bu'thira* transmits a striking image of littering, casting, and scattering of the utterly helpless.[50] Their helplessness and vulnerability is animated further by the expression *huṣṣila* of v. 10. Its semantic and acoustic qualities intensified by the *shadda* of the *ṣād* transmit a palpable picture of strenuous but careful extracting of well concealed possessions: man's hidden dark side.

The terrifying images of these two verses (9–10) transform reality into an absurd alienating setting reminding man of his mortality and helplessness vis-à-vis the All-Powerful, All-Knowing God. The emotions of sorrow over man's destiny and his inescapable doom are evoked by the *madd* convention of the *ūr* sound of the verses' last words: *al-qubūr* and *al-ṣudūr.* Their phonic resonance is augmented by their semantic assonance: both are places of burial and concealment. Grief and the meditative mood, at this stage of the sūra, are now over a loss that is unavoidable. Acoustically, such sound performance appears to have an antithetical effect to the pictorial images of the volcanic fury of the graves and the forcefully anatomic penetration of man's chest. At first encounter, such sound performance seems to be a paradox. But it is the austerity of the situation, its inevitability, gravity, and sense of warning and sarcasm, conveyed by the rhetorical question, that "determine" such sound performance. For man, who perceives himself as the protagonist of existence, loses his status on *Yawm al-Qiyāma.* He is disintegrated and wiped out as one endowed with reason and free will.

The two verses, however, are not intended to suspend the sense and value of human reason but to convey a vision of the supernatural of the Hereafter. Their purpose is to detach man from his earthly shortcomings and to restrain his trust and reverence of his terrestrial existence. In other words, the Qur'ānic *Yawm al-Qiyāma* exists in the orbit of the Qur'ān's fundamental message: man's spiritual and ethical piety. Or better still, the entire purpose of the Qur'ānic *Yawm al-Qiyāma* is to instill in mankind *al-taqwā*, the self-generated sense of correctness.[51] This comprehensive, deeply impressive and overpowering Qur'ānic expression is indeed the cornerstone and the fundamental note of the religion which the Qur'ān has come into existence to articulate.

Evidently vv. 6–8, or the three sententious maxims of the sūra, are the axis around which the two clusters of vv. 1–5 and 9–10 evolve. These maxims are the centripetal force which unifies the symbol and the symbolized. They represent a moment in man's "history" which plays the decisive role in man's final destiny. But then the entire ten verses reflect the Qur'ānic atemporal linearity. For in vv. 1–5 the scene is presented in temporal process, in vv. 6–8 it is presented as universal transcultural facts, while the eschatological gestalt of vv. 9–10 combines past, present, and future tense. Also the verses' passive voice emphasizes the total and absolute confinement and subjugation of all creation on the Day of Resurrection in the hands of God: Q. 39:67 (*wa 'l-arḍu jamī'an qabḍatuhu yawma 'l-qiyāmati wa 's-samāwātu maṭwiyyātun bi-yamīnihi*).[52] Moreover, this passive voice magnifies the image and the power of the divine commander Who is infinitely beyond human expression.

VERSE 11

inna rabbahum bihim yawma'idhin la-khabīr. (11)

The network of tensions (vv. 1–5), releases (vv. 6–8), and tensions (vv. 9–10) comes to its final resting place with this verse, which in a sense "drops the curtain" on the whole scene of convulsion, rumble, and unrest.

The two successive pronouns in *rabbahum bihim* refer to mankind, treated as singular, *al-insān*, in vv. 6–10. In v. 11, the Qur'ān characteristically shifts to the plural pronoun to refer to human beings. Although classical *tafsīr* literature relates this shift to the lexical definition of the term *al-insān*, the shift plays a phonic emphatic role which contributes to the epilogue of the sūra: its supra-tranquillity. For the two proximate pronouns of *hum* in *rabbahum* and *him* in *bihim* possess a "spondaic weightiness"[53] whose acoustic effect transmits an unmistakable sound of subsidence. Juxtaposed with the *an*, of the introductory verses, which brings forth a rising effect, the two pronouns' particular key gains a stronger charge. More interestingly, when the phonic markings of these two pronouns is augmented by the visual Arabic calligraphic form of their consecutive *hā*s and *mīm*s which tend downward, their reflection of the "sound" of abatement is compelling. Furthermore, the outbreak of forceful movements in vv. 1–5 and 9–10 is balanced by the majestic divine image of assertiveness and the "sound of silence" of the last verse. This final proclamation resolves the tension that has been distributed in different directions throughout the sūra. Its acoustic, semantic and thematic dimensions echo Q. 75:12: *ilā rabbika yawma'idhini 'l-mustaqarr.*[54]

This final verse possesses most of the sound patterns of the sūra and mirrors its semantic comprehensiveness. Its onomatopoeia conveys the sense of subsidence vis-à-vis the sound representation of the powerful movements, eruptions, and strenuous extracting of the preceding verses. The nasalization (*ghunna*) of the affirmative particle *inna* echoes the centre of the sūra vv. 6–8. The concluding term *al-khabīr* is the final part in a chain of echoes of resonance of long syllables and sound patterns of the end-terms of vv. 6–10: *ūd/īd/īd/ūr/ūr/īr.* Significantly, a corresponding long vowel end-syllable occurs in *la-kanūd, al-qubūr,* and *al-ṣudūr* on the one hand, and in *la-khabīr, la-shahīd,* and *la-shadīd* on the other. The semantic markings of these expressions charged with their two different assonances bring forth a vertical conflict between the second Qur'ānic major pole: man "facing up" the principal Qur'ānic pole: God. Specifically, the ungrateful doomed man is confronting the omniscient God whose superior knowledge discloses all human machinations. These series of long syllables create a special sequence of acoustic alliteration: *ū/ū/ū/ī/ī/ī.* This rhythmic quality is in contrast to the rhythmic pattern of vv. 1–5 which is composed of short syllables: *an/an/an/an/an.* The contrast of the short and long end-syllables divides the sūra acoustically and rhythmically into almost two halves.

Although the final word of the sūra (*al-khabīr*) is perhaps the least of the divine attributes in petitioning human emotions, the expression that precedes it *yawma'idhin* charges this attribute with the powerful emotions of awe. For this term, *yawma'idhin,* which originally connoted the simple meaning of "that day", has acquired a new denotation in the Qur'ānic *'Arabiyya.* It has become, as Izutsu quite rightly states, "tinged with a marked eschatological colouring"[55] through its relation and direct reference to the very important Qur'ānic moment of *Yawm al-Dīn.* Consequently, this Qur'ānic expression generates dread and veneration inspired by both the sublimity and the austerity of the eschatological event; its corollary is being in the presence of the All-Powerful, All-Righteous, stern Judge. Furthermore, vv. 9–10 which refer to the forceful plunder and extraction of man's most hidden thoughts, reflecting God's sovereignty and absolute power, lends a strong aura of similar emotions to the abstracted divine attribute: *al-khabīr.*

Significantly, however, even though the tension and apprehensive emotions which have been built up through the sūra are resolved rhythmically and syntactically with the emphatic term *al-khabīr,* the term does not offer any semantic closure. Its transcendent connotations, which refer to a realm above and beyond the boundaries of human reason, elevate this concept above the emotional sphere into the heights and mystery of the unknown, or better still, into the realm of God which is beyond thought, emotions and verbal expression. This emphatic transcendent Qur'ānic expression is the principal climax of the sūra and the core of the whole sublime Qur'ānic concept of *Yawm al-Dīn.*

Sūrat al-'Ādiyāt (Q. 100) typifies the distinctively enchanting discourse and arresting eloquence of the Qur'ānic *'Arabiyya.* It is a paradigm of the Qur'ān's grand symphony of subjects, pseudo-narratives, tenses, rhythms, rhymes, and voices.

The sūra is replete with action, suspense, and state-of-the-art ambiguity. Its extremely condensed verses delve into the realm of a phenomenon that defies conventional explanation. They are not only a sequel of the epic of *Yawm al-Qiyāma*; they are some of the Qur'ān's poignant depictions of the link between man's conduct and the galactic event.

Through the intricacy of metaphor, repetitions of images, phrases, and expressions as well as intertextual associations, the sūra has spiritualized an entire familiar image. It has transposed it from its material level to the atemporal sphere, to the Qur'ānic hour (*al-Sā'a*), where time stops and physical reality is altered. The sūra, in this sense, combines the perceptible (*al-shahāda*) and the unseen (*al-ghayb*). The merger has created a literary action-drama where man's religiosity and morality are its *raison d'être.*

The breathtaking imageries of this drama and its fascinating fusion of sound, meaning, and expression, and their mind-altering powers must have been what stunned, captivated, and alarmed the Meccan Arabs. *Wa 'llāhu a'lam.*

NOTES

Author's note: I would like to record my appreciation to Professor Issa J. Boullata for inviting me to contribute to this volume and to Professor Todd Lawson for his valuable comments on earlier drafts of this article.

1 Q. 74:22–24: "then he contemplated, then he frowned and scowled, then he retreated and waxed proud. He said, 'This is naught but an inherited sorcery.'" All Qur'ānic citations follow numbering of the Egyptian standard edition unless otherwise noted. English renderings are the author's modifications of Arthur J. Arberry, *The Koran Interpreted,* 2 vols. (London: George Allen & Unwin Ltd., 1955). Arberry's interpretation is chosen because it is indeed, as Boullata describes it, "one of the best English renditions and, ... one of the finest rhetorical interpretations." Issa J. Boullata, "The Rhetorical Interpretation of the Qur'ān: *I'jāz* and Related Topics," in *Approaches to the History of the Interpretation of the Qur'ān,* ed. Andrew Rippin (Oxford: Clarendon Press, 1988), 156. Undoubtedly, however, much of the sense and feel of the Qur'ānic *'Arabiyya* is lost in any translation. Al-Jāḥiẓ puts the shortcomings of translation succinctly "*wa matā ḥuwwila taqaṭṭa'a naẓmuh, wa baṭala waznuh, wa dhahaba ḥusnuh, wa saqaṭa mawḍi' al-ta'ajjub minhu.*" Abū 'Uthmān 'Amr ibn Baḥr al-Jāḥiẓ, *al-Ḥayawān,* 7 vols., ed. Yaḥyā al-Shāmī (Beirut: Dār wa Maktabat al-Hilāl, 1986), 1:51. More recent discussions on translating the Qur'ān can be found in

A.L. Tibawi, "Is the Qur'ān Translatable? Early Muslim Opinion," *Muslim World* 52 (1962):4–17; Fazlur Rahman, "Translating the Qur'ān," *Religion and Literature* 20 (1988):23–30.

2 This expression, the Qur'ānic *'Arabiyya*, which is used throughout the article, is intended to refer to what is, by now, quite well established: the Qur'ān stands by itself as an independent genre, and possesses its own style and idioms which express its ethos. Mention should be made here of Izutsu's two important studies in which he demonstrates how classical Arabic is evolved, by the Qur'ān, creating its own conceptual network and semantic field of meaning in order to express its own world view; Toshihiko Izutsu, *God and Man in the Koran: Semantics of the Koranic Weltanschauung* (Tokyo: The Keio Institute of Cultural and Linguistic Studies, 1964); idem, *Ethico-Religious Concepts in the Qur'ān* (Montreal: McGill University Press, 1966).

3 In a long and admittedly interesting article, Gluck attempts to demonstrate the existence of poetry in the Qur'ān. His premise is the fact that the Qur'ān uses rhetorical devices employed by poets. I am inclined to think that his grasp of the original Arabic text needs refinement, and that his article would have acquired more value had he dealt with the Qur'ān as an independent genre with its own stylistic system. J.J. Gluck "Is there Poetry in the Qur'ān?" *Semitics* 8 (1982):43–89. Furthermore, his insistence on attributing the composition of the Qur'ān to the Prophet is redundant, and represents the traditional trend in Western scholarship, in terms of its approach to the Qur'ān. Such stance brings out what Geller describes as the tension between the concept of a prophet being "the mouthpiece of God," and the poet being "a craftsman". See Stephen A. Geller, "Were the Prophets Poets?" *Prooftexts* 3 (1983):211.

4 The term *saj'* refers to a prose/text that exhibits no deviation from a symmetrical order or arrangement with rhyme, assonance, and equal rhythm. See Muḥammad ibn Manẓūr, *Lisān al-'Arab*, 15 vols. (Beirut: Dār Ṣādir, n.d.), 8:150–51; Aḥmad al-Qalqashandī, *Ṣubḥ al-A'shā fī Ṣinā'at al-Inshā'*, 2 vols., ed. Muḥammad Shams al-Dīn (Beirut: Dār al-Kutub al-'Ilmiyya, 1987), 2:302; Ḍiyā' al-Dīn Ibn al-Athīr, *al-Kalām al-Sā'ir fī Adab al-Kātib wa 'l-Shā'ir*, ed. Aḥmad al-Ḥūfī and Badawī Ṭabāna (Cairo: Maktabat Nahḍat Miṣr, 1959), 275. The Qur'ān's stylistic similarities to pre-Islamic *saj'* have caused some Muslim authors to write about the absence of any stylistic relationship between *saj'* and the Qur'ānic verses. See for example 'Alī ibn 'Īsā al-Rummānī, *al-Nukat fī I'jāz al-Qur'ān*, in *Thalāth Rasā'il fī I'jāz al-Qur'ān li 'l-Rummānī wa 'l-Khaṭṭābi wa 'Abd al-Qāhir al-Jurjānī*, ed. Muḥammad Khalaf Allāh and Muḥammad Zaghlūl Sallām (Cairo: Dār al-Ma'ārif bi-Miṣr, 1968), 97; Abū Bakr al-Bāqillānī, "Kitāb I'jāz al-Qur'ān," in Jalāl al-Dīn al-Suyūṭī, *al-Itqān fī 'Ulūm al-Qur'ān*, 2 vols. (n.p.: Dār al-Fikr, n.d.), 1:90–94, 103. Al-Bāqillānī repeats what Abū al-Ḥasan al-Ash'arī held before him. These scholars focused on the Qur'ānic periodic rhymes at the end of verses, rather than any other stylistic similarity between *saj'* and the Qur'ān. Their insistence on calling these periodic rhymes *fawāṣil* is strictly tied to their intent to maintain the transcendence of the Qur'ānic style and hold it above the cryptic pronouncements of the pre-Islamic *kuhhān*. Al-'Askarī, on the other hand, makes an observation on the difference between *al-tasjī'* in the Qur'ān and in the sayings of *al-kuhhān*. The rhyming sound effects of the Qur'ānic verses, he explains, have a semantic significance (*li-tamkīn al-ma'nā*). See al-Ḥasan al-'Askarī, *Kitāb al-Ṣinā'atayn: al-Kitāba wa 'l-Shi'r*, ed. Mufīd Qamīma (Beirut: Dār al-Kutub al-'Ilmiyya, 1981), 285. See also Ibn al-Athīr, *al-Kalām al-Sā'ir*, 277 where he holds that *al-saj'*, which occurs frequently in the Qur'ān, is the highest form of expression. For a recent

discussion of *saj'* in the Qur'ān see Devin J. Stewart, "*Saj'* in the Qur'ān: Prosody and Structure," *Journal of Arabic Literature* 21.2 (September 1990):101–39.

5 An interesting example of *saj' al-kuhhān* is given by al-Baghdādī in his account of pre-Islamic Quraysh. It is interesting because both *Sūrat al-'Ādiyāt* and the following incantations employ a similar introduction and the *ḥā'* as an end-consonant, revealing the differences this article is referring to: "*amā wa rabbi 'l-'Ādiyāti 'ḍ-ḍubbaḥ, mā ya'dilu 'l-ḥurru bi-'abdin naḥnaḥ, bi-man aḥalla qawmahu bi 'l-abṭaḥ.*" Muḥammad ibn Ḥabīb al-Baghdādī, *Kitāb al-Munammaq fī Akhbār Quraysh,* ed. Khūrshīd Fārūq (Haydarabād: Dā'irat al-Ma'ārif al-'Uthmāniyya, 1964), 116.

6 Boullata, "*I'jāz* and Related Topics," 157. To my knowledge, Sayyid Quṭb has been the sole Muslim scholar, so far, whose analysis of the Qur'ānic stylistic eloquence is based on a premise identical to Boullata's quoted statement. I am referring here to Quṭb's two studies *al-Taṣwīr al-Fannī fī al-Qur'ān* (Cairo: Dār al-Ma'ārif, 1966) and *Mashāhid al-Qiyāma fī 'l-Qur'ān* (Cairo: Dār al-Ma'ārif, 1966). His counterpart in Western scholarship is Michael Sells in two studies of Q. 97 and 101, namely "Sound, Spirit and Gender in *Sūrat al-Qadr,*" *Journal of the American Oriental Society* 111, 2 (1991):239–59; "Sound and Meaning in *Sūrat al-Qāri'a,*" *Arabica: Journal of Arabic and Islamic Studies* 40 (November 1993):402–30. However, while Quṭb's approach is that of a literary artist who is fascinated by the arresting aesthetics of the Qur'ānic *'Arabiyya,* Sells' approach is that of a linguist who, through scanning, reveals the implicit understructure of the verses' pulses and their interplay with the verses' expressive performance.

7 I take no particular position here on the question of the chronological order of the Qur'ānic verses or sūras.

8 In his discussion of rhythm in poetry, al-'Ayyāshī defines rhythm and sound in general as being abstract concepts so long as they remain within the confines of a text. They, however, assume a corporeal existence through the oral recitation and the intonations of the reader's voice. See Muḥammad al-'Ayyāshī, *Naẓariyyāt Īqā' al-Shi'r al-'Arabī* (Tunis: al-Maṭba'a al-'Aṣriyya, 1976), 40, 103.

9 Concerning the importance of rhymes in the verses of the Qur'ānic discourse, al-Farrā', who calls them *maqāṭi'* or *ru'ūs al-āyāt,* goes as far as postulating that in its intent to maintain the conformity of *al-maqāṭi',* the Qur'ān appears as though it were acting in accordance with what the Arabs liked "*wa ka'anna 'l-Qur'ān nazala 'alā mā yastaḥibbu al-'Arab.*" Yaḥyā ibn Ziyād al-Farrā', *Ma'ānī 'l-Qur'ān,* 3 vols, ed. 'Abd al-Fattāḥ Shalābī, rev. 'Alī Nāṣif (Cairo: al-Hay'a al-'Āmma li 'l-Kitāb, 1973), 3:224. See also ibid., 3:226, 273–74, 285 where he gives examples from various sūras to demonstrate how the Qur'ān resorts to certain structures and words or omits the final letter of a word in order to maintain *ru'ūs al-āyāt.*

10 Q. 97:5 "Peace it is, till the onset of dawn."

11 Ibn Manẓūr, *Lisān al-'Arab,* 5:45. See also Sells, "Sound, Spirit and Gender," 253.

12 Ibid., 239. The lack of correspondence between the solar days and the Qur'ānic "days" can be distinguished, for example, through the Qur'ānic references to the length of *Yawm al-Qiyāma* where it occupies two starkly different spans of time: Q. 32:5 and 70:4. In the former it occupies one thousand years and in the latter fifty thousand years.

13 Al-Ṭabarī, for example, after giving a detailed account of the disagreement of the commentators on the identity of the *fā'ilāt* in Q. 77:1–5, declines to give them any specific identification. See Ibn Jarīr al-Ṭabarī, *Jāmi' al-Bayān 'an Ta'wīl*

Āy al-Qur'ān, 15 vols. (Beirut: Dār al-Fikr, 1995), 14:283–89. Equally uncertain, al-Rāzī presents the six different identifications of the *fā'ilāt* in Q. 79:1–5, given by the various authorities; he, then, concludes by stating that the verses could be referring to one sort of *fā'ilāt* or to five different *fā'ilāt.* See Fakhr al-Dīn al-Rāzī, *Mafātīḥ al-Ghayb,* 32 vols. (Beirut: Dār al-Kutub al-'Ilmiyya, 1990), 31:26–31. Neuwirth, on the other hand, is more certain. She interprets the *fā'ilāt* of Q. 77:1–5 as winds, and those of Q. 79:1–5 as "animals and riders carrying out a *ghazwa.*" Angelika Neuwirth, "Images and Metaphors in the Introductory Sections of the Makkan *Sūras,*" in *Approaches to the Qur'ān,* ed. G.R. Hawting, and Abdul-Kader Shareef (London: Routledge, 1993), 7–9.

14 It is significant to note that the expression *nazā'i'* which is from the same root of *al-nāzi'āt* (N-Z-') refers to winds that blow from every direction. Further, one of the lexical definitions of *al-nāshiṭāt* is the aimlessly running she-camels. *Al-sābiḥāt* has the connotation of moving stars. See Ibn Manẓūr, *Lisān al-'Arab,* 8:352; 7:414; 2:470 respectively.

15 The above rendering is the author's. The end terms of vv. 1–5 are left in transliteration because of their semantic openness. This will become clear as the discussion proceeds.

16 The Arabic term *al-insān* is rendered, for want of a better term, as 'man' and the pronoun 'he' is used to refer to the rational human being throughout this article, even though *al-insān* in Arabic refers to both feminine and masculine gender.

17 This is the gist of the Sunnī *tafsīr,* several of which have been consulted such as: al-Ṭabarī, *Jāmi' al-Bayān,* 15:345–57; al-Rāzī, *Mafātīḥ al-Ghayb,* 32:60–66 and Maḥmūd al-Zamakhsharī, *al-Kashshāf 'an Ḥaqā'iq Ghawāmiḍ al-Tanzīl* (Beirut: Dār al-Kitāb al-'Arabī, 1966), 4:786–89; Sayyid Quṭb, *Fī ẓilāl al-Qur'ān,* 30 vols. (Beirut: Dār al-Shurūq, 1993), 30:3957–59. One of the Shī'ī exegesis consulted is Muḥammad al-Ṭabāṭabā'ī, *Al-Mīzān fī Tafsīr al-Qur'ān,* 2nd ed. (Beirut: Maktabat al-'Alamī, 1974), 20:344–48. Al-Ṭabāṭabā'ī's identifies the *ghazwa* of the first five verses with *ghazwat Dhāt al-Salāsil* which was led by 'Alī ibn Abī Ṭālib. He also suggests that this sūra must have been revealed in Medina rather than in Mecca. His reasons are based on the Shī'ī *tafsīr* which links the revelation of the sūra with the *ghazwa* and the fact that *jihād* was only ordained by the Qur'ān during the Medinan period. Al-Rāzī also, in his *tafsīr* of the sūra, refers to some accounts which give the possibility that the sūra, based on the *jihād* ordinance, could have been revealed in Medina. However, in my view, its literary qualities, its enigmatic features, and the centrality of *Yawm al-Qiyāma* in its discourse tie it more with the Meccan rather than with the Medinan period.

18 Sells, "Sound and Meaning,"421. In his discussion of the probable meaning of the term *hāwiya* in *Sūrat al-Qāri'a* (Q. 101) Sells suggests that interpreting the term as "the pit"or as any spatially and temporally defined place of punishment is "a taming of the text".

19 Bint al-Shāṭi', *al-I'jāz al-Bayāni li 'l-Qur'ān wa Masā'il Ibn al-Azraq* (Cairo: Dār al-Ma'ārif, 1984), 248. In order to bring home his point of view, Ibn Qayyim al-Jawziyya gives a detailed account of the extraordinary and multi-faceted attributes of horses. See Ibn Qayyim al-Jawziyya, *al-Tibyān fī Aqsām al-Qur'ān.* ed., Ṭāhā Shāhīn (Beirut: Dār al-Kutub al-'Ilmiyya, 1982), 50. Bint al-Shāṭi' explains the Qur'ānic oath by saying the oath uses perceptible phenomena to introduce imperceptible ones; however, she gives Ibn Qayyim al-Jawziyya's view without acknowledging him and attributes it to herself. The reasoning given by both is that the Qur'ān's oaths affirm (*tawkīd, taqrīr*) the existence of the unseen (*al-ghaybiyyāt*) by swearing by the seen phenomena. Ibid., 248; Ibn

Qayyim al-Jawziyya, *al-Tibyān*, 6. This view does hold well with oaths that employ identifiable phenomena such as in *Sūrat al-'Ādiyāt.* But the dense ambiguity and supra semantic openness of the sworn-by phenomenon in Q. 77; 79; 51; 37 render such a view unconvincing.

20 Such connotation of the particle *fa* is discussed clearly by Ibn al-Athīr in the context of Q. 74: 2–4: *Qum fa-andhir, wa rabbaka fa-kabbir, wa thiyābaka fa-ṭahhir.* Ibn al-Athīr, *al-Kalām al-Sā'ir*, 412.

21 Like the terms *qadḥan* of v. 2, *naq'an* of v. 4, and *kanūd* of v. 6, *ḍabḥan* has a solitary use in the Qur'ān. These four words appear only in this form, in *Sūrat al-'Ādiyāt.* According to ibn Manẓūr, *ḍabḥ* denotes sounds that are neither neighing nor whinnying emitted by horses when in the rapid movement of running. It also means the sound of their inhaling and exhaling when engaged in the same action. Ibn Manẓūr, *Lisān al-'Arab*, 2:523.

22 "The Hour is indeed coming, that I would almost conceal it".

23 In his comprehensive study of Qur'ānic recitation, Gouda explains that *qalqala* is realized in *tajwīd* through making more pressure on voiceless consonants such as *Ṭ* in order to protect their "sounds from acquiring voicelessness." Ahmad Gouda, "Qur'ānic Recitation: Phonological Analysis," Ph.D. dissertation (George Washington University, 1988), 163–64. Interestingly, for our purpose, the root Q-L-Q-L means "to remove, shake, convulse or agitate." Ibid., 161. See also Ibn Manẓūr, *Lisān al-'Arab*, 11:566–67.

24 The particle *bi* and the pronoun *hi* in vv. 4–5 gave rise to speculations as to what they are intended to refer to. Al-Suyūṭī, for example, finds the *bi* in v. 4 to be either a temporal or spatial adverb, consequently the pronoun *hi* refers to either a time of day or a place. Curiously, however, he understands the *bi* of v. 5 to mean 'with' and links it to the term *al-naq'*, concluding that the horses cleaved the centre of the enemy with the dust. See Jalāl al-Dīn al-Suyūṭī, *Tafsīr al-Jalālayn*, rev. 'Alī al-Ḍabba (Cairo: al-Maṭba'a al-Yūsufiyya, n.d.), 517. See also al-Rāzī, *Mafātīḥ al-Ghayb*, 32:63. Even though the semantic openness of these two *bihi*s slightly increases the sense of suspense and ambivalence of the introduction of the sūra, they do not in my view, warrant a detailed discussion. The reasons are, first, their impact on the basic meaning of the five verses is not significant, and second, it appears to me quite logical that the *bihi*s refer to the act of the vigorous movement of the mares (*al-'adw*) and then to their action of raiding (*al-ighāra*).

25 Muḥammad al-Qurṭubī, *Mukhtaṣar Tafsīr al-Qurṭubī*, ed., Muḥammad Rajab (Beirut: Dār al-Kitāb al-'Arabī, 1986), 5:423.

26 *Encyclopaedia Britannica*, 1984 edition, s.v. "horses". It is noteworthy here that, as pre-Islamic poetry tells us, the 7th century Arabs possessed an extraordinary knowledge of their animals and their behaviour, particularly of camels and horses. For further discussion of this subject through *al-Mu'allaqāt*, see Ṭāhā Ḥusayn, *Ḥadīth al-Arbi'ā'*, 3 vols. (Beirut: al-Sharika al-'Ālamiyya li 'l-Kitāb, 1980), 2 *passim.* See also Shawqī Ḍayf, *Tārīkh al-Adab al-'Arabī*, 2 vols. (Cairo: Dār al-Ma'ārif, 1960), 1:221–23.

27 Al-Zamakhsharī gives the following verse by Labīd ibn Rabī'a in support of his definition: *fa-matā yanqa' ṣurākhun ṣādiqun yuḥlibūhā dhāta jarsin wa zajal.* Al-Zamakhsharī, *al-Kashshāf*, 4:787.

28 Ibn Manẓūr, *Lisān al-'Arab*, 8: 359–63.

29 "By the morning when it shines forth, it is indeed one of the greatest things, (This is) a warning to mankind".

30 "What, do they seek to hasten our punishment? When it descends in their courtyard, how evil will be the morning of them that are warned".

31 "They said: 'Woe unto us! Who roused us out of our sleeping-place? This is what the All-Merciful promised, and the messengers spoke truly'".

32 Jonathan Culler, *The Pursuit of Signs: Semiotics, Literature, Deconstruction* (London: Routledge & Kegan Paul, 1981), 54. Culler refers to literary signals in his discussion of the interaction between a written work and the reading public.

33 "... and so that you warn of the Day of Congregation, of which there is no doubt – a party in Paradise, and a party in the Blaze".

34 Sells, "Sound, Spirit and Gender," 250. Sells uses the above expression to refer to the acoustic breaking down in Q. 97:4 of the tightly constructed hymnic rhythm of the preceding verses.

35 Ibid., 247. Sells is describing, here, the acoustical effects of *ghunna* and *ā* vowels in Q. 97:1.

36 This key Qur'ānic term is used more than one thousand times in the Qur'ān where it is drawn from the context of hierarchical relationships and responsibility. It is used to connote absolute power Q. 37:5, sovereignty Q. 55:27, bounty Q. 34:15, and guardianship Q. 7:151 and 93:5. For more definitions of the term *rabb* see Ibn Manẓūr, *Lisān al-'Arab,* 1:399–409. Morris sees the term *rabb* as being devoid of what he calls "the strong and predominantly negative associations of any of the English equivalents such as 'Lord'". Joseph Morris, "The Dramatizing of the *Sūra* of Joseph: An Introduction to the Islamic Humanities," *Journal of Turkish Studies* 18 (1994):6.

37 Ibn Manẓūr, *Lisān al-'Arab,* 3:381–82.

38 Q. 17:83 "And when We are bountiful to man, he turns away, and withdraws aside".

Q. 14:7 "If you are thankful, I will surely increase you, but if you are ungrateful My punishment is terrible indeed".

39 The auditory experience is acquired here through listening to the well-known Egyptian reciter 'Abd al-Bāsiṭ 'Abd al-Ṣamad, *Tajwīd Sūrat al-'Ādiyāt,* cassette 435 (Cairo: n.p., n.d.).

40 Northrup Frye, *The Great Code: The Bible and Literature* (New York: Harcourt Brace Jovanovich Publishers, 1982), 209.

41 Some of the exegetes who have been referred to earlier such as al-Ṭabarī, al-Rāzī, and Ibn Qayyim al-Jawziyya grappled with this problem using various techniques to resolve it. However, the approach used here is completely independent of theirs.

42 Ibn Manẓūr, *Lisān al-'Arab,* 3:238–39. Ibn Manẓūr explains that when the absolute divine knowledge (*al-'ilm al-ilāhī al-muṭlaq*) is referring to His knowledge of esoteric (*al-bāṭina*) matters, God in such a case is described as *al-khabīr.*

43 Q. 4:72 and 2:282 refer to man in the context of mundane affairs; in Q. 50:37 man is described as a *shahīd* to divine revelation; in Q. 41:47 the unbelievers refuse to testify, on *Yawm al-Dīn,* to the existence of co-partners to God.

44 "And be pious; for surely God is witness of everything".

45 Al-Rāzī, for example, offers a similar reading for the pronominal suffix *hu* of v. 7. He, however, indicates that attributing the second *hu* of v. 8 to God, which – from a syntactical point of view would naturally follow – creates a problem, i.e., God cannot be associated with a negative connotation of *al-khayr.* Therefore these two pronouns *hu* in vv. 7–8 must refer to man. Al-Rāzī, *Mafātīḥ al-Ghayb,* 32:64. This may be true; however, there are Qur'ānic verses where two consecutive *hu* pronouns refer to two different entities. See, for example, Q. 11:46; 29:26–27; 2:130; 17:1. The bottom line here is clear: it is the

Qur'ānic *'Arabiyya* that determines the structure of its passages. Moreover such shifts in the reference of pronouns and voices are so fundamental a characteristic of the Qur'ānic *'Arabiyya* that it is superfluous to give further examples.

46 Q. 50:24–25 "Ye twain, cast into *jahannam* every forward-most unbeliever, every hinderer of good, transgressor, disquieter".

47 Ibn Manẓūr, *Lisān al-'Arab*, 3:232–36.

48 Al-'Ayyāshī, *Naẓariyyat Īqā' al-Shi'r*, 103.

49 See endnote no. 31.

50 It is noteworthy at this juncture to observe that the Qur'ān consistently uses the term *mā* to refer to all creation, rational and irrational, vis-à-vis God, such as Q. 2:116; 5:17; 4:131–32.

51 Fazlur Rahman, in my view, gives the best interpretation of this most crucial Qur'ānic expression. He describes it as being the "inner torch [that] enables [man] to distinguish between right and wrong ... [it is a] development of the conscience of man to a point where this inner torch is lit". See Fazlur Rahman, *Major Themes of the Qur'ān* (Minneapolis: Bibliotheca Islamica, 1980), 120 and *passim.*

52 "And the earth altogether shall be His fist on the Day of Resurrection, and the heavens shall be rolled up in His right hand".

53 Sells, "Sound, Spirit, and Gender," 249. Sells uses this expression to describe the semantic and pivotal role of the term *khayr* in Q. 97:2.

54 "Upon that Day the ultimate and final recourse shall be to thy Lord".

55 Izutsu, *God and Man in the Koran*, 21.

PART III

LITERARY APPRECIATION OF THE QUR'ĀN: PAST AND PRESENT

Chapter 11

The Aesthetic Reception of the Qur'ān as Reflected in Early Muslim History

Navid Kermani

One may examine the language of the Qur'ān and appreciate its style or its rhetorical means as they are presented objectively in the text. If it seems of interest, one may also argue whether the Qur'ān is of divine beauty, as Muslims think, or whether Muḥammad was a "mediocre stylist", as Nöldeke and Schwally thought.[1] Yet, there can hardly be any doubt that throughout its history of reception, the Qur'ān has been reported to have an aesthetic effect uncontested by any other text in world literature. Until today, declarations of fascination with the language of the Qur'ān, reports about various situations in which its recitation caused ecstatic reactions, or praise for particular reciters are known throughout Muslim – and especially Arabic-speaking – literary and theological history. They surface in the most diverse genres, contexts and epochs, and every scholar of Islamic studies will inevitably and regularly encounter them in his work (and as much when travelling). Thus, it can hardly be denied that the Muslims' experience of the Qur'ān, as a poetically structured text and recital, is also aesthetic in its nature. At least in the Arabic- speaking world, the treatment of the Holy Book as an aesthetic phenomenon should be seen as an important part of Islamic religious practice.

Even so, the significance of this obvious fact is still so disproportionate to its resonance in Islamic studies that – while having noticed it early on and mentioning it now and then – they turn to it only gradually and occasionally. The limited impact of such efforts can hardly be detected in the fact that general accounts of Islam touch only in passing on the aesthetic fascination that for many Muslims emanates from the Qur'ān. On the other hand, in the self-perception of the Muslim community it represents a constitutive element, if only because the greatest and, for many theologians, sole confirming miracle of the Muslim prophet is the beauty and perfection of the Qur'ānic language. While in Western treatises on Islamic history one may find mainly ideological, political, psychological, social or military reasons for the success of Muḥammad's prophetic mission, Muslim authors over the ages have emphasized the literary quality of the Qur'ān as a decisive factor for the spread of Islam among seventh-century Arabs. They refer to the numerous stories in Muslim literature that recount the overwhelming effect of Qur'ān recitation on Muḥammad's contemporaries, tales about people spontaneously converting, crying, screaming, falling into ecstasy, fainting or even dying while hearing verses from the Qur'ān. From the *sīra* and the ḥadīth-compendia, the commentaries on the Qur'ān and the treatises on the prophethood of Muḥammad, as well as from modern, partly devotional, partly scientifically-orientated writings about the Prophet and his life, a past is constituted in which the linguistic composition of the Qur'ān becomes a principal element in the history of salvation: a past in which the Qur'ān's metaphysical beauty appears as a historic fact.

It is legitimate to question the authenticity of reports on the reception of the Qur'ān in early Islamic history or to doubt the Qur'ānic effect maintained by Muslims, although it is comparatively banal to do so. Only someone considering the rigid dualism of fiction and reality will fail to recognize the validity of even the most subjective and implausible testimonies of faith, and hence precisely of the reports about the reception of the Qur'ān, in cultural history and religious phenomenology. From such a perspective, the stories about Qur'ān listeners must appear as something like fairy tales, possibly delightful, but unimportant in their informational content and transparent in their pious intention, as they only serve to ascribe miracles to Islam. It is overlooked that they do give access to the specific, such as revelation and faith, and to their own history as it appears to Muslims.

Thus, the following compilation of reports about the reactions of Muḥammad's contemporaries to the recitation of the Qur'ān is not intended as a historico-critical approach to "what really happened" in those days. A picture will be drawn as it derives from Muslim sources. Regarding the founding period of Islam, this means an examination of a phenomenon that the Egyptologist Jan Assman has described as "the cultural memory" (*das kulturelle Gedächtnis*). Assman has pointed out that the collective "memory of a shared inhabited past"[2] is essential for the identity of a community. Independent of its historical validity, such a memory is always a social construct whose properties result from the need to make sense and from the referential framework of particular realities.[3] That the cultural memory particularly preserves events that stabilize a certain identity, adorns them with new details or even entirely fabricates them does not modify their relevance. For the comprehension of a culture, even historically invalid narratives have to be seen as "past" when they are perceived as such by the community. In this context, the significance of narratives is measured less by their historical factuality than by their function within the cultural memory. This should be pointed out especially with reference to the discussion about the doctrine of *i'jāz*, the miraculous character of the Qur'ān, as Islamic studies have been questioning the roots of this dogma in the Qur'ān for some time. Apparently, the passages that mainly serve as documentary evidence for the *i'jāz* (the so-called *taḥaddī* verses, in which God "challenges" the infidels to produce a sūra that would be like the sūras of the Qur'ān)[4] did not originally refer to the stylistic perfection of the Qur'ānic language.[5] Nevertheless, in religio-historical and cultural terms it remains remarkable that latter-day Muslims understood the *taḥaddī* verses as an aesthetic challenge; the various traditions about Arab poets trying in vain to create a work like the Qur'ān tell us a great deal about the cultural memory of the Muslim community – and thus about its identity – which is historically accurate. "One only has to realise," as Assman states, "that memory has nothing to do with historical sciences."[6]

Two premises are fundamental for the early history of Qur'ān reception as it is preserved in the cultural memory of the Muslim community: firstly, the perception that pre-Islamic Arabs were a cultural community, distinguished and identified essentially through its language and poetry; and secondly, the tremendous fascination that was said to emanate from the recitation of the Qur'ān – a fascination nobody could resist. These two premises form the basis for all reports about individual situations of reception, in which in turn particular patterns or figures of remembrance can be identified. There are the opponents who publicly denounce the Prophet, yet secretly yearn to listen to the Qur'ān. There are the villains who cannot defend themselves against the power emanating from the Qur'ān other than by attacking anyone reciting it. There are the poets who cannot succeed in countering the Qur'ān with poetry of equal linguistic perfection and secretly hang around the Ka'ba when the Prophet recites the Qur'ān. There are the supporters of the Prophet who outdo each other in their love for Qur'ān recital; there are the anecdotes about the art of individual reciters, and there is of course the Prophet himself to whom the most beautiful voice is attributed, yet who himself never misses an opportunity to listen to a skillful recitation. Another central element of the early history of reception is the irritation caused by the language of the Qur'ān, as it does not correspond to any known genre of metrical speech and yet is of extraordinary but, at the same time, inexplicable attraction. Interrelated is the curiosity that brings people from all over the Arabian peninsula and even from distant lands to Mecca or Medina so as to listen to the Qur'ān themselves, and simultaneously the frantic attempt of the Quraysh to discourage locals and foreigners alike from doing just that.

As it would go beyond the scope of this essay to annotate or provide examples for all of these motives found in the early history of the reception the Qur'ān,[7] I would like to introduce a particular type of listener: the spontaneous convert. "Anyone who heard it had no option but to surrender to the Qur'ān," said the Egyptian Muṣṭafā Ṣādiq al-Rāfi'ī (d. 1937), explaining this frequently discussed phenomenon, and he gave the following reasons for it:

> Every single part of his mind was touched by the pure sound of the language's music, and portion by portion, note by note, he embraced its harmony, the perfection of its pattern, its formal completion. It was not so much as if something was recited to him but rather as if something had burned itself into him.[8]

In order to realize remembered history as it is presented today, the subsequent account will not only be based on a defined body of source texts from the ḥadīth and the *sīra.* In addition, I want to draw on a selection of later accounts of early Islamic history, that is, explicit Muslim readings of Muslim sources. These include, on the one hand, theological texts from the ninth to the thirteenth century when the relevant doctrines and historical perceptions of Islam were already established, and when reports about the founder's time were not only reproduced but also already arranged much more clearly and embedded in a religious concept. On the other hand, these are modern and in theological and traditional-religious circles generally accepted books about the Qur'ān and early Islamic history which analyze and evaluate the actual sources and either embellish them in parts psychologically or paraenetically or use them to support a particular interpretation.[9] It follows, that – strictly speaking – at least three different layers of memory should be distinguished. For the moment, however, they will not be treated separately to avoid confusion and repetition.[10] However, at the end of this essay, I would like to point out how, with a view to the history of Qur'ān reception, a transformation of particular contents within the cultural memory can be perceived.

It is obvious that the following account illuminates only a few motives of the history of reception – those that are aesthetically relevant. This should not lead to the assumption that in the cultural memory the Qur'ān was only perceived as 'beautiful' by Muḥammad's audience and that the linguistic excellence alone is credited with the success of the Prophet's mission. A series of very important conversions – amongst them the very first, the one of Khadīja – are recorded that make no reference whatsoever to the aesthetic reception of the Qur'ān. In Muslim literature it is never overlooked that other factors such as the charisma of the Prophet[11] or the justice of the Qur'ānic message[12] have played a role; however, they are not the subject of this essay.

According to Muslim literature on the life of the Prophet, neither his arguments nor his sermons, his manner or his charisma alone were crucial factors for the conversions in the early period of Islam. As far as tradition informs us, in most cases the Arabs converted when they heard the

Qur'ān, whether recited or as part of the ritual prayer, the *ṣalāt*.[13] "God's Apostle spoke, and he recited the Qur'ān (*talā 'l-qur'āna*) and invited people to God and commended Islam" – in these and similar words Ibn Isḥāq (d. 767) frequently sketched Muḥammad's courting.[14] Ibn Sa'd (d. 845) writes likewise, "He sat with them, invited them to God and recited the Qur'ān to them, whereupon they joined him"; he relates in the shortest words possible Muḥammad's encounter with envoys of the Khazraj at the first pledge of 'Aqaba.[15] The description remains silent about the impression the recited text made on the Khazraj or whether it was decisive for the conversion. A similar experience is handed down from 'Uthmān b. Maẓ'ūn, to whom the Prophet recited Q.16:90 ("God commands justice, the doing of good"), when he is quoted as saying, "There, faith took root in my heart, and I began to love Muḥammad."[16] In other cases the converted are quoted with general exclamations of joy; an example is a bedouin to whom a Muslim recites the Qur'ān and who exclaims: "I testify that nothing created is capable of producing such speech."[17] One could also think of the anecdote about the young Jew Iyyās b. Mu'ādh, a member of the Banū 'Abd al-Ashhal, who had come with Abū l-Ḥaysar Anas b. Rāfi' from Yathrib to Mecca in order to win the Quraysh for an alliance against the Khazraj. When Muḥammad called on them and recited to them from the Qur'ān, Iyyās exclaimed, "By God, people, this is better than what you came for," and converted to Islam.[18]

The judgement of the healer Ḍimād remains equally vague. He tried to heal Muḥammad who, in the opinion of his compatriots, was obsessed. His attempt ended when Muḥammad recited three times the confession of faith to him. Ḍimād exclaimed, "I have heard already many words of sorcerers, fortunetellers and poets, but never something like this," and converted to Islam.[19] Although it is obvious that Muḥammad's speech is considered better than the verses of other inspired people, it remains open in what this superiority originates. In another version, Ḍimād at least speaks of 'beauty', but without specifying it, "Never have I heard a speech more beautiful (*aḥsan*) than this," he exclaims and asks Muḥammad to repeat it. Finally, he converts to Islam.[20]

From these rather general descriptions of conversions can be guessed rather than deduced the fact that the Qur'ān was received as an aesthetic phenomenon as well. But it becomes more apparent when they are placed in a context of traditions that specifies the impression of the listener, at least to some extent. Thus, in several other stories of converts the recitation is described as *ḥasan* or *aḥsan*, for example by the poet Suwayd b. al-Ṣāmit, a dignitary of the city of Yathrib, who was called the 'perfect' for his strength, poetry, dignity and descent. Some months before the Hijra he had gone on the (pagan) pilgrimage to Mecca where the Prophet sought him out specially to invite him to Islam. In the biographies of the Prophet by Ibn Hishām and Ibn Kathīr (d. 1372), one reports:

> "Perhaps you've got something like that which I have," Suwayd said.
> "And what is that?" the Apostle asked.
> "The roll of Luqmān," meaning the wisdom of Luqmān, he answered.
> "Hand it to me," the Apostle said, and he handed it over. And the Apostle said, "This discourse is beautiful (*ḥasan*), but that which I have is better still (*afḍal*), a Qur'ān which God has revealed to me which is a guidance and a light." And he recited the Qur'ān to him and invited him to Islam. Suwayd did not withdraw from it but said, "This is a fine saying." Then he went off and rejoined his people in Medina and almost at once, the Khazraj killed him. Some of his family used to say, "In our opinion he was a Muslim when he was killed"; he was in fact killed before the battle of Bu'āth.[21]

Occasionally, the recitation is called *jamīl* or *ajmal* [22] which can only be understood as a tribute to its linguistic form; while the root *ḥ-s-n* contains a variety of meanings between (morally) good and (outwardly) beautiful, *jamīl* is more distinctly an aesthetic category, as it almost always refers to the sensual impression of a phenomenon. That the audience's reaction to the Qur'ān originates indeed in an aesthetic experience, is perhaps best described in the following episode:

> Abū 'Ubayd mentions that a Bedouin listened to a man reciting *fa 'ṣda' bi-mā tu'mar* ("So shout that thou art commanded").[23] After this, he threw himself onto the ground worshipping and said: "I threw myself down for the eloquence of this speech (*sajadtu li-faṣāḥatih*)."[24]

In this series of reports, which let us assume an aesthetic experience, belongs moreover the most famous of all conversions known in Islamic history, the conversion of the caliph-to be, 'Umar b. al-Khaṭṭāb. Initially, he was one of the most dangerous opponents of the young Muslim community, a man of 30 or 35, of enormous physical strength and energy, who loved gambling, wine and poetry and was considered as emotional as he was wild-tempered.[25] "We could not pray at the Ka'ba until 'Umar became a Muslim, and then he fought the Quraysh until he could pray there and we prayed with him."[26] This statement of the Prophet's Companion 'Abd Allāh b. Mas'ūd shows what importance 'Umar's conversion held for the cause of Islam.[27] In fact, on this very day he had intended to kill the Prophet; but just as he made for him, he heard that his sister Fāṭima and her husband Sa'īd b. Zayd had become Muslims. Infuriated, he went to their house. On the street, just in front of the entrance, he heard someone reciting the Qur'ān to them. 'Umar stormed into the room. The reciter went for hiding as fast as he could, while Fāṭima took the pages of the Qur'ān and put them under her thighs.

"What is this balderdash I heard," 'Umar shouted at her.

"You have not heard anything," Fāṭima and her husband tried to calm him.

'Umar exclaimed: "By God, I have, and I have been told that you have followed Muḥammad in his religion."

He wanted to go after his brother-in-law, but Fāṭima stepped between them and 'Umar – unintentionally – hit her badly.

"Yes, we are Muslims and we believe in God and His Apostle, and you can do what you like," Fāṭima and Sa'īd exclaimed. 'Umar, however, already regretted his behaviour, the blood on his sister's face touched his heart. Softly he asked her about the scriptures. After Fāṭima got his promise to return the sheet undamaged, and moreover convinced him to undergo a ritual washing, as no unclean person was allowed to touch the Qur'ān. Then she handed it over to him. 'Umar commenced reciting *Sūrat Ṭāhā*. After only a few verses he stopped and exclaimed: "how beautiful and noble is this speech (*mā aḥsana hādha 'l-kalāma wa akrama*)!" When he had finished reading, he immediately went to Muḥammad to convert to Islam in front of him. "The Apostle gave thanks to God so loudly that the whole household knew that 'Umar had become a Muslim," it says in the tradition which has been recounted here, somewhat shortened, as handed down by Ibn Hishām and Ibn Kathīr.[28]

According to another report quoted in both biographies, 'Umar, after searching in vain for his drinking companions and the wine seller, passed by the Ka'ba where he ran into Muḥammad performing his *ṣalāt*. Out of curiosity, he sneaked behind the Black Stone of the Ka'ba without the Prophet realizing it. "When I heard the Qur'ān my heart was softened and I wept, and Islam entered into me," 'Umar's own description is recorded. When Muḥammad had concluded his prayer and went home, 'Umar followed him to convert to Islam before him.[29]

Although rather different in their course of action, both versions have essential aspects in common. In both cases, the recitation of the Qur'ān causes the sudden and unexpected conversion of one of the most important opponents of Muḥammad, and in both cases 'Umar's own comment points towards a subjective experience of an aesthetic nature. Indeed, 'Umar does not say that he had comprehended the truth, that the message had convinced him, or that after prolonged pondering or through sudden insight he had finally understood it or something similar. Rather he talks about "beauty" and about his heart "softening", about him crying when listening to the Qur'ān and about something "entering" him – which, when all these descriptions are taken together, can mean nothing but an emotional and sensual process, not an intellectual decision or a moral-ethical key experience.

In this episode, just as in others, it does not seem to be important *who* recites the revelation; the tradition records spontaneous conversions to Islam and eruptions of joy and pleasure in audiences without Muḥammad being present. The contrast between his own language – which he uses when inviting to Islam – and the Qur'ān is striking already in the early sources. Only the latter explicitly is awarded an aesthetic quality. Muḥammad's missionary sermons, on the other hand, appear to provoke almost dismissive reactions in most people, as is suggested by his own statement.[30]

In marked regularity, conversion reports concern poets, or at least – as in the case of ʻUmar – it is mentioned that the person concerned is quite famous for his rhetorical gift. Tradition treasures it when the superiority and uniqueness of the Qur'ānic language is attested by "experts" such as al-Walīd b. al-Mughīra, al-Ṭufayl b. ʻAmr al-Dawsī, Ḥassān b. Thābit, Labīd b. Rabīʻa, Kaʻb b. Mālik, or Suwayd b. al-Ṣāmit.[31] An example is the conversion of the poet Labīd. According to a later legend (already proven historically wrong by Nöldeke),[32] sheets with his poems were fastened to the entrance of the Kaʻba. None of his poet colleagues dared take on the challenge and hang his verses next to Labīd's poems. But one day some supporters of Muḥammad approached. They attached a piece of the second Qur'ānic sūra to the entrance and asked Labīd to recite it. Confident about himself and the quality of his poetry, the king of poets accepted and recited the verses. Overwhelmed by their beauty, he converted to Islam then and there.[33]

The following anecdote also belongs to this genre of poets' conversions. It recounts the story of al-Ṭufayl b. ʻAmr al-Dawsī who was a wealthy poet and nobleman of the Banū Daws. Ibn Isḥāq records that some men of the Quraysh called on him when he arrived in Mecca, warning him about Muḥammad's magic speeches that only planted discord among men. If al-Ṭufayl came close to the Prophet and listened to his recital, then he and his people also would get involved in arguments and quarrel (through the powerful effect of Muḥammad's recitation, as the contemporary Iranian author Maḥmūd Rāmiyār adds, who retells this episode from the *sīra*). They urgently advised him not to exchange a word with the Apostle and especially not to listen to his recitations. "By God, they were so persistent that I indeed decided neither to listen to anything he said nor to speak to him," al-Ṭufayl is quoted by Ibn Isḥāq. He even stuffed wool in his ears, "fearing that some of his words might still get through, whereas I did not want to hear any of it."[34] In the Kaʻba, al-Ṭufayl eventually met the Prophet performing his prayer. Unintentionally, he picked up some of the recital. While Ibn Isḥāq merely notes that al-Ṭufayl heard a beautiful speech (*fa-samiʻtu kalāman ḥasanan*), in Rāmiyār's re-narration al-Ṭufayl's impression reads as follows: "It was a gentle and soulful recital. It bewitched the heart and caressed the mind. Such an attraction was in the recitation that no man of poetry and letters could resist. In it, he found a wave of tenderness and a spiritual wealth in its meaning, which he never had heard in human speech before."[35]

In any case, the recitation was attractive enough for al-Ṭufayl to give up his intention and to resolve to listen more carefully. "Here I am, an intelligent man and poet, I can distinguish between the beautiful and the repulsive," he said to himself. "So what is to prevent me from listening to what this man is saying? If what he presents is beautiful, I accept it; if it is ugly, I reject it."[36] He followed Muḥammad to his house and asked him to recite something. "By God, never before had I heard a word more beautiful than this, and never had I heard a cause more just than this, and so I converted to Islam and pledged myself to the confession of truth," his reaction is reported by Ibn Hishām. Al-Ṭufayl returned to his clan and won the majority of his companions over to Islam.[37]

Another group besides the poets appears, according to the tradition, to have been particularly receptive to the beauty of the Qur'ān: Muḥammad's most aggressive enemies, Meccans like Unays or, once again, 'Umar b. al-Khaṭṭāb who at first fiercely fought the Prophet, yet spontaneously joined him when they heard his recitation. "Let us only take the effect which the hearing of the verses had on his adversaries," Maḥmūd Rāmiyār remarks. "As regards that alone, we know dozens of people by name and with their biographical data who had come to the Apostle to argue with him, to dispute with him and protest against him, and scarcely had they sat with him, heard his speech and God's verses, when they became Muslims."[38] A well-known example is Muṭ'im b. 'Adī who, after the Battle of Badr where his closest relatives had died, came to the Prophet to ransom his cousin and two of his companions. Just then, the Prophet was in prayer and recited *Sūrat al-Ṭūr,* which warns about Judgement Day and heralds the bliss of Paradise. When he came to the last verse, Muṭ'im converted to Islam.[39] "It was as if my heart split open," Abū Nu'aym quotes him as saying.[40] In al-Wāqidī's version (d. 822), Muṭ'im falls asleep in the mosque of Medina and is awakened by the recitation of the Prophet. "This was the day on which Islam entered my heart for the first time," he says according to this version.[41]

The course of 'Uthmān b. Maẓ'ūn's conversion is similar. In rage, he came to the Prophet who invited him to sit down. Their conversation was suddenly interrupted when a revelation overwhelmed the Prophet. When he came out of it, 'Uthmān asked him, "What has been said to you?" The Prophet recited the Qur'ānic verse 16:90 ("Surely God bids to justice and good-doing"). "Thus faith entered my heart, and I loved Muḥammad," the tradition quotes 'Uthmān.[42]

Even more spectacular are the conversions of Sa'd b. Mu'ādh and Usayd b. al-Ḥuḍayr, the leaders of the Banū 'Abd al-Ashhal. They heard that two of Muḥammad's supporters had arrived in Yathrib, one of them a cousin of Sa'd. Sa'd asked his companion Usayd to go and drive them out of the quarter. To prevent them from seducing the weak members of the clan, Usayd was to forbid them to enter the territory of the Banū 'Abd al-Ashhal ever again. He took his lance and went to the two strangers, full of rage. How dared they deceive his comrades, he exclaimed and threatened to kill them.

"Won't you sit down and listen?" Muṣ'ab b. 'Umayr, one of the two Muslims, asked. "If you like what you hear you can accept it, and if you don't like it you can leave it alone."

Usayd agreed, put his lance on the ground and sat down. Muṣ'ab spoke to him about Islam and recited from the Qur'ān. Even before Usayd replied, his face relaxed and he beamed, and the two Muslims could already see "Islam in his face by its peaceful glow."

"What a wonderful and beautiful discourse this is," he exclaimed. "What does one do if he wants to enter this religion?"

Shortly afterward, Usayd returned to his brother and asserted that nothing evil could be found with the two strangers. What is more, he mentioned that the Banū Ḥāritha had set out to kill As'ad, Sa'd's cousin, so as to expose the leader of the clan and punish him for protecting the two Muslims. Furiously, Sa'd got up, alarmed about the intentions of the Banū Ḥāritha.

"By God, I see that you have been utterly ineffective," he said and went to the two Muslims. But with the same words that had won over Usayd, Muṣ'ab convinced him to sit down first and consider the recitation. When he recited from the Qur'ān, Sa'd too converted to the new religion. With a blissful expression on his face, the clan leader returned to his people who then immediately and unanimously joined Islam.[43]

"Those who were the most stubborn and hostile came to the faith the fastest when the Qur'ān was recited to them," as the Egyptian scholar Muḥammad Abū Zahra comments.[44] It is of course a confirmation of the supernatural effect of the Qur'ān that can hardly be surpassed, when – of all people – the most bitter enemies, and precisely poets, were bewitched by it in a moment.

Conversions initiated through the sound of the Qur'ān are mentioned for adherents of other religions of the Book as well. Some twenty Christians, for example, who had come to Mecca to take back news about the new Prophet, are said to have converted after the very first encounter with him. "When they heard the Qur'ān their eyes flowed with tears, and they accepted God's call, believed in Him, and declared His truth," it says in the tradition. "God, what a wretched band you are," the outraged Quraysh scolded them, "Your people at home sent you to bring them information about the fellow, and as soon as you sat with him you renounced your religion and believed what he said. We don't know a more asinine band than you!"[45]

The Qur'ān recitation is said to have been so irresistible that even non-Arabs fell under its spell. For instance, it is said that a Byzantine general, who had heard a Qur'ān verse from a Muslim prisoner, travelled to Mecca for the express purpose of converting to Islam in front of 'Umar.[46] The Abyssinian Negus together with his bishops is said to have broken down in tears, "until his beard was wet and the bishops wept until their scrolls were wet, when they heard what he recited to them,"[47] when Muslim emigrants recited an excerpt of *Sūrat Maryam.* Apart from this account, Abū Nu'aym (d. 1038) offers a slightly different version:

> When he heard about it, the Negus recognized it as the truth and he said:
>
> "Recite us some more of this good speech!"
>
> And they recited another sūra, and when he heard it, he knew the truth and he said:
>
> "I believe you and I believe your Prophet."[48]

The episode shows how important the pure sound of the Qur'ān is considered to be, as it can neither be assumed that the Negus spoke Arabic nor can it be suggested that the Muslims presented him with a translation – the problematic nature of understanding the content is simply not mentioned in the traditions. The Qāḍī 'Iyāḍ (d. 1149) recounts a similar anecdote about a Christian who "neither understood the meanings of the Qur'ān nor knew its interpretations," but who cried anyway when he heard the Qur'ān. Asked why he cried, he answered, "Because it is moving (*li 'l-shajā*) and because of its linguistic composition (*naẓm*)."[49] Muḥammad Abū Zahra has such reports in mind when he states:

> The Qur'ān was of such musicality (*mūsīqā*) and such a quality of composition that it caused a shiver in every listener, even when he could not understand Arabic at all. For the words with their stretching, nasal sounds, rhymes, verses and pauses were arranged in such a way as to also hold an attraction to the non-Arab although he didn't understand the meaning of the words. It was the melody (*nagham*) that created a wonderful image in him.[50]

In this century, other Muslim authors such as Muṣṭafā Ṣādiq al-Rāfi'ī,[51] Labīb al-Sa'īd,[52] Moḥammad Taqī Sharī'atī Mazīnānī[53] and Maḥmūd Bustānī[54] emphasize the tonal dimension of the Qur'ānic miracle – an aspect mentioned only in passing in the classical *i'jāz* tractates, yet an aspect of which Maḥmūd Rāmiyār says:

> With every beautiful sound that is characteristic to it, with that attraction and that lure found in its rhymes, with the deep and light tones of its words and the density of its melody, Qur'ān recital causes in the listener a state of tenderness and creates a movement in his soul which never appear in another speech or another canto. Its miraculous attraction is effective and moves deeply even those who do not comprehend Arabic and do not know Islam.[55]

Even the devils (*shayāṭīn*) let themselves be converted by the "wonderful recital" (*Qur'ānan 'ajaban*),[56] as did the Jinn when they heard the Prophet say the ritual prayer at night in the desert between Ṭā'if and Mecca.[57] "We have heard a wonderful recital which guides to rectitude, so we believe in it," they are quoted in the Qur'ān.[58] The Prophet is said to have known that they, like the angels,[59] gathered around him every time he recited the revelation. It is said that one time he wanted to give his Companions the chance to see the Jinn and thus went with them outside the gates of Mecca. When they arrived there, he sat apart from the group and recited the Qur'ān. The report of 'Abd Allāh b. Mas'ud goes as follow:

> In this moment, large black creatures were surrounding him. They obstructed our view and I couldn't even hear the voice of the Prophet. After a while, they dispersed like a cloud, but a group of them remained. When day broke, the Prophet ended the recitation and set off. He came to me and asked about the group that had stayed behind. "There they are," I said. The Prophet took a bone and some camel dung and gave it to them as provision and he said that these things were unclean for humans.[60]

As a last example for a conversion effected in an instant through Qur'ān recitation I would like to introduce a tale that I could not find in this form in any of the Prophet's biographies but have heard years ago in Iran. Since then, it has been narrated to me several times.[61] I would like to introduce it not only because it made an indelible impression on me but because it also stands for the fact that not nearly all stories about the life of the Prophet have been included in the canon of biographies and traditions. The story is about a messenger from Yathrib who came to Mecca so as to investigate the mysterious news about the appearance of a new prophet. He had been warned strongly about the Prophet's magic tricks and been urged to plug his ears before he met people reciting his revelation. In any case, the man walked through the streets of Mecca and met a group of believers listening to a Qur'ān recital. He thought to himself: I am a man of intelligence and experience, why do I make a fool of myself and plug my ears just because someone is reciting a text? He unplugged his ears, heard the sound of the Qur'ān, and converted to Islam then and there.

The peculiarity of such – always uniformly structured – tales of conversions (one or more protagonists, who are hostile to the Prophet or do not know him, hear some verses from the Qur'ān and instantly convert to Islam) becomes especially clear when one searches for counterparts in other religions. The phenomenon of conversion initiated by an aesthetic experience in the stricter sense, frequently proclaimed in Islam in later centuries as well,[62] is hardly known in Christianity. Neither about the Gospels nor about other parts of the Bible do we find corresponding reports. As far as autobiographical testimonies inform us, the great conversions and incidents of initiation in Christian history – Paul,[63] Augustine,[64] Pascal,[65] and Luther[66] are the most famous names in this context – are initiated by different, for the outsider possibly likewise remarkable, yet not primarily aesthetic experiences. In the perception of the individual, the pre-eminent aspect is not the beauty of divine revelation, but its moral-ethical message for the individual. This does not imply that the development and religious practice in Christianity or other religions could be imagined without the aesthetic fascination of particular spaces, rituals, texts, sounds, songs, pictures, or even colors, acts, fragrances, gesture,[67] or that for example Protestantism could have spread so tremendously fast in the German-speaking areas without the linguistic power of the Lutheran Bible. Yet in the perception which Christian and especially Protestant communities have of their own past, the aesthetic momentum plays a subordinate role, however relevant it may be for the religious practice. Few Christians would maintain that his disciples gathered around Jesus because they received his speech as formally perfect, and nowhere in Christian religious education is one taught to causally relate the triumphant advance of Christianity to the linguistic beauty of the Gospels. Among the several examples, which William James has cited and analyzed in his prominent collection of accounts of christianization, there is none that would be comparable with, for example, the stories about Labīd's or 'Umar's conversion.[68] While spontaneous confessions of faith cited by James are "all with a sense of astonished happiness and of being wrought by a higher contol,"[69] a description that probably could relate just as well to 'Umar's subjective condition, in James's collection the decisive event is of moral or emotional relevance. People who arrive at point zero or pass through exceptional circumstances recognize the irrelevance of their former existence through an event or an emotion and from one moment to the next begin a new life. The alcoholic abstains from his addiction, the dispirited turns happy, the wealthy becomes a benefactor, the doubtful becomes calm, the corrupt reformed – just as it is demonstrated in Augustine's repentance, in his renunciation of sensual pleasures that tore "on the clothes of my flesh", and in his turn towards pure "dignity of chastity, gently cheerful, but not boisterous, modestly luring me to come and doubt no longer."[70]

James does not record conversions whose immediate cause is the aesthetic experience of the Holy Scripures. When its reading leads to such a reaction, then it is the "overpowering impression of the *meaning* of suddenly presented scripture texts,"[71] but not verses that provide such *delight* that one spontaneously assumes them to be divine. Certainly, there will be conversions to Christianity that are caused directly by the aesthetic quality of the scripture reports; but these do not represent a significant part of the body of Christian testimonies about Christianity's expansion; they do not form a topos of salvation literature, are no figure of memory.

In Muslim self-conception, on the other hand, the aesthetic fascination emanating from the Qur'ān is constitutive of its own religious tradition. This act of collective realization and interpretation is specific to the religious world of Islam – not the experience of beauty occurring in the reception of other sacred texts.

It is noteworthy that in the course of time the significance of the history of salvation, which is attributed to the aesthetic effect of the Qur'ān, is increasingly emphasized. For the triumphant advance of Islam, modern authors such as Abū Zahra, Muṣṭafā Ṣādiq al-Rāfi'ī, Rashīd Riḍā, Sayyid Quṭb, or Maḥmūd Rāmiyār regard the literary supremacy of the text at least as crucial as the actions and speeches of Muḥammad; this is not preconceived in the Qur'ān and not even in the early tradition. In the course of Muslim history, a gradual change in awareness took place; and in the cultural memory individual aspects were accentuated in a very peculiar way. Although some verses in the Qur'ān are documents of its own reception (which includes its aesthetic component), it still leaves unanswered the role that its literary quality has played in Muḥammad's mission. In the *sīra* the attraction supposedly emanating from Qur'ānic recitation is explained in greater detail. But the subtext of – at least – the reports from the Meccan period is that the Prophet meets with rejection mainly; the Hijra, as is well known, is a consequence of this rejection. Except for some followers mostly from the lower strata of society (*qalīlan min al-mustaḍ'afīn*), the Meccans refused any acknowledgement of Muḥammad's recitation.[72] In this phase, the effect of the Qur'ān in the described way is rather the exception than the norm.

In retrospect the perception changes, the irresistibility of the Qur'ānic recitation moves to the fore. This, of course, can be observed particularly well, where texts from different contexts refer to the same event: in the comparison between Qur'ān and exegesis, for example. Characteristic for the (not necessarily wrong, but not readily deductible) interpretation of the original situation of recitation in the collective memory is the interpretation of individual verses which by themselves appear non-specific, but which in the Qur'ānic commentaries or the *asbāb al-nuzūl* works are transformed into an indication about the aesthetic effect of the Qur'ān. As for instance in Q. 41:26:

> The unbelievers say, Do not give ear
> to this Qur'ān, and talk idly about it,
> haply you will overcome![73]

At first, the verse seems to reflect the request of the infidels not to listen to the Qur'ān: not to obey its commandments and to reject its message. At closer look it becomes obvious that the verse refers to a particular situation. It contains not only the appeal of the Meccans not to listen to a certain recital (*lā tasma'ū li-hādhā 'l-Qur'āni*) but also their appeal to disturb it with noise and loud chatter (*wa 'lghaw fīhi*).[74] According to the Muslim commentators, the Qur'ān points here to the fact that the Meccans, after a series of conversions caused by the sound of the Qur'ān, had tried to lessen the effect of Muḥammad's recitations in the Ka'ba through clapping, singing and loud chatter (*laghw*),[75] and, according to al-Rāzī (d. 1210), also through loud reciting of poems and fairytales.[76] Looked at from that angle, it would explain why the Qur'ān urged the faithful repeatedly not to pay attention to the *laghw* of the unbelievers.[77] Muḥammad Abū Zahra's contemporary commentary of the verse sums up the traditional Muslim reading:

> The greatest among Muḥammad's enemies feared that the Qur'ān would have a strong effect on them, while they preferred lack of faith to faith and aberration to right guidance. Thus, they agreed not to listen to this Qur'ān. They knew that everyone listening was moved by its solemn expressive force that exceeded human strength. They saw that the people – even the great personalities, the notables and mighty – one after another believed it, that Islam grew stronger, that the faithful became more numerous, polytheism became weaker, and their supporters became less.[78]

Muslim commentators interpret the following verse likewise as an indication of the attractive power of the Qur'ānic recitation:

> Behold, they fold their breasts, to
> Hide them from Him;
> behold, when they wrap themselves in
> their garments He knows what they secrete
> and what they publish;
> surely He knows all the thoughts
> within the breasts.[79]

At first the verse seems to have nothing to do with the recitation of the Qur'ān. Apparently it alludes to a certain event within Muḥammad's opposition without naming it. Without a commentary, the passage seems barely comprehensible. Here it is interesting *how* Muslim scholars explain it. Muḥammad Rāmiyār writes in his "History of the Qur'ān" that the Meccan poets bent double to avoid being seen and recognized when they slinked around the Ka'ba and listened to Muḥammad's recitations there – in his opinion one of many pieces of evidence for "the forcefulness and impact of the divine message."[80]

In the light of Muslim exegesis, numerous verses in the Qur'ān appear like this one as evidence for its aesthetic spell. The scholars try to supplement the often not very specific allusions to episodes in Muḥammad's milieu with tales about the reactions of individual Meccans to the recitation. However they appeared "in reality", only in the tradition

– and therefore one could say in *remembered* history – is it recorded how much the language of the Qur'ān cast its spell over the first listeners.

As the later community interprets its own sources and tries to understand the aesthetic effectiveness of the Qur'ān in the course of reception history, this effectiveness becomes increasingly important for its own history. This is evident not only in the comparison of Qur'ānic passages and later commentaries and biographical works. Apart from the Qur'ān, the traditions about individual situations of recitation demonstrating the irresistibility of the Qur'ān are increasingly embellished. While the *sīra* – and ḥadīth–works could be designated as the first layer of memory, only in the second layer is the present image of the aesthetic miraculous effect of the Qur'ān formed. The development of the *iʿjāz* doctrine in the ninth and tenth centuries, the reference to the linguistic perfection of the Qur'ān, and the claim that nobody but the Arabs with their talent for language had managed to accept the Prophet's challenge to counter the Qur'ān with something better, more beautiful, more enchanting, all these belong to the elements of identity of the Muslim community. The linguistic perfection and the historical superiority of the Qur'ān, which as a subjective feeling surely existed and was frequently expressed in the earlier centuries, are now taken as plain evidence that what unites the individuals in this community and distinguishes them from individuals of other communities is objectively true and forever valid.

In this respect, the so-called *nubuwwa* works are especially significant, such as for example Abū Nuʿaym's or al-Bayhaqī's (d. 1066) treatises or the *Shifā'* by al-Qāḍī 'Iyāḍ still very popular in the Islamic world. They function as a recollection and description of the history of salvation while structuring and commenting on the scattered traditions about the effect of the Qur'ān. In the surviving *iʿjāz* compendia, on the other hand, the earliest of which date from the late tenth century, the tales about the first listeners of the Qur'ān are found only occasionally and often in a fragmentary form, although from a Muslim perspective they are the most conclusive proof of the miraculous character of the Qur'ān. However, within them the remembered history is present – although it is different, rather shortened, and sketchier than in the *nubuwwa* works. Knowledge of the Qur'ān's reception in earlier Muslim history is required, at least in rough outline. Thus, authors like al-Rummānī, al-Bāqillānī (d. 1013) or al-Jurjānī (d. 1078) do not have to reconstruct the events or the period of foundation, but can content themselves with the invocation of its memory through particular indications of obviously known events or with using them as evidence for the correctness of their own theories.[81]

In contemporary treatises dealing with the Qur'ān, the traditions about individual acts of recitation, which already give testimony to the irresistibility of the Qur'ān, are further adorned. Moreover, conversions like the one of the Christian 'Addās, which in the *sīra* do not yet contain an indication about an aesthetic key experience,[82] are quoted as proof of "that enormous and deep impact," as can be read in Rāmiyār's "History of the Qur'ān".[83] This example is characteristic insofar as the author is an altogether very scrupulous scholar who only uses (from a Muslim perspective) credible sources which are supported carefully by footnotes. While his work is therefore rather free of ornament and transfigurations with which the popular belief embellishes the episodes of the Prophet's life, in his chapter about the "effect of the Qur'ān" (*ta'thīr-e Qor'ān*) he cannot avoid exuberance in ductus.

Even if the sources about the effect of the Qur'ān on its listeners are denied any authenticity and are seen as pure imagination of a later time, as an apologetic construct, the effect attributed to the Qur'ān remains exceptional in cultural history. Although generally disregarded in Western Islamic studies,[84] it is a basic assumption of Muslim historiography and even more of contemporary Muslim scholarship that hardly anyone could escape the gravitation of Qur'ānic recitation and that opponents as much as adherents attributed the success of the new prophet not only to his charisma or to the message of the Qur'ān, but explained it with the unexpected attraction of its recitation. Muslim authors commonly claim that Muḥammad succeeded against the physical strength of his adversaries especially because of the linguistic powers of his recitation. "Muḥammad is the one whose tongue God has made into a sword, and this sword is clear Arabic," asserts for example 'Alī b. Rabban al-Ṭabarī (d. est. 857).[85] "It is certainly undisputed that the glory and the power that Islam has achieved was nothing but a consequence of its [the Qur'ān's] linguistic miraculous character (*i'jāz*), and everything that happened is owed to the brilliance and splendour of the Qur'ān," Maḥmūd Rāmiyār remarks in this century.[86] In a similar way, Sayyid Quṭb, the later intellectual leader of Islamism, identifies the Qur'ān – and he did not mean the effect of its recitation – as the "decisive factor or at least one of the decisive factors for the persuasion of those who found their way to the faith in the early period of the mission, in those days when Muḥammad had neither power nor authority and Islam had neither strength nor power of resistance."[87] Rashīd Riḍā even widens the sphere of its impact. The beautiful and powerful words of the Qur'ān "have changed the souls of the Arabs, and the Arabs, on their part, have changed the foreign nations," he states; and he concludes that the frequent recitation of the Qur'ān has led to "the strongest spiritual and social revolution in history."[88] And Muḥammad Abū Zahra writes:

> The Qur'ān attracted the Arabs to faith on the strength of its stirring magnificence (*raw'a*) and the power of its rhetoric (*bayān*), on the strength of its marvellous conciseness and because it has at its

> disposal lasting words, long and short stories as well as many small and important instructions, because its long expressions cause joy and its short phrases neglect nothing in their transparent expression and their clear indications. Indeed their faith did not emerge from a desire for revolt or from their weakness, weak as they were. When their faith was strong, then this came from the Qur'ān. The Qur'ān was what drove them to faith on the strength of its rhetoric, which exceeded the talents of man as was obvious to all."[89]

Western Qur'ānic studies, especially in Germany, have for decades been dominated by approaches that put in the center either the intentions, influences, and motives of Muḥammad as the assumed author, or analyze what the Qur'ān, "objectively examined,"[90] *is,* or discuss which genre it belongs to, and whether it is complete, authentic, full of mistakes, ethically acceptable or well written.

As more and more contributions by scholars of Islamic studies show, it is at least equally exciting to inquire what the revelation *is for those who are its main recipients* and thus to understand the Qur'ān as a structure: not as a concrete object, but as a system of relations, including those between the text and its recipients in whose mind alone it updates itself as an aesthetic object.

NOTES

1 *Geschichte des Qorāns,* 2nd rev. ed. (Leipzig: Deutsche Verlagsbuchhandlung, 1909), 1:143, n 2.

2 Jan Assmann, *Das kulturelle Gedächtnis. Schrift, Erinnerung und politische Identität in frühen Hochkulturen* (Munich: Beck, 1992), 17.

3 Cf. ibid., 48. Assman derives this argument partly from the French sociologist Maurice Halbwachs who in the 1920s developed the concept of 'mémoire collective'; see Halbwachs's books *Les cadres sociaux de la mémoire* (Paris: Mouton, 1976) and *La mémoire collective* (Paris: PUF, 1969).

4 See Q. 2:23; 10:38; 11:13; 18:88; 52:34.

5 See Nöldeke-Schwally, *Geschichte des Qorāns,* 1:55; John Wansbrough, *Quranic Studies: Sources and Methods of Scriptural Interpretation* (Oxford: Oxford University Press, 1977), 78f.; Vicente Cantarino, *Arabic Poetics in the Golden Age* (Leiden: Brill, 1975), 13; Matthias Radscheidt, "'I'ǧāz al-Qur'ān' im Koran?" in Stefan Wild, ed., *The Qur'ān as Text* (Leiden: Brill, 1996), 113–23; idem, *Die koranische Herausforderung. Die taḥaddī-Verse im Rahmen der Polemikpassagen des Korans* (Berlin: Klaus Schwarz, 1996); Josef van Ess, *Theologie und Gesellschaft im 2. und 3. Jahrhundert Hidschra. Eine Geschichte des religiösen Denkens,* 6 vols. (Berlin/New York: de Gruyter, 1991–1997), 4:607.

6 *Das kulturelle Gedächtnis,* 77.

7 This I have tried in the first chapter of my *Gott ist schön. Das ästhetische Erleben des Koran,* (Munich: Beck, 1999), that also includes a detailed version of this essay and a complete bibliography of all sources analyzed for it. The book is an extended examination of the aesthetic reception of the Qur'ān throughout Muslim history.

8 Muṣṭafā Ṣādiq al-Rāfi'ī, *I'jāz al-Qur'ān wa 'l-Balāgha al-Nabawiyya* (Cairo: Dār al-Kitāb al-'Arabī, 1345/1926), 212f. On al-Rāfi'ī and his work see Carl Brockelmann, *Geschichte der arabischen Litteratur,* 2nd rev. ed., 2 vol. + 3 supl. (Leiden: Brill, 1937–1949), S. 3:71ff.

9 I have deliberately left out works by modernist authors and by others usually considered controversial in religious circles, such as Bint al-Shāṭi', Naṣr Ḥāmid Abū Zayd, Adūnīs, and 'Alī Sharī'atī.

10 A fourth and for the aesthetic reception of the Qur'ān very revealing discourse is the mystical one with its very particular view of the Muslim founding period. However, for lack of space this discourse is not taken into account and I have to refer to my *Gott ist schön.*

11 See al-Qāḍī Abū l-Faḍl 'Iyāḍ, *Al-Shifā' bi-Ta'rīf Ḥuqūq al-Muṣṭafā* (Beirut: Dār al-Kutub al-'Ilmiyya, n.d.), 1:247.

12 See Abū Muḥammad 'Abd al-Malik Ibn Hishām, *al-Sīra al-Nabawiyya,* 4 vols. ed. Muṣṭafā al-Saqqā, Ibrāhīm al-Abyārī and 'Abd al-Ḥafīẓ Shalabī (Cairo: Dār al-Ma'rifa, 1355/1937), repr. Beirut: 1391/1971, 1:383; *The Life of Muhammad,* transl., by Alfred Guillaume (Karachi: Oxford University Press, 1967), 176 (the following translations from Ibn Hishām's work do not always follow Guillaume entirely).

13 It remains unclear in the *sīra* what exactly *ṣalāt* or the accompanying verb means and to what degree it is similar to the ritual prayer that is customary today. However, it is almost certain that in some form or other a kind of ritualized Qur'ān recitation took place.

14 See Ibn Hishām, *Sīra,* 1:442 (transl., 202). The translation of the notion *qur'ān* is problematic. It is known that in the Qur'ān itself it is used in most cases not as a proper name for a collection of texts but simply in the sense of 'recitation'. Later on, however, the expression was established firmly as the name for the revelation recited by Muḥammad and taken down in writing; only retrospectively, the name 'Qur'ān' is read into the concept *qur'ān* (and as only such 'projections' are the topic of this study, it cannot be oriented simply towards the historical meaning of the word without taking into account the history of interpretation). The prophetic transmissions mark the moment of semantic change: *qur'ān* may be used either for mere recitation or for a proper name, and frequently one can hardly decide which of the two possibilities is accurate. It becomes especially complicated when the Qur'ān is quoted within a later text; in the Qur'ān, the reciter uses *qur'ān* as in 'recitation', while the reciter of the later text understands *al-Qur'ān,* the name of the Holy Script. Presumably, this problem cannot be solved in translation, or rather only if one would use the Arabic transcriptions in every case, that is if one would write *qur'ān* instead of Qur'ān. This would hardly illuminate the problem, as an interpretation would still be necessary. With reference to this remark, I will therefore continue to write Qur'ān where *qur'ān* is used in the Arabic, if only for the sake of comprehensibility. However, it should be pointed out that the word in Qur'ānic quotations usually means 'recitation'.

15 Muḥammad Ibn Sa'd, *al-Ṭabaqāt al-Kubrā (= Biographien Muhammeds, seiner Gefährten und der späteren Träger des Islams bis zum Jahre 230 der Flucht),* ed. Eduard Sachau, 9 vols. (Leiden: Brill, 1905–1917), 1/i:146; similar in Ibn Hishām, *Sīra,* 1:428.

16 Ibn Sa'd, *al-Ṭabaqāt,* 1/i:115.

17 'Iyāḍ, *Shifā',* 1:262.

18 See Ibn Hishām, *Sīra,* 1:427f. (transl., 197); Ibn Sa'd, *al-Ṭabaqāt,* 3/ii:14, Abū l-Fidā' Ismā'īl Ibn Kathīr, *al-Sīra al-Nabawiyya,* 4 vols. ed., Muṣṭafā 'Abd al-Wāḥid

(Beirut: Dār al-Rā'id al-'Arabī, 1987), 2:174; Abū Ja'far Muḥammad b. Jarīr al-Ṭabarī, *Tārīkh al-Rusul wa 'l-Mulūk*, ed. M. de Goeje, 15 vols. (Leiden: Brill, 1879–1901), 1208f.

19 Abū Bakr Aḥmad b. Ḥusayn al-Bayhaqī, *Dalā'il al-Nubuwwa*, 2 vols. ed. 'Abd al-Raḥmān Muḥammad 'Uthmān (Cairo: Dār al-Nashr li 'l-Ṭibā'a, 1969), 2:17; also Ibn Kathīr, *Sīra*, 1:452; Ibn Sa'd, *al-Ṭabaqāt*, 1/ii:44.

20 See Abū Nu'aym Aḥmad b. 'Abd Allāh b. Aḥmad al-Iṣfahānī, *Dalā'il al-Nubuwwa* (Beirut: 'Ālam al-Kutub, 1988), 163.

21 Ibn Hishām, *Sīra*, 1:427 (transl., pp. 196f.); also in Ibn Kathīr, *Sīra*, 2:182; Ṭabarī, *Tārīkh*, 1:1208.

22 For example by Usayd b. al-Ḥuḍayr (see Ibn Hishām, *Sīra*, 1:436 [transl.,, 200]; Ibn Kathīr, *Sīra*, 2:182), whose conversion I will examine subsequently and in more detail; and by the poet Hawdha b. 'Alī (see Ibn Sa'd, *al-Ṭabaqāt*, 1/ii:18).

23 Q. 15:94 (Arberry).

24 'Iyāḍ, *Shifā'*, 1:262.

25 That 'Umar loved poetry even before his conversion, is apparent from al-Ṭabarī, *Tārīkh*, 1:1144f. He confesses his passion for wine in a quotation handed down by Ibn Sa'd; one of the most difficult obligations in Islam, he is quoted saying on his deathbed, is abstinence from wine; *al-Ṭabaqāt*, 3/i:261.

26 Ibn Hishām, *Sīra*, 1:342. (transl., 155).

27 See also Muḥammad b. Ismā'īl al-Bukhārī, *Kitāb al-Jāmi' al-Ṣaḥīḥ*, ed., Ḥasūna al-Nawawī, 9 vol. (Cairo: Maktabat al-Bābī al-Ḥalabī wa Awlādih, 1958), 63/ 35 (no. 3863).

28 Ibn Hishām, *Sīra*, 1:343ff. (transl., 155ff.); Ibn Kathīr, *Sīra*, 2:33ff.

29 Ibn Hishām, *Sīra*, 1:346ff. (transl., 157); Ibn Kathīr, *Sīra*, 2:37f.

30 Cf. Ibn Hishām, *Sīra*, 1:252 (transl., 116).

31 For this cf. Abū Bakr Muḥammad b. al-Ṭayyib al-Bāqillānī, *I'jāz al-Qur'ān* (Beirut: 'Ālam al-Kutub, 1988), 272.

32 See his *Beiträge zur Kenntnis der Poesie der alten Araber* (Hannover: Rümpler, 1864, repr. Hildesheim: Olms, 1967).

33 Cf. Edward William Lane, *Selections of the Ḳur-ān with an Interwoven Commentary* (London: H. Bohn, 1843), 88, Edward Sell, *Faith of Islam*, 3rd ed. (Madras: SPCK, 1907), 8; R. Bosworth Smith, *Mohammed and Mohammedanism: Lectures Delivered at the Royal Institution of Great Britain in February and March 1874* (London: Smith, Elder and Company, 1876), 179.

34 Ibn Hishām, *Sīra*, 1:382 (transl., 175).

35 Cf. Maḥmūd Rāmiyār, *Tārīkh-e Qor'ān* (Tehran: Amīr Kabīr, 1984), 214f.

36 Ibn Hishām, *Sīra*, 1:383 (transl., 176).

37 Ibid.; also in Ibn Kathīr, *Sīra*, 2:73; Ibn Sa'd, *al-Ṭabaqāt*, 4/i:175.

38 Rāmiyār, *Tārīkh-e Qor'ān*, 213f.

39 Cf. Bāqillānī, *I'jāz*, 43.

40 Abū Nu'aym, *Dalā'il*, 164.

41 Muḥammad b. 'Umar al-Wāqidī, *Kitāb al-Maghāzī*, 3 vols. ed. Marsden Jones (London: Oxford University Press, 1966), 128; also in 'Iyāḍ, *Shifā'*, 1:274.

42 Aḥmad b. Muḥammad Ibn Ḥanbal, *Al-Musnad*, ed. Aḥmad Muḥammad Shākir, 15 vols. (Cairo: Dār al-Ma'ārif, 1956), 1:318 (no. 2922).

43 Taken from Ibn Hishām, *Sīra*, 1:435ff. (transl., 200f.); also in Ibn Kathīr, *Sīra*, 2:181ff.; Ṭabarī, *Tārīkh*, 1:1214f. Another version of Usayd's conversion is offered by Ibn Sa'd, *al-Ṭabaqāt*, 1/ii:68.

44 Muḥammad Abū Zahra, *Al-Mu'jiza al-Kubrā* (Cairo: Dār al-Fikr al-'Arabī, n.d.), 67.

45 Ibn Hishām, *Sīra*, 1:392 (transl., 179); see also Rāmiyār, *Tārīkh-e Qorān*, 220.

46 See 'Iyāḍ, *Shifā'*, 1:262f.
47 Ibn Hishām, *Sīra*, 1:336 (transl., 152.)
48 Abū Nu'aym, *Dalā'il*, 171.
49 *Shifā'*, 2:274. Already similar in al-Jāḥiẓ; he, however, attributes the statement to the Jewish physician and translator Māsarjawayh; see *Kitāb al-Ḥayawān*, 8 vols. ed. 'Abd al-Salām Muḥammad Hārūn (Cairo: Maktabat al-Bābī al-Ḥalabī wa Awlādih), 4:192.
50 *Al-Mu'jiza al-Kubrā*, 88.
51 *I'jāz al-Qur'ān*, 46f.
52 *Al-Taghannī bi 'l-Qur'ān* (Cairo: al-Hay'a al-'Āmma li 'l-Ta'līf wa 'l-Nashr, 1970), 67ff.; *Al-Jam' al-Ṣawtī al-Awwal aw al-Muṣḥaf al-Murattal* (Cairo: Dār al-Ma'ārif, 1967), 221ff.
53 *Waḥy wa-Nobuwwat dar Partow-e Qor'ān* (Mashhad: Hoseyniyye Ershād, 1970), 420f.
54 *Al-Islām wa-l-Fann*; only the Persian translation by Hosain Ṣāberī was available to me, *Eslām wa-Honar* (Teheran: Bonyād-e Pažūheshhā-e Eslāmī, 1993), 242ff.
55 Rāmiyār, *Tārīkh-e Qor'ān*, 221.
56 Cf. Bukhārī, *Ṣaḥīḥ*, 10:105 (no. 771).
57 Cf. Ibn Hishām, *Sīra*, 1:422 (transl., 193f.).
58 Q. 72:1–2; for this cf. also 'Iyāḍ, *Shifā'*, 1:277.
59 Abū 'l-Ḥusayn Muslim b. al-Ḥajjāj, *Ṣaḥīḥ Muslim*, ed. Muḥammad Fu'ād 'Abd al-Bāqī, 5 vols. (Cairo: Dār Iḥyā' al-Kutub al-'Arabiyya, 1955), 6:36 (no. 796).
60 Bayhaqī, *Dalā'il*, 2:15.
61 I quoted this anectode in "Revelation in Its Aesthetic Dimension. Some Notes about Apostles and Artists in Islamic and Christian Culture," in Wild, *The Qur'ān as Text*, 213–24; I assume that it originally goes back to the report about al-Ṭufayl's conversion; see *supra*.
62 The most famous of the later adherents who supposedly converted to Islam because of the linguistic quality of the Qur'ān is probably 'Alī b. Rabban al-Ṭabarī who writes about the conversion in his *Kitāb al-Dīn wa l-Dawla* (= *The Book of Religion and Empire*, ed. A. Mingana (Manchester: University Press/ Longmans, Green and Company, 1923), 44f.). When asked, a lot of Muslims or people in contact with Muslims report about cases where such a conversion amongst their acquaintances has allegedly taken place even today. Kristina Nelson, who researched for her book about the *The Art of Reciting the Qur'ān* (Austin: University of Texas Press, 1985) in Cairo, made similar observations (94): 'One of several stories which were told to me is that of an American who, hearing a five minute excerpt of Shaykh Rif'at's reciting over the radio, was so moved that he came to Egypt, took instruction, and became a Muslim.' Cf. also Sa'īd, *Al-Jam' al-Ṣawtī*, 255.
63 Cf. *Acts* 9:1ff.; 23:3ff; 26:12ff.
64 See Aurelius Augustinus, *Bekenntnisse*, transl., by Wilhelm Thimme (Zürich and Stuttgart: Artemis, 1950), 190–216 (Book 8).
65 See the *Mémorial* in Blaise Pascal, *Über die Religion und über einige andere Gegenstände (Pensées)*, transl., by Ewald Wasmuth (Heidelberg: Schneider, 1954) (= *Werke* I); cf. Romano Guardini, *Christliches Bewußtsein. Versuche über Pascal* (Munich: dtv, 1962), 17–39.
66 Cf. Karl Holl, *Gesammelte Aufsätze zur Kirchengeschichte. I. Band: Luther*, 6th rev. ed. (Tübingen: Moll, 1932), 27ff.; Hans Lilje, *Luther* (Reinbek bei Hamburg: Rowohlt, 1965), 67f.
67 Cf. Horst Wenzel, *Hören und Sehen. Schrift und Bild. Kultur und Gedächtnis im Mittelalter* (Munich: Beck, 1995); Jan Mukařovsky, *Kapitel aus der Ästhetik*, transl., by Walter Schamschula, 4th ed. (Frankfurt a. M.: Suhrkamp, 1982), 27ff.

68 William James, *The Varieties of Religious Experience: A Study in Human Nature, Being the Gifford Lectures on Natural Religion Delivered at Edinburgh in 1901–1902* (New York: Random House/The Modern Library, n.d.), 186–253.
69 Ibid., 192.
70 Augustinus, *Bekenntnisse*, 212f.
71 James, *Religious Experience*, 233 (italics mine).
72 See Ibn Hishām, *Sīra*, 1:422 (transl., 194).
73 Translation follows Arberry.
74 Cf. Jalāl al-Dīn al-Maḥallī & Jalāl al-Dīn al-Suyūṭī, *Tafsīr al-Jalālayn* (Beirut: Dār al-Qalam, n.d.), commentary on Q. 41:26.
75 See Rāmiyār, *Tārīkh-e Qor'ān*, 217.
76 See Fakhr al-Dīn al-Rāzī, *al-Tafsīr al-Kabīr*, 30 vols. (Tehran: Dār al-Kutub, n.d.), commentary on Q. 41:26.
77 See Q. 28:55; 23:3; 25:72.
78 Abū Zahra, *Al-Mu'jiza al-Kubrā*, 62f.
79 Q. 11:5 (Arberry).
80 Rāmiyār, *Tārīkh-e Qor'ān*, 218.
81 Cf. Chapter Four of my *Gott ist schön.*
82 See Ibn Hishām, *Sīra*, 1:421 (transl., 193); Ṭabarī, *Tārīkh*, 1:1201.
83 Rāmiyār, *Tārīkh-e Qor'ān*, 214.
84 So far, only G.H.A. Juynboll has pointed to this very motive of early Mulim history; cf. his "The Position of Qur'ān Recitation in Early Islam," in *Journal of Semitic Studies* 19 (1974):240–51. Angelika Neuwirth has, in a fundamental essay, dealt with the Qur'ān as a recited text and as the nucleus of Muslim worship in early Muslim history; see her "Vom Rezitationstext über die Liturgie zum Kanon. Zu Entstehung und Wiederauflösung der Surenkomposition im Verlauf der Entwicklung eines islamischen Kultus," in Wild, *The Qur'ān as Text*, 69–105.
85 Ṭabarī, *Kitāb al-Dīn wa 'l-Dawla*, 90.
86 Rāmiyār, *Tārīkh-e Qor'ān*, 214.
87 *Al-Taṣwīr al-Fannī* (Beirut-Cairo: Dār al-Shurūq, 1987), 11.
88 Muḥammad Rashīd Riḍā, *Al-Waḥy al-Muḥammadī* (Beirut: al-Maktab al-Islāmī, 1391/1971), 154.
89 Abū Zahra, *al-Mu'jiza al-Kubrā*, 64; from a different point of view and explained in a different language, a secular author like Adūnīs ('Alī Aḥmad Sa'īd) – to give one example from a discourse which does not consider itself as pious – principally follows this interpretation; cf. his *al-Naṣṣ al-Qur'ānī wa Āfāq al-Kitāba* (Beirut: Dār al-Ādāb, 1993), 21, *et passim.*
90 Rudi Paret, *Mohammed und der Koran. Geschichte und Verkündigung des arabischen Propheten* (Stuttgart: Kohlhammer, 1957), 90.

Chapter 12

Ellipsis in the Qur'ān: A Study of Ibn Qutayba's *Ta'wīl Mushkil al-Qur'ān*

Yusuf Rahman

I

In volumes seventeen and eighteen of the journal *Hamdard Islamicus*, we find a discussion between Salah Salim Ali and Anthony H. Johns on the problem of translating ellipsis in the Qur'ān.[1] Ali in his article states his belief that M.M. Pickthall and A. Yusuf Ali, two Muslim translators of the Qur'ān, misunderstood the ellipted phrases in the Qur'ān and must have, accordingly, mistranslated them. Johns in his turn defends the efforts of both translators in rendering the ellipted terms in the Qur'ān and argues that their translations are "faithful to the exegetical tradition"; in this case he supports his argument with the *Tafsīr al-Jalālayn* and the *Tafsīr al-Kabīr* of Fakhr al-Dīn al-Rāzī (d. 606/1209). At the end of his article, Johns warns modern scholars of the Qur'ān that:

> "[w]hile no one would suggest that all philological problems in the Qur'ān are resolved, or that there are no new and fruitful insights to be gained from a continuing study of the text, it is unwise (if not blasphemous) to take the Qur'ān as one might take a piece of modern Arabic writing, without reference to the tradition of interpretation that lies behind it. A contemporary scholar may indeed discover new insights, but has the responsibility of pointing out in what respects and why, a well-established view has been put aside, and at the very least recognize that one has been put aside. It is hardly appropriate to look at an English rendering of the Qur'ān, to draw attention to solecisms occurring in it, and attempt to redress them by unargued assertions, and the arbitrary use of the concept of ellipsis to solve non-existent problems, disregarding the methodology and insights achieved by tradition, and thereby diluting rather than clarifying the text."[2]

Although Johns has consulted *tafsīr* traditions, he does not refer to the earliest works treating the subject on which later *mufassirs*, like al-Zamakhsharī (d. 538/1144), al-Jalālān, i.e., Jalāl al-Dīn al-Maḥallī (d. 864/1459), Jalāl al-Dīn al-Suyūṭī (d. 911/1505) and others depended. Therefore, in this paper the writer will discuss ellipsis as it was explained in the earliest extant works, particularly Ibn Qutayba's (d. 276/889)[3] *Ta'wīl Mushkil al-Qur'ān,*[4] focussing on the different kinds of ellipsis, and its conditions and interpretations.

II

Actually, Floyd W. MacKay in his "Ibn Qutayba's Understanding of Quranic Brevity"[5] and John Wansbrough in his *Quranic Studies: Sources and Methods of Scriptural Interpretation*[6] have dealt with some aspects of this issue. But since there seem to be certain misunderstandings on the part of MacKay in his study of *Ta'wīl,* this paper may be regarded as a corrective. In his work, Wansbrough quotes 'Abd al-Qāhir al-Jurjānī's (d. 471/1078) statement that many instances of "ellipsis (*ḥadhf*) were not, when unaccompanied by a change in *i'rāb,* considered to qualify as figurative usage. . . ."[7] Basing himself on this thesis, Wansbrough argues that only the ellipsis which fits this condition can be considered as *majāz.* The question is then, not only what is *majāz* but also what do Ibn Qutayba and Abū 'Ubayda (d. 209/824), the author of *Majāz al-Qur'ān,*[8] who lists many kinds of ellipsis under the heading of *majāz,* mean by the term?

There are many studies that discuss the earliest meaning of *majāz.*[9] They have shown that its definition, as well as that of other terms such as *isti'āra* and *badī',* develops from one author to another, and that it took some time before it became a technical term in Arabic literary criticism.[10]

Ibn Qutayba himself defines *majāz(āt)* as *ṭuruq al-qawl wa ma'ākhidhuh* "the ways (methods) of speech and the modes of handling it."[11] To illustrate this, he compares the language of the Qur'ān with the speech of the preacher (*al-khaṭīb*), who delivers it in a variety of ways (*ṭuruq*) depending on the place, occasion or audience (*fayakhtaṣiru tāratan irādat al-takhfīf wa yuṭīlu tāratan irādat al-ifhām, wa yukarrir tāratan irādat al-tawkīd*).[12] The *majāzāt* in the Qur'ān, however, according to Ibn Qutayba, are naturally superior to those of any human. This is due to the fact that the Qur'ān has more methods of speech, which include among other things metaphor (*isti'āra*), inversion (*maqlūb*), ellipsis and abbreviation (*ḥadhf wa ikhtiṣār*), repetition and pleonasm (*takrār al-kalām wa al-ziyāda fīh*), metonymy and allusion (*al-kināya wa 'l-ta'rīḍ*), and idiom (*mukhālafat ẓāhir al-lafẓ ma'nāhu*).[13] Because of these *madhāhib,*[14] it is impossible, Ibn Qutayba argues, to translate the Qur'ān into other languages since the *'ajam,* non-Arabs, lack the variety of *majāz* that Arabs have at their disposal.[15]

The idea of the superiority of the Qur'ān, which later came to be known as *i'jaz al-Qur'ān* or the miraculous nature of the Qur'ān,[16] emerged from the theological discussion of *mu'jiza*. The theory was that in order to test the truth of the claim of prophethood, the claimant had to offer a sign or proof from God. This sign, which was sent to each *bona fide* messenger of God as a *dalīl* (proof) of his prophethood, was always appropriate to the time in which he lived. For example, Moses' staff being transformed into a snake was suited to the era of magic (*zaman al-siḥr*) to incapacitate his opponents; similarly, Jesus' miracles in curing lepers emerged during the period of healing (*zaman al-ṭibb*) ; and finally, Muḥammad who was sent in the era of eloquence (*zaman al-bayān*) was given the Qur'ān, with which neither *jinn* nor human could compete.[17]

However, Ibn Qutayba does not elaborate on this issue of *mu'jiza* as fully as the later theologians do;[18] nor does he discuss the idea of *i'jāz al-Qur'ān* systematically. To be precise, the technical meaning and discussion of Qur'ānic *i'jāz* developed only in the fourth/tenth century with the emergence of the Mu'tazilite al-Rummānī's (d. 386/996) *al-Nukat fī I'jāz al-Qur'ān*[19] and that of the *Bayān I'jāz al-Qur'ān*[20] of the traditionalist al-Khaṭṭābī (d. 388/998); it was to develop further still in the fifth/eleventh century with the appearance of the *I'jāz al-Qur'ān* of the Ash'arite al-Bāqillānī (d. 403/1013), and in the work by the same name of the Mu'tazilite al-Qāḍī 'Abd al-Jabbār (415/1025).[21]

Ibn Qutayba, however, lists some features which later become significant aspects of Qur'ānic *i'jāz*. As a traditionalist, he saw that the *i'jāz* in the Qur'ān lies in the composition of the Qur'ān (*mu'jiz al-ta'līf*). More to the point of our discussion, he also considers brevity, *ījāz*, which he defines as *jam' al-kathīr min ma'ānīh fī 'l-qalīl min lafẓih* (collection of many ideas in a few words), as one aspect of Qur'ānic *i'jāz*.[22] Therefore, contrary to Abū 'Ubayda's usage of *majāz*, in Ibn Qutayba the term includes idiomatic and figurative expression.[23]

Even though al-Jurjānī does not consider all ellipsis to be included in *majāz*, he still considers *ḥadhf* as one *dalīl* or proof of Qur'ānic *i'jāz*. In his *Dalā'il al-I'jāz*, al-Jurjānī discusses ellipsis and its kinds, and comments at the outset that:

> "This chapter [on *ḥadhf*] is a finely-honed method, a delicate mode of handling, a remarkable matter and similar to magic; in it you see that not mentioning something is more eloquent than mentioning it, refraining from expression more informative than indulging in it, and you find yourself more articulate on something if you do not speak it, and the explanation more complete if you do not announce it ... [24]

III

Ibn Qutayba's views expressed in his *Ta'wīl* on the ellipted structures of the Qur'ān are contained in the chapter on ellipsis (*ḥadhf*) and abbreviation (*ikhtiṣār*).[25] MacKay in his work tries to systematize Ibn Qutayba's discussion of ellipsis by distinguishing between these two figures of speech which come under the heading of brevity. For MacKay, ellipsis involves the insertion of a term or phrase required for its syntactic function while abbreviation involves the insertion of a term or phrase that fulfils a semantic purpose.[26]

But does Ibn Qutayba in fact distinguish *ḥadhf* from *ikhtiṣār*? From the types of ellipsis and the Qur'ānic examples[27] that he cites, it would seem that he does not divide brevity into ellipsis and abbreviation. A comparison with works previous to his, as well as those of his contemporaries and successors, will likewise make it clear that *ḥadhf* was but one type of *ikhtiṣār*. This will be shown below.

Ibn Qutayba divides his chapter on ellipsis into eight sections.[28] The first section deals with ellipsis whose function is "to delete the construct noun (*al-muḍāf*) and let the genitive noun (*al-muḍāf ilayh*) take its place, making the verb govern the latter."[29] The simplest example of this is found in Q. 12:82: *wa-s'ali 'l-qaryata* 'Ask the city' – whose real meaning is 'ask [*the people*] of the city (*ahlahā*).' This kind of ellipsis is the only one that is qualified later by al-Jurjānī as *majāz*, because it involves changes of *i'rāb*, that is from the genitive (*wa-s'al ahla 'l-qaryati*) to the accusative case (*wa-s'ali 'l-qaryata*).

Other examples of this kind of ellipsis are Q. 2:93 *wa ushribū fī qulūbihimu 'l-'ijla* and Q. 2:197 *al-ḥajju ashhurun ma'lūmātun*. By inserting the ellipted terms *ḥubb* and *waqt*, respectively, into those passages, they come to mean 'and they drank into their hearts [*the love of*] the calf' and '[*the period of*] pilgrimage is the months well-known.'[30] This process of inserting terms into the verse is known as *taqdīr*, "suppletive insertion"[31] or "reconstruction or restoration of a scriptural context or passage."[32]

MacKay furthermore has drawn attention to the fact[33] that Sībawayh (d. 177/793) in his *al-Kitāb* identifies these passages as examples of ellipsis at one point and of concision and abbreviation at another.[34] Similarly, Abū 'Ubayda considers them to have been ellipted at one point and abbreviated at another.[35] But, this does not mean that there were inconsistencies in their categorization. It simply means that these examples were included in the kind of ellipsis which is a subdivision of *ikhtiṣār/ījāz*. Geert Jan van Gelder has for instance discovered that *ījāz* and *ikhtiṣār* mean the same thing in the early works.[36] Furthermore, al-'Askarī (d. 395/1005), whom the editor of Ibn Qutayba's *Ta'wīl*, Aḥmad Ṣaqr, draws upon in quoting Ibn Qutayba's phrases and examples without acknowledgment,[37] identifies these examples as simply one kind of ellipsis.[38]

In another section on ellipsis it is defined as meaning "to let one verb govern two things when it is only appropriate for one of them and to conceal the verb for the other.[39] Here, he uses the term *iḍmār,* concealment, which together with other terms, such as *tark, isqāṭ,* is supposed to mean *ḥadhf.* Naphtali Kinberg, who has completed an extensive study of the *Ma'ānī al-Qur'ān* of al-Farrā' (d. 207/822), also concludes that the latter's use of many terms was only for stylistic variety and not in order to introduce any real distinctions.[40]

One example which is quoted by Ibn Qutayba to illustrate this type is Q. 10:71 *fa'ajmi'ū amrakum wa shurakā'akum.* In this passage, the verb *ajmi'ū* governs two objects, *amrakum* and *shurakā'akum,* the verb for the latter having been ellipted. He identifies this missing verb to have been *ud'ū.* Al-Farrā' and al-'Askarī also supply the same verb in their treatment of this verse.[41] Furthermore, al-'Askari uses almost the same language as Ibn Qutayba: *an yūqi' al-fi'l 'alā shay'ayn wa huwa li-'aḥadihimā wa yuḍmir li 'l-ākhar.*[42]

The third type of ellipsis in the *Ta'wīl* is "to produce a phrase which should have an apodosis (*jawāb*) but [where] the apodosis is elided for the sake of abbreviation (*ikhtiṣāran*) because of the hearer's awareness of it."[43] MacKay is correct when he ranges the examples of this type cited by Ibn Qutayba into two classes: first the deletion of the *jawāb* in a conditional sentence; and second, its omission in the case of comparison.[44]

Two examples are given by Ibn Qutayba in illustration of ellipsis in a conditional sentence. The first of these is Q. 13:31 'And if there were (*wa-law anna*) a reading (*qur'ānan*) by which the mountains would be moved or the earth would be torn apart or the dead would be made to speak. But, the matter is with God entirely.' In this passage, as can be clearly seen, there is a deletion of the apodosis expected to balance *law anna,* the construction of which would be something like *la-kāna hādha 'l-Qur'ān,* 'it would be this Qur'ān.'[45] Another example of this first type is Q. 24:20 which is introduced by the conditional clause *law lā* (if it were not): *wa law lā faḍlu 'llāhi 'alaykum wa raḥmatuhu wa anna 'llāha ra'ūfu 'r-raḥīm.* Here again the apodosis to *law lā* is omitted because, as Ibn Qutayba tells us, "the hearer is cognizant of the *jawāb.*" The complete statement might have read 'if it were not for the grace and mercy of God toward you [*he would punish you, la-'adhdhabakum*], and indeed God is the Most Merciful and Compassionate.'[46]

If we compare Ibn Qutayba's treatment of these verses with that of al-Farrā', we will find that the latter also says that the apodosis of these conditional clauses are left out (*matrūk*) because the meanings are known.[47] It is interesting to note here that al-Farrā' uses the term *ījāz* instead of *ikhtiṣār* in his explanation of this kind of ellipsis. His phrase is that 'the Arabs omit the answer to a thing, when it is known, for the sake of concision (*ījāz*).'[48] This is another indication that *ījāz* and *ikhtiṣār* effectively meant the same thing to them and that ellipsis was used for the purpose of brevity.

'Izz al-Dīn 'Abd al-'Azīz b. 'Abd al-Salām al-Sulamī (d. 660/1262) who lists nineteen types of ellipsis in his *Majāz al-Qur'ān,*[49] divides the deletion of apodosis in conditional clauses into *ḥadhf jawāb law* and *ḥadhf jawāb law-lā.*[50] Furthermore, according to al-Rummānī, the omission of the apodosis in conditional clauses is more eloquent (*ablagh*) than its retention, "since," he argues, "the mind is left to pursue every possible meaning. Were the answer to be provided, it would be confined to the manner contained in the expression."[51]

The omission of the *jawāb* in instances of comparison – the second of the two classes of this type of ellipsis referred to earlier – may be remarked in two examples cited by Ibn Qutayba, i.e. Q. 3:113 and 39:9. The first reads 'Not all of them are alike (*sawā'*). Some of the People of the Book are an upright community, rehearsing the signs of God all night long and they prostrate themselves.' This verse mentions only one community while the word *sawā'* is used to compare two or more things. Similarly, Q. 39:9, which reads 'Is one who worships devoutly all night long, prostrating and waking up?', does not mention the opposite of the one who worships submissively, while in the next passage we find a comparison drawn between the one who knows and the one who does not know, *qul hal yastawī 'l-ladhīna ya'lamūna wa 'l-ladhīna lā ya'lamūna.*[52]

The fourth type of ellipsis according to Ibn Qutayba lies in "the deletion of a word and [or] two" (*ḥadhf al-kalima wa al-kalimatayn*).[53] Ibn Qutayba gives many examples of this type. The first three examples, to borrow al-Sulamī's typology, involve ellipsis of verbs denoting speech (*hadhf al-aqwāl*),[54] since the elided terms are *qāla* and its derivatives. The Qur'ānic examples of this type, with their *loci probantes,* are Q. 3:106 *fa-ammā 'l-ladhīna 'swaddat wujūhuhum [fa yuqāla lahum] a-kafartum?* 'And as for those whose faces will be black, [*it will be said to them*] do you not believe?'[55] Similarly, Q. 32:12 '*wa law tarā idhi 'l-mujrimūna nākisū ru'ūsihim 'inda rabbihim [yaqūlūna] rabbanā abṣarnā wa sami'nā.* 'And if you could see when the guilty ones lower their heads before their Lord, *[they say]* Our Lord, we have seen and heard.'

The other examples cited by Ibn Qutayba include the omission of one word or two, such as Q. 17:23 *wa qaḍā rabbuka allā ta'budū illā iyyāhu wa [waṣṣā] bi 'l-wālidayni iḥsānan* ('And your Lord has decreed that you worship none but Him and [*commanded*] [you] to be kind to [your] parents')[56] and Q. 29:22 *wa mā antum bi-mu'jizīna fī 'l-arḍi wa lā [man] fī 's-samā'i [bi-mu'jiz]* ('And you will not be able to incapacitate [God's decree] on earth nor [*the one*] in the heaven [*will you be able to weaken*]).'[57]

After discussing the fourth type of ellipsis, Ibn Qutayba cites a kind of phrase, which MacKay counts as the fifth type, stating that it is sometimes the case that the phrase is ambiguous and obscure because of abbreviation and concealment (*wa qad yushkil al-kalām wa yaghmuḍ bi 'l-ikhtiṣār wa 'l-iḍmār*).[58] Interestingly, al-'Askarī, who for the most part follows Ibn Qutayba in the division of ellipsis and citation of examples, does not mention this particular type.[59] Moreover it seems that this is not really a form of ellipsis, but rather an example of an abbreviated statement and the solution offered to understand it.

The example which he provides of this statement is the abbreviated verse in Q. 27:10–11 *innī lā yakhāfu ladayya 'l-mursalūna illā man ẓalama thumma baddala ḥusnan ba'da sū'in fa-innī ghafūru 'r-rahīm* ('The apostles need not be afraid in My presence, except those who have done wrong then substituted good for evil, for I am the Most Forgiving and Merciful'). To explain this verse, Ibn Qutayba first of all quotes the interpretation of al-Farrā' who opines that *al-istithnā',* the exception indicated by the word *illā,* does not apply to the apostles of God but rather to "the concealed meaning in the verse" (*ma'nā muḍmar fī 'l-kalām*). The overall sense of the verse, according to al-Farrā', is that 'The apostles need not be afraid in My presence, [*bal ghayruhum al-khā'if (but other than apostles are in fear)*], except those who have done wrong then repented – they do not fear.'[60] This interpretation, however, is rejected by Ibn Qutayba (*wa hādhā qawl al-Farrā', wa huwa yab'ud*),[61] for, according to Ibn Qutayba's understanding, "the Arabs delete from the phrase that which has been indicated by the obvious phrase. And in the apparent [meaning] of this phrase there is no proof (*dalīl*) of its inner [meaning]."[62] Therefore, the sense of the verse, according to Ibn Qutayba, must be looked for in the beginning of the verse, where it is declared that the apostle, i.e., Moses, was afraid of snakes, so God told him *yā Mūsā lā takhaf innī lā yakhāfu ladayya 'l-mursalūna.* But God also knew that Moses felt afraid because of his sin in having struck another person, and so God said: *illā man ẓalama thumma baddala ḥusnan ba'da sū'in.*[63] The pronoun following *illā* therefore refers to Moses himself.

In addition to this explanation, Ibn Qutayba presents the opinions of "some grammarians" who interpreted *illā* to mean *wa* (and), so that the construction of the verse becomes *wa lā yakhāfu ladayya 'l-mursalūna [wa] lā man ẓalama thumma baddala ḥusnan.* This is also the case with Q. 2:150 *li'allā yakūna li 'n-nāsi 'alaykum ḥujjatun illā 'l-ladhīna ẓalamū,* whose intended meaning is 'so that there be no argument against you among the people [*and*] those who did wrong.'[64]

Al-Farrā' also quotes this interpretation of some grammarians, but he does not agree with it, since he argues, "I do not find that the Arabic language (*al-'Arabiyya*) tolerates what they say, and for this reason I will not accept (the saying) *qāma 'n-nāsu illā 'Abda 'llāh* to mean he ('Abd Allāh) is standing." The exception (*al-istithnā'*), according to al-Farrā', involves excluding the name which comes after *illā* from the names which are understood to come before *illā.*[65]

Another example offered by Ibn Qutayba in illustration of how to interpret ellipsis in the Qur'ān is Q. 8:5 *kamā akhrajaka rabbuka min baytika bi 'l-ḥaqqi* ('Just as your Lord ordered you to go out of your house in truth'). The term *kamā* does not mean that God is comparing here the story of the believers in Q. 8:2–4 with His command to go to Him, but refers rather to the meaning of Q. 8:1, namely, that many believers asked the Prophet about the spoils of the battle. Therefore, God revealed *yas'alūnaka 'ani 'l-anfāli, quli 'l-anfālu li 'llāhi wa 'r-rasūli.* But, since some believers did not like the way the Prophet distributed the spoils, God compares this dislike with their reluctance to go to the battle: *kamā akhrajaka rabbuka min baytika bi 'l-ḥaqqi wa inna farīqan min al-mu'minīna la-kārihūna.* "Their dislike for what you did with the spoils," Ibn Qutayba interprets, "is the same as (*kamā, ka-mithli*) their dislike to go out with you,"[66] i.e., to the battle.

Ibn Qutayba's interpretation of this passage reveals that in order to understand an ambiguous or obscure verse on the basis of ellipsis, one has to find its extra-textual indication from an obvious phrase (*mā yadull 'alayhi ẓāhiruh*),[67] either in the preceding verse[68] or in the subsequent one. This is explained in his presentation of the fifth type of ellipsis.

There, he says that "under [the heading of] abbreviation is the oath without complement when in the following phrase there is an indication of the complement" (*wa min al-ikhtiṣār al-qasam bilā jawāb idhā kāna fī 'l-kalām ba'dahu mā yadull 'ala 'l-jawāb).*[69] MacKay thinks that this phrase connotes another division of brevity besides ellipsis, i.e., abbreviation. But, as was pointed out earlier, the usage of the term *ikhtiṣar* here is not technical in nature. This statement is simply meant to indicate another kind of ellipsis, as can be seen from the fifth *wajh* of ellipsis discussed by al-'Askarī in his *Kitāb al-Ṣinā'atayn.*[70]

The first example of this type is Q. 50:1: '*Qāf*, by the glorious Qur'ān but they wonder that a warner came to them from among themselves so the unbelievers said "This is a wonderful thing. What, when we are dead and become dust?".'[71] In this phrase, the *jawāb* is not mentioned, but it might be understood from the following sentence, i.e., *dhālika raj'un ba'īdun* 'that is impossible return.' From this phrase, we can determine that the *jawāb* of 'What, when we are dead?' is *nub'ath* 'we will be resurrected.' Similarly, in Q. 79:1–6 the complement of each oath is not mentioned until it comes to Q. 79:11 which gives a clue to the *jawāb*. The Qur'ānic verses and their ellipted complement run as follows: *wa 'n-nāzi'āti gharqan, wa 'n-nāshiṭāti nashṭan, wa 's-sābiḥāti sabḥan, fa 's-sābiqāti sabqan, fa 'l-mudabbirāti amran, yawma tarjufu 'r-rājifa [la-tub'athunna].* This elision is evident from the subsequent verse which contains the comment of the unbelievers: 'What, when we are rotten bones? [*we will be resurrected*].'[72]

The sixth type of *ḥadhf* is "to omit 'not' from the phrase even though the meaning asserts it (*an taḥdhif "lā" min al-kalām wa 'l-ma'nā ithbātuhā*)."[73] One such example is Q. 12:85 'By God, you will cease (*tafta'u*) remembering Joseph' which actually means 'you will [*not*] cease remembering Joseph,' or, Q. 4:176 'God makes [things] clear to you so that you stray (*an taḍillū*)' whose meaning is 'so that you [*do not (li'allā)*] stray.'[74]

The next type of ellipsis is "to provide a pronoun (*tuḍmir*) for the term not being mentioned (*wa min al-ikhtiṣār an tuḍmir li-ghayr madhkūr*)."[75] For example, Q. 38:32 *ḥattā tawārat bi 'l-ḥijāb* 'Until it was hidden by the veil.' What is covered by the veil is not mentioned but the verse provides the personal pronoun (*ḍamīr*) of the verb *tawārat* which refers to the sun (*al-shams*). Another example is Q. 35:45 *wa-law yu'ākhidhu 'llāhu 'n-nāsa bimā kasabū*[76] *mā taraka 'alā ẓahrihā min dābbatin* ('If God were to punish people according to what they did, He would not leave one animal on its surface'). Although the location of the animal is not mentioned here, it is known that the *ḍamīr "hā"* affixed to the end of *ẓahrihā* refers to the earth (*al-arḍ*). Similarly, the *ḍamīr "hu"* in Q. 97:1 *Innā anzalnāhu fī laylati 'l-qadr* refers to the ellipted noun "the Qur'ān."

The eighth and last type of ellipsis, according to Ibn Qutayba, is *ḥadhf al-ṣifāt*[77] or, the ellipsis of *ḥurūf al-jarr,* according to other scholars.[78] One example of this type is Q. 83:3 *wa idhā kālūhum aw wazanūhum yukhsirūn* ('When they give them by measure or weigh them, they give less than is due'). The actual construction of this verse means 'when they measure [*to*] them (*kālū lahum*) or weigh [*to*] them *(wazanū lahum)*.' In Q. 7:155, likewise, the verse *wa 'khtāra Mūsā qawmahu sab'īna rajulan* ('And Moses chose his people seventy men') is intended to mean 'he chose [*from*] his people.'[79]

It is interesting to note that al-'Askarī does not mention this type of ellipsis in his *Kitāb al-Ṣinā'atayn.* But, he cites one example, i.e., *wa 'khtāra Mūsā qawmahu,* to mean '[*from*] his people' under the phrase *wa ḍarb minhu ākhar.*[80] Contrary to the assertion of MacKay, who takes this expression to mean "similar [*ḍarb*] to the expression"[81] of the previous example, for the present writer, this statement merely indicates another kind of ellipsis (*naw' ākhar min al-ḥadhf*). If this is the case, the Qur'ānic example Q. 7:155 which is quoted by al-'Askarī in this *ḍarb ākhar* of ellipsis still follows the line of Ibn Qutayba.

IV

These are the eight types of ellipsis introduced by Ibn Qutayba.[82] From the above discussion, we see that ellipsis usually takes place in constructions when the original construction can be understood by some extra-textual indication, either in the phrase previous to it or in the one following.[83] The purpose of ellipsis is to shorten the phrase (*ikhtiṣāran* or *ījāzan*). Furthermore, in the discussion we also find that the conditions of ellipsis are that the hearer should know its intended meaning and that there should be an indication of the ellipted term in the phrase. Al-Rummānī adds another requirement of ellipsis, i.e., that it must not impair the intended meaning.[84]

Since some scholars, like Kinberg and Rippin, have demonstrated that there was no consistent differentiation between the terms and that their technical senses were not fixed until the fourth century of Islam, it might be said that Ibn Qutayba had no intention of distinguishing between *ḥadhf* and *ikhtiṣār.* MacKay's differentiation of the two terms seems to be based, firstly, on his assertion that the two terms had become technical terms in Ibn Qutayba's period, and, secondly, on his simple inference of the usage of the term by Ibn Qutayba. The use of the word *ikhtiṣār,* however, does not necessarily imply that it falls under the heading of abridgment. The third kind of ellipsis, which MacKay classifies as the type of *ikhtiṣār* because of the presence of the term in it, clearly indicates that brevity is the purpose, but not the form, of the omission of the apodosis, *fa-yuḥdhaf al-jawāb ikhtiṣāran.*[85] Similarly, the terms *wa min al-ikhtiṣār* in the fifth type of ellipsis, or the sixth according to MacKay, are not to be understood as a type of abbreviation. Furthermore, we may ask why MacKay categorizes the omission of *lā* and of the qualitative clause (*ḥadhf al-ṣifāt*) as types of ellipsis, when Ibn Qutayba uses the phrases *minhu* and *min dhālik,* which actually refer to the term *ikhtiṣār* discussed beforehand. Even MacKay's conclusion that the ellipsis is related to syntax whereas abbreviation is a form of semantic expression does not fully explain the differences between the two. For example, the seventh kind of ellipsis *an tuḍmir li-ghayr madhkūr,* which is classified by MacKay as a kind of abbreviation, actually falls into the category of use of the *ḍamīr* or a pronoun.

Instead of trying to distinguish *ḥadhf* from *ikhtiṣār,* Ibn Qutayba discusses the second kind of *ījāz/ikhtiṣār,* in addition to ellipsis. Although he does not refer to it by its technical term, this is *qaṣr/qiṣar.* At the beginning of his *Ta'wīl,* he quotes many Qur'ānic examples to illustrate this type.[86] Al-Rummānī, whom van Gelder considers as the first scholar to have made *ījāz* a technical term in *'ilm al-balāgha,*[87] distinguishes two types of *ījāz* : *al-ījāz bi 'l-ḥadhf* and *al-ījāz bi 'l-qiṣar.*[88] The former introduces brevity by means of deleting some words whose original construction might be known through the context, while the latter does so by means of reducing the words and augmenting the meaning (*taqlīl al-lafẓ wa takthīr al-ma'nā*) without deleting any word.[89]

One example cited by Ibn Qutayba to explain the second kind of brevity is Q. 7:199 *khudhi 'l-'afwa wa 'mur bi 'l-'urfi wa a'riḍ 'ani 'l-jāhilīn* ('Take forgiveness, command goodness, and turn away from the ignorant'). There is no ellipsis in this verse, but in its few phrases, according to Ibn Qutayba, many ideas are to be found. It commands a re-connecting of relations with those who cut them off, and it prescribes showing forgiveness to the sinner, observing *taqwā 'llāh,* avoiding telling lies, patience, gentleness, etc.[90] Another example is the Qur'ānic verse

2:179 *wa lakum fi 'l-qiṣāṣi ḥayātun yā ulī 'l-albāb* ('There is life for you in just punishment, O men of understanding').[91] Here, Ibn Qutayba cites also the saying *al-qatl aqall li 'l-qatl* (killing is [cause for] less killing),[92] whose meaning is close to the sense of the verse. Although Ibn Qutayba does not explain the reason for this citation, it seems clear that he would like to demonstrate the superiority of the verses of the Qur'ān over the literature produced by humans. Al-Rummānī gives four reasons for Qur'ānic superiority in this case: firstly, the Qur'ānic statement contains more benefit (*akthar fī 'l-fā'ida*) ; secondly and thirdly, it is more concisely expressed (*awjaz fī 'l-'ibāra*) and more remote from repetition; and finally, it is better in terms of composition.[93]

Although Ibn Qutayba did not elaborate systematically the idea of *i'jāz al-Qur'ān,* he did, as Claude Gilliot writes, "prépara la voie aux grands traités du IV/XIe siècle sur «l'inimitabilité du Coran»."[94] In his *Ta'wīl,* instead of *i'jāz al-Qur'ān,* Ibn Qutayba uses the term *faḍl al-Qur'ān,*[95] the meaning and the content of which can only be known to the more well-versed of the *majāzāt* and the *madhāhib* (methods of speech) of the Arabs. As with the works on *i'jāz,*[96] Ibn Qutayba reports the accusations made by the unbelievers (*mulḥid*s) against the Qur'ān, such as their claims about its inherent contradictions, the imperfections in its composition (*fasād al-naẓm*), and the grammatical mistakes (*laḥn*) in its text, in addition to their accusation that the Qur'ān is the speech of soothsayers or the fables of the ancients.[97] Because of these claims and accusations and in order to deny them, the Prophet Muḥammad, according to Ibn Qutayba, challenged them to produce one *sūra* like the Qur'ān's. The Qur'ān, however, states conclusively that 'if humans and *jinn* were to gather together to produce something similar to this Qur'ān, they would not be able to produce anything similar to it even if they helped one another' (*la'ini 'jtama'ati 'l-insu wa 'l-jinnu 'alā an ya'tū bi-mithli hādha 'l-Qur'āni lā ya'tūna bi-mithlihi wa law kāna ba'ḍuhum li-ba'ḍin ẓahīran*) (Q. 17:88).[98] Many of Ibn Qutayba's discussions of the features of the Qur'ān were developed and elaborated by later generations of scholars in their studies of Qur'ānic *i'jāz.*

NOTES

1 See, Salah Salim Ali, "Misrepresentation of Some Ellipted Structures in the Translation of the Qur'ān by A.Y. Ali and M.M. Pickthall," *Hamdard Islamicus* 17, 4 (1994): 27–33; and A.H. Johns, "Ellipsis in the Qur'ān: A Response to Salah Salim Ali." *Hamdard Islamicus* 18, 2 (1995): 15–23.

2 Johns, "Ellipsis," 22.

3 For his life and works, see, among others, Gérard Lecomte, *Ibn Qutayba (mort en 276/889): l'homme, son oeuvre, ses idées* (Damascus: Institut Français de Damas, 1965); idem, "Ibn Ḳutayba," *EI*^{2}, III:844–7; Isḥāq Mūsā Ḥuseini, *The Life and Works of Ibn Qutayba* (Beirut: The American Press, 1950); Muḥammad Zaghlūl Sallām, *Ibn Qutayba* (Cairo: Dār al-Ma'ārif, 1957).

4 Ed. al-Sayyid Aḥmad Ṣaqr (Cairo: Dār al-Turāth, 1973). This work will be cited in the following simply as *Ta'wīl.*
5 M.A. thesis, McGill University, 1991.
6 Oxford: Oxford University Press, 1977, especially, 227ff.
7 Ibid., 229; idem, "*Majāz al-Qur'ān*: Periphrastic Exegesis." *Bulletin of the School of Oriental and African Studies* 33 (1970): 255, 265; al-Jurjānī, *Asrār al-Balāgha* (Istanbul: Government Press, 1954), para. 26.2 "*bi anna 'l-ḥadhf idhā tajarrad 'an taghyīr ḥukm min aḥkām mā baqiya ba'da 'l-ḥadhf lam yusamma majāzan.*" See also Hellmut Ritter's "Introduction" to 'Abd al-Qāhir al-Jurjānī's *Asrār al-Balāgha*, 24.
8 Ed. Fuat Sezgin. Cairo: al-Khānjī, 1954, 2 vols.
9 See for example, Wansbrough, "*Majāz al-Qur'ān,*" 247–266; Ella Almagor, "The Early Meaning of *Majāz* and the Nature of Abū 'Ubayda's Exegesis," in *Studia Orientalia Memoriae D.H. Baneth Dedicata,* ed. J. Blau, S. Pines, M.J. Kister and S. Shaked (Jerusalem: The Magnes Press, 1979), 307–326; Wolfhart Heinrichs, "On the Genesis of the *Ḥaqīqa-Majāz* Dichotomy," *Studia Islamica* 59 (1984): 111–140; idem, "Contacts between Scriptural Hermeneutics and Literary Theory in Islam: the Case of *Majāz,*" *Zeitschrift für Geschichte der Arabisch-Islamischen Wissenschaften,* 7 (1991/92): 253–84; and B. Reinert, "Madjāz," EI^2, V:1025–6.
10 Heinrichs, "Scriptural Hermeneutics," 255 ff.; G.J.H. van Gelder, "Brevity: the Long and the Short of it in Classical Arabic Literary Theory," in *Proceedings of the Ninth Congress of the Union Européenne des Arabisants et Islamisants,* ed. Rudolph Peters (Leiden: E.J. Brill, 1981), 78–88; and Naṣr Ḥāmid Abū Zayd, *al-Ittijāh al-'Aqlī fī 'l-Tafsīr: Dirāsa fī Qadiyyat al-Majāz fī 'l-Qur'ān 'inda 'l-Mu'tazila* (Beirut: Dār al-Tanwīr wa 'l-Nashr, 1982), 91 ff. Heinrichs also discusses the original meaning and development of the term *isti'āra* in *The Hand of the Northwind. Opinions on Metaphor and the Early Meaning of Isti'āra in Arabic Poetics* (Wiesbaden: Deutsche Morgenländische Gesellschaft, 1977); and idem, "*Isti'ārah* and *Badī'* and Their Terminological Relationship in Early Arabic Literary Criticism," *Zeitschrift für Geschichte der Arabisch-Islamischen Wissenschaften,* 1 (1984): 180–211.
11 *Ta'wīl,* 20; See also Heinrichs, "*Ḥaqīqa-Majāz* Dichotomy," 130; and idem, "Scriptural Hermeneutics," 257.
12 Ibid., 13.
13 Ibid., 20, 134 ff.
14 Ibid., 21.
15 Ibid.
16 See Issa J. Boullata, "I'jāz," in *Encyclopedia of Religion,* ed. Mircea Eliade (New York: Macmillan, 1987), 7:87–8; idem, "The Rhetorical Interpretation of the Qur'ān: *I'jāz* and Related Topics," in *Approaches to the History of the Interpretation of the Qur'ān,* ed. Andrew Rippin (Oxford: Clarendon Press, 1988), 139–57; Gustave E. von Grunebaum, "I'djāz," EI^2, III:1018–20; Angelika Neuwirth, "Das islamische Dogma der 'Unnachahmlichkeit des Korans' in literaturwissenschaftlicher Sicht," *Der Islam* 60 (1983): 166–83; and Naṣr Ḥāmid Abū Zayd, *Mafhūm al-Naṣṣ: Dirāsa fī 'Ulūm al-Qur'ān* (Cairo: al-Hay'a al-Miṣriyya al-'Āmma li 'l-Kitāb, 1990), 155–78.
17 *Ta'wīl,* 12.
18 For further discussion of the doctrine of *mu'jiza* in the classical period, see the present writer's "The Doctrine of *Mu'jiza* According to the Schools of *Kalām* in the Classical Period," *Islamic Quarterly* 40,4 (1996): 235–57.
19 In *Thalāth Rasā'il fī I'jāz al-Qur'ān,* ed. M. Zaghlūl Sallām and M. Khalaf Allāh (Cairo: Dār al-Ma'ārif, 1956), 67–104. For the translation of this text, see Awad

al-Jemaey, "al-Rummānī's al-Nukat fī I'jāz al-Qur'ān: an Annotated Translation with Introduction" (Ph.D. dissertation, Indiana University, 1987), 101–94; or an abridged translation in Andrew Rippin and Jan Knappert, (eds.) *Textual Sources for the Study of Islam* (Manchester: Manchester University Press, 1986), 49–59.

20 Ibid., 17–65. Claude-France Audebert has translated this work into French as *al-Ḫaṭṭābī et l'inimitabilité du Coran: Traduction et introduction au* *Bayān I'ǧāz al-Qur'ān* (Damascus: Institut Français de Damas, 1982), 115–55.

21 Al-Bāqillānī, *I'jāz al-Qur'ān,* ed. Sayyid Aḥmad Ṣaqr (Cairo: Dār al-Kutub, 1954). A section of this book has been translated into English by Gustave E. von Grunebaum as *A Tenth-Century Document of Arabic Literary Theory and Criticism* (Chicago: The University of Chicago Press, 1950). For 'Abd al-Jabbār's work, see his *al-Mughnī fī Abwāb al-Tawḥīd wa 'l-'Adl,* vol. 16, ed. Amīn al-Khūlī (Cairo: Maṭba'at Dār al-Kutub, 1960). As the present writer has shown, the original title of the work should not be *I'jāz al-Qur'an* but *al-Tanabbu'āt;* see his article, "The Miraculous Nature of Muslim Scripture: A Study of 'Abd al-Jabbār's *I'jāz al-Qur'ān,*" *Islamic Studies* 35,4 (1996): 411.

22 *Ta'wīl,* 3. See also 'Abd al-'Azīz 'Abd al-Mu'ṭī 'Arafa, *Qaḍiyyat al-I'jāz al-Qur'ānī wa Atharuhā fī Tadwīn al-Balāgha al-'Arabiyya* (Beirut: 'Ālam al-Kutub, 1985), 214.

23 See also, Heinrichs, "Scriptural Hermeneutics," 255, 257–8, 282; and Wansbrough, *Quranic Studies,* 231.

24 "*Huwa bāb daqīq al-maslak, laṭīf al-ma'khadh, 'ajīb al-amr, shabīh bi 'l-siḥr, fa-innaka tarā bihi tark al-dhikr afṣaḥ min al-dhikr, wa 'l-ṣamt 'an al-ifāda azyad li 'l-ifāda, wa tajiduka anṭaq mā takūn idhā lam tanṭuq, wa atamm mā takūn bayānan idhā lam tubin* . . ." See al-Jurjānī, *Dalā'il al-I'jāz* (Cairo: Maktabat Sa'd al-Dīn, 19870), 162 ff. See also Ceza Kassem-Draz, "Tawālud al-Nuṣūṣ wa Ishbā' al-Dalāla: Taṭbīqan 'alā Tafsīr al-Qur'ān," *Alif* 8 (1988), 50.

25 *Ta'wīl,* 210 ff.

26 MacKay, "Ibn Qutayba's Understanding of Quranic Brevity," 107.

27 Besides Qur'ānic verses, Ibn Qutayba also illustrates his case by citing passages of poetry. The present writer, however, will not discuss the latter. The translation of the Qur'ān is the writer's. The ellipted terms in the Qur'ān will be put in brackets and italicized.

28 *Ta'wīl,* 210–31; 'Arafa, *Qaḍiyyat al-I'jāz al-Qur'ānī,* 140; Wansbrough, *Quranic Studies,* 230; Muḥammad Zaghlūl Sallām, *Athar al-Qur'ān fī Taṭawwur al-Naqd al-'Arabī ilā Ākhir 'l-Qarn al-Rābi' al-Hijrī.* (Cairo: Dār al-Ma'ārif, 1961), 139–40. Cf. MacKay, who lists ten sections in "Ibn Qutayba's Understanding of Quranic Brevity," 56.

29 "*An taḥdhif al-muḍāf wa tuqīm al-muḍāf ilayhi maqāmahu wa taj'al al-fi'la lahu.*" Ibn Qutayba, *Ta'wīl,* 210–2; Heinrichs, "Scriptural Hermeneutics," 263.

30 Ibid., 210.

31 R. Baalbaki, "Some Aspects of Harmony and Hierarchy in Sībawayhi's Grammatical Analysis," *Zeitschrift für Arabische Linguistik* 2 (1979): 7.

32 Wansbrough, "*Majāz al-Qur'ān,*" 247.

33 MacKay, "Ibn Qutayba's Understanding of Quranic Brevity," 61–62.

34 Sībawayh, *Kitāb Sībawayh* (Baghdad: Maktabat al-Muthannā, n.d.; reimpression of Bulaq, 1316 A.H.), 1:108 and 2:25; and Gelder, "Brevity," 83.

35 Abū 'Ubayda, *Majāz al-Qur'ān,* I:8, 47.

36 Gelder, "Brevity," 83.

37 See Ibn Qutayba, *Ta'wīl,* 214, n. 3.

38 Al-'Askarī, *Kitāb al-Ṣinā'atayn,* ed. 'Alī Muḥammad al-Bijāwī and Muḥammad Abū al-Faḍl Ibrāhīm (Cairo: 'Īsā al-Bābī al-Ḥalabī, 1971), 214.

39 "*An tūqi' al-fi'l 'alā shay'ayn wa huwa li-aḥadihimā, wa tuḍmir li 'l-ākhar fi'lahu.*" Ibn Qutayba, *Ta'wīl,* 212–4.
40 N. Kinberg, *A Lexicon of al-Farrā''s Terminology in His Qur'ān Commentary* (Leiden: E.J. Brill, 1996), 19. See also A. Rippin, "Tafsīr,"*EI*[2], X:84
41 Al-Farrā', *Ma'ānī al-Qur'ān,* 1:473; al-'Askarī, *Kitāb al-Ṣinā'atayn,* 187. See also MacKay, "Ibn Qutayba's Understanding of Quranic Brevity," 67–68.
42 Al-'Askarī, *Kitāb al-Ṣinā'atayn,* 187.
43 "*An ya'tiya bi 'l-kalām mabniyyan 'alā anna lahu jawāban, fa-yuḥdhaf al-jawāb ikhtiṣāran li-'ilm al-mukhāṭab bih.*" Ibn Qutayba, *Ta'wīl,* 214–6.
44 MacKay, "Ibn Qutayba's Understanding of Quranic Brevity," 69–70.
45 *Ta'wīl,* 214.
46 Ibid.
47 Al-Farrā', *Ma'ānī al-Qur'ān,* 2:63, 247.
48 Ibid. 2:63: "*al-'Arab taḥdhif jawāb al-shay' idhā kāna ma'lūman irādat al-ījāz.*"
49 *Majāz al-Qur'ān wa yusammā al-Ishāra ilā 'l-Ījāz fī Ba'ḍ Anwā' al-Majāz.* ed. M. Muṣṭafā b. al-Ḥājj (Tripoli: Manshūrāt Kulliyyat al-Da'wa al-Islāmiyya, 1992), 92–142.
50 Ibid., 125–7.
51 Al-Rummānī, *al-Nukat,* 70–1; al-Jemaey, "Al-Rummānī's al-Nukat," 107. See also al-Khaṭṭābī, *Bayān,* 47; and Audebert, *al-Ḫaṭṭābī et l'inimitabilité du Coran,* 141.
52 *Ta'wīl,* 215.
53 Ibid., 216–8.
54 Al-Sulamī, *Majāz al-Qur'ān,* 121–2.
55 *Ta'wīl,* 216.
56 Ibid., 217.
57 Ibid.
58 Ibid., 218–23. See MacKay, "Ibn Qutayba's Understanding of Quranic Brevity," 77 ff.
59 Al-'Askarī, *Kitāb al-Ṣinā'atayn,* 189. Cf. MacKay, "Ibn Qutayba's Understanding of Quranic Brevity," 83.
60 *Ta'wīl,* 219. See also al-Farrā', *Ma'ānī al-Qur'ān,* 2:287, where the author gives two interpretations of this verse. The first is that the apostles are *ma'ṣūm* and are forgiven their sins till the last day, whereas he who combines good deeds and bad deeds will be in fear; the second is that *al-istithnā'* (exception) is for those people who are omitted (*turikū*) in the passage, meaning those who are sent need not fear but all other people (*ghayr al-mursalīn*) ought to.
61 *Ta'wīl,* 219. MacKay seems to mistranslate the word *yab'ud* which he translates as "who continues". MacKay, "Ibn Qutayba's Understanding of Quranic Brevity," 78. This expression actually means "(this opinion) is far from correct."
62 "*Al-'Arab innamā taḥdhif min al-kalām mā yadull 'alayhi mā yaẓhar, wa laysa fī ẓāhir hādhā 'l-kalām dalīl 'alā bāṭinih.*" Ibn Qutayba, *Ta'wīl,* 219. This statement belongs to Ibn Qutayba, not to al-Farrā'. See also, Aḥmad Ṣaqr's note 3 in *Ta'wīl,* 219. Cf. MacKay, "Ibn Qutayba's Understanding of Quranic Brevity," 78 ff.
63 *Ta'wīl,* 220.
64 Ibid.
65 See al-Farrā', *Ma'ānī al-Qur'ān,* 2:287.
66 *Ta'wīl,* 221.
67 Ibid., 219.
68 See our discussion above.
69 *Ta'wīl,* 223–4.
70 *Wa minhā (wujūh al-ḥadhf) al-qasam bilā jawāb.* Al-'Askarī, *Kitāb al-Ṣinā'atayn,* 189–90. Cf. MacKay, "Ibn Qutayba's Understanding of Quranic Brevity," 87.

71 *Ta'wīl,* 223–4.
72 Ibid., 224.
73 Ibid., 225. Al-'Askarī uses the term *isqāṭ* instead of *ḥadhf.* See *Kitāb al-Ṣinā'atayn,* 190. See also MacKay, "Ibn Qutayba's Understanding of Quranic Brevity," 89.
74 *Ta'wīl,* 225.
75 Ibid., 226. Al-'Askarī, *Kitāb al-Ṣinā'atayn,* 190, *an tuḍmir ghayra madhkūr.* Cf. MacKay's translation of the phrase in "Ibn Qutayba's Understanding of Quranic Brevity," 90. "concealment because of a term not being mentioned."
76 The text in *Ta'wīl* inadvertently reads *bi-ẓulmihim* instead of *bi-mā kasabū.* See *Ta'wīl,* 226.
77 *Ta'wīl,* 228–30.
78 Al-Sulamī, *Majāz al-Qur'ān,* 133–4. See also Muḥammad Ramaḍān al-Jarbī, *Ibn Qutayba wa Maqāyīsuh al-Balāghiyya wa 'l-Adabiyya wa 'l-Naqdiyya.* (Tripoli: al-Munsha'a al-'Āmma li-'l-Nashr wa al-Tawzī' wa 'l-I'lān, 1984), 118.
79 *Ta'wīl,* 229.
80 Al-'Askarī, *Kitāb al-Ṣinā'atayn,* 191.
81 MacKay, "Ibn Qutayba's Understanding of Quranic Brevity," 99.
82 MacKay adds one more section under the chapter of ellipsis and abbreviation, through his inference of the Qur'ānic phrases which Ibn Qutayba cites in each small heading "under abbreviation." See "Ibn Qutayba's Understanding of Quranic Brevity," 100 ff. It is not clear whether Ibn Qutayba includes these phrases as another section on ellipsis, because, compared with the other sections, here he does not elaborate on its idea or criteria. The Qur'ānic phrases quoted in those remaining pages might also be understood as other examples of the eight kinds of ellipsis.
83 See also Kinberg, *A Lexicon of al-Farrā"s Terminology,* 165
84 *Lā ikhlāl fīh bi 'l-ma'nā al-madlūl.* Al-Rummānī, *al-Nukat,* 70, 72; al-Jemaey, "al-Rummānī's al-Nukat," 106, 112; and Abū Zayd, *al-Ittijāh al-'Aqlī fī 'l-Tafsīr,* 101.
85 *Ta'wīl,* 214.
86 Ibid., 4 ff.; and al-Jarbī, *Ibn Qutayba,* 114, 118–20.
87 Gelder, "Brevity," 84.
88 Al-Rummānī, *al-Nukat,* 70. See also al-Jemaey, "Al-Rummānī's al-Nukat," 54, 106; al-'Askarī, *Kitāb al-Ṣinā'atayn,* 181 *al-ījāz* : *al-qiṣar* and *al-ḥadhf.*
89 Al-Rummānī, *al-Nukat,* 70; al-Jemaey, "al-Rummānī's al-Nukat," 106; Gelder, "Brevity," 85.
90 *Ta'wīl,* 4–5; and al-'Askarī, *Kitāb al-Ṣinā'atayn,* 183.
91 Ibid., 6.
92 Ibid., 7. Al-'Askarī and al-Rummānī cite *al-qatl anfā li 'l-qatl* in their *Kitāb al-Ṣinā'atayn,* 181 and *al-Nukat,* 71.
93 Al-Rummānī, *al-Nukat,* 71; al-Jemaey, "al-Rummānī's al-Nukat," 109. Cf. Al-'Askarī, *Kitāb al-Ṣinā'atayn,* 181.
94 C. Gilliot, "Coran," in *Encyclopaedia Universalis,* ed. Jacques Bersani (Paris: Encyclopaedia Universalis, 1995), 6:545. See also Wansbrough, *Quranic Studies,* 228, "Ibn Qutayba's monograph on the style of scripture exhibits the transitional employment of *majāz*: from an interpretational device to an aesthetic category."
95 *Ta'wīl,* 12.
96 See, Boullata, "Rhetorical Interpretation of the Qur'ān," 139 ff.
97 *Ta'wīl,* 22.
98 Ibid., 12, 22. For more discussion of the *taḥaddī* verses, see Matthias Radscheit, "'I'ǧāz al-Qur'ān' im Koran?" in *The Qur'ān as Text,* ed. S. Wild (Leiden: E.J. Brill, 1996), 113–23; idem, *Die koranische Herausforderung. Die taḥaddī-Verse im Rahmen der Polemikpassagen des Korans* (Berlin: Klaus Schwarz Verlag, 1996).

Chapter 13

Literary Exegesis of the Qur'ān: The Case of al-Sharīf al-Raḍī

Mahmoud M. Ayoub

I. PRELIMINARY OBSERVATIONS

The Qur'ān may be regarded as the most important literary document in the Arabic language. Its vocabulary and idiom have, moreover, permeated all Islamic languages, thus giving it a unique place in world literature. Through the words of the Qur'ān, Muslims have expressed their joys and sorrows, and their deepest thoughts and emotions.

However, the literary significance of the Qur'ān is not limited to its immense influence on Arabic and other Islamic languages and literatures. It is, according to Islamic faith and tradition, an inimitable literary miracle authored by God Himself. In the Qur'ān theology and literature merge, so that the Qur'ān's literary excellence has been adduced as one of its strongest claims to truth and to authenticity as a divine revelation.

In addition to its literary-theological significance, the Qur'ān can be appreciated as pure literature of a high order, for it contains in a unique way all the elements and qualities of good classical literature: poetic imageries, metaphors and similes, stories, anecdotes and parables, moral precepts and religious injunctions. The Qur'ān admirably utilizes these elements and expressions to present its worldview and philosophy of history.

The Qur'ān's abiding miracle with which it has challenged humankind's intellectual abilities in all ages[1] is its literary eloquence (*faṣāḥa*), rhetorical excellence (*balāgha*) and lucid expression (*bayān*). These and other elements of the Qur'ān's literary style and idiom have been studied and elaborated through a special science dealing with the inimitability (*i'jāz*) of the Qur'ān. Muslim intellectuals of every epoch have added new arguments for the miraculous character of their sacred Book. While in the early centuries of Muslim history such arguments centered on the Qur'ān as a miracle of divine speech, in modern times it has been regarded as a miracle of scientific knowledge as well. Many educated Muslims hold that the Qur'ān contains clear allusions to natural laws and phenomena which modern science discovered centuries after its revelation.

In the early decades of this century, the well known Egyptian exegete, Ṭanṭāwī Jawharī (d. 1940), included pictures of various minerals, plants, and constellations in his commentary to corroborate modern scientific discoveries with what he considered to be allusions to such discoveries in the Qur'ān.[2] Likewise, Aḥmad Muṣṭafā al-Marāghī (d. 1945), the *Shaykh al-Azhar* and foremost authority on the Qur'ān of his time, presented in his rationalistic Qur'ān commentary long medical and scientific excursuses on Qur'ānic verses dealing with the formation of the human embryo and other natural phenomena.[3] There is at present a proliferation of centers in Muslim countries dedicated to the study of modern science in light of the Qur'ān. Nevertheless, the Qur'ān remains for Muslims the peerless literary miracle vouchsafed to the "last prophet" Muḥammad, and which shall endure till the end of time.

The purpose of this essay is to investigate the early developments of literary approaches to the exegesis of the Qur'ān. Although literary Qur'ān exegesis has traditionally been considered as a branch of the science of *i'jāz al-qur'ān*, this study will not deal with this general science. It will rather focus on the contribution of al-Sharīf al-Raḍī to the field of literary Qur'ān interpretation. Al-Sharīf was one of the most celebrated literary figures of his time. He was also a noted religious scholar. In order for us to place al-Sharīf's thought in its proper perspective, we shall begin with a brief discussion of his life, time, and intellectual milieu. This will be followed by an illustrative examination of al-Sharīf's work on the metaphors and other figures of speech in the Qur'ān. We shall also examine al-Sharīf's exegetical methodology as evidenced in his interpretation (*ta'wīl*) of the multivalent (*mutashābih*) verses of the Qur'ān.

As a prominent Shī'ī intellectual and religious scholar, al-Sharīf al-Raḍī was a good representative of the Mu'tazilī/ Shī'ī school of thought. We shall therefore select for consideration verses that demonstrate both his literary and theological orientation. Of special interest to this study will be his interpretation of some of the Christological verses of the Qur'ān, notably those which deal with the nature of Christ and his relationship to God. Apart from the dialogical significance of such verses, the Qur'ānic designation of Christ as the "Word and spirit of God,"[4] had a direct bearing on the Mu'tazilī/Shī'ī concept of Divine Oneness (*tawḥīd*). Special attention will also be paid to verses whose literary exegesis served as primary arguments for al-Sharīf's theological standpoint.

II. AL-SHARĪF AL-RAḌĪ: HIS LIFE AND TIME

The fourth Islamic century has been aptly characterized as the Shī'ī century. Under the Buyids, a Perso-Daylamite Shī'ī dynasty which ruled most of the Eastern heartland of Islam – from the middle of the 10th to the middle of the 11th century including Baghdād, Islam's great cultural and religious center – Twelver Imāmī Shī'ism crystalized with a rich theological, juristic and philosophical tradition. Buyid rulers themselves patronized poets, grammarians, bellettrists and religious scholars. They actively participated in the making of a veritable intellectual renaissance. Their active encouragement of cultural activities led them to appoint well known poets, litterateurs and other intellectuals to high government offices, such as ministers and secretaries.[5]

Abū al-Ḥasan Muḥammad b. al-Ḥusayn, known as al-Sharīf al-Raḍī, was born in Baghdād in 359/970 and died on Muḥarram 6, 406/1015, barely forty-seven years old.[6] Both on his father's and mother's side, al-Sharīf al-Raḍī was a descendant of the Prophet Muḥammad through his daughter Fāṭima and his cousin 'Alī ibn Abī Ṭālib. Al-Sharīf's father was a highly respected scion of the seventh Twelver Shī'ī Imām Mūsā al-Kāẓim. His mother was the daughter of the well-known Zaydī Imām al-Nāṣir who was a descendant of the fourth Imām 'Alī Zayn al-'Ābidīn, grandson of 'Alī and Fāṭima.[7]

Fourth/tenth-eleventh century Baghdād was at one and the same time a city torn by Shī'ī-Sunnī sectarian strife and a center of intellectually open and vibrant activity. In both his intellectual formation and religious orientation, al-Sharīf was a product of this unique milieu. He studied with the best Shī'ī as well as Sunnī religious and literary scholars of his time. Around the age of ten, he was tutored by the famous Sunnī grammarian Abū Sa'īd Ḥasan ibn al-Sīrāfī who, it is reported, asked him one day: "If we say I saw 'Amr (*ra'aytu 'amran*), what is the sign of the accusative ending (*naṣb*) in him?" Al-Sharīf answered, "Hatred (*bughḍ*) of 'Alī." This is a clever play on words, as Shī'īs pejoratively call Sunnī opponents of 'Alī and his descendants *nawāṣib*, that is those who manifest (*naṣabū*) hostility towards the Imams. 'Amr ibn al-'Āṣ was one of the bitterest opponents of 'Alī, hence the grammatical pun.[8]

Unlike the majority of the religious scholars of his time who began their studies with the memorization of the Qur'ān at an early age, al-Sharīf learned the Qur'ān by heart when he was about thirty years old. In spite of his noble lineage, he appears to have lived in poverty. This was largely due to his self-respect which made him often decline gifts from the rich and mighty for his panegyrics. His Qur'ān teacher Abū Isḥāq Ibrāhīm ibn Aḥmad al-Ṭabarī, a noted Mālikī jurist, asked him one day, "O Sharīf, where is your domicile?" "In my father's house," he answered. The teacher said, "A man like you should not live in his father's home," and offered him a house. Al-Sharīf declined saying, "I have never accepted anything from anyone except my father." His teacher retorted, "But I have a greater claim upon you because I taught you the Book of God." Al-Sharīf then accepted the gift.[9]

Al-Sharīf's noble ancestry and the high social status of his own father, as well as his great poetic talents and religious learning earned him the respect of both the political and intellectual leaders of society. He enjoyed intimate relations with two of the 'Abbasid caliphs, al-Ṭā'i' (r. 363–81/974–91) and al-Qādir (r. 381–422/991–1031).[10] In 388/998 al-Qādir appointed al-Sharīf chief judge over the *maẓālim* courts of Baghdād, as well as leader of the *ḥajj* pilgrimage. In the same year he was also appointed as chief (*naqīb*) of the 'Alids of Baghdād, an office which he occupied on five different occasions until his death.[11]

Al-Sharīf enjoyed the favor of the Buyid ruler Bahā' al-Dawla (d. 403/1012), who was a great patron of thinkers, artists and religious scholars. He bestowed on al-Sharīf the high titles of *al-Sharīf al-Ajall* (high-honored most venerable man), *Dhū al-Manqabatayn* (the man of the two noble qualities, i.e., as leader of the *ḥajj* pilgrimage and chief representative of the 'Alids), and finally, *al-Raḍī Dhū al-Ḥasabayn* (the man of true contentment and two noble genealogies).[12] All this gave al-Sharīf an exaggerated sense of self-pride, which in the end led him to covet the caliphate. Thus he addressed al-Qādir with the verses: "You and I are alike in the garden of glory. Only the caliphate has distinguished you, for I am deprived of it and you wear it like a necklace." The Caliph answered, "... despite al-Sharīf's turned-up nose."[13] However, perhaps wisely, al-Sharīf did nothing to realize his ambition, and thus was spared the tragic fate of many 'Alid claimants to this office.

Al-Sharīf was a prolific writer. Beside his large and richly diversified collection of poetry (*dīwān*), which he himself arranged and circulated, he compiled three other books of the poetry of the best poets of his time. He wrote a biography of his father and a history of the judges of Baghdād. He was also the author of several works on jurisprudence and Arabic linguistics, as well as *Khaṣā'iṣ al-A'imma*, a book on the lives and special characteristics of the Twelve Shī'ī Imāms. Unfortunately, none of these books appears to have survived.

Among his most important extant writings is *Nahj al-Balāgha*, a compendium of the orations and sayings of the Imām 'Alī ibn Abī Ṭālib. Next are two works on the metaphors of the Qur'ān – *Talkhīṣ al-Bayān fī Majāzāt al-Qur'ān* – and metaphors of Prophetic ḥadīth traditions – *Majāzāt al-Āthār al-Nabawiyya.* Al-Sharīf wrote a voluminous Qur'ān commentary in ten volumes. Only volume five has been discovered and published. It is chiefly with the last two of these four important works that the rest of this study will be concerned.

III. METAPHORS OF THE QUR'ĀN

Ever since the time of the Prophet, Muslims have attempted to understand and interpret the Qur'ān's metaphorical and figurative expressions. It is reported that 'Adī ibn Ḥātim, a well-known Companion, told the Prophet during the month of Ramaḍān that he placed side by side two hair threads one white and the other black, and looked at them to determine the time when he should stop eating before the break of dawn (in reference to Q. 2:187). The Prophet laughed and said, "O son of Ḥātim, it is the whiteness of day and blackness of night!"[14] Later traditionists, such as Qatāda ibn Di'āma al-Sadūsī (d. 117/735) and Abū 'Amr ibn al-'Alā' (d. 154/771), are credited with interpretations of Qur'ānic metaphors, but only a few general accounts of their interpretations have reached us.

The first extant study of the synonyms (*ashbāh*) and parallel expressions (*naẓā'ir*) of the Qur'ān was written by the famous commentator and traditionist Muqātil ibn Sulaymān al-Balkhī (d. 150/767). Muqātil's work is concerned with related meanings and contexts of certain Qur'ānic terms and phrases. It cannot therefore be said to deal specifically with the symbolic language of the Qur'ān.

The first book to actually bear the title *Majāz al-Qur'ān* (metaphors of the Qur'ān) was by Abū 'Ubayda Ma'mar ibn al-Muthannā al-Taymī (d. 209/824–5). But Abū 'Ubayda's approach to the subject was no more than lexical explications of the meanings of uncommon or obscure Qur'ānic terms.[15] The first traditionist to treat this subject systematically was 'Abd Allāh b. Muslim b. Qutayba (d. 276/889–90) in his important book, *Ta'wīl Mushkil al-Qur'ān*. In this work Ibn Qutayba laid the foundations of this field of Qur'ānic studies. Although Ibn Qutayba dealt with all aspects of this subject, his primary aim was to elucidate recondite Qur'ānic terms rather than clarify their symbolic meanings.[16]

In linguistic usage, the term *majāz* signifies the opposite of reality (*ḥaqīqa*). That is to say, it is a figure of speech used metaphorically to denote a different condition from that which the literal sense of the original words connotes. In this sense, it is a literary device, a borrowed expression. Hence, al-Sharīf calls *majāz*, *isti'āra*, meaning, borrowed speech. He employs this distinctive and precise term consistently in his book *Talkhīṣ al-Bayān fī Majāzāt al-Qur'ān*, which is the first and only known attempt in classical Islam to take the Qur'ān from beginning to end, sūra by sūra and verse by verse, and interpret and analyze its metaphors and other figures of speech.

Al-Sharīf's purpose, as will be seen in what follows, appears to be twofold: to present his Mu'tazilī/Shī'ī theological ideas, and to display his literary acumen. The first he achieved through a sharp contrast of the real meaning behind the metaphor, or 'borrowed expression', with the apparent meaning of the metaphor itself. The second aim is clearly discernable in his literary style and wide knowledge of Arabic poetry, proverbs, and wise aphorisms. These he freely invokes in support of his often critical and independent ideas and interpretations.

The book under discussion was published three times within a few years: in Teheran, Cairo, and Beirut respectively.[17] The book was written at the request of a friend of the author, as he states in his introduction. The author's aim was to undertake a concise but comprehensive presentation of all the metaphors (*majāzāt*) of the Qur'ān, "towards which hearts would be inclined."[18] That this aim was realized may be judged by the enthusiasm with which the famous biographer Ibn Khallikān describes it. He asserts that "It remains a rare book of its kind."[19]

Among the controversial issues in early Islamic theology was the Qur'ānic attribution of anthropomorphic actions to God. The first occurrence of such attributions is in Q. 2: 27 which reads in part, "...Then He [God] turned (*istawā*) to the heaven and fashioned them seven heavens. ..." The word *istawā* implies motion, either in the sense of "ascending" or "turning towards", as used in this verse, or in the sense of "sitting up" as in Q. 20:5, which states, "The All-Merciful sat up upon the throne." Al-Sharīf interprets the word *istawā* in the verse under consideration as follows:

> That is to say, He turned (*qaṣada*) to their creation. This is because the reality (*ḥaqīqa*) of turning towards (*istiwā'*), which implies completeness after deficiency and straightness after crookedness are characteristics of bodies and signs of created things.[20]

Al-Sharīf explains this point at greater length in his analysis of Q. 10:3, "...Then He sat (*istawā*) upon the throne. ..." The act of sitting (*istiwā'*), al-Sharīf avers, can only be ascribed to bodies that rise up and go down, recline, and sit up straight. Thus, *istiwā* here signifies, seizing control (*istīlā'*), by means of power and dominion, and not by means of occupying a place and resting therein. This is like saying, the author further argues, "The king sat upon the throne of his dominion, even though there may not be an actual throne for him to sit upon." He then counters the objection that since God has dominion over all things, why should the throne be mentioned at all, by simply citing Qur'ānic verses affirming God to be "Lord of the great throne."[21]

Another point at issue between Shī'īs and Mu'tazilīs with their allegorical interpretations of the Qur'ān, on the one hand, and Ash'arīs, Ḥanbalīs and Ẓāhirī literalists on the other, is the Qur'ānic attribution of such bodily members as hands, side, face, and eyes to God. On the face of it, verse 71 of Sūra 36 is unqualifiedly anthropomorphic. It reads, "Do they not see that We created for them of what Our own hands have made cattles which they control?" Al-Sharīf categorically rejects any literal or anthropomorphic understanding of this and similar verses. He argues that by hands is here meant one of two senses of the term hand (*yad*) in the Arabic language, either the sense of divine power, or the sense of a real hand. But since the latter is impossible of God, the verse must be interpreted to mean, "Do they not see that We created for them beasts which We originated by means of the power of our determination (*taqdīr*) and our perfect management (*tadbīr*)?" It may also be interpreted to mean that "these beasts are among the things which We undertook to create without any of the creatures aiding Us in this task."[22]

The attribution of side (*janb*) to God is far more problematic than that of hands. The Qur'ān states: "That a soul may say, 'Alas for me for what I have neglected in the side of God. For I am surely among the losers'" (Q. 39:56). Al-Sharīf first asserts that the word *janb* here is a "borrowed figure of speech (*isti'āra*)." He then presents several views of the meaning of this enigmatic term. According to some, it means obedience to God, as well as His command. The word *janb* would signify proximity rather than the side of a body. It may be said in common parlance, "This matter (*amr*) is small beside (*fī janb*) that matter." Others said that the phrase, "in the side of God," means, "in the way or cause (*sabīl*) of God." It means the side or direction nearest to the attainment of His pleasure. "This is because this way divides into paths of right guidance and going astray, and each has its side or direction." Al-Sharīf appears to favor this interpretation.[23]

The ascription of hands and side to God stands in clear theological contrast to the attribution of face (*wajh*) to Him. The expression *wajh Allāh* (face of God) has been a far less problematic issue, as it is generally interpreted to denote God's nearness and infinite grace. In the Qur'ān, this expression also signifies person or self. Thus al-Sharīf interprets the phrase, "Everything shall perish except His face," in Q. 28:88, as follows: "This is a metaphor (*isti'āra*), for face here signifies the essence (*dhāt*) of a thing and its self." The author cites in support of this interpretation the Qur'ānic proclamation: "The face of your Lord of majesty and magnanimity alone shall endure (Q. 55:27)." He comments on this verse at some length, arguing:

> That is to say, the essence or self (*dhāt*) of your Lord alone shall endure. This is clear from the use of the possessive pronoun *dhū*, because it qualifies the face which is the essence or self. Had an actual face been intended, as foolish men think, God would have said, "*dhī al-jalāl*," where *dhī* would qualify the entire phrase, and not only an actual face with its particular complexions.

The author presents still another interpretation, namely, that the face here signifies righteous works by means of which one seeks nearness to God. He cites in support of this view a verse of poetry, "I beg God's forgiveness for sins which I cannot enumerate, the Lord of all creatures, for to Him belong the *wajh* (i.e., quest) and all good works." The verse thus means, "Everything shall perish except the essence (*wajh*) of His religion by means of which people can draw near to Him and attain His grace, and which He made the means for His good pleasure and forgiveness."[24]

The Qur'ān employs such anthropomorphic terms as hands, side, and eyes to portray a vivid and dynamic picture of God's active role in human affairs. In this vein, it dramatically declares that those who pledged allegiance (*bay'a*) to the Prophet in fact were pledging allegiance to God, for "... God's hand was over their hands. ..." (Q. 48:10). In the same tone, God orders Noah in Q. 23:27, "Make the ark under [lit. in] our eyes and our direct inspiration (*waḥy*)."

The expression *'ayn Allāh* (God's eye) has come to signify God's watchful care. Al-Sharīf offers this as the primary meaning of the verse. He says: "It is as though God said, 'Make the ark wherewith We shall watch over you, keep you, and protect you from anyone who wishes you ill'." Perhaps al-Sharīf realized that this interpretation is itself a metaphor needing interpretation. He thus offers another, somewhat far-fetched explanation, but one which strictly safeguards God's absolute transcendence. The verse may also be interpreted to mean, he argues,

> Make the ark under the watchful eyes of our intimate friends (*awliyā'*) of the angels and people of faith. For by means of them We shall protect you, so that no one who intends you ill or plots against you will ever come near you.[25]

We shall end this discussion with a Qur'ānic literary metaphor which the author uses to explain a similar expression in a Prophetic ḥadīth tradition. The Prophet is reported to have declared, "I dissociate myself from any Muslim [who allies himself] with an Associator (*mushrik*)." "Why?" he was asked. "Because their fires should never see one another," he answered. Al-Sharīf interprets fire here to mean war. He then explicates in support of this view the Qur'ānic verse, "Whenever they kindle a fire for war, God extinguishes it" (Q. 5:64). Likening war to fire, al-Sharīf observes, may be done in two ways. The first expresses "the heat of the blows of swords, the heavyheartedness (*karb*) accompanying the dawning of heavy coats of mail, and the heat of battle from constant movement and combat." The second reason is that, as fire devours its kindlings and burns its firewood, war devours men and destroys its great warriors."[26]

Immediately after citing the Prophetic ḥadīth just quoted, the author again asserts that fire here is a metaphor for war. "This is because," he continues, "people metaphorically call war fire on account of the thick dust its battle raises, as well as the heat of the clatter of arms." He then cites in support of this interpretation the poetic verse, "These are two tribes that have set ablaze a war, wherein the garment of death shall for ever remain new between them."[27]

IV. MULTIVALENT MEANINGS OF THE QUR'ĀN

Al-Sharīf's magnum opus, which is also his major work on the Qur'ān, is his ten-volume commentary entitled *Ḥaqā'iq al-Ta'wīl fī Mutashābih al-Tanzīl*.[28] The work is reported to be larger in size and greater in scope than the famous commentary, *al-Tibyān fī Tafsīr al-Qur'ān* of the Shī'ī jurisdoctor (*Shaykh al-Ṭā'ifa*) Abū Ja'far al-Ṭūsī (d. 440/1048–9).[29] But as has already been observed, only volume 5 of this important work has so far been discovered and published.

The book appears to have been extant in its entirety for some time after the author's death. It is reported that the famous genealogist, Abū al-Ḥasan al-'Umarī, saw it and praised it saying: "I saw a handsome and praiseworthy tome of *Tafsīr* attributed to him [al-Sharīf al-Raḍī] which is as large as Ṭabari's *Tafsīr*."[30] In his biography of the author, Ibn Khallikān says that al-Sharīf wrote an exegesis of the noble Qur'ān, the like of which is difficult to find, for it demonstrates clearly the breadth of his knowledge of the sciences of [Arabic] grammar and linguistics."[31]

The principal manuscript of the published volume is a copy made early this century by the well-known Shī'i traditionist, Mīrzā Ḥusayn Nūrī, of an old manuscript which he found in the Imām Riḍā shrine library in Mashhad, Iran. This manuscript was copied in 533 A.H. from a manuscript which was read to the author in 402, three years before his death. Beside this copy, the editor relied on a late eleventh century A.H. imperfect copy of a manuscript found in a private library in Isfahan.[32]

Al-Sharīf's style and methodology reflect the analytical and literary approaches of his time. In both *Ḥaqā'iq al-Ta'wīl* and *Talkhīṣ al-Bayān*, he selects for analysis verses which present theological or linguistic problems. He does not analyze every word or phrase of a verse, as does al-Ṭabarī for example, but rather discusses what he considers to be its central theme, literary or theological issue. Since, however, he follows the accepted order of the Qur'ān, his commentary combines both the thematic and sequential approaches to Qur'ānic exegesis.

Al-Sharīf employs the classical method of organizing his discussion under distinct queries or questions (*masā'il*). This gives the work a clear and lucid organization. There is some disagreement as to whether or not he imitated in this approach his better-known brother, al-Sharīf al-Murtaḍā, in his literary dictations (*amālī*) entitled *Ghurar al-Fawā'id*, as the two works closely resemble one another in style and organization.[33]

The volume under discussion covers all but the first four verses of Sūra 3, *Āl 'Imrān*, and the first 51 verses of Sūra 4, *al-Nisā'*. Consequently, any useful prefatory materials in which the author may have discussed the aim and methodology of the work are lost. This gap, however, is partially filled through somewhat lengthy and rhetorical digressions. In the first of these, al-Sharīf praises his work and apologizes for repeating points in one volume that were clearly and fully presented in a previous one. This shortcoming, he explains, is due to the fact that the book took many years to complete due to difficult circumstances which interrupted his work.

Al-Sharīf makes reference to this book in both his works on the metaphors of the Qur'ān and metaphors of Prophetic ḥadīth traditions.

But he often describes it as a work in progress. This further indicates that this major commentary was begun relatively early in the author's career, and may have been completed after *Talkhīṣ al-Bayān.* Besides the apologetic aim of this long digression, the author appears to have used it to display his literary eloquence, which he does in highly polished, but untranslatable rymed prose (*saj'*). Perhaps a few lines may give some flavor of al-Sharīf's rhetorical erudition:

> Our exclusive attention to it was possible only in stolen moments and our interest in augmenting it could only be realized in fleeting opportunities. [Such moments were] like those of a frightened man stooping to catch a drink, the feverish activity of a pursued man, the grabbing of a firebrand by a man on the run, or the temporary arrest of a patient man against his will.[34]

We shall in the remaining pages of this study examine a few queries (*masā'il*) of the book under discussion in order to illustrate, as we did in the previous section, al-Sharīf's theological orientation and literary talents. While the latter is quite obvious in the Arabic original, the former is not easy to determine because, as the author himself explains, of the length of time required for elucidating obscure issues and erroneous opinions. Thus, al-Sharīf concludes, "A reader of the beginning of our book may surmise that we incline towards Murji'ism. But when he reaches its middle, he may conclude that we profess belief in the divine threat (*wa'īd*)."[35] The reason behind this confusion, the author argues, is the complexity of the beliefs and ideas of the various theological schools and the time and effort required to elucidate them.[36]

The volume begins with a lengthy discussion of the decisive (*muḥkamāt*) and multivalent (*mutashābihāt*) verses. His commentary on Q. 3:5–7, which deal with this much debated and highly significant subject, is rather traditional, as he presents and analyzes the various readings and interpretations of the two terms and whether God alone, or God and "those who are firmly rooted in knowledge" know the Qur'ān's interpretation (*ta'wīl*). Of greater relevance to the purpose of this study is al-Sharīf's discussion of verse 8, in which "those who are firmly rooted in knowledge" humbly pray God not to cause their hearts to swerve after He had guided them.

The author begins by presenting the argument of the opponents of the "people of [divine] justice (*'adl*) and oneness (*tawḥīd*)", that is the Mu'tazilites, then counters the argument with Mu'tazilī rebuttals. It seems, however, that the majority of these counter arguments are fictitious; but for rhetorical reasons, he ascribes them to anonymous contenders. This is the case throughout the book, except where he directly cites a renowned Mu'tazilī thinker, such as his own mentor al-Qāḍī 'Abd al-Jabbār.

The verse under consideration reads: "Our Lord, cause not our hearts to swerve after You have guided us. Grant us mercy from You, for You surely are the Bestower." The argument of the opponents runs thus: "Had this verse not implied an actual swerving of their hearts by God, their supplication to God not to cause their hearts to swerve would have no meaning or benefit." Al-Sharīf counters with ten possible Mu'tazilī interpretations, where the act of leading astray, or causing the hearts of righteous people to swerve cannot be imputed to God.

The first is that this supplication means for God not to know their hearts to be in a state of deviancy after right-guidance. It is as though they prayed:

> Shower upon us Your continuous graces and Your guidance, and grant us Your protection from error, so that our hearts may not swerve, and thus You would not know them to be in the state of deviancy.

The author supports this interpretation with similar expressions in common discourse, as when one says, "I caused so and so to stray" (*aḍlaltu fulānan*), meaning, "I found him to be in the state of straying," or "I caused him to be cowardly" (*ajbantuhu*), meaning, "I found him to be in the state of cowardice."[37]

Another possible interpretation of the verse is that the prayer here is for God not to try them with obligations which they cannot fulfill, and which may thus become the cause of their deviancy. God, the author continues, ascribed the act of swerving to Himself because He it is Who enjoins obligations upon human beings that may be a source of temptation (*fitna*) for them, but not a direct cause of their deviancy. Yet they are the agents of their actions, not God.

Thirdly, according to others, the prayer here means, "Protect us from the whisperings of Satan, so that we do not swerve, and you would not cause our hearts to swerve." This is because God would not cause anyone to fall into error until the person himself first chooses to do so, as God says, "But when they deviated, God caused their hearts to swerve." (Q. 61: 5)

The fourth view is that they prayed God to help them to stand firm on the right way, so that they would not swerve after he had guided them. Consequently, they asked God not to judge them as people of deviancy. For, al-Sharīf argues, "It is possible, when God withholds His grace from a people to say metaphorically that He caused them to deviate, even though God did not wish deviancy for them."

The fifth possibility represents the view of the famous Mu'tazilī theologian Abū 'Alī al-Jubbā'ī,who said:

> They asked God not to cause their hearts to swerve from the great reward (*thawāb*) and the increase of guidance and other Divine graces. They asked God to favor them with the increase of intuitions (*khawāṭir*) of faith and the strength of deterrents (*zawājir*) from

> committing acts of unfaithfulness, and that they abide in faith so long as they live. This is because it is not possible for them to ask God not to chastise them, if they are truly people of faith, except in this sense.

Al-Jubbā'ī interprets the swerving of hearts in this verse to mean tightness of the breast and heaviness of the heart, which is a form of God's chastisement. Inner peace, lightness of the heart, and expansion of the breast, on the other hand, represent Divine reward.

The sixth view is that God enjoined them to utter this prayer in the spirit of servitude and humility before Him. "For, if they so pray with humility, utter helplessness, certainty, and constant turning to God with repentance (*ināba*), God would reward them well for their supplication." The seventh interpretation is similar to this one, except for the assertion that God does not cause faith to inhere in a person's heart; "rather He guides his heart", meaning "He rewards him for his faith."

Some have even interpreted the swerving of hearts in this verse to mean deformation (*maskh*), as a punishment for unbelief. The author admits that this eighth view is strange and far-fetched, and that for this reason he presented it. The ninth is the view of al-Qāḍī 'Abd al-Jabbār, who argues: "It is not necessarily the case that everyone who asks God not to cause something in him that his prayer implies that God chooses this thing and causes it." Hence, the meaning of this prayer is, "Make not our trial arduous through difficult obligations (*taklīf*)."[38]

Finally, al-Sharīf proffers an interpretation which appears to represent his own view of the verse. He begins by asserting the universally accepted principle of interpreting the multivalent verses in light of the decisive ones. There are, he avers, both decisive and multivalent verses which deal with the issue of swerving (*zaygh*) in the Qur'ān. The verse under consideration is multivalent, and thus it must not be taken literally, "for this would lead us to say that God, glorified be He, arbitrarily leads certain people astray from faith (*īmān*)." But God would not do that because it is evil (*qabīḥ*), and God is in no need of so doing. Rather He enjoined faith upon us and made our hearts incline towards it. He likewise warned us against willfully accepting unfaithfulness (*kufr*). "It is therefore rationally imperative that God not lead us astray from what He enjoined upon us or lead us to what He commanded us to forsake."[39]

Our discussion thus far has focused on the principle of God's justice, and whether the All-Just (*'adl*) God could do or wish anything but the best (*al-aḥsan*) for His servants. The act of leading astray, or causing human hearts to swerve, is inherently bad (*qabīḥ*), and therefore cannot be imputed to God. But God is not only just, He is also All-Forgiving, All-Merciful. Forgiveness is inherently good (*ḥasan*), and therefore God must do it both as an act of grace (*tafaḍḍul*) and as a manifestation of His justice towards His obligated (*mukallafūn*), but weak and imperfect servants. Yet the verse with which we shall conclude this part of our discussion seems to contradict the Mu'tazilī-Shī'ī principle of justice as well as the principle of Divine threat (*wa'īd*) of eternal punishment for the unrepentant grave sinners.

Q. 4:48 reads in part: "Surely God will not forgive [the sin] of associating anything with Him, but He forgives [all sins] other than this of whomever He will." The objection of the alleged opponents is that the literal sense of this verse clearly counters the Mu'tazilī principle of Divine threat, as it implies that God would forgive the wicked (*fussāq*, pl. of *fāsiq*) and those who commit grave sins even persistently, as well as all other grave sins other than the sin of association (*shirk*). In fact, the verse supports the Murji'ite position, which is that no sin, however grave, would consign a person of true faith to the fire of Hell. Understandably, therefore, this verse has been the subject of much debate between the theologians of the two schools.

Al-Sharīf argues in answer to this objection that since God says "He forgives whomever He will", and not "He forgives if He so will", it means that God will forgive some, but not all sinners. Thus there must be among them those whom He will forgive, and others whom He will not forgive. He elaborates this point further:

> Since the verse indicates that God will forgive some of those who commit grave sins, apart from the sin of association, we know that it is not possible in His wisdom and justice that among those He will forgive are grave sinners, and among those whom He will not forgive are those who commit only minor sins. Nor is it possible that He forgive one servant and punish another, where the two sins are equal in gravity. For, this is precisely the meaning of bias, which God is far too exalted to show.[40]

This means, al-Sharīf further argues, that God will only forgive those grave sinners who repent, and He will also forgive those who commit small or venial sins; He will not, however, forgive those who persist in sin until they die. Al-Sharīf finally defines forgiveness as follows:

> For us, forgiveness includes good recompense (*ithāba*), because God forgives sins through acts of recompense. He thus becomes as the one who covers up the sins of disobedience, and this is in fact the root meaning of the word *ghāfir* (forgiver) in linguistic usage.

One of the points of contention between Mu'tazilī-Shī'ī and Ash'arī-orthodox Sunnī theology is the relationship of God's attributes (*ṣifāt*) to His essence (*dhāt*). Of special significance in this controversy is God's attribute of speech (*kalām Allāh*), particularly as this relates to the issue of the eternity and temporality of the Qur'ān. However, neither the scope nor purpose of this study allows any detailed discussion of this important theological issue. We shall therefore limit our investigation to al-Sharīf's exegesis of a Qur'ānic verse that speaks of Christ as the Word and spirit of God.

As mentioned earlier, the Qur'ān refers to Jesus Christ as the "Word of God and His spirit." The first occurrence of this designation is in Q. 3:45, which reads in part: "O Mary, surely God gives you glad tidings of a Word from Him whose name is Christ." The term *kalima* (word) in Arabic is feminine, while the epithet Christ (*al-Masīḥ*) is masculine. Thus the main points at issue are:

1. the meaning of the term *kalima* in this verse;
2. the reason for calling Christ Word of God;
3. the use of the masculine possessive pronoun *hu* in *ismuhu* (whose name) to qualify the feminine noun *kalima.*

Al-Sharīf's discussion here is addressed to no particular opponent, but to anyone who asks, "What is the meaning of the term *kalima* here, why did God call Christ *kalima* and why did He not observe the correct grammatical usage of [feminine] gender by saying *ismuhā* (her name), so that the narrative would flow smoothly and the meaning would be well ordered?" The author presents an allegorical interpretation of the phrase "Word of God" in this verse. God, he argues, repeatedly mentioned Christ in previous scriptures, announcing his coming long before his birth. Thus when He sent him as an apostle, He said, "This [apostle] is my Word", meaning "the apostle whose coming I foretold." This is like when a man predicts an event, and it happens as he had predicted, would say, "My speech has reached you, and now you see my words."[41]

The words "God gives you glad tidings of a Word" may also mean that God gave Mary the glad tidings of a son and a prophet who guides to the right, just as God's words guide to the truth. For this reason, the author argues, God called Christ Word, likening him to the word of proof and elucidation. "This is because", he continues, "a word in reality is actual speech; yet Jesus is neither speech nor is he of the genus of speech." It is in like manner that God called Jesus spirit, "because God's servants find life in him for their faith as they have life in their spirits for their bodies."[42]

A third possible interpretation of the verse is that the Word here means promise. This is to say, "God gives you glad tidings of that which He had already promised you." This interpretation is no doubt far-fetched. Therefore, the author comments, "If *kalima* is used here to mean promise, then its application to Christ is only a metaphor. This is because we cannot say that Christ is God's promise unless we mean that He was the promised one (*maw'ūd*) of God." In support of this view, he cites a verse of poetry, "My hope in you, in spite of your slow labor, is like the hope people have in the wombs of pregnant women."[43]

According to the famous Mu'tazilī thinker Abū Hudhayl al-'Allāf, the term *kalima* here signifies the Divine fiat "Be, and it is." Because Jesus was not born from a mother and father, it is possible, al-'Allāf further asserts, to call him "Word of God." Al-Sharīf prefers to interpret *kalima* to mean "the promised one", or that it refers to a messenger with a new religious law (*sharī'a*).

Al-Sharīf then discusses at some length the reason for using the masculine pronoun to qualify *kalima*, which is a feminine noun. It is because the personal pronoun here refers to Jesus, who is a male. In support of this argument, he refers to Q. 39:56–59, as well as a verse of the famous poet al-A'shā: "A tongue (*lisān*) has come to me from on-high in which there is neither wonderment nor mockery." By *lisān* the poet means a word (*kalima*), and so he uses the feminine pronoun with the verb *atatnī* (has come to me) which is the predicate of *lisān*, a masculine noun.

The reason behind this unusual grammatical construction, al-Sharīf explains, is to remove any doubt regarding Christ's personality and mission. Since this is the first mention of Christ as the Word of God, the feminine *kalima* was qualified by the masculine noun *al-Masīḥ*. Thus when this epithet occurred again in Q. 4:171, God said, "Surely Jesus Christ, son of Mary, is an apostle of God and His Word which he cast (*alqāhā*) [cast her] to Mary..."[44]

We shall end this study with al-Sharīf's commentary on a Qur'ānic verse, which in his view combines in a marvelous way religious devotion and literary metaphor. The verse reads in part: "And those who came to dwell in the abode (*al-dār*)[45] and in the faith (*īmān*) before them ..." (Q. 59:9). First al-Sharīf observes that this is a metaphor, because coming to dwell in or occupy an abode means making it a permanent home, which in reality cannot apply to the faith. Therefore, it must be taken as a general figure of speech, meaning, "they abided in faith (*īmān*) as they would abide in their homes (*awṭān*)." He then comments:

> This [metaphor] is of the heart of rhetorical eloquence (*balāgha*) and the inner core of elegant speech (*faṣāḥa*). For a metaphor can add greater resplendence to the meaning of the narrative. I say that words (*alfāẓ*) are always servants to meanings, for they beautify their narrations and bestow order on their significations.[46]

CONCLUDING REMARKS

Literary writing differs essentially from other kinds of expository writing in that it is born out of the imagination: of feelings and emotions, which may arise out of ordinary experiences. It may therefore be argued that the primary framework of literature is metaphor, allegory, or what our author calls "borrowed speech." Al-Sharīf's definition of the function of words in relation to meanings is significant in that it eloquently describes his own literary approach.

Al-Sharīf was not only a prolific and gifted poet, but also a sensitive soul. On account of the delicacy and sensitivity of his poetry, he was nicknamed by the litterateurs of his time, "the bereaved woman mourner."[47] His poetic talents and religious learning added to his exaggerated self-esteem. This is clearly reflected in his frequent prosaic, but nonetheless highly eloquent digressions.

Al-Sharīf discerns in the Qur'ānic metaphor of Christ as "the Word of God" a great literary figure of speech. He then goes on to expatiate at some length on the great literary marvels of the Qur'ān and concludes:

> I may, with God's help, present in this work such meanings, noble wonders, and piercing flashes as would allow me to lead others to some of the Qur'ān's inner secrets. I shall point out the places of these mysteries in ways never discovered; nor shall anyone have cast the arrows of his intellect and hit such targets as I.[48]

Whether al-Sharīf achieved this ambitious goal or not, we may never know; and God knows best.

NOTES

1 The Qur'ān reiterates this challenge in a number of verses, but most emphatically in the declaration: "Were humankind and the jinn to come together to produce the like of this Qur'ān, they could not do so even if they were to stand back to back [in this endeavor]" (Q. 17:88; see also Q. 2:23; 12:13; 10:38).

2 The title of the work is itself a telling comment on his approach: *al-Jawāhir fī Tafsīr al-Qur'ān al-Karīm, al-Mushtamil 'alā 'Ajā'ib Badā'i' al-Mukawwanāt wa Gharā'ib al-Āyāt al-Bāhirāt* [Jewels of the exegesis of the noble Qur'ān, which contains marvels of the beauties of the creation and wonders of dazzling Divine signs]. See *al-Jawāhir*, 25 vols. (Cairo: Muṣṭafā al-Bābī al-Ḥalabī, 1350/1932), xxvi, passim.

3 See his commentary, *Tafsīr al-Marāghī*, 30 vols. (Cairo: Muṣṭafā al-Bābī al-Ḥalabī, 1365/1946), and especially his medical discussion of Q. 86:7.

4 The Qur'ān uses the possessive pronoun in reference to Christ as His (God's) Word (*kalimatuhu*); see Q. 4:171. However, it uses the phrase "*wa rūḥun minhu*" (and a spirit from Him) in reference to Christ as the spirit of God.

5 Among the most active Buyid rulers in this regard was 'Aḍud al-Dawla (d. 372/983) to whose court famous grammarians, poets and other literary figures flocked, seeking his generous patronage. See 'Abd al-Ghanī Ḥasan's edition of *Talkhīṣ al-Bayān fī Majāzāt al-Qur'ān* by al-Sharīf al-Raḍī (Cairo: Dār al-Aḍwā', 1957) [introduction], 71; see also 65–79.

6 Khayr al-Dīn al-Ziriklī, *al-A'lām*, 3rd ed., 13 vols. (published by the author, n.d.), 6:329. See also Abū al-'Abbās Shams al-Dīn Aḥmad ibn Muḥammad ibn Abī Bakr ibn Khallikān, *Wafayāt al-A'yān wa Anbā' Abnā' al-Zamān*, ed. Iḥsān 'Abbās, 8 vols. (Beirut, Dār al-Thaqāfa, 1971), 6:414.

7 Ibid. See also Abū al-Faraj ʿAbd al-Raḥmān b. ʿAlī b. Muḥammad b. al-Jawzī, *al-Muntaẓam fī Taʾrīkh al-Mulūk wa ʾl-Umam*, eds. Muṣṭafā and Muḥammad ʿAbd al-Qādir ʿAṭā, 16 vols. (Beirut: Dār al-Kutub al-ʿIlmiyya, 1415/1995), 15:115.

8 Ibn Khallikān, *Wafayāt*, 4:414; see also Ṣalāḥ al-Dīn Khalīl ibn Aybak al-Ṣafadī, *al-Wāfī fī ʾl-Wafayāt*, 29 vols. (Beirut: German Oriental Institute, 1381/1962–1997), 2:374; first published in Istanbul: Wizārat al-Maʿārif, ed. Helmut Ritter.

9 Ibn al-Jawzī, *al-Muntaẓam*, 15:38; see also ʿAbd al-Ghanī Ḥasan, *Talkhīṣ*, 83.

10 Zakī Mubārak, *ʿAbqariyyat al-Sharīf al-Raḍī*, 4th ed., 2 vols. (Cairo: Ḥijāzī, 1371/1952), 1:139ff.

11 Al-Sharīf al-Raḍī, *Ḥaqāʾiq al-Taʾwīl fī Mutashābih al-Tanzīl*, ed. Muḥammad Riḍā Āl Kāshif al-Ghiṭāʾ (Beirut: Dār al-Muhājir, n.d.), [reprint of the Najaf edition of 1355, with a long introduction by ʿAbd al-Ḥusayn al-Ḥillī], 81.

12 Āl Kāshif al-Ghiṭāʾ, *Ḥaqāʾiq* [Introduction], 47.

13 See Abū ʿAbd Allāh Yāqūt ibn ʿAbd Allāh al-Rūmī al-Ḥamawī, *Muʿjam al-Udabāʾ aw Irshād al-Arīb ilā Maʿrifat al-Adīb*, 5 vols. (Beirut: Dār al-Kutub al-ʿIlmiyya, 1411/1991), 1:186.

14 This tradition is reported by many classical Qurʾān commentators. See M. Ayoub, *The Qurʾān and Its Interpreters*, 2 vols. (Albany: State University of New York Press, 1984), 1:198. For al-Sharīf's interpretation of this metaphor, see *Talkhīṣ al-Bayān fī Majāzāt al-Qurʾān*, 21 (full bibliographic information in footnote 17).

15 The book was published in Cairo by Maktabat al-Khānjī, 197?. See the author's introduction p. 8 where he argues that the Prophet's audiences knew the meanings of the Qurʾān, as it was revealed in their native tongue. He was therefore writing for later generations of Muslims many of whom were not Arabs and others who were far removed from the original Qurʾānic milieu. See also ʿAbd al-Ghanī Ḥasan, *Talkhīṣ*, 5–6.

16 The title of the book means, "Interpretation of difficult or obscure (*mushkil*) terms or phrases of the Qurʾān". The book has been published many times: in 1954, ed. al-Sayyid Aḥmad Ṣaqr (Cairo: ʿĪsā al-Bābī al-Ḥalabī); 1973, ed. al-Sayyid Aḥmad Ṣaqr (Cairo: Dār al-Turāth); 1989, eds. ʿUmar Muḥammad Saʿīd ʿAbd al-ʿAzīz & ʿAbd al-Ṣabūr Shāhīn. See ʿAbd al-Ghanī Ḥasan, *Talkhīṣ*, 14ff.

17 The Tehran edition is simply a phototype reproduction of an old but imperfect manuscript going back to the fifth century A.H., not long after the death of the author. Ed. al-Sayyid Muḥammad al-Mishkāt (Tehran: Muḥammad al-Mishkāt, 1953). The second edition, edited by ʿAbd al-Ghanī Ḥasan, is a version of the first publication, with the former's many lacunae. The third publication, on which we base our discussion, is edited by Makkī al-Sayyid Jāsim and published in Beirut by Maktabat al-Nahḍa al-ʿArabiyya, 1406/1986.

18 Al-Sharīf, *Talkhīṣ*, 10.

19 Ibn Khallikān, *Wafayāt*, 4:416.

20 Al-Sharīf, *Talkhīṣ*, 15.

21 Ibid., 80–81. See Q. 9:129; 23:86; 27:26.

22 Ibid., 231. See also his interpretation of Q. 38:75, ibid., 236.

23 Ibid., 238.

24 Ibid., 204–5.

25 Ibid., 175–76.

26 Al-Sharīf al-Raḍī, *al-Majāzāt al-Nabawiyya aw Majāzāt al-Āthār al-Nabawiyya*, eds. Marwān ʿAṭiyya and Muḥammad Riḍwān al-Dāya (Damascus: al-Mustashāriyya al-Thaqāfiyya li ʾl-Jumhūriyya al-Islāmiyya, 1408/1987), 40.

27 Ibid., 251–52.
28 Aghā Buzurg Ṭihrānī reports an alternative title, *Ḥaqā'iq al-Tanzīl wa Daqā'iq al-Ta'wīl.* See his voluminous bibliographical work, *al-Dharī'a ilā Taṣānīf al-Shī'a,* s.v. *ḥaqā'iq al-ta'wīl* [entry 260].
29 Āl Kāshif al-Ghiṭā', *Ḥaqā'iq al-Ta'wīl* [Intro.], 91.
30 Ibid. [Intro.], 91.
31 Ibn Khallikān, *Wafayāt,* 4:416.
32 Al-Sharīf, *Ḥaqā'iq* [Intro.], 10–12.
33 See Ṭihrānī, *Dharī'a,* s.v. *ḥaqā'iq;* and al-Sharīf, *Ḥaqā'iq al-Ta'wīl* [Intro.], 13–4.
34 Ibid., 16. All references hereafter are to the text's pagination.
35 The term *irjā'* (Murji'ism) refers to the Murji'a, those who chose to postpone judgment regarding the fate of a grave sinner who professes Islam, leaving the matter to God in the Hereafter. *Al-Wa'd* (the Divine promise) and *wa'īd* (threat) together constitute one of the five principles of Mu'tazilī theology.
36 Ibid., 16–7.
37 Ibid., 17.
38 It should be noted that this prayer is similar to that of Q. 2:286, which reads in part, "Our Lord, lay not upon us a burden, as You laid on those who were before us." This verse provides the basis for this and the second interpretation.
39 Ibid., 17–24; see also 24–8.
40 Ibid., 362.
41 Ibid., 94–5; see also al-Sharīf, *Talkhīṣ,* 27.
42 Al-Sharīf, *Ḥaqā'iq,* 95; see also al-Sharīf, *Talkhīṣ,* 36.
43 Al-Sharīf, *Ḥaqā'iq,* 95–6.
44 Ibid., 101–2. See also *Talkhīṣ,* 36.
45 This is a reference to Medina, which is called *dār al-hijra* (abode of the migration).
46 Al-Sharīf, *Talkhīṣ,* 285.
47 Al-Ṣafadī, *al-Wāfī,* 2:374.
48 Al-Sharīf, *Ḥaqā'iq,* 103.

Chapter 14

Studies in the *Majāz* and Metaphorical[1] Language of the Qur'ān: Abū 'Ubayda and al-Sharīf al-Raḍī

Kamal Abu-Deeb

I. SOME INTRODUCTORY OBSERVATIONS

It is widely recognized that the position of the Qur'ān in the life of the early Arabs and the intense interest they took in its supreme qualities generated most of the important questions about language, literature and religious belief. It has been argued that the Qur'ān was the most powerful force behind the rise and development of literary criticism and the theorizing about *balāgha* and *faṣāḥa*.[2] What is less widely acknowledged is that the intense interest in the Qur'ān also generated the first profound contemplations of the nature of poetic imagery and the birth of the very notion of two modes of using language: one real, or literal (*ḥaqīqī*), the other non-real, or non-literal (*majāzī*)[3]. In very early work of mine, I tried to demonstrate that the notion of *majāz* crystallized in the context of questions about the nature of God and man's relationship to Him, specifically with reference to such issues as free will and predestination.[4] Another factor provided a further powerful impulse, namely the notion that the Qur'ān was inimitable (*mu'jiz*). Not that the Qur'ān itself proclaimed this explicitly, but interpretations of its challenge to the people of Quraysh to "bring (compose or produce) anything like it,"[5] steered the debate in this direction: the Qur'ān is *mu'jiz*, that we acknowledge, but where exactly does its *i'jāz* lie, in its words, its meanings or in *ṣarfa* (God purposefully turning people away from competing with it altogether)?[6] It is in attempts to answer questions of this nature that the wonderful work of a figure like 'Abd al-Qāhir al-Jurjānī was produced and the works of many of his predecessors took shape; of these al-Khaṭṭābī, al-Bāqillānī, al-Rummānī and, especially, al-Qāḍī 'Abd al-Jabbār al-Asadī are of special significance.

Many important questions related to the nature and function of metaphorical language were discussed by these writers and others like them as part of their overall enquiries into the inimitability of the Qur'ān, but there were scholars who devoted their attention entirely to the study of *majāz* in this great text. Most prominent amongst these are Abū 'Ubayda Ma'mar b. al-Muthannā (died some time between 208 and 213 A. H.) and al-Sharīf al-Raḍī (died 406 A. H.)

The pioneering nature of Abū 'Ubayda's work has been widely acknowledged although some scholars have argued that his study of *majāz* does not belong to the category of works concerned with *majāz* as a feature of the non-literal use of language. M.A.G. Ḥasan[7] considers it a work of commentary and interpretation (*tafsīr*) in the general sense of the word. Ṭāhā Ḥusayn thinks that it is a book on language, in which Abū 'Ubayda "aimed at collecting those words which were used in meanings other than their original/conventional (*waḍ'ī*) ones".[8] In what follows I shall examine the multiple ways in which Abū 'Ubayda discusses *majāz*, paying special attention to the way in which he handles some of the verses that would fall properly within the scope of *isti'āra* in its technical sense.

II. ABŪ 'UBAYDA ON THE *MAJĀZ* OF THE QUR'ĀN

1.

About the end of the second[9] century A. H., Abū 'Ubayda wrote a book on the *Qur'ān*, which he is said to have called *al-Majāz*,[10] and which is known to us today as *Majāz al-Qur'ān*.[11] The book is reported by many writers to be the first book in Arabic written on *majāz*,[12] and some go even further to claim that Abū 'Ubayda was the first person to have used the word *majāz*.[13] This, however, is doubtful.[14]

Not only has the position of Abū 'Ubayda's book as the earliest work on *majāz* been a subject for controversy,[15] so has the nature of the book itself. The dispute over these questions existed in works by critics relatively near in time to Abū 'Ubayda's, as well as in works by modern Arab critics.[16]

The significance of the word *majāz* has also been a point on which one rarely finds two critics agreeing. It is not entirely due to the vagueness of the book itself that all these ideas have been put forward. It is also due to the methods of analysis adopted by various writers, none of whom looks closely at the word *majāz* in its immediate linguistic context. Moreover, these writers, except for Ibn Taymiyya and, to some extent, Amīn al-Khūlī who adopts his views on the nature of the book, always have in mind traces of the word *majāz* as we conceive of it now. Ṭāhā Ḥusayn has already been quoted as saying, in connection with the nature of the book, that it is "a book on language, in which Abū 'Ubayda aimed at collecting those words which were used in meanings other than their original/conventional (*waḍ'ī*) ones, without making any distinction between the various types of *majāz*."[17] This seems to be responsible not only for Ḥusayn's misinterpretation of the book, but also for the probably unconscious slip which makes him change Abū 'Ubayda's words and replace them with words that coincide with his own concept of *majāz*. The words in question are those which occur in the anecdote relating the reason for Abū 'Ubayda's writing of the book. When asked by skeptics who did not share the view that the Qur'ān was faultless, how it was that the Qur'ān compared things unknown to people with other things equally unknown to them, as is the case of "*shajarat al-Zaqqūm*, (Q. 37:62), described as *ṭal'uhā ka'annahu ru'ūsu 'sh-shayāṭīn*," (*al-Ṣāffāt*, Q. 37:65)[18] he said: "God addressed the Arabs in the way they themselves used in their speech [or discourse]. Have you not heard Imru' al-Qays's line: *ayaqtulunī wa 'l-mashrafiyyu muḍāji'ī / wa masnūnatun zurqun ka-anyābi aghwālī?*"

Ṭāhā Ḥusayn narrates this story as follows:

> Abū 'Ubayda was asked once about [the verse] '... the heads of Satans ...' and he replied: 'This is a *majāz*, like Imru' al-Qays's line: '... the sharpened blue spears which are like the teeth of the *aghwāl*.' Had Abū 'Ubayda been asked about the detailed nature of this *majāz* and its various forms, he would not have been able to answer, for this science [*majāz*] was not yet known in his time.[19]

The importance I attach to the fact that Abū 'Ubayda did not say that the verse (or the line of poetry) was a *majāz* has a specific function: to show that one should not take it for granted that the word *majāz* in his book is used in the sense which later rhetoricians attached to it, namely, that it is a word which is used in a meaning other than its original one. The usage of the word *majāz* itself must be closely examined in order to define accurately Abū 'Ubayda's concept of *majāz*. In what follows when examining the usage of the word *majāz* by Abū 'Ubayda, the meaning of the word in its later development will be deliberately ignored (except for purposes of comparison, where this might be useful).

Abū 'Ubayda's usage of the word *majāz* in both his introductory chapter and his study proper of the *Qur'ān* reveals a basic feature of his concept of *majāz*, a feature which, if ignored, will almost certainly result in serious flaws in any interpretation of the book. Already in this introductory chapter, a distinction should be made between his usage of *majāz* when it is applied to a *single* word and its usage in application to a *phrase*.

The dominant feature of the first part of the chapter is that the word *majāz* in it is applied only to single words, and it can be seen from this application that *majāz* stands primarily for *ma'nā*. Another secondary feature, but one which has important bearings on the arguments of those critics who take the book to be one of *tafsīr*, is that points other than *majāz* are discussed in this part like, for instance, the names of certain sūras. Also, there are a number of explanations of certain words without applying the word *majāz* to them.[20] It must also be noted that Abū 'Ubayda already uses the terms "*majāzuhu*" and "*ma'nāhu*" in a way that may suggest some differences between them.[21]

In this part, the linguistic usage of the word *majāz* does not raise any problems with regards to its syntactic relation to the other words in the context. The importance of noticing the linguistic position of the word *majāz* will be fully realized if it is pointed out that this word means *the original usage* or etymological form or meaning of the word under consideration rather than *the later form or meaning* that *has* resulted from the usage of such a word "for a meaning other than its original one." This is exactly the opposite of the concept of *majāz* which was to develop later on in Arabic studies. The difference can be shown clearly if one compares Abū 'Ubayda's formula "*majāzuhu*" with the formulae of later writers.[22]

Al-Suyūṭi, for instance, says: "They say: 'someone mounted (*istawā 'alā*) the road', while the road doesn't have a back, and 'someone is on the wing [of travel]' and 'the war stood on a leg.' All these are *majāzāt.*"[23]

Abū 'Ubayda would not have called these expressions *majāzāt.* He will, in fact, look for what he calls the *majāzāt* of these expressions: *their original form.*

The second part of the introductory chapter consists of a list of expressions which were used in the *Qur'ān* in an unfamiliar way and Abū 'Ubayda's theoretical formulation of the "type of structure" to which each expression belongs. The phrase "type of structure" is deliberately used here, instead of "type of *majāz*" for reasons which will be explained.

The first reason is the difficulty which faces one here in trying to decide what the word *majāz* means. That is because the linguistic usage is certainly different from that in the first part, not only in the linguistic formulae "*majāz sūra*", "*majāzuhu*" or the syntactic relations between *majāz* and the other words in the phrases, but also in the semantic signification of the word *majāz.* The most common formula of the word *majāz* here is: "*wa min majāzi mā.*"[24] A less common formula is: "*wa min majāzi*" followed by the name of the change of style itself, for instance: "*wa min majāzi al-muqaddami wa al-mu'akhkhari,*" "*wa min majāzi al-maṣdari alladhī.*"[25]

There is also a third formula which can be related to the first one as regards the position of the word *majāz,* but it has an addition presenting some difficulties which are peculiar to it; it is: "*wa min al-muḥtamal min majāzi mā.*"[26]

These three formulae are applied not to single words[27] but to phrases, the comment being one on the structural side, mostly from a semantic[28] point of view, but also sometimes from the point of view of the grammatical[29] relations between the vocabulary. Here it seems certain that *majāz* cannot possibly mean *ma'nā,* for if the latter were substituted for the former, the formulae would become meaningless, as for instance, in the case of the type: "*wa min majāzi mā jā'at lahu ma'ānin ghayru wāḥidin mukhtalifatun fa-ta'awwalathu 'l-'ulamā'u bi-lughātihā fa-jā'at ma'ānīhi.*"[30]

These three formulae are used to introduce the types of structure whose *majāzāt* Abū 'Ubayda is anxious to find out. It is noticeable that the formula "*majāzuhu*" is thus used in the sense "its original form". It occurs like this six times in this part; thus the interpretation suggested earlier can be further developed to say that the word *majāz* stands for the original form of what is being commented on, both in the phrase and the single word, with the original form of the single word being, sometimes, its meaning (*ma'nā*). In the third part of the introductory chapter, Abū 'Ubayda summarizes in about four pages[31] his views on *majāz*. He gives one example of *majāz* applied to the single word,[32] which is one of his examples in the first part, namely the word "*Qur'ānuhu*,"[33] and discusses briefly the question of foreign words in the *Qur'ān*,[34] then enumerates the types of structures to which he had applied the word *majāz*, but here without any examples at all, only listing them.[35]

Abū 'Ubayda's introductory analysis is thus completed and from here onwards he initiates a systematic analysis of the *Qur'ān* commenting on the sūras as they are arranged in it, which reveals a high degree of systematic thinking on his part. His work on *majāz* here, although slightly more complex than in the introductory parts, is essentially of the same nature. In view of this fact, it seems unnecessary to discuss the usage of *majāz* in this part.

2.

The evidence produced so far has been based on the linguistic analysis of the word *majāz* and how it is used in its various contexts. One must also consider whether or not Abū 'Ubayda actually refers to *majāz* in the sense of transference. In this respect, it is noticeable that Abū 'Ubayda fails to take account of the two most important aspects of *majāz* as a rhetorical concept and a term.

I) *The similarity relation* (i.e., *majāz* which is a transference based on similarity). At least 27 verses which are based on *isti'ārī* usage are quoted in the book, but the *isti'ārī* element in them is completely ignored. Most of them are not even called *majāz*. Moreover, when the word *majāz* is applied to some of them, it obviously refers to something other than *isti'ārī* relations. For instance, the *isti'ārī* expression "*fa-dhūqū 'l-'adhāba,*" in the verse: "*fadhūqū 'l-'adhāba bi-mā kuntum takfurūn,*" (*Āl 'Imrān*, Q. 3:106)[36] is commented on as follows: "Its *majāz* (*majāzuhu*) is: try, (experience); it has nothing to do with tasting [lit. tasting by the mouth]."[37] It is curious to observe that "*'adhāb*", the word which renders the verse metaphorical, is dropped.

A more evident comment is made on the verse: "*wa arsalnā 'r-riyāḥa lawāqiḥa*" (*al-Ḥijr*, Q. 15:22).[38] Abū 'Ubayda says: "*majāzuhā majāz malāqiḥ, li-anna al-rīḥa mulqiḥatun li al-saḥābi, wa al-'Arabu qad taf'alu hādhā fa-tulqī al-mīma li-annahā tu'īduhu ilā aṣli al-kalāmi.*"[39]

Similarly, the verse: *"wa ushribū fī qulūbihimu 'l-'ijla"* (*al-Baqara*, Q. 2:93)[40] is described as follows: "They were made to drink it up to the point where it overwhelmed them completely. Its *majāz* is the *majāz* of *al-mukhtaṣar* [probably omission]: they were made to drink the Calf; the love of the Calf".[41]

And the verse: "*hunna libāsun lakum*" (*al-Baqara*, Q. 2:187)[42] is simply explained in the following way: "A man's wife [woman] may be described as being his bed, his clothes, his garment ..."[43] A number of other verses are described in a similar manner without any reference to their *isti'ārī* nature.[44]

It is interesting to note how different Abū 'Ubayda's comments are from those made by later authors for whom *majāz* was based on transference. The way he handles the phrase "*ummu 'l-Kitāb*" (*Āl 'Imrān*, Q. 3:7), is a good example. He does not comment on the *isti'ārī* relation here at all,[45] while al-Jāḥiẓ, for instance, gives a detailed account of this relation.[46] Further, the word *isti'āra* is not used in Abū 'Ubayda's book at all, although in another book of his he uses the phrase "*wa hādhā min al-musta'āri*" a number of times.[47]

II) *The contiguity relation* (together with any other type of *majāz* based on a relation other than similarity). For instance the verse: "*alzamnāhu ṭā'irahu*"[48] (*al-Isrā'* (*Banū Isrā'īl*), Q. 17:13) is commented on with a simple word: "His luck."[49] It is also important to note that Abū 'Ubayda fails to discuss the most obvious instance of *isti'āra* and some of the most artistic images in the *Qur'ān*.

All this represents sufficiently strong evidence that Abū 'Ubayda was not thinking of the transference in the word, or the metaphoric relations in it, when he was thinking of its *majāz*. And on the basis of such evidence, it is perfectly legitimate to argue that Ṭāhā Ḥusayn's description of the book is entirely mistaken.

A final piece of evidence lies in Abū 'Ubayda's attitude towards those verses which evoke anthropomorphic associations. He does not seem to have been aware of what bearings *majāz* can have on anthropomorphism. It will be illuminating to explore what interests him in a verse which was to cause fierce arguments within the community of believers: "*ar-Raḥmānu 'alā 'l-'arshi 'stawā*", (*Ṭā Hā*, Q. 20:5). He comments on this verse as follows:

"... [*istawā*]: meaning (*ay*) sat upon (*'alā*). It can be said "*istawaytu* on the animal and on the mountain, and on the house, meaning: sat upon it (*'alawtu 'alayhi*). Its *majāz* is : "*istawā al-Raḥmānu 'alā al-'arshi.*"[50]

His interest lies in the original form of the expression or the meaning of the words[51] and not in *majāz* in its rhetorical sense. The *majāz* of the phrase, as he sees it, is not whether God can sit or not, but whether or not the word order is normal. Such an important issue can be taken as a criterion for his concept of *majāz*, and it confirms that he is not concerned with the question of the literal and non-literal (*waḍ'ī* and *majāzī*) usage of words at all, but in questions of an entirely different nature. At the same time, his work cannot be described as a work of *tafsīr*, in the general sense of the word, although many of his comments present us with useful tools in the process of interpretation.

In conclusion, it is probably accurate to say that Abū 'Ubayda used the word *majāz* itself in its original, ordinary, linguistic sense that is generated by its morphology and etymology: i. e., as the *ism al-makān* derived from the verb *jāza* (crossed over, passed from to) to mean 'the original point from which a certain word or phrase *jāza* (crossed over) from its original or more familiar mode of formulation to the different mode in which it appears in the Qur'ān.' The idea that *majāz* is a process which involves transferences that generate *isti'āra* as well as contiguity-based modes of expression was totally unfamiliar to him. This was to develop in the works of other scholars.

III. AL-SHARĪF AL-RAḌĪ ON *MAJĀZ* AND *ISTI'ĀRA* IN THE QUR'ĀN

3.

Al-Sharīf al-Raḍī is best known as a fine poet. He is probably the most significant figure in Arabic poetry to emerge in that space which separated al-Mutanabbī (d. 354 A. H.) and Abū al-'Alā' al-Ma'arrī (d. 449 A. H.). But a major aspect of his literary achievement, which has been largely overlooked over the centuries, resides in his outstanding studies of the language of *majāz* and *isti'āra* in the two great sources of religious texts in Islam: the Qur'ān and the traditions of the Prophet (*ḥadīth*). In what appears to be a unique effort in any culture at least up to his own time, al-Raḍī devoted his energies to a detailed enquiry into metaphorical language in an entire, unified body of linguistic material, producing two remarkable books: *Talkhīṣ al-Bayān fi Majāzāt al-Qur'ān* and *al-Majāzāt al-Nabawiyya.*[52] Abū 'Ubayda, as we have just seen, had attempted to offer a systematic and comprehensive study of the *majāz* in the Qur'ān, but his was not a study of metaphorical language or *majāz* in the sense adopted by al-Raḍī and other scholars. Moreover, the two were very different in religious outlook, temperament and intellectual makeup. Abū 'Ubayda was first and foremost a *rāwiya*, a genealogist, a historian and a linguist, who wrote his book in response to a specific challenge. Al-Raḍī was a poet and a Shī'ite *imām*, well immersed in *bāṭinī* interpretation and contemplation of what lies beyond the surface of discourse in all its forms, from an oral text like the *ḥadīth* of the Prophet, to a tightly composed, written text, like the Qur'ān. In addition, they were separated by almost two hundred years during which a great deal of analysis and exploration of the Qur'ānic text and of *majāz* and its categories had taken place and had already produced some remarkable individual works and a complex body of ideas. However, whereas Abū 'Ubayda's reputation as the author of the first study of *majāz* in the Qur'ān has guaranteed him a lasting place within the Arabic and Islamic galaxy of Qur'ānic scholars, al-Raḍī has not been so fortunate. Does the fact that he was a Shī'ite, living in an age of tragic conflict between the Sunnīs and the Shī'ites, have anything to do with this? I am inclined to believe that it does. For his work, purely on merit, deserves to be positioned alongside a select few outstanding works which culminated in al-Jurjānī's great achievement only a few decades after al-Raḍī's death.

4.

Al-Raḍī took great pride in his achievement and the pioneering nature of his work;[53] other scholars also acknowledged that achievement, including some modern Arab writers[54] who have considered it categorically the first of its kind in Arabic. This fact gives it a special status and makes it of particular importance for the study of the Qur'ānic text, the development of *balāgha* and *bayān* (loosely translatable as the science of rhetoric), and literary criticism. Moreover, the qualities of his analysis make it of considerable value not only because of the exhaustive and skilful search for the merits of the figures of speech he identifies, but also because of his penetrating explanations of the aesthetic effects of many such figures, explanations which go beyond anything achieved in the works of his predecessors. Al-Raḍī's essentially poetic sensibility and his capacity to appreciate the beauty and power of many of the figures he discusses enhance the appeal of his analysis and his contribution to the development of the study of figurative language.[55]

I shall examine al-Raḍī's work from two perspectives: first, the way in which he approaches *majāz* and *isti'āra* in the Qur'ān, the characteristics of his analysis, the aesthetic and critical principles underlying it, the light it throws on some fundamental aspects of *majāz* and *isti'āra* as linguistic and imaginative processes, and the implications of his way of identifying them in the Qur'ānic text for a general theory of metaphorical language and its cultural, ideological and anthropological significance. Secondly, the position his exploration of the processes of *majāz* and *isti'āra* occupies in Arabic studies and his contribution to the evolution of critical discourse in this key area of literary inquiry.

5.

The first striking feature of al-Raḍī's work is its *systematic* and *comprehensive* nature. He seems to have set out with a definite plan and a highly organized scheme: to write a comprehensive study of the *majāz* in the

Qur'ān, and to follow this by a similar study of *majāz* in the *ḥadīth.* The scheme he developed for both texts was the same: he went through the Qur'ān sūra by sūra, detailing in each sūra, verse by verse, every usage he believed to belong to a non-literal way of expression. First he would quote the verse, indicate where the *majāzī* or *isti'ārī* usage occurs, explain the reasons for considering this an instance of *majāz* offering a detailed discussion of the way the expression works: the basis for its construction (the point of similarity in the instances based on similarity or the other relations underlying it in different cases), the multiplicity of interpretations possible in dealing with it and the way some interpretations would place the expression outside the space of *majāz* and *isti'āra.* In the process, he would explore some aesthetic aspects of the use of *majāz* and *isti'āra* and reveal the degree of intensification achieved in a given instance. Having applied this scheme throughout the Qur'ānic text, he then devoted his energies to the *ḥadīth* of the Prophet and applied the same scheme to it. It is obvious, however, that al-Raḍī revised his work at various points, as there are cross-references in each of the two books to the other. His statement in the introduction to *al-Majāzāt al-Nabawiyya* that he composed this book in response to a request by somebody who had thought very highly of the book on the Qur'ān might be literally correct or might be his way of taking credit for initiating something truly novel. In either case, it in no way invalidates the suggestion that he sets out with a clear design for what he intended to achieve.

One initial observation needs to be made: due to the fact that al-Raḍī's study is concerned with the figures of the Qur'ān rather than an ordinary secular text, his analysis of the verses concentrates on their merits, their power of expression and their positive effects. It could hardly have been otherwise; one cannot easily conceive of a person of his background and position making negative statements about the language of the holy Book. His positive attitude is well reflected in the variety of phrases of admiration he uses[56] as well as in his search for the traits which render the verses he deals with most eloquent and capable of achieving the highest degree of intensification (*mubālagha*) of the meanings they express.

Intensification is held by al-Raḍī to be the purpose, and function, of creating a figure of speech[57] and the factor which enhances its semantic and aesthetic impact. And his study naturally enough devotes a great deal of attention to the way the verses he examines achieve that supreme function. Intensification also represents the 'added value' that is derived from using a figure of speech in a certain position by comparison with a literal expression that might have otherwise been used in that position.

Al-Raḍī's profound interest in intensification and additional connotations have generated what is perhaps the most rewarding aspect of his entire analysis: the unrelenting and highly intelligent search for the point of similarity which justifies holding a comparison between two objects or aspects of experience and creating an *isti'āra* on the basis of such a comparison. In many instances, the depth of this analysis reveals the origin of an *isti'āra* which might have otherwise gone unnoticed and been treated as a literal statement. An interesting example is his study of the verse: "*qad jā'akum rasūlunā yubayyinu lakum 'alā fatratin mina 'r-rusuli*" (*al-Mā'ida*, Q. 5:19).[58] He considers this an *isti'āra* and analyzes the point of similarity as follows:[59] "[Here there is] a comparison of the sending of messengers to their nations and then their death after delivering their messages to the blazing of fire and its fading away."[60]

The word *fatra* is analyzed here as being a description of fire applied to the prophets, through a perceived similarity. This analysis has entirely revitalized the *isti'āra* in this word. The effectiveness of the *isti'āra* would be lost if, for instance, the word *fatra* was taken in its dictionary sense.[61] The *isti'āra* in *fatra*, as it is analyzed by al-Raḍī, conveys not only the meaning of "interval" between the prophets, but adds to that rich associations of a sensuous nature. The image of the fire burning out, spreading light, heat, and even aesthetic pleasure, is associated here with the image of the prophets who are sent by God at intervals, carrying to the world guidance, love, security, and describing the beauty of heaven. Similarly the "interval" between two rounds of fire dying away, which is full of darkness, cold, ash, vanishing beauty and warmth, is associated with the interval between two prophets, when neither guidance, security nor heavenly beauty is given or revealed. The image of darkness and ash filling the space between each two prophets is particularly powerful in heightening the significance and importance of the sending of a prophet into this desolate space.

In other examples, al-Raḍī's analysis of the point of similarity reveals in a metaphorical expression a wider range of associations which enrich the image and add to its aesthetic effect. For instance, his comments on the verse: "*li-nuḥyiya bihi baldatan maytan*" (*al-Furqān*, Q. 25:49)[62] suggest two points of similarity, the second of which enriches the image with elements that belong to the space of human emotions. Al-Raḍī says:

> [His] description of the town as being dead may, here, be interpreted in either of two ways: first the town may have been compared to a dead [person] in view of its barrenness because it has been devastated by drought, or [it may have been said to be dead] because before there had existed in it plenty of plants and trees which then died because of the drought, and as such it has become possible to describe the land itself as being dead when its children have died, for it is like a mother for them feeding them with its milk.[63]

Further examples of this remarkable aspect of his work will be presented throughout this paper.

6. Subtlety of Analysis: Syntactic Structures, Position and Context

Another dimension of al-Raḍī's work is the attention he pays to the position of *isti'āra* within a given structure, thus by examining the metaphorical expression not as an isolated element but as part of a network of relations. Although generally he contents himself with making brief comments on this aspect, some of his remarks are strikingly perceptive. His comment on the verse: *"bal naqdhifu bi 'l-ḥaqqi 'alā 'l-bāṭili fa-yadmaghuhu, fa-idhā huwa zāhiqun wa lakumu 'l-waylu mimmā taṣifūn"*[64] (*al-Anbiyā'*, Q. 21:18) is a clear instance of his awareness of the importance of the context for the creation of an *isti'āra.* He says, commenting particularly on the phrase *"fa-yadmaghuhu"*:

> As God began by describing the hurling of the truth against falsehood, He went on to perfect the *isti'āra* and expand it in the most appropriate way, saying 'truth stamps falsehood on the brain' rather than 'truth makes falsehood vanish' because stamping is a characteristic of heavy objects and it expresses their force and overwhelming impact [on things against which they are hurled]. It is as if truth kills falsehood when it is hurled against its brain because to hit [any living being] on the brain is fatal. It is due to this that God then said, *"Fa-idhā huwa zāhiqun"*.[65]

His study of the verse *"fa-mā rabiḥat tijāratuhum"* (*al-Baqara*, Q. 2:16) is another fine example of this contextual view of *majāzī* and *isti'ārī* usage. Having explained how the *isti'āra* in the verse operates, he says that God has here called the actions of the unbelievers a trade because at the beginning of the verse He had said, *"ishtarawu 'ḍ-ḍalālata bi 'l-hudā,"* as the word of *shirā'* was used here, the words *"mā rabiḥat tijāratuhum"* were used later, aiming to harmonize the jewels of the system and organization, and to intertwine and coalesce the limbs of discourse.[66]

Of a similar nature are his comments on the verse *"wa man khaffat mawāzīnuhu fa-ulā'ika 'lladhīna khasirū anfusahum."* (*al-A'rāf*, Q. 7:9):

> Loss in reality is decrease in the price of goods sold, and that applies to money not to souls. But as He mentioned scales and their heaviness and lightness He then brought the mention of loss, in order that the *kalām* (discourse) be in agreement and that narration of the situation be harmonious and congruous. He thusby has placed their souls in the position of owned goods, as they are described as possessing their souls, as they are described to possess their moneys. Mentioning their loss of them is because they exposed their souls to loss and made it inevitable that they suffer the agony of hell. Their souls have thus become like possessions wasted and they have gone beyond the limit of losing in prices to the loss of themselves.[67]

Related to al-Raḍī's view of the impact of the context on *isti'āra* are his numerous remarks on the possibility of interpreting certain verses in two different ways, one of which will "remove the verse from the sphere of *isti'āra* to that of *ḥaqīqa*," as such differing interpretations will clearly depend on the context to acquire any validity or legitimacy.[68] His work in this area will be dealt with a little later.

Another striking feature of al-Raḍī's concern for the contextual dimensions of *majāzī* expressions is his occasional interpretations of a verse with reference to another occurring in an entirely different context and position in the Qur'ān. This cross-referencing enables him to look at a verse which appears to be a simple statement on a literal level in a totally different light. The verse "*wa thiyābaka fa-ṭahhir*" (*al-Mudddaththir*, Q. 74:4) appears to be a simple command telling the Prophet to keep his clothes clean; but to al-Raḍī it functions in much more complex ways: According to some interpretations, he says, this is an *isti'āra*, whereby clothes are a *kināya* for self or deeds or acts relating to the self. He then quotes three lines from major poets (Imru' al-Qays, al-Farazdaq and al-Ashja'ī) to support the view that clothes can refer to self. As such the verse will mean: purify yourself. However, he goes on to say that clothes can have another meaning: as God has called couples clothing in "*hunna libāsun lakum wa antum libāsun lahunna*" (*al-Baqara*, Q. 2:187) it is as though God has commanded the Prophet to choose pure women, those who have not been touched by the dirtiness of *kufr* because they are the givers of children and the agents of procreation.[69]

7.

A further, and most interesting, dimension of al-Raḍī's work which deserves close attention is his discussion of the linguistic structures in which a metaphorical process is embodied. His study of the verse "*bal hum minhā 'amūn*" (*al-Naml*, Q. 27:66) is a remarkable example of the subtlety of his work and recognition of the fine differences that minute linguistic details and syntactic relations create in literary expression. Having said that blindness here is not used to indicate the physical loss of sight but ignoring the truth and avoiding contemplation and thinking, either intentionally or out of ignorance, he goes on to say that ignorance was treated here like blindness because each of them prevents people from recognizing something as it really is, as ignorance is the opposite of knowledge, and blindness negates seeing. God has said "*bal hum minhā 'amūn*" rather than *'anhā* because the *murād*[70] is that they are skeptical and doubtful, that they dispute its validity and correctness, so they are *'amūna minhā*; it is not accurate here to say *'anhā*, because the *murād* is to say that they do not look at it and see it but that they are blind because they doubt it. This is one of the subtlest of meanings.[71]

Another useful example occurs in the verse "*idh qāla Mūsā li-ahlihi innī ānastu nāran* (*al-Naml*, Q. 27:7), in which *ānastu nāran* is described by al-Raḍī as 'an *isti'āra* by way of inversion (*'alā al-qalb*).' The *murād* is to say "I have found a fire which has granted me comfort and intimacy and removed my feeling of loneliness (*ānasatnī*). The action of *īnās* was reversibly applied to himself, thusby producing the shift to *ānastu nāran*, meaning: "*wajadtu al-nāra mu'nisatan lī*" (I found the fire to be a source of comfort and intimacy to me).[72]

Al-Raḍī's work abounds in manifestations of his subtle and discerning poetic alertness to the slightest shifts in language as evident, for instance, in his comments on the verse in *Sūrat Maryam* which says, "*fa-ajā'ahā 'l-makhāḍu ilā jidh'i 'n-nakhlati*" (Q. 19:23). This is an *isti'āra*, he says, the meaning being that labour pains brought her to, or forced her to seek refuge in, the trunk of the palm tree, in order to find support or rest her back. She is the one who sought refuge in the palm tree, but as the labour pains were the cause of that, it was good to attribute the verb (the action) to them in making her seek refuge.[73] Only a poet with a great deal of sensitivity to the minute details in which language reveals its power could have discerned the metaphorical element in this verse.

But it is in his study of the verse "*wa najjaynāhu mina 'l-qaryati 'llatī kānat ta'malu 'l-khabā'itha, innahum kānū qawma saw'in fāsiqīn*" (*al-Anbiyā'*, Q. 21:74) that he displays his skilful and penetrating sensitivity to the syntactic and linguistic structure of *isti'āra* and creative language in general at its most impressive and exciting. Here is his analysis of this verse, which reveals at the same time his sense of enchantment and thrill *vis-à-vis* the Qur'ānic text:

> The word *qarya* is here *musta'ār*, the *murād* by it is the group of the people of the village which was performing evil deeds. God has revealed that by saying, "*innahum kānū qawma saw'in fāsiqīn.*" In this discourse there is a wonderful *khabar*, because He made what follows the word *qarya* feminine, as the *qarya* is feminine, saying *allatī kānat ta'malu 'l-khabā'itha*, and made the rest of the discourse masculine, saying "*innahum kānū qawma saw'in fāsiqīn*", because the *murād* by this [last part] is masculine; as such the discourse in this verse has become of two divisions: one pertaining to *al-lafẓ* [the actual wording or surface structure, as Chomsky might call it], and the other pertaining to *al-ma'nā* [meaning or deep structure]. And this is one of the wonders (*'ajā'ib*) of the Qur'ān.[74]

Al-Raḍī's interest in the linguistic structure in which an *isti'ārī* process is embodied directs his attention to another type of *isti'āra*, that which results from a genitive-link (*iḍāfa*) construction where an object, abstract or concrete, is related as a genitive to another object, abstract or concrete, where no immediate similarity can be observed. For instance, in the verse:

"*wa mā 'l-ḥayātu 'd-dunyā illā matā'u 'l-ghurūr* (*Āl 'Imrān,* Q. 3:185)," which al-Raḍī calls an *isti'āra,* there is no direct point of similarity between two given objects. "This is an *isti'āra,*" he says, "because conceit cannot have possessions (*matā'*) in reality. The meaning conveyed is that all the pleasures of this life are only shadows which will vanish."[75] In this type of expression, recognizing similarity can be of varying degrees of immediacy. In the quoted example the similarity is less immediately recognized than in the following example: "*kullamā awqadū nāran li 'l-ḥarbi aṭfa'ahā 'llāhu*" (*al-Mā'ida,* Q. 5:64).[76]

"This is an *isti'āra,*" al-Raḍī says, "because war does not in reality possess a fire. War is here compared to fire in view of its force and horror when it flares up and its devouring of people as fire devours the wood thrown into it".[77]

8. Novelty of Interpretation

In much of al-Raḍī's work, his way of interpreting *isti'āra* is original and often striking. At times, his sensitive touches turn what appears to be a normal formulation of an idea into a metaphorical structure pulsing with freshness, novelty and aesthetic appeal. Although this is true of much of what he does, the following two examples are particularly revealing.

8.1.

In the verse, "*wa laqad khalaqnā 'l-insāna min sulālatin min ṭīn*" (*al-Mu'minūn,* Q. 23:12), he considers the use of *sulāla* to be an *isti'āra,* because *sulāla* in truth is to extricate (*yasullu*) something from another; it is as though when Adam was created out of the soil of the earth he was extricated (*insalla*) from it, and extracted out of its very essence and mysterious being. That has become an expression of the very essence and purity of an object and its extraction and heart. In reality nothing has been extricated (*insalla*) from something else. The sperm may be called *sulāla* in this sense, and a man's offspring can be called *sulāla* too.[78]

8.2.

In the verse "*wa laqad khalaqnā fawqakum sab'a ṭarā'iqa*" (*al-Mu'minūn,* Q. 23:17), there is an *isti'āra,* he says, because the *murād* by *ṭarā'iqa* are the seven heavens, similized here to *ṭarā'iq* of shoes, whose singular is *ṭarīqa,* which can also be in the plural *ṭariq.* They are the pieces of leather which are placed one on top of another and strung with beads. It is said *ṭaraqtu al-na'la,* on the basis of that.[79]

9. Revitalization of Dead Metaphors

His perceptive approach often reveals the metaphoric origins of expressions which usage and familiarity have turned into non-metaphorical expressions. Such is the case in his discovery of the *isti'āra* in the verse "*fa-quṭi'a dābiru 'l-qawmi*" (*al-An'ām*, Q. 6:45), as the origin as far as this word is concerned is *dābirat al-faras*, which is the part immediately behind its heel from the outside, the *dābira* of a bird is the bit which is behind its leg, the *murād* of this verse being that those who come after the people who have been unjust have been severed or that their children have been destroyed and none of their offspring left.[80]

Another fine example of this rekindling of a faded metaphor is his comment on the verse "*thumma ja'alnāka 'alā sharī'atin mina 'l-amri fa 'ttabi'hā*" (*al-Jāthiya*, Q. 45:18). "This is an *isti'āra*," he says, "because the *sharī'a* in *aṣl al-lugha* is a sign (*ism*) for the path which leads to the water being sought for drinking. Religions were called *sharā'i'* because they are the paths which lead to the drinking places of rewards and the useful points for *al-'ibād*, by way of comparison with the *sharā'i'* of springs which are the ways leading to water and the quenching of thirst."[81]

Another example of this search for the metaphoric dimension in what appears to be on the *ẓāhir* (the outward, apparent, surface plane) no more than a simple, literal usage, is his treatment of the verse: "*wa 'ḍ-ḍuḥā / wa 'l-layli idhā sajā*" (*al-Ḍuḥā*, Q. 93:1–2) which he describes as an *isti'āra. Sajā*, he says, means to settle down (*sakana*), and the night does not settle down, what settle down are the movements of people in it.[82]

But perhaps the most striking piece of work he does in this respect is the way in which he excavates the *isti'ārī* nature of the word *fatra* in the verse: "*qad jā'akum rasūlunā yubayyinu lakum 'alā fatratin mina 'r-rusul*" (*al-Mā'ida*, Q. 5:19) which I have already considered in a slightly different context.[83]

10. Concreteness and Vividness

Al-Raḍī's analysis often brings out the concrete and sensuous – visual and otherwise – aspects of metaphorical language and sharpens our awareness of the originality and inventiveness of the imagination responsible for the construction of the metaphorical process; without such evocation of these concrete aspects, the metaphor is likely to be missed altogether or imagined and responded to in a much less concrete and vivid fashion. Here is his working out of the *isti'āra* in the beautiful verse: "*wa huwa 'lladhi maraja 'l-baḥrayni hādhā 'adhbun furātun wa hādhā milḥun ujājun*" (*al-Furqān*, Q. 25:53):

"This is an *isti'āra*, the *murād* – and God is more knowledgeable – is that He lets them loose out of their places and released them into their courses, as horses *tamruj* i.e., are left loose with their pastures. The point of the miracle in this is that despite leaving them to criss-cross and co-operate in their benefits, the salty water mixes not with the fresh water, and saltiness mixes not with freshness."[84] As concrete in his reading and description is the verse "*wa huwa 'lladhi ja'ala lakumu 'l-layla libāsan, wa 'n-nawma subātan, wa ja'ala 'n-nahāra nushūran*" (*al-Furqān*, Q. 25:47). He points out that there are two *isti'āras* here, the first in *ja'ala 'l-layla libāsan*, the second in *ja'ala 'n-nahāra nushūran*; the *murād* of *al-libās* is the covering by the night of all places, high and low, and the bodies of animals (meaning creatures, human and non-human) as wide clothes and large protective covers cover things. This expression is one of the most eloquent ways of expressing this meaning. As for *nushūr* he says, *nushūr* in reality is giving life after death, it is here borrowed for the behaviour of the living being and his expansiveness, by way of comparing sleep to death and waking up to life; and this is one of the most effective and striking [acts of] *tashbīh* and one of the best [acts of] *tamthīl*.[85]

Even in what appears to be a simple, immediately recognizable *isti'āra*, al-Raḍī presents alternatives which do one important thing: they increase the degree of concreteness and the vividness and liveliness of our perception of the metaphorical process. Take for instance his comments on "*li-nuḥyiya bihi baldatan maytan*" (*al-Furqān*, Q. 25:49) which he has discussed apparently in a part of the book that has been lost and on which he offers some elaboration here; he says:

> describing the town as dead is done on one of two interpretations or bases: either it was compared to the dead because of its extreme barrenness and dryness as barrenness completely dominates it, and rain comes not to it, or that there are trees and grass in it which have died and as such it has become good to describe the town itself as dead because of the death of its children, as it is like a mother which cares for children and a deer which suckles its babies.[86]

Another excellent example is his study of the famous verse, "*wa 'shta'ala 'r-ra'su shayban*" (*Maryam*, Q. 19:4) which he describes as being "*min al-isti'āra al-'ajība*," an amazing *isti'āra*. The *murād*, he says, is to depict the spreading and proliferation of hoariness in the head to a point where its whiteness becomes vivid and its blackness withers. And there is here evidence of the speed of the spread and multiplication of hoariness and the continuation of its tide, so much so that it becomes like fire in the speed of its spreading which will cause somebody trying to extinguish it to fail to do so and somebody trying to avoid it to be incapable of avoiding it.[87]

One of the finest examples of his work is his discussion of the *isti'āra* in the verse "*wa law tarā idhi 'ẓ-ẓālimūna fī ghamarāti 'l-mawti*" (*al-An'ām*, Q. 6:93). Again he says that this is an *isti'āra 'ajība*, going on to reveal the impact of describing death in terms of mountains of water hurling a person about.[88] Of similar quality are his studies of verses 96, 95 and 94 of this sūra.[89] But perhaps the most striking example of this aspect of his analysis is the following:

> ... God narrates that the queen of Saba' has said: "*mā kuntu qāṭi'atan amran ḥattā tashhadūni*" (*al-Naml*, Q. 27:32) and this is an *isti'āra*; the *murād* by *al-qaṭ'* – and God knows best – is returning after the consideration of various views and the churning of different interpretations, to one view which it is proper to resolve to execute and act on its basis rather than any other, similizing this to the warp in the weaving of clothes then the *qaṭ'* (cutting) after finishing the weaving. It is as though she had thought much of different options when she received the invitation from Solomon to believe in him and follow him and she was skeptical and wavered between refusing and responding positively, between being rough or tender, until the desire to be gentle overwhemed her and she resolved to act in that fashion, thus it became good to express that by the *qaṭ'* of a matter.[90]

11. Multiplicity of Interpretations: Open and Closed Readings

On a different level, al-Raḍī reveals the open-endedness of language when he explore a number of ways of interpreting the same verse: one of which only is metaphorical, the other(s) is (are) not; most significantly, he considers both – or all – of them valid and correct, which was a major step towards breaking away from a tradition which had tended to confine discourse to having one meaning which can be either immediate or non-immediate, but reachable as a single, well-defined entity through the immediate meaning. Al-Raḍī, perhaps because he was first and foremost a poet who experienced the fluidity of language, opens up this new direction for critical studies which advocate a view of language as multiple, as a space of possibilities. Only Sufism and Shī'ism were to take this path in the interpretation of texts and to some extent in their production. The principle underlying al-Raḍī's views has been crucial not only for modern literary theories but also for modern literary production everywhere.

While discussing "*wa zurū'in wa nakhlin ṭal'uhā haḍīm*," (*al-Shu'arā'*, Q. 26:148) he considers three, not two, alternative meanings. First he calls this an *isti'āra*, suggesting that the *murād* by *haḍīm* according to some interpretations is that which has gathered together as some of its parts got intertwined with other parts, as such some parts would look as though they have swallowed others, because of its thickness and entwining. It was also said that *haḍīm* means *laṭīf*, which is more expressive as a description of the growth intended for eating. This is taken from their saying "*haḍīmu al-ḥashā*." It was also said *haḍīm* means ripened. It was also said that *haḍīm* is that which if touched would fall because it is so supple and watery. The last two meanings would place the expression outside the space of *isti'āra*.[91]

One of the best examples is the way he deals with *ighwā'* (temptation, seduction) in verses which attribute *ighwā'* to God. Ideological reasons prevent him from accepting the use of temptation as a quality of God, but beyond that he explores four different meanings of "*ghayy*" in order to enable himself to handle this expression in ways which, either through a *majāzī* interpretation or a literal one, denies that it is a literal description of God. All the meanings he explores appear to him possible.[92]

At times he goes beyond explaining how the *isti'āra* works to reveal what he refers to as *fā'ida ukhrā laṭīfa* (another subtle benefit and added connotation), as is the case in his study of "*wa qīla yā arḍu 'bla'ī mā'aki,*" (*Hūd*, Q. 11:44) which he views as being *ablagh* than saying "take your water away," as the act of swallowing indicates the speed of the disappearance of the water. And in the study of this verse he once more explores the metaphor as part of a wider structure and examines the relationship between it and other parts of its context. "All this," he says, "comes in addition to what lies in the act of pairing of the two verbs "*ibla'ī*" and "*yā samā'u aqli'ī*" an act that produces *balāgha 'ajība and faṣāḥa sharīfa.* There is much in the Qur'ān of this type of thing."[93]

Another fine example is his analysis of "*yukawwiru 'l-layla 'alā 'n-nahāri wa yukawwiru 'n-nahāra 'alā 'l-layl*" (*al-Zumar*, Q. 39:5). He considers four different possibilities here, supporting each case with references to poetry and prose. The four possibilities are widely different, but al-Raḍī accepts all of them as interpretations of the verse and the metaphorical process in it.[94] His entire approach here represents a break with a dominant tendency in much work in Arabic criticism and commentary on texts to seek a single, well-defined and final meaning of discourse.

It is illuminating to contrast al-Raḍī's open approach with views which often sought a literal, final and tightly defined meaning in verses of the Qur'ān; he himself quotes some examples of such approaches and denounces them, as he does in his study of the verse "*khuliqa 'l-insānu min 'ajalin*" *(al-Anbiyā'*, Q. 21:37) where he says there is an *isti'āra.* Having explained the basis for this *isti'ārī* usage, he goes on to say that some people of *tafsīr* said that *'ajalin* here is one of the names of mud (*ṭīn*) and quoted a line of poetry in support of their interpretation; this is to be ignored, and the line of poetry discarded as it is *muwallad* and corrupt.[95]

12. Complexity of Interpretation

If one epithet is to be used to describe al-Raḍī's analysis of *majāz* in the Qur'ān by comparison with all his predecessors, it will perhaps be 'complexity and sophistication.' This has already been demonstrated, I hope, in some of the examples quoted above, but might still need some further elaboration. One of the most complex examples of his analysis of *isti'āra* is his detailed study of the verse "*fa-adhāqahā 'llāhu libāsa 'l-jū'i wa 'l-khawfi*" (*al-Naḥl*, Q. 16:112). In this striking verse, the *isti'āra* goes beyond the standard ways of metaphorical usage in Arabic poetry of the time, as it involves mixing two senses: taste and sight. Al-Raḍī says that the tasting in reality is only applicable to food and drink, not to clothing and attiring. He first argues that the way the Qur'ān used *adhāqa libāsa* here is in harmony with the natural mode of expression in Arabic; the Arabs say to somebody who has been punished for a crime "taste the consequences of your action," although his punishment is not something that can be realized by taste. God said *libāsa 'l-jū'*, rather than *madhāqa 'l-jū'* because He wanted to show that their punishment was all inclusive and comprehensive as clothes cover the body comprehensively, and as the consequences of terrible hunger and painful fear that they suffer imprint onto them signs of awful states of being, of wretchedness and paleness and meagreness of bodies, appearing thus like a garment attiring them covering them."[96]

Another example will hopefully suffice to demonstrate the complexity of al-Raḍī's interpretations and his working out of metaphorical usage in the Qur'ān; I have deliberately chosen an example which appears on the surface to present no problem for interpretation. In the verse, "*alam tara ilā rabbika kayfa madda 'ẓ-ẓilla wa law shā'a la-ja'alahu sākinan, thumma ja'alnā 'sh-shamsa 'alayhi dalīlā*" (*al-Furqān*, Q. 25:45) al-Raḍī points out two *isti'āras*, one is "*alam tara ilā rabbika*," which means "*alam tara ilā fi'li rabbika*" or "*ilā ḥikmati rabbika*" (the action or wisdom of your Lord) in extending the shade, so He deleted this word as the discourse indicates its presence, as God cannot be perceived by feelings or seen by sight. It is also possible here that *ru'ya* means *'ilm* (knowledge). It is as though God has said "Haven't you come to know the wisdom of your Lord in extending the shadow? substituting *ru'ya* for *'ilm* because the addressee, who is the Prophet himself knows God's aim of extending the shadow and thus the knowledge he has in his heart is as good as that he would have through his sight as far as total certainty and complete absence of doubt are concerned. The other *isti'āra* is in His saying, "*thumma ja'alnā 'sh-shamsa 'alayhi dalīlan*"; it is, according to al-Raḍī, an *isti'āra* by way of inversion (*al-qalb*), because in reality it is the shade which acts as a cue or evidence to the presence of the sun, as shade cannot exist except when there is a shining sun, in which case what the sun does not shine over because of some barrier to its shining over it, is described as shade. It has been said that shadow (*ẓill*) is what is formed in the morning and shade (*fay'*) is what forms in the evening. It has also been said that *ẓill* is what the sun nullifies and *fay'* is what nullifies the sun, according to which view the meaning of His saying' "*wa law shā'a la-ja'alahu sākinan*" is that he would have made it permanent whereby the sun does not shine unto it and nullify it or remove it, then we made the sun a guide (*dalīlan*) to it, meaning we guided the sun to it, so it erases parts of it, eats out its endings until it covers the whole of it and replaces it completely. This is the meaning of "*thumma qabaḍnāhu ilaynā qabḍan yasīra*" (*al-Furqān*, Q. 25:46).[97]

13. *Isti'āra* Between Normality and Deviation

One salient feature of al-Raḍī's work on the metaphors of the Qur'ān is his constant reference to the way the Arabs use their language in normal speech; by so doing, he anchors the Qur'ānic expressions in real life situations of language use and brings the effectiveness of the metaphor into focus; his references at times go far beyond to explore the cultural background in which a certain use of language is rooted, as he does in the study of "*wa najjaynāhum min 'adhābin ghalīẓ*" (*Hūd*, Q. 11:58).[98]

Al-Raḍī appears to have gone further than anybody else in anchoring the Qur'ānic language and especially metaphorical language in everyday speech and the ancient traditions of the Arabs; it is as though he was echoing and further elaborating Ibn al-Mu'tazz's argument that the first element of *al-badī'*, namely *isti'āra,* existed in the Qur'ān and Arabic poetry and prose. Al-Raḍī at times seeks out one interpretation as better than another on the grounds that the first is *ablaghu fī al-faṣāḥa wa a'raqu fī uṣūl al-'Arabiyya,*[99] commenting on the omission of the preposition in *la-aq'udanna lahum ṣirāṭaka,* (*al-A'rāf,* Q. 7:16) and saying that it is more eloquent. But in a certain way, by carrying this principle to an extreme degree, al-Raḍī appears sometimes to be stripping some Qur'ānic metaphors of there striking and adventurous qualities as he refers them back to normal speech. In modern poetics, we have come to believe a metaphor represents a process of deviation from normal modes of language, but al-Raḍī shows beyond doubt that *isti'āra* is not deviation, it is very much part and parcel of ordinary language and it partakes of the common modes of expression; its power is not thus measurable by its unfamiliarity but by the complexity and effectiveness and degree of intensification and harmony with the system, as he calls it, in the texts in which it is used.

One expression he describes as being "*min ghawāmiḍ asrār al-Qur'ān,*"[100] as he reveals its *isti'ārī* nature. In the verse "*a-ṣalawātuka ta'muruka an natruka mā ya'budu ābā'unā*" (*Hūd*, Q. 11:87), al-Raḍī argues that it is inaccurate in terms of the *ẓāhir* of this discourse that Shu'ayb should be ordered that his folk should give up something they practice; the meaning, he says, is: Does your prayer command you to command us to give up what our fathers worship? The Qur'ān used only the first command and did not mention the second because the context clarifies it and makes it easy to anticipate.

14. Metaphysical, Ideological and Cultural Dimensions of *Majāz* and *Isti'āra*

Al-Raḍī's work demonstrates most eloquently and coherently that *isti'āra* is a much more complex and intriguing process than was generally assumed and is still often assumed in literary discourse; the Aristotelian definition of metaphor in terms of transference, or the use of a word to denote a meaning for which it was not set in the language convention, is totally inadequate for the understanding of *isti'āra*; for the process of *isti'āra* is not a product of playing around with a fixed convention of language; it is in the main a function of ideological, cultural and psychological precepts and beliefs. As I said earlier, the very conception of a *majāzī* way of expression in Arabic originated in conflicts about religious and metaphysical questions, especially the nature of God and free will and predestination. The ideological basis for arguing that a phrase like: "The tree blossomed" is *majāzī* is pretty obvious. By al-Raḍī's time, these issues had acquired great potency and caused acute schisms within the community. Al-Raḍī, more than anybody else before al-Jurjānī, pushed these points to their most extreme position in a systematic, unflinching manner in that he went through the Qur'ān verse by verse revealing in each relevant case how one interpretation will border on blasphemy, another will be valid and proper, as the first involves assigning to God attributes (*ṣifāt*) which should not be attributed to Him, while the second does not do so. The measure of whether one interpretation is of this or that nature has very little to do with any 'objective' characteristics of the Qur'ānic text itself; it has everything to do with the ideological point of view of the interpreter. Texts have no objective reality of their own, and conflicts are hardly ever conflicts between texts; they are conflicts between interpretations and interpreters; in other words, they are worldly conflicts even when they appear to revolve around metaphysical notions and beliefs. Al-Raḍī's work abounds in sophisticated instances of analysis which demonstrate the validity of this point, if not always explicitly, then at least by implication. For the sake of brevity, I shall quote only three such examples here:

14.1.

In the verse "*alam tara ilā rabbika kayfa madda 'ẓ-ẓilla wa law shā'a la-ja'alahu sākinan*" (*al-Furqān*, Q. 25:45), the expression "*alam tara ilā rabbika*" is an *isti'āra*, meaning "don't you see the action of your Lord or the wisdom of your Lord," as God "cannot be perceived by the senses (*mashā'ir*), or seen by the eyes; seeing here can also mean knowing."[101]

14.2.

Of a similar nature is his reading of the verse "*wa qadimnā ilā mā 'amilū min 'amalin fa-ja'alnāhu habā'an manthūrā*" (*al-Furqan*, Q. 25:23) as an *isti'āra*, because the attribute of coming can only be correctly applied to someone who can also be correctly described as being absent or away, so he can be said to return. God is always there, never absent, eternally present (*qā'im*) never transient.[102]

14.3.

"God mocks them" in the verse "*allāhu yastahzi'u bihim*" (*al-Baqara*, Q. 2:15), is also an *isti'āra* because God cannot be in truth and literally described as mocking, because mocking is contrary to the qualities of one who has forbearance (*ḥalīm*), and is in opposition to the ways of the wise.[103]

All of the verses which involve anthropomorphic conceptions of God are treated in the same way, e.g. "*ani 'ṣna'i 'l-fulka bi-a'yuninā wa waḥyinā*" (*al-Mu'minūn*, Q. 23:27) spoken by God.[104] The same conceptual process is applied to other metaphysical notions connected with the divine world. In the verse "*aṣḥābu 'l-jannati yawma'idhin khayrun mustaqarran wa aḥsanu maqīlā*" (*al-Furqān*, Q. 25:24), we may fail to recognize a metaphorical usage, but not al-Raḍī. He argues that there is an *isti'āra* here, because *al-maqīl* is an attribute of places where people sleep, and in the *Janna* (Paradise) there is no sleep. This is like describing *Janna* in another verse as "*lahum rizquhum fīhā bukratan wa 'ashiyyā*," (*Maryam*, Q. 19:62) i. e., like the times of morning and the times of evening known to people in this world. For *Janna* cannot be described in temporal terms involving days and nights, as these are attributes of time which is recurred upon by the sun as it rises and sets, so it is called daylight with its rising and night with its resting.[105]

What applies to *Janna* applies to *Jahannam* (Hell); the verse "*idh ra'athum min makānin ba'īd*," (*al-Furqān*, Q. 25:12) referring to Hell is said to be an *isti'āra* and described as "*min laṭā'if al-ta'wīl wa gharā'ib al-tafsīr*," as seeing cannot be attributed to *Jahannam*, the *murād* is when it became close to them in distance at a point where, if somebody who could see was standing, he would see them.[106]

15. Cultural Roots of Responses: Mythological Structures

Some of the interpretations al-Raḍī offers demonstrate how deeply rooted responses to artistic expression are in mythological conceptions of the world. The verse "*innā lammā ṭaghā 'l-mā'u ḥamalnākum fī 'l-jāriyati*" (*al-Ḥāqqa*, Q. 69:11) he describes as an *isti'āra* by which is intended the comparison of water as its waves build up and rise high with a tyrannical man who has risen high and exercised great power. Then al-Raḍī goes on to say: some have suggested that *ṭaghā al-mā'u* means that it became too plentiful for its keepers, who became unable to control its flow, because water has keepers and the winds have keepers of the blessed angels, they release as much of them as God finds beneficial for his worshippers and the earth, as the traditions have informed.[107]

This purity of belief, indeed this purging of the Qur'ān of all anthropomorphic beliefs and conceptions, no matter how minute, produces on some occasions brilliant interpretations which challenge our conception of the world in which we live and present entirely different perceptions of our human and divine 'realities'. One such case is al-Raḍī's intellectually daring suggestion that there is an *isti'āra* in the verse "*ilayhi yaṣ'adu 'l-kalimu 'ṭ-ṭayyibu wa 'l-'amalu 'ṣ-ṣāliḥu yarfa'uhu*" (*Fāṭir*, Q. 35:10). His argument is this, "the *murād* is not in reality that there is something which can be described as rising or going up from a lower place to a higher place; the *murād* is that good words and deeds are accepted and liked by God, and that they will reach Him, meaning they will reach his pleasure and approval and that He will not ignore them or fail to reward them. ... Another way this can be interpreted is to say that as God was described in terms of height by way of greatness and not distance and space, everything that seeks to come close to Him in words or deeds will be talked about in terms of height and rising, by way of *majāz* and *ittisā'* (expansion, extension)."[108]

This shatters a deeply enshrined human conception of the divine world as being '*up there*' and plays havoc with so much in human language that addresses Divinity in terms of height and space and distance in an upward direction. "*Naḥnu narfa'u ilayka ṣalawātinā wa qarābīnanā yā Rabb*" has been heard and practiced by human communities for countless centuries. For al-Raḍī to treat all this as metaphorical is, to say the least, dizzying, as it wrecks an age-old, and coherently designed world view and a deeply rooted human conception of the divine world and of man's position in relation to it: where is God then if he is not *up there*, and where are heaven and hell if they are not up there and down there? Where do our prayers, our souls, and longings go if not *upwards*? To a direction-less void? How traumatizing!

In each of the cases discussed above, and in tens like them, there is no point in talking about an original meaning which the words have in the language convention; the word is not a fixed sign, with an objective existence *out there*, autonomous and immobile and eternal; a word is a mercurial entity, in a state of flux, heavily immersed in subjective, personal and communal views of the world, in beliefs, feelings and mythologies, in fears and hopes which man experiences in his confrontation with his terrifyingly complex world. Al-Raḍī feels passionately that utterances like the ones quoted above should be treated as metaphors not because their meaning in the language convention was originally fixed as a, b and c, and they are now being used of other objects, which they were not meant to denote, but because not to interpret them as metaphorical will generate dangerous beliefs and lead to *ḍalāla*, as al-Jurjānī was to say categorically a few decades later.

And far beyond that: al-Raḍī's analysis demonstrates that metaphor is not only a function of ideological principles, but of a whole view of the world, of man and nature, of man's position in relation to God and the nature of human feelings and affections. Few of us today will consider a sentence like "I love this landscape" as metaphorical; much less "I love my cat" in a culture where cats and dogs are treated almost like idols or totems. To al-Raḍī, however, love as a human emotion can only be bestowed upon *an other* as an expression of certain attitudes; when these are not compatible with that which is said to be loved, the expression is metaphorical. The Prophet says in a *ḥadīth* of his: "*hādhā 'l-jabalu nuḥibbuhu wa yuḥibbunā*";[109] al-Raḍī comments that it is clear that "*yuḥibbunā*" is metaphorical but it is equally true that "*nuḥibbuhu*" is metaphorical, for man's love for *an other* is an expression of the desire to benefit that other or to glorify him in the fashion appropriate to him as we explained in many places in our two famous books on the *'ulūm* of the Qur'ān, and both aspects are not valid with reference to the inanimate – neither the glorification that is appropriate to it nor the benefit bestowed on it ... what is *murād* is that the people of the mountain love us and we love them.[110]

Such treatment of love is applied to God himself; consequently, in the verse "*fa- sawfa ya'tī 'llāhu bi-qawmin yuḥibbuhum wa yuḥibbūnahu*" (*al-Mā'ida*, Q. 5:54); al-Raḍī suggests that there is an *isti'āra*. Love which is the inclination of temperaments cannot be ascribed to God.[111]

One last example which demonstrates that *isti'āra* is deeply rooted not only in ideological systems but in anthropological realities made up of mythology, legend, cultural history and systems of belief as well as psychological structures, is his treatment of the verse "*ḥattā yatawaffāhunna 'l-mawtu*" (*al-Nisā',* Q. 4:15), where he says there is an *isti'āra* "because the agent who performs the act indicated by *yatwaffā* is the angel of death, not death itself; the verse transferred the verb to death by way of *majāz* and *ittisā'* (extension and expansion), because the reality of [the action of] that who *yatawaffā* is the clinching of the soul from the body."[112]

16. Ideological Roots of *Isti'āra*

Conflicts over the nature of God have thus been the source of much of what al-Raḍī does in his identification of *isti'āra* and *majāz* in the language of the Qur'ān; but this is not the only governing principle of his analysis. The ideological roots of conceiving of *isti'āra* are further revealed in his comments on verses relating to the Prophet Muḥammad, rather than to God Himself. The Qur'ān says addressing Muḥammad: "*a-lam nashraḥ laka ṣadrak, wa waḍa'nā 'anka wizrak, alladhī anqaḍa ẓahrak*" (*al-Inshirāḥ*, Q. 94:1–3), which appears to be a direct statement of the attitude of God to His Prophet but, according to al-Raḍī, is not as direct as we tend to think. This is a *majāz* and *isti'āra*, he says, because it cannot be the case that the Prophet's sins were so great that they would cause the snapping or crackling of his back (*inqāḍ*), as *inqāḍ* is the sound of the bones snapping under a heavy load. Such a statement can only be made by way of *kināya* denoting great sins and ugly deeds, and all this cannot be attributed to prophets neither according to those who believe that prophets do not commit either *ṣaghā'ir* or *kabā'ir* nor according to those who believe that prophets may commit *ṣaghā'ir* but not *kabā'ir*, because God has purified all his prophets of all bad sins and deadly actions as they are the keepers of His revelation, and the tongues of His commands and prohibitions, and His ambassadors to His creatures. What is intended here by "*waḍ' al-wizr*" has nothing to do with sin, but with the difficulties the Prophet faced and the dangers he encountered and the harm caused him by his folks in the course of spreading his message. All of which caused him pain in his chest and heaviness on his back, so God pointed out that He had relieved the Prophet of all these fears and burdens and granted him security and restfulness after long worries and dangers.[113]

From a different angle, it is interesting to note that verses which do not involve God or His divine world but the Qur'ān are also treated in the same fashion. The verse "*wa ladaynā kitābun yanṭiqu bi 'l-ḥaqqi*" (*al-Mu'minūn*, Q. 23:62) receives a lot of attention; first al-Raḍī calls it an *isti'āra*, on the basis that utterance (*nuṭq*) can only be attributed to those who speak with a tool/ means/ instrument of speech; then he quotes in support of his argument al-Qāḍī Abū al-Ḥasan saying in answer to somebody who asked him whether it is permissible to describe the Ancient (God) as *nāṭiq* as He is said to speak (*yatakallam*), and giving the explanation al-Raḍī has already given. God has thus described the Qur'ān as *nāṭiq* by comparison with the tongue as far as its revelation of what is contained within it and expression of what is hidden inside it are concerned.[114]

In summary, it is possible to say that al-Raḍī's exploration of the Qur'ānic text demonstrates that metaphysical, mythological, ideological and cultural conceptions are at least as powerful as language conventions in determining whether a certain expression is metaphorical or not. And much depends on the recipient's response to language, a response that is deeply rooted in individual as well as communal 'realities', perceived to have 'objective' existence, or constructed purely imaginatively.

17. *Isti'āra* and the Resolution of Problematic Issues

Resorting to a metaphorical interpretation of the text is often a means of resolving questions which appear, to say the least, problematic. This, as I have suggested more than once, was at the very heart of the emergence and crystallization of a metaphorical conception of language in Arabic. But al-Raḍī's study on a number of occasions goes beyond the general problems of anthropomorphism and free will and predestination to tackle issues which would cause serious doubts and create problems for the very notion of a divine order and purposefully constructed universe if read in a non-metaphorical way. One such real problem emerges in the verses in the Qur'ān which refer to the believers inheriting *al-Janna* (Paradise). Of these there are many; for instance, "*wa nūdū an tilkumu 'l-jannatu ūrithtumūhā bi-mā kuntum ta'malūn*" (*al-A'rāf*, Q. 7:43). Al-Raḍī devotes a couple of pages to this verse, quoting other verses which refer to God giving land as inheritance to some people in preference to others. The idea of inheritance implies the presence of more than one time and the succession of A by B but that, al-Raḍī says, cannot be correct with reference to *al-Janna*, because *al-Janna* cannot be inhabited by one people after another or one generation after another once the latter has departed from it. As such His saying "*ūrithtumūhā*" is an *isti'āra*, the meaning which justifies constructing this *isti'āra* is that as these people did good in their worldly life and deserved reward for their deeds and this could not be given them except in *al-Janna*, which belongs in the other world, and so it is as though they deserved now to enter it. As such from this perspective it has become good to say that they have inherited it although their lodging in it does not come after another people who had lived in it and departed from it. Another justification also is the difference between the states of the two worlds and the transposition of the believers from the one to the other as though what they did in the first world were the reason for what they attained in the last, as inheritance is deserved by causality (*bi al-sabab*).[115]

In a similar fashion, an *isti'ārī* interpretation can resolve contradictions which would otherwise create cracks in the logic of the divine universe. In the Sūra of *Ḥā Mīm* (*Fuṣṣilat*, Q. 41:11), a verse depicts God at the very outset of the act of creation performing further acts. It says, "*thumma 'stawā ilā 's-samā'i wa hiya dukhānun*" (Q. 41:11) at a point prior to the existence of anything else specifically sky and earth; the verse then goes on to say "*fa-qāla lahā wa li 'l-arḍi 'tiyā ṭaw'an aw karhan, qālatā ataynā ṭā'i'īn.*" Quite clearly, this is an impossible situation: God addresses the sky and the earth and commands them to come, when they do not yet exist: they have not been created. Al-Raḍī is fully aware of the problem and he acknowledges that, without his *isti'ārī* interpretation, this verse depicts a command being made to a non-existent and an address to nothingness, which is an impossible act to expect from the Wise One – God. Al-Raḍī, therefore resolves this issue by arguing that the verse is an *isti'āra*, embodying the lightning speed of the formation of the sky and the earth, as is indicated in the verse "*innamā qawlunā li-shay'in idhā aradnāhu an naqūla lahu kun fa-yakūn*" (*al-Naḥl*, Q. 16:40).[116]

Another example is his treatment of the verse "*allāhu yatawaffā 'l-anfusa ḥīna mawtihā wa 'llatī lam tamut fī manāmihā*" (*al-Zumar*, Q. 39:42) which appears to state that God grasps the souls at death as well as the souls of those who are asleep. Al-Raḍī argues that there is a hidden *isti'āra* here, namely that God stops the sleeping souls from performing discriminating and wilful acts involving intention and will and organization of getting up and sitting down. As we know people can still perform certain actions in their sleep, proving that God has not taken their souls away as they fell asleep.

And a third and excellent example is his discussion of the verse "*yakhruju min buṭūnihā sharābun mukhtalifun alwānuhu*" (*al-Naḥl*, Q. 16:69). Scientifically, al-Raḍī recognizes, honey does not come out of the bellies of bees; which might appear troublesome for the explicit Qur'ānic statement that honey comes out of the bellies of bees. Al-Raḍī resolves this by arguing that the verse means that honey comes out from the direction of the bellies of bees; the direction of their bellies is their mouth; they are known to collect honey and carry it with their mouths to their beehives. This way of expression he admires greatly and calls "*wa hādhā min ghawāmiḍi hādhā al-bayān wa sharā'ifi hādhā al-kalām.*"[117]

Furthermore, one major problem, with both metaphysical and worldly implications, relates to the nature of Christ and his relationship to God. Quite clearly, there are always serious consequences for holding one view rather than another over these issues, not only for the question of faith and religious doctrine but also for actual relationships between human beings and groups within society. Much depends on how the word *rūḥ* (soul, spirit) is interpreted. And al-Raḍī appears fully aware of the seriousness of the issue. Some commentators have treated *rūḥ* as simply indicating a close relationship between God and Christ basing their argument on the everyday usage of the word *rūḥ* in such phrases as "you are my soul" meaning you are close to me. Al-Raḍī sees another dimension of the problem: does God have a *rūḥ* in the first place to blow it into Maryam's vagina? What is it that He actually blew into that sacred place? How did He blow it? Does He have a mouth? etc., etc. And in order to resolve the problems, al-Raḍī argues ingeniously that the verse "*wa 'llatī aḥṣanat farjahā, fa-nafakhnā fīhā min rūḥinā*" (*al-Anbiyā'*, Q. 21:91) is an *isti'āra*; the *murād* here by *rūḥ* is: running / releasing (*ijrā'*) the *rūḥ* of Christ *'alayhi 's-salām* in *Maryam 'alayhā 's-salām*, as air runs by blowing, because this has happened to Maryam without contact with a male, or movement from one *ṭabaq* to another *ṭabaq*; God has attributed the *rūḥ* to Himself, in order to specify the glorification, and the selection and assignment of honouring, as His creation of Christ was without the mediation of a *munākaḥa* (sexual intercourse) or being proceeded with a *mulāmasa*, touching.[118] Quite interestingly, al-Raḍī had explained *rūḥ* in another verse, "*innamā 'l-masīḥu 'Īsā 'bnu Maryama rasūlu 'llāhi wa kalimatuhu alqāhā ilā Maryama wa rūḥun minhu*" (*al-Nisā'*, Q. 4:171) as meaning "that people benefit from His guidance and comeback to life out of the death of *ḍalāla* by His guidance, as bodies live by their souls (*arwāḥ*) and act with the help of their movements."[119]

As problematic for Islam is the death of Christ. Al-Raḍī faces the problem once more with an ingenious *isti'ārī* interpretation that impresses with its cleverness and novelty. In "*wa mā qatalūhu wa mā ṣalabūhu wa lākin shubbiha lahum*" (*al-Nisā'*, Q. 4:157), he resolves the problem simply by stating that "*shubbiha lahum* is an *isti'āra*, the *tashbīh* here not being an act performed by an external agent upon them, but an act that they performed themselves, i.e., they *shabbahū 'alā anfusihim*, as it is said "*ayna yudhhabu bika*, meaning *ayna tadhhabu*."[120]

In the verse "*mā lahum bihi min 'ilmin illā 'ttibā'a 'ẓ-ẓanni, wa mā qatalūhu yaqīnā*," (*al-Nisā'*, Q. 4:157) he resolves the problem, by saying that *qatalūhu* refers not to Christ but to conjecture (*al-ẓann*), quoting a whole series of statements which show how "*qatala 'l-amra 'ilman*" can mean to think about something thoroughly.[121]

18. Cultural Roots of *Majāz* and *Isti'āra*

As is the case in all types of texts, *isti'āra* in the Qur'ān derives from cultural as well as physical realities. This is recognized by many scholars including al-Raḍī (his comments on using trade (*tijāra*) to describe man's relationship with God, which leads him to say that all religions and forms of worship are types of trade exchanges, are most interesting in this connection). Furthermore, it is common knowledge that the Qur'ān is not merely a Book about metaphysical beliefs and spiritual concerns but is deeply involved in worldly matters. Many of its verses raise issues of a legal and social nature and, depending on the way in which they are interpreted, social organization can take one form or another. By virtue of all this, al-Raḍī's work on *majāz* in the Qur'ān was bound to touch on such matters and some of the interpretations he offers give us insight into interesting aspects of the life of the community and its views on the world. Indeed, in many instances, his comments go far beyond the aesthetic dimensions of language to produce readings that illuminate the cultural basis for metaphorical interpretation and have serious consequences on the worldly level of human existence. Some of these readings are highly controversial.

None is more so than his reading of the verse, "*inna hādhā akhī lahu tis'un wa tis'ūna na'jatan wa lī na'jatun wāḥidatun*" (*Ṣād*, Q. 38:23). This falls within the space of *isti'āra*, al-Raḍī says, "because the *na'ja* here is a *kināya* for a woman; using a sheep as a *kināya* for a woman occurs in their [the Arabs] poetry, as al-A'shā says ... and as 'Antara says ... They may also call a deer a *na'ja*, and a deer is like a woman, so the word will be an *isti'āra* on this construction ... women are compared to *ni'āj* because *ni'āj* are tied up and kept for milking and procreation, and women are chosen and elected for pleasure and producing children."[122] Only in a culture where women are elected for pleasure and procreation can an *isti'āra* like this be constructed and interpreted in a meaningful fashion; in a modern world like ours, in which feminism has come to erect an image of the female as a challenging, strong creature empowered by The Pill, a *na'ja* would be much less likely to be interpreted as a metaphorical reference to a woman.

No less controversial is his reading of *taḥta* in the verse which refers to the wives of Noah and Lot as being "*taḥta 'abdayni min 'ibādinā ṣāliḥayni fa-khānatāhumā,*" (*al-Taḥrīm,* Q. 66:10) as an *isti'āra.* While some scholars argue that *taḥta* simply indicates a marriage relationship, al-Raḍī says that *taḥta* here has nothing to do with a real situation of spatial dimensions, of below and above, but that the position of the female is lower than that of the male, as the male supervises the female and is more powerful than she is, as evident in God's statement that "*ar-rijālu qawwāmūna 'alā 'n-nisā',*" (*al-Nisā',* Q. 4:34); in the same way, al-Raḍī explains, someone might say "so and so the soldier is under (*taḥta*) the hands of the prince" and another might say "I do not take my livelihood from under (*taḥta*) the hands of so and so."[123]

At times the readings he offers raise purely legal questions as is the case in the verse "*wa 's-sāriqu wa 's-sāriqatu fa-'qṭa'ū aydiyahumā*" (*al-Mā'ida,* Q. 5:38); the obvious meaning here is 'cut off their hands'; al-Raḍī, however, points out that this means cut off the right hand of the thief, male or female, and that this is a very common way of expression in Arabic.[124]

19. Al-Raḍī's Attitude and Response to the Metaphorical Language of the Qur'ān

Al-Raḍī's comments on some of the Qur'ān's most beautiful and dramatic *isti'āras* are sensitive, full of admiration and a sense of wonder. He says on many occasions "*wa hādhihi isti'āratun 'ajībatun.*"[125] The Qur'ān says: "*tūliju 'l-layla fi 'n-nahāri wa tūliju 'n-nahāra fī 'l-layli*" (*Āl 'Imrān,* Q. 3:27) and al-Raḍī says: "This is an *isti'āra;* it is a fantastic expression of [the idea of] inserting this into that and that into this. The meaning is that what God takes away from daylight he adds to night, and what he takes away from night he adds to daylight. The word *īlāj* here is *ablagh,* (more expressive, more intense) because it connotes the interjection of each of them into the other, with subtlety of mixing and intensity of coalescing (*laṭīf al-mumāzaja wa shadīd al-mulābasa*).[126]

We might have now lost our sensitivity to the word *'ajība,* but clearly to him it was just about the most powerful word he could use to describe the fascination and power of an *isti'āra.* Here is one such use, commenting on "*wa 'ṣ-ṣubḥi idhā tanaffas,*" (*al-Takwīr,* Q. 81:18) "this is one of the fantastic metaphors, breathing here is an expression of the emergence of the light of dawn out of the overall darkness of the night, as though it was breathing and sighing in relief of worry or departure from concern ... the meaning could also be 'as it [morning] breaks out'; this second interpretation takes the expression out of the scope of *isti'āra*."[127]

Phrases like "*wa hādhā min al-aghrāḍ al-sharīfa wa al-asrār al-laṭīfa*"[128] occur frequently in his work; they indicate a great degree of fascination by the power of the *isti'āra* in the Qur'ān, a fascination, however, that is not always accompanied by detailed analysis, as though the enchantment with the power of language does not easily lend itself to concrete description.

Occasionally, he extends his admiration and elaborates on the aesthetic value of a given metaphor, such as is the case in his comments on the verse "*wa 'lladhīna tabawwa'ū 'd-dāra wa 'l-īmāna min qablihim*" (*al-Ḥashr*, Q. 59:9); having explained that *tabawwa'ū 'd-dāra* means inhabiting a house and settling down well in it and that this could not be said of faith except metaphorically, he says: "*wa hādhā min ṣamīm 'l-balāgha wa lubāb al-faṣāḥa*," and goes on to say that the borrowed word here "has increased the *rawnaq* of the discourse. Can't you see how much difference there is between saying 'they settled into their house' and saying 'they settled into their faith?' And I always say that words are servants for meanings, because they contribute to the enhancement of their *ma'āriḍ* and bestow elegance on their *maṭāli'*".[129] On one occasion, as he describes the verse "*ṣibghatu 'llāhi*" (*al-Baqara*, Q. 2:138) he says: "this is pure *isti'āra*."[130]

Although he rarely extends his observations to such a point, he on one occasion goes on to theorize the very need to use metaphor. This comes in the course of his comments on the verse "*huwa 'l-awwalu wa 'l-ākhiru, wa 'ẓ-ẓāhiru wa 'l-bāṭinu, wa huwa bi-kulli shay'in 'alīm*" (*al-Ḥadīd*, Q. 57:3). He says that "this is an *isti'āra* onto Him, *subḥānahu*, as we say this of somebody else, because He does not use words which are *musta'ār* and *majāz* unto Himself but because these words reach a much further point of *balāgha* and more dazzling place of *faṣāḥa*, and one of us usually borrows the more difficult words and deviates from truth and literalism to *majāzāt* because ways of saying might get too tight for one and thus one turns away to ... the rest of the discourse. Some of it [thought, ideas?] might be too obstinate and refuse to yield itself to his mind, so he turns back to what yields itself (*ilā al-muṭāwa'a*.). The sum of the meaning of *al-ẓāhir* and *al-bāṭin* is that He knows what is manifest just as He knows what is hidden, what is secret and what has been revealed."[131]

Thus the sense of wonder, the belief that Qur'ānic language represents a world of *asrār* and *ghawāmiḍ* permeate al-Raḍī's encounter with the language of metaphor in the Qur'ān. Indeed, the creation of a sense of wonder appears to have been for him a key function of great discourse. In one instance at least, al-Raḍī considers one interpretation he is offering as advantageous by comparison with another possible interpretation on the basis of the recipient's response to the first and the sense of wonder that overcomes him as he receives it. This relates to the verse, "*wa yunazzilu mina 's-samā'i min jibālin fīhā min baradin*," (*al-Nūr*, Q. 24:43) where he considers at length whether the mountains are in the sky or on the earth and concludes by saying, "if we consider the pronoun to refer to the sky the ambiguity will be removed; in addition this will create a sense of wonder in us at the description of mountains in the sky by way of comparison, because mountains in reality only exist on earth."[132]

Yet, overall, al-Raḍī's language is measured and rather restrained in its depiction of the aesthetic power of the Qur'ān and its effect on the recipient. He does not use flowery or over-excited words to describe the material he is dealing with. His language is as clear, as precise and as dispassionate in its assessment as critical language can ever be. By comparison with al-Jurjānī a little later on, al-Raḍī is far less given to writing about the Qur'ān (and poetry) in a *poetic* style and with an overwhelming sense of enchantment by the magic of metaphorical language. Compared with the Sufis and other adherents to the *bāṭinī* view of texts, he is as sharply defined and clear as they are ambiguous and mysterious. It is perhaps his Mu'tazilite intellectual makeup that distinguishes him most, despite his upbringing within the *bāṭinī* traditions of interpretation.

His balanced, dispassionate attitude and response can be seen in such phrases as: "*wa hādhihi al-'ibāratu min afṣaḥ al-'ibārati 'an hādhā al-ma'nā,*" and "*wa dhālika min awqa'i al-tashbīhi wa aḥsani al-tamthīli*",[133] which he uses on many occasions. That he says "*min afṣaḥi*" and "*min awqa'i*" reveals a tendency to avoid hyperbolic, superlative expressions and over-excited reactions. After all, the Qur'ān in whole and part is believed by many to be the *most* eloquent, the *most* powerful and the *mu'jiz*; for a leading *imām* to describe some of its metaphors in relative terms, as *among the most* beautiful, is genuinely interesting and revealing.

Indeed, al-Raḍī's comments on one of the most striking *isti'āra*s in the Qur'ān are illuminating of his balanced approach. The verse "*wa ushribū fī qulūbihimu 'l-'ijla*" (*al-Baqara*, Q. 2:93) is said to be an *isti'āra*, "the *murād* is the intensification of their love for the calf; it is as though their hearts had drunk its love which has mixed with those hearts and fused with them, the way something drunk and pleasurable and enjoyable mixes and fuses with the heart. He deleted the word 'love' because the discourse suggests it, as the hearts cannot be correctly described as drinking the calf in reality and in truth."[134] On the other hand, it is of genuine interest that he, at least on one occasion, uses a formula, which he often uses to express his admiration of the Qur'ānic language, to describe a line of poetry he admires, adding the epithet *badā'i'* to it, which radiates an even greater degree of admiration.[135]

The overall effect of al-Raḍī's work is to reveal the Qur'ān as a highly metaphorical text and a universe permeated with some bewildering, magical metaphors, although some of its sūras are entirely free of *isti'āra*. But the critical text itself appears to keep this magic under the control of a contemplative mind rather than intensify its magic. The clarity and lucidity of the critical text contrasts sharply with the ambiguity, multiple possibilities and problematic structures that the studied text creates. A fine balance is thus achieved between religious, poetic and highly emotional language and worldly, critical and tightly controlled discourse.

20. Concepts and Terminology

I shall now briefly consider al-Raḍī's concept of *majāz* and *isti'āra* and his contribution to the development of these aspects of literary language. And here I shall take into account his work in *al-Majāzāt al-Nabawiyya* in addition to his study of the *majāz* of the Qur'ān.

The concentration on intensification as being the function of figures of speech and on similarity as being the main basis for *majāz* and *isti'āra* is very likely to have been responsible for one of the most important features of al-Raḍī's work, namely, his identification of all figures which are apparently based on non-literal usage of words. Thus *majāz, isti'āra, kināya,* and *tamthīl* are identified with one another. For al-Raḍī, the only distinction which seems to matter is the distinction between the literal and non-literal usage of words. As such there is the category of *ḥayyiz al-ḥaqīqa*[136] and the category of *ḥayyiz* (or *ḥadd*) *al-majāz,*[137] including *majāzī, isti'ārī, kinā'ī* and *tamthīlī* senses. The following points will illustrate this suggestion:

a) *Mubalāgha* is said to be the purpose of all the figures of speech in the following examples, taken from the Qur'ān, the *ḥadīth* and popular speech:
   i) "[The verse], "*wa idh hum najwā*" (*al-Isrā',* Q. 17:47)[138] is an *isti'āra. Al-najwā* is similar to *al-taqwā*; the *maṣdar* is used to describe them [the evil-doers] in view of its capacity to intensify and heighten [their qualities and] their state of conspiring (*tanājī*)"[139]
   ii) "[The tradition], "*al-ḥummā kīru jahannam*"[140] is a *majāz,* the purpose being to intensify the description of the high temperature at the height of the fever."[141]
   iii) "[The verse], "*kataba 'llāhu la-aghlibanna anā wa rusulī*" (*al-Mujādila,* Q. 58:21)[142] is an *isti'āra.* The purpose of the *kināya* here . . . is to intensify and heighten the [characteristics attributed to] Fate."[143]

In the three examples *mubalāgha* is attributed to *isti'āra, majāz* and *kināya,* respectively.

b) The similarity relation is viewed as being the relation involved in the figures *majāz, isti'āra* and *kināya* in numerous places in al-Raḍī's books. The following examples illustrate this point:
   i) "[The verse], "*alladhī ja'ala lakumu 'l-arḍa firāshan wa 's-samā'a binā'a,*" (*al-Baqara,* Q. 2:22)[144] is an *isti'āra,* for God has compared

the earth in its flatness to a bed and the sky in its height to a building."[145]

ii) "[The tradition], "*al-'ilmu khazā'inu wa miftāḥuhā al-su'ālu,*"[146] is a *majāz*, the *murād* being to similize knowledge in the hearts of the *'ulamā'* to cupboards which are locked and doors which do not open. All of these may be opened only by the questioning of the seekers of knowledge and the quest of searching minds."[147]

iii) "[The popular saying], "*fulānun min biṭānati fulānin*" is a *kināya* for [i.e., expressing] the closeness of one person to another by way of similizing the first to the lining (*biṭāna*) of a dress which is the closest thing to the body."[148]

The fact that al-Raḍī believes these figures to share the two aspects under consideration suggests that he views them as representing the same phenomenon.[149] In fact, sometimes the same expression is described as being an *isti'āra*, *majāz* or *kināya*. This generally happens in different places, as with the traditions, "*bayna yaday mawtihi*" (between the hands of his death),[150] and "*bayna yaday al-sā'a*" (between the hands of the hour [of judgement]),[151] but it may also happen in the same passage commenting on an example, as is clear in his comment on the verse: "*wa 'indahum qāṣirātu 'ṭ-ṭarfi 'īn / ka-annahunna bayḍun maknūn,*" (*al-Ṣāffāt*, Q. 37:48–49).[152]

In addition to such examples, al-Raḍī uses *majāz* and *isti'āra* interchangeably or in conjunction with each other, even when the verse he is commenting on represents a type of *majāz* not based on similarity.

In the course of his analysis of some examples of the first type, he points out very clearly three relations of the non-*isti'ārī majāz* (which were to form the basic criterion for the distinction between *isti'āra* and *majāz* in later works) on the subject. Nevertheless al-Raḍī calls such examples *isti'āra.*[153]

Al-Raḍī's identification of the terms *majāz, isti'āra* and *kināya* is also evident in the plan he sets for his study and in his execution of this plan. In both of his books, he states unequivocally that his work is confined to *isti'āra,*[154] whereas both books include Qur'ānic verses and *ḥadīth* traditions which he calls *majāz* or *isti'āra*, and which he describes also in terms of *kināya*.

The factors responsible for al-Raḍī's identification of the figures mentioned above may be also responsible for his identification of another figure with *majāz* and *isti'āra*, namely the *tashbīh* (simile) of the type "Zayd is a lion". Throughout his books, al-Raḍī has called this type of simile *majāz* or *isti'āra* as he does, for instance, in his comments on the following examples:

i) "[The verse], "*innakum wa mā ta'budūna min dūni 'llāhi ḥaṣabu jahannam*" (*al-Anbiyā'*, Q. 21:98)[155] is a *majāz.*"[156]

ii) "The tradition, "*al-hummā kīru jahannam,*" is a *majāz*"[157]

iii) "The tradition, "*al-mu'minu mir'ātun li-akhīhi,*" is a *majāz* and *isti'āra.*"[158]

It is likely that al-Raḍī identifies this type of simile with *isti'āra* and *majāz* because it achieves a higher degree of intensification than the simile of the type, "Zayd is like a lion", on the one hand, and, on the other, because it expresses complete identity between the objects involved. As the difference between these two types of expression is generated by the use of "like" in the latter, al-Raḍī considers the particle the only criterion for differentiating between *tashbīh* on the one hand and *majāz* and *isti'āra* on the other. Thus he says that "the introduction of the particle *kāf* (as, like) into an expression removes it from the sphere of *majāz.*"[159]

The identification of *isti'āra* with *majāz, kināya* and *al-tashbīh al-balīgh,* is probably responsible for the lack of theoretical definitions and analysis of the nature of any of these figures. For what seems to have been al-Raḍī's underlying criterion for them is the distinction between the literal and extra-literal sense of a word or an expression. In the very rare places where he has produced any theoretical discussion of *isti'āra* or *majāz,* his comments revolve around the same idea, namely that these figures involve transferring a word, or an expression, to be used in another sense than its literal one.[160] It is significant that al-Raḍī applies the formula which describes this process to *isti'āra, majāz*[161] *tamthīl,*[162] *kināya*[163] and the *tashbīh* of the type "Zayd is a lion".[164] No further theoretical work on *isti'āra* is produced in either of his books.[165]

The fundamental role which similarity plays in al-Raḍī's concept of figurative language has already been pointed out. It must be emphasized that his best contribution to the study of the images of the Qur'ān, and to poetic imagery generally, arises from this aspect of his work. For, in his analysis of the points of similarity in a number of the figures he considers we encounter some of the most profound remarks on *isti'āra* made by anybody before al-Jurjānī arrives on the critical scene later in the fifth/eleventh century. In this respect, the various types of relations between the two extremes of *isti'āra* which al-Raḍī has pointed out are interesting. Although he has not produced any classification of *isti'āra* based on the nature of its two extremes or constituents (*arkān*), his practical analysis can be taken as an adequate basis for such a classification. The relations which he is clearly aware of can be organized in the following categories:

i) Abstract-Concrete.[166]
ii) Personification of an abstract or concrete object.[167] (In this category falls the inanimate-animate relationship.)
iii) Genus-Species.[168]
iv) Animate-Inanimate.[169]
v) Analogy, where the constituents are either abstract or concrete.[170]
vi) The synaesthetic *isti'āra* (based on the interfusion of senses).[171]

Nevertheless, it remains true that al-Raḍī's major contribution to the study of *isti'āra* lies in his analysis of the points of similarity in the figures he discusses.[172] His gift for revealing the hidden similarities in figures which were generally believed to be instances of the literal usage of language, his revitalization of a number of what seem to be dead *isti'ārāt*, and finally, the sensitive and refined poetic sensibility evident throughout his work, make him closer in spirit to the critical approach of al-Jurjānī than any other figure in Arabic criticism. Where al-Raḍī appears to stand almost alone, however, is in the identification of all the figures involving a non-literal way of expression and *al-tashbīh al-balīgh*. For these categories had been, ever since al-Jāḥiẓ and Ibn al-Mu'tazz and throughout the critical production in the third and fourth centuries A.H., almost always separated and analyzed with a fine degree of discrimination and awareness of the differences between them. Al-Raḍī's work from this point of view appears to fall outside the main stream of Arabic studies of *majāz* and *isti'āra* and other aspects of figurative language. It was probably due to the fact that he approached these issues first and foremost as a creative poet who was not brought up in the traditions of rhetorical studies but within the literary circles and close to the environment of the linguists. As such, his work represents a return to the very embryonic notions about *majāz, isti'āra, kināya, tashbīh* and other phenomena of creative language, which had burgeoned probably in the second century of the Hijra. Despite the superficial similarity between his conception of *majāz, isti'āra,* and *tashbīh* and the Aristotelian definitions – which had been current in his background – I tend to think that the determining force behind his work was his being first and foremost a poet, rather than any adherence to Aristotelian thought. Evidence from the work of modern poets today may help to support this hypothesis; the best and most theoretically aware of them at times treat symbol, metaphor, simile, and other figures interchangeably and discuss them sometimes in opposition to the term image and at other times as incorporated into this generic term.

IV. EPILOGUE

In his keenness to anchor the Qur'ān in the linguistic and imaginative traditions of the Arabs, a keenness he inherited from scores of scholars before him, going back especially to Abū 'Ubayda, al-Raḍī, like other scholars, has deprived the Qur'ānic text of some of its most poignant qualities: its inventiveness, creativity and sense of unbound freedom, its breaking away from the traditions of the Arabs *imaginatively and linguistically* as it broke away from their traditions *morally and metaphysically*. By insisting that the Qur'ān used Arabic just as the Arabs had done, al-Raḍī and others were subconsciously seeking legitimacy in the past and the established order of things; it is as though even the Word of God derives its legitimacy only or mainly from its conformity to the words of man. By so doing, they were setting the first *fundamentalist* rules in the culture; they failed to see and appreciate the novelty and adventurous nature of much metaphorical language in the Qur'ān. But this created a problematic for them: as on other levels, particularly in grammar, they found linguistic features which they could not easily anchor in the established traditions and they resolved the problem either by saying that these were dialects or *qirā'āt* or just exclusively Qur'ānic modes that should not be emulated, as is the case in "*in hādhāni la-sāḥirāni*," (*Ṭā Hā*, Q. 20:63) or they sought to show why it is more effective and eloquent to use the particular forms the Qur'ān has used, despite the fact that they do not fit into the normal grammar of the language, as is the case in "*fa-innahā lā ta'mā 'l-abṣāru*." (*al-Ḥajj*, Q. 22:46).

On the other hand, they emphasized that the Qur'ān is unique and *mu'jiz*, and that, as al-Raḍī himself attributes to some interpreters, "*lā yushbihuhu shay'un min al-kalāmi 'l-mutaqaddimi 'alayhi ... wa lā min al-kalāmi al-wāridi ba'dahu*"[173] because if any discourse before it was like it, this would nullify its *mu'jiza* and undo its *ḥujja*. The truth, however, is that some Qur'ānic metaphors are truly astonishing: they border on the surreal. A verse like "*wa ushribū fī qulūbihimu 'l-'ijla*" (Q. 2:93) is more adventurous than anything that even Abū Tammām was later to produce. And this is true of verses like "*wa āyatun lahumu 'l-laylu naslakhu minhu 'n-nahāra*" (Q. 36:37); "*yūliju 'l-layla fī 'n-nahāri* (Q. 57:6); *hunna libāsun lakum wa antum libāsun lahunna*" (Q. 2:187); "*nisā'ukum ḥarthun lakum*" (Q. 2:223); "*yukawwiru 'l-layla 'alā 'n-nahāri*" (Q. 39:5); "*wa 's-samāwātu maṭwiyyātun bi-yamīnihi*" (Q. 39:67); "*la-yuzliqūnaka bi-abṣārihim*" (Q. 68:51)); "*wa huwa 'lladhī maraja 'l-baḥrayni*" (Q. 25:53); "*fa-wajadā fīhā jidāran yurīdu an yanqaḍḍa*" (Q. 18:77); "*wa hiya khāwiyatun 'alā 'urūshihā*" (Q. 18:42), and countless others.

It is in the face of such wonderful metaphors, whereby a boundless imagination breaks away from all conventions and restrictions, cultural or linguistic, and roams freely in the world, connecting what cannot be connected and inventing linguistic and imaginative structures never before contemplated, that al-Raḍī's analysis shows its limitations. His keenness to interpret and offer clearly defined meanings renders his work less capable of exploring the imaginative richness and the boundless energy in the metaphors that are most fascinating in the Qur'ānic text. But perhaps it would be a little too much to expect such explorations of metaphorical language from a critic of his temperament and concerns writing early in the eleventh century A.D.

Al-Raḍī's analysis is often brilliant and always enriching, but on the whole, his emphasis is more on the semantic structure of the verses he is discussing; his is part of a drive to offer interpretations that articulate coherent meanings, even where he accepts a wide range of possible meanings. What matters to him most is to show what a verse means, how an *isti'ārī* usage functions as a semantic structure; insufficient emphasis is placed on the overall aesthetic, imaginative, poetic dimensions of the verses or their emotional and intellectual impact or the recipient's response to them. The process is controlled by a rationalism that often ignores the other dimensions of metaphor and its power and beauty. Al-Raḍī could describe in a rational way how the word *ṭarā'iqa* (Q. 23:17) related the seven heavens to a pair of shoes by way of *isti'āra*, but it did not occur to him to explore the associations and psychological factors which emerge out of this relationship. This rationalism lay behind many of the great achievements in Arabic studies, but it often deprived literary contemplation of that extra dimension: the wayward, irrational, adventurous, and above all ambiguous and mysterious mode of experiencing the world as well as language and writing. One cannot but be struck by the fact that, despite the flourishing of Sufism and the literature of the fantastic in prose writings up to the end of the fifth century A.H., there was a dominant rationalist, *ẓāhirī* tone to most contemplations of the Qur'ān in scholarly circles. One of the rare exceptions was 'Abd al-Qāhir al-Jurjānī who was to reveal some of the more mysterious and irrational aspects of the imagination in his study of *isti'āra, takhyīl* and similar aspects of artistic creation.

NOTES

1 I should make clear at the outset that I use the word 'metaphorical' here in a liberal fashion to approximate it to the terms used by al-Sharīf al-Raḍī such as *majāz, isti'āra* and *kināya.* For a precise definition of *isti'āra* and whether or not it corresponds to the Aristotelian notion of metaphor and to modern ways of using this term in Western discourse, see my *al-Jurjani's Theory of Poetic Imagery* (Warminster: Aris and Phillips, 1979), esp. Ch. 5.

2 See, for instance, Muḥammad Zaghlūl Sallām's *Athar al-Qur'ān fi Taṭawwur al-Naqd al-Adabī* (Cairo: Dār al-Ma'ārif, 1955).

3 See Jābir 'Uṣfūr's important study of the influence of the discussions within the various 'circles' of learning on the development of the study of imagery in *al-Ṣūra al-Fanniyya fi al-Turāth al-Naqdī wa al-Balāghī* (Cairo: Dār al-Thaqāfa, 1974).

4 In the first part of my D.Phil. dissertation, "Al-Jurjānī's Theory of Poetic Imagery and Its Background" (Oxford University, 1970), only the second part of which has been published.

5 In the verse, *"fa 'tū bi-sūratin min mithlihi"* (*al-Baqara,* Q. 2:23 and, in a slightly different form, *Hūd,* Q. 11:13).

6 The argument in favour of *ṣarfa* was put forward powerfully in a treatise attributed to 'Abd al-Qāhir al-Jurjānī, the very critic who was to do more than anybody else to show that the *i'jāz* of the Qur'ān resided neither in its words nor in its meanings but in its *naẓm.* See "al-Risāla al-Shāfiya fi I'jāz al-Qur'ān," in *Thalāth Rasā'il fī I'jāz al-Qur'ān,* eds. by Muḥammad Khalaf Allāh Aḥmad and Muḥammad Zaghlūl Sallām (Cairo: Dār al-Ma'ārif, 1956) and my *al-Jurjānī's Theory of Poetic Imagery,* especially Ch. 1.

7 In his excellent introduction to his edition of al-Sharīf al-Raḍī's *Talkhīṣ al-Bayān fī Majāzāt al-Qur'ān* (Cairo: 'Īsā al-Bābī al-Ḥalabī, 1955), 5.

8 *Dhikrā Abī al-'Alā'* (Cairo, 1915), 116.

9 According to the story related by Yāqūt, amongst many other writers, who quoted Abū 'Ubayda himself, the book was written after the year 188 A. H. It could be understood from the story that the book was written in 188 A.H. itself. See Yāqūt, *Irshād al-Arīb* (*Mu'jam al-Udabā'*), 2nd ed. (Cairo: Maṭba'at Hindiyya, 1923–1932), 7:166–67 and al-Khaṭīb al-Baghdādī, *Tārīkh Baghdād* (Cairo: Maktabat al-Khānjī, 1931), 13:254.

10 Ibid. See also Ibn Khallikān, *Wafayāt al-A'yān* (Būlāq: Maṭba'at Būlāq, 1298/1880), 2:139 and Ibn al-Anbārī, *Nuzhat al-Alibbā'* (Baghdad, 1294/1877), 143.

11 See F. Sezgin's edition of the book, 2 vols. (Cairo: Khānjī, 1955, 1962).

12 See Nāṣir al-Ḥillāwī, "Abū 'Ubaida Ma'mar b. al-Muthannā," (Ph.D. thesis S.O.A.S., University of London, January, 1966), 325, quoting al-Suyūṭī in his *al-Wasā'il ilā Musāmarat al-Awā'il* (Baghdad: Maṭba'at al-Najāḥ, 1950), 127.

13 Ibn Taymiyya, *Kitāb al-Īmān* (Cairo, 1325 A. H.), 35.

14 It is not certain that Abū 'Ubayda was the first person to use the word *majāz* as a "technical term" and although Ibn Taymiyya states categorically that none of Abū 'Ubayda's predecessors had used the word, it is possible to suggest that at least one of them had done so, namely Abū 'Amr (possibly Ibn al-'Alā'), who is quoted by Abū 'Ubayda himself (See *Majāz*, 2:274.).

15 See al-Anṣārī, *Abū Zakariyyā al-Farrā'* (Cairo: al-Majlis al-A'lā li-Ri'āyat al-Funūn wa al-Adab wa al-'Ulūm al-Ijtimā'iyya, 1964), 271. The dispute is over the question whether the book is a book on *tafsīr* or *balāgha*.

16 For an account of the opinions of Abū 'Ubayda's contemporaries of the book, see al-Ḥillāwī, "Abū 'Ubaida Ma'mar b. al-Muthannā," 316. See also Amīn al-Khūlī, *Manāhij Tajdīd* (Cairo: Dār al-Ma'rifa, 1961), 107, who concludes that the nature of these opinions show clearly that those contemporaries regarded the book as a book on *tafsīr*. Al-Khūlī, however, produced a passage from a later writer, Abū Isḥāq Ibrāhīm b. 'Alī al-Shīrāzī al-Shāfi'ī (d. 476 A. H.) who considers the book a book on *majāz* in its rhetorical sense. See also al-Khūlī's adoption of Ibn-Taymiyya's opinion of the book: that it is a book on *tafsīr*, ibid., 108. A third view of the nature of the book is held by Sallām (*Athar al-Qur'ān*, 36), which is shared by M. S. al-Juwaynī (see *Manhaj al-Zamakhsharī fī Tafsīr al-Qur'ān* (Cairo: Dār al-Ma'ārif, 1959), 283, and al-Anṣārī (*Abū Zakariyyā al-Farrā'*, 327). These writers consider the book as a representative of "*al-manhaj al-lughawī fī al-tafsīr*" (the linguistic approach to interpretation), though Sallām says that *majāz* in it does not mean *ma'nā* absolutely (*Athar al-Qur'ān*, 41). There is also Ṭāhā Ḥusayn's interpretation, with which al-Khūlī partly agrees and describes as the nearest interpretation, put forward by "the academics" to the truth (*Dhikrā Abī al-'Alā'*, 112–113), whereas al-Ḥillāwī rejects it entirely. Another view of the book is Ibrāhīm Muṣṭafā's who seems to consider it to be a study in the syntactic structures of the *Qur'ān* (see *Iḥyā' al-Naḥw*, Cairo, 1937, 11–12). Al-Khūlī describes this view as "*ḍarbun min al-takalluf* (an artificial view?)", (*Manāhij Tajdīd*, 113.) It is very curious that al-Khūlī, Muṣṭafā and Ḥusayn read only fragments of the manuscript of the book and gave their final judgements. However, Al-Khūlī did not change his interpretation of the book after he read it. (Ibid., 113, n.).

17 None of the sources which reproduce the story mentions the words "*huwa majāz.*" I have tried to find any reference which quoted Abū 'Ubayda saying "*huwa majāz*" but I have failed. See for a detailed discussion of this matter, the unpublished part of my thesis referred to in note 4, above, 205–206.

18 (... the tree of *Zaqqūm* (Q. 37:62), its fruits are like the heads of Satans (Q. 37:65)). In a study of this nature, much of the material needs to be quoted in Arabic; translating metaphorical language has been recognized for centuries as an almost impossible task. An *isti'āra* often loses its metaphorical nature as well as its power and effectiveness when rendered in another language. That is a major obstacle for all translations of the Qur'ān.

19 Ṭāhā Ḥusayn, *Dhikrā Abī al-'Alā'.*

20 See *Majāz,* 1:9 : "*al-āyatu", "al-surādiqu."*

21 See, for instance, ibid., 3.

22 Compare with later critics who lived in different periods. See *al-Muzhir,* 3rd ed. (Cairo: Dār Iḥyā' al-Kutub al-'Arabiyya, n. d.), 1:355–364. Ibn Fāris, for instance, is quoted as saying: "*qawlunā 'aṭā'u fulānin muznun wākif, fa-hādhā tashbīh, wa qad jāza majāza qawlihi: 'aṭā'uhu kathīrun wāfin.*" Ibid., 355. Al-Rāzī is reported to have said: "*al-Majāzu khilāfu al-aṣli, li-annahu yatawaqqafu 'alā al-waḍ'i al-awwali.*" Ibid., 361. Al-Subkī says "*al-gharaḍu anna al-aṣla al-ḥaqīqatu, wa al-majāzu khilāfu al-aṣli.*" Ibid.

23 Ibid., 364.

24 See *Majāz,* 1:8–16, where this formula occurs in 30 out of 39 types of structure discussed by Abū 'Ubayda.

25 Ibid., 1:11–16.

26 Ibid., 1, 7, 8.

27 Probably types 8 (1:10) and 28 (ibid., 13) can be considered examples where this formula is applied to the single words. But even here there are possible interpretations which prove that it is due to structural reasons that this formula is applied.

28 Ibid., 12, lines 12, 16; 10, lines 6, 8, 10, 13, 15, and other places.

29 Ibid., 14, lines 3, 10; 15, lines 1, 3; 16, lines 1, 5.

30 Ibid., 13. Other examples on 13, line 11; 14, line 3.

31 Ibid., 1:16–19.

32 Ibid., 17.

33 Ibid.

34 Ibid., 17–18.

35 Ibid., 18–19.

36 "Then taste the chastisement for that you disbelieved." (*Āl 'Imrān,* Q. 3:106).

37 Ibid., 246. See also 2:168.

38 "And We loose the winds fertilizing," (*Al-Ḥijr,* Q. 15:22).

39 Ibid., 1:348.

40 "... and they were made to drink the Calf in their hearts," (*Al-Baqara,* Q. 2:93).

41 Ibid., 47

42 "They are a vestment for you ...," (*Al-Baqara,* Q. 2:187).

43 Ibid., 67

44 See, for instance, ibid., 68, 77, 110, 229.

45 Ibid., 20

46 See "Risāla fī Fakhr al-Sūdān," in *Rasā'il al-Jāḥiẓ,* ed. 'Abd al-Salām Muḥammad Hārūn (Cairo: Maktabat al-Khānjī, 1964), 1:186 and compare their comments on "*nuzulan min 'indi 'llāhi, Majāz,* 1:112 and *al-Ḥayawān,* ed. 'Abd al-Salām Muḥammad Hārūn (Cairo: Maktabat Muṣṭafā al-Bābī al-Ḥalabī, 1938–1945), 1:153.

47 See *al-Naqā'iḍ,* ed. A. S. Bevan (Leiden: Brill, 1908–1909), 1:275.

48 "And every man – We have fastened to him his bird," (*Al-Isrā',* Q. 17:13).

49 *Majāz,* 1:372.

50 Ibid., 2:15.

51 See ibid., 1:273 where he says: "*thumma 'stawā 'alā 'l-'arshi: majāzuhu: ẓahara 'alā al-'arshi wa 'alā 'alayhi.*" Here the structure of the expression is normal, i.e., there is no inversion, therefore Abū 'Ubayda applies the word *majāzuhu* not to the expression as a whole but to the single word, explaining its meaning. There is no interest whatsoever in the *isti'ārī* nature of the verse and the anthropomorphic implications in the word *istawā.*
52 Baghdad, 1328 A. H.
53 Ibid., 3, for instance.
54 Ḥasan, *Talkhīṣ,* Introduction, 30– 38. Ḥasan suggests also that this book is the only book of its type in Arabic. Ibid., 30– 31.
55 Examples are available in both of al-Raḍī's books. See, for instance, *Talkhīṣ,* 240, 241, 250, 313 and *Majāzāt,* 25, 26–27, 88–89. See also Ḥasan, "Introduction," 46–54 where a comparison between Abū 'Ubayda, Ibn Qutayba and al-Raḍī is made, quoting examples of their analysis of the same verses, and showing the merits of al-Raḍī's analysis.
56 For instance, the epithets he uses in *Talkhīṣ,* 118, 119, 150, 156, 171, 240, and *Majāzāt,* 5.
57 See, for instance, *Talkhīṣ,* 230, 249, 120, 123, 138. The function of *mubālagha* was first developed by al-Rummānī. It is interesting that both authors were dealing, when they discussed this concept, with the figures of the *Qur'ān.*
58 "There has come to you Our Messenger, making things clear to you, upon an interval between the Messengers," (*Al-Mā'ida,* Q. 5:19).
59 The editor's reading of the word "*bi-ḥāli*" in this passage appears to be wrong. It should be read "*li-ḥāli.*"
60 *Talkhīṣ,* 131.
61 See *Lisān al-'Arab* where "*fatra*" is said to mean "*mā bayna kulli nabiyyayni,*" which renders the usage of "*fatra*" in the quoted verse a literal one. The nearest meaning to the one suggested by al-Raḍī is "*fatara al-mā'u: sakana ḥarruhu*" which makes the *isti'āra* in the verse, if "*fatra*" is interpreted in this way, much less beautiful, if not dull.
62 "So that we might thereby revive a dead land," (*Al-Furqān,* Q. 25:49).
63 *Talkhīṣ,* 253. Also 178, where the comment on the verse "*ka-dhālika yaḍribu 'llāhu 'l-amthāla*" (*al-Ra'd,* Q. 13:17) offers two interpretations.
64 In Arberry's inappropriate translation, "Nay, We hurl the truth against falsehood and it prevails over it, and behold, falsehood vanishes away." *The Koran Interpreted* (Oxford: Oxford University Press, 1964), 324.
65 *Talkhīṣ,* 228. See also 214: "*fa-lā tuẓlamu nafsun shay'an,*" (*al-Anbiyā',* Q. 21:47), 222, 229.
66 Ibid., 114.
67 Ibid., 142.
68 See, for instance, ibid., 214: "*wa sā'at murtafaqā,*" (*al-Kahf,* Q. 18:29).
69 Ibid., 353–54.
70 *Murād* means 'wanted', "that which is wanted," which can be rendered as 'purpose, goal'; in order to avoid the pitfalls of what William Wimsatt has called 'the intentional fallacy,' however, I shall use the Arabic word regularly rather than translating it as 'intention, purpose, etc..'
71 Ibid., 261–62.
72 Ibid., 260.
73 Ibid., 220.
74 Ibid., 231.
75 *Talkhīṣ,* 126.
76 "As often as they light a fire for war, God will extinguish it," (*Al-Mā'ida,* Q. 5:64).

77 *Talkhīṣ,* 133–34. It must be noted that the similarity is not established between fire and war, as al-Raḍī suggests. War is said to have a fire. The *arkān* of *isti'āra* are not easy to define. The *mushabbah* could be "*shiddat al-ḥarb*" for instance, which is similized to fire. In general, this type of expression does not establish similarity between the two words which are linked by *iḍāfa.* Al-Raḍī himself realizes this in other examples. See, for instance, his comment on "*wa 'indahu mafātiḥu 'l-ghaybi,*" (Q. 6:59). Ibid., 136.
78 Ibid., 241.
79 Ibid.
80 Ibid., 136.
81 Ibid., 305.
82 Ibid., 367.
83 One is strongly reminded here of T. S. Eliot's brilliant revitalization of the metaphor of vision in his famous use of vision and re-vision for which he has been praised lavishly by some modern critics. Al-Raḍī deserves no less lavish a praise for his handling of *fatra.*
84 Ibid., 253.
85 Ibid., 252.
86 Ibid., 253.
87 Ibid., 220. There is every possibility that this detailed and concrete analysis was familiar to 'Abd al-Qāhir al-Jurjānī while writing his work and contemplating this particular verse with great profundity and brilliance.
88 Ibid., 137.
89 Ibid., 138.
90 Ibid., 260–61.
91 Ibid., 257–58.
92 Ibid., 160–61.
93 Ibid. 161–62.
94 And in a similarly detailed fashion, he offers four possible interpretations of "*la-aḥtanikanna dhurriyatahu illā qalīlan*" (*Banū Isrā'īl / al-Isrā',* Q. 17:62), *Talkhīṣ,* 202–03.
95 Ibid., 230.
96 Ibid., 196–97.
97 Ibid., 251–52.
98 Ibid., 162.
99 Ibid., 143.
100 Ibid., 166 "Does your prayer command you that we leave what our fathers worship?" (*Hūd,* Q. 11:87).
101 Ibid., 251–52.
102 Ibid., 249.
103 Ibid., 113–14.
104 Ibid., 241.
105 Ibid., 250.
106 Ibid., 248.
107 Ibid., 343.
108 Ibid., 269.
109 "This mountain, we love it/him and it/he loves us."
110 See this in *Majāzāt,* 6.
111 *Talkhīṣ,* 133.
112 Ibid., 127.
113 Ibid., 367.
114 Ibid., 242.

115 Ibid., 146.
116 Ibid., 293, the verse can be rendered roughly as "when We want something We say to it be and it is," in order to embody the immediacy of response al-Raḍī is trying to depict.
117 Ibid., 193.
118 Ibid., 232.
119 Ibid., 130; see also 190; also 290 where *rūḥ* is said to mean *al-waḥy.*
120 Ibid., 128–29.
121 Ibid., 129.
122 Ibid., 279.
123 Ibid., 338.
124 Ibid., 337.
125 See, for instance, ibid., 120.
126 Ibid., 123.
127 Ibid., 360.
128 See, for instance, ibid., 200.
129 Ibid., 330.
130 Ibid., 118.
131 Ibid., 326–27 "He is the first and the last, the *ẓāhir* and the *bāṭin,* and He is knowledgeable of all things" (*al-Ḥadīd,* Q. 57:3).
132 Ibid., 247.
133 See, for instance, ibid., 252, 253.
134 Ibid., 117.
135 See ibid., 222. "*wa qawlu al-shā'iri 'akhfiyat al-karā' min al-isti'ārāt al-'ajība wa al-badā'i' al-gharība.*"
136 Ibid., 140.
137 Ibid., 191.
138 "We know best what they listen for, when they listen to thee, and when they conspire," (*Al-Isrā',* Q. 17:47).
139 *Talkhīṣ,* 201.
140 "Fever is the bellows of Hell."
141 *Majāzāt,* 271.
142 "God has written 'I shall assuredly be the victor, I and My Messengers'."
143 *Talkhīṣ,* 329.
144 "Who assigned to you the earth for a couch, and heaven for an edifice," (*Al-Baqara,* Q. 2:22).
145 *Talkhīṣ,* 115. Also 120,122,124,125, 226, 356–357.
146 "Knowledge is a cupboard and its key is questioning."
147 *Majāzāt,* 132. Also 195–96 and 25: "*Hādha al-qawlu majāz wa hādhā min al-tashbīh al-wāqi' wa al-tamthīl al-nāfi'.*"
148 Ibid., 23–24. Also 74, 167–168 and *Talkhīṣ,* 126, 231, 341.
149 Further evidence for this suggestion is available in other aspects of his treatment of those figures. First, it is interesting to note that each of those figures is used in contrast with *ḥaqīqa.* See *Talkhīṣ,* 140 and *Majāzāt,* 10–11, 75, 88, 230. Secondly, each of the three figures *majāz, isti'āra, kināya,* is described in various places by the expression: "*fa-aqāma ta'ālā dhikrā (al-amri hāhunā) maqāma dhikri (al-targhībi wa al-ḍalālati) 'alā ṭarīqi al-majāzi wa al-isti'ārati.*" See ibid., 278 and *Talkhīṣ,* 117. Thirdly, al-Raḍī uses each of the terms *majāz, isti'āra, kināya,* and *tamthīl* in relation to the others. See ibid., 245, 264, 200, 341, 265, 278–279, 261.
150 See *Majāzāt,* 11–12.
151 Ibid., 95.

152 "And with them are wide-eyed maidens restraining their glances." (Q. 37:48). See his analysis of the *majāz* in *Qāṣirāt al-ṭarf, Talkhīṣ*, 277. Another useful example is his comment on 368, 369 and in *Majāzāt*, 22.
153 Ibid., 53, 155–156, 195–96.
154 *Talkhīṣ*, 333, and *Majāzāt*, 2–4, 223. The suggestion made in the present study is in disagreement with Badawī Ṭabāna's suggestion that al-Raḍī "means by *majāz* one of its elements [or forms] only, namely *isti'āra* which is, according to rhetoricians, a type of *majāz* based on similarity. Al-Raḍī's whole book is [a study] of this figure [i.e., *isti'āra*]." See *Al-Bayān al-'Arabī*, 3rd ed. (Cairo, 1962), 30. On the other hand, Ḥasan's view that al-Raḍī's failure to distinguish between the various forms of *majāz* was due to the fact that the terms designating these forms were not yet known or invented in his time, is invalid. (Ḥasan, "Introduction," *Talkhīṣ*, 57). My early work has demonstrated that *majāz, isti'āra, mathal*, and *tashbīh* and many relations of *majāz* were clearly defined in the works of al-Raḍī's predecessors.
155 "Surely you, and that you were serving apart from God, are fuel for Gehenna; you shall go down to it," (*Al-Anbiyā'*, Q. 21:98).
156 *Talkhīṣ*, 233.
157 "Fever is the bellows of Hell", *Majāzāt*, 271.
158 "The believer is a mirror for his brother," Ibid., 49. These examples show also the complete identification of *majāz* with *isti'āra*. The same type of phrase is described as being "*isti'āra*", "*majāz*" *and* "*majāz wa isti'āra*".
159 Ibid., 180–81.
160 This is expressed in a variety of phraseology, such as:
"*wa hādhihi isti'āra, li-anna al-ẓulma hāhunā laysa 'alā aṣlihi fī al-lughati, wa lā 'alā 'urfihi fī al-sharī'ati,*" "*wa hādhihi isti'āra, wa 'alā al-qawli al-ākhari yakūnu al-ṭayyu hunā 'alā ḥaqīqatihi.*" *Talkhīṣ*, 214, 234 respectively. See also 222, 278. It is of genuine interest to note here that the notion of original meaning is paired with the notion of "*'urf fī al-sharī'a*" as defining factors of the literal use of language. This is certainly worth exploring, but it has to be left for another occasion.
161 *Majāzāt*, 131.
162 Ibid., 88.
163 *Talkhīṣ*, 133, 200.
164 Ibid., 277.
165 Apart from a brief quotation from "another writer" who is almost certainly al-Rummānī, some of whose remarks are quoted in other places of al-Raḍī's work without his name being mentioned. See, for instance, *Talkhīṣ*, 207, 249, 322–23 and cf. al-Rummānī's "al-Nukat fī I'jāz al-Qur'ān," in *Thalāth Rasā'il* (referred to above, note 6), 78–87. Al-Raḍī makes a general remark on the nature of *isti'āra* in *Majāzāt* (116–117) saying:
" *al-isti'āra 'alā ḍarbayni: ẓāhiratun tu'rafu bi-ḥilyatihā, wa ghāmiḍatun yuḍṭarru ilā istinbāṭi khabī'ihā.*"
166 See *Talkhīṣ*, 137–38 "*taqaṭṭa'a baynukum,*" (Q. 6:94). Also 136 "*mafāṭiḥu al-ghaybi,*" (Q. 6:59); 165 "*yawmin muḥīṭ,*" (Q. 11:84).
167 Ibid., 166 "*aṣalātuka ta'muruka,*" (Q. 11:87). Also 206 "*wa lam yaj'al lahu 'iwaja,*" (Q. 18:1), and 215 "*li-yadḥaḍū bihi 'l-ḥaqqa,*" (Q. 18:56). In this category all the verses which describe God in terms of human beings can be classified. Al-Raḍī is strongly anti-anthropomorphist. He offers non-literal interpretation of any anthropomorphic verse or tradition. See, for instance, ibid., 124, 133, 137, 145, 153, 160, 347, 361, and *Majāzāt*, 27, 30, 225.
168 *Talkhīṣ*, 275–276: "*man ba'athanā min marqadinā,*" (Q. 36:52). See also 214–15.

169 Ibid., 217. "*wa taraknā ba'ḍahum yawma'idhin yamūju fī ba'ḍin,*" (Q. 18:99).
170 *Majāzāt*, 100 "*al-waladu ...majhalatu thamarāti al-qulūbi wa qurratu al-'ayni.*" Also, 223 "*wa 'ḍmum yadaka ilā janāḥika,*" (Q. 20:22).
171 *Talkhīṣ*, 190–197: "*fa-adhāqahā 'llāhu libāsa 'l-jū'i wa 'l-khawfi,*" (Q. 16:112).
172 An interesting aspect of his work is his study of the role played by *isti'āra* in semantic change as manifested in a good number of Qur'ānic verses. See, for instance, ibid., 177 where he studies "*al-sujūd,*" and 210–11 where he studies "*al-rajīm.*"
173 Ibid., 295.

Chapter 15

Sayyid Quṭb's Literary Appreciation of the Qur'ān

Issa J. Boullata

One of the most influential and radical ideologues of Islamic resurgence in the second half of the twentieth century, Sayyid Quṭb (1906–1966) had a noted writing career as a litterateur in Egypt in the 1930s and 1940s and a very promising future ahead of him in this field. It was only in the late 1940s that he changed course and in the 1950s produced works, latterly in prison, projecting his vision of a reinvigorated Islamic society based on what he viewed as the perennial tenets of original Islam found in the Qur'ān, and aiming to replace the secularized modern society he impugned as *jāhilī*, that is, ignorant of God and His prescriptions for a morally good life.[1]

However, literary appreciation of the Qur'ān was a constant factor throughout his adult life, even before he became an Islamic activist in the 1950s. As a literary critic, in his early writing career, he wrote two important and ground-breaking books expressing his literary appreciation of the Holy Book of Islam. The first was *al-Taṣwīr al-Fannī fī al-Qur'ān* (1945)[2] and the second, *Mashāhid al-Qiyāma fī al-Qur'ān* (1947).[3] These were two books in what he planned to be a literary series on the Qur'ān by him, which was to contain titles like "al-Qiṣṣa bayn al-Tawrāh wa al-Qur'ān", "al-Namādhij al-Insāniyya fī al-Qur'ān", "al-Manṭiq al-Wijdānī fī al-Qur'ān", and "Asālīb al-'Arḍ al-Fannī fī al-Qur'ān".[4] But he never wrote the remaining books in the series, mostly because Egyptian political life after the 1952 Revolution carried him away to other intellectual concerns related to political activism and religious radicalism. Yet he wrote a commentary on the whole Qur'ān in thirty volumes entitled *Fī Ẓilāl al-Qur'ān* (1952–1959),[5] in which he made reference to these earlier two books and in which his literary appreciation of the Qur'ān continued unabated and was even developed.

The aim of this paper is to study Sayyid Quṭb's literary appreciation of the Qur'ān and how he believes it continues to affect the minds and hearts of human beings and win them over to its message. Its method will be phenomenological in eliciting facts from Sayyid Quṭb's life and literary writings, and making them shed light on his understanding and expression of religious meaning in the literary structures of the Qur'ān.

As a child growing up in a pious Muslim family in the village of Mūshā, in the District of Asyūṭ in Upper Egypt, Sayyid Quṭb was continually exposed to recitations of the Qur'ān, especially in the month of Ramadan.[6] Its words, its images, its rhythms, its music enchanted him before he even knew its meaning – as he admits.[7] By the time he was ten years old, he had learned the Qur'ān by heart. But as he grew older and entered institutions of higher learning, where he read books of *tafsīr* and heard Qur'ānic exegesis from his professors, he was disappointed not to find the same thrill as that of his childhood in what he read and heard – as he likewise admits.[8] So he went back primarily to the Qur'ān itself and studied it on his own as a young adult in the late 1930s, far from the innocence of impressionable childhood, in order to understand its meaning and learn the secrets of its literary spell. That is when he regained his early enchantment with the Qur'ān and decided to share it publicly by writing a couple of articles in 1939 for *al-Muqtaṭaf*[9] and a few more in 1945 for *al-Risāla*,[10] articles he later developed into his book *al-Taṣwīr al-Fannī fī al-Qur'ān*.[11]

In this book, Sayyid Quṭb states that the Qur'ān has a specific and very effective way of using language, and he calls it *taṣwīr fannī*, i.e., artistic portrayal, representation, or depiction. He says that Muslim exegetes of the past missed it because they were engrossed in discussions of a legalistic, grammatical, philosophical, or historical nature about the Qur'ān.[12] He singles out al-Zamakhsharī (d. 1144) among them as one who occasionally had some success in perceiving artistic beauty in the Qur'ān but who failed to clarify it analytically and was understandably limited to the discourse of his time.[13] As for past Muslim rhetoricians and those dealing with the *I'jāz* of the Qur'ān, Sayyid Quṭb thinks that they were bogged down in useless discussions on whether rhetorical beauty lay in the wording or in the meaning of the text, and that they often sank to unbearable levels of triviality in their efforts to make technical rules for rhetorical beauty.[14] In his view, only 'Abd al-Qāhir al-Jurjānī (d. 1078) among them was about to achieve something great in his book *Dalā'il al-I'jāz*, had he not succumbed to the polarity of wording and meaning in his analysis, despite his perceptive sensibility unequalled by all those dealing with the subject, even in modern times.[15] Sayyid Quṭb concedes, however, that al-Jurjānī's theory of *naẓm* offered, albeit in a complicated way, the most decisive understanding of the indivisible unity of wording and meaning in producing a specific intellectual or emotive effect, the meaning being invariably circumscribed by the particular *naẓm*, i.e., by the particular organization of the wording.[16]

One further point Sayyid Quṭb decries about past Muslim exegetes and, in particular, rhetoricians dealing with the Qur'ān is their disjointed method, which considered each discrete text of a Qur'ānic verse individually and analyzed it apart from the whole Book, thus losing sight of the general literary qualities unifying the whole Qur'ān. Within their limited and deficient tools of analysis, they arrived at disparate perceptions of the different loci of beauty in the Qur'ān, he thinks, but not at a perception of its unitary way of expression irrespective of the variety of purposes it addresses.[17] This unitary way, according to Sayyid Quṭb, is *al-taṣwīr al-fannī.*

Explaining his concept of it, he says:

> *Taṣwīr* is the preferred tool in the style of the Qur'ān. By palpable fancied images, it designates intellectual meanings, psychological states, perceptible events, visual scenes, human types, and human nature. It then elevates these images it draws, and grants them living presence or regenerating movement; whereupon intellectual meanings become forms or motions, psychological states become tableaux or spectacles, human types become vivid and at hand, and human nature becomes visible and embodied. As for events, scenes, stories, and sights, it renders them actual and immediate, pulsating with life and movement. When it adds dialogue to them, it brings into full play all the elements of imaginative representation in them.[18]

Sayyid Quṭb points out that when a person reads the Qur'ānic text or listens to it, he is transported, through its words, to another level of reality in which he forgets that he is being exposed to words; he imagines he sees actual scenes as they unfold, watches real events as they happen, and witnesses existing persons as they act. In his view, the Qur'ānic text offers life and not an imitation of life.[19]

Expanding the concept of *taṣwīr,* Sayyid Quṭb adds it also appeals to the rhythm and sound of words, to the music and sequential flow of expression, as well as to color and movement in order to highlight images for contemplation by the eyes and the ears, by the senses and the imagination, by the intellect and the emotion; it calls upon the imaginal power and often permits all these elements to cooperate in the creation of a desired effect.[20] In addition, there is what Sayyid Quṭb calls *tanāsuq fannī,* artistic harmony or symmetry, in the *taṣwīr* style of the Qur'ān. This is evident in its choice of words to represent specific ideas, in its selection of the rhyme word at the end of a verse to reflect and strengthen the verse's content, in its balancing of ideas or images in a passage to highlight semantic opposition, in its sequential layout of words in a text to show the flow of movement, in its use of alternative grammatical structure or its resort to alternative choice of words in a sentence to emphasize a desired rhetorical meaning, in its systematic arrangement of words in composition to energize a particular intention, and in sundry other ways which he richly documents by citing and elaborately studying a large number of proof-texts from the Qur'ān.[21] Furthermore, in order to persuade, the Qur'ān uses what Sayyid Quṭb calls *al-manṭiq al-wijdānī*, emotive logic.[22] It does not resort to intellectual ratiocination, which later Muslim theologians resorted to, but rather seeks to convince by always appealing to common sense, by awakening feeling, and by aiming to directly reach one's intuitive insight, one's emotion,[23] and ultimately one's soul, to which the intellect is merely one of many channels and not the only one.[24]

Sayyid Quṭb believes that this quality of the Qur'ān was what impressed the Arabs when they first heard Prophet Muḥammad utter the earliest revealed texts of it. He cites the reactions of such stalwart opponents of the Prophet as 'Umar ibn al-Khaṭṭāb[25] and al-Walīd ibn al-Mughīra:[26] how the former was converted to Islam under the spell of the Qur'ānic text and how the latter turned away from Islam but recognized the Qur'ān's powerful effect and, when asked by Muḥammad's enemies to publicly criticize it, advised after deep thought that they should say, "This is nothing but magic handed down from of old."[27]

Sayyid Quṭb argues against those who attribute the early fascination of the Arabs with the Qur'ān to other aspects of it, such as its legislation or its prophecies of future events or its scientific information about the universe. He says that these other aspects of it are to be found in parts of the Qur'ān mostly revealed much later. Depending on the traditional Muslim chronology of revelation and on his own preponderating judgment, he states without claiming certainty that the text which al-Walīd ibn al-Mughīra heard was probably that of *Sūrat al-Muzzammil* (Q. 73), the second sūra to be revealed,[28] and that the one by which 'Umar ibn al-Khaṭṭāb was influenced was – according to one report – the beginning of *Sūrat Ṭā Hā* (Q. 20), the forty-fifth sūra to be revealed.[29] He asserts there is generally no scientific information about the universe, and likewise there is no legislation and there are no prophecies of future events in those early sūras.[30] He concludes that it is the Qur'ān's artistic beauty as an independent element that gives sufficiency by itself when contemplated and he adds that, when seen in the interrelated context of the Qur'ān's religious purpose, it is appreciated even more highly.[31]

Sayyid Quṭb's study has led him to believe that his concept of *al-taṣwīr al-fannī* applies to the greater part of the Qur'ān. He excludes from it only those parts of the Holy Book that deal with legislation, and those that contain debate and other themes requiring pure intellectual statement, all of which – at any rate – are limited to about one quarter of the Qur'ān in his opinion.[32]

There is no doubt that Sayyid Quṭb hit on a powerful idea when he came upon the concept of *al-taṣwīr al-fannī* in the Qur'ān. Earlier Muslim writers like 'Abd al-Qāhir al-Jurjānī, al-Khaṭṭābī (d. 998),[33] al-Rummānī

(d. 996),[34] and a few others, including Muṣṭafā Ṣādiq al-Rāfi'ī (d. 1937) in modern times,[35] dealt with some of the literary aspects of the Qur'ān that Sayyid Quṭb concerned himself with.[36] But they never conceived of them in the same forceful way as he did, nor did they see them integrated in a unitary theory in the manner he did, despite their undeniable contributions to understanding the style and rhetoric of the Qur'ān, notably al-Jurjānī.

However, Sayyid Quṭb himself felt it necessary to expand his initial concept of *al-taṣwīr al-fannī*, first elaborated in his two articles of 1939, because it did not fully do justice to the Qur'ānic style. Six years later, he included in it the concept of *al-tanāsuq al-fannī* as part of its manifestation as well as the concept of *al-manṭiq al-wijdānī.* And when he sat down to produce a book on the subject, he added to it themes on *al-qiṣṣa fī al-Qur'ān* and *namādhij insāniyya,* among other things, in order to deal with aspects he had left out. He averred that behind the horizon of *al-taṣwīr* and its two prominent ways of expression, *al-takhyīl* (imaginative representation) and *al-tajsīm* or *al-tashkhīṣ* (embodiment or personification), there were other horizons to the Qur'ānic style.[37] He did not say so only as a humble scholar facing an overwhelming task in studying the Qur'ānic style, but also as one recognizing his human limitations and inviting others to pursue and develop his line of investigation. In fact, he expressed his joy in a postscript, in the third edition of the book published in 1952, on seeing his approach being adopted by others to uncover other applications of *al-taṣwīr al-fannī* not mentioned in his book.[38]

Yet despite its originality and genuine perceptiveness, his book suffers from some unnecessary repetition and avoidable overlapping, not because it lacks an organizing principle but probably because its chapters, conceived as integral units, were written on separate occasions over a period of several years interrupted by other concerns. Furthermore, many of the technical terms used in his literary analysis are taken for granted and are not always defined. Their meanings often remain slippery and a cause of ambivalent connotation, though not of any insurmountable obscurity.

On the other hand, Sayyid Quṭb's other work, *Mashāhid al-Qiyāma fī al-Qur'ān,* was conceived as a book. On reading it, one feels the unity of purpose that pervades it. It offers itself as an application of the concept of *al-taṣwīr al-fannī* explained in the earlier book and it aims, like its predecessor, to recover for the modern reader what Sayyid Quṭb believes to be the original powerful charm of the Qur'ān that the Arabs felt on first receiving it and falling under its spell.[39]

After a preface, the book begins with an essay on "The Other World in Human Conscience," which deals generally with the concept of the Other World in earlier religions practiced before Islam; this is followed by another essay on "The Other World in the Qur'ān." Then comes the remainder of the book, which is the major part of it, and presents Qur'ānic scenes of the Day of Resurrection and of the Afterlife. These are organized in sections, each of which contains a study of one eschatological scene or more from one specified sūra of the Qur'ān at a time.

Sayyid Quṭb surveys 150 scenes taken from 80 of the Qur'ān's 114 sūras: 63 from the Meccan period and 17 from the Medinan period,[40] some of the sūras containing more than one scene. The length of each scene varies depending, in his view, on the context of the religious purpose of the sūra and the principles of artistic exposition.[41]

What he calls "scene" is one which he characterizes as having graphic representation, movement, and rhythm. He overlooks a few short scenes and does not deal with the many Qur'ānic instances where there is only mere mention of the Last Day, Paradise, or punishment without depicting a vivid or moving scene.[42] He concedes that the texts of the Qur'ānic eschatological scenes should be read in their contexts so that their beauty may be appreciated fully, and he says that he has tried to provide a modicum of connections between these scenes and their contexts without unduly lengthening the book.[43] He finally advises the reader of his book to carefully read each scene with the sūra containing it and within the context of the Qur'ān as a whole, including its other eschatological scenes, for that is more enjoyable in his view and more akin to the nature of the Holy Book.[44]

As for his organization of the scenes in the chronological order of the revelation of the sūras containing them, he admits that there is no certainty about the authenticity of that order, which he acknowledges is only approximate and not definitive; and he adds that even if there was certainty, the fact is that many sūras were not revealed as wholes but rather piecemeal at diverse occasions, of which there is no full or exact historical record agreed upon by scholars. Hence, the only option available to him, he says, is that of assumption and preponderation in this matter.[45]

In his chronological presentation of the eschatological scenes, Sayyid Quṭb first quotes the chosen Qur'ānic text as a whole (without verse numbers) and mentions in a footnote the chronological order of the sūra from which the scene is taken. He then proceeds to study this text in detail to show its literary beauty and psychological effect. His approach is partly analytical and partly consisting of a running exegetical paraphrase, sequentially quoting again parts of the text, elaborating their meaning, and clarifying their intent. While doing so, he interjects assertions showing his admiration for the beauty of expression and its effect on the psyche. Sometimes he offers a cross-reference for rhetorical comparison, stops at a particular word to highlight its onomatopoeic contribution to the sense or its semantic effect as one preferred over alternative ones; or he comments on the oppositional structure of the imaginative representation of the scene, explains the transitional shifts in its sentence composition and the speech attribution shifts with varying pronouns which the Qur'ānic style employs for dramatic effect; or he remarks on the general atmosphere of fear, shame, regret, hope or bliss which the text of the eschatological scene creates. He often refers to his own concept of *taṣwīr* and its concomitant elements of *tanāsuq fannī* and *manṭiq wijdānī* or its other horizons of *tajsīm*, *tashkhīṣ*, and *takhyīl*, as the text allows, and he makes frequent footnote references to his earlier book *al-Taṣwīr al-Fannī fi al-Qur'ān*.

Sayyid Quṭb makes a good effort in analyzing the Qur'ān's depiction of the scenes of Resurrection and Judgment, and of the ensuing Afterlife in Hell and in Paradise. He shows how the Qur'ān has described the Other World as a living and moving reality in a perceptible and graphic way and how it has rendered it perpetually present and visible to human beings at all times. He says that Muslims have lived with these scenes in their minds, alternately frightened and comforted by them, but always knowing this Other World well before its promised day arrives.

In his analysis, he shows how the eschatological scene in some texts portrays life beginning in this world and continuing in the next without interruption, and how in other texts it shows this world and the next contemporaneously. He points out that the style at times is that of statement and description, and at others it is that of dialogue and commands. In some scenes it is God who addresses the human beings in them, and in others it is the devils or the angels who do so. In some scenes, the tone of the dialogue is one of incrimination and chastisement, in others it is one of rueful remorse and bitter sarcasm, and in others still it is one of blissful acceptance and rewarding joy, depending on who voices these feelings or ideas.

The physical world is shown to disintegrate in a fearful way on the Day of Resurrection, and the usually stable laws of nature are seen to be disrupted by uncontrollable chaos in the ensuing cosmic cataclysm. Human relations of parentage and filiation are shown to be of no help to defend oneself, and intercession with God is of no avail. The powerful human beings of this world are shown in the next to be as powerless as the weak ones, when everyone is brought before the dread judgment seat of God. However, Sayyid Quṭb emphasizes that everyone receives justice, and no one is treated unfairly or with any special favor.

He shows how eternal happiness and punishment in the Other World are at times described in the Qur'ān as physical and amenable to the senses, at other times as spiritual and perceived by the soul, and at others still as a combination of both physical and spiritual experience.

The examples chosen from the Qur'ān portraying eschatological scenes are some of the most moving in the Holy Book and, through them, Sayyid Quṭb aptly demonstrates his concept of *al-taṣwīr al-fannī* with all its artistic manifestations. He points out that the religious purpose of such scenes is to call upon human beings to lead a morally good life in this world knowing that there is a just God who rewards and punishes them according to their faith and deeds in the end. The scenes of the Day of Resurrection and of the Afterlife are constant emotive reminders of this reality. Although similar in some ways, they are presented by Sayyid Quṭb to show that each of them really adds new details and standpoints so that, apart from occasional common words or images, each is shown to be an utterly new representation with different points of emphasis, the better to affect the minds and hearts of human beings and offer them a most comprehensive view of the eschaton.

In his magnum opus, *Fī Ẓilāl al-Qur'ān* (1952–1959), Sayyid Quṭb took up some of the literary issues he had discussed in his former books, *al-Taṣwīr al-Fannī fī al-Qur'ān* (1945) and *Mashāhid al-Qiyāma fī al-Qur'ān* (1947), and he referred his reader in footnotes to the relevant chapters in these two books for further details. Since his purpose in *Fī Ẓilāl al-Qur'ān* was mainly a commentary on the Qur'ān, his literary appreciation of its text was not given the prominence it had in his former two books.

Initially, *Fī Ẓilāl al-Qur'ān* began to appear in 1952 as a series of articles under the same title in *al-Muslimūn*, a periodical edited in Cairo by Sa'īd Ramaḍān.[46] After the seventh article, Sayyid Quṭb announced he would write a thirty-volume book under the same title dealing with the whole Qur'ān, one volume to appear every two months and to be published by Dār Iḥyā' al-Kutub al-'Arabiyya in Cairo. Between October 1952 and January 1954, sixteen volumes were published including, in volume 1, the materials originally published in *al-Muslimūn.* Sayyid Quṭb was arrested in January 1954 as a leading member of the Society of the Muslim Brothers when it was dissolved but he managed to publish volumes 17 and 18 while in prison. Upon his release in April 1954, he was busy as editor in chief of *al-Ikhwān al-Muslimūn* weekly until it ceased publication in August 1954. He was arrested in November 1954 during the Egyptian government's crackdown on the Society of the Muslim Brothers after the failed attempt at President 'Abd al-Nāṣir's life. He was sentenced to 15 years of hard labor in July 1955 and completed his work in prison on the remaining 12 volumes of his commentary in 1959, his publisher having successfully obtained court permission for him to meet his contract obligation. A second edition was published in 1961, with a revision of the first 13 volumes to match the more activist spirit with which the latter volumes of the book had been written under incarceration. Sayyid Quṭb was released in May 1964 upon the intervention of Iraqi President 'Abd al-Salām 'Ārif with the Egyptian authorities, only to be imprisoned again in August 1965 under new charges. After trial, he was sentenced to death on August 21, 1966 for his alleged attempt to overthrow 'Abd al-Nāṣir's regime by force and, despite pleas for mercy, he was hanged on August 29, 1966.[47]

As in his former two books on the Qur'ān, Sayyid Quṭb in *Fī Ẓilāl al-Qur'ān* does not involve himself in complex linguistic, theological, or legal discussions that overly engaged past Qur'ān exegetes, although he often digresses at the least Qur'ānic suggestion in order to treat social conditions. At such instances, he compares the conditions of the early Muslims at the time of revelation with the conditions of contemporary Muslims and others in modern times,[48] and he strongly condemns what he views as the rampant *jāhiliyya* of the secularized modern world. He repeatedly calls Muslims to be inspired by their Holy Book and act to change the world and shape it according to Qur'ānic principles and live what he considers to be a true Islamic life under God "in the shades of the Qur'ān."[49]

However, he remains interested in the concept of *taṣwīr fannī* and offers much of his commentary in its light and refers the reader to his former two books dealing with it. Moreover, he is now able to introduce a new literary concept he did not have to deal with in his earlier books, namely, the coherent unity of each of the Qur'ān's sūras and of the Qur'ān as a whole.

Early in his *Fī Ẓilāl al-Qur'ān,* Sayyid Quṭb says the following in his general introduction to *Sūrat al-Baqara* (Q. 2):

> Hence, whoever lives in the shades of the Qur'ān notices that each of its sūras has a distinctive personality, a personality that has a soul with which one's heart lives as though with a living soul possessing distinctive features and traits. It [each sūra] has a main topic or several main topics tightly bound to a special theme; it has a special atmosphere enveloping all its topics and helping it to deal with them from specific angles to achieve harmony among them accordingly; it has a special musical rhythm which, if it changes in the course [of the sūra], changes for a specific consideration related to the topic. This is a general characteristic of all the sūras of the Qur'ān.[50]

The Arabic word for theme that Sayyid Quṭb uses in the above-quoted text is *miḥwar* (literally: axis). In his understanding, this is the core or the central point of the sūra around which its meaning revolves. The sūra may have one main topic (*mawḍū'*), which will then be the locus of its theme, or it may have several main topics (*mawḍū'āt*) that are tightly bound to its theme. Furthermore, he says that the sūra has a special atmosphere (*jaww*) that helps integrate its topics harmoniously; and it also has musical rhythm (*īqā' mūsīqī*) related to its topic and changing only when the topic changes. All these unifying traits endow each sūra with what Sayyid Quṭb calls personality (*shakhṣiyya*) that has a soul (*rūḥ*) and makes the sensitive reader feel it is a living being.[51]

Sayyid Quṭb was aware of the call for unity in the modern Arabic poem that Arab literary critics of his generation emphasized in their attack on neo-classical Arab poets like Aḥmad Shawqī (1868–1932) who, they claimed, lacked it; and Sayyid Quṭb's former mentor, 'Abbās Maḥmūd al-'Aqqād (1889–1964), was one of the foremost critics of Shawqī[52] and quite influential among modern Arab poets and critics in inculcating the idea of the need for unity in the Arabic poem.[53] Under the power of this idea, Sayyid Quṭb's appreciation of the unity of the Qur'ānic sūra must have been strengthened. A few pre-modern Muslim exegetes had particularly attempted some Qur'ānic analysis indicating verbal and textual interconnectedness.[54] On the other hand, some Western writers have also been known to criticize the Qur'ān because of its perceived lack in this respect: from Thomas Carlyle who said, "It is as toilsome reading as I ever undertook, a wearisome, confused jumble, crude, incondite"[55] to R. A. Nicholson who referred to "the opinion almost unanimously held by European readers that it is obscure, tiresome, uninteresting; a farrago of long-winded narratives and prosaic exhortations . . ."[56] to W. Montgomery Watt who spoke of "its disjointedness" as "a characteristic . . . which has often been remarked on."[57] Sayyid Quṭb may have known of writings by Muslims and others on the subject of the unity of the Qur'ānic sūra, both on the positive and the negative side of it; but he additionally had a genuine personal need to appreciate the Qur'ān's literary qualities in a new light. His own findings as a literary critic in earlier books, his belief as a committed Muslim who had latterly joined the Society of the Muslim Brothers, and his activism as a radical ideologue calling for change based on a vision in which he did see unity – all these factors helped to shape his view in this regard. And his findings have led him to believe that each sūra of the Qur'ān has one theme he usually calls *miḥwar* and that the whole Qur'ān has one coherent aim he usually calls *hadaf* (goal).[58]

While he had no iron-clad certainty about the authenticity of the traditional chronological order of the Qur'ān's sūras, he never doubted the tradition that ascribed to Prophet Muḥammad himself the organization of the verses of each of them in the sequence they now have in the received text.[59] This organization of the verses, therefore, is for him inseparable from the truth of divine revelation itself and is expressed in the tradition that Muḥammad recited to Jibrīl the entire Qur'ān and that Jibrīl recited it likewise to Muḥammad. "This means," Sayyid Quṭb concludes, "that they both recited it as its verses are arranged in its sūras."[60]

He, therefore, felt the obligation to ponder the wisdom of this very arrangement of verses and probe the reasons behind it. The few premodern exegetes who had engaged themselves in such exercise had come forth with theories of *naẓm* (organization) or of *munāsabāt* (interrelationships) between Qur'ānic verses,[61] but were either mostly concerned with grammatical-rhetorical considerations within the verses regarding relations between wording and meaning or with mere linear connections between one verse and the next, and sometimes between one sūra and the next.[62] Sayyid Quṭb, on the other hand, arrived at a theory of coherence in each sūra as a unit of meaning and he based it on the idea that each sūra revolved around a single *miḥwar* (axis) giving it thematic and semantic unity enhanced by a certain psychological atmosphere, a special musical rhythm, and harmony.[63]

Let us look, for example, at his analysis of the unity of *Sūrat al-Baqara* (Q. 2), which is the longest sūra of the Qur'ān and contains a variety of topics. This sūra is Medinan, for it consists of some of the first revelations of the Qur'ān to have been received by Prophet Muḥammad after his *hijra* (emigration) from Mecca to Medina. Its 286 verses were not all revealed at once but rather over a long period of time; verses from several later sūras were revealed before it was itself completed and, as Sayyid Quṭb says, this sūra contains verses that are among the last of the Qur'ān's to be revealed, such as the verses on *ribā* (usury),[64] namely, vv. 275–276. Yet according to tradition, Prophet Muḥammad purposefully arranged all the verses of this sūra, as of the whole Qur'ān, in the particular sequence they now have in the canonical, received text.

Sayyid Quṭb says that *Sūrat al-Baqara* (Q. 2) consists of several topics (*mawḍū'āt*) united by one double-lined theme (*miḥwar*) whose two main lines (*khaṭṭān*, singular *khaṭṭ*) are strongly bound together. On the one hand, it revolves around the hostile attitude of the Jews to Islam in Medina and their strong friendly relations with the Arabian polytheists and hypocrites. On the other hand, it revolves around the attitude of the Muslim community at the beginning of its growth in Medina and deals with the process of its preparation to carry the responsibility of God's call after the Jews have rejected it. Sayyid Quṭb asserts that all the topics of this sūra revolve around this double-lined axis.[65] His commentary on the sūra attempts to prove his point and he cleverly negotiates his way through its diverse details, bringing them into line with one or the other of its double-lined theme, until he reaches the end of the sūra which, he says, harmoniously harks back to its beginning in its exhortation of human beings to belief in all God's prophets and scriptures as well as in the metaphysical Unseen World.

As Sayyid Quṭb goes from one sūra of the Qur'ān to the next, interpreting its various topics, he continually returns to the concept that each has unity based on a *miḥwar*, to which all its topics are tightly bound. This unity is often made to appear as though it were an organic unity, a unity of a living being whose body parts are organically related to one another and who has a will, an intention, a personality. In the introduction to *Sūrat al-Nisā'* (Q. 4), for example, he says:

> Yet each sūra of the Qur'ān has its special personality, its distinguishing features, and its theme (*miḥwar*) to which all its topics are tightly bound. And among the requisites of the special personality is that each sūra's topics gather themselves in a

> harmonious array around its theme in a system particular to it, in which its features are prominent and by which its personality is made distinct, like a living being with distinct traits and features who – nevertheless – is generally one of his kind.
>
> In this sūra [Q. 4], we see – we almost feel – that it is a living being aiming at a specific purpose, exerting effort for it, and seeking to achieve it by all means. The paragraphs, the verses, the words of this sūra are the means through which it attains what it wants. Hence, we have a feeling of affection and harmony toward it as toward all other sūras of this Qur'ān, a feeling similar to that we experience with a living being of known characteristics and distinct features, who has an intention and a viewpoint, who has life and movement, who has sensation and emotion.[66]

Even when Sayyid Quṭb does not use the word *miḥwar* for theme in his analysis of the sūra's structure, his belief in its unity is clear by his use of other terms. In the introduction to *Sūrat al-Aḥqāf* (Q. 46), for example, he says: "The course (*siyāq*) of the sūra proceeds in four interconnected rounds (*ashwāṭ*, singular *shawṭ*) as though they were one round of four divisions (*maqāṭi'*, singular *maqṭa'*)." Then he goes on to analyze each round and show how they are thematically united.[67]

Unlike other modern Muslim writers on the unity of the sūra in the Qur'ān, and especially unlike Iṣlāḥī (1906–1997) who sees that sūras go together in complementary pairs and that the whole Qur'ān falls into seven groups, each of which is composed of a block of Meccan and a block of Medinan sūras dealing respectively with theoretical and practical aspects of its theme,[68] Sayyid Quṭb does not schematize his literary appreciation of the Qur'ānic text in any manner. He is satisfied with showing the unity in each of the Qur'ān's sūras: this unity is mostly shown to be thematic and semantic, but it is often shown to be also structural as enhanced by the sūra's choice of words and images and their specific grammatical construction, particularly when this choice is highlighted by the sound of words, the rhyme of verses, and the rhythm of sentences to reflect the signification or the intention of the content and sometimes the mood or the atmosphere of the sūra.[69]

As Sayyid Quṭb goes through each sūra of the Qur'ān commenting on its particular theme, he often relates it to the total message of the Holy Book. For he also believes that the Qur'ān as a whole has a coherent unity inasmuch as it has a unitary message, of which the sūras are the blocks that build it up. In his commentary he often refers to what he calls *al-taṣawwur al-islāmī,* i.e., the Islamic conceptualization of existence, which is the basic message of the Qur'ān with all its concomitants of doctrine, outlook, and aspirations.[70] This is evident right from the Opening Chapter of the Qur'ān, *Sūrat al-Fātiḥa* (Q. 1), which – he says – contains the fundamental universals of this Islamic conceptualization despite the sūra's shortness, hence the Islamic duty of reciting it daily in ritual prayers.[71] Faith in God – Sayyid Quṭb asserts – is the basis of this Islamic conceptualization, the basis of the Islamic way of life, the basis of its ethics and economics, the basis of every act the believing Muslim undertakes anywhere.[72]

In his commentary on *Sūrat Āl 'Imrān* (Q. 3), after Sayyid Quṭb analyzes the three lines of its theme, he adds, "And these broad three lines (*khuṭūṭ*, singular *khaṭṭ*) are well-coordinated and complementary in establishing the Islamic conceptualization and in clarifying the reality of the unicity [of God] and its requirements in the life of human beings ..."[73]

In his commentary on almost every sūra, Sayyid Quṭb relates it to this unitary message of the Qur'ān, not merely to show the literary coherence of the Holy Book as a whole, but to emphasize its religious goal and purpose. At one point in his commentary on *Sūrat al-Mā'ida* (Q. 5), he says:

> "Hence we find in this sūra – as we have found in the three previous long ones before it – that it deals with various topics and the link between them is this original *hadaf* (goal, purpose), which the whole Qur'ān came in order to attain, namely, to raise a community, to establish a state, and to organize a society on the basis of a special doctrine, a definite conceptualization, and a new structure ..."[74]

It is not that he confuses the theme of the sūra with the objective of the entire Qur'ān, but that he sees both to be of one kind, like one seeing the whole ocean in a drop of water or the whole universe in a grain of sand. The themes of individual sūras may be different, just as the topics within one sūra may be different. But as these topics within the single sūra are united in producing one theme, the themes of all the sūras of the Qur'ān are likewise united in producing one Qur'ānic message which, in Sayyid Quṭb's brief designation, is the Islamic conceptualization of existence.

This conceptualization is a comprehensive worldview, an all-inclusive apprehension of the universe and of life, to which believers should attune themselves in total commitment to God and in full submission to His will by holding certain beliefs, doing certain things, and abstaining from certain others, if they truly aspire to live a morally good and meaningful life on earth and a blissful one in the Hereafter. It is the Qur'ān's all-encompassing weltanschauung, valid for all times and places because humanity continues to be the same despite change, much as the universe continues to be the same despite movement. To explain this basic idea, Sayyid Quṭb says the following, which is quoted at length because of its importance in explaining his understanding of the objective of the Qur'ān's message:

> This Qur'ān is a reality with an enduring existence, much like this universe itself. The universe is God's book to see and the Qur'ān is

> God's book to read. Each is evidence of its creating Author and a guide to Him, and both exist to do work. The universe continues to move according to its laws and it continues to play the role its Creator decreed for it: the sun continues to run in its orbit and play its role; and the moon, the earth, and the rest of the planets and the stars are not prevented from playing their role by time's lengthy stretch. The newness of this role is in the circumvolution of the universe. Likewise, the Qur'ān has played its role for humankind and continues to be what it always is. Man, too, continues to be what he always is, he continues to be himself in his reality and in the origin of his nature. And this Qur'ān is God's speech to this man – among others God addressed in it. It is a speech that does not change because man himself has not changed in nature, however much the conditions and circumstances around him have changed, and however much these conditions and circumstances have influenced him and he has influenced them. The Qur'ān speaks to him, [as constituted] in his original nature and in his original reality, which are not subject to change or transformation; and it can direct his life today and tomorrow because it has been prepared for that, inasmuch as it is God's last speech and inasmuch as its nature is like that of this universe: unchangeable, moving, without transformation.[75]

This powerful message that Sayyid Quṭb reads in the Qur'ān is the more compelling because, in the Holy Book, it is couched in what he does his best to demonstrate as an unmatchable, unique language with a variety of relevant vocabularies, topics, themes, rhythms, rhymes, tones, moods, styles, structures, and other aesthetic, rhetorical, and psychological modalities of literary expression which, nonetheless, preserve and enhance the unitary character of its conceptualization of existence.

Sayyid Quṭb's Qur'ānic commentary is not similar to works of exegesis known as *tafsīr,* a genre which has a long tradition in the history of Islam. It is rather a free expression of his feelings and thoughts as he religiously reads the Holy Book he loves. When he comments on it, his literary acumen as a critic is coupled with his commitment as a believing Muslim seeking its religious meaning while fathoming its literary structures. Living in the shades of the Qur'ān, as he says, he finds spiritual comfort and inspiration as well as a comprehensive program for life and action within a cogent conceptualization of existence.[76]

Sayyid Quṭb's literary appreciation of the Qur'ān as evidenced in his *al-Taṣwīr al-Fannī fī al-Qur'ān*, his *Mashāhid al-Qiyāma fī al-Qur'ān*, and his *Fī Ẓilāl al-Qur'ān* remains one of the deepest a Muslim has written in modern times. As in all writing on religions by their committed practitioners, there are many religious and ideological assumptions in his thought, with which this paper has not been planned to deal because it has adopted a phenomenological approach in studying Sayyid Quṭb's literary appreciation of the Qur'ān. But for many generations to come, his contributions will remain classical examples of how literary studies of religious scriptures can shed light not only on the nature of religion and its hold on the minds and hearts of its adherents but also on the nature of religious language itself and its ceaseless effort to deal with the ineffable.

NOTES

1 For brief information on Sayyid Quṭb's life and thought, see Shahrough Akhavi, "Qutb, Sayyid" in *The Oxford Encyclopedia of the Modern Islamic World*, 3:400–4 with bibliography.
2 Cairo: Dār al-Ma'ārif, 1945. There are many printings of this book. The one used in this paper is the 14th, that of Cairo-Beirut: Dār al-Shurūq, 1993.
3 Cairo: Dār Sa'd Miṣr bi l-Fajjāla, 1947. There are many printings of this book. The one used in this paper is the 7th, that of Cairo: Dār al-Ma'ārif, 1981.
4 Quṭb, *al-Taṣwīr,* 254, in his comment in 1952 on the third edition of the book. However, in Quṭb, *Mashāhid,* 8, only three further books of the series are mentioned and their titles (with a little variance) are "al-Qiṣṣa fī al-Qur'ān," "al-Manṭiq al-Wijdānī fī al-Qur'ān", and "Asālīb al-'Arḍ al-Fanniyya fī al-Qur'ān". It should be noted, however, that in *al-Taṣwīr,* there is a long chapter on narratives in the Qur'ān entitled "al-Qiṣṣa fī al-Qur'ān," 143–215; there is also a short chapter on human types in the Qur'ān entitled "Namādhij Insāniyya," 216–25; and there is another short chapter on emotive logic in the Qur'ān entitled "al-Manṭiq al-Wijdānī," 226–38. For a study of Quṭb's aesthetics, see John Calvert, "Qur'anic Aesthetics in the Thought of Sayyid Quṭb," *Religious Studies and Theology* 15, 2–3 (Dec. 1996):61–7. See also Leonard Binder, *Islamic Liberalism* (Chicago: University of Chicago Press, 1988), 170–205.
5 Cairo: Dār Iḥyā' al-Kutub al-'Arabiyya, n.d.; second revised edition, 1961. The edition used in this paper is the 15th, that of Cairo-Beirut: Dār al-Shurūq, 1988 in six tomes, with a preface by Muḥammad Quṭb, Sayyid's younger brother. For a study of Quṭb's approach in this book, see Ahmad Shboul, "A New Approach to the Qur'ān: The Work of Sayyid Quṭb," a paper presented at the Second International Congress on the Qur'ān, New Delhi: Indian Institute of Islamic Studies, 1982.
6 For autobiographical information on his childhood, see Sayyid Quṭb, *Ṭifl min al-Qarya* (Beirut: Dār al-Ḥikma, n.d.).
7 Quṭb, *al-Taṣwīr,* 5–8.
8 Ibid., 8.
9 See Sayyid Quṭb, "al-Taṣwīr al-Fannī fī al-Qur'ān," *al-Muqtaṭaf* 94, 2 (Feb. 1939):206–22 and 94, 3 (Mar. 1939):313–18.
10 Sayyid Quṭb wrote seven articles for *al-Risāla* on this subject including "al-Taṣwīr al-Fannī fī al-Qur'ān," *al-Risāla* 13, 601 (1945): 43–6; and "al-Tanāsuq al-Fannī fī Taṣwīr al-Qur'ān," *al-Risāla* 13, 610 (1945): 278–81.
11 Quṭb, *al-Taṣwīr,* 8–10.
12 Ibid., 27.
13 Ibid., 28.
14 Ibid., 29.
15 Ibid., 31.

16 Ibid., 240. See also Sayyid Quṭb, *al-Naqd al-Adabī: Uṣūluh wa Manāhijuh* (Cairo: Dār al-Fikr al-'Arabī, 1960), 129–132 for a brief discussion of al-Jurjānī, to whom the book is dedicated.
17 Quṭb, *al-Taṣwīr*, 34–35.
18 Ibid., 36.
19 Ibid.
20 Ibid., 37.
21 See particularly the long chapter entitled "al-Tanāsuq al-Fannī" in his *al-Taṣwīr*, 87–142. The citations of Qur'ānic proof-texts in this chapter of the book and in others are too many to reproduce in translation.
22 See the chapter entitled "al-Manṭiq al-Wijdānī" in Quṭb's *al-Taṣwīr*, 226–38.
23 Ibid., 229.
24 Ibid., 242.
25 Ibid., 11–13. See also Ibn Hishām, *al-Sīra al-Nabawiyya*, eds. Muṣṭafā al-Saqqā, Ibrāhīm al-Abyārī, and 'Abd al-Ḥafīẓ Shalabī, 2nd edn. (Cairo: Muṣṭafā al-Bābī al-Ḥalabī, 1955), 342–46.
26 Quṭb, *al-Taṣwīr*, 13–14. See also Ibn Hishām, *al-Sīra al-Nabawiyya*, 270–71.
27 Quṭb, *al-Taṣwīr*, 13. This incident is reflected in the Qur'ān (Q. 74:19–26).
28 In *Mashāhid*, 50 n. 1, Sayyid Quṭb mentions that *Sūrat al-Muzzammil* was the third sūra to be revealed although in *al-Taṣwīr*, 23, he mentions it as the second.
29 Ibid., 22–3. See footnote 1, ibid., 19, regarding the chronology of Qur'ānic revelation Quṭb goes by, while admitting there is no certainty in the matter.
30 Ibid., 24.
31 Ibid.
32 Quṭb, *Mashāhid*, 8.
33 See al-Khaṭṭābī, *Bayān I'jāz al-Qur'ān*, published in *Thalāth Rasā'il fī I'jāz al-Qur'ān*, eds. Muḥammad Khalaf Allāh and Muḥammad Zaghlūl Salām (Cairo: Dār al-Ma'ārif, n.d.), 17–65.
34 See al-Rummānī, *al-Nukat fī I'jāz al-Qur'ān*, published in *Thalāth Rasā'il*, 67–104.
35 See Muṣṭafā Ṣādiq al-Rāfi'ī, *I'jāz al-Qur'ān wa al-Balāgha al-Nabawiyya*, 6th edn. (Cairo: Maṭba'at al-Istiqāma, 1956).
36 For a general conspectus of their contributions, see Issa J. Boullata, "The Rhetorical Interpretation of the Qur'ān: *I'jāz* and Related Topics," in Andrew Rippin, ed., *Approaches to the History of the Interpretation of the Qur'ān* (Oxford: Clarendon Press, 1988), 139–57.
37 Quṭb, *al-Taṣwīr*, 87. For *al-tashkhīṣ*, see ibid., 73–5, 95, et passim.
38 Ibid., 254.
39 Quṭb, *Mashāhid*, 9.
40 *Sūrat al-Ra'd* (Q. 13) is considered by Sayyid Quṭb to be among the 17 Medinan period sūras but, based on internal evidence, he later considers it to be Meccan. See *Mashāhid*, 213, n. 1.
41 Ibid., 10.
42 Ibid.
43 Ibid., 11.
44 Ibid., 229.
45 Ibid., 11.
46 See *al-Muslimūn*, 1, 3–9, 1952.
47 For details on the stages of Sayyid Quṭb's writing of *Fī Ẓilāl al-Qur'ān*, see 'Abd Allāh 'Awaḍ al-Khabbāṣ, *Sayyid Quṭb al-Adīb al-Nāqid* (Algiers: Sharikat al-Shihāb li al-Nashr wa al-Tawzī' /and/ al-Zarqā', Jordan: Maktabat al-Manār, n.d. [1983?], 311–13. For details on his imprisonment, trial, and execution, see ibid., 102–9; see also Adnan Ayyub Musallam, "The Formative Stages of Sayyid

Qutb's Intellectual Career and his Emergence as an Islamic Dā'iya, 1906–1952," Ph.D. diss., University of Michigan, 1983, 270–5.

48 Sayyid Quṭb's interest in Muslim societal conditions begins in his book *al-'Adāla al-Ijtimā'iyya fī al-Islām* (Cairo: Lajnat al-Nashr li al-Jāmi'iyyīn, 1949) where he offers his views on the theoretical foundations of the Islamic social system, says where it has gone wrong in history, and suggests what it should do to achieve its ideals; but he does not use the term *jāhilī* to denounce secularized modern society, as he does in later writings.

49 See Yvonne Yazbeck Haddad, "The Qur'anic Justification of an Islamic Revolution: The View of Sayyid Qutb," *The Middle East Journal* 37, 1 (Winter 1983):14–29.

50 Sayyid Quṭb, *Fī Ẓilāl al-Qur'ān*, 1:27–8.

51 For a good study on the sūra as a unity, see Mustansir Mir, "The *Sūra* as a Unity: A Twentieth Century Development in Qur'ān Exegesis," in *Approaches to the Qur'ān*, eds. G. R. Hawting and Abdul-Kader A. Shareef (London-New York: Routledge, 1993), 211–24. See also his *Coherence in the Qur'ān: A Study of Iṣlāḥī's Concept of* Naẓm *in* Tadabbur-i Qur'ān (Indianapolis: American Trust Publications, 1986), esp. 64–74.

52 See, for example, *al-Dīwān: Kitāb fī al-Naqd wa al-Adab* by 'Abbās Maḥmūd al-'Aqqād and Ibrāhīm 'Abd al-Qādir al-Māzinī, 2 vols. (Cairo: Maktabat al-Sa'āda, 1921–1922).

53 Among the new critics, Muḥammad Mandūr, esp. in *Fī al-Mīzān al-Jadīd* (Cairo: Maṭba'at Lajnat al-Ta'līf wa al-Tarjama wa al-Nashr, 1944), called attention to other qualities in the poem in addition to unity, such as tone, imagery, and sensibility.

54 See a brief account on attempts by pre-modern Muslim writers in Mir, *Coherence in the Qur'ān*, 10–19, concentrating on concepts of *naẓm*, *munāsaba*, and *i'jāz*.

55 Thomas Carlyle, *Sartor Resartus and On Heroes and Hero Worship* (London: Everyman, 1908), 299; also quoted in H. A. R. Gibb, *Muhammedanism* (Oxford: Oxford University Press, 1968), 36.

56 R. A. Nicholson, *A Literary History of the Arabs*, 1st paperback edition (Cambridge: At the University Press, 1969; 1st printing: T. Fisher Unwin, 1907), 161; also cited by A. J. Arberry in *Oriental Essays: Portraits of Seven Scholars* (London: George Allen & Unwin Ltd., 1960), 207.

57 See, *Bell's Introduction to the Qur'ān*, rev. and enl. by W. Montgomery Watt (Edinburgh: Edinburgh University Press, 1970), 22.

58 Mustansir Mir says Sayyid Quṭb "does not always make a distinction between the *miḥwar* of a particular sūrah and the *hadaf* of the Qur'ān as a whole." See Mir, *Coherence in the Qur'ān*, 69.

59 Quṭb, *Fī Ẓilāl al-Qur'ān*, 1:27.

60 Ibid.

61 See Mir, *Coherence in the Qur'ān*, 10–19.

62 For modern attempts to study the unity of the Qur'anic sūra, see Mir, *Coherence in the Qur'ān*, 19–24; for details on the contributions of Farāhī (1863–1930) and Iṣlāḥī (1906–1997), see ibid., esp. 25–63. See also Issa J. Boullata, "The Rhetorical Interpretation of the Qur'ān," esp. 149.

63 For other modern exegetes who viewed a sūra as a unity, see Mir, "The *Sūra* as a Unity: A Twentieth Century Development in Qur'ān Exegesis," 211–24; and idem., *Coherence in the Qur'ān*, esp. 25–75.

64 Quṭb, *Fī Ẓilāl al-Qur'ān*, 1:27.

65 Ibid., 28.

66 Ibid., 1:555.

67 Ibid., 6:3252–4.
68 Mir, *Coherence in the Qur'ān*, 75–98. See also Neal Robinson, *Discovering the Qur'an: A Contemporary Approach to a Veiled Text* (London: SCM Press Ltd, 1996), 271–3.
69 See, for example, Quṭb, *Fī Ẓilāl al-Qur'ān*, 1:547–8 or 6:3957–9.
70 For details of this conceptualization, see Sayyid Quṭb, *Khaṣā'iṣ al-Taṣawwur al-Islāmī wa Muqawwimātuh* (Cairo: Dār Iḥyā' al-Kutub al-'Arabiyya, 1962).
71 Quṭb, *Fī Ẓilāl al-Qur'ān*, 1:21, 26
72 Ibid., 1:341.
73 Ibid., 1:358.
74 Ibid., 2:825.
75 Ibid., 1:349.
76 See Sayyid Quṭb's emotional introduction to his *Fī Ẓilāl al-Qur'ān*, 1:13–8.

Bibliography

'Abd al-Bāqī, Muḥammad Fu'ād. *Al-Mu'jam al-Mufahras li-Alfāẓ al-Qur'ān al-Karīm.* Cairo: Kitāb al-Sha'b, n.d.; Beirut: Dār al-Fikr, 1992.

'Abd al-Jabbār. *Al-Mughnī fī Abwāb al-Tawḥīd wa 'l-'Adl.* Vol. 16. Ed. Amīn al-Khūlī. Cairo: Maṭba'at Dār al-Kutub, 1960.

'Abd al-Ṣamad, 'Abd al-Bāsiṭ. *Tajwīd Sūrat al-'Ādiyāt.* Cassette 435. Cairo: n.p., n.d.

Abdel Haleem, M.A.S. "Context and Internal Relationships: Keys to Quranic Exegesis. A Study of *Sūrat al-Raḥmān* (Qur'ān Chapter 55)." In *Approaches to the Qur'ān.* Ed. G.R. Hawting and A. Shareef. London: Routledge, 1993, 71–98.

——. "The Face, Divine and Human, in the Qur'ān." *Islamic Quarterly* 34 (1990):164–79.

'Abduh, Muḥammad and Muḥammad Rashīd Riḍā. *Tafsīr al-Qur'ān al-Ḥakīm,* known as *Tafsīr al-Manār.* 2nd ed. 12 vols. Beirut: Dār al-Ma'rifa, n.d. First publ., Cairo, 1325–53/1907–34.

Abu-Deeb, Kamal. "Al-Jurjānī's Theory of Poetic Imagery and Its Background." Ph.D. dissertation, Oxford University, 1970.

——. *Al-Jurjani's Theory of Poetic Imagery.* Warminster: Aris and Phillips, 1979.

Abū Nu'aym al-Iṣfahānī, Aḥmad b. 'Abd Allāh b. Aḥmad. *Dalā'il al-Nubuwwa.* Beirut: 'Ālam al-Kutub, 1988.

Abū 'Ubayda, Ma'mar ibn al-Muthannā al-Taymī. *Majāz al-Qur'ān.* Cairo: Maktabat al-Khānjī, n.d.; Ed. F. Sezgin. 2 vols. Cairo: Khānjī, 1954, 1955, 1962; Ed. Muḥammad Fu'ād Sizkīn. Beirut: Mu'assasat al-Risāla, 1401/1981.

——. *Al-Naqā'iḍ.* Ed. A. S. Bevan. Leiden: Brill, 1908–1909.

Abū Zahra, Muḥammad. *Al-Mu'jiza al-Kubrā.* Cairo: Dār al-Fikr al-'Arabī, n.d.

Abū Zayd, Naṣr Ḥāmid. *Al-Ittijāh al-'Aqlī fī 'l-Tafsīr: Dirāsa fī Qaḍiyyat al-Majāz fī 'l-Qur'ān 'inda 'l-Mu'tazila.* Beirut: Dār al-Tanwīr wa 'l-Nashr, 1982.

——. *Mafhūm al-Naṣṣ. Dirāsa fī 'Ulūm al-Qur'ān.* Cairo: al-Hay'a al-Miṣriyya al-'Āmma li 'l-Kitāb, 1990.

——. *Naqd al-Khiṭāb al-Dīnī.* Cairo: Sīnā li 'l-Nashr, 1992.

Adūnīs ('Alī Aḥmad Sa'īd). *Al-Naṣṣ al-Qur'ānī wa Āfāq al-Kitāba.* Beirut: Dār al-Ādāb, 1993.

Akhavi, Shahrough. "Qutb, Sayyid." In *The Oxford Encyclopedia of the Modern Islamic World.* 3:400–4.

'Ali, 'Abdullāh Yusuf. *The Holy Qur'ān: Text, Translation and Commentary.* 3rd ed. Lahore: Muḥammad Ashraf, 1979. First publ., Lahore, 1934; Kuwait: Dhāt al-Salāsil, 1984.

Ali, Ahmed. *Al-Qur'ān: a Contemporary Translation*. Princeton: Princeton University Press, 1988.
'Alī, Maulawī Sher. *The Holy Qur'ān*. Rabwah, Pakistan: Quran Publications, 1971.
Ali, Salah Salim. "Misrepresentation of Some Ellipted Structures in the Translation of the Qur'ān by A.Y. Ali and M.M. Pickthall." *Hamdard Islamicus* 17, 4 (1994):27–33.
Almagor, Ella. "The Early Meaning of *Majāz* and the Nature of Abū 'Ubayda's Exegesis." In *Studia Orientalia Memoriae D.H. Baneth Dedicata*. Eds. J. Blau, S. Pines, M.J. Kister, S. Shaked. Jerusalem: The Magnes Press, 1979, 307–26.
Alter, Robert and Frank Kermode, eds. *The Literary Guide to the Bible*. Cambridge, MA: The Belknap Press of Harvard University Press, 1987; first Harvard University Press paperback edition, 1990.
al-Anṣārī, Aḥmad Mālikī. *Abū Zakariyyā al-Farrā'*. Cairo: al-Majlis al-A'lā li-Ri'āyat al-Funūn wa al-Adab wa al-'Ulūm al-Ijtimā'iyya, 1964.
al-'Aqqād, 'Abbās Maḥmūd and Ibrāhīm 'Abd al-Qādir al-Māzinī. *Al-Dīwān: Kitāb fī al-Naqd wa al-Adab*. 2 vols. Cairo: Maktabat al-Sa'āda, 1921–1922.
'Arafa, 'Abd al-'Azīz 'Abd al-Mu'ṭī. *Qaḍiyyat al-I'jāz al-Qur'ānī wa Atharuhā fī Tadwīn al-Balāgha al-'Arabiyya*. Beirut: 'Ālam al-Kutub, 1985.
Arberry, Arthur J. *The Koran Interpreted*. 2 vols. London: George Allen & Unwin Ltd., 1955; Oxford: Oxford University Press, 1964.
——. *Oriental Essays: Portraits of Seven Scholars*. London: George Allen & Unwin Ltd., 1960.
Arkoun, Mohammad. *Lectures du Coran*. Paris: Maisonneuve and Larose, 1982.
——. *Ouvertures sur l'Islam*. 2nd ed. Paris: Jacques Grancher, 1992.
——. *Pour une critique de la raison islamique*. Paris: Maisonneuve and Larose, 1984.
Asad, Muhammad. *The Message of the Qur'ān*. Gibraltar: Dār al-Andalus, 1980.
al-'Askarī, al-Ḥasan. *Kitāb al-Ṣinā'atayn*. Eds. 'Alī Muḥammad al-Bijāwī and Muḥammad Abū al-Faḍl Ibrāhīm. Cairo: 'Īsā al-Bābī al-Ḥalabī, 1971; Ed. Mufīd Qamīma. Beirut: Dār al-Kutub al-'Ilmiyya, 1981.
Assmann, Aleida and Jan Assmann. "Kanon und Zensur als kultursoziologische Kategorien." In *Kanon und Zensur. Archäologie der literarischen Kommunikation II*. Eds. Aleida and J. Assmann. Munich: Fink, 1987.
Assmann, Jan. *Das kulturelle Gedächtnis. Schrift, Erinnerung und politische Identität in frühen Hochkulturen*. Munich: Beck, 1992.
Audebert, Claude-France. *Al-Ḫaṭṭābī et l'inimitabilité du Coran: Traduction et introduction au Bayān I'ğāz al-Qur'ān*. Damascus: Institut Français de Damas, 1982.
Augustinus, Aurelius. *Bekenntnisse*. Transl. by Wilhelm Thimme. Zürich and Stuttgart: Artemis, 1950.
Awn, Peter J. *Satan's Tragedy and Redemption. Iblis in Sufi Psychology*. Leiden: E.J. Brill, 1983.
Ayoub, Mahmoud M. *The Awesome News, Interpetation of Juz' 'Amma – The Last Part of the Qur'ān*. N.p.: World Islamic Call Society, second edition, 1997.
——. *The Qur'ān and Its Interpreters*. 2 vols. Albany: State University of New York Press, 1984.
al-'Ayyāshī, Muḥammad. *Naẓariyyat Īqā' al-Shi'r al-'Arabī*. Tunis: al-Maṭba'a al-'Aṣriyya, 1976.
al-Azmeh, Aziz. "The Muslim Canon from Late Antiquity to the Era of Modernism." Unpublished.
Baalbaki, R. "Some Aspects of Harmony and Hierarchy in Sībawayhi's Grammatical Analysis." *Zeitschrift für Arabische Linguistik* 2 (1979):7–22.
al-Baghdādī, Muḥammad ibn Ḥabīb. *Kitāb al-Munammaq fī Akhbār Quraysh*. Ed. Khūrshīd Fārūq. Haydarabād: Dā'irat al-Ma'ārif al-'Uthmāniyya, 1964.

Bal, Mieke. *Narratology: Introduction to the Theory of Narrative.* Trans. Christine van Boheemen. Toronto: University of Toronto Press, 1985. From the 2nd ed. of *De theorie van vertellen en verhalen.* Muiderberg: Coutinho, 1980.

Balentine, Samuel E. *The Hidden God. The Hiding of the Face of God in the Old Testament.* Oxford: Oxford University Press, 1983.

Baljon, J. M. S. "'To Seek the Face of God' in Koran and Hadith." *Acta Orientalia* 21 (1953):254–66.

Baneth, D. Z. H. "What Did Muhammad Mean When He Called His Religion 'Islam'? – the Original Meaning of *Aslama* and Its Derivatives." *Israel Oriental Studies* 1 (1971):183–90.

al-Bāqillānī, Abū Bakr Muḥammad b. al-Ṭayyib. *I'jāz al-Qur'ān.* Ed. al-Sayyid Aḥmad Ṣaqr. Cairo: Dār al-Ma'ārif, [1954], 1981; Beirut: 'Ālam al-Kutub, 1988.

——. "Kitāb I'jāz al-Qur'ān." In Jalāl al-Dīn al-Suyūṭī, *al-Itqān fī 'Ulūm al-Qur'ān.* 2 vols. N.p.: Dār al-Fikr, n.d.

Bauer, Thomas. "Liebe und Liebesdichtung in der arabischen Welt des 9. und 10. Jahrhunderts. Eine literatur- und mentalitätsgeschichtliche Studie des arabischen Gazal." Unpublished habilitation thesis submitted to the University of Erlangen, 1996.

al-Bayḍāwī, 'Abd Allāh ibn 'Umar al-Shīrāzī. *Anwar al-Tanzīl wa Asrār al-Ta'wīl,* known as *Tafsīr al-Bayḍāwī.* 5 vols. (bound in two). Beirut: Dār al-Jīl, n.d.; Beirut: Mu'assasat Sha'bān li 'l-Nashr wa 'l-Tawzī', n.d.

al-Bayhaqī, Abū Bakr Aḥmad b. Ḥusayn. *Dalā'il al-Nubuwwa.* 2 vols. Ed. 'Abd al-Raḥmān Muḥammad 'Uthmān. Cairo: Dār al-Nashr li 'l-Ṭibā'a, 1969.

Bell, Richard. *A Commentary on the Qur'ān.* Ed. C.E. Bosworth and M.E.J. Richardson. 2 vols. Manchester: Manchester University Press, 1991.

——. *The Qur'ān, Translated, with a Critical Re-arrangement of the Surahs.* 2 vols. Edinburgh: Edinburgh University Press, 1937–39, 1960.

Ben Milad, Mahjoub. "Ambiguïté et *mathani* coraniques." In *L'ambivalence dans la culture arabe.* Ed. P. Alexandre, R. Arnaldez et al., Paris: Éditions Anthropos, 1967, 366–81.

Bennabi, Malik, *Le Phénomène coranique.* Kuwait: International Islamic Federation of Student Organizations, 1977.

Bennett, Tony. "Texts, Readers, Reading Formations." In *Modern Literary Theory: A Reader.* Eds. Philip Rice and Patricia Waugh. 2nd ed. London: Edward Arnold, 1992. Originally published in *The Bulletin of the Midwest Modern Language Association* 16 (1983):3–17.

Binder, Leonard. *Islamic Liberalism.* Chicago: University of Chicago Press, 1988.

Bint al-Shāṭi'. *Al-I'jāz al-Bayānī li 'l-Qur'ān wa Masā'il Ibn al-Azraq.* Cairo: Dār al-Ma'ārif, 1984.

Blachère, Régis. *Introduction au Coran.* 2nd ed. Paris: G.-P. Maisonneuve et Larose, 1977. 1st ed., 1947.

——. *Le Coran (al-Qor'ân), traduit de l'arabe.* Paris: G.-P. Maisonneuve & Larose, 1966.

——. *Le Coran, traduction nouvelle. Traduction selon le reclassement des Sourates d'après les quatre phases successives de la prédiction de Mahomet, accompagnée d'une annotation et de commentaires philologiques.* 2 vols. Paris: G.-P. Maisonneuve, 1949–50.

——. *Le Coran, Traduction selon un essai de reclassement des sourates.* Paris: Maisonneuve & Co, 1949.

Booth, Wayne. *The Rhetoric of Fiction.* 2nd ed. Chicago: University of Chicago Press, 1983.

Bosworth, C.E. "Madyan Shu'ayb in Pre-Islamic and Early Islamic Lore and History." *Journal of Semitic Studies* 29 (1984):53–64.

Boullata, Issa J. "I'jāz." *Encyclopedia of Religion.* Ed. Mircea Eliade. New York: Macmillan, 1987. 7: 87–8.

——. "The Rhetorical Interpretation of the Qur'ān: *I'jāz* and Related Topics." In *Approaches to the History of the Interpretation of the Qur'ān.* Ed. Andrew Rippin. Oxford: Clarendon Press, 1988, 139–57.

Böwering, Gerhard. "The Scriptural 'Senses' in Medieval Sufi Qur'ān Exegesis." Forthcoming in *With Reverence for the Word: Medieval Scriptural Exegesis in Judaism, Christianity and Islam.* Ed. J. McAuliffe et al.

Bravmann, Meir M. "Arabic *Aslama* (*Islām*) and Related Terms." In Meir M. Bravmann *Studies in Semitic Philology.* Leiden: E. J. Brill, 1977, 434–54.

——. *The Spiritual Background of Early Islam. Studies in Ancient Arab Concepts.* Leiden: E. J. Brill, 1972.

Brockelmann, Carl. "Abū Bakr Muḥammad b. al-Qāsim b. al-Anbārī." *EI*[2]. s.v.

——. *Geschichte der arabischen Litteratur.* 2nd rev. ed. 2 vols. + 3 supls. Leiden: Brill, 1937–1949.

al-Bukhārī, Muḥammad b. Ismā'īl. *Kitāb al-Jāmi' al-Ṣaḥiḥ.* Ed. Ḥasūna al-Nawawī. 9 vols. Cairo: Maktabat al-Bābī al-Ḥalabī wa Awlādihi, 1958; *Ṣaḥīḥ.* Cairo: Muṣṭafā al-Bābī, 1953; *Ṣaḥīḥ al-Bukhārī.* Cairo: 'Abd al-Salām Ibn Muḥammad Ibn Shaqrūn, 1314 H.

Burton, John. *The Collection of the Qur'an.* Cambridge: Cambridge University Press, 1977.

Bustānī, Maḥmūd. *Eslām wa-Honar.* Trans. Ḥosain Ṣāberī. Teheran: Bonyād-e Pažūheshhā-e Eslāmī, 1993.

Cachia, P.J.E. "Bayḍāwī on the *Fawātiḥ.*" *Journal of Semitic Studies* 13 (1968):218–31.

Calinescu, Matei. *Rereading.* New Haven: Yale University Press, 1993.

Calverley, E.E. "Doctrines of the Soul (*Nafs* and *Rūḥ*) in Islam." *Moslem World* 33 (1943):254–65.

Calvert, John. "Qur'anic Aesthetics in the Thought of Sayyid Quṭb." *Religious Studies and Theology* 15, 2–3 (Dec. 1996):61–7.

Cantarino, Vicente. *Arabic Poetics in the Golden Age.* Leiden: Brill, 1975.

Carlyle, Thomas. *Sartor Resartus and On Heroes and Hero Worship.* London: Everyman, 1908.

Carpenter, David. *Revelation, History, and the Dialogue of Religions: A Study of Bhartrhari and Bonaventure.* Maryknoll, NY: Orbis Books, 1995.

Chatman, Seymour. *Story and Discourse: Narrative Structure in Fiction and Film.* Ithaca: Cornell University Press, 1978.

Childs, B.S. *Biblical Theology of the Old and New Testaments. Theological Reflection on the Christian Bible.* London: SCM Press, 1992.

Cornis-Pope, Marcel. *Hermeneutic Desire and Critical Rewriting: Narrative Interpretation in the Wake of Poststructuralism.* Basingstoke: Macmillan Press, 1992.

Cortes, Julio. *El Coran, edición, traducción y notas.* Madrid: Editora Nacional, 1979.

Cragg, Kenneth. *The Mind of the Qur'ān.* London: George Allen and Unwin, 1973.

Culler, Jonathan. *The Pursuit of Signs: Semiotics, Literature, Deconstruction.* London: Routledge & Kegan Paul, 1981.

Ḍayf, Shawqī. *Tārīkh al-Adab al-'Arabī.* 2 vols. Cairo: Dār al-Ma'ārif, 1960.

Darnton, Robert. "First Steps Toward a History of Reading." *The Kiss of Lamourette: Reflections in Cultural History.* New York: Norton, 1990.

Darwaza, M. 'I. *Al-Tafsīr al-Ḥadīth.* Cairo: 'Īsā al-Bābī al-Ḥalabī, 1962.

Dohmen, Chr. and M. Oeming. *Biblischer Kanon warum und wozu?* Freiburg: Herder, 1992.

Ehlich, K. "Text und sprachliches Handeln. Die Entstehung von Texten aus dem Bedürfnis nach Überlieferung." In *Schrift und Gedächtnis. Archäologie der*

literarischen Kommunikation I. Eds. A. Assmann, J. Assmann and Chr. Hardmeier. Munich: W. Fink, 1983, 24–44.
Encyclopaedia Britannica. 1984 edition s.v. "horses".
van Ess, Josef. "Review of Wansbrough's *Quranic Studies.*" *Bibliotheca Orientalis* 35 (1978):349–53.
——. *Theologie und Gesellschaft im 2. und 3. Jahrhundert Hidschra. Eine Geschichte des religiösen Denkens.* 6 vols. Berlin/New York: de Gruyter, 1991–1997.
al-Farāhī, Ḥamīd al-Dīn 'Abd al-Ḥamīd. *Dalā'il al-Niẓām.* Azamgarh, India: Al-Dā'ira al-Ḥamīdiyya wa Maktabatuhā, 1968.
——. *Majmū'a-yi Tafāsīr-i Farāhī.* Tr. Amīn Aḥsan Iṣlāḥī. Lahore: Anjuman-i Khuddāmu'lqur'ān, 1973.
——. *Al-Takmīl fī Uṣūl al-Ta'wīl.* Azamgarh, India: Al-Dā'ira al-Ḥamīdiyya wa Maktabatuhā, 1968.
al-Farrā', Yaḥyā ibn Ziyād. *Ma'ānī 'l-Qur'ān.* 3 vols. Ed. 'Abd al-Fattāḥ Shalābī, rev. 'Alī Nāṣif. Cairo: al-Hay'a al-'Āmma li 'l-Kitāb, 1973.
Fish, Stanley. *Doing What Comes Naturally: Change, Rhetoric, and the Practice of Theory in Literary and Legal Studies.* Durham: Duke University Press, 1989.
——. *Is There a Text in This Class? The Authority of Interpretive Communities.* Cambridge: Harvard University Press, 1980.
Flügel, Gustav. *Concordantiae Corani arabicae.* Leipzig, 1841.
Frye, Northrup. *The Great Code: The Bible and Literature.* New York: Harcourt Brace Jovanovich Publishers, 1982.
Furrer, Priska. "Fenster zur Welt oder selbstreflektierender Spiegel? Referentialität und Textualität in der modernen türkischen Erzählliteratur." *Asiatische Studien* 50/2 (1996):321–38.
van Gelder, G.J.H. "Brevity: the Long and the Short of it in Classical Arabic Literary Theory." In *Proceedings of the Ninth Congress of the Union Européenne des Arabisants et Islamisants.* Ed. Rudolph Peters. Leiden: E.J. Brill, 1981, 78–88.
Geller, Stephen A. "Were the Prophets Poets?" *Prooftexts* 3 (1983):211–21.
Genette, Gérard. *Palimpsestes: la littérature au second degré.* Paris: Seuil, 1982. English trans., Channa Newman and Claude Doubinsky. Lincoln: University of Nebraska Press, 1997.
al-Gharnāṭī, 'Abd al-Ḥaqq b. 'Aṭiyya. *Al-Muḥarrar al-Wajīz fī Tafsīr al-Kitāb al-'Azīz.* Ed. Aḥmad Ṣāriq al-Mallāḥ. Cairo: al-Majlis al-A'lā li 'l-Shu'ūn al-Islāmiyya, 1399/1979.
Gibb, H.A.R. *Muhammedanism.* Oxford: Oxford University Press, 1968.
Gilliot, Claude. "Coran (l'exégèse du Coran)." In *Encyclopaedia Universalis.* Ed. Jacques Bersani. Paris: Encyclopaedia Universalis, 1995. 6:543–8.
——. "Muqātil, grand exégète, traditionniste et théologien maudit." *Journal Asiatique* 279 (1991):39–92.
Gluck, J.J. "Is there Poetry in the Qur'ān?" *Semitics* 8 (1982):43–89.
Goldziher, Ignaz. *Die Richtungen der islamischen Koranauslegung.* Leiden: Brill, 1920.
Good, Edwin M. *Irony in the Old Testament.* Philadelphia: The Westminster Press, 1965.
Gouda, Ahmad. "Qur'ānic Recitation: Phonological Analysis." Ph.D. dissertation, George Washington University, 1988.
von Grunebaum, Gustave E. "I'djāz." EI^2. III:1018–20.
——. *A Tenth-Century Document of Arabic Literary Theory and Criticism.* Chicago: The University of Chicago Press, 1950.
Guardini, Romano. *Christliches Bewußtsein. Versuche über Pascal.* Munich: dtv, 1962.
Guillaume, A. *The Life of Muhammad.* London, New York and Toronto: Oxford University Press, 1955.

Haddad, Yvonne Yazbeck. "The Qur'anic Justification of an Islamic Revolution: The View of Sayyid Qutb." *The Middle East Journal* 37, 1 (Winter 1983):14–29.

Halbwachs, Maurice. *La mémoire collective.* Paris: PUF, 1969.

——. *Les cadres sociaux de la mémoire.* Paris: Mouton, 1976.

Hawting, G.R. and Abdul-Kader A. Shareef, eds. *Approaches to the Qur'ān.* London-New York: Routledge, 1993.

Heinrichs, Wolfhart. "Contacts between Scriptural Hermeneutics and Literary Theory in Islam: the Case of *Majāz.*" *Zeitschrift für Geschichte der Arabisch-Islamischen Wissenschaften* 7 (1991/92):253–84.

——. *The Hand of the Northwind. Opinions on Metaphor and the Early Meaning of Isti'āra in Arabic Poetics.* Wiesbaden: Deutsche Morgenländische Gesellschaft, 1977.

——. "*Isti'ārah* and *Badī'* and Their Terminological Relationship in Early Arabic Literary Criticism." *Zeitschrift für Geschichte der Arabisch-Islamischen Wissenschaften* 1 (1984):180–211.

——. "On the Genesis of the *Ḥaqīqa-Majāz* Dichotomy." *Studia Islamica* 59 (1984):111–40.

Highet, Gilbert. *The Anatomy of Satire.* Princeton: Princeton University Press, 1962.

al-Ḥillāwī, Nāṣir. "Abū 'Ubaida Ma'mar b. al-Muthannā." Ph.D. thesis, S.O.A.S., University of London, January, 1966.

Holl, Karl. *Gesammelte Aufsätze zur Kirchengeschichte. I. Band: Luther.* 6th rev. ed. Tübingen: Moll, 1932.

Holub, Robert. *Crossing Borders: Reception Theory, Poststructuralism, Deconstruction.* Madison: University of Wisconsin Press, 1992.

——. *Reception Theory: A Critical Introduction.* London: Methuen, 1984.

Horovitz, J. *Koranische Untersuchungen.* Berlin: de Gruyter, 1926.

Humphreys, W. Lee. *Joseph and His Family: A Literary Study.* Columbia, South Carolina: University of South Carolina Press, 1988.

Ḥusayn, Ṭāhā. *Dhikrā Abī al-'Alā'.* Cairo, 1915.

——. *Ḥadīth al-Arbi'ā'.* 3 vols. Beirut: al-Sharika al-'Ālamiyya li 'l-Kitāb, 1980.

——. *Min Ḥadīth al-Shi'r wa 'l-Nathr.* 10th printing. Cairo: Dār al-Ma'ārif, 1969. First printing, 1936.

Ḥuseini, Isḥāq Mūsā. *The Life and Works of Ibn Qutayba.* Beirut: The American Press, 1950.

Ibn al-'Arabī, Muḥammad b. 'Abdallāh. *Aḥkām al-Qur'ān.* Ed. Muḥammad 'Abd al-Qādir 'Aṭā'. Beirut: Dār al-Kutub al-'Ilmiyya, 1408/1988.

——. *'Āriḍāt al-Aḥwadhī bi-Sharḥ Ṣaḥīḥ al-Tirmidhī.* Beirut: Dār al-'Ilm li 'l-Jamī', 1972.

Ibn al-Anbārī. *Nuzhat al-Alibbā'.* Baghdad, 1294/1877.

Ibn 'Āshūr, Muḥammad al-Ṭāhir. *Tafsīr al-Taḥrīr wa al-Tanwīr.* 17 vols. Tunis: al-Dār al-Tūnisiyya li-al-Nashr, 1971.

Ibn al-Athīr, Ḍiyā' al-Dīn. *Al-Kalām al-Sā'ir fī Adab al-Kātib wa 'l-Shā'ir.* Eds. Aḥmad al-Ḥūfī and Badawī Ṭabāna. Cairo: Maktabat Nahḍat Miṣr, 1959.

Ibn Ḥanbal, Aḥmad b. Muḥammd. *Al-Musnad.* Ed. Aḥmad Muḥammad Shākir. 15 vols. Cairo: Dār al-Ma'ārif, 1956.

Ibn Hishām, Abū Muḥammad 'Abd al-Malik. *Al-Sīra al-Nabawiyya.* 4 vols. Eds. Muṣṭafā al-Saqqā, Ibrāhīm al-Abyārī and 'Abd al-Ḥafīẓ Shalabī. Cairo: Dār al-Ma'rifa, 1355/1937. Repr. Beirut: 1391/1971; 2nd ed. Cairo: Muṣṭafā al-Bābī al-Ḥalabī, 1955.

——. *The Life of Muhammad.* Transl. by Alfred Guillaume. Karachi: Oxford University Press, 1967

Ibn al-Jawzī, Abū al-Faraj 'Abd al-Raḥmān b. 'Alī b. Muḥammad. *Al-Muntaẓam fī Ta'rīkh al-Mulūk wa 'l-Umam.* Eds. Muṣṭafā and Muḥammad 'Abd al-Qādir 'Aṭā. 16 vols. Beirut: Dār al-Kutub al-'Ilmiyya, 1415/1995.

——. *Zād al-Masīr fī 'Ilm al-Tafsīr.* Beirut: al-Maktab al-Islāmī, 1404/1984.

Ibn Kathīr, Abū l-Fidā' Ismā'īl b. 'Umar. *Al-Sīra al-Nabawiyya.* 4 vols. Ed. Muṣṭafā 'Abd al-Wāḥid. Beirut: Dār al-Rā'id al-'Arabī, 1987.

——. *Mukhtaṣar Tafsīr Ibn Kathīr (Tafsīr al-Qur'ān al-'Aẓīm).* 2 vols. Beirut: Dār al-Ma'rifa, 1983, 1987; *Tafsīr al-Qur'ān al-'Aẓīm.* Beirut: Dār al-Fikr, 1966, 1389/ 1970.

Ibn Khallikān, Abū al-'Abbās Shams al-Dīn Aḥmad ibn Muḥammad ibn Abī Bakr. *Wafayāt al-A'yān wa Anbā' Abnā' al-Zamān.* Būlāq: Maṭba'at Būlāq, 1298/ 1880; Ed. Iḥsān 'Abbās. 8 vols. Beirut: Dār al-Thaqāfa, 1971.

Ibn Manẓūr, Muḥammad ibn Mukarram. *Lisān al-'Arab.* 6 vols. Cairo: Dār al-Ma'ārif, n.d.; 15 vols. Beirut: Dār Ṣādir, n.d.

Ibn Qayyim al-Jawziyya. *Al-Tibyān fī Aqsām al-Qur'ān.* Ed. Ṭāhā Shāhīn. Beirut: Dār al-Kutub al-'Ilmiyya, 1982.

Ibn Qutayba, 'Abdallāh b. Muslim al-Dīnawarī. *Ta'wīl Mushkil al-Qur'ān.* Ed. al-Sayyid Aḥmad Ṣaqr. Cairo: 'Īsā al-Bābī al-Ḥalabī, 1954; Ed. al-Sayyid Aḥmad Ṣaqr. Cairo: Dār al-Turāth, 1973; Ed. al-Sayyid Aḥmad Ṣaqr. Beirut: Dār al-Kutub al-'Ilmiyya, 1401/1981; Eds. 'Umar Muḥammad Sa'īd 'Abd al-'Azīz & 'Abd al-Ṣabūr Shāhīn, 1989.

Ibn Sa'd, Muḥammad. *Al-Ṭabaqāt al-Kubrā (= Biographien Muhammeds, seiner Gefährten und der späteren Träger des Islams bis zum Jahre 230 der Flucht).* Ed. Eduard Sachau. 9 vols. Leiden: Brill, 1905–1917.

Ibn Taymiyya. *Kitāb al-Īmān.* Cairo, 1325 A. H.

Iṣlāḥī, Amīn Aḥsan. *Tadabbur-i Qur'ān.* 8 vols. [vols. 1–2: Lahore: Dār al-Ishā'āt al-Islāmiyya, 1387–1391/1967–1971; vols. 3–4: Lahore: Anjuman-i Khuddām' ulqur'ān, 1393–1396/1973–1976; vols. 5–8: Lahore: Fārā Foundation, 1398–1400/1977–1980].

Iser, Wolfgang. *The Act of Reading: A Theory of Aesthetic Response.* Baltimore: Johns Hopkins University Press, 1978. Originally published as *Der Akt des Lesens. Theorie ästhetischer Wirkung.* Munich: Wilhelm Fink, 1976.

——. *The Implied Reader: Patterns of Communication in Prose Fiction from Bunyan to Beckett.* Baltimore: Johns Hopkins University Press, 1974. Originally published as *Der Implizite Leser: Kommunikationsformen des Romans von Bunyan bis Beckett.* Munich: Wilhelm Fink, 1972.

'Iyāḍ, al-Qāḍī Abū 'l-Faḍl. *Al-Shifā' bi-Ta'rīf Ḥuqūq al-Muṣṭafā.* Beirut: Dār al-Kutub al-'Ilmiyya, n.d.

Izutsu, Toshihiko. *Ethico-Religious Concepts in the Qur'ān.* Montreal: McGill University Press, 1966.

——. *God and Man in the Koran: Semantics of the Koranic Weltanschauung.* Tokyo: The Keio Institute of Cultural and Linguistic Studies, 1964.

al-Jāḥiẓ, Abū 'Uthmān 'Amr ibn Baḥr. *Al-Ḥayawān.* 7 vols. Ed. Yaḥyā al-Shāmī. Beirut: Dār wa Maktabat al-Hilāl, 1986; *Kitāb al-Ḥayawān.* 8 vols. Ed. 'Abd al-Salām Muḥammad Hārūn. Cairo: Maktabat al-Bābī al-Ḥalabī wa Awlādihi, n.d.; Ed. 'Abd al-Salām Muḥammad Hārūn. Cairo: Maktabat Muṣṭafā al-Bābī al-Ḥalabī, 1938–1945.

——. "Risāla fī Fakhr al-Sūdān." In *Rasā'il al-Jāḥiẓ.* Ed. 'Abd al-Salām Muḥammad Hārūn. Cairo: Maktabat al-Khānjī, 1964.

James, William. *The Varieties of Religious Experience: A Study in Human Nature, Being the Gifford Lectures on Natural Religion Delivered at Edinbburgh in 1901–1902.* New York: Random House/The Modern Library, n.d.

Jansen, J.J.G. "Polemics on Mustafa Mahmud's Koran Exegesis." *Proceedings of the Ninth Congress of the Union Européenne des Arabisants et Islamisants, Amsterdam, 1st to 7th September 1978.* Ed. R. Peters. Leiden: E.J. Brill, 1981.

al-Jarbī, Muḥammad Ramaḍān. *Ibn Qutayba wa Maqāyīsuh al-Balāghiyya wa 'l-Adabiyya wa 'l-Naqdiyya.* Tripoli: al-Munsha'a al-'Āmma li-'l-Nashr wa 'l-Tawzī' wa 'l-I'lān, 1984.

Jauss, Hans Robert. *Aesthetic Experience and Literary Hermeneutics.* Trans. Michael Shaw. Minneapolis: University of Minnesota Press, 1982. Originally published as *Ästhetische Erfahrung und literarische Hermeneutik I.* Munich: Wilhelm Fink, 1977.

——. *Rhetorical Power.* Ithaca: Cornell University Press, 1989.

——. *Toward an Aesthetic of Reception.* Trans. Timothy Bahti. Minneapolis: University of Minnesota Press, 1982.

Jawharī, Ṭanṭawī. *Al-Jawāhir fī Tafsīr al-Qur'ān al-Karīm, al-Mushtamil 'alā 'Ajā'ib Badā'i' al-Mukawwanāt wa Gharā'ib al-Āyāt al-Bāhirāt.* 25 vols. Cairo: Muṣṭafā al-Bābī al-Ḥalabī, 1350/1932.

Jeffery, Arthur. *The Foreign Vocabulary of the Qur'an.* Baroda: The Oriental Institute, 1938.

——. *Materials for the History of the Text of the Qur'an.* Leiden: Brill, 1937.

——. *The Qur'ān as Scripture.* New York: R.F. Moore Co., 1952.

——. *Two Muqaddimas to the Qur'anic Sciences: the Muqaddima to the Kitab al-Mabani and the Muqaddima of Ibn 'Atiyya to his Tafsir.* Edited from the MSS in Berlin and in Cairo. 2nd ed. revised by 'Abdullāh Ismā'īl al-Ṣāwī. Cairo: Maktabat al-Khānijī, 1392/1972.

al-Jemaey, Awad. "Al-Rummānī's al-Nukat fī I'jāz al-Qur'ān: an Annotated Translation with Introduction." Ph.D. dissertation, Indiana University, 1987.

Johns, A.H. "Ellipsis in the Qur'ān: A Response to Salah Salim Ali." *Hamdard Islamicus* 18, 2 (1995):15–23.

——. "The Quranic Presentation of the Joseph Story." In *Approaches to the Qur'ān.* Eds. G.R. Hawting and Abdel-Kader Shareef. London: Routledge, 1993, 37–70.

Johnson, Aubrey R. "Aspects of the Use of the Term [penim] in the Old Testament." In *Festschrift Otto Eissfeldt zum 60. Geburtstag 1. September 1947.* Ed. Johann Fück. Halle: Max Niemeyer Verlag, 1967, 155–9.

Joyce, Paul. *Divine Initiative and Human Response in Ezekiel.* Sheffield: JSOT Press, 1989.

al-Jurjānī, 'Abd al-Qāhir. *Asrār al-Balāgha.* Ed. Helmut Ritter. Istanbul: Government Press, 1954.

——. *Dalā'il al-I'jāz.* Damascus: Maktabat Sa'd al-Dīn, 1987.

——. "Al-Risāla al-Shāfiya fi I'jāz al-Qur'ān." In *Thalāth Rasā'il fī I'jāz al-Qur'ān.* Eds. Muḥammad Khalaf Allāh Aḥmad and Muḥammad Zaghlūl Sallām. Cairo, 1956.

al-Juwaynī, Muṣṭafā al-Ṣāwī. *Manhaj al-Zamakhsharī fī Tafsīr al-Qur'ān.* Cairo: Dār al-Ma'ārif, 1959.

Juynboll, G.H.A. "The Position of Qur'ān Recitation in Early Islam." *Journal of Semitic Studies* 19 (1974):240–51.

Kassem-Draz, Ceza. "*Tawālud al-Nuṣūṣ wa Ishbā' al-Dalāla: Taṭbīq 'alā Tafsīr al-Qur'ān.*" *Alif* 8 (1988):31–81.

Kermani, Navid. "Revelation in Its Aesthetic Dimension. Some Notes about Apostles and Artists in Islamic and Christian Culture." In *The Qur'ān as Text.* Ed. Stefan Wild. Leiden: Brill, 1996, 213–24.

——. *Gott ist schön. Das ästhetische Erleben des Koran.* Munich: Beck, 1999.

——. *Offenbarung als Kommunikation. Das Konzept waḥy in Naṣr Ḥāmid Abū Zayd, Mafhūm an-naṣṣ.* Frankfurt: Lang, 1996.

al-Khabbāṣ, 'Abd Allāh 'Awaḍ. *Sayyid Quṭb al-Adīb al-Nāqid.* Algiers: Sharikat al-Shihāb li al-Nashr wa al-Tawzī' /and/ al-Zarqā', Jordan: Maktabat al-Manār, n.d. [1983?].

Khan, Geoffrey. *Studies in Semitic Syntax.* London Oriental Series, 38. New York, Oxford, Toronto: Oxford University Press, 1988.

al-Khaṭīb al-Baghdādī. *Tārīkh Baghdād.* Cairo: Maktabat al-Khānjī, 1931.

al-Khaṭīb, Abd al-Karīm. *I'jāz al-Qur'ān.* Cairo: Dār al-Fikr al-'Arabī, 1964.

al-Khaṭṭābī. *Bayān I'jāz al-Qur'ān*. In *Thalāth Rasā'il fī I'jāz al-Qur'ān*. Eds. M. Zaghlūl Sallām and M. Khalaf Allāh. Cairo: Dār al-Ma'ārif, 1956, 17–65.
al-Khūlī, Amīn. *Manāhij Tajdīd*. Cairo: Dār al-Ma'ārif, 1961.
Kinberg, Leah. "*Muḥkamāt* and *Mutashābihāt* (Koran 3/7): Implication of a Koranic Pair of Terms in Medieval Exegesis." *Arabica* 35 (1988):143–72.
Kinberg, N. *A Lexicon of al-Farrā"s Terminology in His Qur'ān Commentary*. Leiden: E.J. Brill, 1996.
Labid Ibn Rabiah. *The Golden Ode*. Translated with an Introduction and Commentary by William R. Polk. Chicago: University of Chicago Press, 1974.
Lagarde, Michel. "De l'ambiguïté (mutašābih) dans le Coran: tentatives d'explication des exégètes musulmans." *Quaderni di studi arabi* 3 (1985):45–62.
Lane, Edward William. *Selections of the Ḳur-ān with an Interwoven Commentary*. London: H. Bohn, 1843.
Lassen, Eva Maria. "Family as Metaphor: Family Images at the Time of the Old Testament and Early Judaism." *Scandinavian Journal of the Old Testament* 6 (1992):247–62.
Lecomte, Gérard. "Ibn Ḳutayba." EI^2, III:844–7.
——. *Ibn Qutayba (mort en 276/889): l'homme, son oeuvre, ses idées*. Damascus: Institut Français de Damas, 1965.
Leemhuis, F. 'A Koranic Contest Poem in Sūrat al-Ṣāffāt.' In *Dispute Poems and Dialogues in the Ancient and Medieval Near East*. Eds. G.J. Reinink and H.L.J. Vanstiphout. Leuven: Departement Orientalistiek: Uitgeverij Peeters, 1991. Series Orientalia Lovaniensia Analecta 42, 165–77.
Lilje, Hans. *Luther*. Reinbek bei Hamburg: Rowohlt, 1965.
Luckmann, Th. "Kanon und Konversion." In *Kanon und Zensur. Archäologie der literarischen Kommunikation II*. Eds. Aleida and J. Assmann. Munich: Fink, 1987, 38–46.
MacDonald, D.B. "The Development of the Idea of Spirit in Islam." *Acta Orientalia* 9 (1931):307–51.
MacKay, Floyd W. "Ibn Qutayba's Understanding of Quranic Brevity." M.A. thesis, McGill University, 1991.
Mailloux, Steven. *Interpretive Conventions: The Reader in the Study of American Fiction*. Ithaca: Cornell University Press, 1982.
——. "Learning to Read: Interpretation and Reader-response Criticism." *Studies in the Literary Imagination* 12 (1979):93–108.
——. "Power, Rhetoric, and Theory: Reading American Texts." In *Making Sense: The Role of the Reader in Contemporary American Fiction*. Ed. Gerhard Hoffmann. Munich: Wilhelm Fink, 1989.
Mandūr, Muḥammad. *Fī al-Mīzān al-Jadīd*. Cairo: Maṭba'at Lajnat al-Ta'līf wa al-Tarjama wa al-Nashr, 1944.
al-Marāghī, Aḥmad Muṣṭafā. *Tafsīr al-Marāghī*. 30 vols. Cairo: Muṣṭafā al-Bābī al-Ḥalabī, 1365/1946.
Massey, Keith. "A New Investigation into the Mystery Letters of the Qur'ān." *Arabica* 43 (1996):497–501.
Mawdūdī, Abū 'l-A'lā. *Tafhīm al-Qur'ān* [Urdu; "Explaining the Qur'ān"]. 6 vols. Lahore: Maktaba-i Ta'mīr-i Insāniyat/Idāra-i Tarjumānu'l-Qur'ān, 1369–1392/1949–72.
McAuliffe, Jane Dammen. "The Abrogation of Judaism and Christianity in Islam: A Christian Perspective." *Concilium* (1994/3), 154–63.
——. "Assessing the Isrā'īliyyāt: An Exegetical Conundrum." In *Story-telling in the framework of non-fictional Arabic literature*. Ed. S. Leder. Wiesbaden: Harrassowitz Verlag, 1998.

——. "Creating a Genre: Explorations in *Muqaddimāt al-Tafāsīr.*" Forthcoming in *Qur'ānic Studies on the Eve of the 21st Century.* Ed. J.J.G. Jansen and Naṣr Abū Zayd.

——. "'Debate with Them in the Better Way': The Construction of a Qur'ānic Commonplace." Forthcoming in *Aspects of Literary Hermeneutics in Arabic Culture: Myths, Historical Archetypes and Symbolic Figures in Arabic Literature, Beiruter Texte und Studien.* Eds. A. Neuwirth, S. Gunther, M. Jarrar. Wiesbaden: Franz Steiner.

——. "The Genre Boundaries of Qur'ānic Exegesis." Forthcoming in *With Reverence for the Word: Medieval Scriptural Exegesis in Judaism, Christianity and Islam.* Ed. J. McAuliffe et al.

——. "Ibn al-Jawzī's Exegetical Propaedeutic: Introduction and Translation [of the *Muqaddima* to *Zād al-Masīr fī 'Ilm al-Tafsīr*]" *Alif: Journal of Comparative Poetics* 8 (1988):101–13.

——. "Ibn Taymiyya's *Muqaddimatun fī Uṣūl al-Tafsīr.*" In *Windows on the House of Islam: Muslim Sources on Spirituality and Religious Life.* Ed. John Renard. Berkeley: University of California Press, 1998, 35–43.

——. "The Qur'ānic Context of Muslim Biblical Scholarship." *Islam and Christian-Muslim Relations* 7 (1996):141–58.

——. "Qur'ānic Hermeneutics: The Views of al-Ṭabarī and Ibn Kathīr." In *Approaches to the History of the Interpretation of the Qur'ān.* Ed. A. Rippin. Oxford: Clarendon Press, 1988, 46–62.

——. "Ṭabarī's Prelude to the Prophet." Forthcoming in *Al-Ṭabarī: A Medieval Muslim Historian and His Work.* Ed. Hugh Kennedy. Princeton: Darwin Press.

McGinn, Bernard. *The Presence of God: The Foundations of Mysticism.* New York: Crossroad, 1991.

Mir, Mustansir. "Bāqillānī's Critique of Imru' al-Qays." In *Studies in Near Eastern Culture and History in Memory of Ernest T. Abdel-Massih.* Ed. James A. Bellamy. Ann Arbor: Center for Near Eastern and North African Studies, University of Michigan, 1990, 118–31.

——. *Coherence in the Qur'ān: A Study of Iṣlāḥī's Concept of* Naẓm *in* Tadabbur-i Qur'ān. Indianapolis, IN: American Trust Publications, 1986.

——. "The Qur'ānic Story of Joseph: Plot, Themes, and Characters." *Muslim World* 76, 1 (1986):1–15.

——. "The Qur'an as Literature." *Religion and Literature* 20 (1988):49–64.

——. "The *Sūra* as a Unity. A Twentieth Century Development in Qur'ān Exegesis." In *Approaches to the Qur'ān.* Eds. G.R. Hawting and Abdul-Kader A. Shareef. London: Routledge, 1993, 211–24.

Morris, Joseph. "The Dramatizing of the *Sūra* of Joseph: An Introduction to the Islamic Humanities." *Journal of Turkish Studies* 18 (1994):201–24.

Mubārak, Zakī. *'Abqariyyat al-Sharīf al-Raḍī.* 4th edition. 2 vols. Cairo: Ḥijāzī, 1371/1952.

Mujāhid b. Jabr. *Tafsīr Mujāhid.* Ed. 'Abd al-Raḥmān al-Ṭāhir b. Muḥammad al-Sūrtī. Islamabad: Majma' al-Buḥūth al-Islāmiyya, n.d.

Mukařovsky, Jan. *Kapitel aus der Ästhetik.* Transl. by Walter Schamschula. 4th ed. Frankfurt a. M.: Suhrkamp, 1982.

Muqātil b. Sulaymān. *Tafsīr al-Khams Mi'at Āya min al-Qur'ān.* Ed. I. Goldfeld. Shfaram: Dār al-Mashriq, 1980.

——. *Tafsīr Muqātil ibn Sulaymān.* Ed. 'Abdallāh Maḥmūd Shiḥāta. 5 vols. Cairo: al-Hay'a al-Miṣriyya al-'Āmma li 'l-Kitāb, 1979, 1984.

Musallam, Adnan Ayyub. "The Formative Stages of Sayyid Qutb's Intellectual Career and his Emergence as an Islamic Dā'iya, 1906–1952." Ph.D. dissertation, University of Michigan, 1983.

Muslim b. al-Ḥajjāj, Abū 'l-Ḥusayn. *Ṣaḥīḥ Muslim.* Ed. Muḥammad Fu'ād 'Abd al-Bāqī. 5 vols. Cairo: Dār Iḥyā' al-Kutub al-'Arabiyya, 1955.

Muṣṭafā, Ibrāhīm. *Iḥyā' al-Naḥw.* Cairo, 1937.

Nelson, Kristina. *The Art of Reciting the Qur'ān.* Austin: University of Texas Press, 1985.

Neuwirth, Angelika. "Erste Qibla – Fernstes Masǧid? – Jerusalem im Horizont des historischen Muhammad." In *Zion – Ort der Begegnung. Festschrift für Laurentius Klein.* Eds. F. Hahn, F.L. Hossfeld, H. Jorissen and A. Neuwirth. Bodenheim, Hain: Athenäum; Hainstein, 1993, 227–70.

——. "Der historische Muhammad im Spiegel des Koran – Prophetentypus zwischen Seher und Dichter?." In *Biblische Welten. Festschrift für Martin Metzger zum 65.Geburtstag.* Ed. W. Zwickel. Göttingen: Vandenhoeck & Ruprecht, 1993, 83–108.

——. "Der Horizont der Offenbarung. Zur Relevanz der einleitenden Schwurserien für die Suren der frühmekkanischen Zeit." In *Gottes ist der Orient – Gottes ist der Okzident. Festschrift für Aboldjavad Falaturi zum 65. Geburtstag.* Ed. U. Tworuschka. Köln: Böhlau, 1991, 3–39.

——. "Images and Metaphors in the Introductory Sections of the Makkan *Sūras.*" In *Approaches to the Qur'ān.* Eds. G.R. Hawting and Abdul-Kader Shareef. London: Routledge, 1993, 3–36.

——. "Intertextuality and 'Intrinsic Exegesis': Sūrat ar-Raḥmān between its Biblical Pretext and its Implied Audience." Forthcoming in *With Reverence for the Word: Medieval Scriptural Exegesis in Judaism, Christianity and Islam.* Ed. J. McAuliffe et al.

——. "Das islamische Dogma der 'Unnachahmlichkeit des Korans' in literaturwissenschaftlicher Sicht." *Der Islam* 60 (1983):166–83.

——. 'Koran'. In *Grundriß der arabischen Philologie, II: Literaturwissenschaft.* Ed. Helmut Gätje. Wiesbaden: Dr. Ludwig Reichert Verlag, 1987, 96–130.

——. "Review of Burton's *The Collection of the Qur'an.*" *Orientalische Literaturzeitung* 76 (1981):372–80.

——. "Vom Rezitationstext über die Liturgie zum Kanon. Zu Entstehung und Wiederauflösung der Surenkomposition im Verlauf der Entwicklung eines islamischen Kultus." In *The Qur'ān as Text.* Ed. S. Wild. Leiden: E.J. Brill, 1996, 69–105.

——. *Studien zur Komposition der mekkanischen Suren.* Studien zur Sprache, Geschichte und Kultur des islamischen Orients, Neue Folge, Band 10. Berlin and New York: Walter de Gruyter, 1981.

——. "Zur Struktur der *Yūsuf*-Sure." In *Studien aus Arabistik und Semitistik Anton Spitaler zum 70. Geburtstag.* Eds. W. Diem and S. Wild. Wiesbaden: Harrassowitz, 1980, 123–52.

——. "*Sūrat al-Fātiḥa.* 'Eröffnung' des Text-Corpus Koran oder 'Introitus' der Gebetsliturgie?." In *Text, Methode und Grammatik. Wolfgang Richter zum 65. Geburtstag.* Eds. W. Gross, H. Irsigler and T. Seidl. St. Ottilien: EOS Verlag, 1991, 331–57.

——. "Symmetrie und Paarbildung in der koranischen Eschatologie. Philologisch-Stilistisches zu *Sūrat al-Raḥmān.*" In *Mélanges M. Allard et P. Nwyia.* Ed. Louis Pouzet. Beirut: Dar el-Machreq, 1985

Newman, N.A. *Muhammad, the Qur'ān and Islam.* Hatfield, PA.: Interdisciplinary Biblical Research Institute, 1996.

Nicholson, R. A. *A Literary History of the Arabs.* 1st paperback edition. Cambridge: At the University Press, 1969; 1st printing: T. Fisher Unwin, 1907.

Nöldeke, Theodor. *Beiträge zur Kenntnis der Poesie der alten Araber.* Hannover: 1864. Repr. Hildesheim: Olms, 1967.

—— and Friedrich Schwally. *Geschichte des Qorāns.* 2nd rev. ed. 2 vols. Leipzig: Deutsche Verlagsbuchhandlung, 1909, 1919, 1938; Repr. in one vol. Hildesheim: Georg Olms Verlag, 1970.

Noth, A. "Früher Islam." In *Geschichte der arabischen Welt.* Ed. Ulrich Haarmann. Munich: C.H. Beck, 1987, 11–100.

Nwyia, Paul. *Exégèse coranique et langage mystique.* Beirut: Dar el-Machreq, Recherches Série 1: Pensée Arabe et Musulmane, Tome xlix, 1970.

O'Leary, de Lacy. *Arabic Thought and its Place in History.* London: Luzac, 1922.

O'Shaughnessy, Thomas. *The Development of the Meaning of Spirit in the Koran.* Rome: Pont. Institutum Orientalium Studiorum, 1953.

Paret, Rudi. "Furḳān." *EI*[2]s.v.

——. *Der Koran. Kommentar und Konkordanz.* Stuttgart: W. Kohlhammer, 1977, 1980.

——. *Der Koran: Übersetzung.* Stuttgart: W. Kohlhammer, 1962. Reprinted with corrections, 1966.

——. *Mohammed und der Koran. Geschichte und Verkündigung des arabischen Propheten.* Stuttgart: Kohlhammer, 1957.

Parunak, H. Van Dyke. "Oral Typesetting: Some Uses of Biblical Structure." *Biblica* 62 (1981):153–68.

——. "Transitional Techniques in the Bible." *Journal of Biblical Literature* 102 (1983):525–48.

Pascal, Blaise. *Über die Religion und über einige andere Gegenstände (Pensées).* Transl. by Ewald Wasmuth. Heidelberg: Schneider, 1954 (= *Werke* I)

Pautz, Otto. *Muhammeds Lehre von der Offenbarung. Quellenmässig Untersucht.* Leipzig: J. C. Hinrichs'sche Buchhandlung, 1898.

Pickthall, Marmaduke. *The Meaning of the Glorious Coran.* (Bilingual edition). Beirut: Dār al-Kitāb al-Lubnānī, 1970; *The Glorious Koran, a Bi-lingual Edition with English Translation, Introduction and Notes.* Albany: State University of New York Press, 1976. First publ., Hyderabad-Deccan, 1930.

al-Qalqashandī, Aḥmad. *Ṣubḥ al-A'shā fī Ṣinā'at al-Inshā'.* 2 vols. Ed. Muḥammad Shams al-Dīn. Beirut: Dār al-Kutub al-'Ilmiyya, 1987.

Quasem, Muhammad Abul. *The Recitation and Interpretation of the Qur'ān: Al-Ghazālī's Theory.* London: Kegan Paul, 1982.

al-Qummī, 'Alī b. Ibrāhīm. *Tafsīr.* Ed. Ṭayyib al-Mūsawī al-Jazā'irī. Qumm: Dār al-Kitāb li 'l-Ṭibā'a, 1202 [solar].

al-Qurṭubī, Abū 'Abdallāh Muḥammad b. Aḥmad al-Anṣārī. *Al-Jāmi' li-Aḥkām al-Qur'ān.* Cairo, n.p., 1962; 20 vols. in 10. Cairo: Dār al-Kātib al-'Arabī li-'l-Ṭibā'a wa-'l-Nashr, 1387–1967; Teheran reprint 1364 S.

——. *Mukhtaṣar Tafsīr al-Qurṭubī.* Ed. Muḥammad Rajab. Beirut: Dār al-Kitāb al-'Arabī, 1986.

Quṭb, Sayyid. *Al-'Adāla al-Ijtimā'iyya fī al-Islām.* Cairo: Lajnat al-Nashr li al-Jāmi'iyyīn, 1949.

——. *Fī Ẓilāl al-Qur'ān.* 6 vols. Cairo: Dār al-Shurūq, 1402/1982; 30 vols. Cairo: Dār Iḥyā' al-Kutub al-'Arabiyya, n.d.; second revised edition, 1961; 30 vols. in 6 tomes. Cairo-Beirut: Dār al-Shurūq, 1988; 30 vols. Beirut: Dār al-Shurūq, 1993.

——. *Khaṣā'iṣ al-Taṣawwur al-Islāmī wa Muqawwimātuh.* Cairo: Dār Iḥyā' al-Kutub al-'Arabiyya, 1962.

——. *Mashāhid al-Qiyāma fī 'l-Qur'ān.* Cairo: Dār al-Ma'ārif, 1966, 1981.

——. *Al-Naqd al-Adabī: Uṣūluh wa Manāhijuh.* Cairo: Dār al-Fikr al-'Arabī, 1960.

——. "Al-Tanāsuq al-Fannī fī Taṣwīr al-Qur'ān." *al-Risāla* 13, 610 (1945):278–81.

——. "Al-Taṣwīr al-Fannī fī al-Qur'ān." *al-Muqtaṭaf* 94, 2 (Feb. 1939):206–22 and 94, 3 (Mar. 1939):313–18.

——. "Al-Taṣwīr al-Fannī fī al-Qur'ān." *al-Risāla* 13, 601 (1945):43–6.

——. *Al-Taṣwīr al-Fannī fī al-Qur'ān.* Cairo: Dār al-Ma'ārif, 1966; Beirut and Cairo: Dār al-Shurūq, 1987, 1993.

——. *Ṭifl min al-Qarya.* Beirut: Dār al-Ḥikma, n.d.

von Rad, Gerhard. *Genesis, A Commentary.* Philadelphia: The Westminster Press, 1972.

al-Raḍī, al-Sharīf. *Al-Majāzāt al-Nabawiyya.* Baghdad, 1328 A. H.

——. *Talkhīṣ al-Bayān fī Majāzāt al-Qur'ān.* Ed. ʿAbd al-Ghanī Ḥasan. Cairo: ʿĪsā al-Bābī al-Ḥalabī, 1955.

Radscheidt, Matthias. "'Iʿǧāz al-Qur'ān' im Koran?" In *The Qur'ān as Text.* Ed. Stefan Wild. Leiden: Brill, 1996, 113–23.

——. *Die koranische Herausforderung. Die taḥaddī-Verse im Rahmen der Polemikpassagen des Korans.* Berlin: Klaus Schwarz, 1996.

al-Rāfiʿī, Muṣṭafā Ṣādiq. *Iʿjāz al-Qur'ān wa 'l-Balāgha al-Nabawiyya.* 6th ed. Cairo: Maṭbaʿat al-Istiqāma, 1956; Beirut: Dār al-Kitāb al-ʿArabī, 1410/1990.

Rahbar, Daud. *God of Justice: A Study in the Ethical Doctrine of the Qur'ān.* Leiden: E. J. Brill, 1960.

Rahman, Fazlur. *Major Themes of the Qur'ān.* Minneapolis: Bibliotheca Islamica, 1980.

——. "Translating the Qur'ān." *Religion and Literature* 20 (1988):23–30.

Rahman, Yusuf. "The Doctrine of *Muʿjiza* According to the Schools of *Kalām* in the Classical Period." *Islamic Quarterly* 40, 4 (1996):235–57.

——. "The Miraculous Nature of Muslim Scripture: A Study of ʿAbd al-Jabbār's *Iʿjāz al-Qur'ān.*" *Islamic Studies* 35, 4 (1996):409–24.

Rāmiyār, Maḥmūd. *Tārīkh-e Qor'ān.* Tehran: Amīr Kabīr, 1984.

al-Rāzī, Fakhr al-Dīn. *Al-Tafsīr al-Kabīr.* 32 vols. Tehran: Dār al-Kutub al-ʿIlmiyya, n.d.; 32 vols. Cairo: Al-Maṭbaʿa al-Bahiyya al-Miṣriyya, 1934–1962; Tehran reprint; 30 vols. Tehran: Dār al-Kutub, n.d.; 33 vols. Cairo: al-Maṭbaʿa al-Bahiyya, 1938; *Mafātīḥ al-Ghayb.* Cairo: Iltizām ʿAbd al-Raḥmān Muḥammad, n.d.; 32 vols. Beirut: Dār al-Kutub al-ʿIlmiyya, 1990; *Mafātīḥ al-Ghayb.* 32 vols. Beirut: Dār al-Fikr, 1401/1981.

Redford, Donald B. *A Study of the Biblical Study of Joseph (Genesis 37–50).* Leiden: E. J. Brill, 1979. Supplements to Vetus Testamentum, XX.

Reinert, B. "Madjāz." EI^2, V:1025–6.

Ricoeur, Paul. *Hermeneutics and the Human Sciences.* Ed. and trans. John B. Thompson. Cambridge: Cambridge University Press, 1981.

——. *Time and Narrative.* Trans. Kathleen Blamey and David Pellauer. Chicago: University of Chicago Press, 1988.

Riḍā, Muḥammad Rashīd. *Al-Waḥy al-Muḥammadī.* Beirut: al-Maktab al-Islāmī, 1391/1971.

Riffaterre, Michael. *Semiotics of Poetry.* Bloomington: Indiana University Press, 1978.

Ringgren, Helmer. *Islām, 'Aslama and Muslim.* Uppsala: Almqvist, 1949.

Rippin, Andrew. "'God is King': Studying the Qur'ān and talking of God." Unpublished paper presented at a colloquium in honour of Mohammed Arkoun, Carthage, 1993.

——. "Muhammad in the Qur'ān. Reading Scripture in the 21st Century." Unpublished.

——. "The Qur'ān as Literature: Perils, Pitfalls and Prospects." *British Society for Middle Eastern Studies Bulletin* 10 (1983):38–47.

——. *Reading the Qur'ān.* Forthcoming from Darwin Press, Princeton.

——. "Tafsīr." EI^2, X:83–8.

——, ed. *Approaches to the History of the Interpretation of the Qur'ān.* Oxford: Clarendon Press, 1988.

—— and Jan Knappert, eds. *Textual Sources for the Study of Islam.* Manchester: Manchester University Press, 1986.

Robinson, Neal. *Discovering the Qur'ān: A Contemporary Approach to a Veiled Text.* London: SCM Press, 1996.

Rubin, Uri. *The Eye of the Beholder: The Life of Muḥammad as Viewed by the Early Muslims.* Princeton: Darwin Press, 1995.

al-Rummānī, ʿAlī ibn ʿĪsā. *Al-Nukat fī Iʿjāz al-Qurʾān.* In *Thalāth Rasāʾil fī Iʿjāz al-Qurʾān li ʾl-Rummānī wa ʾl-Khaṭṭābi wa ʿAbd al-Qāhir al-Jurjānī.* Eds. Muḥammad Khalaf Allāh and Muḥammad Zaghlūl Sallām. Cairo: Dār al-Maʿārif bi-Miṣr, 1968; Cairo: Dār al-Maʿārif, n.d., 67–104.

al-Ṣābūnī, Muḥammad ʿAlī. *Ṣafwat al-Tafāsīr: Tafsīr al-Qurʾān al-Karīm.* 3 vols. Beirut: Dār al-Qurʾān al-Karīm, 1980.

al-Ṣafadī, Ṣalāḥ al-Dīn Khalīl ibn Aybak. *Al-Wāfī fī ʾl-Wafayāt.* 29 vols. Beirut: German Oriental Institute, 1381/1962–1997; first published in Istanbul: Maṭbaʿat al-Dawla, 1931. Ed. Helmut Ritter.

Said, Edward. *The World, the Text, and the Critic.* Cambridge: Harvard University Press, 1983.

al-Saʿīd, Labīb. *Al-Jamʿ al-Ṣawtī al-Awwal aw al-Muṣḥaf al-Murattal.* Cairo: Dār al-Maʿārif, 1967.

——. *Al-Taghannī bi ʾl-Qurʾān.* Cairo: al-Hayʾa al-ʿĀmma li ʾl-Taʾlīf wa ʾl-Nashr, 1970.

Sakhr CD-ROM. *Bāḥith al-Nuṣūṣ: Wasīlat al-Baḥth al-Muthlā. al-Nuṣuṣ al-ʿArabiyya wa l-Inglīziyya* (also called *Sakhr Find*). Cairo: Sakhr Products, 1997.

——. *Al-Qurʾān al-Karīm* (also called *The Holy Qurʾān*). Version 7. Cairo: Sakhr Products, 1997.

Sale, George. *The Koran Translated into English from the Original Arabic.* London and New York: Frederick Warne and Co., n.d.

al-Ṣāliḥ, Ṣubḥī. *Mabāḥith fī ʿUlūm al-Qurʾān.* Beirut: Dār al-ʿIlm li ʾl-Malāyīn, 1982.

Sallām, Muḥammad Zaghlūl. *Athar al-Qurʾān fī Taṭawwur al-Naqd al-Adabī.* Cairo: Dār al-Maʿārif, 1955, 1961.

——. *Ibn Qutayba.* Cairo: Dār al-Maʿārif, 1957.

—— and M. Khalaf Allāh, eds. *Thalāth Rasāʾil fī Iʿjāz al-Qurʾān.* Cairo: Dār al-Maʿārif, 1956.

al-Ṣanʿānī, ʿAbd al-Razzāq b. Hammām. *Tafsīr al-Qurʾān.* Ed. Muṣṭfafā Muslim Muḥammad. Riyadh: Maktabat al-Rushd, 1410/1989.

Schoeler, George. "Writing and Publishing. On the Use and Function of Writing in the First Centuries of Islam." *Arabica* 44 (1997):423–35.

——. "Schreiben und Veröffentlichen. Zu Verwendung und Funktion der Schrift in den ersten islamischen Jahrhunderten." *Der Islam* 69 (1992):25.

Segre, Casare. *Introduction to the Analysis of the Literary Text.* Trans. John Meddemmen. Bloomington: Indiana University Press, 1988.

Sell, Edward. *Faith of Islam.* 3rd ed. Madras: SPCK Depot, 1907.

Sells, Michael. *Approaching the Qurʾān: The Early Revelations.* Ashland: White Cloud Press, 1999.

——. *Desert Tracings: Six Classic Arabian Odes.* Middletown: Wesleyan University Press, 1989.

——. *Early Islamic Mysticism.* New York: Paulist Press, 1996.

——. *Mystical Languages of Unsaying.* Chicago: University of Chicago Press, 1994.

——. "Sound and Meaning in *Sūrat al-Qāriʿa.*" *Arabica: Journal of Arabic and Islamic Studies* 40 (November 1993):402–30.

——. "Sound, Spirit and Gender in *Sūrat al-Qadr.*" *Journal of the American Oriental Society* 111, 2 (1991):239–59.

Shahîd, Irfan. "Another Contribution to Koranic Exegesis: the Sūra of the Poets." *Journal of Arabic Literature* 14 (1983):1–21.

——. "The *Hijra* (Emigration) of the Early Muslims to Abyssinia: The Byzantine Dimension." *To Hellenikon, Festschrift Speros Vryonis, Jr.* Ed. Milton v. Anastos. New Rochelle, New York: Aristide D. Caratzas, 1993, 2:203–13.

——. "Medieval Islam: the Literary-Cultural Dimension." In *Religion and Culture in Medieval Islam.* Eds. Richard G. Hovanissian and Georges Sabagh, Cambridge University Press, (forthcoming).
——. "The Sūra of the Poets Re-visited: Some Final Observations. (forthcoming).
Shaltūt, Maḥmūd. *Tafsīr al-Qur'ān al-Karīm* [on Sūras 1–9]. 11th ed. Cairo and Beirut: Dār al-Shurūq, 1988.
Sharī'atī Mazīnānī, Moḥammad Taqī. *Waḥy wa-Nobuwwat dar Partow-e Qor'ān.* Mashhad: Ḥoseyniyye Ershād, 1970.
al-Sharīf al-Raḍī. *Ḥaqā'iq al-Ta'wīl fī Mutashābih al-Tanzīl.* Ed. Muḥammad Riḍā Āl Kāshif al-Ghiṭā'. Beirut: Dār al-Muhājir, n.d. [reprint of the Najaf edition of 1355, with a long introduction by 'Abd al-Ḥusayn al-Ḥillī].
——. *Al-Majāzāt al-Nabawiyya aw Majāzāt al-Āthār al-Nabawiyya.* Eds. Marwān 'Aṭiyya and Muḥammad Riḍwān al-Dāya. Damascus: al-Mustashāriyya al-Thaqāfiyya li 'l-Jumhūriyya al-Islāmiyya, 1408/1987.
——. *Talkhīṣ al-Bayān fī Majāzāt al-Qur'ān.* Ed. al-Sayyid Muḥammad al-Mishkāt. Tehran: Muḥammad al-Mishkāt, 1953; Ed. 'Abd al-Ghanī Ḥasan. Cairo: Dār al-Aḍwā', 1957; Ed. Makkī al-Sayyid Jāsim. Beirut: Maktabat al-Nahḍa al-'Arabiyya, 1406/1986.
Shboul, Ahmad. "A New Approach to the Qur'ān: The Work of Sayyid Quṭb." A Paper presented at the Second International Congress on the Qur'ān, New Delhi: Indian Institute of Islamic Studies, 1982.
Sībawayh. *Kitāb Sībawayh.* 2 vols. Baghdad: Maktabat al-Muthannā, n.d.; reimpression of Bulaq, 1316 A.H.
Smith, R. Bosworth. *Mohammed and Mohammedanism: Lectures Delivered at the Royal Institution of Great Britain in February and March 1874.* London: Smith, Elder and Company, 1876.
Speiser, E. A. *Genesis.* Garden City, New York: Doubleday, 1982. The Anchor Bible Series, 1.
Speyer, Heinrich. *Die biblischen Erzählungen im Koran.* Gräfenhainichen o.J., ca. 1936, reprint Hildesheim: G. Olms, 1961.
Spitaler, A. *Die Verszählung des Korans nach islamischer Überlieferung.* Munich: Verlag der Bayerischen Akademie der Wissenchaften, 1935.
Stanzel, F. K. *A Theory of Narrative.* Trans. Charlotte Goedsche. Cambridge and New York: Cambridge University Press, 1984. From the 2nd ed. of *Theorie des Erzählens.* Göttingen: Vandenhoeck and Ruprecht, 1982.
Stern, M.S. "Muhammad and Joseph: A Study of Koranic Narrative." *Journal of Near Eastern Studies* 44 (1985):193–202.
Stetkevych, Jaroslav. *Muḥammad and the Golden Bough: Reconstructing Arabian Myth.* Bloomington: Indiana University Press, 1996.
Stetkevych, Suzanne. *The Mute Immortals Speak.* Ithaca: Cornell University Press, 1993.
Stewart, Devin J. "*Saj'* in the Qur'ān: Prosody and Structure." *Journal of Arabic Literature* 21.2 (September 1990):101–39.
Sufyān al-Thawrī. *Tafsīr Sufyān al-Thawrī.* Ed. Imtiyāz 'Alī Arshī. Beirut: Dār al-Kutub al-'Ilmiyya, 1403/1983.
al-Sulamī. *Majāz al-Qur'ān.* Ed. M. Muṣṭafā b. al-Ḥājj. Tripoli: Manshūrāt Kulliyyat al-Da'wa al-Islāmiyya, 1992.
Suleiman, Susan R. and Inge Crossman, eds. *The Reader in the Text: Essays on Audience and Interpretation.* Princeton: Princeton University Press, 1980.
Surty, Muhammad. *A Course in 'Ilm at-Tajwīd. The Science of Reciting the Qur'ān.* Leicester, UK: Islamic Foundation, 1988.
al-Suyūṭī, Jalāl al-Dīn 'Abd al-Raḥmān. *Al-Itqān fī 'Ulūm al-Qur'ān.* Ed. Muḥammad Abū Faḍl Ibrāhīm. Cairo: Dār al-Turāth, 1985/1405; 2 vols. Cairo: al-Ḥalabī and Sons, 1951.

——. *Al-Muzhir.* 3rd ed. Cairo: Dār Iḥyā' al-Kutub al-'Arabiyya, n.d.
——. *Al-Wasā'il ilā Musāmarat al-Awā'il.* Baghdad: Maṭba'at al-Najāḥ, 1950.
—— and Jalāl al-Dīn al-Maḥallī. *Tafsīr al-Jalālayn.* Beirut: Dār al-Qalam, n.d.; Rev. 'Alī al-Ḍabba. Cairo: al-Maṭba'a al-Yūsufiyya, n.d.; Beirut: Dār Ibn Kathīr, 1994
al-Ṭabarī, Abū Ja'far Muḥammad b. Jarīr. *Jāmi' al-Bayān 'an Ta'wīl Āy al-Qur'ān.* Ed. Maḥmūd Muḥammad Shākir and Aḥmad Muḥammad Shākir. Cairo: Dār al-Ma'ārif, 1954–68; 30 vols. in 12. Būlāq, 1327 H; Beirut reprint; 15 vols. Beirut: Dār al-Fikr, 1995.
——. *Tārīkh al-Rusul wa 'l-Mulūk.* Ed. M. de Goeje. 15 vols. Leiden: Brill, 1879–1901.
al-Ṭabarī, 'Alī b. Rabban. *Kitāb al-Dīn wa l-Dawla* (= *The Book of Religion and Empire*). Ed. A. Mingana. Manchester: University Press/Longmans, Green and Company, 1923.
al-Ṭabarsī, al-Faḍl b. al-Ḥasan. *Majma' al-Bayān fī Tafsīr al-Qur'ān.* Intr. Muḥsin al-Amīn al-Ḥusaynī al-'Āmilī. Beirut: Dār Maktabat al-Ḥayā, 1380/1961.
al-Ṭabāṭabā'ī, Muḥammad. *Al-Mīzān fī Tafsīr al-Qur'ān.* 2nd ed. Beirut: Maktabat al-'Alamī, 1974.
Ṭihrānī, Aghā Buzurg. *Al-Dharī'a ilā Taṣānīf al-Shī'a.* s.v. *ḥaqā'iq al-ta'wīl* [entry 260].
Terrien, Samuel. *The Elusive Presence. Toward a New Biblical Theology.* San Francisco: Harper and Row, 1978.
Theissen, Gerd. "Mythos und Wertrevolution im Urchristentum." In *Revolution und Mythos.* Ed. Dietrich Harth and Jan Assmann. Frankfurt: Fischer Taschenbuch Verlag, 1992, 2–81.
Tibawi, A.L. "Is the Qur'ān Translatable? Early Muslim Opinion." *Muslim World* 52 (1962):4–17.
Tompkins, Jane P., ed. *Reader-Response Criticism: From Formalism to Post-Structuralism.* Baltimore: Johns Hopkins University Press, 1980.
Trible, Phyllis. *God and the Rhetoric of Sexuality.* Philadelphia: Fortress Press, 1978.
——. *Texts of Terror: Literary-Feminist Readings of Biblical Narratives.* Philadelphia: Fortress Press, 1984.
al-Ṭūsī, Muḥammad b. al-Ḥasan. *Al-Tibyān fī Tafsīr al-Qur'ān.* Ed. Aḥmad Ḥabīb Qaṣīr al-'Amalī. Beirut: Dār Iḥyā' al-Turāth al-'Arabī, n.d.
'Uṣfūr, Jābir. *Al-Ṣūra al-Fanniyya fī al-Turāth al-Naqdī wa al-Balāghī.* Cairo: Dār al-Thaqāfa, 1974.
Wansbrough, John. "*Majāz al-Qur'ān*: Periphrastic Exegesis." *Bulletin of the School of the Oriental and African Studies* 33 (1970):247–66.
——. *Quranic Studies, Sources and Methods of Scriptural Interpretation.* Oxford: Oxford University Press, 1977.
al-Wāqidī, Muḥammad b. 'Umar. *Kitāb al-Maghāzī.* 3 vols. Ed. Marsden Jones. London: Oxford University Press, 1966.
Watt, W.M. *Bell's Introduction to the Qur'ān, Completely Revised and Enlarged.* Islamic Surveys Series, No. 8. Edinburgh: Edinburgh University Press, 1970. Repr. in 1990 with the title *Introduction to the Qur'ān* on the cover, although not on the title page.
——. *Muḥammad at Medina.* Karachi, Oxford, New York, Delhi: Oxford University Press, 1981.
Webster. *Webster's Ninth New Collegiate Dictionary.* Springfield, MA: Merriam Webster, 1986.
Welch, A.T. "Ḳur'ān." *EI*[2] 5:400–29.
——. "Muḥammad's Understanding of Himself: The Koranic Data." In *Islam's Understanding of Itself.* Ed. Richard G. Hovannisian and Speros Vryonis, Jr. Levi della Vida Series. Publ. for the Center for Near Eastern Studies, University of California, Los Angeles. Malibu: Undena, 1983, 15–52.

——. "Sūra." *EI*[2] 8:885–89.
Wensinck, A.J. "*Nafs.*" *EI*[1] 3:827–30.
—— and C.E. Bosworth. "Lawḥ." *EI*[2]. s.v.
Wenzel, Horst. *Hören und Sehen. Schrift und Bild. Kultur und Gedächtnis im Mittelalter.* Munich: Beck, 1995.
Widengren, Geo. *The Accadian and Hebrew Psalms of Lamentation as Religious Documents.* Uppsala: Almqvist 1936.
Wild, Stefan. "Die andere Seite des Texts. Naṣr Ḥāmid Abū Zaid und der Koran." *Die Welt des Islam* 33, 2 (1993):256–61.
——. "The Self-Referentiality of the Qur'ān: Sūra 3,7 as an Exegetical Challenge." Forthcoming in *With Reverence for the Word: Medieval Scriptural Exegesis in Judaism, Christianity and Islam.* Ed. J. McAuliffe et al.
——, ed. *The Qur'ān as Text.* Leiden: E.J. Brill, 1996.
Worton, Michael and Judith Still, eds. *Intertextuality: Theories and Practice.* Manchester: Manchester University Press, 1990.
Yāqūt, Abū 'Abd Allāh ibn 'Abd Allāh al-Rūmī al-Ḥamawī. *Mu'jam al-Udabā' aw Irshād al-Arīb ilā Ma'rifat al-Adīb.* 2nd ed. Cairo: Maṭba'at Hindiyya, 1923–1932; 5 vols. Beirut: Dār al-Kutub al-'Ilmiyya, 1411/1991.
Zahniser, A. H. Mathias. "Discourse Analysis and the Qur'ān." (forthcoming).
——. "Sūra as Guidance and Exhortation: The Composition of *Sūrat al-Nisā'.*" In Asma Afsaruddin and A. H. Mathias Zahniser, eds. *Humanism, Culture, and Language in the Near East: Studies in Honor of Georg Krotkoff.* Winona Lake, Indiana: Eisenbrauns, 1997, 71–85.
——. "The Word of God and the Apostleship of 'Īsā: A Narrative Analysis of Āl 'Imrān (3):33–62." *Journal of Semitic Studies* 37 (1991):77–112.
al-Zamakhsharī, Jār Allāh Maḥmūd ibn 'Umar. *Al-Kashshāf 'an Ḥaqā'iq Ghawāmiḍ al-Tanzīl wa 'Uyūn al-Aqāwīl fī Wujūh al-Ta'wīl.* Beirut: Dār al-Kitāb al-'Arabī, 1947; Beirut: Dār al-Kitāb al-'Arabī, 1966; Ed. Muḥammad Mūsā 'Āmir. Cairo: Dār al-Muṣḥaf, 1397/1977; 4 vols. Beirut: Dār al-Ma'rifa, n.d.; *Al-Kashshāf 'an Ḥaqā'iq al-Tanzīl Aqāwīl fī Wujūh al-Ta'wīl.* 4 vols. Cairo: al-Ḥalabī and Associates, 1972.
al-Zarkashī, Badr al-Dīn Muḥammad b. 'Abdallāh. *Al-Burhān fī 'Ulūm al-Qur'ān.* Ed. Muḥammad Abū al-Faḍl Ibrāhīm. Cairo: Dār al-Turāth, n.d.; 4 vols. in 2. Ed. Muḥammad Abū Faḍl Ibrāhīm. Cairo: 'Īsā al-Ḥalabī wa Shurakā'uhu, 1957–58.
Zenger, E. and H.L. Hossfeld. *Kommentar zum Alten Testament mit der Einheitsübersetzung. Die Psalmen. Psalm 1–50.* Würzburg, 1993.
al-Ziriklī, Khayr al-Dīn. *Al-A'lām.* 3rd edition. 13 vols. Published by the author, n.d.
Zayd Ibn 'Alī. *Tafsīr Zayd b. 'Alī al-Musammā Tafsīr Gharīb al-Qur'ān.* Ed. Muḥammad Taqı al-Ḥakīm. Cairo: Dār al-'Ālamiyya, 1412/1992.
Zysow, Aron. "Two Unrecognized Karrāmī Texts." *Journal of the American Oriental Society* 108 (1988):577–87.

Index